Lecture Notes in Computer Science 5971

Commenced Publication in 1973
Founding and Former Series Editors:
Gerhard Goos, Juris Hartmanis, and Jan van Leeuwen

T0181551

Matthias Müller-Hannemann
Stefan Schirra (Eds.)

Algorithm Engineering

Bridging the Gap
between Algorithm Theory and Practice

 Springer

Volume Editors

Matthias Müller-Hannemann
Martin-Luther-Universität Halle-Wittenberg, Institut für Informatik
Von-Seckendorff-Platz 1, 06120 Halle, Germany
E-mail: muellerh@informatik.uni-halle.de

Stefan Schirra
Otto-von-Guericke Universität Magdeburg, Fakultät für Informatik
Universitätsplatz 2, 39106 Magdeburg, Germany
E-mail: stschirr@ovgu.de

Library of Congress Control Number: 2010931447

CR Subject Classification (1998): F.2, D.2, G.1-2, G.4, E.1, I.3.5, I.6

LNCS Sublibrary: SL 1 – Theoretical Computer Science and General Issues

ISSN   0302-9743
ISBN-10   3-642-14865-4 Springer Berlin Heidelberg New York
ISBN-13   978-3-642-14865-1 Springer Berlin Heidelberg New York

springer.com

© Springer-Verlag Berlin Heidelberg 2010

Typesetting: Camera-ready by author, data conversion by Scientific Publishing Services, Chennai, India
Printed on acid-free paper   06/3180

Preface

The systematic development of efficient algorithms has become a key technology for all kinds of ambitious and innovative computer applications. With major parts of algorithmic theory and algorithmic practice developing in different directions since the 1970s a group of leading researchers in the field started about 15 years ago to coin the new paradigm "Algorithm Engineering". Its major goal is to bridge the gap between theory and practice.

This book is a collection of survey articles on different aspects of Algorithm Engineering, written by participants of a GI-Dagstuhl seminar held during September 3-8, 2006. Dorothea Wagner and Peter Sanders came up with the idea for the seminar, and approached us to organize it. In general, the concept of the GI-Dagstuhl seminars is to provide young researchers (mostly PhD students) with the opportunity to be introduced into a new emerging field of computer science. Based on a list of topics collected by the organizers, the participants prepared overview lectures they presented and discussed with other participants at the research seminar in Dagstuhl. Each contribution was elaborated afterwards and carefully cross-reviewed by all participants.

Chapter 1 gives an introduction into the emerging field of Algorithm Engineering and describes its main ingredients. It also serves as an overview for the remaining chapters of the book.

The editing process took much longer than expected, partially due to the fact that several aspects of Algorithm Engineering have never been written up before, which gave rise to lengthy internal discussions. But for the major part of the delay, the editors take their responsibility. Since the field of Algorithm Engineering has developed rapidly since the seminar took place, we made an effort to keep the contents up to date. Ideally, our book will be used as an introduction to the field. Although it has not been written as a textbook, it may well serve as accompanying material and as a reference in class.

As this book project now comes to an end, we are indebted to many people and institutions. First of all, we would like to thank the Gesellschaft für Informatik e.V. (GI) for their generous support of the GI-Dagstuhl seminar, funding the stay of all participants at Schloss Dagstuhl. We thank the Schloss Dagstuhl Leibniz-Zentrum für Informatik GmbH for their excellent workshop facilities and its hospitality, which provided the basis for a successful seminar. Alfred Hofmann and his team made it possible to smoothly publish this volume in the LNCS series of Springer. Special thanks go to Annabell Berger, Holger Blaar, and Kathleen Kletsch for their help in the editing process.

March 2010
Matthias Müller-Hannemann
Stefan Schirra

List of Contributors

Editors

Matthias Müller-Hannemann
Martin-Luther-Universität
Halle-Wittenberg
Institut für Informatik
Von-Seckendorff-Platz 1
06120 Halle, Germany
muellerh@informatik.uni-halle.de

Stefan Schirra
Otto-von-Guericke Universität
Magdeburg
Fakultät für Informatik
Universitätsplatz 2
39106 Magdeburg, Germany
stschirr@ovgu.de

Authors

Heiner Ackermann
Fraunhofer Institute for
Industrial Mathematics
Fraunhofer-Platz 1
67663 Kaiserslautern, Germany
heiner.ackermann@itwm.fraunhofer.de

Daniel Delling
Microsoft Research Silicon Valley
1065 La Avenida
Montain View, CA 94043, USA
dadellin@microsoft.com

Deepak Ajwani
Aarhus University
MADALGO - Center for Massive
Data Algorithmics
IT-parken, Aabogade 34
8200 Aarhus N, Denmark
ajwani@cs.au.dk

Roman Dementiev
Universität Karlsruhe (TH)
Department of Computer Science,
Algorithmics II
Am Fasanengarten 5
76131 Karlsruhe, Germany
dementiev@ira.uka.de

Markus Geyer
Universität Tübingen
Wilhelm-Schickard-Institut für
Informatik, Paralleles Rechnen
Sand 14
72076 Tübingen, Germany
geyer@informatik.uni-tuebingen.de

Eric Berberich
Max-Planck-Institut für Informatik
Algorithms and Complexity
Campus E1 4
66123 Saarbrücken, Germany
eric@mpi-inf.mpg.de

Matthias Hagen
Bauhaus Universität Weimar
Faculty of Media, Web Technology
and Information Systems Group
Bauhausstr. 11
99423 Weimar, Germany
matthias.hagen@uni-weimar.de

Maria Kandyba
Technische Universität Dortmund
Fakultät für Informatik
Lehrstuhl für Algorithm Engineering
Otto-Hahn-Str. 14
44227 Dortmund, Germany
maria.kandyba@cs.uni-dortmund.de

Sabine Helwig
Universität Erlangen-Nürnberg
Department of Computer Science
Hardware-Software-Co-Design
Am Weichselgarten 3
91058 Erlangen, Germany
helwig@cs.fau.de

Sascha Meinert
Karlsruhe Institute of Technology
(KIT)
Institute of Theoretical Informatics,
Algorithmics I
Am Fasanengarten 5
76131 Karlsruhe, Germany
meinert@kit.edu

Benjamin Hiller
Konrad-Zuse-Zentrum für
Informationstechnik Berlin (ZIB)
Department Optimization
Takustr. 7
14195 Berlin-Dahlem, Germany
hiller@zib.de

Henning Meyerhenke
Universität Paderborn
Department of Computer Science
Fürstenallee 11
33102 Paderborn, Germany
henningm@upb.de

Roberto Hoffmann
Martin-Luther-Universität
Halle-Wittenberg
Institut für Informatik
Von-Seckendorff-Platz 1
06120 Halle, Germany
hoffmaro@informatik.uni-halle.de

Marc Mörig
Otto-von-Guericke Universität
Magdeburg
Fakultät für Informatik
Universitätsplatz 2
39106 Magdeburg, Germany
marc@moerig.com

Falk Hüffner
Humboldt-Universität zu Berlin
Institut für Informatik
Rudower Chaussee 25
12489 Berlin, Germany
hueffner@informatik.hu-berlin.de

Hannes Moser
Friedrich-Schiller-Universität Jena
Institut für Informatik
Ernst-Abbe-Platz 2
07743 Jena, Germany
hannes.moser@uni-jena.de

Matthias Müller-Hannemann
Martin-Luther-Universität
Halle-Wittenberg
Institut für Informatik
Von-Seckendorff-Platz 1
06120 Halle, Germany
muellerh@informatik.uni-halle.de

Heiko Röglin
Maastricht University
Department of Quantitative
Economics
6200 MD Maastricht, The Netherlands
heiko@roeglin.org

Ivo Rössling
Otto-von-Guericke Universität
Magdeburg
Fakultät für Informatik
Universitätsplatz 2
39106 Magdeburg, Germany
ivo.roessling@ovgu.de

Ulf Schellbach
Technische Universität Ilmenau
Institut für Theoretische Informatik
Helmholtzplatz 1
98684 Ilmenau, Germany
ulf.schellbach@tu-ilmenau.de

Stefan Schirra
Otto-von-Guericke Universität
Magdeburg
Fakultät für Informatik
Universitätsplatz 2
39106 Magdeburg, Germany
stschirr@ovgu.de

Sven Scholz
Freie Universität Berlin
Institut für Informatik
Takustr. 9
14195 Berlin, Germany
scholz@inf.fu-berlin.de

Anna Schulze
Universität zu Köln
Zentrum für Angewandte Informatik
(ZAIK)
Gyrhofstr. 8c
50931 Köln, Germany
schulze@zpr.uni-koeln.de

Nils Schweer
Technische Universität Braunschweig
Institute of Operating Systems
and Computer Networks
Mühlenpfordtstr. 23
38106 Braunschweig, Germany
n.schweer@tu-bs.de

Johannes Singler
Universität Karlsruhe (TH)
Department of Computer Science,
Algorithmics II
Am Fasanengarten 5
76131 Karlsruhe, Germany
singler@ira.uka.de

Tobias Tscheuschner
Universität Paderborn
Department of Computer Science
Fürstenallee 11
33102 Paderborn, Germany
chessy@upb.de

Maik Weinard
Johann Wolfgang Goethe-Universität
Frankfurt am Main
Theoretische Informatik
Robert-Mayer-Str. 11-15
60325 Frankfurt am Main, Germany
weinard@thi.informatik.uni-frankfurt.de

Contents

Chapter 1. Foundations of Algorithm Engineering

Matthias Müller-Hannemann and Stefan Schirra

1.1 Introduction

Efficient algorithms are central components of almost every computer application. Thus, they become increasingly important in all fields of economy, technology, science, and everyday life. Most prominent examples of fields where efficient algorithms play a decisive role are bioinformatics, information retrieval, communication networks, cryptography, geographic information systems, image processing, logistics, just to name a few.

Algorithmics—the systematic development of efficient algorithms—is therefore a key technology for all kinds of ambitious and innovative computer applications. Unfortunately, over the last decades there has been a growing gap between algorithm theory on one side and practical needs on the other. As a consequence, only a small fraction of the research done in Algorithmics is actually used. To understand the reasons for this gap, let us briefly explain how research in Algorithmics has been done traditionally.

1.1.1 Classical Algorithmics

The focus of algorithm theory are simple and abstract problems. For these problems algorithms are designed and analyzed under the assumption of some abstract machine model like the "real RAM". The main contributions are provable worst-case performance guarantees on the running time with respect to the used model or on the quality of the computed solutions. In theoretical computer science, efficiency usually means polynomial time solvability.

Working with abstract problems and abstract machine models has several advantages in theory:

- Algorithms designed for such problems can be adapted to many concrete applications in different fields.
- Since most (classical) machine models are equivalent under polynomial time transformations, efficient algorithms are timeless.
- Worst-case performance guarantees imply efficiency also for problem instances of a kind which have not been expected at design time.
- It allows for a machine-independent comparison of worst-case performance without a need for an implementation.

From the point of view of algorithm theory, the implementation of algorithms is part of application development. As a consequence, also the evaluation of algorithms by experiments is only done by practitioners in the application domain. However, we should note that for many pioneers in the early days of Algorithmics, like Knuth, Floyd and others, implementing every algorithm they designed

M. Müller-Hannemann and S. Schirra (Eds.): Algorithm Engineering, LNCS 5971, pp. 1–15, 2010.

was standard practice. This changed significantly the more progress in the design of algorithms was made, and the more complicated the advanced data structures and algorithms became. Many people realized that the separation of design and analysis from implementations and experiments has caused the growing gap between theory and practice. Since about fifteen years, a group of researchers in Algorithmics started initiatives to overcome this separation.

1.1.2   The New Paradigm: Algorithm Engineering

In a much broader view of Algorithmics, implementation and experiments are of equal importance with design and analysis. This view has led to the new term *Algorithm Engineering*.

Is Algorithm Engineering just a new and fancy buzzword? Only a new name for a concept which has been used for many years? Here we argue that the departure from classical Algorithmics is fundamental: Algorithm Engineering represents a new paradigm. Thomas Kuhn [502] analyzed the structure of scientific revolutions and used the notion *paradigm* to describe a "coherent tradition of scientific research". According to Kuhn a paradigm shift takes place when a paradigm is in crisis and cannot explain compelling new facts.

What are the facts which require a new paradigm? Here we mention just a few examples, many more will be given in the following chapters of this book.

- The classical von-Neumann machine model has become more and more unrealistic, due to instruction parallelism, pipelining, branch prediction, caching and memory hierarchies, multi-threading, processor hierarchies, and parallel and distributed computing models.
- Design of algorithms focused on improving the asymptotical worst-case running time or the performance guarantee of approximation algorithms as the primary goals. This has led to many algorithms and to the design of data structures which contain some brilliant new ideas but are inherently impractical. Sometimes it is not clear that these algorithms are not implementable, however, their implementation seems to be so challenging that nobody ever tried to realize them.

  The disadvantage of studying asymptotical running times is that they may easily hide huge constant factors. Similarly, often huge memory requirements are simply ignored as long as they are polynomially bounded.

  As concrete examples we may cite some of the masterpieces in classical Algorithmics:

  1. Many (if not most) polynomial time approximation schemes (PTAS) like Arora's [48] or Mitchell's [577] for the traveling salesman problem (TSP) and related problems suffer from gigantic constant factors.
  2. Robins and Zelikovsky [677, 678] presented a family of algorithms which approximates the Steiner tree problem in graphs with a running time of $O(n^{2k+1} \log n)$, where k is a parameter which influences the performance guarantee. For large k, their algorithm achieves the currently best known approximation guarantee of 1.55. To improve upon the previously best

approximation guarantee of 1.598 by Hougardy and Prömel [414], it is necessary to choose $k > 2^{17}$. Moreover, an instance is required to have also more than 2^{17} terminals. Thus also n must be at least in this order.

3. The question whether a simple polygon can be triangulated in linear time was one of the main open problems in computational geometry for many years. In 1990 this problem was finally settled by Chazelle [163,164] who gave a quite complicated deterministic linear time algorithm. To the best of our knowledge this algorithm has never been implemented.

4. A geometric construction, known as an ϵ-cutting, provides a space partitioning technique for any finite dimension which has countless applications in computational geometry [165]. However, algorithms based on ϵ-cuttings seem to provide a challenge for implementation.

In practice constant factors matter a lot: in applications like computer assisted surgery, information retrieval by search engines, vehicle guidance, and many others, solutions have to be computed in almost real time. In other applications, the productivity of the user of a software tool is closely positively related to the tool's performance. Here any constant factor improvement is worth its investment. Thus, constant factor improvements often make the difference whether a tool is applied or not.

- The notion of efficiency as polynomial time solvability is often inappropriate. Even running times with small, but superlinear, polynomial degree may be too slow. Realistic applications in VLSI design, bioinformatics, or spatial data sets require to handle huge data sets. In such cases we usually can afford at most linear running time and space, often we need even sublinear time algorithms. In fact, the study of sublinear algorithms has recently emerged as a new field of research. Sublinear algorithms either look only at a small random sample of the input or process data as it arrives, and then extract a small summary.

- As stated above, the primary goal of algorithm design by theoreticians is efficiency. This has stimulated the development of highly sophisticated data structures—for many of them it is questionable or at least unclear whether they are implementable in a reasonable way.

  However, in practice, other design goals than efficiency are of similar, sometimes even higher importance: flexibility, ease of use, maintainability, ... In practice, simpler data structures and algorithms are preferred over very complex ones.

- Theoretical work on algorithms usually gives only a high-level presentation. The necessary details to start with an implementation are left to the reader. The transformation from a high-level description to a detailed design is far from trivial.

- The easiest start to study and to develop new algorithmic ideas is from problems which can be stated in a simple way. However, hand in hand with general progress in Computer Science and the availability of increased computational power, the applications themselves become more and more complex. Such applications require a careful modeling. It is often questionable whether insights gained for simplistic models carry over to more complex ones.

- Real-world input data has typically not the structure of the worst-case instances used in the theoretical analysis. Hence chances are high that the predicted performance is overly pessimistic.
- Good experimental work requires a substantial effort (time, manpower, programming skills, experience, ...).

    In many experimental setups, one performs experiments with randomly generated instances only. This can be strongly misleading. For example, random graphs have some nice structural properties which make them very different from real-world graphs. Another example arises in computational geometry: a uniformly sampled set of points will almost surely be in arbitrary position. In practice, however, instance are very likely not to fulfill this assumption.

    Unfortunately, working with real-world input data also has its problems: Such data may be unavailable for researchers or it may be proprietary. It is often extremely tedious to prepare such data for use in experiments.

In order to bridge the gap between theory and practice, Algorithm Engineering requires a broader methodology. However, Algorithm Engineering will have to keep the advantages of theoretical treatment:

- generality,
- reliability, and
- predictability from performance guarantees.

A central goal of Algorithm Engineering, or of good experimental algorithmic work, is to tease out the trade-offs, parameters and special cases that govern which algorithm is the right one for a specific setting. The hope is that Algorithm Engineering will increase its impact on other fields significantly. It will do so if the transfer to applications is accelerated.

1.1.3   Towards a Definition of Algorithm Engineering

Some of the spirit of Algorithm Engineering has already been present in the DIMACS Implementation Challenges (http://dimacs.rutgers.edu/Challenges/):

> "The DIMACS Implementation Challenges address questions of determining realistic algorithm performance where worst case analysis is overly pessimistic and probabilistic models are too unrealistic: experimentation can provide guides to realistic algorithm performance where analysis fails. Experimentation also brings algorithmic questions closer to the original problems that motivated theoretical work. It also tests many assumptions about implementation methods and data structures. It provides an opportunity to develop and test problem instances, instance generators, and other methods of testing and comparing performance of algorithms. And it is a step in technology transfer by providing leading edge implementations of algorithms for others to adapt."

Since 1990, where the First Challenge started with network flows and matching [438], a total of nine implementation challenges have been conducted. The term Algorithm Engineering was first[1] used with specificity and considerable impact in 1997, with the organization of the first Workshop on Algorithm Engineering (WAE'97) [56]. A couple of years ago, David Bader, Bernard Moret, and Peter Sanders define in [56]:

> "Algorithm Engineering refers to the process required to transform a pencil-and-paper algorithm into a robust, efficient, well tested, and easily usable implementation. Thus it encompasses a number of topics, from modeling cache behavior to the principles of good software engineering; its main focus, however, is experimentation."

We agree that all mentioned topics are important parts of Algorithm Engineering, but prefer a much broader view. A more general definition already appeared in the announcement of the ALCOM-FT Summer School on Algorithm Engineering in 2001:

> "Algorithm Engineering is concerned with the design, theoretical and experimental analysis, engineering and tuning of algorithms, and is gaining increasing interest in the algorithmic community. This emerging discipline addresses issues of realistic algorithm performance by carefully combining traditional theoretical methods together with thorough experimental investigations."

(posted in DMANET on May 17, 2001 by Guiseppe Italiano)

1.1.4 Methodology

The scientific method has its origin in the natural sciences. It views science as a cycle between theory and experimentation. Theory can inductively[2] and partially deductively—by means of a *theory* which is based on specific *assumptions*—build *experimentally falsifiable hypotheses* which are tested with experiments. The outcome of the experiments in turn may lead to new or refined hypotheses or theories, and so forth.

Just like software engineering, Algorithm Engineering is not a straight line process. Ideally, one would design an algorithm, implement it, and use it. However, the ultimate algorithm, i.e., the best algorithm for the task to be solved in an application, and the ultimate implementation are not known in advance. In Algorithm Engineering, a theoretical proof of suitability for a particular purpose is replaced by an experimental evaluation. For instance, such an experimental

---

[1] Peter Sanders [694] recently pointed out that the term Algorithm Engineering has already been used by Thomas Beth, in particular in the title of [98], but without a discussion.

[2] Inductive reasoning draws general conclusions from specific data, whereas deductive reasoning draws specific conclusions from general statements.

part checks whether the code produced is sufficiently efficient or in the case of approximation algorithms, sufficiently effective. Usually, the results of the experimental evaluation ask for a revision of design and implementation. Thus, as stated in the call for the DFG Priority Program 1307 [556]:

"The core of Algorithm Engineering is a cycle driven by falsifiable hypotheses." [www.algorithm-engineering.de]

Often, analysis is considered a part of this cycle, resulting in a cycle that consist of design, analysis, implementation and experimental evaluation of practicable algorithms. However, since the results of the analysis of the design will immediately give feedback to the designer and not go through implementation and experimentation first, it seems more appropriate to let the analysis phase be part of a cycle of its own together with the algorithm design. Thus, in Fig. 1.1, the core cycle in the center consists of design, implementation, and experimentation only.

Algorithm Engineering is always driven by real-world applications. The application scenario determines the hardware which has to be modeled most realistically. In a first phase of Algorithm Engineering not only a good machine model has to be chosen, but also the problem itself has to be modeled appropriately, a task, that is usually excluded from algorithm design. The results of an experimentation phase might then later on ask for a revision of the modeling phase, because the chosen models are not well suited. Sometimes an analysis of the chosen model can already reveal its inadequacy. This gives rise to another cycle consisting of applications, modeling, and analysis. The applications also provide real-world data for experimental evaluation and the experimental evaluation might reveal a need for particular type of data to further investigate certain aspects. Reliable components from software libraries can significantly ease the implementation task. Having said that, well engineered code that is sufficiently generic and reusable should be provided in a software library for future projects. For this purpose designing and implementing for reuse is important right from the beginning. Obviously, this is another cyclic dependency in Algorithm Engineering. We close our discussion with another quote from the call for the DFG Priority Program 1307:

"Realistic models for both computers and applications, as well as algorithm libraries and collections of real input data allow a close coupling to applications." [www.algorithm-engineering.de]

1.1.5 Visibility of Algorithm Engineering

Several conferences invite papers on Algorithm Engineering, but most of them only as one topic among many others. The first refereed workshop which was explicitly and exclusively devoted to Algorithm Engineering was the Workshop on Algorithm Engineering (WAE) held in Venice (Italy) on September 11-13, 1997. It was the start of a yearly conference series. At the 5th WAE in Aarhus,

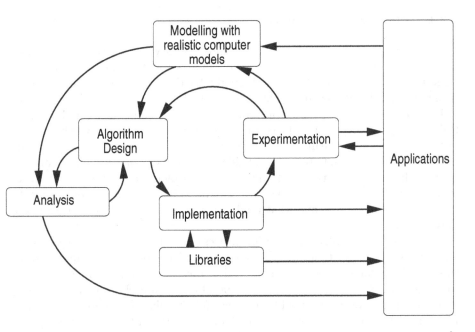

Fig. 1.1. The Algorithm Engineering process

Denmark, 2001 it was decided to become part of the leading European conference on algorithms ESA. Since then, the former WAE has been established as track B, the "Engineering and Applications" track. Only slightly after the WAE, the ALENEX (Algorithm Engineering and Experiments) conference series has been established. The ALENEX takes place every year, and is colocated with SODA, the annual ACM-SIAM Symposium on Discrete Algorithms. A relatively new conference devoted to Algorithm Engineering is SEA, the International Symposium on Efficient and Experimental Algorithms, until 2009 known as WEA (Workshop on Experimental Algorithms).

The primary journal for the field is the ACM Journal of Experimental Algorithmics (JEA) founded in 1996. The INFORMS Journal on Computing publishes papers with a connection to Operations Research, while more specialized journals like the Journal of Graph Algorithms and Applications invite papers with experiences (animations, implementations, experimentations) with graph algorithms. In 2009, the new journal Mathematical Programming Computation has been launched which is devoted to research articles covering computational issues in Mathematical Programming in a broad sense.

1.2 Building Blocks of Algorithm Engineering

This section is intended to provide a brief overview on the chapters of this book.

1.2.1   Modeling of Problems

Traditionally theoretical work on algorithms starts with a problem statement like this: "Given a set of points in the plane in arbitrary position, compute some structure X", where the structure X might be the convex hull, the Delaunay triangulation, the Steiner minimum tree, or the like.

Practitioners, however, work on problems of a very different kind: They typically face very complex problems. In many cases it is not clear which features of the application are really relevant or which can be abstracted away without sacrificing the solution. Often relevant side constraints are not formalized or may be difficult to formalize rigorously. Thus, given problems may be ill-posed. Moreover, quite often several objectives are present which are usually conflicting. In such cases we have to define what kind of trade-off between these goals we are looking for.

Hence, before the algorithm design process can start, a careful requirement analysis and formalization of the problem is needed. For complex applications, this modeling phase is a non-trivial and highly demanding task. In contrast to Algorithmics, its sister disciplines Operations Research and Mathematical Programming have a long tradition in careful modeling of complex problems. Finding or selecting an appropriate model can be crucial for the overall success of the algorithmic approach. Sometimes the borderline between polynomial time solvability and NP-hard problems is hidden in a small innocent-looking detail. The presence or non-presence of a single side constraint may lead to a switch in the complexity status. This, in turn, heavily influences the kind of algorithmic approaches you are considering in the design phase.

The question which side constraints should be incorporated into a model are sometimes more subtle than you may think. Let us give a concrete example from our own experience. Several years ago, the first author was faced with the problem of generating finite element meshes. Given a coarse surface mesh described by a set of triangular and quadrilateral patches the task was to create a refined all-quadrilateral mesh of a certain mesh density. Our cooperation partners— experienced engineers—advised us to use certain patterns (templates) for the refinement of the given original patches. We developed a model for this problem and realized quite soon that it turned out to be strongly NP-hard [581]. It took us a couple of years until we realized that the problem can be modeled in a much more elegant way if we drop the restrictions imposed by using templates. These side constraints only became part of the problem formulation because the engineers *thought* that they would help in solving the problem. After making this observation, we changed our model, and got nicer theoretical as well as improved practical results [596, 580].

Chapter 2 is intended to discuss which aspects have to be considered within the problem modeling process. It gives some general guidelines on how to model a complex problem, but also describes some inherent difficulties in the modeling process.

Modeling goes beyond a formalization of the problem at hand. Two models may be equivalent in their solution sets, but can behave very differently when we try to solve them. For example, this is a quite typical observation for integer linear programming problems. Which model performs best, also often depend on the algorithmic approach. Thus a model should be formulated (or reformulated) so that it best fits to the intended approach in the algorithm design phase. Here, modeling and design have to interact closely. Moreover, insights into the structure of the problem and its solution space may be required.

The art of modeling includes reformulation in a special framework like (mixed) integer linear programming, convex programming, constraint programming, or in the language of graph models. Algebraic modeling languages are helpful tools to formalize problems from practice.

1.2.2 Algorithm Design

Chapter 3 discusses some aspects of algorithm design, more precisely, simplicity, scalability, time-space trade-offs, and robustness issues. The chapter does not cover classical algorithm design paradigms as these are discussed in virtually every textbook on algorithms and data structures, at least implicitly. Among the many textbooks we recommend, for example, [191, 475, 562].

Simplicity of an algorithm has positive impact on its applicability. The section on simplicity describes several techniques how to achieve this goal. In view of the fact that we have to deal in many areas with rapidly growing data sets and instance sizes, scalability is another important feature. The corresponding section therefore presents fundamental techniques for developing scalable algorithms.

Time and space efficiency allow quite often for a trade-off, which can be exploited in Algorithm Engineering if it is possible to sacrifice one of these key performance parameters moderately in favor of the other. You invest a bit extra space and gain a nice speed-up. General techniques like lookup tables or preprocessing are typical applications of this idea. The tremendous power of preprocessing will also become visible in a case study on point-to-point shortest paths in Chapter 9.

The development of algorithms is usually based on abstraction and simplifying assumptions with respect to the model of computation and specific properties of the input. To make sure that an implemented algorithm works in practice, one has to take care on robustness issues. The section on robustness includes numerical robustness and related non-robustness issues in computational geometry. A discussion of such aspects is continued in Chapter 6 on Implementation.

1.2.3 Analysis

The purpose of algorithm analysis is to predict the resources that the algorithm requires. Chapter 4 briefly reviews and discusses the standard tools of algorithm analysis which one can find in any textbook on algorithms: worst-case and average-case analysis, as well as amortized analysis. Unfortunately, all these techniques have their drawbacks. Worst-case analysis is often too pessimistic with respect to instances occurring in practice, while average-case analysis assumes a certain probability distribution on the set of inputs which is difficult to choose so that it reflects typical instances.

Algorithm Engineering is interested in the analysis of algorithms for more realistic input models. If we allow arbitrary input, our analysis proves for many algorithms a poor worst-case performance. However, in practice some of these algorithms may perform pretty well while others confirm our poor predictions. To narrow the gap between theoretical prediction and practical observation, it is often helpful to study the structure of the input more carefully.

A possible compromise between worst and average case analysis is formulated in semi-random models, where an adversary is allowed to specify an arbitrary input which is then slightly perturbed at random. This has led to the development of so-called *smoothed analysis*. Chapter 4 gives a detailed exposition of this recent technique.

Another thread of research concerning realistic input models is to restrict the input by additional constraints. These constraints, motivated by insight into the nature of the application, then often lead to tighter predictions of the performance. It may also show that even with restricted input we have to expect a poor algorithmic worst-case performance.

The restriction of the input may also be parameterized. A parameter specifies by which extent a certain property is fulfilled. The analysis then depends also on such a structural parameter and not only on the size of an instance. Chapter 4 explains this idea for several applications in Computational Geometry.

The last part of the chapter on analysis is concerned with the analysis of experimental performance data (all other issues of experiments are postponed to Chapter 8). If we are interested in improving the performance of an algorithm, we should try to identify those operations which dominate the running time. Knowing the bottleneck operations will then guide us how we should redesign our algorithm. The concept of *representative operation counts* is one such technique to identify bottleneck operations through experiments.

Finally, Chapter 4 discusses how finite experiments can be used to study asymptotic performance in cases where a complete theoretical analysis remains elusive.

1.2.4 Realistic Computer Models

The RAM model has been a very successful computer model in algorithm theory. Many efficient methods have been designed using this model. While the RAM model was a reasonable abstraction of existing computers it is not a good model for modern computers anymore in many cases. The RAM model is basically a single processor machine with unlimited random access memory with constant access cost. Modern computers do not have a single memory type with uniform access cost anymore, but memory hierarchies with very different access costs. Nowadays data sets are often so huge that they do not fit in main memory of a computer.

Research on efficient algorithms gave rise to new models that allow for better designing and predicting practical efficiency of algorithms that exploit memory hierarchies or work with data sets requiring external memory usage. Disadvantages of the RAM with respect to modern computer architectures and new better, more realistic computer models and related algorithmic issues are discussed in Chapter 5. Especially, the chapter discusses models for external memory algorithms, I/O-efficiency, external memory data structures, and models for and algorithms exploiting caches.

Furthermore, modern computer architectures are not single processor machines anymore. Consequently, Chapter 5 also treats parallel computing models, less realistic ones like the PRAM as well as more realistic ones. We also look at simulating parallel algorithms for designing efficient external memory algorithms.

The models presented all address certain deficiencies of the RAM model and are more realistic models for modern computers. However, the models still do not allow for perfect prediction of the behavior of algorithms designed for those models in practice and thus can not render experiments unnecessary. Chapter 5 closes with highlighting some relevant success stories.

1.2.5 Implementation

Implementation is the lowest level and usually visited several times in the Algorithm Engineering process. It concerns coding the outcome of the algorithm design phase in the chosen programming language. Chapter 6 addresses correctness and efficiency as implementation aspects.

Of course, when we start with the implementation phase we assume that the algorithm we designed is correct, unless we aim for experiments that give us more insight into the correctness of a method. Thus Chapter 6 discusses preserving correctness in the implementation phase by program testing, debugging, checking, and verification. Especially program checking has proven to be very useful in Algorithm Engineering. However, it is not a pure implementation detail, but affects the algorithm design as well. As for numerical and geometric computing, preserving correctness is challenging because algorithm design often assumes exact real arithmetic whereas actual development environments only offer inherently imprecise floating-point arithmetic as a substitute. Therefore, a section of its own is devoted to exact geometric computation. Alternatively, one could design the algorithm such that it can deal with the imprecision of floating-point arithmetic, but this is not an implementation issue, but must be taken into account in the algorithm design phase already.

Efficiency in the implementation phase is treated in different ways. On one hand Chapter 6 considers the efficiency of the code produced, on the other we consider the efficiency of the coding process itself. While the first aspect is basically related to implementation tricks and issues regarding code generation by the compiler, implementing efficiently involves issues like programming environment and code reuse. Code reuse is two-sided. First, it means reusing existing code, especially using components of existing libraries, and second, it means implementing for reuse. The latter embraces flexibility, interface design, ease of use, and documentation and maintenance. The role of software libraries in Algorithm Engineering is discussed in the next chapter.

1.2.6 Libraries

Software libraries are both a very useful tool and a subject of its own in Algorithm Engineering. Good libraries provide well-tested, correct and efficient, well-engineered software for reuse in your projects and thus ease your implementation task. On the other hand, designing and engineering good software libraries is a primary goal of Algorithm Engineering. Software libraries have the potential to enhance the technology transfer from classical Algorithmics to practical programming as they provide algorithmic intelligence. Algorithm Engineering for software libraries is more difficult since you do not a priori know the application context of your software and hence can not tailor it towards this context. Therefore, flexibility and adaptability are important design goals for software libraries.

There are software libraries for various programming levels, from I/O libraries via libraries providing basic algorithms and data structures to algorithm libraries for special tasks. The former lower level libraries are often shipped with the compiler or are part of the development platform. Libraries also come in various shapes. Sometimes, collections of software devoted to related tasks is already called a library. However, a loose collection of programs does not make an easy-to-use, coherent and extendible library. Usually, in order to call a software collection a library you at least require that its components also seamlessly work together. Chapter 7 presents selected software libraries in the light of Algorithm Engineering, in particular the STL, the Boost Libraries, CGAL and LEDA. Of course, providing a comprehensive overview of the functionality provided by these libraries is way beyond the scope of this chapter. Besides a quick overview on the areas addressed by these libraries, e. g., data structures, graph algorithms, and geometry, the role of Algorithm Engineering in the design of the libraries is discussed. Let us exemplify the latter for LEDA.

Initially, the designers of LEDA did not think that the development of the library would involve any additional research in Algorithmics. However, soon they learned that the gap between theory and practice is not that easy to close. While their first implementation of geometric algorithms often failed because of rounding errors, the present code implements exact geometric computation and handles all kinds of degeneracies.

1.2.7 Experiments

As we have explained earlier, experiments have a key role in the Algorithm Engineering cycle. The design and planning of insightful experiments, the running of experiments and their evaluation are challenging tasks which contain many pitfalls.

Jon Bentley has pointed out at several occasions[3] that sometimes already little experiments can uncover surprising insights. In general, however, experimentation requires some careful planning and systematics. The first step is to define

---

[3] For example, at an invited talk of WEA 2006.

the goals of an experiment to find out what type of experiment is needed, what to measure and which factors shall be explored. Usually, our implementation has to be adapted slightly to report the information we are interested in (by adding operations counts, timing operations or extra output messages). The next step is to select suitable test instances. Since results of experiments on random input data are often of very little relevance for real applications one needs benchmark test sets of a wide variety. Thus, test data generation and the set-up and maintenance of test data libraries are very important.

One crucial although all to often neglected issue when conducting experiments in Computer Science is to ensure the reproducibility. At the very least this means to document *all factors* which may have a direct or indirect influence on the computation and to use version control to store the whole computational environment (including not only programming source code but also the compiler and external software libraries).

The final important step in the experimentation process is to analyze the collected data, to draw conclusions by statistical methods and to report the findings. Chapter 8 is devoted to all these issues.

In contrast to the natural sciences and to neighboring fields like Mathematical Programming and Operations Research, Computer Science has no long-standing tradition of doing experiments. Although much cheaper than in natural sciences, experimentation is a very time consuming process which is often underestimated. In fact, a systematic treatment of the issues discussed in Chapter 8 is usually not contained in the curriculum for students in Computer Science. Thus, it is no surprise that also many research papers that report on experimental results do not follow the state-of-the-art. With new courses on Algorithm Engineering this will hopefully change in the future.

1.2.8 Success Stories of Algorithm Engineering

By now, there are already many well-known, highly competitive companies like Google Inc., Akamai Technologies, Inc., and Celera Genomics Group which owe their strong position in the market to a large extent also from Algorithm Engineering.

One of the most impressive examples for steady progress over the years— due to Algorithm Engineering methodology—is Linear Programming and the simplex algorithm. Let us briefly review some milestones of our ability to solve Linear Programs [103]. In 1949, when George B. Dantzig invented the simplex algorithm, it took 120 man days to compute by hand the optimal solution for a problem instance with 9 constraints and 77 variables (a famous "diet problem"). In 1952, one was able to solve a problem with 48 constraints and 71 variables in 18 hours at the National Bureau of Standards. About twenty years later, in 1970, the record was to solve a linear program with about 4000 constraints and 15000 variables. For about additional twenty years, there was only marginal progress.

In 1987, Bob Bixby cofounded CPLEX Optimization, Inc., a software company marketing algorithms for linear and mixed-integer programming and started to work on CPLEX. Two years later, a famous problem from the netlib, degen4, with 4420 constraints and 6711 variables was not solved on a supercomputer of that time, a CRAY, after 7 days by CPLEX 1.0. It is interesting to note that the very same code can solve this problem on a current desktop in 1.5 days. But with the following versions of CPLEX, a dramatic and steady improvement could be achieved. Already in 1992, degen4 was solved in 12.0 seconds by CPLEX 2.2. In 2000, a huge test model with 5,034,171 constraints and 7,365,337 variables was solved in 1880.0 seconds by CPLEX 7.1. Bob Bixby reports speed-up due to improvements of algorithms from CPLEX 1.0 to the CPLEX 10.0 by a factor of > 2360 [4]. An additional speed-up by a factor of about 800 comes from improved machine performance. This is not the end of the story. Similar achievements can be reported as to the solution of Integer Linear Programs.

What have been the key factors of CPLEX' success? Progress become possible by the integration of new mathematical insights (improvements of pricing, ratio test, update, simplex phase I, numerical stability, and perturbation) and cutting-edge preprocessing. Many ideas lay already around, but have first been rigorously engineered. With continuous testing on benchmark libraries of test instances, a large number of variants, heuristics and parameter settings have been evaluated systematically. Of course, such progress is driven by individuals and their enthusiasm for their work.

In Chapter 9 on Case Studies three other success stories are presented. Two of them stem from combinatorial optimization (shortest paths and Steiner trees), and one from computational geometry (Voronoi diagrams). Each case study traces the "historical development"—what has been achieved since the beginning of intensive study on some particular problem? The purpose of this chapter is to illustrate all aspects of Algorithm Engineering and their mutual interaction.

Let us sketch these ideas for the geometric case study which is about Voronoi diagrams, more precisely, about Voronoi diagrams for point sites and its dual, the Delaunay diagram, and for Voronoi diagrams of line segments. In both cases we consider standard Euclidean metric only. Since these diagrams have many applications they have been the subject of many implementation efforts. As discussed above in Chapters 3 and 6, precision caused robustness problems are a major issue in the implementation of geometric algorithms. Voronoi diagrams are among the few geometric problems where both main stream approaches to handle the robustness problem have been applied successfully.

On one hand, we know by now how to compute Voronoi diagrams of points and line segments exactly, handling all degenerate cases. Thanks to the Algorithm Engineering in exact geometric computation techniques have been developed that allow us to compute Voronoi diagrams of points efficiently. Such techniques are used in the Voronoi code provided by software libraries CGAL and LEDA. The computation of Voronoi diagrams of line segments involves non-linear geometric objects, and thus the slow down due to exact computation is more noticeable. CGAL and a LEDA extension package provide code for the exact computation of Voronoi diagrams of line segments.

---

[4] Private communication.

On the other hand, topological approaches have been successfully applied to Voronoi diagrams, initially especially by Sugihara and its co-workers [765, 764, 619]. These topological approaches use fast floating-point arithmetic to compute something meaningful, but not necessarily the topologically exact diagram for the given input, in particular with respect to the numerical part of the output. But they do guarantee certain properties of the combinatorial part of the output, for example, the underlying graph of the computed diagram is always planar. The approach has been applied to Voronoi diagrams of points at first and then been extended to Voronoi diagrams of line segments. The algorithm engineering work now culminates in Held's VRONI software [385], which is a master piece of algorithm engineering in the context of robust geometric software. However, it does not compute the exact solution nor does it handle degenerate cases, but whenever the guaranteed properties of the only approximately correct diagram suffice, it is the matter of choice because of its efficiency.

1.2.9 Challenges

In view of the mentioned success stories of Algorithm Engineering there is no doubt that this discipline has the potential to "shape the world". However, since Algorithm Engineering is still a relatively young, but evolving discipline, there are many challenges: research problems on methodology that are worthy to invest a significant effort. The last chapter of the book tries to point out some of them. It discusses challenges for Algorithm Engineering as a new discipline as well as challenges related to different phases of the Algorithm Engineering cycle.

1.2.10 Further Topics — Not Covered in This Book

A book like ours cannot cover every topic related to Algorithm Engineering which deserves attention. We clearly had to make a choice to keep the size of this book within reasonable limits.

Fortunately, several special topics have already been covered in a survey collection on Experimental Algorithmics [288]. This made our decision easier to leave out some of them. For *parallel computing* which is likely to have an increasing importance in the coming years we refer to the survey by Bader, Moret and Sanders [56]. Likewise, *distributed computing* has been surveyed by Spirakis and Zaroliagis [750]. Further interesting topics in relation with Algorithm Engineering include randomized and online algorithms, sublinear algorithms, high performance computing and the huge field of (meta-)heuristics.

Finally, we recommend the recent essays by Peter Sanders who presents the general methodology of Algorithm Engineering and illustrates it by two striking case studies on minimum spanning trees [694] and sorting [695].

Chapter 2. Modeling

Markus Geyer, Benjamin Hiller*, and Sascha Meinert

2.1 Introduction

The very first step in Algorithm Engineering is to get a thorough understanding of the problem to be solved. This understanding can then be used to construct a formal model of the problem, which is the starting point for further investigations.

To get an idea of modeling in this context imagine three developers meeting at the coffee machine and talking about their new tasks they have to complete. In a brief version their tasks are as follows.

1. The first developer takes part in a *Sudoku* challenge, where different companies present their software to solve this problem as fast as possible. The Sudoku puzzle game consists of a 9-by-9 grid of cells, which is divided into nine 3-by-3 subsquares. Some of the cells contain numbers from 1 to 9. The task is now to complete the remaining cells such that each number occurs exactly once in each row, column, and 3-by-3 subsquare. Figure 2.1 shows an example of a Sudoku puzzle.

	5		9		6		3	
4	6		5		1		7	8
			4		7			
3	2	1				7	4	9
7	4	6				8	5	1
			8		2			
2	7		1		5		8	6
			8		3		9	2

Fig. 2.1. An example of a Sudoku puzzle

2. The second developer works in a project whose aim is to plan printed circuit board assembly. The software should optimize the time the robot arm needs to put all electronic components on their specific place on the board.

---

* Supported by the DFG research group "Algorithms, Structure, Randomness" (Grant number GR 883/10-3, GR 883/10-4).

M. Müller-Hannemann and S. Schirra (Eds.): Algorithm Engineering, LNCS 5971, pp. 16–57, 2010.

3. The last developer works on a *scheduling* software for a company that runs garages. This software should help the technicians of these garages, who usually look at the cars waiting for repair in the morning and determine in which order they are going to repair them. When the customers put their cars in the garage, they are told the time when the repair of the car is expected to be finished. The technician has to take these times into account when making his plan, since he does not want to upset the customers.

By the time all three developers finished explaining their tasks to each other, they had all drunk their fourth cup of coffee. But why did it take so long? To explain his tasks each developer had to describe his respective application and the algorithmic problem derived from it, namely, which data is available, which requirements exist, how the problem was solved up to now, what should be improved, and how this goal can be achieved. Furthermore, the explanation of a task's background and its description involve highly specific elements and certain special cases, which all require a long while of explaining.

Now let us review the problems. All three tasks involve making decisions subject to problem-specific requirements in order to solve the problem. The goal is to create models that capture these requirements but can be applied to a wider range of situations. Thus, *modeling is the procedure of abstracting from actual problem instances at hand to problem classes that still contain the essential details of the problem structure.* Hence, *models* should describe the given problem, be an abstraction of the instances at hand, and contain no contradictions. Such a model constitutes the input of the next phase in the process of Algorithm Engineering, sparing others from unnecessary problem details.

The emphasis here is that the model should really be useful to actually solve the underlying problem. In particular, this implies that important aspects of the problem must not be abstracted away or oversimplified. Classical algorithm theory tends to consider rather artificial problems and models which are more or less contrived in order to get analytical results. One purpose of Algorithm Engineering is to overcome this artificial gap and contribute to solving real problems. On the other hand, building a model that takes into account every aspect in detail may not be of help either, since it may be too complicated to design an algorithm for. Therefore, modeling boils down to finding an appropriate level of abstraction that captures the essential real structure and omits less important aspects.

We see, modeling is in general a challenging task and strongly relies on experience. To have a common ground, modelers should be acquainted with some basic modeling frameworks presented later in this chapter. Namely, these are graphs (see Section 2.3.1), mixed integer programming (see Section 2.3.2), constraint programming (see Section 2.3.3), and algebraic modeling languages (AML, see Section 2.3.4).

Many books have been written concerning the design and the performance analysis of algorithms. Unfortunately, classical algorithm literature assumes an existing formal model. At best, modeling is taught by presenting a flood of specific examples and case studies. Of course some experience is gained studying these approaches. But in general they lack a description or discussion of

1. the model's development process,
2. how appropriate a model is, according to a problem,
3. a rating of model selection, according to chosen algorithmic approaches.

As mentioned before, textbooks on algorithms usually assume that models already exist and omit a discussion of these points. For many specific models solutions exist which are well analyzed and documented.

Advantages of models are generalization, faster explanation of problems to others and possibly the availability of well analyzed solutions. Standard models used in theoretical research often do not reflect properties which are inherent to practical applications. Some reasons for this might be over-general modeling and unrealistic assumptions. This has contributed to the gap between theory and practice as described in Chapter 1.

Consequently, Algorithm Engineering places more emphasis on modeling. Being the first step in the Algorithm Engineering process, modeling needs to be carried out carefully. It is crucial to follow some guidance and to avoid pitfalls. Otherwise, if done in an *ad hoc* way, successive steps of the Algorithm Engineering process may fail. Note that it is not possible to establish a sharp border between modeling and designing. Depending on the problem instance the model brings forward design decisions or at least strongly influences them. An example where the border is blurred due to decisions made in modeling affecting design is given in Section 2.4.1. The impact of modeling decisions on the design phase can be estimated by looking at the example which we present in Section 2.4.2.

Before starting with the modeling process some fundamentals, that modelers should be aware of, are presented in Section 2.2. The modeling process itself can be subdivided into three phases.

First, the problem has to be understood and formalized. It is very important to spend quite some time and effort on this topic as all following steps rely on this first one. Thus, in Section 2.2.2 several ideas are collected as well as suggestions on how to deal with common problems. Applying them, the problem can be abstracted and a formal problem specification is gained.

Second, starting from the precise specification of the problem — the problem model found in the first phase —, the problem is reformulated towards one or more candidates of solution approaches which we simply call *"solution approach models"*. A checklist of questions arising here is given in Section 2.2.4. To formulate solution approaches knowledge about common modeling frameworks is indispensable. Hence, Section 2.3 gives a brief introduction to four modeling frameworks out of the many existing ones. They allow for the application of many solution approaches or techniques that have already been developed. In addition, discussing problems become easier when all participants are familiar with modeling techniques.

Finally, the results have to be evaluated and verified (see Section 2.2.5). In the case of unsatisfactory results, the procedure has to start over again with the feedback gained up to then. In general, we can say modeling is the first step in the process of Algorithm Engineering, which is to understand the problem, get a formalized version of it and create a model which allows the application of solution approaches.

The process of modeling will be clarified by some examples, which are used throughout this chapter. In particular, we will look at the well-known Sudoku puzzle, the traveling salesman problem, a scheduling problem from [452] and a car manufacturing problem described in [15].

Modeling is a process which cannot be done in a straight forward way. Hence, Section 2.4 deals with some further issues one needs to be aware of. First, some unrealistic assumptions often found in theoretical research are discussed. Next, a problem decomposition approach is presented. If problems get too complex, they are decomposed into easier ones which are still challenging. Furthermore, we indicate the relationship to algorithm design and try to point out the border between modeling and design, which is not always clear. Section 2.5 concludes this chapter.

2.2   Modeling Fundamentals

Before solving a problem much work has to be done. There are essential steps every algorithm engineer should be aware of. In modeling these are often a little vague. Nevertheless, besides describing these steps, this section gives checklists which should help modelers in fulfilling their tasks. To have a common ground, the basic concepts used throughout this chapter are presented in Section 2.2.1. Having read this part, we can start with the modeling process.

First, the problem has to be analyzed. Section 2.2.2 gives the modeler some pointers for asking the right questions about the problems at hand. These questions should provide a basis for further examinations of the problem, until a satisfactory understanding of the given application is achieved. With this knowledge we specify the problem or the *requirements* and thus gain the *problem model*. The next step is to model one or more *solution approaches* using the problem model as a source. Hence, in Section 2.2.4 some fundamental guidelines for the second modeling step are given. Additionally, some possible pitfalls for this stage are shown. Often the modeling process itself will take some time to complete and the resulting model should be appropriate for the given application. This verification process is discussed in Section 2.2.5. Concluding with Section 2.2.6 some inherent difficulties and pitfalls for the modeling process will be addressed. All points in this section could be covered in more detail, but since this book is not solely about modeling, we rather give the reader some overview of the used techniques and refer to further literature at the appropriate places.

2.2.1   Fundamentals

As mentioned before, one property of a model is its abstraction from the former original application. Another property is the purpose of the model. Models may either specify a problem, describe a solution approach, or both. Obviously, a problem model has to specify the *requirements* of the application. For each problem class, e. g., decision-, construction-, counting-, and optimization problems, the model has to specify what a valid solution looks like. In the case of an optimization problem the objective function, which indicates the quality of a solution, must be defined. A model can be specified using one of the following three formalisms.

Informal specification is colloquial where no formal concept is used. Anyway, it should be as precise as possible. In most cases, this is the first step in practice, e. g., when talking with a customer.

Semi-formal specification is again colloquial but uses some formal concepts, e. g., graphs or sets. This is the first step towards abstraction from the underlying problem.

Formal specification uses mathematical concepts to describe requirements, valid solutions, and objective functions.

Obviously, increasing the formalism leads to an increasing abstraction level. When specifying a model we use the following concepts.

Variable is used to denote certain decision possibilities.

Parameter is a value or property of a problem instance, which is used as an abstraction in the model.

Constraint is an abstract description of a given requirement.

For clarification consider the following example where two workers have to produce an item on a certain machine. Because they are differently skilled working on these machines Bill needs 30 minutes to produce one item, whereas John only needs 15 minutes. We now want to answer the question: How many items can be produced in an eight hour shift by each worker? The number of items that can be created is denoted by the variable x. The question was how many items can be produced in one eight hour shift. We introduce a model parameter w which stands for the working time needed to complete one item. Combining these elements, we get the constraint

$$w \cdot x = 8.$$

In this example, one worker corresponds to one instance. Putting them into the model and caring about the minutes and hours we arrive at

$$\text{Bill} \quad 0.5 \cdot x = 8,$$
$$\text{John} \quad 0.25 \cdot x = 8.$$

Thus, we exactly modeled, what has been described as the problem earlier. But in a certain way we abstracted from reality. We did not and maybe cannot model everything. For example, we assumed an average working speed and do not consider fluctuations in the worker's productivity.

Now having introduced the concepts that are necessary to create a model, we next want to discuss the problem analysis phase of the modeling process.

2.2.2 Problem Analysis

One of the most important steps in the process of Algorithm Engineering is a good comprehension of the problem. Each successive step builds upon the prior ones. Faults, particularly during the first step, may pervade the whole modeling process.

The following overview is inspired by Skiena's book on Algorithm Design [742]. It should be considered when facing a problem. Of course this list is not exhaustive, but gives some good starting points. Some aspects of this section will not be very important for the modeling of the problem itself, but they become important in the design phase of the engineering process.

1. What exactly does the input consist of?
2. What exactly are the desired results or output?
3. Is it possible to divide constraints into hard and soft ones?
   The difference is the following: Hard constraints have to be fulfilled, whereas soft constraints should be fulfilled, i. e., they are goals. Often, soft constraints can be formulated as part of the objective function.

In these first points the very basic structure of the problem is studied, and it is quite clear that any omissions in this stage may render all following steps more or less futile.

4. Can variables or parameters of the problem be divided into important and unimportant ones?
   This will serve two different goals. At first, the problem can be understood more easily, which makes it more convenient to handle subsequent algorithm engineering phases. Second, the correlation between input and output becomes more meaningful. Removing an important input will in most cases result in an output that doesn't correspond to a solution of the original problem. Often tests and experiments have to be done to decide whether the right parameters and variables were chosen or not.
5. Is the problem of a certain problem class, or does it imply a certain solution approach?
   Examples might be solving a numerical problem, graph algorithm problem, geometric problem, string problem, or set problem. Check if the problem may be formulated in more than one way. If so, which formulation seems to be the easiest one to actually solve the problem?

Answering all these questions will provide the essential aspects of a given problem. They will mostly impact how the problem is modeled, but might also suggest solution approaches. Note that it is not necessarily clear how to obtain input and output parameters or constraints. Thus, check whether a small input example can be constructed, which is small enough to solve by hand, and analyze what exactly happens when it is solved. Obviously, for complex problems, e. g., the public railroad transportation problem (see Section 2.4.2), the large number of choices and requirements related to the problem makes it difficult to distinguish between important aspects and less important ones.

Another important aspect of the problem analysis is the imprecision of data. It will impact the quality of any solution quite strongly. To highlight this aspect, we will address two major cases where imprecision of data is likely to be encountered in the modeling process. The first one is a discrepancy between the model of computation which is being used in classical algorithm theory and the reality of actual hardware and operating systems. In theory an arbitrary precision for any kind of computation is assumed, while real computers can efficiently handle only computations with fixed precision. This problem is covered in more detail in Section 2.4.1 and in Chapter 5. But we should always be aware of the level of precision we can guarantee.

The second scenario where imprecision matters comes into play when imperfect information in general affects the problem in question. This could be the problem of imperfect input data, but also the problem of very imprecise problem-settings has to be addressed. We will give some examples of the latter in Section 2.4.1.

If we are dealing with real-world applications it can happen quite easily that we have only imperfect input data or imperfect constraints. For example if the input data is some kind of measured data it is almost certain to contain some kind of error, depending on the measurement process, or more extreme, if certain input data is just gained by a process like polling some customers, it is assured that the resulting data is a little vague. Another important point is that in real-world applications the parameters of the problems change quite fast over time. For example the cost for some raw materials or insufficient availability of employees due to ill health is not a fixed number, but changes over time. Often these changes are very limited, but all such data has to be handled with care and it should be ensured (or at least analyzed) that no small perturbation of the input, regarding the imperfect data, should yield a huge difference in the solution. This connection between input and output is analyzed in the field of sensitivity analysis, which we will not cover in this section. For more information on this topic we refer to a comprehensive book by Satelli et al. [689].

In order to handle vague and uncertain data in the model, there are several approaches that could be taken. One could try to obtain new sharpened versions of the vague and imperfect data. But, in general, this is either not possible or too expensive to obtain. Additionally, dependencies between the relevant variables are often only known approximately [122]. In reality, vague data or constraints are often sharpened artificially. But such artificial sharpening can distort the image of reality up to a complete loss of reality [384]. In such cases it is necessary to integrate some kind of vagueness into the model formulation itself. But of course we must guarantee a precise and mathematically sound processing for sharp and vague information. The theory of fuzzy sets is very well suited for this task, since it is possible to model and process not only sharp information, but also not exactly measurable or vague information in a uniform way. The fundamental approach is to provide the means to take into account vague, uncertain and sharp data into a common decision basis, on which every decision in the solution of the problem is founded. In fuzzy theory such a possibility is provided by using fuzzy approximate reasoning methods, like the fuzzy decision support system described in [324]. For further details on this topic we refer the reader to some examples for the application of this methods in [324] or [272]. More general information for information modeling with fuzzy sets can be found in [271]. Finally, it should be noted that by using vague information and avoiding highly detailed specifications it is in some cases possible to actually reduce the complexity of certain problems in comparison to the sharp version [384].

In modeling, the wheel does not need to be reinvented. Many problems are well studied. Thus, the first task is to check similar problems for existing approaches that might be applicable to the given problem. Therefore, it is important to know classical and generic models that have been developed so far. A short overview of popular types of models can be found in Section 2.3.

Hopefully, the above checklist and discussion helps in getting an understanding of the structure and the requirements of the problem. After analysis is completed, a model for the problem needs to be specified.

2.2.3 Problem Specification: Examples

Let us come back to the developers' problems presented in the introduction. Namely, these are Sudoku, printed circuit (PC) board assembly and scheduling a garage. In the following we present specification models for these problems in order to give an impression on how a specification model might look like.

Before starting with the specification models, we introduce an additional problem that will be used for explaining various modeling frameworks in Section 2.3, too. The problem arises in a *car manufacturing company*, which operates several plants, each of which may produce some of the car models out of the company's product range. The plants need to organize their production such that they meet the stock requirements of the retail centers to which the company is bound by contract. The car company is also responsible for delivering the manufactured cars to the retail centers. The management requires the production and delivery to be as cost-efficient as possible.

In the following, these four problems are formalized into simple mathematical models.

Sudoku. Let $N := \{1, \ldots, 9\}$ and $N' := \{1, \ldots, 3\}$. An instance of a Sudoku puzzle can be described by a set S of triples $(i, j, n) \in N^3$, meaning that the value n is prescribed at position (i, j). A solution can then be modeled as a function $f : N^2 \to N$, which provides for each row-column pair the value at this position. For instance, the requirement that all cells in row 1 have distinct values is equivalent to stipulating that the image of row 1 is exactly N, i. e., f has to satisfy

$$\{f(1, j) \mid j \in N\} = N.$$

To express this requirement for the subsquares, we introduce the set C_{ij} for $i, j \in N'$ that exactly contains the cells corresponding to subsquare (i, j)

$$C_{ij} := \{(3(i-1) + i', 3(j-1) + j') \mid (i', j') \in N' \times N'\}.$$

The model can then be written as

$$
\begin{aligned}
f(i,j) &= n & \forall (i,j,n) \in S, \\
\{f(i,j) \mid j \in N\} &= N & i \in N, \\
\{f(i,j) \mid i \in N\} &= N & j \in N, \\
f(C_{ij}) &= N & (i,j) \in N' \times N'.
\end{aligned}
$$

The sets C_{ij} will also show up in later models. Finally, note that the Sudoku puzzle is a pure feasibility problem.

Traveling Salesman Problem (TSP) and Board Assembly. We consider n cities, numbered from 1 to n. Every round trip through all cities can be expressed as a permutation $\pi \colon \{1, \dots, n\} \to \{1, \dots, n\}$. Naturally, the cost for traveling between two cities can be put in a matrix $C = (c_{i,j})_{1 \le i,j \le n}$. The cost $c(\pi)$ for a round trip π is then given by

$$
c(\pi) := \sum_{i=1}^{n-1} c_{\pi(i),\pi(i+1)} + c_{\pi(n),\pi(1)}.
$$

The task is to find a permutation π with minimum cost. Note that throughout this chapter we assume symmetric costs and thus a symmetric matrix. When looking at the problem of printed circuit board assembly, we observe that it can be interpreted as a TSP. The mounting holes are the "cities" to be visited, the robot arm corresponds to the salesman, and the cost matrix reflects the time needed for the robot arm to be moved between mounting holes.

Scheduling (a garage). We first observe that although the company runs several garages, they can be scheduled separately (assuming that jobs are not transferred between different sites). The interesting objects here are the cars that need to be repaired, so let us number them in some way and put them into the set J. We will call each car to be repaired a *job*. Each job j can be described by its (estimated) duration p_j and the agreed due date d_j, which is the time the customer wants to fetch the repaired car. For simplicity, we also assume that each garage can handle only one job at each point of time. Then, the order of repair jobs can again be expressed as a permutation, and we are looking for one that respects all due dates. Each permutation corresponds to a sequence of starting times s_j for each job.

However, it may not always be possible to come up with such a permutation, and the fact that there is no feasible solution is of no help to the technician. A way out of this problem is to allow the due dates to be violated if necessary but requiring them to be respected as much as possible. This can be done by introducing a *soft constraint*, i. e., by penalizing the violation of each due date and trying to minimize overall violation. To this end, we introduce the *tardiness* t_j for each job j, which is exactly the violation of its due date

$$
t_j := \max(0, s_j + p_j - d_j).
$$

We also introduce weights w_j for each tardiness, allowing the technician to express which customers are more important than others. All in all, we want to minimize the following objective

$$\sum_{j \in J} w_j t_j.$$

Note that introducing the soft constraints converted the problem from a feasibility problem to an optimization problem.

This problem is known as the single-machine weighted tardiness scheduling problem.

Car manufacturing. Abstracting from the general description, we can identify the following relevant entities:
- a set M of all car models that are build by the car company,
- a set of plants P,
- for each plant $p \in P$ a set of car models $M_p \subseteq M$ that can be produced at this plant,
- a set of retailers R,
- for each retailer $r \in R$ a vector $d_r \in \mathbb{Z}^{|M|}$ specifying the retailer's demand for each car model.

We look for
- a matrix $X = (x_{p,m})_{p \in P, m \in M}$ that prescribes the number of cars for model m that are to be produced at plant p, and
- a matrix $Y = (y_{p,m,r})_{p \in P, m \in M, r \in R}$, where $y_{p,m,r}$ indicates how many cars of model m will go to retailer r from plant p.

The matrices X and Y have to satisfy the following requirements:
1. the demand of each retailer has to be met, and
2. the number of cars of model m leaving plant p must be exactly $x_{p,m}$.

The goal is to fulfill the requirements of the retailers at minimum cost. But what are the costs? Presumably the production of a car at a plant incurs some cost, which may be different for each plant. Moreover, transportation from a plant to a retailer will also incur some cost. Assuming that the cost for producing a car at a plant is constant for each car model and that the cost for transporting a car from the plant to the retailer is also fixed and does not depend on the car model, we can model the total cost as follows. Given
- a matrix $A = (a_{p,m})_{p \in P, m \in M}$ describing the cost for producing one unit of car model m at plant p, and
- a matrix $B = (b_{p,r})_{p \in P, r \in R}$ providing the cost for transporting one car from plant p to retailer r

we look for matrices X and Y that minimize the total cost $c(X, Y)$ defined by

$$c(X, Y) := \sum_{p \in P, m \in M} a_{p,m} x_{p,m} + \sum_{m \in M} \sum_{p \in P, r \in R} b_{p,r} y_{p,m,r}.$$

Note that this model may be a drastic simplification of the original problem which may feature much more complex constraints or possibilities. For instance, there may be more than one way to transport cars from a plant to a retailer, and each such way may have a limited capacity or a complex cost structure.

These are the four problem specification models we will use as an input for modeling solution approaches respectively. Note that *no best way to model* exists. These formulations strongly depend on the requirements someone has for a specific problem. The same holds for modeling a solution approach. Nevertheless, the following subsection provides checkpoints, which should be considered when advancing to the next step of modeling.

2.2.4   Modeling a Solution Approach

So far, the problem has been analyzed and it was specified using some formalisms. The next step is to transform or use this problem model to gain a solution approach model. Again we provide a checklist that should be processed carefully. The points are bundled into three themes. First, constraints have to be identified.

1. What constraints have to be considered to solve the problem?
2. How do these constraints affect the solution of the problem?
3. Is it possible to apply some simple post-processing to take them into account or do they change the solution space fundamentally?
4. Is the approach adequately chosen to formulate all necessary constraints with reasonable certainty?

Answering these questions often implies a certain model depending on the modeler's knowledge on certain domains. Modelers tend to be focused on models they are used to (see Section 2.3).

Second, the problem has to be analyzed again. Now the aim is to find properties a solution approach may possibly exploit. Often the same questions arise in the design or even the implementation phase. However, as they sometimes have an impact on the modeling phase too and modeling cannot be strictly separated from designing, they should be considered anyway.

5. Can the problem be decomposed into subproblems?
   Usually the decomposition of problems will be handled in the design phase of the Algorithm Engineering process. But facing very complex problems, it might be useful to split them early, if possible. These still challenging subproblems need to be modeled separately (see Section 2.4.2).
6. How does accuracy impact the application? Is the exact or optimal answer needed or would an approximation be satisfactory?
   This point usually has to be taken into account in the design or even in the implementation phase. There, an algorithm or approach will be selected for solving the problem.
7. How important is efficiency for the application? Is the time frame in which an instance of the problem should be solved one second, one minute, one hour, or one day?

8. How large are typical problem instances? Will it be working on 10 items, 1,000 items or 1,000,000 items?
9. How much time and effort can be invested in implementing an algorithm? Will there be a limit of a few days such that only simple algorithms can be coded? Or is the emphasis on finding sophisticated algorithms such that experiments (see Chapter 8) could be done with a couple of approaches in order to find the best one?

The last two items belong to the field of real-world constraints. Even if they come into effect at a later phase in the Algorithm Engineering process, they will impact the modeling process quite strongly.

Hence, in practice real-world constraints, like time constraints or budget constraints, have quite a great influence on the modeling process. In general, finding a model quickly is a good thing. But finding a simple model that is easy to understand and appropriate, is much more important.

Thus, if more than one model has been requested and was built, the question arises which models should be chosen that proceed to the designing phase. At this point the introduction of several common types of models is deferred to Section 2.3. For now, the following list contains points which help rating a given model. Depending on this rating a decision has to be made about which models to discard and which to work out. Taking common practice into account, some points are derived which can usually be found in the field of software engineering.

Simplicity. The easier the structure of a model, the easier it might be to understand. Furthermore, deciding which methods to choose in the design step might be accomplished more easily.

Existing solutions. It might be easier to use an existing algorithm or a library rather than writing all things anew from scratch. There might be some well analyzed algorithms that perform very good. Furthermore, libraries tend to have less bugs. Nevertheless, they often do not perform as good as customized solutions. The main reason is that libraries are usually general-purpose tools, implying that they cannot exploit problem specific properties.

Complexity of implementation. The implementation of a model should not be too complex. People might get deterred when seeing a very difficult specification. Another example are algorithms which perform well in theory but are too complex to implement to achieve the theoretical performance.

Time line. How much time, according to project requirements, can be spent to implement a model?

Costs. The costs of realizing a certain model should roughly be estimated. Maybe certain models are too expensive to take a deeper look into them. Overall project costs can be measured as a monetary budget, as the effort in man months or years, or as the required know-how.

Patents. More and more countries impose laws concerning software patents. So models need to be checked for an idea or rather an approach that is patent covered. If so, licensing the idea and a solution might be a fast but expensive idea. If not possible, the model has to be skipped.

2.2.5   Model Assessment

After a model has been developed it has to be verified and rated. Depending on the outcome a decision has to be made, whether to continue with the next step of Algorithm Engineering using the current models or to start over again and improve them. There are several points to keep in mind at this stage:

1. Have all necessary aspects of the underlying problem been considered? If not, the model fails in its field of application and may come up with useless solutions.
2. Are all modelled aspects really necessary for the problem? If not, removing unnecessary parts from the model might reduce solving time. This does not hold in general. In the case of constraint programming redundant constraints are added to improve running time significantly (see Section 2.3.3).
3. Is the model consistent?

One important approach is to test the model with small instances if possible or to use a standard solver if available. Another very difficult decision is to determine the appropriate level of abstraction or degree of specification for the model. Consider the following example which arises in throughput optimization of assembly lines. A workpiece has to undergo different assembly phases. After a phase is finished it advances to the next machine until it is completed. In this example a robot arm picks up components and mounts them on a prescribed position [775]. The problem is to minimize the total duration of all phases a workpiece needs to be worked on. One way to model this problem at a high detail is to solve the TSP on the lowest level. Unfortunately, TSP is a well known NP-hard problem. In this example the cities would be the points where components should be mounted on the workpiece. But the authors decided to omit the TSP modeling. The goal was to develop a very fast algorithm, that could be used as a substage in another algorithm using this part very frequently. Finding the exact solution of the TSP with typically a few hundred cities could not be done efficiently in the required time frame. Furthermore, the potential gain in processing time did not seem to be very significant when compared to the scale of potential gain of other variables and decisions in the problem.

The appropriate level of detail for any application is not measurable and often hard to achieve. It depends to a very high degree on soft constraints given by the environment of the application. As some concluding remark, a modeler should always try to achieve a deep insight into the problem structure, such that he will be able to tell how and to what extent the solution of the different aspects of the task will influence the solution of the whole problem. Only then it will be possible to reduce the level of detail by abstracting from such subproblems that influence the solution least.

2.2.6   Inherent Difficulties within the Modeling Process

Even if we follow the guidelines and take the different points for a good model into account, there will always be problems for which a fully satisfactory model cannot be found. Most of the difficulties we are facing here are caused by the inability to formalize the criteria for assessing the quality of a solution. Sometimes new insights in the field of the problem can help to overcome these difficulties. But usually they cannot be solved in the modeling phase of the algorithm engineering process.

The inability to come up with a correct and formal objective function for an optimization problem is the most prominent difficulty. Even if all constraints are modeled properly, we would not be able to come up with an optimal solution. This is due to the fact that two given solutions can hardly be compared without an optimization function. Hence, there is no possibility to reason the optimality of the results. However, based on given constraints valid solutions can still be generated. Such difficulties appeared in the following examples.

Consider a company whose aim is to build 3D CAD models of objects they get delivered. These objects need to undergo a scan to get sampling points of the surface. Afterwards the samples should serve as an input for building 3D models. One approach is to build a mesh consisting of triangles which approximates the surface. Hence, a good triangulation of the given samples has to be found. Note that the quality of a triangulation is a vague concept. Depending on the application the 3D model is needed for, triangulations have to be rated differently. For instance, in visualization acute angles should be prevented and other esthetic criteria preserved. If the application is in the field of mathematical analysis, for instance solving partial differential equations on the model, numerical stability and accuracy are very important. This can be achieved by letting each triangle have angles much larger than 0 and much lower than 180 degrees, for instance larger than 30 and lower than 150 degrees. Accuracy may be increased by shrinking the space which triangles may occupy, thus increasing their total number. Even being aware what a triangle should look like to be considered good, it is unknown how a distribution of angles over the mesh should look like to get a good overall rating. Most triangulation applications are faced with this problem [827]. Furthermore, another problem arises in the area of mesh generation. Inputs of instances can hardly be checked in terms of whether they meet some topological properties. For example, given sample points only, it is impossible to check if the input surface is a closed 2-manifold. Even worse, if the surface may contain borders or holes, then it is impossible to check the input for topological correctness.

Another example can be found in the biological research field of proteins. Proteins take part in almost every process occurring in cells. Thus it is very important to analyze their functionality to help understanding how cells behave and how potential drugs should work. Such proteins are arranged in chains of amino acids. The number of elements in such a chain varies from two up to 30,000. These elements are taken from a set of 20 standard amino acids which are encoded by the genetic code. Each amino acid is represented by a one-letter code. Hence, any protein can be seen as a string over the alphabet of the amino acids. These pieces of information are stored in databases open to researchers, for example the protein database UniProt [788].

Researchers are mainly interested in relationships or similarities between proteins. Thus, they have to search the databases and compare protein information with each other. This is in fact a key application area of bioinformatics. To create sequence alignments, two or more sequences are compared with each other and a scoring function is applied that indicates the similarity.

One very simple comparison method is the *edit distance*. The edit distance is used to measure the distance between two strings, given by the minimum number of operations needed to transform one string into the other. Allowed operations are deletion, substitution and insertion. Usually, the main application areas are spell checkers, but it can be applied to sequence alignment, too. Consider the following example where we want to transform 'RQGKLL' into 'RCGGKL'.

1. RQGKLL (initial string)
2. RCGKLL (substitute Q with C)
3. RCGGKLL (insert G)
4. RCGGKL (delete L)

So the edit distance is at most three assuming every operation was assigned uniform cost of 1. Note that this is not the only way to transform the sequences with an edit distance of three.

Unfortunately, similarity has to be more differentiated. Proteins may have structural, evolutionary or functional similarity. In most cases, applied methods only allow for the checking of structural similarities. Hence, evolutionary and functional similarities should be derived. Regrettably, this deduction does not always hold. Therefore, many methods and scoring functions were developed, each to be applied in its very specific field of research. Hence, no model could be built to satisfy the request of finding similarities between proteins in general.

So we see that each problem might have some ambiguities which the modeler needs to be aware of. Special care should be exercised when dealing with metaheuristics, where such objective functions are an integral part of the selection process.

2.3   Modeling Frameworks

Once the problem is understood and some intuition is gained about it, the next step is to formalize the problem and to build a model that describes solutions and their desired properties.

Various general frameworks for modeling and solving problems have been developed. In this section we will give an overview on the most prominent ones, namely graph-based models, linear and mixed integer programs (LPs/MIPs), constraint programming (CP), and algebraic modeling languages (AMLs). As a rule of thumb, these frameworks are becoming more general and powerful in this order.

We will illustrate the frameworks using the example problems already introduced, by providing models for them in the different frameworks. This allows us to highlight the special features of each framework and provides a comparison of their modeling philosophies.

The focus will be on modeling for solving the problem, rather than only specifying it. We will highlight the properties of a good model in the sense that the model can be solved quickly.

2.3.1   Graph-Based Models

Graph-based models are used for a very broad range of problems. Most prominent are combinatorial problems, which can often be easily formulated as a graph-based model.

A central point for modeling any problem as a graph problem is the formulation of the underlying graph structure. Graphs are combinatorial structures that can be used to model a set of objects together with pairwise relations between these objects.

More formally, a *graph* G is an ordered pair $G := (V, E)$ of a set V of *vertices* and a set $E \subseteq \binom{V}{2}$ of *edges*, where $\binom{V}{2}$ denotes the set of 2-element subsets of V. An edge between two vertices indicates a relation between these vertices and is interpreted in various ways, depending on the graph problem considered.

This is only the most basic notion of an undirected graph. There are many variations and more advanced notions, for instance directed graphs, in which the edges are ordered pairs of the vertices (called *arcs*) or multigraphs which may possess more than one edge between two vertices. Often there will be additional information assigned to the vertices or edges. For example, if the edges correspond to connections between the objects (i. e., vertices), they can be weighted by assigning distance values to them, so the graph becomes a *weighted graph*. More formally, the additional information will be described by functions of the type $f\colon V \to I$ or $f\colon E \to I$ where I is the set of information to be assigned.

For modeling, it is useful to be familiar with basic concepts from graph theory, like paths, flows, matchings, stable sets and connectivity. These concepts can be used to capture the problem structure in a graph-theoretic setting. There are many textbooks on graph theory, which introduce these and other concepts, graph problems, and algorithms, e. g., [242, 116]. For a more algorithmic perspective, see [500, 15] or the chapters on graph algorithms in the book of Cormen et al. [191].

Graph-based models have three main advantages: First, they are often quite intuitive and thus easy to grasp. Second, due to their combinatorial structure they enable the design of direct and — in many cases — efficient algorithms. Third, there is much theory that might help in modeling or designing algorithms.

A graph-based description is also often at the heart of other, more sophisticated models. Actually, graph formulations are used as a first model to further investigate the problem and in a later step some LP/MIP formulation is chosen to benefit from strong general-purpose solvers for LP/MIP formlations. Such a decision is often made in the design phase. This is one example that it is often necessary to repeat some parts of the modeling phase. In such a reiteration the model is improved to achieve a better performance or easier implementation. A first glance of such a possible translation of a graph problem into an LP formulation is given in Section 2.3.2.

However, graph-based models often cannot cope with more complicated constraints which may be needed for modeling the problem accurately. Although it may be possible to formulate these constraints in a model, existing algorithms may not be adaptable to deal with the constraints. It should also be noted that there is no formalism for specifying graph-based models as is the case for LP/MIP, CP, and AML. This approach makes graph formulations more flexible, but has the drawback that there can be no generic "graph solver", which can compute solutions for any graph problem. There are, however, many libraries of graph algorithms available, see Section 7.8 in Chapter 7.

We will now model some of our problems based on graphs. All necessary notions will be introduced as needed.

TSP. The TSP is one of the classical combinatorial optimization problems which can be formulated as a graph problem. It is straightforward to model a TSP instance as a weighted complete graph, where vertices of the graph represent the cities and the weights c_{ij} are the distances between the cities. If there is no connection between cities i and j this can be modeled by a sufficiently large weight c_{ij}. A solution is a cycle that visits all the vertices (known as *Hamiltonian cycle*) and the cost of a cycle $C = (v_1, \ldots, v_n)$ is

$$c(C) := \sum_{i=1}^{n-1} c_{v_i,v_{i+1}} + c_{v_n,v_1}.$$

Sudoku. Sudoku can be modeled as a graph problem in various ways, two of which we will give here. Both ways use edges to represent conflicts, i. e., forbidden assignments of numbers to the cells.

The first model is based on *vertex coloring*. Given a graph $G = (V, E)$, a vertex coloring is a function $c \colon V \to \mathbb{N}$ that assigns vertices connected by an edge different numbers (colors). Thus an edge indicates a conflict between the vertices, requiring distinct colors at the vertices. The vertex coloring problem is to find a vertex coloring that uses the minimum number of colors.

For Sudoku, the idea to make use of the vertex coloring problem is simple: We use a set of 81 vertices, one for each square and the assignment of numbers to the squares as a vertex coloring. The only thing we need to do is to insert edges such that they reflect the rules of Sudoku. This is easy: We just connect all vertices corresponding to a line, a row, and a subsquare, respectively. In this way we express that they should be numbered differently. Figure 2.2(a) shows the resulting graph for a smaller Sudoku of size 2.

Another way to model Sudoku is to create 9 vertices for each square, where each vertex corresponds to assigning the square the number of the vertex. We insert an edge between every pair of vertices belonging to the same square to model that only one of these vertices can be selected. Similarly, we pairwise connect all vertices with number i in a row, column, and subsquare by an edge, for each $i \in N$. Thus we manage to encode a solution as a stable set: A *stable set* is a set S of vertices such that for any two vertices $v_1, v_2 \in S$ there is no edge $\{v_1, v_2\}$ in E. The specific instance of Sudoku has a solution if and only if there is a stable set of size 81 that contains the vertices corresponding to the prescribed numbers. A subset of the graph is depicted in Figure 2.2(b), again for a smaller Sudoku of size 2.

Car Manufacturing. It is quite natural to formulate the car manufacturing problem as a network flow problem. Network flows are maybe the most important and the most generally applicable graph problems, since a lot of transportation and assignment problems, as well as performance problems in real-world networks can be modeled using this concept. We just recollect the basic definitions for network flows and then formulate a model for the car manufacturing problem.

A good intuition for network flow problems is to think of water that needs to flow from some sources to some sinks through a network of pipelines to satisfy the demand at the sinks. Formally, a network $N = (V, A)$ is a directed graph with lower and upper bounds for the flow on each arc given by the functions $l \colon A \to \mathbb{R}_{\geq 0}$ and $u \colon A \to \mathbb{R}_{\geq 0}$, respectively [15]. The demand and supply at the vertices is specified by a function $b \colon V \to \mathbb{R}$. A vertex v with $b(v) > 0$ is called *source* and one with $b(v) < 0$ *sink*, all others are *transshipment vertices*. A flow is a function $f \colon A \to \mathbb{R}_{\geq 0}$ that respects the lower and upper bounds and satisfies the demand and supplies specified by b at every vertex v, i.e., one that satisfies

$$\sum_{u \colon (u,v) \in A} f(v, u) - \sum_{u \colon (v,u) \in A} f(u, v) = b(v) \quad \forall v \in V.$$

Note that the first sum is the amount of flow that leaves vertex v (the outflow), whereas the second sum gives the amount of flow entering it (the inflow).

There are many variants of network flow problems which impose further properties on the flow. The most important one is the *minimum cost flow problem*. In this problem there is an additional cost function $c \colon A \to \mathbb{R}$ that gives the cost per unit flow for each arc, i.e., the total cost of a flow is given by

$$\sum_{a \in A} c(a) f(a).$$

The task is then to find a flow with minimum cost.

We can model the car manufacturing problem as a minimum cost flow problem as follows [15]. We introduce four types of vertices (confer Figure 2.3).

– A source vertex s represents the total production (i.e., total demand) over all car models and provides a corresponding amount of flow, i.e., $b(s) = \sum_{r \in R, m \in M} d_{r,m}$.
– Plant vertices p_i represent the various plants. These vertices are transshipment vertices.

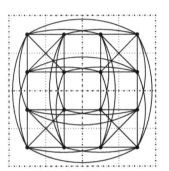

(a) Sudoku as a vertex coloring problem.

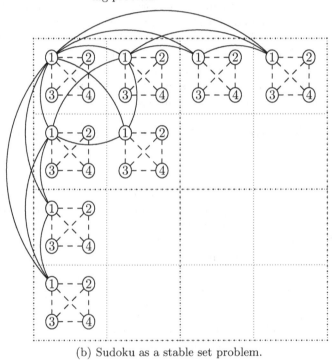

(b) Sudoku as a stable set problem.

Fig. 2.2. Two different graph-based models for a Sudoku of size 2 (instead of 3)

- Plant/model vertices p_i/m_j correspond to each car model built at a specific plant. These vertices are transshipment vertices, too.
- Retailer/model vertices r_i/m_j correspond to each car model required by a specific retailer. These vertices are sinks and have a demand corresponding to the demand of the retailer for the specific car model, i. e., $b(r_i/m_j) = -d_{i,j}$.

Furthermore, our network will contain three different types of arcs.

- Total production arcs: These arcs go from the source vertex s to the plant vertices and are used to decide how the total production is distributed among the plants. The cost for these arcs is zero, the lower bound for the flow is also 0. We will assume that the upper bound is infinite, but a different value could be used to express overall capacity limitations at a plant.
- Production arcs: These arcs connect a plant node with the different plant/-model vertices that represent the car models built at the given plant. The costs assigned to these arcs are the production costs of the corresponding car model at the plant. Furthermore, the upper bound for the flow on each arc is the production capacity for the car model at the plant.
- Transportation arcs: These arcs connect plant/model vertices to the retailer/model vertices such that the corresponding car models of the source and target vertices are equal. They describe which share of the retailers' demand for a car model is produced at the respective plants. The capacity of such an arc could be given either by restrictions imposed by the used infrastructure or by some contracts with local transportation firms.

Obviously, any feasible flow on this network corresponds one-to-one to a production and transportation schedule for the manufacturer. Therefore, a *minimum* cost flow corresponds to an *optimal* production and transportation schedule. Figure 2.3 shows an example instance together with the network arising from this construction.

For a much more detailed and exhaustive view on network flows and their applications we recommend the book of Ahuja et al. [15].

2.3.2   Mixed Integer Programming

Mixed integer programs (MIPs) are a very successful tool in the field of decision making and optimization, since it is possible to model and solve a broad range of problems.

A MIP describes the set of feasible solutions by linear constraints, which may be linear equations or inequalities. The objective is also a linear function of the variables used to model the solutions. There are two kinds of variables that

$P = \{A, B\}$

$M = \{a, b, c\}$

$R = \{1, 2\}$

$$(d_{rm})_{r \in R, m \in M} = \begin{pmatrix} 3 & 1 & 0 \\ 1 & 1 & 3 \end{pmatrix}$$

$$(a_{pm})_{p \in P, m \in M} = \begin{pmatrix} 10 & 15 & 30 \\ 8 & 13 & 33 \end{pmatrix}$$

$$(b_{pr})_{p \in P, r \in R} = \begin{pmatrix} 1 & 2 \\ 3 & 1 \end{pmatrix}$$

(a) Example instance data.

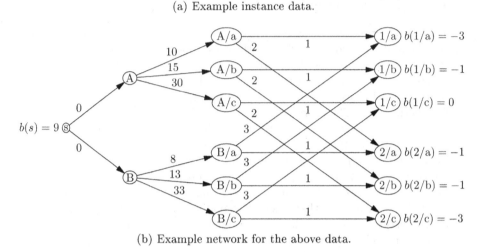

(b) Example network for the above data.

Fig. 2.3. An example network for an instance of the car manufacturing problem. The arc labels indicate the cost per unit flow. Lower and upper bounds for the flow are 0 and ∞ on all edges. For the sake of simplicity we did not consider capacity constraints of the plants, which can be included in the network model by appropriately modifying the upper bounds on the respective edges.

can be used for modeling: real variables and integer variables. Formally, a MIP written in matrix notation looks as follows.

$$\begin{aligned} \min \quad & c_1^T x + c_2^T y \\ \text{s.t.} \quad & A_{11}x + A_{12}y = b_1 \\ & A_{21}x + A_{22}y \leq b_2 \\ & x \in \mathbb{R}^{n_1} \\ & y \in \mathbb{Z}^{n_2} \end{aligned}$$

In this MIP, x denotes the n_1 real variables and y the n_2 integer variables. Moreover, the entries of c_1, c_2, b_1, b_2, A_{11}, A_{12}, A_{21}, and A_{22} are arbitrary real numbers, which are the parameters of the model.

Depending on the type of the variables, one distinguishes several types of special MIPs.

Linear programs (LP) All variables are real variables.
Integer programs (IP) All variables are integer variables.
Binary integer programs (BIP) All variables are *binary* integer variables,
i. e., variables with range $\{0, 1\}$.

When constructing a MIP model for a problem, the task is to identify variables that encode the decisions and that can be used to express both the problem's requirements and the objective. Sometimes it may be necessary to introduce variables that do not reflect an actual decision (but rather decision consequences) in order to model the problem.

From the computational viewpoint, LPs are the easiest MIPs. They are known to be solvable in polynomial time [472, 463] and there are several efficient implementations available. IPs and even BIPs on the other hand are known to be NP-hard. However, there are several MIP solvers available that perform very well in practice, e. g., the commercial ones ILOG CPLEX [422] and Dash Xpress [203] and the open-source framework SCIP [5]. For our purposes it is sufficient to know that they are based on a concept called *LP relaxation*, which amounts to omitting the integrality constraints for obtaining lower bounds. We will highlight the impact of this technique on modeling in the following examples.

Car Manufacturing. The minimum cost flow problem for the car manufacturing problem discussed in Section 2.3.1 can readily be formulated as a MIP model. In fact, every minimum cost flow problem can easily be written as an LP. Since the conditions a flow has to satisfy are linear and the cost function is linear, too, we only need to model the function $f: A \to \mathbb{R}_{\geq 0}$ describing the flow by real variables $x_a \geq 0$ to obtain an LP formulation of the general minimum cost flow problem:

$$\min \quad \sum_{a \in A} c(a) x_a$$

$$\text{s. t.} \quad \sum_{u : (u,v) \in A} x_{(u,v)} - \sum_{u : (v,u) \in A} x_{(v,u)} = b(v) \quad \forall v \in V$$

$$l_a \leq x_a \leq u_a \quad \forall a \in A$$

$$x_a \in \mathbb{R} \quad \forall a \in A$$

It is well-known that this type of LPs has integral optimal solutions. This implies that the car manufacturing problem can be solved by the simplex algorithm. However, there are more efficient algorithms for solving the minimum cost flow problem. In Section 2.3.4, we will come back to the minimum cost flow formulation of the car manufacturing problem and also provide a more customized LP model.

Sudoku. The initial mathematical model for Sudoku on page 23 used a function $f: N^2 \to N$ with $N := \{1, \ldots, 9\}$ to model a solution to the puzzle. It is not possible to translate the requirements for this function to IP constraints by just replacing the function value $f(i,j)$ by an integer variable $x_{ij} \in N$. The reason is that we cannot express the condition that each number should appear exactly once as we did for the mathematical model.

To resolve this issue, we use binary variables x_{ijn} with $x_{ijn} = 1$ meaning that n is put in cell (i,j). We have to select exactly one number for cell (i,j), which can be ensured by the constraints

$$\sum_{n \in N} x_{ijn} = 1 \quad \forall i, j \in N.$$

The condition that the first row contains each value exactly once can similarly be written as

$$\sum_{j \in N} x_{1jn} = 1 \quad \forall n \in N.$$

The entire IP reads

$$
\begin{aligned}
\min \quad & 0 \\
\text{s.t.} \quad & x_{ijn} = 1 & \forall (i,j,n) \in S, & \quad \text{(fixed)} \\
& \sum_{n \in N} x_{ijn} = 1 & \forall i,j \in N, & \quad \text{(nums)} \\
& \sum_{j \in N} x_{ijn} = 1 & \forall i,n \in N, & \quad \text{(rows)} \\
& \sum_{i \in N} x_{ijn} = 1 & \forall j,n \in N, & \quad \text{(columns)} \\
& \sum_{(i',j') \in C_{i,j}} x_{i'j'n} = 1 & \forall (i,j) \in N' \times N', \forall n \in N, & \quad \text{(squares)} \\
& x_{ijn} \in \{0,1\} & \forall i,j,n \in N. &
\end{aligned}
$$

The model uses the sets C_{ij} containing the indices for the cells in one subsquare, as defined on page 23. Note that the objective can be taken as "0" since Sudoku is a pure feasibility problem. Also notice the conceptual similarity to the graph-based Sudoku model using stable sets.

Scheduling. In the scheduling problem, the task is to find an execution sequence for the jobs which is described by the starting times s_j and tardiness t_j. We defined the tardiness t_j of a job j as

$$t_j := \max(0, s_j + p_j - d_j),$$

where p_j and d_j are the job's parameters. Obviously, this is a nonlinear relation between s_j and t_j, which needs to be expressed as a linear one in order to get a MIP model. This can be accomplished with the two inequalities

$$t_j \geq 0 \quad \text{and}$$
$$t_j \geq s_j + p_j - d_j.$$

Of course, the same trick can be applied to model the maximum or minimum of an arbitrary number of variables.

Given two jobs i and j, the essential decision is whether to process job i or job j first. This decision can be modeled by binary variables x_{ij} which are 1 if and only if job i is processed before job j. Of course, if $x_{ij} = 1$ then x_{ji} should be 0 and vice versa. This kind of negation is modeled easily by $x_{ij} = 1 - x_{ji}$. We also need to ensure transitivity: if $x_{ik} = 1$ and $x_{kj} = 1$, then $x_{ij} = 1$. This can be modeled by constraints of the form $x_{ij} \geq x_{ik} + x_{kj} - 1$.

We still need to cover the connection between the x_{ij} variables and the starting times of the jobs. If job i is selected to be processed first, then the starting time s_j of job j is at least $s_i + p_i$. Thus we need to express the following implication:

$$x_{ij} = 1 \implies s_j \geq s_i + p_i.$$

Implications like this can be modeled using so-called *big-M-formulations*. The idea is to use a large constant M to "disable" the constraint for one of the values of a binary variable. In our case a big-M-formulation of the above implication is

$$s_j \geq s_i + p_i - M(1 - x_{ij}).$$

Clearly, if $x_{ij} = 1$ the inequality holds. For $x_{ij} = 0$ and M large enough, the right hand side becomes negative and thus meaningless. We therefore succeeded in modeling the implication. The full MIP model for the scheduling problem then becomes

$$\min \quad \sum_{j \in J} w_j t_j$$

s. t.	$t_j \geq s_j + p_j - d_j$	$\forall j \in J$	(tardiness.1)
	$t_j \geq 0$	$\forall j \in J$	(tardiness.2)
	$s_j \geq s_i + p_i - M(1 - x_{ij})$	$\forall i \neq j \in J$	(precedence)
	$x_{ij} = 1 - x_{ji}$	$\forall i > j \in J$	
	$x_{ij} \geq x_{ik} + x_{kj} - 1$	$\forall i, j, k \in J, i > j$	(transitivity)
	$x_{ij} \in \{0, 1\}$	$\forall i \neq j \in J$	
	$s_j, t_j \in \mathbb{R}$	$\forall j \in J.$	

Using big-M-formulations to convert logic or non-convex constraints to binary variables, as we do here, has some drawbacks. The first has to do with how MIPs are solved. Recall that the integrality constraints are relaxed (i. e., ignored) to get lower bounds. These lower bounds become worse as M gets larger. As an example, consider the following constraints, which may be part of a scheduling model as above:

$$s_j \geq s_i + 5 - M(1 - x_{ij})$$
$$s_i \geq s_j + 3 - M x_{ij}$$

and suppose that $s_j = 7$ and $s_i = 5$ are values which would be good for the entire problem, i. e., gives a good objective value. If M is at least 8, it is possible to achieve $s_j = 7$ and $s_i = 5$ by choosing $x_{ij} = 5/M$. Since these starting times cannot be realized in any integer solution, this means that the LP relaxation has not much to do with the original MIP model, which is bad for standard MIP solvers. In particular, there may be no integer solution with a similar objective value, which means that the lower bound is weak. The effect gets worse for larger M, since the range of values realizing these starting times increases.

Another drawback of using big-M-formulations is that they may lead to numerical instability. The advice to cope with both issues is to avoid big-M-formulations if possible. If they need to be used, always choose the value of M as small as possible and individually for each constraint. However, as the size of the problem increases the values required for M usually grow, too. Therefore, big-M-formulations are most attractive for small instance sizes.

Further Modeling Aspects. Since many formulations modeling the same problem may exist, the models have to be compared with each other. One might think that minimizing the number of constraints or variables yields a better model. This is because inexperienced modelers expect solvers to perform better if they have to cope with less variables or constraints.

Consider the following facility location problem [611] where we are given a set of $C := \{1, \ldots, m\}$ customers and $W := \{1, \ldots, n\}$ possible locations of warehouses. We need to decide at which of the possible locations to build a warehouse and which warehouse serves each customer. To this end, we introduce binary variables x_{ij} and set $x_{ij} = 1$ to denote that customer j is assigned to warehouse i, and set binary variables $y_i = 1$ to indicate that warehouse i is available. The cost for actually building warehouse i are f_i. If customer j is assigned to warehouse i the costs incurred are c_{ij}. Warehouses should be opened in such a way that the total cost is minimized.

This leads to the following formulation

$$\min \quad \sum_{i \in W, j \in C} c_{ij} x_{ij} + \sum_{i \in W} f_i y_i$$

$$\text{s.t.} \quad \sum_{i \in W} x_{ij} = 1 \qquad\qquad j \in C$$

$$x_{ij} \leq y_i \qquad i \in W, j \in C \qquad \text{(single)}$$

$$x_{ij}, y_i \in \{0, 1\} \quad i \in W, j \in C.$$

Another, very similar formulation is as follows

$$\min \quad \sum_{i \in W, j \in C} c_{ij} x_{ij} + \sum_{i \in W} f_i y_i$$

$$\text{s.t.} \quad \sum_{i \in W} x_{ij} = 1 \qquad\qquad j \in C$$

$$\sum_{j \in C} x_{ij} \leq m y_i \qquad\qquad i \in W \qquad \text{(agg)}$$

$$x_{ij}, y_i \in \{0, 1\} \quad i \in W, j \in C.$$

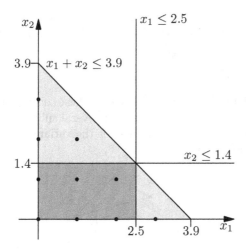

Fig. 2.4. Illustration of the tightness of an LP relaxation

In fact, the only difference is that the inequalities (single) of the first formulation have been aggregated by summing over all customers to obtain inequalities (agg) in the second formulation.

Obviously, inequality (single) generates many more constraints than inequality (agg). One is tempted to prefer the second model. Unfortunately, this would not be a good decision and the reason is again the LP relaxation which is much *tighter* for the first formulation. This means that a fractional solution of the LP relaxation for the first relaxation is closer to an integral solution (which is a solution to the IP) than a solution of the LP relaxation for the second formulation. Formally, the reason is that the set $\{x_{ij}, y_i \in [0,1] \mid x_{ij} \leq y_i, i \in W, j \in C\}$ is contained in the set $\{x_{ij}, y_i \in [0,1] \mid \sum_{j \in C} x_{ij} \leq m y_i, i \in W\}$. An illustration of this relation is given in Figure 2.4 where a lose formulation corresponds to the triangular region defined by $x_1, x_2 \geq 0$ and $x_1 + x_2 \leq 3.9$, and the tighter relaxation with additional constraints $x_1 \leq 2.5$ and $x_2 \leq 1.4$ to the dark grey region.

In Mixed Integer Programming there are even more extreme cases where a large number of constraints or variables does not indicate a bad model. On the contrary, such a model may be a suitable one since there are special techniques for dealing with them, in particular techniques like *cutting planes* and *column generation* [612, 531].

A famous example for the application of cutting planes is the symmetric TSP, i.e., a version of the traveling salesman problem where the distance between any two cities is independent of the direction. The symmetric TSP can be modeled by introducing binary variables x_{ij} that indicate whether or not the edge between city i and j belongs to the tour or not. Thinking in terms of graphs, this means that edge ij is selected to be in the cycle visiting all the vertices. Note that we need only variables x_{ij} for $j > i$, since the direction of an edge does not matter. It is clear that every city i has exactly two neighbors, giving the constraints

$$\sum_{j<i} x_{ji} + \sum_{j>i} x_{ij} = 2 \quad \text{for } 1 \le i \le n.$$

However, there are integer solutions that satisfy these constraints and that do not correspond to tours. Instead, they consist of several subtours. For instance, the following picture for n cities shows values for the variables x_{ij} that are feasible w. r. t. to the constraints above.

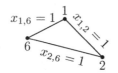

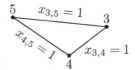

To avoid these subtours, one can use the following *subtour elimination constraints*, see e. g., [611]:

$$\sum_{i,j\in S, i\neq j} x_{ij} \le |S| - 1 \quad \forall S \subseteq \{1,\ldots,n\}, 2 \le |S| \le n - 1.$$

In order to get an intuition for the subtour elimination constraints, look at the set $S = \{1, 2, 6\}$ in the picture. Since

$$x_{1,2} + x_{2,6} + x_{1,6} = 3 > |S| - 1 = 2,$$

the above situation cannot occur anymore.

Although there are exponentially many constraints, this formulation can be used within a cutting plane framework. The basic idea is to start the solution process with a subset of all constraints. If an optimal solution to the reduced constraint set yields an overall feasible solution, one is done. Otherwise, the task is to identify one or more violated constraints (the name-giving cutting planes) and to add them to the active constraints. Searching for cutting planes is called *separation*. The drawback of this approach is that such models cannot be solved using an MIP solver out-of-the-box, but require customized algorithms. Indeed, to make this approach work in practice, a number of sophisticated enhancements is necessary. For the TSP this is nicely illustrated in the recommendable book by Applegate et al. [33].

Many available MIP solvers support further so-called "modeling objects", which are special kinds of variables, e. g., semi-continuous variables and specially ordered sets (SOS). These may be used to obtain simpler models and are mostly targeted towards the needs of business users.

Another aspect of modeling are the *presolving* capabilities of existing MIP solvers. Presolving is a process that aims at converting the model to an equivalent one that is better suited for the subsequent solution process. The fact that the solvers employ presolving techniques like variable substitution can be exploited by the modeler to obtain models that are easier to write down. For instance, in our scheduling problem it would have been possible to introduce completion time variables c_j by the constraint

$$c_j = s_j + p_j$$

and to use c_j instead of the right hand side in the remaining constraints. The presolver converts this model to the one given before.

There are many more useful MIP modeling tricks and techniques that can be found in e. g., [611] and [840].

2.3.3 Constraint Programming

Constraint programming (CP) is a declarative modeling formalism similar to mixed integer programs. A survey on CP related research and its applications is given in [680]. For deeper insights and a reasonably complete coverage of all lines of work in the field of constraint programming take a look into the Handbook of Constraint Programming [682].

A constraint programming model basically consists of

1. a set of variables $X = \{x_1, \ldots, x_n\}$,
2. for each variable x_i, a (potentially infinite) set D_i of possible values called its *domain*,
3. and a set of *constraints* restricting the values variables can take simultaneously. For a set of variables $\{x_{i_1}, \ldots, x_{i_k}\}$, a constraint is an arbitrary subset of $D_{i_1} \times \cdots \times D_{i_k}$.

A solution is an assignment of values to the variables, such that

- the value of a variable is from the variable's domain, and
- every constraint is satisfied by the assignment.

Such an assignment is called *labeling*.

Notice that a CP model is very general. Variable domains can be chosen arbitrarily, for instance intervals of real, integer or natural numbers. In contrast to MIP models domains need not be intervals, but can contain holes. Furthermore, domains are not restricted to numbers, also enumeration types like colors or names can be used. The same generality is possible for the constraints: They can be any relation on the domain.

Clearly, the constraint set of a MIP model is also a CP model. However, due to its generality CP is much more powerful regarding expressiveness, which is useful for modeling. Of course, no solver can be implemented that deals with arbitrary domains and arbitrary constraints. Modeling is therefore restricted to those type of domains and constraints that are available in the solver. Usually, these include equality, inequality, and comparison of numerical expressions (in particular non-linear expressions) as well as logical expressions. Examples are

$$x^2 + y \neq 5,$$
$$x + y \geq 5 \implies z = 2,$$
$$x \leq 2 \vee x \geq 4.$$

There are different approaches for solving CPs. An overview is given in [64]. Standard solvers like ILOG Solver [424] employ an enumeration scheme, which makes use of backtracking to systematically search for solutions, by extending a partial labeling towards a labeling of all variables. Many CP frameworks like ECL^{i}PS^e [265] are based on or are implemented in Prolog exploiting the inherent back-tracking of this programming language. The main point for our purposes is that they use some kind of implicit enumeration.

.This enumeration is, of course, an exponential algorithm. In order to get acceptable running times it is therefore important to reduce the search space and detect partial labelings that cannot be extended to feasible ones early, so that they can be pruned. The idea is to use the structure of a constraint to delete inconsistent values, i. e., values that cannot participate in any feasible labeling, from the domains of the variables involved in the constraint. Such techniques are known as *consistency techniques* or *domain reduction*. In order to allow for efficient domain reduction, the constraints may not be arbitrary but have to be of certain types.

The most basic technique builds up a constraint graph for unary and binary constraints, i. e., constraints involving only one or two variables. It can be shown that any arbitrary constraint can be transformed into a binary constraint using dual encoding [211] or hidden variable encoding [681], so this can in principle be done for all CPs. In the constraint graph a node represents a variable and an edge represents a constraint. The resulting graph can be traversed and relying on the constraints inconsistent values in the domains of the affected variables can be deleted. This possibly reduces the search space significantly. However, there still might be inconsistencies regarding longer paths in the graph. Surveys on more advanced techniques can be found in [64, 34].

CP techniques can also be used to solve optimization problems. To this end, the search for an optimal solution is modeled with additional constraints that forbid solutions that are inferior to the currently best one. The goal is to reduce the search space to find an optimal solution and not to search for all solutions and then iterate to find the best one.

So far, we gave an overview on Constraint Programming. We will now turn to real models for our example problems. We will use a notation that is similar to the Mathematical Programming notation already used for mixed integer programs in order to keep models compact and general. The syntax to implement these models differs strongly from solver to solver.

In the remainder of this section, we will only consider problems with finite domains. As discussed before, it is important to reduce the search space which has to be considered during modeling. Therefore, we will address this important aspect of CP modeling in greater detail.

Sudoku. The Sudoku puzzle (recall the notation introduced on page 23) can be cast into a CP model in very intuitive way. We use variables $x_{ij} \in \{1, \ldots, 9\} =: N$ to represent the values in the corresponding cells. We still need to express that all the values in a row, column, and subsquare are different. This can be done by simply using pairwise inequality constraints $x_{ij} \neq x_{kl}$ as follows:

$$
\begin{aligned}
x_{ij} &\neq x_{ik} & \forall k \neq i, j \in N, & \quad \text{(rows)} \\
x_{ij} &\neq x_{kj} & \forall k \neq i, j \in N, & \quad \text{(columns)} \\
x_{i_1 j_1} &\neq x_{i_2 j_2} & \forall (i_1, j_1) \neq (i_2, j_2) \in C_{ij}, \forall i, j \in N', & \quad \text{(subsquares)} \\
x_{ij} &\in N & \forall i, j \in N. &
\end{aligned}
$$

There is a more convenient and also more powerful formulation using the global `alldifferent` constraint. A *global constraint* is a constraint capturing a relation between an arbitrary number of variables.

For instance, the `alldifferent`(X) constraint imposes that all variables in the variable set X take distinct values. Obviously, this constraint is very useful for modeling Sudoku, since the above model can now be written as

$$
\begin{aligned}
\texttt{alldifferent}\,(\{x_{ij} \mid j \in N\}) & \quad \forall i \in N, & \quad \text{(rows)} \\
\texttt{alldifferent}\,(\{x_{ij} \mid i \in N\}) & \quad \forall j \in N, & \quad \text{(columns)} \\
\texttt{alldifferent}\,(C_{ij}) & \quad \forall i, j \in N', & \quad \text{(subsquares)} \\
x_{ij} \in N & \quad \forall i, j \in N. &
\end{aligned}
$$

This model is not only more compact, but also gives better search-space pruning. The reason is that, in general, domains of variables involved in an `alldifferent` constraint can be reduced stronger than if a set of equivalent inequality constraints is used.

We illustrate this with the following example taken from [34]. Consider the CPs

$$\texttt{alldifferent}(x_1, x_2, x_3); x_1, x_2, x_3 \in \{1, 2\}$$

and

$$x_1 \neq x_2; x_1 \neq x_3; x_2 \neq x_3; x_1, x_2, x_3 \in \{1, 2\},$$

which are obviously equivalent and cannot be satisfied. Domain reduction is done by considering each constraint, reduce the domains of some variable if possible and then considering other constraints that involve these variable in order to *propagate* the reduction. For the inequality constraints, however, no domain reduction can be performed, since the domains of both variables have two elements. The `alldifferent` constraint for three variables implies that the union of the domains of the variables has to contain at least three elements, so we can directly conclude that there is no solution. This conclusion can also be drawn in the inequality representation, but then we need to consider more than one constraint at a time, which is more complicated. For a CP solver it is easier to detect the group of inequality constraints and convert it to an equivalent alldifferent constraint in a preprocessing step.

TSP. A solution of the TSP, i.e., a tour, can be interpreted as a permutation of the cities. This view can be directly transformed to a CP model by using a variable x_i giving the number of the city at position i in the sequence, i.e., a permutation. We can make use of the alldifferent constraint to ensure that the variables indeed constitute a permutation. CP allows to use variables as indices to other variables, which is known as *variable indexing*. This modeling technique can be used to express the objective function just as we did for permutations.

$$\min \quad \sum_{i=1}^{n-1} c_{x_i,x_{i+1}} + c_{x_n,x_1}$$
$$\text{s.t.} \quad \text{alldifferent}\left(\{x_1,\ldots,x_n\}\right),$$
$$x_i \in \{1,\ldots,n\}.$$

Scheduling. The scheduling problem, the following CP models and their discussion are taken from [452].

The first model for the minimum weighted tardiness scheduling problem is very similar to the MIP model introduced in Section 2.3.2. The main difference is that we can model the disjunction

job j is processed before job i $\lor$ job i is processed before job j

directly, which is due to the greater generality of the CP approach. In the MIP model, we had to use big-M-constraints to model this disjunction. The CP model uses only the variables s_j giving the start time and c_j giving the completion time of a job j. The completion time variables are used for convenience only.

$$\min \quad \sum_{j \in J} w_j \max(0, c_j - d_j) \qquad \qquad \text{(Sched1)}$$
$$\text{s.t.} \quad c_j = s_j + p_j \qquad \qquad \forall j \in J,$$
$$\left(s_i \geq s_j + p_j\right) \lor \left(s_j \geq s_i + p_i\right) \quad \forall j \in J,$$
$$s_j, c_j \in \{0, \ldots, \textstyle\sum_{j \in J} p_j\}.$$

Note that we could also use the max-function directly in the objective function, since there is no restriction to linear objective functions. Moreover, we used $\sum_{j \in J} p_j$ as an upper bound for any completion and start time, to get finite domains for the variables.

We now turn to another kind of model in order to discuss how modeling can help to reduce the search space. The basic idea for this kind of model is to use a permutation to encode the order of job processing similar as we did for the TSP. The model uses variables x_j giving the position of the job j in the sequence (this is just the other way around than in the TSP model) and completion time variables c_j. Now the question is how to relate the position information to the completion time. The key to this is the realization that they should define equivalent orderings of the jobs, i. e., if job j is processed after job i then the completion time of job j is greater than the completion time of job i. Making this more precise, we get the following model.

$$\min \quad \sum_{j \in J} w_j \max(0, c_j - d_j) \qquad \text{(Sched2)}$$

$$
\begin{aligned}
\text{s. t.} \quad & \texttt{alldifferent}(\{x_j \mid j \in J\}), \\
& x_j > x_i \iff c_j \geq c_i + p_j && \forall j \neq i \in J, \\
& x_j = 1 \implies c_j = p_j && \forall j \in J, \\
& c_j \in \{0, \ldots, \sum_{j \in J} p_j\} && \forall j \neq i \in J, \\
& x_j \in J && \forall j \neq i \in J.
\end{aligned}
$$

The constraints $x_j = 1 \implies c_j = p_j$ are needed to ensure that the job processed first has the correct completion time.

Model (Sched2) is correct in the sense that all solutions to this model are in fact solutions to the scheduling problem. We now consider additional *redundant* constraints, which may help to reduce the search space. A constraint is redundant, if it is not necessary in order to guarantee a correct solution.

First we note that the constraint

$$x_j > x_i \iff c_j \geq c_i + p_j \quad \forall j \neq i \in J$$

can be strengthened in the case that $x_j = x_i + 1$. In this case job j is processed immediately after job i, giving the constraints

$$x_j = x_i + 1 \iff c_j = c_i + p_j \quad \forall j \neq i \in J, \qquad \text{(successive)}$$

using the fact that in an optimal schedule, the machine is never idle.

Another set of redundant constraints arises as follows. Suppose that the jobs are ordered non-decreasingly according to their processing times. If job j is now processed as the k-th job, the completion time of job j is at least the sum of the processing times of the k shortest jobs. In the case that job j is not among the k shortest ones, its completion time is at least the sum of p_j and the $k-1$ shortest jobs, which is somewhat stronger. To formalize these observations in the model, let $\tilde{p}_l$ be the duration of the l-shortest job and let J^k denote the set of the k shortest jobs.

$$
\begin{aligned}
& x_j = k \implies c_j \geq \sum_{l=1}^{k} \tilde{p}_l && \forall j \in J^k \; \forall k \in J \\
& && \qquad \qquad \qquad \text{(LB)} \\
& x_j = k \implies c_j \geq \tilde{p}_j + \sum_{l=1}^{k-1} \tilde{p}_l && \forall j \neq J^k \; \forall k \in J \; .
\end{aligned}
$$

Table 2.1. Data of the scheduling instance used to compare the CP models. The data for the first 7 jobs is taken from [452] and has been extended arbitrarily to obtain 11 jobs.

j	1	2	3	4	5	6	7	8	9	10	11
p_j	3	3	2	1	5	4	4	3	2	5	5
d_j	2	5	6	8	10	15	17	19	20	21	21
w_j	1	3	4	1	2	3	1.5	1	1	2	2

Table 2.2. Comparison of search tree size and total running times for various versions of the Constraint Programming model for minimum tardiness scheduling.

#jobs	number of choice points / running time in seconds							
	(Sched1)		(Sched2)		(Sched2) + (successive)		(Sched2) + (LB) + (successive)	
7	507	0.02	4.070	0.27	3.528	0.40	356	0.04
8	1.924	0.10	20.282	1.67	17.369	2.36	1.016	0.15
9	5.397	0.34	103.903	10.21	89.195	14.18	4.136	0.68
10	103.366	6.93	956.123	129.85	847.842	179.73	37.296	7.47
11	1.7×10^6	113.83	12×10^6	2128.28	11×10^6	2934.80	433.887	92.64

Now let us look at how much these redundant constraints contribute to reducing the search space. To this end, we use an instance of 7 jobs which was used for a similar comparison in [452] and has been extended for this small study to 11 jobs. The precise data of this instance is given in Table 2.1. Table 2.2 presents measurements of four different CP models solved by ILOG Solver 6.3 [424]. The four models considered are

1. Model 1: (Sched1)
2. Model 2: (Sched2)
3. Model 3: (Sched2) + (successive)
4. Model 4: (Sched2) + (successive) + (LB)

The first column for each model gives the number of *choice points*, which is some measure for the search space size reported by ILOG Solver. Clearly, the number of choice points decreases from Models 2 to 4, as more constraints are in the model. The most effective constraints in this respect seem to be the lower-bound constraints (LB). However, adding only constraints (successive) to the model (Sched2) *increases* the running time, although it does decrease the number of choice points. The reason is that the search space reduction achieved by the redundant constraints needs some computation time itself. It is therefore worthwhile to investigate whether including certain redundant constraints pays off in a reduced running time as well. Comparing Models 1 and 4 we see that it does pay off to use the position-based model, *if* we include the constraints (LB). Model 4 has both significantly fewer choice points than Model 1 and a comparable or shorter running time. In particular, the running time is much shorter for larger instances.

The data of Table 2.2 seem to indicate that the running times for all four models increase quite fast with instance size. In order to solve larger instance using CP it is often necessary to use some problem-specific search strategy. This is one reason why many CP solvers are no "model-and-run" solvers, but rather some kind of framework for solving CP models that can be customized to the problem at hand.

2.3.4 Algebraic Modeling Languages

So far we introduced many mixed integer programming and constraint programming models. The question how to really use these models was not addressed. Usually, one needs to create a program that generates the model in a solver or framework-specific way, solves the model and interprets the solution. For MIP models, there are also two quasi-standard file formats, the MPS file format [601] and the CPLEX LP file format [423]. However, it is still quite laborious to generate models for larger instances by hand, or a custom generator program is still needed.

Algebraic modeling languages (AML) aim to overcome these issues. They are high-level languages that are quite close to the standard set-based notation used in Mathematical Programming and thus provide quite compact input files and are more or less solver-independent. These languages pose a powerful way to convert a Mathematical Programming model into one that can be solved by a solver program. Most Algebraic Modeling Languages support a subset of the modeling formalisms linear programs, mixed integer programs, quadratic programs, non-linear programs, and constraint programs and thus cover a large range of problems. Examples are the commercial AMLs GAMS [139, 542] and AMPL [304] and the academic ZIMPL [487, 488, 486], which is also available as open source. The real power of AMLs is due to the fact that they support *rapid Mathematical Programming* [487], i. e., quick evaluation and comparison of different models, enabling the identification of a suitable model for the problem at hand. They support an iterative process that is very similar to the Algorithm Engineering cycle described in Chapter 1.

1. Collect data that defines one ore more specific problem instances.
2. Formulate a model, i. e., the abstract system of variables, constraints, and objectives that represent the general form of the problem to be solved.
3. Instantiate the model for each problem instance, using the data and parameters specified for the problem instance.
4. Solve the model corresponding to a problem instance by running a suitable solver to find optimal solutions.
5. Analyze the solutions, answering question such as "Does the solution correspond to a feasible solution for the original problem?", "Does the solution exhibit some specific structure that all solutions should have?", or "Does the solution fulfill the goals specified in the problem?".
6. Refine the model and the data as necessary and start over again at Step 1. For instance, if the solution is not feasible w. r. t. the original problem, we need to add further constraints that ensure feasibility.

AMLs allow to strictly separate the model from the data. Thus, the data collected in Step 1 can be stored in one fixed format that is used by a variety of models. To this end, AMLs provide methods for using this instance data to instantiate the general model for the problem instance. Separating the model and the data makes it easy to investigate various models and model variants.

Although AMLs are very powerful and in many cases sufficient to solve real-world problems, they do have limitations. For instance, it is hard to exploit special structure in the data or in the model. Therefore, a solution process based on the use of an AML will not give the best performance, which might be important for large-scale problems. However, AMLs are a valuable tool to guide the design and selection of promising solution approaches, which is their main role in the Algorithm Engineering cycle.

As an example for the use of an AML, we will have a closer look at the open-source AML ZIMPL [486, 488], which has successfully been used in various research projects [487] as well as in several university courses. In its stand-alone version, ZIMPL takes an input file describing a MIP model and generates a corresponding LP or MPS file, which in turn can be solved using any MIP solver. More recently, ZIMPL has been integrated with the academic MIP solver SCIP [5, 6] into the ZIB Optimization Suite [859]. Hence, models formulated in ZIMPL can be solved directly.

Sudoku. The MIP model for the Sudoku puzzle introduced in Section 2.3.2 can readily be coded as a ZIMPL program, see Figure 2.5. The ZIMPL language is rather simple and allows to describe the model based on sets and numerical parameters. Sets in ZIMPL are defined using the keyword **set**. They consist of tuples that are delimited by < and >, which may be omitted for unary tuples. Sets can be constructed using the usual set-theoretic operations like intersection, union, cross product and so on. In the Sudoku program, we use an explicit construction to set up the set S of fixed numbers and the cross product of sets, e. g., when defining the variables. Variables are usually indexed by some set and it is possible to specify lower and upper bounds, as well as the type of variable (real, binary, integer). For the Sudoku model, we only need binary variables.

Constraints are introduced by the keyword **subto**, followed by a name and a colon. A **subto** statement can be used to generate a set of constraints by using the **forall** expression similar to the mathematical notation used for MIPs. Similarly, there is a syntax for summing variables over a set of indices, since sums are very common in MIP models. The name provided for a class of constraints can be helpful when debugging the model. Figure 2.6 shows the solution for the Sudoku puzzle presented in Figure 2.1 computed using the ZIMPL program.

In our initial attempt at modeling the Sudoku puzzle using Mixed Integer Programming, we did not include constraints ensuring that each cell contains exactly one number, erroneously assuming that this would implied by the constraints for rows, columns, and subsquares. However, this is not the case and such constraints are needed. We recognized this when looking at the solution to the ZIMPL program produced by SCIP, which in fact set both $x_{1,8,1}$ and $x_{1,8,3}$

```
1   # instance data
2   set S:= { <1,2,5>, <1,4,9>, <1,6,6>, <1,8,3>,
3            <2,1,4>, <2,2,6>, <2,4,5>, <2,6,1>, <2,8,7>, <2,9,8>,
4            <3,4,4>, <3,6,7>,
5            <4,1,3>, <4,2,2>, <4,3,1>, <4,7,7>, <4,8,4>, <4,9,9>,
6            <6,1,7>, <6,2,4>, <6,3,6>, <6,7,8>, <6,8,5>, <6,9,1>,
7            <7,4,8>, <7,6,2>,
8            <8,1,2>, <8,2,7>, <8,4,1>, <8,6,5>, <8,8,8>, <8,9,6>,
9            <9,2,8>, <9,4,3>, <9,6,9>, <9,8,2> };

11  # sets for modeling
12  set N  := { 1 .. 9 };
13  set N2 := { 1 .. 3 };
14  set C[ <i,j> in N2*N2 ] :=
15       { <i2,j2> in N2*N2: <3*(i-1)+i2,3*(j-1)+j2> };

17  # variables
18  var x[ N*N*N ] binary;

20  # the model
21  subto fixed:
22       forall <i,j,n> in S do
23       x[i,j,n] == 1;

25  subto nums:
26       forall <i,j> in N*N do
27       sum <n> in N: x[i,j,n] == 1;

29  subto rows:
30       forall <i,n> in N*N do
31       sum <j> in N: x[i,j,n] == 1;

33  subto cols:
34       forall <j,n> in N*N do
35       sum <i> in N: x[i,j,n] == 1;

37  subto squares:
38       forall <i,j,n> in N2*N2*N do
39       sum <i2,j2> in C[i,j]: x[i2,j2,n] == 1;
```

Fig. 2.5. A ZIMPL program corresponding to the MIP model for the Sudoku puzzle

1	5	7	9	8	6	4	3	2
4	6	2	5	3	1	9	7	8
9	3	8	4	2	7	6	1	5
3	2	1	6	5	8	7	4	9
8	9	5	7	1	4	2	6	3
7	4	6	2	9	3	8	5	1
6	1	3	8	7	2	5	9	4
2	7	9	1	4	5	3	8	6
5	8	4	3	6	9	2	2	7

Fig. 2.6. The solution to the example Sudoku puzzle from Figure 2.1 computed using the ZIMPL program from Figure 2.5

to 1. This could easily be resolved by just adding the constraints, now leading to a feasible solution. Once again this emphasizes the usefulness of AMLs in developing models.

Car Manufacturing. As a last example, we shortly discuss a ZIMPL program for the car manufacturing problem, see Figure 2.7. The goal is to solve the instance given in Figure 2.3 on page 36. To do this, we first need a more concrete version of the general MIP formulation for the minimum cost flow problem. We use the following variables (confer Figure 2.3)

x_p flow on arcs leaving the source vertex s and entering the plant vertex p,

$y_{p,p,m}$ flow on arcs leaving the plant vertex p and entering the plant/-model vertex p/m,

$z_{p,m,r,m}$ flow on arcs leaving the plant/model vertex p/m and entering the retailer/model vertex r/m.

This gives the LP model

$$\min \quad \sum_{p\in P, m\in M} A_{p,m} y_{p,p,m} + \sum_{m\in M, p\in P, r\in R} B_{p,r} z_{p,m,r,m}$$

$$\text{s. t.} \quad \sum_{p\in P} x_p = \sum_{r\in R, m\in M} d_{r,m} \qquad\qquad\qquad \text{(source)}$$

$$\sum_{m\in M} y_{p,p,m} = x_p \qquad\qquad \forall p \in P \qquad \text{(plant)}$$

$$\sum_{r\in R} z_{p,m,r,m} = y_{p,p,m} \qquad\qquad \forall p \in P, m \in M \qquad \text{(plant/model)}$$

$$\sum_{p\in P} z_{p,m,r,m} = d_{r,m} \qquad\qquad \forall r \in R, m \in M \qquad \text{(retailer/model)}$$

$$x_p, y_{p,p,m}, z_{p,m,r,m} \geq 0 \qquad \forall p \in P, m \in M, r \in R.$$

Constraint (source) "generates" the flow, i. e., production capacity, that is necessary to satisfy the demand, whereas constraints (retailer/model) ensure that the retailers' demands are satisfied. The remaining constraints just distribute the flow in the network.

In the ZIMPL program in Figure 2.7, we first specify the parameters defining the instance to be solved. Note that the sets for plants, models, and retailers actually consist of strings, i. e., symbolic names. The data specifying the demand and the cost are given using ZIMPL's parameter table syntax. The model that follows these data declarations uses the information only in a very abstract way, thus effectively separating the data from the model. This separation could be enhanced by putting the input data in an external file.

In the Sudoku example, we did not need to give an objective function, since Sudoku is just a feasibility problem. For the minimum cost flow formulation of the car manufacturing problem, the cost is determined by the amount of flow on each edge. The objective is introduced in ZIMPL by the keywords **minimize** or **maximize** and otherwise similar to constraints.

2.3.5   Summary on Modeling Frameworks

In this section we gave an overview on the most common modeling frameworks. We saw that all of these frameworks had their specific advantages and disadvantages and are more or less suited for certain applications.

One main advantage of the MIP and CP approaches was that the models can directly be solved by suitable solver programs. This holds especially for MIPs, since all models have the same, fixed structure and very powerful solvers are available. Being able to solve models directly is a huge benefit, since it may sometimes be possible to get by without having to implement something. If this is not possible, it helps to identify promising approaches to implement. In particular, special-purpose implementations will be necessary when it comes to solving large-scale instances.

In order to get a model solved reasonably fast, we had to model with the way the solver works in mind. Hence, modelers need to be aware of different techniques solvers may use and adapt their models accordingly.

2.4   Further Issues

Before concluding the modeling chapter and continuing with the design phase of Algorithm Engineering we discuss by example some special situations where the border between modeling and design is blurred. Furthermore, these situations also provide insights into some of the difficulties encountered in modeling. The first example described in Section 2.4.1 deals with special modeling requirements for the input of a problem. In Section 2.4.2, a setting is analyzed in which a first decomposition of the problem already in the modeling phase seems necessary.

```
 1  # instance data
 2  set P:= { "A", "B" };
 3  set M:= { "a", "b", "c" };
 4  set R:= { 1, 2 };

 6  param d[ R*M ]:=      | "a", "b", "c" |
 7                        |1|   3,   1,   0 |
 8                        |2|   1,   1,   3 |;

10  param A[ P*M ]:=      | "a", "b", "c" |
11                        |"A"|  10,  15,  30 |
12                        |"B"|   8,  13,  33 |;

14  param B[ P*R ]:=      |  1,  2 |
15                        |"A"|  1,  2 |
16                        |"B"|  3,  1 |;

18  # variables
19  var x[ P ] real >= 0;
20  var y[ P*P*M ] real >= 0;
21  var z[ P*M * R*M ] real >= 0;

23  # auxiliary parameters
24  param D:= sum <r,m> in R*M: d[r,m];

26  # the model
27  minimize cost :
28      sum <p,m> in P*M: A[p,m] * y[ p, p,m ]
29      + sum <m,p,r> in M*P*R: B[p,r] * z[ p,m, r,m ];

31  subto flow_s :
32      sum <p> in P: x[ p ] == D;

34  subto flow_p :
35      forall <p> in P do
36      x[ p ] == sum <m> in M: y[ p, p,m ];

38  subto flow_pm :
39      forall <p,m> in P*M do
40      y[ p, p,m ] == sum <r> in R: z[ p,m, r,m ];

42  subto flow_rm :
43      forall <r,m> in R*M do
44      sum <p> in P: z[ p,m, r,m ] == - d[r,m];
```

Fig. 2.7. A ZIMPL program corresponding to the MIP model for the minimum cost flow formulation of the car manufacturing problem. The data of the instance used here is that given in Figure 2.3.

2.4.1   Specific Input Characteristics

Some difficulties of the modeling process are caused by characteristics of the given input. The problems we are referring to are based on some unrealistic input requirements in specific models. Whenever the specific input characteristics of the instances do not match the requirements of the theoretical model, or more precisely of the algorithms within this model, the modeler has to ensure to give a valid translation between these two worlds.

For example, many geometric algorithms assume in 2D the property that *all points are in general position*. Hence, no three points of the input are lying on a straight line. Obviously, this requirement is violated by real-world instances quite often. Usually, it is possible to perturb the points of the input somewhat to guarantee this requirement. But after doing this, the final output of the algorithm only guarantees valid, or optimal respectively, solutions for the perturbed input. It is up to the algorithm engineer to analyze if and how the solution is fitting to the original non-perturbed input.

Another discrepancy between theoretical computation models and available computers is the assumed computational precision of the model. As before, this may lead to misused algorithms and eventually to faulty results. In most cases, theory assumes full precision of its computations, while computers can only use fixed precision if efficiency matters. An example where the input has to be modeled in a special way to circumvent erroneous computations can be found in the field of *interval geometry*. Here the standard geometric objects will simply be replaced by so-called *fat geometric objects*. A fat point could be a disc, but it can generally be any simply connected bounded region. A fat line could be any region that is bounded by two infinite polygonal paths, with some additional properties as well. Now, the basic operations are a lot more sophisticated and have to be defined for this new geometry. But since all objects have some kind of error tolerance for rounding, finite precision arithmetic can compute correct solutions. This is done at the price of a more sophisticated algorithm design and a significantly increased running time. This kind of discrepancy is covered in a lot more detail in a later chapter in this book (Chapter 5).

2.4.2   Problem Decomposition for Complex Applications

Problem decomposition is one of the most central points in Algorithm Engineering and a meeting point between the modeling and the design aspect. Identifying subproblems and exploring how they are linked up is a first important step in the design phase of Algorithm Engineering. This may lead to a remodeling of certain subproblems to ease handling. These decisions are usually done in the design phase. It is easy to see, that different choices of decompositions often yield quite different algorithm performances. Nonetheless, situations occur where a first decomposition is very helpful for modeling as well as for the following design phase. In the case of highly complex applications, it is often a good idea to do a first top level decomposition. In most cases these subproblems are still challenging. Each of these problems has to be modeled on its own, before continuing with the design part of Algorithm Engineering.

As an example we consider the highly complex field of public railway transportation planning. Given the needs and demands of the passengers and the requirements of a profitable company, the problem is to find an optimal solution for all these conflicting requirements. Obviously, the enormous size of this problem recommends a division of the planning process into several steps. A hierarchical approach to problem decomposition seems to be reasonable [527,145]. It consists of the following five main steps.

1. Analysis of passenger demand
2. Line Planning
3. Train Schedule Planning
4. Planning of Rolling Stock
5. Crew Management

In the first step, the demands of the customers have to be modeled. This is often done with a so-called *origin destination matrix*. The second step poses the problem of choosing the lines through the railway network and how often each line should be served. During step three the actual departure and arrival times for each train on each line have to be computed, thereby fixing the train schedule for this network. The last two steps address assignment problems. Scheduled trips have to be performed by engines and wagons, scarce resources which must provide the necessary capacity for the connection, and by some crew, like conductors, drivers or cleaning staff.

Each of these subproblems is still a quite challenging problem on its own. But in contrast to the original problem, each of these subproblems is now of feasible size. The major drawback of this approach is that each solution is the (unchangeable) input for the next step. Thus, it is unlikely that the optimal solution for the whole problem can be computed. Moreover, at a later step it might be realized that some former decision is not only suboptimal, but is blocking all feasible solution. Therefore, the previous steps might have to be repeated. Nevertheless, with this approach a feasible solution can in fact be computed at all. There are more possibilities to decompose such problems into manageable parts and a lot more analysis comparing them. We refer the interested reader to [527] for further details in this field.

2.5   Conclusion

This chapter gave an overview of steps necessary to arrive at a model formulation of a given problem. In summary: modeling is not a skill, that can be grasped quickly. Far from it! Modeling relies strongly on experience and discipline. Thus, a good overview of standard techniques and formulations is as important as acquirements of skill in the modeling process itself.

Modeling has always been an integral part of the sister disciplines Operations Research and Mathematical Programming. In contrast, the modeling aspect of algorithm design has been neglected in the classical algorithmic theory but plays a crucial part then theory is transferred into practice.

Following the modeling phase the next step in the Algorithm Engineering process is the design phase. It includes decisions that are required for constructing correct, fast and robust algorithms for already modeled problems. Nevertheless, while advancing in the Algorithm Engineering process, one should keep in mind that the process of modeling is not necessarily finished. It is common experience that developments in the design phase, or even at a later step, make it necessary to revisit the modeling phase.

Chapter 3. Selected Design Issues

Sabine Helwig, Falk Hüffner*, Ivo Rössling, and Maik Weinard

3.1 Introduction

In the cycle of Algorithm Engineering, the design phase opens after the modeling phase. We may assume that the algorithmic task to be performed is well understood, i. e., that the desired input-output relation is specified, and an agreement has been reached as to what makes a solution to the problem a good solution. These questions must be settled in cooperation with representatives from fields of application.

Once the problem specification has been successfully translated into the language of computer science, we must design an appropriate algorithm. We seek a construction plan for the algorithm to be developed, starting with choices about very fundamental algorithmic concepts and iteratively enhancing this picture, until the plan is sufficiently convincing to move it forward to the implementation phase. If there are several alternatives and a theoretical analysis does not reveal a clear winner, design decision should be based on an experimental evaluation.

This chapter discusses selected aspects of the design phase. However, we do not discuss classical algorithm design paradigms like divide & conquer, dynamic programming, prune & search, or greedy approaches, because textbooks on algorithms like [191, 742, 475, 14, 348, 520, 562] usually provide very instructive examples on how to use and combine these design paradigms.

While classical algorithm design mainly considers asymptotic worst-case performance in a certain model of computation, Algorithm Engineering now deals with algorithms exposed to a real-world environment like real-world data, real-world computers, and real-world requirements as to performance and reliability. In Algorithm Engineering, an algorithm *and* an implementation is sought. Hence, in the big picture of Algorithm Engineering the sublime task of algorithm design is to bridge the gap from the first abstract algorithmic ideas to the implementation by anticipating questions that arise during the implementation phase and providing sufficiently detailed answers to them.

A first important step in that direction is to recognize the inherent limitations of the models used. Abstraction is and will remain one of the fundamental approaches to science and everything from the asymptotical $O(\cdot)$ notation to the simplifying PRAM model has been developed for a good and justified reason. However, awareness is advised. When designing an algorithm for real world applications, it is crucial to recognize the potential dangers, e. g., the imprecision resulting from the finite representation of *real* numbers in a computer. Hence,

---

* Supported by DFG Emmy Noether research group PIAF (fixed-parameter algorithms), NI 369/4.

M. Müller-Hannemann and S. Schirra (Eds.): Algorithm Engineering, LNCS 5971, pp. 58–126, 2010.
© Springer-Verlag Berlin Heidelberg 2010

the task of algorithm design is being extended by a couple of important issues arising from reasonable practical needs.

In order to complement standard textbooks on algorithms with respect to Algorithm Engineering we concentrate on the following design issues, which have turned out to be of quite practical importance:

Simplicity. We explain how simplicity of an algorithm is not just a nice feature, but has wide-ranging effects on the applicability. We give several techniques that can help in developing simple algorithms, among them randomization and the use of general purpose modelers.

Scalability. Algorithm designers have to deal with rapidly growing data sets, large input sizes, and huge networks, and hence, they have to develop algorithms with good *scalability* properties. We will introduce some basic ideas, ranging from the pure definition of scalability to scalability metrics used in parallel algorithm design. Moreover, some fundamental techniques for improving the scalability properties of an implementation are presented. Finally, we will discuss techniques for designing highly scalable systems such as decentralization, content distribution in peer-to-peer networks, and self-organization.

Time-space trade-offs. The time and space requirements of algorithms are key parameters of an algorithms performance. How easily one measure of quality can be improved by moderately sacrificing the other one is the central question in the analysis of time-space trade-offs. We discuss formal methods to analyze the capability to exchange time for space and vice versa. Typical application of time-space trade-offs in the context of storing data or supporting brute force methods are discussed, as well as general techniques like lookup tables and preprocessing.

Robustness. Conventional algorithm design is a development process that is often based on abstraction and simplifying assumptions – covering things like the model of computation, specific properties of the input, correctness of auxiliary algorithms, etc. Such assumptions allow the algorithm designer to focus on the core problem. Yet, resulting implementations and runtime environments are not generally able to meet all of these assumptions, at times leading us to the sobering conclusion: In theory, the algorithm works provably – in practice, the program fails demonstrably. The section on robustness discusses the various aspects of this issue, points out focal problems and explains how to consciously design for robustness, i. e., making algorithms able to deal with and recover from unexpected abnormal situations.

Reusability is another design goal. The benefits of reuse are obvious: using a building block that is already available saves implementation time and one inherits the correctness of the existing implementation. This limits the chances to introduce new bugs during the coding and everything that has been done in terms of testing or proofs of correctness is of immediate use. Furthermore, if at a later time a part of the required functionality needs changes or extensions, it suffices to change the one building block every algorithm is using, rather than making similar changes in similar codes.

The issue of reusability arises at two occasions during the algorithm design stage. At an early stage it arises as an opportunity. It should be checked whether the entire algorithm to be designed or algorithms performing subtasks of the given problem are already available. Using a top down approach in designing algorithms the designer will eventually arrive at building blocks that perform a functionality that has been required before. Public software libraries should be checked as well as components of previously completed projects.

At a later stage reusability arises as a strategic option. Newly developed algorithms should be decomposed into building blocks performing functionalities that are easy to grasp and document. The more thoroughly this decomposition is performed and dependencies between the blocks are minimized, the higher is the chance that some of them will come in handy at a later project.

Design for reusability is supported by functions, procedures and modules in imperative programming languages or to a higher degree by objects and classes in object oriented languages. The smaller the degree of interdependence between the building block, the higher the likelihood that a building block can be reused.

3.2   Simplicity

Simplicity is a highly desirable property of an algorithm; a new algorithm that achieves the same result as a known one, but in a simpler way, is often an important progress. Although the simplicity of an algorithm seems to be an intuitively clear concept, it probably cannot be defined rigorously. A reasonable approximation is "concise to write down and to grasp". However, this clearly depends on "cultural" factors: for example, using sorting as a subroutine would certainly not be considered to make an algorithm complicated nowadays, since library functions and knowledge about their behavior are readily available. This might have been different 50 years ago.

Also, much of the perceived simplicity of an algorithm lies in its presentation. For example, Cormen et al. [191] define red-black trees (a dictionary data structure) based on five invariants, and need about 57 lines of code to implement the *insert* function. In contrast, a presentation by Okasaki [620] uses two invariants and requires 12 lines of code. The reason is that Okasaki focuses on simplicity from the start, chooses a high-level programming language, and omits several optimizations.

Because of these inherent difficulties, and to avoid getting tangled in semantic snares, we will do without a formal definition of "simplicity" and rely on the intuition of the concept.

Advantages of simplicity will be further discussed in Section 3.2.1. Section 3.2.2 shows some general design techniques that can help in keeping algorithms simple. Finally, Section 3.2.3 examines the interplay between simplicity and analyzability of algorithms.

3.2.1 Advantages for Implementation

The most obvious reason to choose a simple algorithm for practical applications is that it is quicker to implement: an algorithm that is more concise to describe will take fewer lines of code, at least when using a sufficiently high-level language. This means simple algorithms can be implemented more quickly. Moreover, since the number of bugs is likely to increase with the number of lines of code, simple algorithms mean fewer bugs. Also, the effort for testing the implementation is reduced.

Another major factor is maintainability. A smaller and simpler code base is easier to understand and debug. Also, if the specification changes, simple methods are more likely to be adaptable without major efforts.

A third factor is employment in resource constrained environments, such as embedded systems, in particular pure hardware implementations. An even moderately complicated algorithm has no chance of being implemented in an application-specific integrated circuit (ASIC) or a field-programmable gate array (FPGA).

As an example for the importance of simplicity, the Advanced Encryption Standard (AES) process, which aimed to find a replacement algorithm for the aging DES block cipher, required "algorithm simplicity" as one of the three major criteria for candidates [238].

Lack of simplicity in an algorithm may not only be a disadvantage, but even make implementation infeasible. A famous example is the algorithm for four-coloring planar graphs by Robertson, Sanders, Seymour, and Thomas [674]. The algorithm works by finding one of 633 "configurations" (subgraphs), and then applying one of 32 "discharging rules" to eliminate them. Even though this is the only known efficient exact algorithm for four-coloring, it has to the best of our knowledge never been implemented.

On the other hand, algorithms initially dismissed as too complicated sometimes still find uses; for example Fibonacci heaps, a priority queue data structure, have been described as "predominantly of theoretical interest" [191], but have still found their way into widely used applications such as the GNU Compiler Collection (gcc) [754].

3.2.2 How to Achieve Simplicity?

Clearly, one cannot give a recipe that will reliably result in a simple algorithm. However, several general principles are helpful in achieving this goal.

Top-Down Design. A standard way of simplifying things is to impose a hierarchical, "top-down" structure. This means that a system is decomposed into several parts with a narrow intersection, which can then independently designed and understood, and be further subdivided. Possibly the most simple example are algorithms that work in phases, each time applying a transformation to the input, or enforcing certain invariants. For example, compilers are usually divided

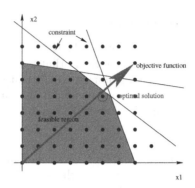

Fig. 3.1. Example Integer Linear Program (ILP)

into a *lexing*, a *parsing*, and a *translation* phase, even though in principle lexing and parsing could be done at the same time. The translation phase is usually broken down further; for example gcc chains more than 100 separate optimization passes.

This concept is well-explored (although typically at the somewhat lower programming language level) in software engineering, for example as *modularity*, but can equally be applied in algorithm design, where one still thinks in terms of pseudo-code. Another benefit of this approach is increased robustness, as explained in Section 3.5.1.

In addition to straightforward phases, there are several more standard algorithm design schemes which can simplify algorithms by reducing them to smaller steps. Examples are divide & conquer, dynamic programming, greedy, and branch & bound. A particular advantage of choosing such a standard scheme is that they are well-known and thus simpler to grasp, and much knowledge about implementing and analyzing them has been accumulated.

General-Purpose Modelers. Often, it is possible to cast a problem in terms of a general problem model. Particularly successful models are linear programs (LPs) and integer linear programs (ILPs) [710, 191], constraint satisfaction problems (CSPs) [34], and boolean satisfiability problems (SAT) [522, 191]. The chapter on modeling, Section 2.3, gives an extended introduction to this topic; we here focus on an example that demonstrates the simplicity of the approach.

LP solvers optimize a linear function of a real vector under linear constraints. ILPs add the possibility of requiring variables to be integral (see Figure 3.1). This allows to express nonlinear constraints, as will be seen in an example below. CSPs consists of variables that can take a small number of discrete values and *constraints* on these variables, where a constraint forbids certain variable allocations. This generalizes a large number of problems, for example graph coloring. Finally, SAT solvers find assignments to boolean variables that satisfy a boolean expression that contains only AND, OR, and NOT.

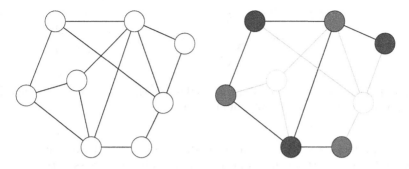

Fig. 3.2. Example GRAPH BIPARTIZATION instance (left) and optimal solution by deleting two vertices (right)

As an example, consider the NP-hard GRAPH BIPARTIZATION, which asks for a minimum set of vertices to delete from a graph to make it bipartite. Given a graph $G = (V, E)$, this problem can be formulated as an ILP with little effort:

$c_1, \ldots, c_n$: binary variables $(c_i \in \{0, 1\})$ *(deletion set)*

$s_1, \ldots, s_n$: binary variables $(s_i \in \{0, 1\})$ *(side)*

$$\text{minimize} \sum_{i=1}^{n} c_i$$

s. t. $\forall \{v, w\} \in E : (s_v \neq s_w) \vee c_v \vee c_w$

which can be expressed as an ILP constraint as

s. t. $\forall \{v, w\} \in E : s_v + s_w + (c_v + c_w) \geq 1$

$\forall \{v, w\} \in E : s_v + s_w - (c_v + c_w) \leq 1.$

Here, $c_v = 1$ models that v is part of the deletion set, and the variables s_v model the side of the bipartite graph that remains after deleting the vertices from the deletion set. The solution space then has $2n$ dimensions (in contrast, the example in Figure 3.1 has only 2 dimensions).

To actually solve an instance, it takes little more than a script containing the above description in a solver-specific syntax. In this way, problem instances could be solved much faster than with a problem-specific branch&bound-algorithm that consists of several thousand lines of code [417], and the size of instance that could be solved within reasonable time was doubled to about 60 vertices.

The power of this approach comes from the many years of Algorithm Engineering that went into the solvers. These solvers are readily available, e. g., GNU GLPK [536] for LPs and ILPs, MINION [326] for CSPs, or MiniSat [270] for SAT, as well several commercial solvers.

When it is possible to formulate a problem in one of these general models without too much overhead, this is usually the quickest way to obtain a solution,

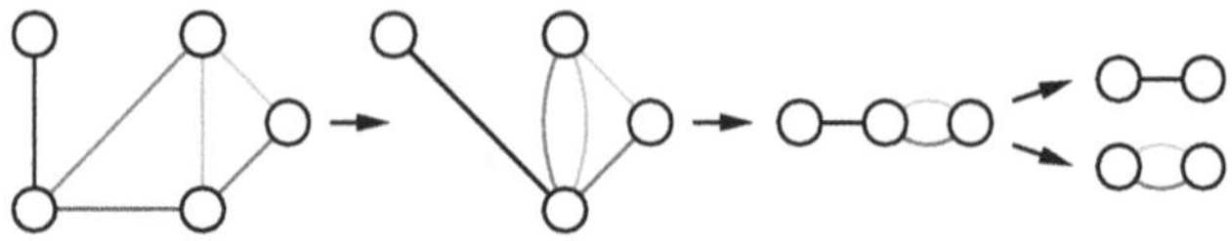

Fig. 3.3. Example for the Monte Carlo algorithm for Min-Cut. In the last step, the top option displayed yields the optimum minimum cut.

and often performance is surprisingly good. Even if it is not satisfactory, there are ways to tune performance and amend the solving process with problem-specific tricks, such as branch&cut for ILPs [185]. Therefore, it is recommendable to try this approach first, if applicable, before thinking about any problem-specific algorithms. An exception are very simple problems that are expected to be solvable in a very good polynomial time bound, since the transformation of the problem representation incurs a noticeable linear-time overhead.

Trade-Off Guaranteed Performance. Sometimes, bad worst-case performance of an algorithm comes from corner case inputs, which would have to be specifically designed by an adversary to thwart the usually good performance of the algorithm. For example, consider quicksort, a sorting algorithm that works by selecting an element as *pivot*, dividing the elements into those smaller than the pivot and those larger than the pivot, and then recursively sorting these subsets. It usually performs very well, except when the choice of the pivot repeatedly divides the subsequence into parts of very unequal size, resulting in a $\Theta(n^2)$ runtime. Even elaborate pivot choice schemes like "median-of-three" cannot eliminate this problem. A very simple solution to this problem is to choose a *random* pivot. In a sense, this thwarts any attempt of an adversary to prepare a particularly adverse input sequence, since the exact behavior of the algorithm cannot be predicted in advance. More formally, one can analyze the *expected* runtime of this algorithm to be $\Theta(n \log n)$. The disadvantage of the approach is that with a small probability, the algorithm takes much longer than expected. An algorithm employing randomness that always produces a correct result, but carries a small probability of using more resources than expected, is called a *Las Vegas algorithm* [589].

A disadvantage of Las Vegas algorithms is that they are often hard to analyze. Still, it is often a good idea to employ randomness to avoid excessive resource usage on corner case inputs, while retaining simplicity.

Trade-Off Guaranteed Correctness. While Las Vegas algorithms gamble with the resources required to solve a problem, *Monte Carlo algorithms* gamble with the quality of the result, that is, they carry some small chance that a solution will not be correct or optimal [589]. Consider for example the Min-Cut problem: given a graph G, find a *min-cut* in G, that is, a minimum size set of edges whose removal results in G being broken into two or more components. We consider the following algorithm: pick a random edge and merge its two endpoints. Remove all self-loops (but not multiple edges between two vertices) and repeat until only two vertices remain. The edges between these vertices then form a candidate min-cut (see Figure 3.3). The whole process is repeated, and the best min-cut candidate is returned. With some effort, one can calculate how often the procedure has to be repeated to meet any desired error probability. This algorithm is much simpler than deterministic algorithms for MIN-CUT, which are mostly based on network flow. In addition, a variant has an expected running time that is significantly smaller than that of the best known deterministic algorithms [589].

Another classical example is the Miller–Rabin primality test [574, 656]. In particular in public-key crypto systems, it is an important task to decide whether an integer is prime. Only recently a deterministic polynomial-time algorithm has been found for this problem [13]. This method is quite complicated and will probably never be implemented except for educational reasons; moreover, it has a runtime bound of about $\tilde{O}(g^{7.5})$, where g is the number of digits of the input [243]. The Miller–Rabin primality test, on the other hand, is quite practical and routinely used in many software packages such as GNU Privacy Guard (GnuPG) [492]. To test a number n for primality, $n - 1$ is first rewritten as $2^s \cdot d$ by factoring out 2 repeatedly. One then tries to find a *witness* a for the compositeness of n. With comparably simple math one can show that if for some $a \in \mathbb{Z}/n\mathbb{Z}$

$$a^{2^r d} \not\equiv -1 \pmod{n} \text{ for all } 0 \le r \le s - 1$$

holds, then n is not prime. By trying many random a's, the probability of failing to detect compositeness can be made arbitrarily small. This algorithm is very simple, can be implemented efficiently, and is the method of choice in practice.

3.2.3   Effects on Analysis

Intuitively, a simpler algorithm should be easier to analyze for performance measures such as worst-case runtime, memory use, or solution quality. As an example, consider the NP-complete VERTEX COVER problem: given a graph, find a subset of its vertices such that every edge has at least one endpoint in the subset. This is one of the most well-known NP-complete problems, and it has found many applications, for example in computational biology. A simple greedy algorithm repeatedly chooses some edge, takes *both* endpoints into the cover, and then deletes them from the graph. Clearly, this gives an approximation factor of 2, that is, the solution is always at most twice the size of an optimal solution. The currently best approximation for VERTEX COVER [456] is based on semidefinite programming and achieves a factor of $2 - \Theta(1/\sqrt{\log n})$, where n is the number of vertices in the graph. This algorithm is quite complicated, and requires advanced concepts to be analyzed.

However, in fact sometimes simplicity and analyzability seem to be excluding properties, and more complicated algorithms are developed to make them more amenable to analysis tools.

This is illustrated by the NP-complete SHORTEST COMMON SUPERSTRING problem: given a set $\mathcal{S} = \{S_1, \ldots, S_n\}$ of strings, find the shortest string that contains each element of $\mathcal{S}$ as a contiguous substring. This problem has important applications in computational biology and in data compression. The standard approach is a simple greedy algorithm that repeatedly merges two strings with the largest overlap, until only one string remains. Here, the *overlap* of two strings A and B is the longest string that is both a suffix of A and a prefix of B. For example:

```
TCAGAGGC GGCAGAAG AAGTTCAG AAGTTGGG
AAGTTCAGAGGC GGCAGAAG AAGTTGGG
AAGTTCAGAGGC GGCAGAAG AAGTTGGG
GGCAGAAGTTCAGAGGC AAGTTGGG
GGCAGAAGTTCAGAGGC AAGTTGGG
AAGTTGGGCAGAAGTTCAGAGGC
```

In the first line, the largest overlap is "TCAG", found at the start of the first string and the end of the third string. Therefore, these strings are merged (second line). After this, the largest overlap is "AAG" (third line), and so on.

One can find an example where the resulting superstring is twice as long as an optimal one, but no worse example is known. This has lead to the conjecture that a factor of 2 is indeed the worst case [828], which is supported by recent smoothed analysis results [532]. However, despite considerable effort, only an upper bound of 3.5 has been proven yet [455].

The currently "best" algorithm for SHORTEST COMMON SUPERSTRING [769] provides a factor-2.5-approximation. In contrast to the 3-line greedy algorithm, it takes several pages to describe it, and, to the best of our knowledge, has never been implemented. However, its design and features allow to derive the better bound.

Another example for the interplay of simplicity and analysis are recent results on exponential-time algorithms for NP-hard problems. As an example, the VERTEX COVER problem can be solved in $O(2^k n)$ time, where n is the number of vertices in the input graph, and k is the size of the cover. For this, one considers an arbitrary edge and branches into two possibilities: the one endpoint is in the cover, or the other is. In a long series of papers, the runtime of this algorithm has been improved to $O(1.274^k n)$ [166]. Most progress was based on an ever increasing number of case distinctions: a list of possible graph substructures, and a corresponding list on how to branch, should they occur. Similar studies were undertaken for other NP-complete problems. The process of finding and verifying such algorithms became somewhat tedious; eventually computer programs were written to automate the task of designing case distinctions [354]. Also, experiments have shown that the numerous distinguished cases do often not lead to a speedup, but in fact to a slowdown, due to the overhead of distinction. Better methods of analyzing the recurrences involved were designed by Eppstein [274]. Using these methods, it was shown that many simple algorithms perform in fact much better than previously proved; for example, an algorithm for DOMINATING SET runs in $O(2^{0.598n})$ on n-vertices graphs instead of $O(2^{0.850n})$ [292]. These examples seed the doubt that some "improvements" to algorithm performance in fact may actually be only improvements to their analyzability. There are several ways how this situation could be ameliorated:

- Experimental results can shed some light on the relative performance. For example, one could generate random SHORTEST COMMON SUPERSTRING instances and see whether the 2.5-approximation fares better than the 3.5-approximation. However, these tests will always be biased by the choice of instances and can never prove superiority of an algorithm.
- Proving lower bounds on the performance of algorithms can give hints on the quality of an upper bound. However, proving good lower bounds can be difficult, and often there remains a large gap between lower and upper bounds. Also, instances used to show the lower bounds are often "artificial" or could easily be handled as special cases in actual implementations.
- Improving the algorithm analysis tool chest. This is clearly the most valuable contribution, as illustrated by the effects of Eppstein's paper [274].

These steps can help to avoid that designers give up simplicity without an actual gain in implementations.

3.3 Scalability

Due to rapid technological advances, system developers have to deal with huge and growing data sets, very large input and output sizes, and vast computer networks. A typical Internet search engine has to find relevant data out of billions of web pages. These large data sets can only be processed by very sophisticated text-matching techniques and ranking algorithms [626]. Car navigation systems have to find shortest paths in graphs with several billions of nodes, ideally with taking traffic jams and road works into account. The graphs used for North America or Western Europe have already about 20,000,000 nodes each [697]. Although the shortest path problem can be solved with the well-known Dijkstra's algorithm [244] in time $O(n^2)$ (where n is the number of nodes), for large road graphs and on mobile hardware with memory constraints, the original Dijkstra algorithm is much too slow. Here, we need new, more specialized, algorithms which can successfully handle real world problems, not only today but also tomorrow, i. e., taking growing data sets into consideration.

Simulation and measurement results of, e. g., car crash tests or computed tomography, produce gigabytes of data which have to be evaluated, analyzed, or visualized. In the "Visible Human Project", the data set representing a human's body is about 40 GB [7]. We certainly expect these data sets to grow larger and larger due to technological progress which allows better and better resolutions of, e. g., computed tomography scans. An algorithm designer must be aware of increasing data sets and larger input and output sizes when approaching a real world problem.

Moreover, not only data sets, but also computer networks are growing. The Internet connects billions of computers which are often sharing the same resources, for instance, a certain web service. The world wide web introduces a lot of new challenges for algorithm designers: Load variations and denial of service attacks must be handled by, e. g., using redundancy and data distribution [247]. The Internet allows its users to share any kind of resources such as data or computational power. Grid computing projects like SETI@home [726] use the idle times of ordinary computers to perform large computational tasks. Coordination between the participants is strongly required in order to solve huge problems jointly in networks whose structure changes permanently. In computer networks, it can be advantageous to spread data over the network in order to decrease space requirements. Distributed data storage has recently become an important research area, and new protocols for efficient data storage and access in large, unreliable, and ever-changing networks have to be invented. The Chord protocol from Stoica et al. [757] proposes a very efficient protocol for distributed data storage.

Summarizing, we have seen that an algorithm designer who wants his or her algorithm to also be used in a few years has to anticipate growing data sets, increasing input and output sizes, and large, permanently changing networks. Such algorithms are said to "scale well". Countless papers propose a "new scalable algorithm" for a certain problem, which suggests that scalability is an important feature of an algorithm. But what is the exact meaning of the term "scalability"? When can we claim our algorithm to "scale well"? The term scalability is used in many different application areas such as data mining, computer graphics, and distributed computing. Thus, giving an overall definition seems to be rather difficult. Nevertheless, in 2006, Duboc et al. [260] presented a "scalability framework", which is a first step towards a formal definition of "scalability". This framework will be presented in Section 3.3.1. In parallel computing, however, the term "scalability" already is widely-used and there exist metrics for evaluating the scalability of a parallel system. Unfortunately, these metrics are too specific to be applied elsewhere. Nevertheless, they give deeper insight into the whole topic, and they might be helpful when an algorithm designer wants to prove his or her system to scale well. Thus, we will show two of these metrics in Section 3.3.2. Afterwards, some basic techniques for designing algorithms with good scaling properties will be presented in Section 3.3.3. Finally, state-of-art strategies for creating highly scalable computer networks such as using decentralization or hierarchies, distributed hash tables, and self-organization, are discussed in Section 3.3.4.

3.3.1   Towards a Definition of Scalability

The term *scalability* is used in many different application areas in order to describe technical systems or algorithms. There exists a variety of different scalability aspects, for example:

- An algorithm should be designed such that it can deal with *small and large input sizes*.

- A database system should be designed such that queries can be answered on *small and large data sets.*
- The running time of a parallel algorithm should decrease in relation to the *number of processing elements.*
- Peer-to-peer networks should be able to deal with a *small and large number of users.*

Usually, a system is said to *scale well* if it can react to modifications (mostly enlargement) of the application or the hardware properties in a way which is acceptable for the system developer as well as for its users. Due to the many aspects of scalability, it is difficult to develop evaluation methods suitable for broad application. But in some research areas the use of specific scalability metrics is well-established, e.g., as already mentioned, in parallel computing. Although the concept of scalability is hard to define, many systems are claimed by their developers to scale well. In 1990, Mark Hill [394] considered the question "What is Scalability?" and concluded with "*I encourage the technical community to either rigorously define scalability or stop using it to describe systems.*" Few studies have been published since then providing more general definitions [368,117], but most of them correspond to the intuitive definition mentioned above. In a recent study, Duboc et al. [260] still argue:

Most uses of the term scalability in scientific papers imply a desired goal or completed achievement, whose precise nature is never defined but rather left to the readers' imagination.

Duboc et al. provide a first step towards expressing scalability more generally. They claim that scalability is about the relationship between cause and effect, i.e., how a system reacts to changes in the environment. Based on this definition, the framework presented in Figure 3.4 has been derived. The application domain and the machine domain are called *independent variables* whereas system requirements such as performance, economics, physical size, security, or reliability are called *dependent variables*. When investigating the scalability properties of a system, single parts of the independent variables, e.g., input size, number of users, size of a database system, or number of processing elements, are changed, and the *effects* on the dependent variables are considered. Accordingly, scalability should never be regarded on its own, but always together with one or more independent and one or more dependent variables. For example, a developer could claim his or her system to scale well in the input size regarding the system's performance. Of course, more precise statements are also possible, e.g., by showing that a parallel system scales well up to 50 processors, but poorly for more than 50 processors. Ideally, the relationship between cause and effect is expressed as a function, but most researchers only present experimental results in order to demonstrate the scalability of their system.

Sometimes, well-scaling systems can be achieved by sacrificing one or more rather unimportant dependent variables for the benefit of one or more other qualities. For example, in many applications it is possible to get faster algorithms by using more space, and vice versa. These so-called *time-space trade-offs* are

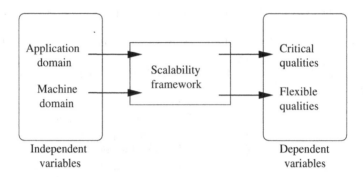

Fig. 3.4. A first step towards a general definition of scalability: the scalability framework [260]

extensively discussed in Section 3.4. Duboc et al. have integrated trade-offs into their framework by dividing the dependent variables into *critical qualities* and *flexible qualities*. Critical qualities are those qualities which are assumed to be very important whereas flexible qualities can be sacrificed. If, for example, performance and quality are critical qualities, and space is a flexible one, we can try to find a time-space trade-off. If performance and space are assumed to be critical qualities, but quality is rather flexible, we might design an approximation algorithm.

Although this framework does not include any concrete scalability metrics, it provides a useful general definition. However, parallel algorithm designers have developed methods for evaluating the scalability of a system. Two of these metrics will be presented in the next section.

3.3.2 Scalability in Parallel Computing

Parallelization can be used to improve the performance of a computer program, and is discussed in detail in Chapter 5. Here, we focus on scalability metrics for parallel systems. The running time of a parallel algorithm does not only depend on the input size, but also on the number of processing elements that are used. Ideally, we would expect a program to run ten times faster if ten processing elements are used instead of a single one. However, for most parallel algorithms, this is not the case due to the following overheads which might occur through parallelization [352]:

Communication overhead. In most parallel systems, the processing elements have to interact with each other to spread intermediate results or to share information.

Idle times. A processing element becomes idle when it must wait for another processor in order to perform a synchronization step, or due to load imbalance.

Poor parallel algorithm. It might be impossible to parallelize the best known sequential algorithm for a given problem. Thus, it might be necessary to use a poorer algorithm, resulting in inherent performance loss.

In the context of parallel algorithm design, scalability is defined as the ability of an algorithm to scale with the number of processing elements, i. e., if more processors are used, the running time should decrease in proportion to the number of the additional processing elements. It is a measure for how efficiently additional processing elements can be used.

There are some broadly applicable techniques to achieve scalability in parallel systems: As communication often is one of the main sources of parallelization overhead, Skiena recommends to design parallel algorithms such that the original problem is split into tasks which can be executed completely independently from each other, and to just collect and put together the results in the end [742]. This strategy is successfully applied in grid computing projects like SETI@home [726]. If communication is necessary for performing the task, Dehne et al. [216] suggest to partition the problem such that only a constant number of global communication steps are required. They show the practicability of this approach on a number of geometric problems such as 2D-nearest neighbor search on a point set, or the calculation of the area of the union of rectangles.

The most challenging part in parallelization is to divide the given problem into appropriate subproblems. Grama et al. [352] identified four decomposition techniques which can serve as a starting point for designing a parallel algorithm:

Recursive decomposition. Problems that can be solved by using a *divide-and-conquer* strategy are qualified for recursive decomposition. The problem is divided into a set of independent subproblems, whose results are then combined to the overall solution. For each of the subproblems, the same algorithm is applied, until they are small enough to be solved efficiently on a single processing element.

Data decomposition. There are several ways for data decomposition: Each processor can compute a single element of the output, if the computation of each output element only depends on the input. Sometimes, the input can be split using a kind of divide-and-conquer strategy: For example, let us assume that the sum of a sequence of numbers has to be computed. It is possible to split the task into summing up the numbers of subsequences and to finally combine the results. If the algorithm is structured such that the output of one step is the input of another, it might be possible to partition the input or the output of one or more such intermediate steps.

Exploratory decomposition. If, for example, the solution of a combinatorial problem is searched for, we might give the problem to an arbitrary number of processors, letting each one apply another search strategy, and finish if a solution has been found.

Speculative decomposition. Some applications are hard to parallelize because a long sequential computation must be performed in order to decide what should be done next. If this is the case, all possible next computation steps can be executed in parallel, and needless computations will be discarded afterwards.

Evaluating the Scalability of a Parallel Algorithm. Until now, we have defined scalability as a measure for a parallel system's capability to utilize additional processing elements efficiently. Grama et al. [352] described the following model for parallel programs which allows a formal definition of a parallel system's scalability.

When analyzing a parallel algorithm, its performance is usually compared with a sequential algorithm which solves the same problem, and has execution time T_S. To provide fair comparison, a parallel algorithm designer should always use the best known sequential algorithm for the analysis and not, if existing, the sequential algorithm which has been the basis of his or her parallel algorithm.

The execution time T_P of a parallel algorithm is the time elapsed between the beginning of the computation until the last processor has finished.

The *overhead* of a parallel program which is executed on p processing elements is defined as

$$T_O = pT_P - T_S$$

which is the time that would have been required in addition to the sequential running time if the parallel algorithm was processed sequentially.

Speed-up is defined as the ratio of the time required to solve a given problem sequentially to the time required to solve the same problem on p processing elements:

$$S = \frac{T_S}{T_P} \ .$$

Theoretically, this assures that $S \leq p$ is always true, but in practice, speedups greater than p have also been observed, referred to as *superlinear speed-up*. This can be due to, for example, cache effects: If the data is too large to fit in the cache of a single processing element, partitioned for parallel computation it might fit. We need two more definitions to complete the model:

– The *efficiency metric* tells us how efficiently the processing elements are used:

$$E = \frac{S}{p} = \frac{T_S}{pT_P} \ .$$

– The *problem size* W is the number of computation steps that is required by the best known sequential algorithm for solving the problem. For example, for matrix addition, the problem size is $\Theta(n^2)$. The problem size is a function of the input size.

With the previous definitions in mind, scalability is now defined as a parallel system's ability to increase speed-up in proportion to the number of processing elements.

Looking at scalability from another point of view (but based on the same definition), a parallel system is called scalable, if the efficiency can be kept constant as the number of processing elements as well as the input size is increased. If we assume that the problem size W is equal to the sequential running time T_S, we can evaluate W to [352]:

$$W = KT_O(W, p) \ , \tag{1}$$

where T_O is the overhead, which depends on the problem size W and on the number of processing elements p, and $K = E/(1 - E)$ is a constant, as we keep the efficiency constant.

Equation (1) is called the *isoefficiency function* of a parallel system. The isoefficiency function is a measure for the scalability of a system: It specifies the growth rate of the problem size (which is a function of the input size) required to keep the efficiency fixed when adding more processing elements. If its asymptotic growth is slow, additional processing elements can be utilized efficiently. For unscalable parallel systems, the isoefficiency function does not exist, since it is impossible to keep the efficiency fixed when p increases.

3.3.3 Basic Techniques for Designing Scalable Algorithms

After having presented the scalability framework and shown some metrics which can be applied in parallel computing, we will now approach scalability from a more general point of view. In this section, we will present some fundamental techniques for designing algorithms with good scaling properties.

In Algorithm Engineering we are supposed to solve a concrete real world problem. Designing algorithms with good asymptotic worst case running times is of great theoretical interest and leads to valuable insights for practical applications. However, when regarding Algorithm Design in the context of Algorithm Engineering, we have to extend our view and consider the specific application. An algorithm with a bad worst case behavior might be a good choice if the worst case seldom or never happens. Consider the simplex algorithm as an example: It has exponential worst case running time, but it is nevertheless a very popular and successful technique for solving linear programming problems.

One of the most-used methods to achieve scalability in a software system is to apply problem-specific heuristics which have proven to scale well in practice. Since Algorithm Engineering means cycling between design, analysis, implementation and experimentation until an appropriate solution is found, heuristic approaches are very common. Their quality can be checked, e. g., in the experimentation step, and further improvements are possible in the next cycle. The major drawback of applying heuristics is that most of the times, only suboptimal outputs are generated, and often, an analysis of the expected output quality does not exist.

When approaching a concrete problem, we first analyze the problem and make assumptions on the expected inputs and system properties. In order to design an algorithm with good scaling properties, we have to decide which concrete scaling properties we want to realize. Certainly, if we have to develop a program for a mobile phone, it is not important for us whether our algorithm scales in the number of processors, because we will not use thousands of them in a single mobile phone. Thus, the expected application domain (e. g., input size, number of users) and the system properties (e. g., number of processing elements, memory size) have to be bounded appropriately. Then, we concentrate on designing algorithms which are efficient within the given restrictions, and thus scale well in their application areas. We are not searching for algorithms with good asymptotic behavior because our concrete problems are bounded. A typical example of bound dependent design is the choice of an appropriate data structure which will be explained in the following subsection, and is also discussed in the context of time-space trade-off in Section 3.4.4.

Using Appropriate Data Structures. The choice of the most efficient data structure for a given application depends on the number of elements which have to be stored as well as on the operations which are expected to be most commonly applied to them. Using appropriate data structures can improve an application's performance significantly.

Dictionaries. One of the most important data structure needed in computer science is dictionaries, which can store data identifiable by one or more keys and provide methods for inserting, deleting, and searching for objects. There exists a variety of different dictionaries such as simple arrays, hash tables, and trees. The following dictionary types are widely used (see, e. g., Skiena [742]):

Unsorted arrays. For very small data sets, i. e., less than 20 records, a simple array is most appropriate. A variant which has been proven to be very efficient in practice is a *self-organizing list*: Whenever an element is accessed, it is inserted at the front of the list in order to provide faster access the next time.

Sorted arrays. In a sorted array, elements can be accessed in logarithmic time by performing binary search. However, they only perform well if there are only very few insertions or deletions.

Hash tables. Often, a hash table with bucketing is good choice, when many elements have to be stored. The keys are transformed to integers between 0 and $m - 1$ via a hash function, and then the objects are stored at the respective position of an array of length m. If two or more elements have been mapped to the same position, they can for example be organized as a linked list. The array size m and the hash function have great impact on the performance of a hash table, and should therefore be chosen carefully.

Binary search trees. Binary search trees provide fast insertions, deletions, and access. There are balanced and unbalanced versions. For most applications, balanced trees such as *red-black trees* or *splay trees* are more efficient since an unbalanced tree might degenerate to a linked list, which performs very poorly.

For large data sets which do not fit in main memory, using a *B-tree* might be appropriate. In a B-tree, several levels of a binary tree are moved into one node in order to process them sequentially before requiring another disk access.

Space Partitioning Trees. In many applications, such as computer graphics, statistics, data compression, pattern recognition, and database systems, many objects in low- or high-dimensional spaces have to be stored. Typical questions to such systems are "which object is closest to another given object" (nearest neighbor search), "which region contains the following object" (point localization) or "which objects lie within a given region" (range search).

The nearest neighbor problem is defined as follows: A set S of n elements in k dimensions is given, and we are searching for the closest element in S to a query object q. Obviously, this query can be answered in linear time by comparing all objects with the given one. This simple approach performs very well for a small number (less than 100) of objects. However, for hundreds or thousands of objects, there are better approaches, based on *space partitioning trees*. The idea is to arrange the objects into a tree structure so that the time for answering queries depends on the height of the tree, which ideally is $\log n$. The most-used space partitioning trees are *kd-trees* [91, 307]: The space is recursively divided into two parts according to a splitting strategy, e. g., such that each subregion contains equally many elements. The recursion stops if the number of elements in a region is below a given threshold [590]. These elements can be processed more efficiently using the simple linear time approach. Of course, it is also possible to divide a region not only along one dimension but along every dimension in every split, resulting in *quadtrees* for two-dimensional data sets and *octtrees* for three dimensions [690]. Figure 3.5 shows a kd-tree and a quadtree. The kd-tree should only be used for less than 20 dimensions since it performs very poorly in higher-dimensional spaces. For such applications, searching for an approximate solution of the given problem might be a good approach [49].

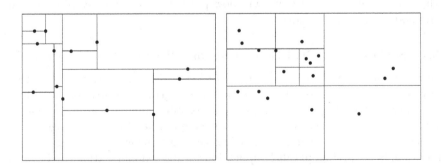

Fig. 3.5. An example of a kd-tree (left) and of a quadtree (right)

The process of analyzing, transforming, and/or reducing data before applying an algorithm is called *preprocessing*, and is discussed in more detail in Section 3.4.4, concentrating on time-space trade-offs. Usually, creating a kd-tree is not a space-critical procedure, but a time-consuming task, and therefore only pays off for large input sizes, or if we expect a large number of queries.

Algorithm Selection. If it is impossible to make any assumptions on the expected application domain, we can design more than one algorithm for a given problem and choose the appropriate one during runtime, when more information is available.

For small input sizes, an algorithm with good asymptotic running time might not be the best choice due to overhead produced by, for example, applying complicated transformations on the input data before solving the problem. These computations (preprocessing operations) are hidden in the O-notation, and might significantly slow down an algorithm for small input sizes. When solving larger problems, however, it pays off to create additional data structures or to do precalculations, since the additional running time is mostly negligible compared to the overall execution time.

An example for algorithm selection is the *introspective sorting algorithm* described by Musser [602]. The median-of-three quicksort algorithm has an average computing time $O(n \log n)$ and is considered to be faster than many other algorithms with equally good asymptotic behavior. However, there are input sequences which lead to quadratic running time. In these cases, a better performance can be achieved by heapsort, with average and worst case running time $O(n \log n)$, but which on average is slower than quicksort. The *introspective sorting algorithm* uses quicksort on most inputs, but switches to heapsort if the partitioning of quicksort has reached a certain depth. The result is an algorithm which works almost exactly like quicksort on most inputs and is thus equally fast, but has a $O(n \log n)$ worst case running time by using heapsort for the critical cases.

After having introduced some fundamental strategies for achieving algorithms with good scaling properties, we will now present some examples of advanced, more modern design techniques.

3.3.4 Scalability in Grid Computing and Peer-to-Peer Networks

In *grid computing* projects, large computational tasks are performed by using many processing elements which can be located geographically far away from each other. Often, they are connected via existing communication infrastructures, mostly the Internet, and try to solve computational problems together by sharing their resources. The number of processing elements can be significantly larger than in traditional parallel applications, while communication can be much slower, and thus, scalability is an important concern here. Special types of grid computing are desktop grids. They have become popular through projects like SETI@home [726], which try to use the idle times of ordinary desktop computers to perform large computations.

Peer-to-peer is a concept which differs from the traditional client-server-approach: Every participant, also called *peer*, acts as both client and server, which means that it provides resources for other peers, but also uses resources of the others. Peer-to-peer networks have become well-known through file sharing, but more generally, each kind of resource can be shared. In peer-to-peer networks, two communicating participants usually establish a direct connection to each other. The scalability question which arises here is whether new participants can be integrated without decreasing the performance of the whole net. For further reading, an overview on peer-to-peer networks and grid computing can be found in [31], and a comparative study has been published by Foster and Iamnitchi [303].

When designing distributed algorithms for grid or peer-to-peer computing, we have to consider two main scalability issues: The system should be able to deal with a large number of participants, and it should use available resources efficiently, even if they are not known beforehand. There exist some techniques to achieve these goals, namely decentralization, making use of hierarchies, and utilizing distributed hash tables, which have been proven to work very well in practice. These techniques will be explained below, in the context of information sharing and content distribution.

Decentralization. Using a central instance which coordinates the whole computation can easily become the bottleneck of a distributed application since the performance of the whole network depends on the performance of this central node. Consider the information sharing application Napster (see, e.g., [31, p. 344ff]): Data is stored in a decentralized manner on the peers, but a central server knows where to find which piece of data. If a peer is searching for something it must ask the central server where to find it. Afterwards, a direct connection to a peer owning the desired information is established. Although data storage takes place decentralized, the existence of a central server slows down the whole application significantly the more users participate.

Gnutella [443] is completely decentralized: A central server does not exist, instead, each peer helps other peers to find information by forwarding incoming requests to its neighbors. The bottleneck caused by centralization vanishes, but Gnutella has another problem, resulting in bad scalability properties: Each request is published randomly in the net, and thus the unintelligent searching strategy can become the bottleneck of this application when too many messages are spread and single nodes become overloaded.

Making Use of Hierarchies. The problem caused by broadcasting requests has been solved by the developers of Kazaa, which is, like Gnutella, fully decentralized, but divides its participants into super nodes and ordinary nodes. This way, Kazaa exploits the heterogeneity of the peers as they can strongly differ in up time, bandwidth connectivity, and CPU power [525]. Each ordinary node is assigned to a super node. Super nodes are fully informed about which information is provided by their children. If a participant searches for data, it asks its super node where to find it. The super node first checks whether another child node has the desired information, otherwise forwards the request to its adjacent super nodes. If an appropriate node has been found, a direct connection between the peers is established for transferring the data.

Besides Kazaa, there exist many other algorithms which exploit the inherent heterogeneity of a problem in order to achieve better scalability. For example, in car navigation systems, the inherent hierarchical structure of road networks can be used in order to develop extremely efficient, problem-specific solutions [224]. Shortest path algorithms are discussed in detail in Chapter 9. Another example is an algorithm for rendering objects in computer graphics, namely *level of detail* [275]: Objects, which are near the viewer are rendered with high resolution whereas objects which are far away are shown less detailed.

Intelligent Data Distribution. Although Kazaa has helped to eliminate some of the bottlenecks of earlier protocols, it has two main disadvantages: The first one is the lookup strategy. Each request is broadcasted in the net, but after passing a specified number of nodes, it is deleted in order to avoid that unanswered requests are rotating in the network forever. This means that it might happen that a data request is removed even if the data is available. Hence, accessibility of data can not be guaranteed. The second disadvantage is the inhomogeneity of the nodes, although helpful to achieve scalability, this property causes larger vulnerability as, for example, the failure of a super node may cause serious problems for the whole net.

More recent protocols like CAN [664], Chord [757], Pastry [683], Tapastry [391], Viceroy [537], Distance Halving [610], and Koorde [445] overcome these two drawbacks by using *distributed hash tables (DHT)*, which have been introduced as *consistent hashing* in 1997 by Karger et al. [460]. All these protocols assume that data does no longer belong to a certain peer, but can be distributed arbitrarily in the net. This is done by hashing data as well as peers into a predefined space. In order to illustrate this principle, Chord will now be presented in more detail.

Here, each piece of data is represented by a unique key which is hashed to an m-bit identifier. The participating nodes also get an m-bit identifier by hashing, for example, their IP address. Thus, every piece of data and every node has an ID in the interval $[0 \ldots 2^m - 1]$. The nodes are arranged into a logical ring structure, sorted by their IDs. Each piece of data is now assigned to the first node whose ID is equal to or follows the data's ID. Figure 3.6 shows a Chord ring with $N = 3$ nodes and $m = 3$, i.e., all IDs are in the interval $[0 \ldots 7]$. Let us assume that our nodes have IDs 0, 1, and 3. Data is always stored in its succeeding node, which means that, in our example, in the node with ID 0 all data with ID 0, 4, 5, 6, and 7, is stored, and in the node with ID 3 all data with ID 2 and 3 is stored. This strategy allows efficient leaving and entering of nodes. If a node leaves the net, all its data is transfered to its successor, while when a node is joining, it might get data from its successor.

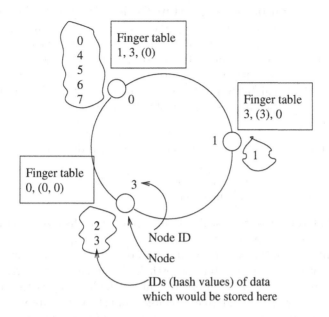

Fig. 3.6. A Chord ring with 3 nodes with IDs 0, 1, and 3. Data is always stored in the node whose ID follows the data's ID, and thus, data with ID 0, 4, 5, 6, 7 is stored in node with ID 0, and data with ID 2 or 3 is stored in node with ID 3.

In order to locate data, each node must have information about other nodes. A Chord node only maintains a very small amount of such routing information; this is the main reason why it scales well in the number of nodes. The routing table of a Chord node, also called *finger table*, consists of at most m entries, which is in $O(\log N)$ where N is the number of nodes. The i-th entry of the finger table of node n contains the ID and the IP address of the first node following $n + 2^{i-1} \bmod 2^m$, for $i = 1 \ldots m$. The finger tables of the nodes in our example are also shown in Figure 3.6. The construction of the finger table assures that each node has more information about the nodes following it than about those located further away in the ring structure, but also has some information about more distant nodes.

If a node wants to look up a piece of data with ID k, it searches its finger table for the node whose ID most closely precedes k and asks this node for more information. By repeating this procedure, the data with ID k will finally be found. Stoica et al. [757] show that with high probability or in steady state, each data can be located using only $O(\log N)$ communication steps. Also with high probability, entering and leaving of nodes only cost $O(\log^2 N)$ messages.

Using Self-Organization as Algorithm Design Strategy. Many biological systems have very good scaling properties, whereby scaling in this context means that the system works well no matter how many individuals are involved. Consider, for example, a fish swarm. There are swarms with only very few fish, but there are also swarms with millions of them. The behavior remains the same which indicates good scalability properties. Reynolds [670] succeeded in visualizing fish swarms by assigning a small set of rules to each fish:

1. Collision Avoidance: Avoid collisions with neighboring fish.
2. Velocity Matching: Try to have the same speed and direction as the neighboring fish.
3. Centering: Try to move towards the center of the swarm, i.e., try to be surrounded by other swarm members.

The reason that this algorithm scales well is that every fish only makes local decisions, and knowledge about the whole swarm is not required.

This is similar to decentralization, but goes one step further: The rules described above are very simple, but nevertheless, complex structures can result [149]. There have been attempts to imitate biological systems in order to develop systems which are simple, scalable, robust, and adaptable, such as ant colony optimization, and genetic algorithms. Only few approaches use self-organization without a concrete natural basis, among them the *organic grid* of Chakravarti et al. [154]. In grid computing, a large number of computers are working together in order to perform expensive calculations. Often, a central instance distributes the tasks among the clients. In the organic grid, however, everyone should be able to use the resources of the whole system by spreading its task over the net. As already mentioned, centralization often becomes the bottleneck of such an application, and thus, Chakravarti et al. developed a fully decentralized system by using self-organized agents which carry the tasks from one node to another. They did not use any biological system as their basis. Instead, they developed their system by first defining the desired goals and by then thinking about the rules each agent must obey in order to achieve these goals. The resulting rules are simple, but provide complex behavior. Thus, they showed that using self-organization as an algorithm design strategy might lead to simple, well-scaling, and robust algorithms.

3.4 Time-Space Trade-Offs

Introductory textbooks about algorithm design usually focus on the time complexity of algorithms and problems, the space requirements are mostly just mentioned in passing. For teaching purposes on an elementary level there is an easy justification for this apparently one-sided approach: using the fundamental model of a Turing machine, it is obvious that an algorithm running for $f(n)$ steps cannot use more than $f(n)$ cells of the working tape. Hence, $DTIME(f) \subseteq DSPACE(f)$ follows and an analysis of time complexity suffices to establish the term of an efficient algorithm.

Space constraints may arise out of system requirements. As nowadays only a vanishing portion of the produced computers are in the shape of multi-purpose computers (e. g., personal computers or laptops) and the major part is embedded in systems as miscellaneous as cell phones, cars, watches or artificial pacemakers, the space requirements of algorithms and problems will likely increase in significance. Technological improvements making it possible to store more and more data at the same cost are usually met by an ever-growing wish to store more and more data creating a permanent shortness.

To pick the most space efficient algorithm among algorithms of the same running time is a first step to include space analysis into algorithm design. When designing algorithms minimizing time and minimizing space may easily be two conflicting goals. Hence, a variety of different algorithmic solutions to one and the same problem may be optimal for different time and space requirements.

The problem of choosing the right algorithm remains relatively simple if one of the resources time or space is by far more crucial than the other one, in a given setting: in an artificial pacemaker, one might be willing to sacrifice orders of magnitude in calculation time to gain a constant factor in space. For a high-end chess computer providing immense extra storing capacities might be acceptable if this enables the system to evaluate 5% more configurations in the time available for a move, because it is able to recognize more configurations which were already evaluated.

The degree to which minimization of time and space are in conflict is the central issue in the discussion of time-space trade-offs. These trade-offs differ immensely in scope: For some problems, the set of time-optimal algorithms and the set of space-optimal algorithms may intersect while in other cases, time-optimality can only be reached by accepting severe space requirements and vice versa. Apart from the scope of the trade-offs also their shape is of interest: For some problems the trade-off between time and space is smooth which means that an increase in time by a factor of $f(x)$ results in a reduction of space by a factor of $g(x)$ with f and g not too different in growth or, in the best case, even asymptotically equivalent. In other cases, the trade-off is rather abrupt which means there is a certain bound of one resource so that even a relatively small step below this bound can only be made by sacrificing the other resource to an extreme extent. We will see examples of these cases in the following discussions.

Time-space trade-offs do not only arise in the comparison of different algorithmic approaches, but may also arise within one algorithm that can be adapted, e. g., by tuning parameters appropriately. A search algorithm can be run with very restricted memory resulting in revisiting the same places over and over again, or it can store its entire search and avoid redundancy completely.

Such an adaption can even be made at runtime if the algorithm itself evaluates parameters like the current processor idle time or the amount of main memory available. The SETI@home [726] project may serve as an example for this line of thought: the system is allowed to use resources (space and time) of participants willing to contribute but it must be ready to clear the resources at all times, should the user require his resources for other purposes.

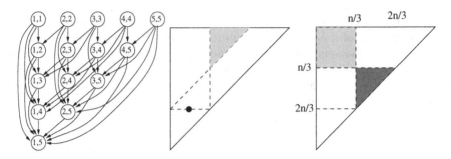

Fig. 3.7. Left: A dependency graph with $G = (V, E)$, $V = \{(i, j) | 1 \le i \le j \le n\}$ and $E = \{((a, b), (a, d)) | b < d\} \cup \{((a, b), (c, b)) | a < c\}$ shown for $n = 5$. **Middle**: An illustration for results no longer needed at a certain point. **Right**: An illustration for the counting argument.

Beyond the application driven motifs to consider time-space trade-offs, there is also a structural insight into the nature of the problem in question and its algorithmic solutions that should not be underestimated. Theory has provided means to establish lower bounds for time-space products and to analyze the important question whether a time-space trade-off for a given algorithm is smooth or abrupt. (See for example [700] for an introduction.)

3.4.1   Formal Methods

Theoretical studies break down into the analysis of *straight line programs* and the analysis of *data-dependent programs*. The latter class is more powerful. In straight line programs, the input does not effect the course of computation – loops (with variable number of executions) and branches are forbidden. Hence, straight line programs for a given input size n may be written as a fixed sequence of input and output steps and operations on previously computed values. A naive bubble sort is a straight line algorithm (it looses this property if a test is added to make the algorithm stop should the array be sorted after some iteration). Prominent straight line algorithms are the Fast Fourier Transformation, computation of convolutions or matrix multiplications.

The dependencies between the different steps of an algorithm can naturally be modeled as a directed acyclic graph. The vertices are the different steps of the algorithm and an edge (u, v) is inserted, if the result of step u is called for in the computation of step v. Input steps have indegree 0, output steps have outdegree 0. Consider for example the dependency graph of Figure 3.7 that we will revisit when discussing dynamic programming in the next section.

The Pebble Game. A fundamental approach to formally studying time-space trade-offs is the so-called *pebble game*, played on these dependency graphs. Pebbles are placed on the vertices and moved from vertex to vertex according to certain rules. A pebble on a vertex indicates that the result of this node is currently stored by the algorithm. The rules follow naturally:

1. A pebble may be placed on an input vertex at any time.
2. A pebble may be placed on an inner vertex, if there is a pebble on every predecessor of the node. (It is allowed that the pebble placed on the node is one of the pebbles of the predecessors.)
3. A pebble can be removed at any time.
4. If all nodes have once carried a pebble, the game is won.

As every move represents an operation or a reading of an input component, the number of moves needed to win the game corresponds to the running time of the algorithm. The maximum number of pebbles that has been in use at the same time is the algorithm's space requirement. (If a distinction between input space and working space is required, input vertices never carry pebbles and an inner node may be pebbled if all its preceding inner nodes carry a pebble.)

In our example we could just pebble the graph row-wise from top to bottom and within each row from left to right. This results in $\Theta(n^2)$ for time and space. Clearly $\Omega(n^2)$ is a lower bound for time, as every node must be pebbled at least once. But what about space? The center part of Figure 3.7 shows that nodes arise that are no longer needed when computing in this order. If the dot resembles the node currently being pebbled, every result in the shaded area will not be needed again. Hence, we could save pebbles by using them over. It turns out however, that the number of pebbles needed remains $\Theta(n^2)$.

The next approach would be to modify the order in which the nodes are pebbled. This freedom cannot be exploited to yield a lower space requirement: Let (a_1, b_1) and (a_2, b_2) with $1 \leq a_i \leq b_i \leq n$ be two nodes and let $X(a_1, b_1, a_2, b_2)$ be an indicator that is 1 iff the result for node a_2, b_2 is stored at the time the result for node (a_1, b_1) is computed, 0 otherwise. Then $\sum_{(a_2, b_2)} X(a_1, b_1, a_2, b_2)$ is the space in use at the time (a_1, b_1) is evaluated. Due to an averaging argument it suffices to verify that $\sum_{a_1, b_1} \sum_{a_2, b_2} X_{a_1, b_1, a_2, b_2} = \Theta(n^4)$ in order to establish a $\Omega(n^2)$ space bound.

Define $\mathrm{Span}((a_1, b_1), (a_2, b_2)) := (\min\{a_1, a_2\}, \max\{b_1, b_2\})$. Now note that if $\mathrm{Span}((a_1, b_1), (a_2, b_2)) \notin \{(a_1, b_1), (a_2, b_2)\}$, both (a_1, b_1) and (a_2, b_2) are predecessors of the span and hence they are both stored when the node of their span is computed. Consequently, $X(a_1, b_1, a_2, b_2) = 1$ or $X(a_2, b_2, a_1, b_1) = 1$ as we do not delete results until we know that they will not be called for again. A counting argument completes the proof: Pick (a_1, b_1) from the pale shaded area in the right diagram of Figure 3.7 and (a_2, b_2) from the dark shaded area. The span of these combinations is below the lowest dashed line and hence all these $\Theta(n^4)$ combinations contribute a 1 in the above sum.

Hence, we cannot save space (asymptotically) without sacrificing time. If we allow results to be computed, deleted and later recomputed, we are actually able to win the game with $2n - 1$ pebbles. The price turns out to be exponential running time: We inductively verify that a node in the i-th layer (counting top-down starting with layer 1) can be pebbled with $2i - 1$ pebbles. This is obviously true for level 1. For a node in level i, proceed from $k = i-1$ down to 1 and pebble its two predecessors recursively. This can be done by the induction hypothesis. At the end of each recursive call remove all pebbles placed during this call except the final one. When all the predecessors are pebbled, the node in level i can be pebbled. For the running time, we obtain the recursion $T(n) = 2 \sum_{i=1}^{n-1} T(i)$ with $T(1) = 1$ which solves to $T(n) = 2 \cdot 3^{n-2}$.

The time-space trade-offs of other graphs can be much smoother. Several graph classes like binary trees, pyramids, lattices and butterflies have been studied. Hence, an algorithm designer even if he does not want to establish trade-off bounds by analyzing pebble games himself, should at least check whether the specific pattern of dependencies in his task is a prominent one and already analyzed.

The total independence between input and course of computation in straight line programs appears to be a rather severe restriction. However, in algorithms that are *mostly straight line* the same formal methods may still give a hint on time-space trade-offs even though they lose the formal assurance of a mathematical proof. We revisit the above graph and this line of thought when discussing dynamic programming.

3.4.2   Reuse and Lookup Tables

On the conceptual level, an important way to save time is avoiding doing the same things over and over again. Storing and reusing results that have been obtained from a time consuming process is an obvious solution requiring space. Some simple examples:

- In a lookup table values previously obtained by a lengthy calculation are stored for later use.
- In caching, a certain amount of pages is kept in main memory to minimize slow hard disk accesses.
- In distributed databases an object may be stored in more than one location in order to keep the communication time small.

An important question in a given application is to what degree the access pattern to data can be predicted. If the designer is dependent on working with probabilities or relying on heuristics, a more redundant storing must be used to obtain the same performance.

Dynamic Programming. In dynamic programming it is known in advance which previously computed result is needed at a given stage of the algorithm. Hence, the necessary space can be figured out in advance and can be made the subject of a minimization process. A graph, like the one to demonstrate the pebble game, modeling the dependencies between the different subproblems, comes in handy.

Consider the following two basic problems, firstly the problem to decide whether a word w of length n is in a language of a context free grammar

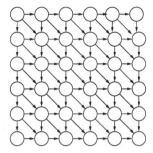

Fig. 3.8. The dependency graph for the longest common subsequence problem

$G = (V, T, P, S)$ given in Chomsky normal form, where V denotes the set of variables, T the set of terminals, P the production rules, and S the start symbol. The well-known Cocke-Younger-Kasami (CYK) method solves $\frac{n \cdot (n+1)}{2}$ problems corresponding to all subwords of w. In fact, the dependency graph in Figure 3.7 is exactly the dependency graph of the subproblems in the CYK-algorithm. Node (i, j) represents the computation of $V_{i,j}$, the set of variables that can produce the subword $x_i, \ldots, x_j$. The dependencies are due to the rule

$$V_{i,j} = \{A \in V | \exists_{i \leq k < j} \exists_{B,C \in V} (A \rightarrow BC) \in P, B \in V_{i,k}, C \in V_{k+1,j}\}$$

for $j > i$.

The second problem we discuss is to find the longest common subsequence of two sequences x and y of length n. A standard dynamic programming algorithm computes the longest common subsequences $Max_{i,j}$ of every pair of prefixes $x_1, \ldots, x_i$ and $y_1, \ldots, y_j$ including the empty prefix ϵ for $i = 0$ or $j = 0$. Hence, $(n+1)^2$ subproblems are solved. The dependency graph (Figure 3.8) reflects the rule

$$Max_{i+1,j+1} = \max\{Max_{i,j+1}, Max_{j+1,i}, Max_{i,j} + 1_{x_{i+1} = y_{i+1}}\}$$

for $i, j \geq 0$.

While the common subsequence problem computes roughly twice as many subproblems, a smart implementation only requires storing $\Theta(n)$ solutions at a time. A glance at the structure of the dependency graph of this algorithm reveals this. If the subproblems are solved in a top-down and left to right manner, the algorithm does only need the results of the last $n + 1$ computations. The older ones may be overwritten. We thus have a case where space improvement can be obtained without a loss in computation time.

Observe that our proof for the CYK-algorithm graph needing $\Omega(n^2)$ pebbles when time is constrained to $O(n^2)$, only proves the necessity of storing $\Theta(n^2)$ subsolutions for CYK, *provided* the task of computing one table entry is not interrupted and no partial solutions are stored. We may conclude however, that if we intend to break the $\Omega(n^2)$ space bound, we must do exactly that. Hence, there is no *easy* way to break this bound, i.e., the bound cannot be broken simply by optimizing the order in which subproblems are solved.

An aspect of dynamic programming that deserves special attention are the two different versions of optimization problems. In many problems which are approached with dynamic programming there is a *value version* and a *construction version*. The value version just asks for the value of the solution, while the construction version also requires producing the solution itself. This solution consists of information gathered during the computation.

In the above example of the longest common subsequence the computation of an internal node consists of picking the maximum among three candidates provided by the predecessors. A constructive solution does not just require the length of the longest common subsequence, but also the sequence itself. This is easily solved by storing after every computation the identity of the predecessor that delivered the maximum value. Then, after the value of the optimal solution is found, one traces these predecessor information back to the origin. This requires storing the whole table even if it is redundant for the value version. In the dependency graph the shift from value- to construction version is reflected in further edges: in the constructive case every internal node has an incoming edge from every node located to its upper left. We loose a factor of n just by switching from the value version to the constructive version.

This problem is addressed in [114] for a variety of interesting cases. It is shown that in the cases they describe, a construction version may be computed with asymptotically the same space as the value version if a slowdown of a logarithmic factor is acceptable. In the cases covered, subproblems are organized in bags and the dependencies are reflected by a constant degree tree with the bags as nodes. A simple case would be the one where the tree is a simply linked list. We can obtain this structure by organizing the different columns of the subsequence graph as a bag. (See Fig. 3.9.)

Bodlaender and Telle point out that this setup arises for many NP-hard problems on graphs that can be solved efficiently, provided the path decomposition or the tree decomposition of the graphs is bounded by a constant. We will only describe the algorithmic idea for the case where the bags constitute a simply linked list. The more general case follows similar ideas.

Assume a sequence of n bags is to be solved. Each subproblem in bag $i + 1$ can be solved using only the results of bag i. Furthermore, assume that for every subproblem a single predecessor *delivers* the optimal solution, hence the constructive solution is a path through the dependency graph. (This assumption is met in the subsequence problem, as we only need to remember which predecessor constituted the maximum. The assumption is not met in the CYK graph, as we need to store a pair of predecessors.)

In a first iteration (Fig. 3.9 top) the optimal value as well as a pointer to the subproblem in the first bag, where the path of the optimal solution starts, are computed. Afterwards the algorithm works recursively on problems $P_{l,r}$ with $l < r$, starting with $P(1, n)$. It is assumed that we know which result in bag

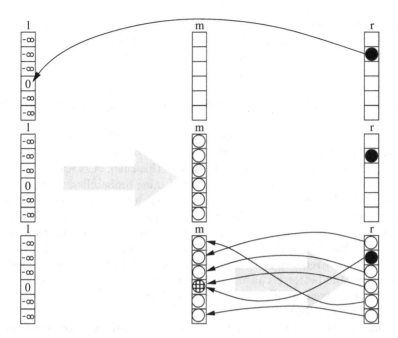

Fig. 3.9. Finding the middle of an optimal path. A method to reconstruct the optimal path in short time, without storing the entire table.

l and which result in bag r is part of the optimal path. We seek to determine which result from bag $m = \lceil \frac{l+r}{2} \rceil$ is on the optimal path.

This is achieved as follows. Assuming a maximization problem, we set the value of the starting point of the optimal path in bag l to 0 and all the other entries of bag l to $-\infty$. That way the optimal path does not change and we do not need to know the real values of bag l. With these fictitious starting values we rerun the dynamic program up to bag m (Fig. 3.9 middle). In the second half of the run from bag m to r we maintain a set of pointers indicating which result in bag m is on the path leading to a specific result. When bag r is reached we follow the pointer from the optimal result to its predecessor in bag m (Fig. 3.9 bottom). The recursion than continues independently for $P(l,m)$ and $P(m,r)$.

We never store more than two bags at a time and have asymptotically the same space requirement as the value version. The time is described by $T(n) = 2T(\frac{n}{2}) + n$ yielding $T(n) = \Theta(n \log n)$.

Online Scenarios. In an online scenario the input and therefore the requests for stored data are revealed at runtime. A web server, for example, has no way of knowing which page a user might request next. The theory of online computation [125] provides formal frameworks for performance guarantees on worst case inputs. We say an approximation algorithm A is c–*competitive* for a minimization problem, if for every legal instance I the inequality $A(I) \leq c \cdot opt(I)$ holds. The paging heuristic *Least-Recently-Used* for example is k-competitive if k is the number of pages which fit into main memory. It is optimal among all deterministic strategies in the worst case analysis [744]. A marking algorithm using random bits is $O(\log k)$-competitive for *oblivious* input (i.e., if the sequence of page requests is independent of the behavior of the paging algorithm) [4, 286] and optimal in this sense.

However, for real world applications, the idea of an adversary generating the input with the intent to hurt the system as bad as possible is overly pessimistic (*denial of service attacks* being an exception to this rule). A stochastic analysis, assuming every page being requested with the same probability, is equally little appealing. More advanced methods have turned out to resemble experiments with real world data pretty well. The idea is to model legal sequences of requests either deterministically in an access graph or more generally allowing randomness in a Markov chain [461]. By the last one it is assumed that a request for page a is followed by a request for page b with a probability $p_{a,b}$. The sparser the Markov chain, the better it can be exploited to figure out a tailor-made paging strategy for the given application. The probability values themselves may arise out of experimental studies.

In online scenarios we usually have a smooth trade-off: the more space we are able and willing to provide in main memory, the more seldomly page misses will occur.

Interpolation. For arithmetic functions, lookup tables may be used in yet a different manner. Assume a complicated function $f(x)$ is to be evaluated many times throughout an algorithm with the x-values neither being known in advance nor sufficiently predictable. Hence, we are facing an online scenario. But if the function is defined over real-valued variables – even given the usually finite representation of a real value in a computer – the odds of luckily having a requested value in store is negligible. Assuming a certain smoothness of the function however, it might be acceptable to work with interpolation: if function f is called for a specific value x the algorithm determines the biggest x-value smaller than x and the smallest x-value greater than x in the lookup table. The result for x is then obtained for example by linear interpolation or, if the first k derivates of f are also stored, by a more advanced method. In this scenario, building a lookup table for interpolation is also an example of a preprocessing phase yielding a time-space trade-off.

In this case of arithmetic functions the time-space trade-off is a conceptual decision and is not smooth. The lookup table is only constructed if the decision is made to totally ban exact evaluations of f from the computation. Once a table is established, the time saved does not increase with the size of the table, but of course, we do have a clear space precision trade-off.

3.4.3   Time-Space Trade-Offs in Storing Data

Crucial properties of **data structures** are their space requirement and their ability to execute specific operations in a given time. Hence, for data structures the time-space trade-off is *the* measure of performance.

An obvious example are B-trees. They are specifically designed to organize data that does not fit into main memory and the space requirements are only measured in the number of hard disk accesses as the operations in main memory are by orders of magnitudes faster. A B-tree is specified by a parameter $t \geq 2$. Every node except for the root contains at least $t - 1$ and at most $2t - 1$ keys. Every inner node containing the keys $x_1 < x_2 < \ldots < x_r$ has exactly $r + 1$ children that correspond to the intervals

$$[-\infty, x_1], [x_1, x_2], \ldots, [x_{r-1}, x_r], [x_r, \infty].$$

Furthermore, every leaf of a B-tree has the same depth. Insertions and deletions are arranged so that they maintain these invariants.

For reasonably high values of t almost every key will be stored in a leaf. Hence, every unsuccessful and almost every successful search requires d hard disk accesses if d is the depth of the tree. The depth d of a B-tree with n keys is bounded by $d \leq \lceil \log_t n \rceil$. Therefore t should be picked as large as possible, that is, t should reflect the amount of main memory one is able and willing to provide for the search. This example also reminds that different measures of time (main memory operation or external memory access) and space must be used properly in order to achieve a useful performance description. Here the $O(\cdot)$ notation poses a specific danger.

As data structures are designed to support specific operations efficiently while keeping space small, an exhaustive discussion of time-space trade-offs in data structures would actually be an exhaustive discussion about data structures, well beyond the scope of this chapter. We thus restrict ourselves to three aspects that are of specific interest in Algorithm Engineering. First, using the example of resizing in hashing schemes, we describe how a scheme with good amortized performance bounds can be enriched to yield good worst-case performance bounds. We then point out that advanced data structures usually use sub-data structures that need to be well chosen. Hence, both observations deal with bridging the gap from theoretical analyzes to practical necessities. We finish with some remarks about data compression.

Hashing. Hashing is almost a scientific field on its own. The more data is stored in a hash table of a given size, the more often collisions will occur. These collisions either result in longer linked lists in the case of hashing with chaining or in multiple hash table accesses when a form of open addressing is used. Hence, densely filled hash tables require less space per item stored but the price is longer lookup times.

Every concept of hashing provides a system of resizing the hash table. Once a certain load factor is exceeded, a larger hash table is created and the data is re-hashed. Should a table become too sparse due to deletions, the table is shrunken.

As the hash function will involve the table size, it becomes necessary to recompute the hash values of every key already stored, whenever a resize measure is undertaken. Usually the change in size of the hash tables will be by a multiplicative factor, as then amortized analysis using the simple accounting method shows constant amortized cost per operation. Hence, even if a single operation, namely the one causing the resizing measure, may take time $\Theta(n)$ where n is the number of elements currently stored, the cost per operation remains constant in the long run.

However, if for a given time crucial operation we cannot afford operations which take linear time in rare peak situations, and therefore an amortized constant time per operation is not good enough, further space can be invested to obtain this goal. One possibility is to setup a new larger hash table in the case of overflow, but to also keep the old one. Lookups are performed on both tables resulting in an increase of a factor 2 in lookup time. Deletions are treated similarly. Whenever a new element is inserted, it is inserted into the larger table and c further elements from the small table are removed from there and hashed into the larger one. The constant c needs to be picked in a manner such that the time needed to rehash c elements is still acceptable. As soon as the old hash table is empty, it can be discarded. The density bounds for enlarging or shrinking tables are picked such that never more than two tables are in use at the same time. Hence, by doubling the space needed, the worst case time of an operation has been reduced from $\Theta(n)$ to constant. So in this case space is used to take the peaks out of the runtime.

Sub-Data Structures. More advanced data structures often include elementary ones as substructures. Here knowledge about the context in which the data structure is to be used, comes in handy. Consider for example a suffix tree [367].

A *suffix tree* T for an m-character string S is a rooted directed tree with exactly m leaves numbered 1 to m. Each internal node, other than the root, has at least two children and each edge is labeled with a nonempty substring of S. No two edges out of a node can have edge-labels beginning with the same character. The key feature of a suffix tree is that for any leaf i, the concatenation of the edge-labels on the path from the root to leaf i exactly spells out the suffix of S that starts at position i. That is, it spells out $S[i \ldots m]$.

Figure 3.10 shows an example of a suffix tree for the word MISSISSIPPI\$. (The unique stop symbol "\$" is used as otherwise there are strings with no suffix trees.) We will briefly describe the use of suffix trees when discussing preprocessing in the next section.

Constructing a suffix tree speeds up algorithms that make use of their structure. However, they clearly require significantly more space than the string itself. Hence, finding a space efficient representation is worth a thought. How should the children of an internal node be represented? In bioinformatics, where the strings are DNA sequences consisting of the four nucleotide bases A, C, G and T, an array providing room for pointers to each of the four possible children makes sense. Every child can be addressed in constant time and the space blowup is acceptable. If in principle the entire ASCII code could be the first character of

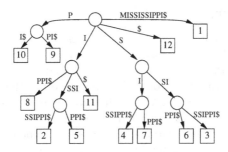

Fig. 3.10. An example suffix tree

an edge label, we will clearly not afford an array of 256 cells for every internal node. Possible alternatives are linked lists (space efficient, slows down lookup), binary trees (more space consuming than linked lists but faster in lookup times) or hash tables.

In fact, practical implementations use a mixture of these schemes. In a suffix tree internal nodes, that are higher in the tree, usually have more children than the ones located closer to the leafs. Hence, one might start with arrays for the first levels and then switch to simple lists further down.

Data Compression. The field of data compression finds ways to save space by investing calculation time. Classical algorithms make only use of statistical properties of the text to be compressed. They rely on redundancies within the text to be compressed and find ways to exploit them. Such redundancies appear in different scope depending on the nature of the compressed file: a text in a natural language has redundancy simply because letters appear with different frequency and e. g., only a small portion of all combinations of 5 letters will ever appear in a text. Is the original file a picture, redundancy arises for example from larger areas having the same color. A random binary string can hardly be compressed as it has by definition no structure, and information theoretic bounds prevent lossless compression of arbitrary input.

Usually the compression is performed to save space when the file in question is currently not used, e.g., the photos on the memory card of a digital camera should take as few space as possible, since one wants to store as many photos as possible and has no problem whatsoever with the time needed to compress and decompress the picture. A new branch of research (e.g. [738]) is dealing with compression methods that allow to execute specific tasks on the compressed file directly, hence making it superfluous to decompress and re-compress it afterwards. First methods of this kind were reported for string problems. Lately, also graph-theoretic questions have been dealt with on compressed representations [107].

3.4.4 Preprocessing

Preprocessing or input enhancement is the process of adding an additional structure to the input, such that the task can then exploit that structure to obtain a better running time. Preprocessing requires anticipating the kind of tasks that are to be performed with the stored data. Quite often the preprocessing will compute partial solutions hoping they will turn out to be useful when the real computation begins. In this case space must be invested.

What constitutes a good preprocessing, obviously depends on the task to be performed. A hint that time-space trade-offs might be obtainable by means of preprocessing is that in a given task the input breaks down into different layers, where the input components of one layer change much more frequently than the components of other layers.

An illustration is a navigation system for cars. The input consists of the *graph* letting us know which streets exist and at what speed we can expect to drive on them. Furthermore, the input consists of the requests, namely origin and destination between which the fastest route is to be found. In a middle layer the input could also include information about current traffic jams, road blocks and so on. As a change in the first layer – the graph – requires building, expanding or redirecting roads in reality, it seldomly appears. More often, traffic jams evolve or vanish, road blocks are established or lifted. Still much more frequently, a new query consisting of origin and destination is brought forward.

It would obviously be unwise if the system reacted to every query as if it had never seen the graph before, hence handling every part of the input equally. A system should at first work on the graph and enrich it with additional structures and information like e. g., the fastest connection between large cities. When a query appears, the system can then first find the closest larger cities to the origin and the destination and use the connection between these cities as a basis for its solution. If a middle layer with current traffic information is used, the system might store additional alternative connections on the graph level, such that if an anticipated scenario of traffic jams occurs, the already developed *backup plan* is immediately available. Chapter 9 has a section devoted to preprocessing techniques for shortest path queries.

It is well possible, that for one and the same problem different preprocessing steps may be useful depending on the context. Let us consider the problem of simple pattern matching: given a text T of length n and a pattern P of length m, find every occurrence of P in T. Clearly $\Omega(n + m)$ is a lower time bound as every algorithm must at least read pattern and text completely. This bound is met by several algorithms. It is possible to preprocess the pattern in time $O(m)$, such that every search for that pattern in a string of length n runs in time $O(n)$. Hence, searching this pattern in r texts of size n each is possible in time $O(rn + m)$ [367].

This approach is advisable if the pattern seldomly changes. For example in bioinformatics a certain sequence of nucleotides in a DNA string may constitute a defect and a lot of DNA samples are to be checked for this defect.

Using suffix trees [333] it is even possible to preprocess the text in time $O(n)$ such that after the preprocessing every request for patterns of length m runs in time $O(m)$. Hence, a sequence of r calls with patterns of length m runs in time $O(n + rm)$.

This setup for example applies to web search engines that store huge databases of web pages. These web pages are comparably seldomly updated. More frequently, requests for web pages containing a certain word are made, and in a preprocessed web page the check for the presence of every search-phrase can be done in time linear in the size of the phrase (which is usually short) and independent of the size of the web page.

These preprocessing steps, again, require additional space. For preprocessing the text, a suffix tree of the text must be constructed. That suffix tree may require $\Omega(n^2)$ space. Hence, it should be made sure, that the number of searches to be expected before the next update of the text justifies the factor of n compared to the naive representation of the string.

Let us stick to the Internet search engine a little longer to illustrate another implicit time-space trade-off. The designers of the search engine may choose to store several web pages in one suffix tree. (This roughly corresponds to creating a suffix tree for the concatenation of the pages and deriving the page with the occurrence from the position in the concatenation). Hence, a query now delivers the results of several searches which may (depending on the degree of similarity between the pages) be faster than iterating independent searches in every single text. However the combined suffix tree may need more space than the sum of the individual ones, as fewer edge label compressions may be possible.

3.4.5   Brute Force Support

Brute force methods are mostly applied when efficient algorithms for a problem do not exist or are not acceptable even though they formally count as efficient. The recognition of a problem's NP-completeness for example does not change anything about the presence of the problem and its relevance in certain applications. If efficient approximation algorithms are not available or ruled to produce results of insufficient qualities, brute force methods may be an option.

Optimization Problems. The A^* algorithm [382] is an optimization algorithm which finds on a weighted graph $G = (V, E)$ the shortest path from a source $s \in V$ to a destination $t \in V$ (see also the case study in Chapter 9.2). Of course, this problem can be solved with Dijkstra's algorithm running for $|V|$ iterations in the worst case. The A^* algorithm is capable of exploiting a heuristic $h : V \to \mathbb{R}$ that delivers a lower bound for the lengths of the paths from a certain node to the destination. If this heuristic is weak, A^* will not perform any better than Dijkstra's algorithm. If the lower bound reflects the real distance rather well, a lot of *unpromising paths* do not have to be examined.

A^* maintains a set S of paths. Initially, the set consists of only the path $[s]$. In each iteration, the path p with minimum priority is removed from S. The priority of a path $p = [v_1, \ldots, v_i]$ is $\sum_{j=1}^{i-1} w(v_j, v_{j+1})$, the sum of the weight of the edges of the path plus $h(v_i)$, the lower bound for the remaining path connecting v_i and t. Hence, A^* is best understood as a *most promising first search*. The possible extensions of p are included into S and it is made sure that further paths in S that end with v_i are ignored.

An obvious example is the computation of shortest routes in traffic guidance systems. The direct line distance between two points (clearly a lower bound for their road distance) serves as heuristic h. Unless the roads of the area in question are heavily distorted, the algorithm will find the fastest route without visiting the entire graph.

The A^* algorithm is not restricted to applications in which the vertices resemble distributed points in space. Another prominent example are solitaire games like the Rubik's cube or the tile game. In the $n \times n$ tile game a set of $n(n-1)$ square shaped tiles numbered 1 to $n^2 - 1$ is arranged in a square frame of side length n, leaving one empty space. Now tiles adjacent to the empty space can be moved into the empty space. The goal is to bring the tiles into a specific order. Here the sum of the distances of each tile to its destination may serve as a heuristic. As every move involves only one tile, the game cannot be won with fewer moves. More moves however may be necessary, as the tiles cannot be moved independently.

Usually the space requirement of the A^* algorithm is severe as A^* quickly proceeds into uncharted areas of the graph creating a huge set of vertices, that the algorithms has *seen* but not yet visited. Several approaches have been used to deal with this problem. One is to search simultaneously starting from the start vertex and from the goal vertex. This turns out to be helpful, if the heuristics typically is more accurate at a long distance from the goal. The straight line distance for navigation systems is clearly of that type. If one is far away from his destination, the straight line gives a good idea about the actual distance. When approaching the destination and being exposed to small labyrinthine alleys and one-way streets the straight line distances value decreases severely.

The concept to iterate A^* is also often used in order to reduce the space requirements at the cost of time. Every run of A^* is executed with a certain bound. Vertices with priorities beyond that bound are ignored and not stored. If a run of A^* fails to reach the goal, the bound is raised and A^* starts all over. This leads to an increase in calculation time, as results are recomputed in every run. This approach is driven to the extreme, if a run of A^* saves the smallest priority above the current bound that it has seen to use this value as the bound for the next run. In this case there is not even a need for a priority queue anymore, as only vertices with minimum priority are considered. This *iterated deepening A^** approach is called IDA^*. If the length of paths from the source to the goal is extremely small in comparison to the number of vertices, this will be a preferable approach. For the Rubik's cube for example the number of configurations is greater than $4.3 \cdot 10^{19}$ but no configuration is further than 26 moves away from the solution.

Non-Optimization Problems. There is also a variety of applications where a search is not for an optimal solution with respect to a given function but just for a *solution with a certain property*. The attack of cryptographic systems is an example (meet in the middle attack or rainbow tables).

In these cases the approach can be abstracted as follows: A universe U is to be searched for an element x having a property $A(x)$. The designer decomposes the universe U to $U_1 \times U_2$, so the search is now for $x_1 \in U_1$ and $x_2 \in U_2$. If one is able to find a domain U' and a function $f : U_1 \to U'$ as well as a relation $A' \subset U' \times U_2$ such that $A'(f(x_1), x_2) \to A(x_1, x_2)$, one can speed up the process of searching the universe naively by computing as many values $f(x_1)$ as possible and storing them.

Let us demonstrate this setup with the example of the Baby Step Giant Step Algorithm to determine discrete logarithms. Let p be prime and $1 \le a, b \le p-1$. We want to find x so that $a^x = b \bmod p$. Many cryptographic schemes are based on the hardness of constructing discrete logarithms. The Baby Step Giant Step Algorithm can be used to attack such a cryptographic system or, from the designers perspective, to reveal the systems vulnerability.

A naive algorithm checks every value from 1 to $p - 1$ and hence needs exponential time in the number of bits of p. The idea is to split x into two components $x = x_2 \cdot m + x_1$ with $x_1 < m$. A good selection for parameter m is $\lceil \sqrt{p} \rceil$. We get $U_2 = \{0, 1, \ldots, \lceil \frac{p-1}{m} \rceil\}$ and $U_1 = \{0, 1, \ldots, m - 1\}$.

The function $f : U_1 \to U'$ in this case is $f(x_1) = a^{x_1} \bmod p$ for $x_1 \in U_1$. We compute these values and store them. Now $x_2 \in U_2$ matches $x_1 \in U_1$ if they combine to the solution we seek. Hence they must fulfil $a^{x_2 \cdot m + x_1} = b \bmod p$ which we can write as $f(x_1) = \frac{b}{a^{x_2 \cdot m}} \bmod p$. So this is the relation A' of the general description.

Using the extended Euclid algorithm we compute $a^{-m} \bmod p$ and set $\beta := b$. For $0 \le x_2 \le m - 1$ we do the following: If β is stored in our table of results (say as $a^{x_1} \bmod p$) we have $x = x_2 \cdot m + x_1$ and are done. Otherwise, we set $\beta := \beta \cdot a^{-m} \bmod p$ and continue. Hence, by iteratively dividing the target value β by powers of a^m we search for a x_2 that, paired with one of the $f(x_1)$ in store, constitutes the solution.

Choosing $m := \lceil \sqrt{p} \rceil$ we gain a factor of $\sqrt{p}$ in time as we first calculate $\lceil \sqrt{p} \rceil$ values of the function f and later divide β by a^m at most $\lceil \sqrt{p} \rceil$ times. We assume that the values of $f(U_1)$ are stored in a data structure that allows quick lookup. On the other hand we invest the space necessary to store $\lceil \sqrt{p} \rceil$ values of the function f. The naive algorithm only needs constant space.

The search scenarios described in this section allow smooth time-space transitions, as every register available for storing a value in principal shortens the search time. Every register saved for other purposes increases the runtime.

3.5 Robustness

Depending on the subject of discourse, the term *robustness* is assigned quite different meanings in pertinent literature. At the bottom line, these various denotations may be subsumed as the degree to which some system shows insusceptible to abnormal conditions in its operational environment.

In computer science, these systems of interest are algorithmic components, the defining units of computational processes. Robustness here is usually defined with respect to a given specification of the desired behavior. Still, even in this restricted field concepts are varying and sometimes rather vague. In the following we will employ the terminology due to Meyer [568, p. 5]. He defines *correctness* as the ability of a software component to perform according to its specification, whereas *robustness* denotes its ability to react appropriately to abnormal conditions not covered by this specification. Following this definition, it must be stressed that correctness and robustness are both relative notions. A software component may thus neither called (in)correct nor (non)robust per se, but always only with respect to a given specification.

Note that the above definition has been still uncommitted as to what the precise meaning of *reacting appropriately* would be. Yet, this is just consequential, as any precise definition of some concrete behavior for certain conditions would ultimately become part of the specification. Robustness in turn by intention concerns those conditions for which the concrete behavior is *not* specified after all. Informally, the overall objective is to maintain the component's usefulness despite possible adverse situations; no condition shall make the algorithm crash, run infinitely or return absolute garbage. In other words, we seek for the algorithm in any case to behave reasonable and compute something meaningful.

Throughout this section we want to provide a survey on most relevant non-robustness issues as well as techniques and tools to deal with them. The following subsection discusses robustness from a more software engineering point of view. Sections 3.5.2 and 3.5.3 in turn address robustness issues that arise due to numerical inaccuracy during computation. There, the term *meaningful* will be re-rendered with regard to numerical, respectively combinatorial properties of computed solutions.

3.5.1   Software Engineering Aspects

Abnormal situations do not just appear from nowhere. Instead, they can generally be traced back to a single or more often a combination of several factors. Henceforth, we will call any such cause a *fault*. Note though that this term may be used quite differently in the literature.

The policy of robustness is twofold: anticipate the faults, the causes of abnormal conditions, or limit their adverse consequences. We will soon go into detail on these two notions, called *fault avoidance* and *fault acceptance*. But first let us have a closer look on the adverse momenta themselves.

Fault Types. Depending on the primary causer, faults may be grouped into two classes: *interaction faults* and *design faults*. The following passage is meant to provide a brief overview on most common faults for each category. The list will certainly be incomplete and the faults mentioned may not always be classified unambiguously.

Interaction faults originate from interaction with other systems, which in turn can be the user, some hardware resource or yet another software component. In case of the user, we can identify *accidental interaction faults*, such as operator mistakes or invalid inputs, and *intentionally malicious interaction faults* like penetration attempts or crashing aimed attacks.

As far as hardware is concerned, we have to deal with *service deliverance faults* in the first line. Typical representatives of this kind are that a given resource is not available at all, still busy in serving further requests or it has reached other limits like memory or storage capacity, for example. The second category are *data flaws*, which may arise in (at least) three different scenarios: the hardware serving for data generation, data storage/transmission, or data processing. To name just one example of each kind, imagine a 3d laser scanner producing extremely noise-polluted measured data, an ill-functioning hard disk or network connection causing data corruptions, or a GPU inducing artifacts in a crucial (e. g., medical) visualization.

The same two subcategories can be observed for the software component domain. In this scope, a service deliverance fault can be a communication to another software resource that could not be established, a service that terminated unexpectedly, or a software component that failed to provide time-critical results duly. Concrete examples are a database connection that cannot be established, a shared library that fails being loaded dynamically, or a tardy nested computation in a real-time application. As before, the second category of issues are again data flaws. In fact, any interaction with another software component bears the risk of adverse data to be transferred in one of both directions. Such a fault can usually be seen in two different ways. From the viewpoint of the component receiving adverse input it may be considered an interaction fault. Yet, regarding the component that produced adverse output despite actually benign input, one may considered it a design fault.

Design faults are faults unintentionally caused by man during the modeling, the design but also the implementation phase. In the modeling phase you try to capture the core of the problem and derive a notion of the desired input-output relation, thereby incorporating fundamental assumptions. Clearly, if one of these assumptions is in actual fact unfounded, the formal or informal specification obtained may not suit all problem instances, making the algorithm run into trouble in case of their incidence.

However, in general the modeling phase very well manages to come up with a proper specification. Instead, it more often happens to be the algorithm designer not playing by the rules. For the sake of easing correctness proofs and human understanding, *simplifying assumptions* are drawn and intricate details are omitted. Not filling the voids at a later point in time, this policy ultimately boils down to in an *incomplete design* at the very end. In the very same way also *hidden assumptions*, unintentionally incorporated at some intermediate step, can give rise to a design that does not fully meet the specification. Every so often we can even encounter algorithms being published that, although a "correctness proof" was provided, eventually turn out to be *incorrect*. Yet, it is sometimes only thanks to the implementation that such a fact gets revealed [373].

Of course, also the implementer can be source of faults. His task is to put the algorithm into practice, thereby filling up all details that have been left open so far. This in particular covers things like *dynamic management of runtime resources* (e. g., memory, (I/O-)streams, locks, sockets, devices and so on), each of which imposing its very own potential for faults. Another problem zone arising in this phase is the realization of *dynamic data structures* and their manipulation, which needs to be crafted carefully to avoid runtime faults. On the other hand, the implementer is given the freedom to locate and make reuse of already existing implementations, e. g., as provided by libraries and frameworks. At this point, however, it is imperative to verify their suitability and to know about their possible restrictions. In both scenarios, own implementation and reuse, the pitfall is to unintentionally impose a *mismatch between the models and specifications* the design is based on, and their counterparts (re)used in the implementation. It is certainly beyond the scope of the algorithm designer to avoid all these potential faults – yet, it is not beyond his scope to treat some of them.

Fault acceptance regards the existence of faults as actually not completely avoidable. It therefore focuses on the resolution of abnormal conditions in case of their incidence, each time seeking for reestablishing some normal condition again. We can distinguish three types of approaches: *detection and recovery, fault masking* and *fault containment*.

Approach 1: Detection and recovery is the most common practice. As the term suggests, it consists of an initial fault detection followed by a subsequent recovery procedure. The detection of faults can be attained by the following mechanisms:

Design diversity relies on several alternative versions of a given component, expected to be of dissimilar design. Derived independently from the same specification, these so-called *variants* allow the detection of design faults that cause the diversified copies to produce distinct results on the same given input. The approach is based on the assumption that sufficiently dissimilar designs may hardly suffer from the very same design fault. It is closely related to the *duplication and comparison* technique in the field of fault-tolerant hardware architectures, which makes use of two or more functional identical (hardware) components as a means against physical faults.

Validity checks are used to test whether the given input, the requested operation or the current internal state is actually valid, i. e., covered by the component's specification. They check for the presence of an observable abnormal condition, yet they do not confirm any correctness of the computation performed so far.

Reasonableness checks assess the current internal state or some computed (intermediate) result w. r. t. plausibility. As opposed to the previous scenario, we do not only check for present abnormality. Instead, additional constraints intrinsic to the specification are exploited, rendering necessary or sufficient conditions entities can be tested against.

Redundancy in representation is introduced to detect integrity faults in the course of data manipulation or exchange. Most well-known realizations are *error detecting codes* such as parities and checksums.

Timing and execution checks are used to detect timing faults or to monitor some component's activity. They are usually implemented by so-called "watchdog" timers and facilitate a mechanism for interception of tasks which fail to provide the result duly or are likely to suffer from an infinite loop.

Once a fault has been detected in the course of performing a requested task, there are basically the following main strategies for a software component to deal with that situation:

Backward recovery tries to return the component from the reached abnormal state back to a previous one, known or supposed to be sane. Afterwards normal service is resumed, proceeding with the next operation.

Forward recovery basically searches for a new state from which the component will be able to resume or restart the requested task.

Graceful degradation can be regarded as a variant of forward recovery where after finding the new state, only that single operation is performed at reduced capability, or the component permanently switches to some degraded operating mode.

Omission of the moot operation is also generally worth considering. The idea is to check first whether the operation would possibly lead to an abnormal state, and simply skip it in that case. Clearly, this technique is only applicable for faults that can actually be detected prior to the execution of the operation. Moreover, omission must be feasible, i. e., we cannot skip operations that are actually vital.

Fault compensation requires sufficient redundancy, either in terms of the internal state's representation or by means of design diversity. Exploiting this additional information provides means to transform the abnormal state into a suitable (usually uniquely corresponding) sane state. It should be noted that in fact more redundancy is required to compensate a fault than to just detect one.

Fault propagation is a matter of releasing competence. The component detects an abnormal condition which it is effectively unable to handle itself. Using some fault notification mechanism, it informs a competent authority, which can also be the calling component or the user, and temporarily or permanently transfers control without conducting any further changes first.

Fail-safe return terminates the execution under control after detecting a fault the component observes to being unable to handle. Based on the assumption that no other component may be capable either, some local or global fail-safe state is entered and possibly a dummy result is returned.

Increasing verbosity is no approach actually aimed for *handling* abnormal situations, yet the minimum to accomplish when concerned about robustness on the long run. The policy is to report or record any abnormality, at least those that cannot be handled – the more severe, the more verbosely. The basic aim is, if ever an abnormal condition occurs, then to be able to locate its cause based on the recordings and to fix the design appropriately.

Approach 2: Fault masking can basically be circumscribed as "fault compensation without prior detection". It can take the following three forms:

Functional redundancy based masking relies on the design diversity principle described above. The individual outcomes of a component's different variants are merged together, e. g., using some weighted or unweighted majority voting model, thereby obtaining a common result.

Representation redundancy based masking exploits   the   redundancy incorporated into the internal state's representation in an implicit way. That is, the fault-induced abnormal fraction of the present state is inherently being superseded by the dominant redundant deal. Using an *error correcting code* for the state representation, simply refreshing (i. e., decoding and encoding) the current state represented automatically removes the supported number of bit errors – a common technique to enhancing integrity of data exchange.

Normalization based masking is another way of returning abnormal states or inputs back into normal domain. It usually involves a more or less simple total mapping that maps every normal element to itself and and a deal of the abnormal states to a corresponding normal element each. A trivial example is, when expecting positive inputs, to accept whatever is passed and simply turn it into its absolute value.

Note the way in which the role of redundancy differs between this *fault masking* and the previous *detection and recovery* scenario. Here, redundancy is used to directly override possible faults without explicitly checking for inconsistency first. In contrast, detection and recovery exploits redundancy to detect abnormal situations first of all. Only in case of incidence action is taken, which may then possibly but not necessarily involve recourse to redundancy again.

Approach 3: Fault containment basically neither tries to prevent faults a priori, nor to recover from abnormal conditions. Instead, it aims at restraining the evolution and propagation of abnormal conditions within a so-called containment area. The overall objective is to prevent any further components to become affected. Two obvious paradigms can be distinguished:

Self containment commits to the detection and containment of abnormal conditions eventuating in the component's internal context. In contrast to the detection and recovery principle, we are not too much interested into maintaining or re-establishing service. That is, even unplugging or shutting down is considered tolerable in the border case, as long as a safe state was established first.

Defensive design follows the inverse idea. Every component shall be designed in a way that it defends itself against its outside. By no means shall a fault of external origin be able to infect the component, if there is any chance to detect it beforehand. We will go into more detail on this strategy later.

Fault avoidance is aimed at designing algorithmic components with effectively less fault potential. Faults shall in the best case never be introduced, or get eliminated before the component or system goes into live operation.

Fault removal concentrates on reducing the number or severity of already existing faults. This clearly involves locating these present faults first in the currently established design.

Inspection of the current design (or implementation) should be the most obvious approach. The (pseudo-)code is being reviewed thoroughly by human hand to verify the correspondence between design and specification, thereby challenging once again any assumptions and conclusions made during the design phase. Yet, this is just half of the picture, in that one would have only checked for correctness then. Seeking for robustness in turn amounts to additionally asking the *"But what if ...?"* question over and over again, and requires the algorithm designer to systematically think beyond the borders of the specification.

Formal verification is the method of choice in fields of inevitably high-reliable software construction like aviation, space flight and medicine. Specifications are expressed by means of some description formalism with well-defined semantic [777]. Based on these descriptions, formal methods allow to some degree to verify correctness or other specifiable properties of a software component. Apart from human-directed proofs, two (semi-)automatic approaches can be distinguished: *Model checking*, which basically consists of an exhaustive exploration of the underlying mathematical model, and *automated theorem proving*, which based on a set of given axioms uses logic inference to produce a formal proof from scratch. Some approaches directly verify the code itself, instead of an abstract model. For functional programming languages, verification is usually done by equational reasoning together with induction. For imperative languages in turn, Hoare logic is used in general. This so-called *program verification* will be discussed in Chapter 6.

Testing is the preferred approach applied in medium- and large-scale design scenarios. It basically relies on a dual design strategy. Parallel to designing the component itself, one develops appropriate test scenarios and documents their expected I/O relation. These test scenarios are intended to capture a representative set of normal and abnormal conditions, as well as border cases. *Black-box testing* thereby only uses the given formal specification of the component, whereas *white-box testing* additionally incorporates knowledge on its design or implementation into the development of the test scenarios. Binder [101] explains in detail how to design for testability, how to generate suitable test patterns and how to finally do the tests. It should yet be noted that, although software testing having proved to be quite successful, not observing any abnormalities does not imply having no faults – this is the curse of testing, as pointed out by Dijkstra [245].

Runtime fault detection should be used to report and/or record any abnormalities caused by faults that were still present as the component went into live operation. The overall goal w. r. t. fault avoidance is that any fault that becomes detected, can be located and removed by making suitable adjustments. The detection should be as rigorous as possible and reporting as verbose as necessary. Basically, the art is to design both fault detection and reporting in a way that renders debugging superfluous.

Fault prevention is concerned about preventing the introduction of faults, or at least limiting their occurrence, from the very beginning. This is usually achieved by starting the design phase with some clear and preferably formal specification of requirements, and by following proven design methodologies. The remaining part of this section tries to give some suggestions on basic rules and methodologies one may follow to achieve empirically more robust designs. Yet, there will certainly be no such thing as an "ultimate answer".

The Role of Specification. The probably most essential ingredient to constructing a software component is a proper specification. This description of the desired behavior is the starting point for any efforts of *validation* ("Am I building the right product?") and *verification* ("Am I building the product right?"). In fact, as pointed out by Meyer [568, p. 334]: Just writing the specification is a precious first step towards *ensuring* that the software actually meets it.

As a specification builds the basis for all subsequent steps of software construction, the resulting design is always as weak as its underlying specification. It is obvious, that latter one should therefore be precise and unambiguous. To achieve this, the best way to express a specification is to make use of some formal systems like Abstract State Machines [366, 123], Hoare logic [397], the B-method [2, 707] or Z-notation [3, 842]. The second of these formalisms will be described into more detail in Section 6.2 of Chapter 6. For a more general introduction on how to create specifications, see [777].

As mentioned before, a formal specification of a component is the basis of its formal verification. At the same time, a specification draws the line between normal and abnormal states. Everything that is not covered by the specification definitely needs to be included into the considerations of how to attain robustness. Moreover, this borderline has coining influence on the design of suitable test scenarios. Last, but not least, specifications are the pivotal elements for reuse. In fact, two designs or implementations can only be exchanged with each other if their corresponding specifications match.

Expressing Expectations. The component's specification is not the only thing that asks for being documented for later purpose. In fact, any assumption and expectation made during the design phase can become crucial at a later point of time. Therefore, it is also a task of the designer to express any such statement in some formal or informal way. Opting for a formal representation has two advantages: First, one clearly avoids ambiguity. And second, these formal statements can later be turned into so-called *assertions*, or can already be designed that way. Assertions are Boolean expressions defined over the values available in the local context of the considered design fragment. They reflect assumptions or expectations on which the fragment is based and are therefore intended to be true. Assertions can be used to check these expectations at runtime. In fact, if an assertion ever proves false, this indicates a possible fault in the overall design.

However, as Meyer [568, p. 334] sums up, assertions convey even further relevance: They force the designer to think more closely and in formal dimensions, thus getting a much better understanding of the problem and its eventual solutions. They provide a mechanism to equip the software, at the time you write it, with the arguments showing its correctness. They document assumptions and expectations drawn throughout the design phase, thus facilitating later understanding and inspection of the design. Finally, they provide a basis for runtime fault detection and for systematic testing and debugging.

Decompose what is Decomposable. According to Meyer [568, p. 332], the probably single biggest enemy of robustness is complexity. In fact, there is just too much monolithic software construction nowadays [803]. The most obvious way out of complexity is proper decomposition. First of all, decomposition usually leads to a much simpler design. And simplicity in general reduces potential error sources considerably (cf. Section 3.2). Accordingly, Raymond [666, p. 13] outlines the *Rule of Robustness*: Robustness is the child of transparency and simplicity. Breaking the design down allows to focus on single parts at a time. Thus, a top-down analysis of the problem followed by a bottom-up synthesis of the algorithmic solution encourages the use of "building blocks", which in turn can much easier be handled (i. e., examined, tested, replaced, etc.).

Apart from the reduction of potential error sources itself, decomposition might support robustness also from another point of view. If applied in a clever way, the resulting design may pay off, in terms of the robustness of the *whole* software component to be implied in a bottom-up-fashion by robustness of its building blocks on the one hand and their interaction on the other.

But how do we guarantee, or at least increase, robustness in these two areas? Are we back again at the same problem as before? Actually not, since firstly, robustness for smaller components may certainly be assumed to be much easier to achieve than for larger ones. And secondly, robustness of sub-components on the one hand and of their interaction on the other may be treated separately and independently.

Reuse what is Reusable. Another basic rule in modern software construction is: Avoid to reinvent the wheel! The past decades gave raise to copious quantities of algorithms and data structures, ranging from most fundamental to highly specialized ones. So, instead of designing from scratch, try to (re)use building blocks for which well-tested implementations already exist. In fact, it is certainly not unwise to let the process of decomposition be guided to some extend by the knowledge about such implementations.

Clearly, this might actually mean a trade-off to be weight out between the risk of inventing faults when designing from scratch and the risk of importing faults from these "well-tested" implementations. Apart from that, the principle of reuse asks for more: Similarly to using what is already available, try to design for reusability in the first place – you may want to reuse parts of the design and/or the implementation once again later on, probably much earlier than expected.

However, it must be stressed that designing for simplicity and for reusability is not straight forward. There is usually no such thing as a "best way of decomposition", and in particular reusability is difficult to achieve [803].

Generating Trust. One all too common backdoor for non-robustness to come into play is too much confidence in computed solutions. In general, when requesting an external algorithm for performing some desired task, the returned output is usually not checked for correctness, or at least plausibility [112]. Certainly, such checks might be performed after receiving the result computed by some external algorithm by treating it like unreliable input. Yet, from the external algorithm's point of view fairness dictates to either verify your results before returning them – or to provide some mechanism that makes it relatively easy for your clients to verify your output.

Regarding the former of both approaches, Weihe [826] suggests letting the software component apply runtime checkers that test its (given) input and its (self-produced) output for conformance with the specification. In case of a negative checking result, the component is obligated to handle the abnormal situation itself, instead of returning the adverse result. Depending on how restrictive the runtime checker is, Weihe [826] distinguishes two types of robustness in his own terminology: *Complete robustness* is achieved, when success of the runtime checkers is both, necessary and sufficient for the computation to satisfy the specification. If computed results are just checked for necessary conditions, Weihe speaks only of *partial robustness*. Certainly, the first of the two options should be expected the better choice with regard to robustness. Unfortunately, complete robustness checking may very well increase the expected asymptotic complexity of the initial computation itself.

Of course, runtime checking may in the very same way also be used to verify results obtained from any auxiliary software component invoked for performing some desired subtask. However, in general external results do not have to pass any but at the most a simple plausibility check. First, complete robustness checking can sometimes turn out to be quite expensive. Second, it can not always be achieved easily. But most of all, the task of verification actually appears rather responsibility of the callee than of the caller. The second promising approach towards result verification is therefore concerned with the provision of a mechanism for externally verifying the correctness of computed solutions. The so-called *certification* policy dictates that an algorithm for solving an instance I

of a problem $\mathcal{P}$ does not solely produce some output O, claiming that $\mathcal{P}(I) = O$. Instead, the algorithm additionally produces some *certificate* or *witness* C that (a) is easy to be verified and (b) whose validity implies that indeed $\mathcal{P}(I) = O$.

The topic of checking the correctness of computed solutions is discussed in more detail in Section 6.2 of Chapter 6.

Defensive Design. The idea of *defensive design* is simple: Take precautions to defend your software component against all external sources. On global program level, such provisions can be for instance: Explicit checking of the values of input parameters, overflow and underflow protection during numerical computations, plausibility checks for intermediate results, or redirection of data transfers in case of hardware breakdown.

However, defensive design calls for not only protecting the program as a whole against the outside, but rather every single entity against any other. In its extreme, there were no such thing as too much checking or precaution. Basically, defensive design advocates the attitude of not trusting clients and demands for the protection of any kind of interface – even internally. What you want is to completely isolate failures from one module to the next, so that a failure in module A cannot propagate and break a second module B [803]. Two examples of this kind are *information hiding*, i. e., delimiting access to any internal data solely to the use of access methods; and *defensive copying*, i. e., not sharing any data with other (untrustable) modules, but instead creating copies, both when receiving input as well as when returning output. Of course, this strategy will often be in conflict with efficiency.

In their book, dedicated to teaching how to construct large programs, Liskov and Guttag [529] emphasize the need to "program defensively". A *robust* program, so they conclude, is one that "continues to behave reasonably even in the presence of errors". After all, this is also (and maybe even in particular) a defense against intentional failures, such as hacking.

Design by Contract. The central idea of this systematic approach, developed by Bertrand Meyer [566], is the metaphor of a business contract. The way in which modules interdepend and collaborate is viewed as a kind of a formal agreement between a *client* and the *supplier* of a service, stating mutual rights and obligations. By demanding both parties to go by the contract, the obligations for one party make up the benefit for the other.

In the terminology of design by contract, the two most important elements in a contract are *preconditions*, expressing constraints under which a routine will function properly, and *postconditions*, expressing properties of the state resulting from a routine's execution [568, p. 340]. With a contract at hand, responsibilities are firmly distributed. The client is responsible for fulfilling the suppliers precondition. The supplier, in turn, is responsible for fulfilling its own postcondition. However, the supplier is bound to the contract only inasmuch as the precondition was being adhered. In fact, if the client (the caller) fails to observe

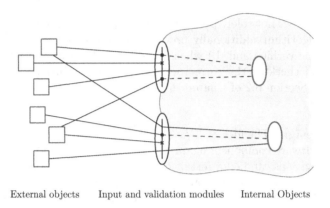

External objects   Input and validation modules   Internal Objects

Fig. 3.11. The principle of *filter modules* (following [568, p. 345 et seq.])

its part of the deal, the supplier (the routine) is left free to similarly do as it pleases [568, p. 343].

Basically, *design by contract* even preaches a so-called *non-redundancy principle*, stating that under no circumstances the routine's body should ever test its own precondition. This is contrary to what *defensive design* advocates, which calls for modules to always check incoming messages and reject those violating its precondition [101, p. 845]. Yet, the non-redundancy principle by no means prohibits consistency checks within the body entirely. It rather postulates assigning the enforcement of those conditions to solely one of the two partners. "Either a requirement is part of the precondition and must be guaranteed by the client, or it is not part of the precondition and must be handled by the supplier" [567]. In this regard, it is up to the designer to choose either for a *demanding* or a *tolerating* type of contract.

Basically, this also answers the question of how to ensure a protection of internal components from, e. g., invalid inputs. Note, that we certainly cannot contract the user. To solve this and related problems, Meyer suggests the principle of *filter modules*. The idea is to let internal and external modules be separated by a layer of specifically designed input and validation modules, featuring tolerant contracts with the external modules and strict contracts with the internal modules (cf. Figure 3.11). It is the task of these filter modules to prohibit all external calls that do not fulfill the precondition of the respective internal module, by handling them in an appropriate way.

Being placed as close to the source of the objects in question as possible, such filter modules go in line with what Meyer calls the principle of *modular protection* [568, p. 45]. A method satisfying modular protection ensures that the effect of an abnormal condition in one module will remain confined to that module, or at worst will only propagate to a few neighboring modules [568, p. 45]. Note that this principle differs from *defensive design* in two points: First, Meyer does not ask for a maximum possible protection for each and every single module. And second, modular protection is not aimed at necessarily letting the modules protect themselves against the outside, but leaves it open how to achieve the desired protection.

Concerning the issue of (non)robustness, it is often claimed that this notion of a contract is so powerful that many well-known failures would certainly have never been caused if design by contract had been applied in the first place. In particular, the Ariane-5 disaster is regularly quoted as an example [434].

Dealing with Adverse Input. There are a couple of reasons why input should not be assumed to be generally good-natured. First, the user should not be expected to be aware of every single aspect that makes up the difference between a valid and an invalid input, not to mention intentional malignity by means of purposeful attacks. Also, the input may not be adverse due to the user's fault, but due to some other origin it results from. In fact, nowadays a multitude of algorithms is actually designed for processing data known to originate from measurements (e. g., in GIS, medicine or bio-science) or previous computations (e. g., in numerical computing, mechanical engineering or computational geometry). Such data cannot be ruled out of being noise-prone, inaccurate, contradictory or even corrupted. Finally, even if the input is in fact valid, it may still be ill-conditioned due to other reasons, e. g., an exceeding complexity of the data or the task requested.

Hence, the question arises, how to deal with an input or request that turns out to be not handleable, based on the current design. To come to the point, there are four obvious answers to this question: *reject it, tolerate it, fix it* or simply *handle it.*

The first and probably easiest solution, of course, is to reject the request by announcing to be incapable of handling the input data or performing the requested task. Although this does not actually solve the user's problem, it is certainly still preferable to the alternative of a crash or garbage to be computed. In fact, this measure reflects a basic principle: If you are not able to handle it, then it is better to stop right away rather than continuing in spite of being aware of the problem. Just a few years ago, Yap and Mehlhorn [849] as well as Du et al. [259] still criticized the instability of modern CAD software, lacking any robustness guarantees whatsoever and crashing even on suitable choices of inputs. Nowadays, current CAD software still sometimes shows unable to perform the user's request on the given data. Yet, they do not crash anymore, but simply notify the user if an operation could not be performed.

The second option is (trying) to be tolerant. One may, for instance, dynamically decide to revert to a different variant of the algorithm that features less strict prerequisites. Or, in particular, if the input is known beforehand to possibly be subject to noise or inaccuracy, one may use a tolerance-based approach from the very beginning. Such approaches will be discussed more extensively in Section 3.5.3 in the context of geometric robustness issues.

If input turns out to be invalid, it might very well be possible to actually correct it by fixing the points of invalidity. This technique is sometimes employed in the field of terrain modeling where meshes are checked for their adjacency and incidence information not reflecting a regular mesh (e. g., being incomplete or inconsistent), and are remeshed where necessary. Correcting input requires substantial knowledge about the domain of interest. Missing information demands for being added and contradictory information needs to be replaced, both in a way that guarantees consistency of the resulting patched version of the input. In fact, the problem amounts to answering the two questions: First, which properties do constitute a "valid input" at all? And second, given some invalid input, how exactly does a corrected version look like that, by some means, "corresponds" to that input?

Last, but not least: If the algorithm is, due to its design or its implementation, yet not capable of handling specific inputs or requests, then one can try to make it capable of doing so. Although this may sound slightly absurd, it is not that out of place actually. After all, the cause for the incapability may very well be remediable. The Sections 3.5.2 and 3.5.3, as for instance, will discuss more closely how to proceed in case numerical inaccuracy is the problem.

3.5.2 Numerical Robustness Issues

The previous section was concerned with robustness in a rather general sense and discussed issues from a software-engineering point of view. The following two sections are meant to complete the picture by considering non-robustness arising due to numerical inaccuracy. In mathematics and in theoretical computer science, one commonly assumes being able to *compute exactly* within the field of all real numbers. It is this assumption based on which algorithms are generally proven to be correct. In implementations however, this exact real arithmetic is usually replaced by some fast but inherently imprecise hardware arithmetic, as provided by the computing device.

This hardware arithmetic is generally based on some specific kind of *finite number system*, intended to mimic its infinite counterpart as good as possible. The finiteness of the co-domain of this mapping, however, inevitably results in an approximation, which in turn involves two inconvenient side-effects: discretization errors (round-offs) and range errors (overflows and underflows). They apply to both, the input representation as well as the following computation. Such numerical errors are basically fully expected and in general considered benign [848]. However, the consequence of using a finite number system is crucial: Basic mathematical laws just do not hold anymore in hardware arithmetic (cf. Chapter 6), which in turn used to form the theoretical basis used for proving relevant algorithm properties, like correctness, convergence, termination and other quality guarantees. In fact, these formerly benign errors may turn into serious ones as soon as one of the following two situations eventuates:

- the numerical error accumulates, causing the (numerical) result to be far off from correct, or
- the numerical error, involved in the computation that determines a branch in the control flow, entails a wrong decision with respect to the program logic, thus leading to an inconsistent state of the algorithm.

The remainder of this section will address the first issue, whereas Section 3.5.3 will discuss the second one in detail.

Numerical Problems and their Sensitivity to Inaccuracy. The influence of numerical errors on the quality of computed solutions has been studied extensively in the field of numerical analysis for a couple of decades already. The overriding concern thereby has been to minimize such errors by studying how they propagate, to determine the sensitivity of problems to minor perturbations in the input, and to prove rigorous error bounds on the computed solutions.

Thereby, two types of errors are generally distinguished. The *absolute error* that results from using an approximation s^* to represent some numerical data s is given by $e(s, s^*) := \|s - s^*\|$. Similarly, for $s \neq 0$ the *relative error* of this approximation is given by $\tilde{e}(s, s^*) := \|s - s^*\| / \|s\| = e(s, s^*) / \|s\|$. A numeric *problem type* $\mathcal{T}$ may generally be expressed by some function $\mathcal{T} : X \rightarrow Y$ from an input space $X \subseteq \mathbb{R}^n$ to an output space $Y \subseteq \mathbb{R}^m$. In this sense, a *problem (instance)* $\mathcal{P}$ can be considered as a pair $\mathcal{P} = (\mathcal{T}, x)$ of a problem type $\mathcal{T}$ and a specific input $x \in X$. Solving this problem instance amounts to determining $y = \mathcal{T}(x) \in Y$.

Imagine now, the input x is subject to error such that (due to whatever reason) only an approximation x^* is at hand. This error in the input will imply a corresponding error in the output, whose size depends on both, x and $\mathcal{T}$. Let's say, someone may guarantee that the absolute error in the input will be definitely less than δ, or that the relative error will be definitely less than ε. Then one may be willing to ask, how much influence such an (absolute or relative) inaccuracy might actually have on the result. This sensitivity to minor perturbations in the input is generally referred to as the *condition of a problem*. We define, the *absolute δ-condition* $\kappa_\delta(\mathcal{P})$ of a problem $\mathcal{P} = (\mathcal{T}, x)$ as

$$\kappa_\delta(\mathcal{P}) := \sup_{e(x,x^*) \leq \delta} \frac{e(\mathcal{T}(x), \mathcal{T}(x^*))}{e(x, x^*)}.$$

There are actually different ways to measure a problem's sensitivity to minor perturbations in the input. In fact, Rice [671] and Geurts [330] as well as Trefethen and Bau [783], choose for an asymptotic version. This *asymptotic condition*, which is sometimes just referred to as the *condition* or the *condition number*, represents the limit of the absolute δ-condition for δ approaching zero.

Historically, the term *condition* was first introduced by Turing [786] in the context of systems of linear equations $Ax = b$. To quantify the *benignity* of such a system, he defined the *condition number of a matrix* with respect to inversion $\kappa(A) := \|A\| \cdot \|A^{-1}\|$. Although Turing's definition seems somewhat different, Geurts [330] showed that, when choosing the matrix norm, κ actually corresponds to the absolute (asymptotic) condition.

Let us briefly illustrate the meaning of condition. Assume, we want to solve the following linear system of equations $A \cdot x = b$

$$\begin{pmatrix} 99 & 98 \\ 100 & 99 \end{pmatrix} \begin{pmatrix} x_1 \\ x_2 \end{pmatrix} = \begin{pmatrix} 197 \\ 199 \end{pmatrix} \tag{2}$$

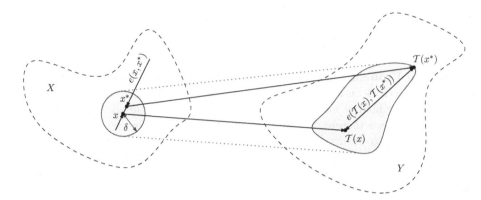

Fig. 3.12. The δ-condition of a problem $\mathcal{P} = (\mathcal{T}, x)$, based on the problem type $\mathcal{T}$: $X \to Y$ and a problem instance $x \in X$. It is the maximum of the ratio of $e(x, x^*)$ to $e(\mathcal{T}(x), \mathcal{T}(x^*))$ over all approximations x^* of x within an absolute distance of δ to x. As the δ-condition here is large, this problem is considered *ill-conditioned*.

This system features the solution $x_1 = x_2 = 1$, whereas the slightly perturbed version $A' \cdot x = b$

$$\begin{pmatrix} 98.99\ 98 \\ 100\ 99 \end{pmatrix} \begin{pmatrix} x_1 \\ x_2 \end{pmatrix} = \begin{pmatrix} 197 \\ 199 \end{pmatrix} \tag{3}$$

has the somewhat completely different solution $x_1 = 100$, $x_2 = -99$. The reason is easily revealed: Applying Turing's formula, we obtain

$$\kappa(A) := \|A\| \cdot \|A^{-1}\| = \left\| \begin{matrix} 99\ 98 \\ 100\ 99 \end{matrix} \right\| \cdot \left\| \begin{matrix} 99\ -98 \\ -100\ 99 \end{matrix} \right\| = 199 \cdot 199 \approx 4 \cdot 10^4$$

This condition number now tells us that if we were to be faced with some specific minor error or variance in the input, we could not get around accepting a variance in the output of up to four orders of magnitude times as much.

Indeed, the condition number for a problem can be seen as some kind of a magnification factor stating the amplification or dilution of variances from the input towards the output space. It is a measure for a given problem's benignity, i. e., a property that is *inherent to that problem*, imposing an inevitable vagueness in computed solutions when dealing with (e. g., due to discretization) perturbed input. A problem instance that exhibits a small condition is generally referred to as *well-conditioned*, whereas a high condition number gives rise to the term *ill-conditioned*. By extending this notion over the whole input space, we may consequently call a problem (type) *well-conditioned*, if all valid input instances are actually well-conditioned, and similarly *ill-conditioned*, if at least one input-instance is ill-conditioned. In the above example, the problem instance given by Equation (2) is obviously ill-conditioned. Hence, the general problem of solving a system of linear equations or determining the inverse of a given matrix, should be considered ill-conditioned.

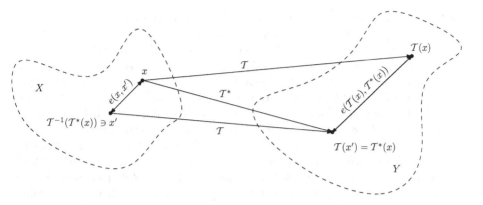

Fig. 3.13. Forward errors (right) and backward errors (left)

Algorithms and Numerical Stability. The quality of computed solutions for a problem does not solely depend on its condition. In fact, it is additionally impaired due to rounding errors that occur during computation. Even for exactly represented input, these round-off errors therefore entail the effective function induced by an algorithm for computing T to deviate from this ideal function by means of an approximation T^*. The error that is introduced due to this approximation is usually measured in one of the two following ways. The *(absolute) forward error* $\underset{\rightarrow}{e}(x)$ with respect to a given input x shall be defined as $\underset{\rightarrow}{e}(x) = \underset{\rightarrow}{e}(T, T^*, x) := e(T(x), T^*(x))$. Assuming the existence of a preimage of $T(x)$ with regard to T^*, the *(absolute) backward error* with respect to a given input x shall be defined as $\underset{\leftarrow}{e}(x) = \underset{\leftarrow}{e}(T, T^*, x) := \inf_{\{x' | T(x') = T^*(x)\}} e(x, x')$. The corresponding *relative* notions are defined similarly by substituting $\tilde{e}$ for e.

Basically, the *forward error* tells us how close the computed solution is to the exact solution, whereas the *backward error* tells us how well the computed solution satisfies the problem to be solved — in other words, how close to the initial problem x there is a similar problem x' for which the exact solution is equal to the computed result. The latter of the two notions allows us to introduce a property for classifying algorithms with regard to their computational quality: An algorithm is called *(numerically) stable*, if it guarantees the backward error to be small for all feasible inputs x. Similarly, an algorithm is called *(numerically) unstable*, if there is at least one feasible input x for which the backward error is large. A (numerically) stable algorithm thus guarantees us that the computed (approximate) solution for a given problem is at least equal to the true solution of a nearby problem. For a more detailed introduction into *numerical stability*, refer to Trefethen and Bau [783] who devote several chapters to this topic and offer the most explicit definition of stability.

Unfortunately, having an algorithm at hand, the exact function T^* induced by this algorithm is usually not easily determined. However, by viewing an algorithm as a finite sequence of elementary operations, one can stepwise determine a bound for the overall computation, if for each of the operations such a bound is known. And indeed, depending on the underlying arithmetic, such bounds are at hand – for fixed precision arithmetic in their *absolute*, for floating point arithmetic in their *relative* notion. In fact, standards such as IEEE 754 [420], for instance, dictate an upper bound on the relative forward error per elementary operation in floating point arithmetic, usually referred to as *machine epsilon*, which can be taken for granted in case the environment fully conforms to that standard.

Based on such guarantees, *forward error analysis* tries to bound the forward error of the whole computation, whereas the *backward error analysis* tries to bound the backward error. The analysis of round-off goes back to the work of von Neumann and Goldstine [813, 346]. Historically, forward error analysis was developed first, but regrettably led to quite pessimistic predictions regarding how numerical algorithms would actually perform, once confronted with larger problems. Backward error analysis is heavily to be credited to Wilkinson who did pioneering work in this field (see [831,832], but also the classical books [833,834]).

Coping With Numerical Inaccuracy. As mentioned, the quality of the computed solution basically depends on three parameters: The *input error*, reflecting the initial quality of the input; the *condition* of the problem instance, reflecting the severity inherent to the problem; and finally the *numerical stability* of the algorithm, reflecting the additional deviation between the round-off error affected implementation and its corresponding model, i. e., the problem type. In fact, seeking for $\mathcal{T}(x)$, actually results in finally computing $\mathcal{T}^*(x^*)$. However, regarding the input, it is most common to assume it to be either error-free or beyond our control; and the condition of the problem can even less be biased. Hence, it remains to address the problem of inaccuracy of computer arithmetic, with the objective of avoiding the overall round-off error to blow up.

Facing the fact, that naively implementing a numerical algorithm in a straight-forward way based on standard hardware arithmetic may easily result in the resulting program to be prone to numerical inaccuracy, the question arises how to cope with this issue. There are two not necessarily mutually exclusive choices: focus on minimizing or controlling the error, or adapt the underlying arithmetic.

When choosing for sticking to the given arithmetic, the overriding challenge is to get a grip on the round-off errors. This objective basically amounts to determining good bounds for numerical errors, locating numerically critical computations, and finding alternative ways for computing the same value that may show less prone to round-off. (Note, however, that a better bound does not necessarily impose a guarantee for better results.) Numerical analysis offers both static and dynamic techniques. For example, given two equivalent one-line expressions, one may statically assess bounds on the corresponding errors and choose for the more accurate version for the implementation. However, only in rare cases it will be possible to show that one way of computing a value will always yield a better bound than any other known one. In most cases, it will be necessary to react dynamically to the values of the arguments passed. Common strategies are, for instance, to reorder the data values, to consciously select the next out of a set of permitted alternatives, to transform the data into a more pleasant equivalent, or to choose between different equivalent implementations – always seeking for the least maximum error for the given input.

For example, when computing the sum of a set of numbers, one may dynamically re-order the sequence of values in a way such that cancellation effects will be minimized. Another example can be found in the context of solving a set of linear equations $Ax = b$ via Gaussian elimination. In each step i the current matrix $A_{n \times n}$ of coefficients is pivoted by one of the entries of the still unprocessed submatrix $A[i..n; \; i..n]$. In theory, this choice does not make any difference on the computed solution. In practice, however, it turns out that selecting a small pivot may introduce large numerical errors. Simply choosing the first non-zero coefficient in the current row as pivot (*trivial pivoting*) appears thus not advisable. In consequence, other pivoting strategies have been developed: In *partial pivoting* one chooses the largest magnitude in the current column as pivot. *Scaled partial pivoting* also chooses the largest magnitude in the current column, but always relative to the maximum entry in its row. Finally, in *total pivoting* one always chooses the absolutely largest coefficient in $A[i..n; \; i..n]$. Although out of these three strategies total pivoting involves the best bound on the numerical error, partial pivoting is usually applied in practice since it is much less computationally expensive.

Apart from delimiting the negative effects of round-off by controlling the accumulation of numerical errors, numerical analysis also helps us in assessing their actual magnitude at runtime. In doing so it allows us to check at runtime whether computed solutions are reliable or not. This is an important part of the basis of reliable computing and will be discussed in Chapter 6. Another question, that chapter deals with, is how to get away from (fast, but) inaccurate hardware arithmetic in those cases where it turns out insufficient.

For a detailed introduction into the field of error analysis, the reader is referred to the classic books [833, 834]. Moreover, the topic of stability is extensively treated in [783], devoting several chapters to this issue. Last, but not least, when looking into the subject of floating-point programming, [819] and [343] should be consulted.

3.5.3 Robustness in Computational Geometry

As mentioned in Section 3.5.2, numerical errors, initially considered benign, may well turn into serious ones as soon as they start changing the control flow in a crucial way. Conditional tests delivering the wrong result impose erring branches the program runs through during computation. Whereas some algorithms are actually immune against such wrong decisions, other algorithms may be highly sensitive to them. This sensitivity in particular arises in the field of computational geometry, as we will see shortly. Afterwards, we will discuss different approaches to cope with the problem of inaccuracy.

Problems that are considered to be of *geometric* nature generally have one property in common. The given input and the desired output are supposed to consist of a combinatorial and a numerical part each. A geometric algorithm solves a given geometric problem if for any given input it computes the output as specified by the problem definition. The algorithm involves so-called *geometric primitives* to progressively transform the given input into the desired output. These fundamental operations are basically each of one of two kinds: *Geometric constructions* create single basic geometric objects out of a constant number of given defining basic objects. *Geometric predicates* in turn test a specific relationship between, again, a constant number of given basic geometric objects. In doing so, they provide a mechanism for querying decisive properties in conditional tests that direct the control flow in geometric algorithms.

Each geometric predicate can be considered to perform in its very last step a comparison of two numbers, which in turn are determined based on the numerical data of the involved geometric object and possibly additional constants. Without loss of generality, one may assume that the second of both numbers is actually zero, which means that a geometric predicate at the bottom line amounts to determining the sign of the value of some arithmetic expression.

The crucial point now is the following. Geometric algorithms are usually designed and proven to be correct in the context of a model that assumes exact computation over the set of all real numbers. In implementations however, this exact real arithmetic is mostly replaced by some fast but finite precision arithmetic as provided by the hardware of the computing device. For some few types of problems with restricted inputs this approach works out well. However, for most of the geometric algorithms, if simply implemented this way, one would have to face adverse effects caused by this finite approximation, which for some critical input could finally result in catastrophic errors in practice.

The reason is that due to the lack of an exact arithmetic, the predicates do not necessarily always deliver the correct answer, but may err if the computed approximation happens to yield the wrong sign. In consequence, the algorithm will branch incorrectly, which in the most lucky case may be masked by some later computation. If not, the algorithm will in the best case compute some combinatorially incorrect or even topologically impossible result. In the worst case, however, an inconsistent state will be entered that causes the algorithm to crash or loop forever.

A simple example of geometrically impossible situation can be observed in the context of computing the intersection point p of two lines l_1 and l_2. Computing $p = l_1 \cap l_2$ and subsequently testing whether p lies on l_i, $i = 1, 2$, both with limited precision floating-point arithmetic, will most of the times result in at least one of the two tests to fail. Schirra [705] points out that even for obviously well-conditioned constellations the intersection point only rarely verifies to actually lie on both lines. Of course, one may argue that these failing tests may just result from p not being exactly representable within the limited precision in most of the cases. However, as it turns out, a direct floating point implementation even fails to always determine correctly for each of the two defining lines, on which side the computed point p actually lies w. r. t. line. Kettner et al. [471] explain in detail, but so that it can be readily understood, how and why an erring sideness test may cause even the most simple convex hull algorithm to fail in various ways.

Similar robustness problems apply for practically most of the algorithms in Computational Geometry. They arise because the approximate substitute for real number arithmetic used in practice just does not behave exactly like its counterpart in theory, i. e., the real RAM model based on which algorithms and data structures were initially designed and proven to be correct. However, not all input data needs to be considered critical. For most of the configurations representable in the available finite precision format, a direct implementation of a geometric predicate will indeed deliver the correct sign. In fact, the approximate arithmetic may fail to yield the correct sign basically only in those situations, where the given configuration is somewhat close to a configuration for which an exact evaluation of the predicate would report zero. The latter configurations are commonly called *degenerate*. Hence, it is the true and near-degenerate configurations that make up the critical inputs.

These scenarios are the ones that call for approaches to deal with numerical inaccuracy. Recalling that the root of the whole issue was the assumption in theory to being able to compute exactly, but the insufficiency of plain hardware arithmetic to do so in practice, there are two obvious ways out: (a) adapt practice to fit the theory, i. e., compute exactly in practice; or (b) adapt theory to fit the practice, i. e., take imprecision into account during design.

Adapt Practice: The Exact Geometric Computation Paradigm. If we are asked for some way to guarantee that our geometric algorithm in practice will always deliver correct results, the most obvious solution would be to ensure that any numerical computation ever performed is actually (numerically) exact. When resorting for some kind of exact arithmetic, correct results are thus automatically achieved. In fact, in such a case, robustness is actually a non-issue. Chapter 6 discusses such approaches in detail, how to compute exactly within the field of rational numbers or algebraic numbers, respectively. However, it should be noted that, in general, off-the-shelf use of exact arithmetic packages may become quite expensive and should therefore be employed cautiously.

Now, in order to make the algorithm behave in practice just as in theory, we do not necessarily need numerical exactness all the time. Instead, all we need to assure is that the program flows are identical in both cases. In fact, this will guarantee a correct combinatorial part of our output. To achieve this, we request that any decision is always made in the same way as if it was done on a real RAM. As mentioned above, the predicates that are evaluated during the branching steps of the algorithm may w. l. o. g. be assumed to deliver just the sign of some arithmetic expression over the numerical values of the geometric objects involved (and possibly additional constants). In effect, what it takes to always guarantee correct decisions is to (a) have a suitable representation for any object which is always sufficient to (b) compute the correct sign of the expression for the inquired predicate. Since compliance with these two requirements enables the geometric algorithm to always compute the correct geometric result, this postulation is called the *exact geometric computation* paradigm.

The term *suitable representation* already suggests that we do not necessarily seek for numerical exactness. So, (a) and (b) can be achieved in further ways, other than exact arithmetic. The applicability of these approaches, however, depends on the class of problem to be solved – more precisely, on the kind of arithmetic operations that are required and the maximum *depth of derivation* for any value that may occur during computation.

In short, a problem that can be solved by using solely the four basic arithmetic operations $+, -, *, /$ is called *rational*. Similarly, one that does not require more than algebraic primitives is called *algebraic*. Moreover, following Yap [845], one may inductively define the *depth* d of a value: given a set U of numbers, x is of depth 0, if $x \in U$; and x is of depth at most $d+1$ if it is obtained by applying one of the rational operations to numbers of depth at most d, or by root extraction from a degree k polynomial with coefficients of degree at most $d - k + 1$. An algebraic problem now is said to be *bounded-depth*, if there exists an algorithm that does not impose any value of more than some fixed depth d, otherwise it is called *unbounded-depth*.

Unbounded-depth problems cannot reliably be solved without employing exact arithmetic. However, such problems are rather rare in traditional Computational Geometry [846]. One example of this kind is a solid polyhedral modeler allowing us to perform rational transformations and Boolean operations on solids. There, each such transformation and operation inherently may increase the depth of derivation. But due to the lack of a well-defined input-output-relation, this kind of problem is often not considered a "computational problem" in algorithmics.

Problems that are bounded-depth but not rational may go beyond an off-the-shelf use of standard (arbitrary precision) rational arithmetic. They require techniques for determining the root of a polynomial of bounded degree, which will be explained in Chapter 6. In contrast, *rational bounded-depth* problems, in short *RBD*, can be solved without arbitrary precision arithmetic. In fact, for any given RBD algorithm there is a constant D such that as long as the input is known to involve only rational numbers of size (at most) s, all intermediate computations involve only rational numbers of size at most $D \cdot s + O(1)$. This fact allows us to limit the needed precision in the context of specific applications if the input precision is known in advance. And indeed, in most of the applications, the input is given as either integers of fixed maximum length or in floating-point format with fixed-precision. A few examples shall be given now.

Many geometric predicates used in prevalent geometric algorithms can be expressed by computing the sign of some determinant. Common representatives include the orientation test in two- or three-dimensional space, the in-circle test in 2D as well as the in-sphere test in 3D, the intersection test of lines in 2D, etc. Not surprisingly, a lot of effort has been done on computing the exact sign of determinants.

Concerning matrices with integral entries of bounded bit length, different authors have proposed algorithms for computing the sign of a determinant. The approaches vary from specializations for 2×2 and 3×3 matrices [52] to general $n \times n$ matrices [177,137] and cover standard integer as well as modular arithmetic [138]. In each case, a bound on the required bit length for the arithmetic is given.

Besides these algorithms for integral instances, further algorithms were suggested for computing the exact sign of a determinant for a matrix given in floating-point format. The ESSA algorithm ("exact sign of sum algorithm") due to Ratschek and Rokne [665] computes the sign of a finite sum for double precision floating-point values. Since the determinant of a 2D orientation test is representable as a sum $\Sigma x_k y_l$ over the coordinates of the three points involved, ESSA can compute the orientation of three points if their coordinates are given in single-precision floating-point format (which simply guarantees that all $x_k y_l$ are exactly computable in double-precision). Shewchuk [731] offers a method for adaptively computing exact signs of matrices of size up to 4×4 with entries in double precision floating-point format, provided that neither overflow nor underflow occurs.

Apart from the sign of a determinant, also its actual value may be of interest sometimes. Whereas testing two lines in 2D for intersection only amounts to determining just the sign of 3×3 determinants, computing the intersection itself amounts to determining their actual values. Hoffmann [401] shows how to compute such an intersection point for two lines in parametric form based on the *exact inner product* and derives a bound on the bit length of the homogeneous coordinates of this point. Sugihara and Iri [763] introduced an algorithm for exactly computing polyhedral intersections. In this method, geometric elements are represented without redundancy, giving only the coefficients of the parametric plane equations of the faces. The key property of Sugihara and Iri's method is that neither edges nor vertices are computed explicitly. Instead, all primitives are represented topologically. Vertices are represented as intersections of three planes, edges by their two endpoints and finally faces by delimiting edge loops. Two important observations shall not stay unmentioned: First of all, the representable polyhedra are not restricted to convex polyhedra only. And second, no digit proliferation takes place when intersecting the polyhedra, since the resulting polyhedron always inherits its surfaces from the two input polyhedra. However, as noted by Hoffmann [401], Sugihara and Iri's proposed approach unfortunately lacks support for exactly representing rotations, which is due to the fact that plane coefficients are not being exactly representable anymore. However, Sugihara and Iri represent their polyhedra in a dual form, based on a CSG (constructive solid geometry) tree of trihedral polyhedra and a history recording the boundary structure for the Boolean operations. Then, rotation of a complex polyhedron is performed by first rotating the trihedral primitives and then reconstructing the rotated polyhedron from the CSG representation.

Adapt Theory: Design for Inaccuracy. When having to rely on potentially inaccurate computations, one has to resign from the assumption of getting exact results to base the decisions on. However, an algorithm may still be quite suitable as long as it guarantees to deliver the exact result for a problem that is (in some sense) close to the original one. This motivates the following definition of robustness which was omitted in this section until now, since in the scope of the exact geometric computation paradigm, robustness was actually a non-issue.

Following Fortune [295], a geometric algorithm shall be called *robust*, if it produces the correct result for some perturbation of the input. In close connection to Section 3.5.2, we want to call the algorithm *stable* if this perturbation is small. Moreover, Shewchuk [731] suggests calling an algorithm *quasi-robust* if it computes some useful information, even though not necessarily a correct output for any perturbation of the input.

Interval Geometry. These approaches can be seen as the geometric counterpart to interval arithmetic (cf. Chapter 6). Numerical inaccuracy is treated by systematically thickening the geometry of processed objects, or by adjusting the geometric meaning of the predicates. The *tolerance-based approach* due to Segal and Sequin [720, 719] associates tolerance regions to geometric objects. The challenge now is to always keep the data in a consistent state. To achieve this consistency and to obtain correct predicates on these "toleranced objects" they enforce a *minimum feature separation*. Features that are too close to each other (i. e., have overlapping tolerance regions) must either be shrunken (by re-computation with higher precision), merged or split. Each of these actions might require backtracking if the new tolerance region of one object happens to start or stop overlapping the tolerance region of an object that has already been processed. In order to enable this kind of consistency checking, tolerance-based approaches usually maintain additional neighborhood information.

Epsilon Geometry due to Guibas, Salesin and Stolfi [688] treats the problem of uncertainty due to numerical inaccuracy from the other side, namely the geometric predicates. An epsilon-predicate returns a real number ε that reflects, how much the input satisfies the predicate. A non-positive outcome states that the input could successfully be verified to satisfy the predicate and, moreover, that the predicate would even be satisfied when perturbing the input by not more than ε. A positive ε in turn states that the input could not be verified to satisfy the predicate. However, ε is the size of the smallest perturbation that would actually produce an input satisfying the predicate. Unfortunately, reasoning in this framework seems to be difficult [704], and until now epsilon geometry has been applied successfully only to a few basic geometric problems, cf. [688, 364].

Axiomatic Approach. Another quite tempting approach was proposed by Schorn [708, 709]. The key idea of what he calls the *axiomatic approach* is to determine properties of primitive operations that are sufficient for performing a correctness proof of an algorithm, and to find invariants that solely base on these properties. Schorn applies his axiomatic approach to the problem of computing a closest pair within a set of points in 2D, but also to the problem of finding pairs of intersecting line segments.

In the former case, he introduces some abstract functions d, d_x, d_y, d'_y of type $(\mathbb{R}^2 \times \mathbb{R}^2) \to \mathbb{R}$ as substitutes for $\|p - q\|$, $p_x - q_x$, $p_y - q_y$, and $q_y - p_y$, respectively. Then he lists some properties that these functions shall fulfill: First, d is to be symmetric and furthermore an upper bound for each of the functions d_x, d_y, d'_y. And second, the functions d_x, d_y, d'_y need to feature some monotonicity properties. Schorn proves that based on these *axioms* his sweep algorithm is guaranteed to compute $\min_{s,t \in P} d(s, t)$ for the given point set P – no matter what d, d_x, d_y, d'_y are, as long as they satisfy the postulated axioms. He also shows that floating-point implementations of the substituted exact distance functions from above would yield a guaranteed relative forward error of at most 8ε, for ε being the machine epsilon.

Consistency Approach. The consistency approach implements robustness by simply demanding that no decisions are contradictory. The requirement of *correct* decisions is weakened towards *consistent* ones. In fact, as long as they are consistent with all other decisions, also incorrect decisions are tolerable. Of course, in the lucky case that an algorithm performs only tests that are completely independent of previous results, it would always deliver consistent results, even for random outcomes for the predicates. Fortune [295] calls such algorithms *parsimonious*. He presumes that – in principle – many algorithms should be capable of being made parsimonious.

An algorithm that is not parsimonious needs to assure consistency in another way. The *topology-oriented approach* due to Sugihara and Iri [765] puts highest priority on topology and combinatorial structure. Whenever a numerical computation would entail a decision violating the current topology, this decision is substituted by a consistent one that actually conforms to the topology. Degeneracies are not treated explicitly. If the sign of a predicate evaluates to zero, it is replaced by a positive or negative one, whatever is consistent. Sugihara's approach ensures topological consistency throughout the whole computation, in particular for the final result. However, there is no guarantee for obtaining topologically *correct* results, and the numerical values computed may be noticeably far away from correct. Usually it is argued at this point that computing with higher precision will make the output getting closer to the correct result – finally being equal to it, once the precision is sufficient. Yet, this argument only holds as long as no true degeneracies are involved. Irrespective thereof, the topology-oriented approach has still proven capable of leading to amazingly robust algorithms. In fact, Sugihara et al. presented several algorithms for polyhedral modeling problems (see p. 117, but also [762]), for computing Voronoi diagrams [764, 619, 765] and for determining the convex hull in 3D [575]. The reader is also referred to Chapter 9, devoting a whole section to Voronoi diagrams, including a topology oriented implementation due to Held [385].

Milenkovic proposes an approach, called the *hidden variable method* [572], which is based on two components: a structure with topological properties and a finite approximation of the numerical values. The topological structure is chosen in such a way that there exist infinite precision numerical values (close to the given finite precision parameter values), for which the problem has the chosen structure. The name *hidden variable method* derives from the fact that the topology of the infinite precision version is known but not its numerical values. In [572], the approach is applied to the computation of line arrangements.

Adapting Input. Milenkovic [572] also proposes a second approach to deal with numerical inaccuracy. His technique called *data normalization* modifies the input in such a way that it will finally be able to be processed with approximate arithmetic. It basically constitutes a preprocessing procedure, in which incidence is enforced for features that are too close together and the subsequent algorithm may not be able to tell apart. After eliminating any near coincidence this way, it is guaranteed that all the finite precision operations performed by the algorithm will yield correct results based on this *normalized* input. Milenkovic exemplifies his approach on the problem of polygonal modeling, based on the two operations permitted to be performed on the input: *vertex shifting*, which merges two vertices that are closer than ε, and *edge cracking*, which subdivides an edge into a poly-edge at all vertices that are too close to that edge. Clearly, introducing incidences definitely changes the local topological structure of the input in terms of connectivity. Yet, Milenkovic proves bounds on the maximum positional displacement introduced by his method.

Controlled perturbation is another approach that adapts the input so as to make it pleasant enough for being processed with approximate arithmetic. Again, one concedes the problem at hand not necessarily to be solved for the given input but for some nearby input. The basic procedure is yet somewhat different to the *data normalization* technique. The idea is to run the algorithm in a supervised manner, and to monitor if any of the predicate invocations is once not guaranteed to deliver a reliable result. In the latter case, the current pass is interrupted, the original input is perturbed and the algorithm is restarted again on the perturbed input. This protection is achieved by augmenting each of the predicate calls with a so-called *guard*. A guard G_E for a geometric predicate E is a Boolean predicate that, if evaluating to true in the given approximate arithmetic, guarantees E to yield the correct sign when evaluated in the same arithmetic. By increasing the size of the perturbation after each unsuccessful run, one increases the probability that none of the guards evaluates to false. However, the larger the perturbation, the less nearby is the finally solved input instance to the original one. Controlled perturbation, as proposed by Halperin et al. [378], therefore calls for controlling over the size of perturbation by means of choosing the perturbed input in a careful manner. Halperin et al. use this technique to compute arrangements of spheres [378], arrangements of polyhedral surfaces [654], and arrangements of circles [376], each in floating point arithmetic. Klein [474] applies the paradigm to the computation of Voronoi diagrams. Finally, Funke et al. [311] compute Delaunay triangulations using controlled perturbation. In each case, the authors derive a relation between the perturbation amount and the quality guarantee of the approximate arithmetic, i.e., the precision of the floating point system intended to be used.

Funke et al. point out that controlled perturbation (as opposed to data normalization) is actually a general conversion strategy for idealistic algorithms designed for the real RAM model and some general position assumption. In addition to this original approach, Klein [474] and Funke et al. [311] also consider so-called *lazy controlled perturbations*, which perturb only those sites that during their incremental insertion caused one of the involved guards to fail. Unfortunately, neither the perturbation bound nor the expected running time could be shown to carry over from the standard scenario.

Representation and Model Approach. This approach is probably the most abstract one to deal with numerical inaccuracy. Basically, an explicit distinction is drawn between mathematical objects, the *models*, on the one hand and their corresponding computer *representations* on the other. Based on this distinction, a geometric problem $\mathcal{P}$ is considered to define a mapping $\mathcal{P} : \mathcal{I} \to \mathcal{O}$ from a set $\mathcal{I}$ of input models into a set $\mathcal{O}$ of output models. In comparison, a computer program $\mathcal{A}$ imposes a mapping $\mathcal{A} : \mathcal{I}_{rep} \to \mathcal{O}_{rep}$ on corresponding sets $\mathcal{I}_{rep} \supseteq \{rep_{\mathcal{I}}(i) | i \in \mathcal{I}\}$ and $\mathcal{O}_{rep} \supseteq \{rep_{\mathcal{O}}(o) | o \in \mathcal{O}\}$ of computer representations.

A computer program $\mathcal{A}$ for a problem $\mathcal{P}$ will be called *correct*, if it holds that $rep_{\mathcal{I}} \circ \mathcal{A} \circ rep_{\mathcal{O}}^{-1} = \mathcal{P}$, i.e., if for any $i \in \mathcal{I}$ we have $rep_{\mathcal{O}}^{-1}(\mathcal{A}(rep_{\mathcal{I}}(i))) = \mathcal{P}(i)$. Obviously, this requires $rep_{\mathcal{I}}$ and $rep_{\mathcal{O}}$ both to be bijections. In other words, it would take a one-to-one correspondence between representations and models. However, because of the infinite character of most mathematical models on the one hand and the finite nature of computer representations on the other, the correspondence between the two is normally not one-to-one.

Taking this issue into account, the term correctness is therefore replaced by robustness as follows: A computer program $\mathcal{A} : \mathcal{I}_{rep} \to \mathcal{O}_{rep}$ for a problem $\mathcal{P} : \mathcal{I} \to \mathcal{O}$ will be called *robust*, if for every computer representation $i_{rep} \in \mathcal{I}_{rep}$ there is a corresponding model $i \in \mathcal{I}$ such that $\mathcal{P}(i) \in \mathcal{O}$ is among the models corresponding to $\mathcal{A}(i_{rep}) \in \mathcal{O}_{rep}$ – or formally, if for any $i_{rep} \in \mathcal{I}_{rep}$ we have $\{\mathcal{P}(i) | i \in \mathcal{I}, rep_{\mathcal{I}}(i) = i_{rep}\} \cap \{o \in \mathcal{O} | rep_{\mathcal{O}}(o) = \mathcal{A}(i_{rep})\} \neq \emptyset$. So, in order to prove that a given computer program is robust in this terminology, one basically has to show that for any given representation there always exists a model for which the computer program takes the correct decisions.

Admittedly, this definition of robustness allows a fairly generous interpretation of the term "correspondence". In particular, if we were to define only a single input representation x and a single output representation y and let $\mathcal{A}$ simply return y for the only possible input x, then $\mathcal{A}$ would be a robust algorithm for any problem $\mathcal{P}$, as all input models are mapped to x and all output models are mapped to y. In fact, this definition of robustness basically rather reflects what Shewchuk [731] suggests to be called quasi-robust.

Hoffmann, Hopcroft, and Karasick [402] introduced this formalization. They also gave an algorithm for intersection of polygons and proved its robustness with respect to their formalism. Hopcroft and Kahn [411] considered robust intersection of polyhedron with a half-space. However, in both cases the interpretation of "correspondence" was actually quite generous, leading to fairly loose relationship between computer representation and its "corresponding" model.

Related Issues. In the remaining part of this subsection, we will look at three issues that are actually closely related to precision-caused robustness problems in computational geometry, namely: inaccurate data, degeneracies and geometric rounding. Each of these issues shall be briefly discussed now in closing.

Inaccurate Data. Approximate arithmetic employed for computation is not the only type of inaccuracy relevant in computational geometry. As Schirra [704] points out, many geometric data arising in practice is actually known or supposed to be inaccurate. Since both types of inaccuracy basically impose a similar kind of uncertainty, there is actually not much of a difference between processing geometric objects that result from inaccurate computations and processing real-world data that is potentially inaccurate by nature.

Now, if we were to directly employ exact geometric computation on this kind of input, we would implicitly treat inaccurate data as exact. This way we would determine the correct result for some possibly inaccurately represented problem instance. Yet, this procedure only works out as long as the given data are actually consistent. Otherwise, we were to face similar problems as discussed in the course of this subsection: The algorithm may happen to enter a state that it was never supposed to be confronted with. In fact, it got actually launched in such a state already. This close relationship was a sufficient natural reason for researchers to address both kinds of inconsistencies in a uniform way. An immediate consequence however is, that any error in the output cannot be identified whether to be caused by inaccuracy of input or during computation.

In order to finally achieve an error-free output, there are two ways to choose between. When sticking to exact geometric computation, one will have to fix the relevant deal of the data – either in advance or on the fly, if possible. Basically, the input needs to be considered as non-benign and asks for being handled in one of the ways discussed in Section 3.5.1. Geometric rounding, as discussed shortly, may turn out one of these possible answers. The second way is to follow one of the approaches of consciously designing for inaccuracy discussed earlier in this section. In particular, tolerance-based and consistency-driven approaches appear naturally promising in this respect.

Degeneracy. As already mentioned in the beginning of this subsection, precision-caused non-robustness is closely related to degeneracy in computational geometry. The nearly degenerate and true degenerate instances are the critical scenarios in computing with numerical inaccuracy. Roughly speaking, degeneracies may be deemed to be points of discontinuity of the input-output-function induced by an algorithm – usually configurations of the input data where one of the predicates involved in the overall computation evaluates to zero, thus entailing a switch-over in the algorithm's control flow.

When designing a geometric algorithm it is common practice to assume the absence of such degeneracies. In fact, in scientific publications authors on a regular base tend to declare them as negligible details "left to the reader". The assumption is usually justified, for in most cases the details can indeed more or less easily be filled up. Yet, the more the phase of implementation approaches, the less pleasant it becomes from the point of robustness to keep hold of any such void in the algorithm's specification.

Following Yap [848], an algorithm is called *generic*, if it is only guaranteed to be correct on generic (i.e., non-degenerate) input. A *general* algorithm in turn is one that works for all (legal) inputs. In order to avoid the final implementation to crash due to degenerate input that could not be handled, it is desirable for the implementer to being delivered a general algorithm. So, if the initial description did not cover all degeneracies, then at one point in time a generic algorithm asks for being turned into a general one. There are basically two (not mutually exclusive) options for doing so: Adapting the algorithm or modifying the input.

Certainly, when following one of the approaches for computing with inaccuracy discussed earlier in this section, true degeneracy is actually kind of a non-issue. Since they cannot reliably determine true degeneracy anyway, these approaches treat any nearly degenerate case like an untrustworthy outcome of a predicate. For example, tolerance-based approaches simply adapt their tolerance information for any (true or) near degeneracy they hit upon. Consistency approaches in turn do not treat degeneracies explicitly at all. If the sign of a predicate evaluates to zero, it is replaced by a positive or negative one, whatever is consistent. In contrast, the controlled perturbation approach perturbs the input until it does not entail any predicate anymore that evaluates too close to zero. In general, approaches adapting the input (like also Milenkovic's data normalization technique) explicitly remove possible degeneracies.

In contrast to that, when applying exact geometric computation true degeneracy becomes an explicit issue. In fact, exact geometric computation guarantees to always yield the correct sign for each of the involved geometric predicates. However, it does not help us any further, once a predicate happens to correctly evaluate to zero, but the algorithm by design doesn't have an answer at hand how to handle this degenerate situation. Again, one could adapt the algorithm, i.e., extend it in a way that allows for degeneracies to being handled. However, apart from really treating them, there is again the second option, namely bypassing.

Edelsbrunner and Mücke [268] were the first ones to introduce the notion of so-called *symbolic perturbation schemes* into the field of computational geometry. The idea of this concept is to perturb the input in a symbolic way in order to remove degeneracies, but at the same time to obtain a result as close as possible to the real solution. In fact, perturbing only in a symbolic manner is the way to ensure that the perturbation does not change the sign of any non-zero predicate result. Edelsbrunner and Mücke [268] introduced a scheme, called *Simulation of Simplicity* (SoS). This technique, that was already known in the context of the simplex method, amounts to adding powers of some indeterminate ε to each input parameter. Emiris and Canny [273] reduced the computational complexity by applying *linear perturbations* only: to each input parameter x_i they add a perturbations $\pi_i \cdot \varepsilon$ where $\pi_i \in \mathbb{Z}$ and ε infinitesimal.

Yap [845] proposes a slightly more generalized concept called *blackbox sign evaluation schemes*. In this approach, every call to a predicate is generally replaced by a call to a sign blackbox which (a) always returns a non-zero sign and

(b) guarantees to preserve any non-zero sign concluded by the original predicate. Yap [845, 844] shows how to formulate a consistency property for the blackbox and offers a whole family of admissible schemes applicable for polynomial functions. This approach is in particular important, as SoS can be applied to determinants only.

Finally, Seidel [722] proposes an approach, based on the following idea. Given a problem $P(x)$ and just a single non-degenerate input x^*, then every other input x can be made non-degenerate by perturbing it in the direction of x^*, leaving us with computing $P(x + \varepsilon x^*)$. He shows that the other perturbation schemes mentioned above are each special cases of his general approach.

Geometric Rounding. Computing geometrically exact results is only worth as much as the computed result can actually be successfully passed on to subsequent stages. In fact, it does not help much, for example, to determine the exact solution of a geometric problem if the output format is yet not capable of representing it without information loss. There may also be a couple of other reasons (e. g., the computational cost) that call for a reduction of the numerical and/or structural complexity of geometric data.

The goal of *geometric rounding* now is to find a *simplification* of a given geometric structure, i. e., a geometric structure of lower complexity that does not deviate too much from its original with respect to some specific geometric or topological criteria. Thereby, two different objectives may be the driving forces, namely combinatorial versus precision simplification [848]. Whereas the former one aims at reducing the number of primitives and their combinatorial relations, the latter objective seeks for reducing the (bit-)complexity of the numerical values themselves.

Greene and Yao [359] were the first authors to introduce the topic of geometric rounding in the field of computational geometry. They considered the problem of rounding line segments consistently to a regular grid. They suggested to break the line segments into polygonal chains by moving any vertex of the subdivision (i. e., every endpoint of a line segment or intersection point of two segments) to its nearest grid point. Their approach moves edges only by a distance of at most half a grid cell's diameter. It may introduce new incidences, but no additional crossings, which is the property that is meant by "consistently". Unfortunately, it may produce a large number of new vertices along the polygonal chains. Since n segments may show $\Theta(n^2)$ intersections, Greene/Yao rounding may end up with quadratically many additional vertices, compared to initially $O(n)$.

Snap rounding, usually attributed to Hobby [398] and Greene [358], overcomes this issue. The general idea is based on the notion of a *hot pixel*, which also gave raise to the name *hot pixel rounding*. A pixel of the grid is called *hot*, if it either contains an endpoint of an original line segment, or an intersection point of two original line segments. The rounding procedure consists of snapping all segments intersecting a hot pixel to the pixel center. As with Greene/Yao rounding, snap rounding guarantees that the resulting arrangement will be contained within the Minkowski sum of the original arrangement and a unit grid cell centered at the origin.

However, Halperin and Packer [377] showed that a vertex of the output computed that way may be very close to an actually non-incident edge. Since this might induce new potential near-degeneracies, they proposed an augmented procedure, called *iterated snap rounding*, aimed to eliminate the undesirable property. Their rounding basically consists of two stages. In a preprocessing stage they compute hot pixels defined by the vertices of the arrangement. Additionally, they prepare a segment intersection search structure that allows to query for all hot pixels that a given segment s intersects. In a second stage they perform a procedure the call *reroute* on each input segment. This recursive procedure produces a polygonal chain s^* as an approximation for a given segment s, such that when s^* passes through a hot pixel, it passes through its center. Halperin and Packer show that their rounding procedure guarantees that any vertex is at least half the width of a pixel away from any non-incident edge.

Milenkovic [573] proposes a scheme called *shortest path rounding*, which introduces even fewer bends than snap rounding. He defines a *deformation* to be a continuous mapping $\pi : [0,1] \times \mathbb{R}^2 \to \mathbb{R}^2$ such that $\pi(0,p) = p$ for all $p \in \mathbb{R}^2$, and for any fixed $t \in [0,1)$ the function $\pi_t(p) := \pi(t,p)$ is a bijection. (Note that π_1 not necessarily needs to be a bijection – distinct points may collapse at time $t = 1$. However, π_1 is clearly the limit of a series of bijections.) π_t represents the state of the deformation at time $t \in [0,1]$. In comparison, $\gamma_p(t) := \pi(t,p)$ reflects the path that p travels through during the whole process of deformation, starting at p and ending at the target position $\rho(p) := \pi(1,p) = \pi_1(p) = \gamma_p(1)$. A geometric rounding of a straight line embedding $G = (V, E)$ to a lattice S is then a deformation of the plane such that the following two properties hold:

(a) For any $v \in V$, γ_v is completely contained in $CELL(S, v)$, i.e., the deformation path of any vertex $v \in V$ always stays within the lattice cell corresponding to v.

(b) Each $(u, v) \in E$ is deformed into a polygonal chain having its vertices in lattice points of vertices of V only.

Such a geometric rounding is called a *shortest path rounding* if every rounded edge results in a polygonal chain with shortest possible paths among all (feasible) roundings. Milenkovic shows that the result of a shortest path rounding is always unique.

Apart from 2-dimensional arrangements and planar subdivisions, geometric rounding has also been studied in 3D. As already mentioned in Section 3.5.3, Sugihara and Iri [763] apply what may be called *CSG rounding* to a geometric object by first rounding all involved CSG primitives and subsequently reconstructing the tree. Fortune [296] in turn rounds geometric objects given in manifold representation. This *manifold rounding* works by first rounding the equations or faces and afterwards, in case the rounded solid is self-intersecting, retaining only the "unburied" portion of the boundary.

In general, rounding geometric data is far more than just rounding numbers, and doing it properly can be very difficult. In fact, the quest for reducing complexity significantly while always keeping the numerical and combinatorial data consistent may turn out highly complicated.

Final Remarks. As we have seen in the second part of this section, computing with inaccuracy obviously seems to impair problems for geometric algorithms. In fact, as pointed out by Fortune [297], it is in general "notoriously difficult to obtain a practical implementation of an abstractly described geometric algorithm". In effect, the number of problems that have been successfully attacked this way is still small (see [524, 401, 704] for surveys on robustness issues in geometric computation). In fact, these approaches entail two major disadvantages: First of all, the respective techniques are highly specific to the considered problem and do hardly generalize to other geometric problems. And second, they do not permit off-the-shelf use of all the various geometric algorithms already available, but require a redesign of practically every single algorithm intended to be used. In short: They force us to redo Computational Geometry [141].

Chapter 4. Analysis of Algorithms

Heiner Ackermann, Heiko Röglin*, Ulf Schellbach, and Nils Schweer

4.1 Introduction and Motivation

Analyzing the properties of algorithms is fundamental for drawing conclusions on their applicability, for the comparison of different algorithms, and for the development of new ideas that help to improve existing algorithms. An algorithm that solves a problem optimally while the time and space it consumes grow not too fast is the ideal case. Unfortunately, such algorithms are not known to exist for many optimization problems that occur frequently in industrial applications. For these problems one can look for trade-offs between different properties like, e. g., the quality of the solution and the running time of the algorithm. Another possibility for coping with these problems is to relax the requirement that an algorithm has to work well on all instances of the considered optimization problem. It is sufficient if the algorithm performs well on those instances that occur typically in the considered application.

Consider, for example, the *traveling salesman problem (TSP)*. In its general form we are given a finite set of points and the cost of travel between each pair of points. A tour visits each point exactly once and returns to its starting point. The task is to find a tour of minimum cost. An approach may be to enumerate all tours and to choose the shortest one. This procedure clearly finds an optimal tour, but we have to evaluate $\frac{(n-1)!}{2}$ tours. If we assume that the computation of a tour can be done in one nanosecond (1 second = 10^9 nanoseconds) it takes approximately 2 years for a set of 20 points and approximately 177 centuries for an instance with 23 points to find an optimal tour. If we relax the condition of finding an optimal tour, i. e., if we are satisfied with a tour that is not optimal but not "too long" and the travel costs satisfy the triangle inequality, then we can for instance use Christofides heuristic [172] to find a tour that is at most 1.5 times longer than an optimal tour; this would take less than 1 second for both instances in the above example. Hence, we can find a trade-off between the quality of the solution and the running time in this case. If the travel costs are not restricted to satisfy the triangle inequality, then even finding a constant factor approximation of the optimal tour is NP-hard. Hence, one can also learn from this example that analyzing and restricting the input space properly is crucial for drawing conclusions about the complexity of a problem. Many TSP instances that occur in industrial applications satisfy the triangle inequality and considering them in the model with arbitrary travel costs leads to too pessimistic conclusions.

We have seen that enumerating all solutions is in general not feasible because too much time is needed. But when do we consider an algorithm to be efficient

---

* Supported by DFG grant Vo889/2.

M. Müller-Hannemann and S. Schirra (Eds.): Algorithm Engineering, LNCS 5971, pp. 127–193, 2010.
© Springer-Verlag Berlin Heidelberg 2010

for a given problem? Cobham, Edmonds and Rabin were one of the first who suggested an answer to this question [655, 269, 178]. They called an algorithm "efficient" if its running time grows polynomially in the input size for all input instances. This definition coincides with what we observed for the TSP. The idea of finding an upper bound on the running time of an algorithm over *all* instances leads directly to the so-called *worst-case analysis*, which is still the predominant type of analysis nowadays. An algorithm whose worst-case running time is polynomially bounded is the ideal case because the running time of such an algorithm never exceeds the corresponding polynomial, regardless of the instance the algorithm is applied to. Hence, this is also a very restrictive requirement, and indeed there is a large class of problems for which such algorithms are not believed to exist, namely the class of NP-hard problems. In their pioneering works, Cook [184] and Levin [519] identified the first NP-hard problem. Based on these results Karp [464] showed the NP-hardness of many other problems, including the TSP. It is not known whether NP-hard problems can be solved in polynomial time, but the existence of a polynomial-time algorithm for one of these problems would imply that all NP-hard problems can be solved in polynomial time. However, most researchers believe that no efficient algorithms for NP-hard optimization problems exist. Let us briefly remark that typically there are three different versions of a problem, the decision version "Is there a TSP tour of length at most b?", the optimization version "What is the length of the shortest TSP tour?", and the construction version "What is the TSP tour of minimum length?". For most problems the three versions are equivalent in the sense that an efficient algorithm for one of the versions also yields efficient algorithms for the other versions.

One way of dealing with the lack of efficient algorithms for NP-hard problems that we have already discussed above is to relax the requirement of solving the problems optimally. Another way is to give up the requirement that an algorithm should be efficient on every input. For many problems heuristics exist which are known to perform poorly in the worst case but work amazingly well on those inputs that occur in practical applications. For instance, the 2-Opt heuristic for the TSP, a simple local search algorithm, which is known to perform very poorly in the worst case with respect to both running time and approximation ratio, runs efficiently on most instances that occur in practice and yields tours whose lengths are typically worse than the optimal tour by only a few percentage points. These observations motivate to study the *average-case behavior* theoretically and to experimentally evaluate algorithms on a set of test instances. A recently developed probabilistic tool that uses advantages of both worst-case and average-case analysis is the so-called *smoothed analysis*. As this type of analysis is relatively new and seems to be an approach towards closing the gap between "pessimistic" worst-case analysis and sometimes too "optimistic" average-case analysis we discuss the most prominent results in detail.

The reader should be aware of the fact that all these measures can lead to completely different results, e. g., an algorithm can be efficient on average and non-efficient in the worst case. The main purpose of this chapter is to present and to discuss the different measures. Depending on the situation one or another of them may be more suitable. We try to point out where a measure is reasonable and where not.

In the remainder of this chapter we mainly deal with both theoretical and experimental analysis of an algorithm's running time, but of course there are also other interesting properties of an algorithm that one can analyze, e. g., the space consumption. Since computers contain a memory hierarchy consisting of a small amount of fast memory and a large amount of slow memory, it is worthwhile to analyze the space consumption of an algorithm and to utilize the memory hierarchy properly (cf. Chapter 5). In particular in computational geometry stating the *space complexity*, that is, the amount of space used while running an algorithm, is very common. Nearly all these analyses consider the worst-case space consumption, but of course, as for the running time, it is also possible and might be useful to study the average or smoothed space consumption in order to obtain more realistic results.

When dealing with distributed systems a fourth property (besides approximation ratio, time, and space), the so-called *message complexity*, is of special interest. For example a sensor network, consisting of a set of small devices (sensors) each equipped with a CPU, a radio interface, a battery, and a small memory, is a distributed system. In order to execute an algorithm, the sensors have to communicate. The number of messages necessary for the execution of an algorithm is called the message complexity. The methods presented in this chapter can also be used to analyze the message complexity; although we do not mention this explicitly in every section.

Before we concretize the term running time we have to make some remarks on the computational model we use. We call an operation *elementary* if the amount of time spent for its execution is bounded by a constant, i. e., if it does not depend on the size of the input. There are two common models for dealing with arithmetic operations like addition, multiplication, division, and comparison. The first one is the *logarithmic model* in which the costs for arithmetic operations depend on the lengths of the representations of the involved numbers, that is, the costs depend logarithmically on the involved numbers. This model is appropriate for algorithms that deal with large numbers, as for instance number-theoretic algorithms for primality testing. Algorithms that do not deal with large numbers can also be considered in the simplified *uniform model* in which also arithmetic operations are assumed to be elementary. In the remainder of this chapter we restrict our discussion to algorithms which fall into the latter category. Thus we use the uniform cost model in the following. We refer to elementary operations also as *(basic) steps*.

When analyzing an algorithm, we are mainly interested in its behavior on large problem instances. This is reasonable because for small instances often simple enumeration techniques work well. If an algorithm needs at most $8n^2 + 4n + 7$ steps to solve an instance, where n is some input parameter, then for large n the term $4n + 7$ is rather small in comparison to $8n^2$. In a theoretical analysis also the constant factors in the running time are not of great interest as they heavily depend on the implementation of the algorithm and since some basic steps can be executed faster than others. Hence, if we theoretically compare the running times of algorithms it is reasonable in most cases just to consider the dominant terms, in this case n^2. However, let us point out that this only makes sense if the constant factors are not too large. An algorithm whose running time depends only linearly on n can still be infeasible in practice if the constant factors in its running time are astronomically large. Of course, one is interested in implementations of algorithms for which the constant factors in the running time are as small as possible (cf. Chapter 6). But, since we consider the theoretical analysis of algorithms and not the implementation, we compare running times only based on the dominant terms in the remainder of this chapter. To make this precise, we introduce next the *set of asymptotic positive functions* $\mathcal{F}^{\oplus}$, and define subsets $O(g)$, $\Omega(g)$, $\Theta(g)$, $o(g)$ and $\omega(g)$ of $\mathcal{F}^{\oplus}$, whose elements are characterized by some relative order of growth with respect to some function g.

Definition 1. *Call $f \colon \mathbb{N} \to \mathbb{R}$ an* asymptotic positive function, *if there exists a natural number n_0 such that $f(n) > 0$ holds for all $n \geq n_0$. Let $\mathcal{F}^{\oplus}$ denote the set of asymptotic positive functions, and let f and g be in $\mathcal{F}^{\oplus}$. Function f belongs to $O(g)$, read f is of growth order g, iff there exist positive constants c and n_0 such that $f(n) \leq c \cdot g(n)$ holds for all $n \geq n_0$. Function f belongs to $\Omega(g)$, iff $g \in O(f)$. Defining $\Theta(g)$ as the set $O(g) \cap \Omega(g)$, $f \in \Theta(g)$ means that f and g have the same order of growth. Function f is said to grow slower than g, denoted by $f \in o(g)$, iff $\lim_{n \to \infty} f(n)/g(n) = 0$. Accordingly, f grows faster than g, iff $f \in \omega(g)$, or equivalently, $\lim_{n \to \infty} f(n)/g(n) = \infty$.*

Sometimes we will abbreviate a statement like *f is in $O(g)$* by *f is $O(g)$*. Obviously, the running time of an algorithm can be described in terms of a function $f \in \mathcal{F}^{\oplus}$. If this running time is in $O(p(n))$ for some polynomial $p(n)$, then we say that the algorithm has a *polynomial running time* and we call the algorithm a *polynomial time algorithm*.

In Section 4.2 we present the *worst-case* and the *average-case analysis*. In Section 4.3 *amortized analysis* is introduced and an application to data structures and online algorithms is presented. A detailed discussion of recent results on the smoothed analysis of algorithms is contained in Section 4.4. In Section 4.5 we discuss *realistic!input models*. Section 4.6 contains a discussion of *computational testing* and in Section 4.7, the method of *counting representative operations* is presented. Finally, the question of how and in how far experiments can be used to study the asymptotic performance of an algorithm is posed and partly answered in Section 4.8.

4.2   Worst-Case and Average-Case Analysis

The classical methods for analyzing the behavior of an algorithm are the *worst-case analysis* and the *average-case analysis*. In Section 4.2.1 we present the worst-case analysis and in Section 4.2.2 the average-case analysis. We discuss their merits and drawbacks at the end of each section.

4.2.1   Worst-Case Analysis

The worst-case analysis yields an upper bound on the running time of an algorithm over all input instances. Suppose we are given an algorithm in pseudocode or any programming language. This code consists of a finite number of lines $1, 2, \ldots, k$, and we assume that the worst-case performance is known for each line. Note that we do not require each line having constant time complexity. In particular a line can contain the call of a subroutine. In order to obtain the worst-case running time we additionally need to know the maximum number of times each line is executed over all valid instances. Consider, e. g., the *minimum weight spanning tree problem* on a graph $G = (V, E)$ with edges $E = \{e_1, \ldots, e_m\}$, n vertices, and a weight function $c : E \mapsto \mathbb{R}$. We are looking for a connected cycle-free subgraph of minimum total weight. *Kruskal's algorithm* is stated in Algorithm 1.

Algorithm 1. Kruskal's algorithm

1: Sort the edges such that $c(e_1) \leq c(e_2) \leq \ldots \leq c(e_m)$.
2: $T \leftarrow (V, \emptyset)$
3: **for** $i \leftarrow 1$ to m **do**
4:     **if** $T + e_i$ contains no cycle **then**
5:         $T \leftarrow T + e_i$

The first line is executed at most once, and sorting the edges according to their weights can be done in $O(m \log m)$ using *mergesort*. The second line is also called only once and can be performed in constant time. The third and the fourth line are both executed m times; the fifth line at most n times. Proving the nonexistence of a cycle (line 4) can, e. g., be done using the *breadth first search algorithm*. Its running time is linear in the number of edges of the graph it is applied to. In this case the graph has at most n edges; so the running time is $O(n)$. Thus, the worst-case running time of Kruskal's algorithm is $O(m \log m + 1 + m + m \cdot n + n) = O(mn)$. Let us mention that the implementation of Kruskal's algorithm can be improved by using special data structures, yielding a bound of $O(m \log n)$ on the worst-case running time.

Next we formalize the concept of worst-case analysis. We denote by $T(i), i = 1, \ldots, k$ the running time of a single execution of line i multiplied with the maximum number of times it is executed over *all* valid input instances. $T(\cdot)$ is expressed in O-notation. Because there are only finitely many lines of code, we only have to care about the lines that *dominate* the running time of the algorithm.

Definition 2. *A line i dominates a line j if $T(i) > T(j)$. A line that is not dominated by any other line is called a bottleneck.*

Note, there may be lines where none dominates the other. This can in particular happen if the size of a problem is described by more than one parameter. Suppose the problem size is described by the two parameters s and t, and there is a line i with $T(i) = s^2$ and a line j with $T(j) = t^3$. If there is no relationship between s and t, then neither i dominates j nor j dominates i. Hence, the running time of these two lines is $O(s^2 + t^3)$. Following the discussion above we define the worst-case running time as follows:

Definition 3. *For fixed input parameters, we define the* worst-case *running time of an algorithm A as the maximal number of steps that algorithm A can perform on instances with the given parameters.*

Corollary 1. *Let S be the set of those lines of algorithm A that are not dominated by other lines. Then the worst-case running time of A can be bounded by* $O(\sum_{i \in S} T(i))$.

In a worst-case analysis of Kruskal's algorithm we obtain line 4 with $T(4) = O(mn)$ as a bottleneck, and this line is the only one that is not dominated by any other line. Hence, the running time of Kruskal's algorithm (in the naive implementation described above) is $O(mn)$.

An obvious disadvantage of the worst-case analysis is that if an algorithm performs badly on a single instance this instance determines the worst-case running time. Although an algorithm usually does not run slow on a single instance only, there are algorithms with exponential worst-case running time that are often used in practical settings. Consider for example the well known *simplex algorithm*. For almost every pivot rule there exists a polytope and an objective function such that the worst-case running time cannot be bounded by a polynomial. But the implementations of the simplex method (e. g., *ILOG CPLEX*) are among the most commonly used programs for solving linear programs.

One advantage of the worst-case analysis is that it yields an upper bound on the running time of an algorithm over *all* instances. If the worst-case bound is a polynomial of small degree we know that the algorithm will solve instances of moderate size in reasonable time.

A second advantage is that the worst-case analysis provides theoretical insights to the behavior of an algorithm. In particular it helps to identify bottleneck operations. If we want to improve the running time of an algorithm it is necessary to look at the operations that are not dominated by others. If one can make these operations faster, e. g., by using another data structure without making other operations slower this enhances the worst-case performance.

A third advantage is that a worst-case analysis can usually be performed easily and fast. In comparison to the *average-case analysis* (compare Section 4.2.2) or the *smoothed analysis* (compare Section 4.4) which both need probabilistic techniques the worst-case analysis requires only the *pseudocode* of an algorithm.

4.2.2   Average-Case Analysis

The next method we describe is the average-case analysis. The basic idea of this technique is to average the running time over all valid instances of the same size. The instances on which the algorithm performs badly may be rare in the set of all instances or they may occur seldom in practical settings, and therefore they should not determine the running time of the algorithm as they do in the worst-case analysis.

Formally, this concept can be defined as follows: Let A be an algorithm, $\mathcal{I}_n$ the set of all instances of length n, $g_A : \mathcal{I}_n \to \mathbb{N}$ a function that maps each instance $I \in \mathcal{I}_n$ to the number of basic steps performed by algorithm A on I, and $f_n : \mathcal{I}_n \to [0,1]$ the density function of a probability distribution on $\mathcal{I}_n$. Then the average-case running time $T_{\text{AVG}}(n)$ on the set of instances of length n can be defined as follows:

$$T_{\text{AVG}}(n) = \int_{I \in \mathcal{I}_n} f(I) \cdot g_A(I)\, dI \ .$$

Note that there are different ways of defining average-case running time and this is only one of them; we present another one at the end of this section.

If $\mathcal{I}_n$ is finite, the density function is a discrete probability function p_I. If we further assume that all instances are equally likely, we get $p_I = \frac{1}{|\mathcal{I}_n|}$. Then the average running time is simply the mean value $\frac{1}{|\mathcal{I}_n|} \sum_{I \in \mathcal{I}_n} g_A(I)$.

The advantage of the average-case analysis is obvious; single instances do not influence the running time by too much. A disadvantage is that one has to know the probability distribution of the input instances. Assuming that all instances occur with equal probability may be convenient from a theoretical point of view but not from a practical one. In general the probability distribution is not known and depends on the concrete application, and therefore a uniform distribution is not a realistic assumption in most cases.

Another disadvantage of the definition of average-case analysis we use is that it is not robust under changes of the computational model. If a worst-case analysis states a polynomial running time for an algorithm, then the algorithm has also a polynomial running time if one replaces the machine model by another machine model that can simulate the former one in polynomial time. Average-case analysis does not preserve polynomial running time when changing the model of computation as the following example shows [820]: Consider the set $\mathcal{I}_n = \{0,1\}^n$ of all instances of a fixed length $n \in \mathbb{N}$. We assume that all instances occur with equal probability $\frac{1}{2^n}$. Let $\mathcal{D} \subseteq \mathcal{I}_n$ with cardinality $2^n(1 - 2^{-0.1n})$. Suppose that algorithm A runs in polynomial time $p(n)$ on every instance from $\mathcal{D}$ and runs in $2^{0.09n}$ time on all other instances. Then the average-case running time T_{AVG}^1 can be computed as follows:

$$T_{\text{AVG}}^1 = \sum_{I \in \mathcal{D}} \frac{1}{2^n} p(n) + \sum_{I \in \mathcal{I}_n \setminus \mathcal{D}} \frac{1}{2^n} 2^{0.09n}$$

$$= \frac{1}{2^n} \left[2^n p(n) - 2^{0.9n} p(n) + 2^{0.99n} \right]$$

$$= p(n) - \frac{1}{2^{0.1n}} p(n) + \frac{1}{2^{0.01n}} \ .$$

Note, T_{AVG}^1 is bounded from above by a polynomial in n. Now consider a quadratic increase in the running time of the algorithm, i. e., the algorithm needs $p^2(n)$ and $2^{0.18n}$ time on instances from $\mathcal{D}$ and $\mathcal{I}_n \setminus \mathcal{D}$, respectively. Then the average-case running time

$$T_{\text{AVG}}^2 = p^2(n) - \frac{1}{2^{0.1n}} p^2(n) + 2^{0.08n}$$

is not polynomially anymore. Hence, an algorithm with average polynomial running time on one machine model can have an average exponential running time on another machine model, even if the former can be simulated by the latter in polynomial time.

Let us consider only the first part of the example. In this case A is efficient under average-case analysis but non-efficient under the worst-case measure because the running time is exponential on instances from $\mathcal{I}_n \setminus \mathcal{D}$. Thus, the distinction between "applicable" and "non-applicable" depends also on the measure we use.

The last disadvantage we want to mention is that although an algorithm may have small average-case running time it still can perform badly on some instances. In particular, depending on the choice of the probability distribution the algorithm can perform badly on those instances that occur in practical applications. So, what seems to be the average case analysis's most obvious advantage turns out to be a disadvantage in some cases.

Furthermore we want to mention briefly that there is another way of defining polynomial average-case complexity, which overcomes the model dependency.

Definition 4. *For $n \in \mathbb{N}$ let μ_n be a probability distribution on the set $\mathcal{I}_n$ of instances of length n. Let A be an algorithm, let $\mathcal{I}$ denote the set of instances, and let $g_A : \mathcal{I} \to \mathbb{N}$ denote a function that maps each instance $I \in \mathcal{I}$ to the number of basic steps performed by algorithm A on instance I. Algorithm A has average polynomial running time* with respect to the sequence $\mu_1, \mu_2, \dots$ *if there exists an $\varepsilon > 0$ such that*

$$\mathrm{E}_{I \xleftarrow{\mu_n} \mathcal{I}_n} [(g_A(I))^\varepsilon] = O(n) \ , \tag{1}$$

where the left hand side of (1) denotes the expectation of $(g_A(I))^\varepsilon$ with respect to the density function μ_n for $n \in \mathbb{N}$.

The drawback of this definition is that average polynomial running time does not imply expected polynomial running time. In order to obtain expected polynomial running time, the exponent ε in (1) has to be placed outside instead of inside the expectation. For further discussions of this definition and the theory of *average-case complexity* we refer the reader to [115].

4.3   Amortized Analysis

Amortized analysis was proposed by Tarjan [773] and is, e. g., used for analyzing online algorithms [287,87,850] and data structures [431,744]. Tarjan characterizes amortized analysis by "to average the running times of operations in a sequence over the sequence". That is, instead of considering only a single operation, one always considers a sequence of operations, e. g., a sequence of paging requests is analyzed. The idea is that even if a single operation is expensive the costs averaged over the whole sequence may still be small.

Definition 5. *The* actual cost *of an operation is the amount of time (number of basic steps) actually consumed by this operation; it is denoted by c_i. The* total actual cost *of a sequence of m operations is $\sum_{i=1}^{m} c_i$.*

The basic idea of amortized analysis is to charge the ith operation *amortized cost* a_i which may be smaller or larger than the actual cost c_i. If the amortized cost of an operation j is larger than the actual cost, the difference is stored and is used to pay for operations with $a_i < c_i$, $i \neq j$. We want the total actual cost of a sequence to be bounded by the sum of the amortized costs of each operation in the sequence. In other words, we require $\sum_{i=1}^{m} c_i \leq \sum_{i=1}^{m} a_i$. The latter is called the *total amortized cost*. The amortized costs a_i, $i = 1, \dots, m$, do not necessarily have to be the same for every operation as we will see in Section 4.3.2. Amortized analysis is often used if the operations in the sequence are related in some way. To point this out: Amortized analysis gives a worst-case bound for a sequence of operations and does not rely on any probability assumptions.

The following analysis [773] is an example where amortized analysis beats classical worst-case analysis by using the relationship between two operations. Consider the manipulation of a stack by the two operations POP and PUSH each consuming one time unit. POP removes the top item on the stack if the stack is not empty, and PUSH adds a new element to the top of the stack. Now we define a new operation MULTI that consists of zero or more POP operations and exactly one PUSH after all POPs. We consider a sequence of m operations each being either a POP, a PUSH or a MULTI operation. We assume that they are executed on an initially empty stack. The worst-case running time for a single operation is bounded by m, and this bound is attained if the first $m - 1$ operations do not contain a POP, and the last operation removes $m - 1$ items from the stack and pushes exactly one element onto the stack. This yields a worst-case running time of $O(m^2)$. But in fact, the running time is bounded by $2m$ because the stack is initially empty, and there are at most m PUSHs and therefore there can be at most m POPs.

This example gives a rough idea of amortization and how to use the relationship between two operations but does not describe a general technique for performing an amortized analysis. In the next sections three different techniques are described, and each is applied to the example of stack manipulation. Section 4.3.1 contains the *aggregate analysis*. Section 4.3.2 introduces the *accounting method* or sometimes called the *banker's view* [773]. The *potential method* also referred to as the *physicist's view* is described in Section 4.3.3. In Section 4.3.4 an application of the potential method to online algorithms and data structures is show.

4.3.1 Aggregate Analysis

The first method we present is the aggregate analysis. In this method the amortized cost per operation is defined as the averaged cost $a_i = \frac{1}{m} \sum_{j=1}^{m} c_j$ for every $1 \leq i \leq m$ where $\sum_{j=1}^{m} c_j$ is the total actual cost, and m is the length of the sequence. Note that the amortized costs are the same for every operation.

Next we apply the aggregate analysis to the example of stack manipulation. The actual cost for POP and PUSH is 1, the actual cost of MULTI is $\min(s, k)+1$ where s is the number of objects on the stack, and k is the number of POPs in MULTI. Since there are at most m PUSHs in a sequence of length m there can be at most m POPs, single POPs, or POPs contained in MULTI. Hence, the total actual cost is bounded by 2m which is $O(m)$, and the amortized cost is $O(1)$.

4.3.2 The Accounting Method

The accounting method also called the banker's view is another technique for performing an amortized analysis. In contrast to the aggregate analysis the accounting method explicitly allows different amortized costs for different operations. Again, the amortized cost per operation can be larger or smaller than the actual cost per operation. If the amortized cost exceeds the actual cost the difference is stored and is used to pay for operations where the amortized cost is less than the actual cost. We call this difference *credit*. The *total credit* of a sequence of length k is $\sum_{i=1}^{k} a_i - \sum_{i=1}^{k} c_i$.

In order to bound the total actual cost by the total amortized cost we require the total credit to be nonnegative. If we know the length of the analyzed sequence in advance this condition is sufficient for obtaining a worst-case bound. If the length of the sequence is not known the total credit has to be nonnegative after every operation; that is $\sum_{i=1}^{k} c_i \leq \sum_{i=1}^{k} a_i$ for every $k \geq 1$.

However, the crucial step of the accounting method is the allocation of the amortized costs. Next we show how this can be done for the example of stack manipulation. We assign amortized cost of 2 to PUSH and amortized cost of 0 to POP. This implies that the amortized cost of MULTI is 2. Note that the actual cost of MULTI may depend on the length of the sequence, but the amortized cost is constant.

Next we prove that $\sum_{i=1}^{k} c_i \leq \sum_{i=1}^{k} a_i$ for every $k \geq 1$ in this example. This is trivial, because the stack is initially empty, and for every PUSH we can store one unit of amortized cost. This credit can be used to pay for the POP operations. Since there are at most as many POPs as PUSHs we can guarantee that the total credit is nonnegative after every operation.

4.3.3 The Potential Method

The third technique and probably the one that has been used most often is the potential method. In the literature this method is also referred to as physicist's view because of the use of potential functions [773]. Like the accounting method the potential method usually assigns different amortized costs to different operations. But this time the difference $c_i - a_i$ (for the ith operation) is not stored directly as a credit. Instead, it is reflected by the change in a potential function. The bound obtained by the potential method depends in particular on the potential function. Therefore it has to be chosen carefully.

The potential method can be described as follows: Consider an object that is modified by a sequence of m operations. One may think of a data structure (a search tree, an unsorted list, etc.) that is modified by a sequence of insertions or deletions.

We denote the initial configuration of the object by D_0, its configuration after the ith operation by D_i for $i = 1, \ldots m$, and the set of all configurations by $\mathcal{D}$. First, we have to choose the potential function $\Phi : \mathcal{D} \to \mathbb{R}$ which maps the current configuration of the object to the real numbers. Then the amortized cost (with respect to the potential function Φ) of the ith operation is defined as

$$a_i = c_i + \Phi(D_i) - \Phi(D_{i-1}) \; . \tag{2}$$

Thus, the amortized cost is the actual cost plus the change in the potential function. If the change in the potential function is positive the difference is stored as "potential energy" in the function; otherwise the stored "energy" is used to perform the operation. From equation (2) we get:

$$\sum_{i=1}^{m} a_i = \sum_{i=1}^{m} c_i + \Phi(D_m) - \Phi(D_0) \; .$$

Note that the terms $\Phi(D_i)$ telescope. As we want the total amortized cost to bound the total actual cost we have to make sure that $\Phi(D_m) - \Phi(D_0)$ is nonnegative. If we do not know the length of the sequence in advance, we require this property for every $k \geq 1$. If the potential function is chosen such that $\Phi(D_0) = 0$, then one has to prove that it is nonnegative for every other D_i.

To make the potential method more concrete we apply it to the example of stack manipulation. We define the potential function to be the number of objects on the stack. Since we start with the empty stack, we get $\Phi(D_0) = 0$ and Φ is clearly nonnegative for all other D_is. Hence the total amortized cost (with respect to Φ) is an upper bound on the total actual cost.

Next we compute the amortized cost for each of the three operations. Let l be the number of items on the stack before the ith operation. Then we can compute the amortized cost if the ith operation is a POP or a PUSH:

POP: $a_i = c_i + \Phi(D_i) - \Phi(D_{i-1}) = 1 + (l - 1) - l = 0$

PUSH: $a_i = c_i + \Phi(D_i) - \Phi(D_{i-1}) = 1 + (l + 1) - l = 2 \; .$

If the ith operation is a MULTI operation that consists of s POPs (and one PUSH), the following amortized cost is obtained:

MULTI: $a_i = c_i + \Phi(D_i) - \Phi(D_{i-1}) = (s + 1) + (l - s + 1) - l = 2 \; .$

Since $a_i \leq 2$ for all $i \in \{1, \ldots, m\}$ the total amortized cost is bounded by $2m$, and because the potential is nonnegative for arbitrary $k \geq 1$, the total actual cost is bounded by $2k$ for every sequence of length k.

4.3.4 Online Algorithms and Data Structures

Amortized analysis has been applied to more complex problems than stack manipulation [125]. In particular it has been used to analyze online algorithms and data structures. Consider, e. g., the situation where a certain property of the data structure has to be maintained while serving a sequence of requests. Usually future requests are not known, and the algorithm has to make its decisions based on former requests. Well studied data structures are for instance different kinds of search trees. The purpose is to keep the depth of the tree bounded by $\log n$ where n is the number of nodes while maintaining an order in the tree such that a new node can be inserted into the tree by only traversing one path in the tree [772].

Another data structure that is often analyzed using amortization are lists (see [287] for a survey). Exemplarily we present the problem of maintaining an unsorted list of maximal length n under an intermixed sequence of m requests. These requests are of the following kind:

- *insert(i)*: Insert item i into the list.
- *access(i)*: Locate item i in the list.
- *delete(i)*: Delete item i from the list.

An insertion is performed by scanning the list from the beginning to the end to make sure the item is not already in the list and to insert the item at the end of the list. The cost of insert(i) is $k + 1$, where k is the length of the list before the insertion. Locating item i in the list or deleting it from the list costs l if i is at the lth position in the list. This is done by scanning the list from the front to the end and stopping at the requested item.

We want to study the problem of how to serve a sequence of requests at minimum cost. Different strategies for this problem arise from the fact that we are allowed to rearrange the items. After every insert(i) or access(i) operation the item i may be moved to any position closer to the front at no cost. These exchanges are called *free*. Other exchanges are also allowed any time; but exchanging two neighbored items, where none was currently requested, costs 1; we refer to them as *paid exchanges*.

Let i be the requested item. Then the most common strategies can be described as follows:

- *Move-To-Front*: Move i to the first position of the list.
- *Transpose*: Flip the position of i and its predecessor in the list.
- *Frequency-Count*: A counter is maintained for every item i, and it is increased by one if the item is accessed or inserted. The counter is set to zero if the item is deleted. The items in the list are rearranged such that they appear in non-increasing order (with respect to their frequency counters) after every operation.

The problem we just described belongs to the class of online problems, and the strategies Move-To-Front, Transpose and Frequency-Count are online algorithms. In general the analysis of online algorithms is different to the analysis of offline algorithms. Since online algorithms do not know future requests, the sequence may always ask for the last element in the list. Such a sequence exists for every strategy and therefore classical worst-case analysis yields the same lower bound on the performance for every algorithm. To overcome this gap Sleator and Tarjan [744] introduced the competitive analysis. The main idea of competitive analysis is to consider the ratio between the algorithms' behavior and the behavior of an optimal offline algorithm on the same sequence.

Definition 6. *Let Σ be the set of all legal input sequences for an algorithm A, $C_A(\sigma)$ the cost of algorithm A for serving $\sigma \in \Sigma$, $C_{OPT}(\sigma)$ the cost of an optimal offline algorithm for σ, and d a constant. Then*

$$\inf\{c \in \mathbb{R} : C_A(\sigma) \leq c \cdot C_{OPT}(\sigma) + d, \forall\, \sigma \in \Sigma\}$$

is called the competitive ratio *of algorithm A. An algorithm with finite competitive ratio c is called c-competitive.*

Sleator and Tarjan showed that the Move-To-Front algorithm is 2-competitive using amortized analysis [744]. Their proof is a straight forward application of the potential method. We restate the proof for the case that the sequence consists of accesses only. The analysis of deletion and insertion can be done similarly.

Theorem 1. *The Move-To-Front algorithm is 2-competitive.*

Proof. Let $\sigma = (\sigma_1, \sigma_2, \ldots, \sigma_m)$ be a sequence of m requests consisting of accesses only. We denote by L_{OPT} or L_{MTF} the list maintained by the optimal offline algorithm OPT or the Move-To-Front algorithm, respectively. We use the potential function $\Phi(s)$ which counts the number of inversions in L_{MTF} with respect to L_{OPT} after the sth request. An *inversion* is a pair of items i and j such that i occurs before j in L_{MTF} and after j in L_{OPT}. We assume w.l.o.g. that OPT and Move-To-Front start with the same initial list. We denote the actual cost and amortized cost incurred by Move-To-Front for serving request σ_t by $c_{MTF}(t)$ and $a_{MTF}(t)$, respectively, and define analogous notation for the cost incurred by OPT. Now suppose item i is accessed. Let k denote the number of items that precede i in L_{MTF} *and* L_{OPT} and l the number of items that precede i in L_{MTF} but follow i in L_{OPT}. Note that $k + l$ is the total number of items preceding i in L_{MTF}. Thus, $c_{MTF}(t) = k + l + 1$ and $c_{OPT}(t) \geq k + 1$. After serving the request, Move-To-Front changes i to the first position in the list. Thereby l inversions are destroyed, and at most k new inversions are created. Now we can bound the amortized cost $a_{MTF}(t) = c_{MTF}(t) + \Phi(t) - \Phi(t-1)$ of request σ_t as follows:

$$c_{MTF}(t) + \Phi(t) - \Phi(t-1) \leq c_{MTF}(t) + k - l = 2k + 1 \leq 2c_{OPT}(t) - 1 \ .$$

Summing this expression for all t we obtain $\sum_{i=1}^{m} c_{MTF}(t) + \Phi(m) - \Phi(0) \leq \sum_{i=1}^{m} 2c_{OPT}(t) - m$, which implies $\sum_{i=1}^{m} c_{MTF}(t) \leq \sum_{i=1}^{m} 2c_{OPT}(t) - \Phi(m) + \Phi(0)$.

As Φ is initially zero (OPT and Move-to-Front start with the same list) and clearly nonnegative at any time we get $\sum_{i=1}^{m} c_{\text{MTF}}(t) \leq 2 \sum_{i=1}^{m} c_{\text{OPT}}(t)$. If OPT makes a paid exchange, this can increase the potential function by 1, but OPT also pays 1. The competitive ratio follows.   □

4.4   Smoothed Analysis

We already discussed that worst-case analyses are often too pessimistic because for many algorithms with "bad" worst-case behavior "bad instances" occur in practical applications very rarely. The most prominent example is the simplex algorithm, which we consider in more detail in Section 4.4.2. Another well known example is the knapsack problem, which we consider in Section 4.4.1. On the other hand, average-case analyses are often problematic because it is not clear how to choose the probability distribution on the input set. Many average-case analyses assume a uniform distribution on the set of instances. However, for most problems uniformly at random chosen instances do not reflect *typical* instances. Consider for example a random graph in which each edge is created independently of the other edges with some fixed probability. Such random graphs have very special properties with high probability, e. g., concerning the number of edges, the connectivity, and the chromatic number. In many applications these properties are not satisfied and hence algorithms that have low average-case complexity can still perform "badly" on typical inputs. That is, average-case analyses tend to be too optimistic.

In order to capture the behavior of algorithms on practical inputs better than it is possible by a worst-case or average-case analysis alone, Spielman and Teng introduce a hybrid of these two models, the so-called *smoothed analysis* [749]. The input model in a smoothed analysis consists of two steps. In the first step, an adversary specifies an arbitrary input. After that, in the second step, this input is slightly perturbed at random. The magnitude of the perturbation is parametrized by some value σ. For $\sigma = 0$, no perturbation occurs, and the larger σ is chosen, the larger is the expected perturbation. The smoothed running time of an algorithm as defined in [749] is the worst expected running time that the adversary can achieve. To make this more precise, let $\mathcal{A}$ denote an algorithm, let I denote an input for $\mathcal{A}$, and let $\mathcal{C}_{\mathcal{A}}(I)$ denote a complexity measure of algorithm $\mathcal{A}$ on input I. Let $\mathcal{I}_n$ denote the set of inputs of length n. The worst-case complexity for inputs of length n is defined by

$$\mathcal{C}_{\mathcal{A}}^{\text{worst}}(n) = \max_{I \in \mathcal{I}_n} \left(\mathcal{C}_{\mathcal{A}}(I) \right) \ .$$

Given a family of probability distributions μ_n on $\mathcal{I}_n$, the average-case complexity of $\mathcal{A}$ for inputs of length n is

$$\mathcal{C}_{\mathcal{A}}^{\text{ave}}(n) = \mathrm{E}_{I \xleftarrow{\mu_n} \mathcal{I}_n} \left[\mathcal{C}_{\mathcal{A}}(I) \right] \ .$$

For an instance I and a magnitude parameter σ, let $\text{per}_\sigma(I)$ denote the random variable that describes the instance obtained from I by a perturbation with

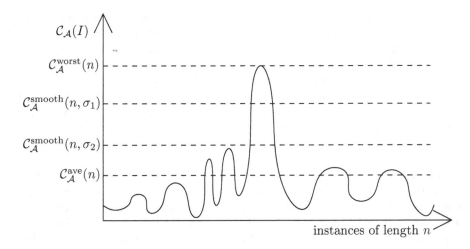

Fig. 4.1. Illustration of the different complexity measures. The horizontal axis ranges over the set of inputs of length n, for some fixed n. It is assumed that $\sigma_1 < \sigma_2$, hence $C_{\mathcal{A}}^{\text{smooth}}(n, \sigma_1) > C_{\mathcal{A}}^{\text{smooth}}(n, \sigma_2)$.

magnitude σ. The smoothed complexity of algorithm $\mathcal{A}$ for inputs of length n and magnitude parameter σ is defined as

$$C_{\mathcal{A}}^{\text{smooth}}(n, \sigma) = \max_{I \in \mathcal{I}_n} \mathrm{E}\left[C_{\mathcal{A}}\left(\mathrm{per}_\sigma(I)\right)\right] \ .$$

These definitions are illustrated in Figure 4.1. From the definition of smoothed complexity, one can see that it is a hybrid between worst-case and average-case analysis and that one can interpolate between these kinds of analyses by adjusting the parameter σ. For $\sigma \to 0$, the analysis becomes a worst-case analysis since the input specified by the adversary is not perturbed anymore. For $\sigma \to \infty$, the analysis becomes an average-case analysis since the perturbation is so large that the initial input specified by the adversary is not important anymore.

Since the invention of smoothed analysis by Spielman and Teng in 2001, many different results on the smoothed analysis of algorithms have been obtained, including results on different algorithms for solving linear programs, various discrete optimizations problems, and the competitive ratio of online algorithms. In this section, we concentrate on two results. We present Spielman and Teng's result on the smoothed running time of the simplex algorithm and some related results. Furthermore, we present a general result on the smoothed complexity of discrete optimization problems due to Beier and Vöcking.

4.4.1   Smoothed Analysis of Binary Optimization Problems

Although smoothed analysis was introduced in Spielman and Teng's seminal article on the *simplex algorithm* [749], we start our discussion with a result on the smoothed complexity of *binary optimization problems* due to Beier and Vöcking [86]. This result is proven by an elegant application of elementary probability theory and in contrast to the analysis of the simplex algorithm, it is possible to present the ideas and also most of the details of its proof in this exposition.

Beier and Vöcking consider optimization problems with randomly perturbed constraints as well as optimization problems with randomly perturbed objective functions. We postpone the discussion of their general result to the end of this section and first present a simplified version for optimization problems in which only the objective function is randomly perturbed.

Problems and Perturbation Model. We consider *linear binary optimization problems*. An instance I of such an optimization problem Π consists of a set of feasible solutions $\mathcal{S} \subseteq \{0,1\}^n$ and a linear objective function $f : \{0,1\}^n \to \mathbb{R}$ of the form maximize (or minimize) $f(x) = c^T x$ for some $c \in \mathbb{R}^n$. Many well known optimization problems can be formulated in this form, e. g., the problem of finding a *minimum spanning tree*, the *knapsack problem*, and the *traveling salesman problem*. Our goal is to study these problems in a probabilistic input model in which the coefficients in the linear objective function are randomly perturbed.

Since the input model which we consider combines adversarial and random decisions, we call it a *semi-random* model. In the first step of this semi-random input model, the coefficients in the objective function are chosen by an adversary. The adversary is allowed to choose real valued coefficients from the interval $[-1, 1]$. Observe that restricting the adversary to this interval is no severe restriction because every objective function can be brought into this form by scaling. In the second step, the numbers specified by the adversary are perturbed by adding independent Gaussian random variables with mean 0 and standard deviation σ to them. The smaller σ is chosen, the more concentrated are the random variables and hence, the better worst-case instances can be approximated by the adversary. Intuitively, σ can be seen as a measure specifying how close the analysis is to a worst-case analysis.

Polynomial Smoothed Complexity. Now we define the term *polynomial smoothed complexity* formally. Of course, one could base this definition on $\mathcal{C}_{\mathcal{A}}^{\text{smooth}}(n, \sigma)$ in the obvious way by defining that algorithm $\mathcal{A}$ has polynomial smoothed complexity if $\mathcal{C}_{\mathcal{A}}^{\text{smooth}}(n, \sigma)$ is polynomially bounded in n and $1/\sigma$. This definition, however, is not sufficiently robust as it depends on the machine model. An algorithm with expected polynomial running time on one machine model might have expected exponential running time on another machine model even if the former can be simulated by the latter in polynomial time (cf. Section 4.2.2). In contrast, the definition from [86], which we present below, yields a notion of polynomial smoothed complexity that does not vary among classes of machines admitting polynomial time simulations among each other.

Fix a linear binary optimization problem Π. We denote by $\mathcal{I}_N$ the set of unperturbed instances of length N. The definition of the input length N needs some clarification as the coefficients in the objective function are assumed to be real numbers. We ignore the contributions of these numbers to the input length and assume $N \geq n$. The bits of these numbers can be accessed by asking an oracle in time $O(1)$ per bit. The bits after the binary point of each coefficient are revealed one by one from the left to the right. The deterministic part of the input can be encoded in an arbitrary fashion. For an instance $I \in \mathcal{I}_N$, let $\mathrm{per}_\sigma(I)$ denote the random instance that is obtained by a perturbation of I with magnitude σ. We say that Π has *polynomial smoothed complexity* if and only if it admits a polynomial P and a randomized algorithm $\mathcal{A}$ whose running time $\mathcal{C}_\mathcal{A}$ satisfies

$$\Pr \left[\mathcal{C}_\mathcal{A} \left(\mathrm{per}_\sigma(I) \right) \geq P \left(N, \frac{1}{\sigma}, \frac{1}{p} \right) \right] \leq p , \tag{3}$$

for every $N \in \mathbb{N}$, $\sigma \in (0,1]$, $p \in (0,1]$, and $I \in \mathcal{I}_N$, where the probability is taken over the random input and the random decisions of the algorithm. That is, with probability at least $1 - p$ the running time of $\mathcal{A}$ is polynomially bounded in the input length N, the reciprocal of the standard deviation σ, and the reciprocal of p. This definition of polynomial smoothed complexity follows more or less the way how polynomial complexity is defined in average-case complexity theory. The drawback of this definition is, however, that polynomial smoothed complexity does not imply polynomial expected running time. A more detailed discussion of this definition can be found in [86], and for a more detailed discussion of polynomial average-case complexity we refer the reader to [115].

We prove the following theorem that characterizes the class of linear binary optimization problems with polynomial smoothed complexity.

Theorem 2 (Beier, Vöcking [86]). *A linear binary optimization problem Π has polynomial smoothed complexity if and only if there exists a randomized algorithm for solving Π whose expected worst-case running time is pseudo-polynomial[1] with respect to the coefficients in the objective function.*

For example, the knapsack problem, which can be solved by dynamic programming in pseudo-polynomial time, has polynomial smoothed complexity even if the weights are fixed and only the profits are randomly perturbed. Moreover, the traveling salesman problem does not have polynomial smoothed complexity when only the distances are randomly perturbed, unless P = NP, since a simple reduction from Hamiltonian cycle shows that it is strongly NP-hard. Let us point out that these results are not only of theoretical interest but that they exactly match the empirical observations. There exist many experimental studies showing that the knapsack problem is easy to solve on typical and on random instances by certain heuristics [638, 85]. On the other hand, there are numerous experimental studies on the TSP which suggest that solving the TSP to optimality is hard

---

[1] An algorithm is said to have *pseudo-polynomial* running time if it runs in polynomial time when the numbers in the input are encoded in unary or, equivalently, if its running time is bounded polynomially in the input size and the largest number occurring in the input.

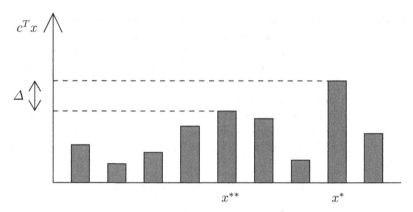

Fig. 4.2. Illustration of the definitions of the winner gap Δ, the winner x^* and the second best solution x^{**}. The horizontal axis ranges over all solutions from $\mathcal{S}$.

even on real-world and on random instances [440]. These examples lead to the conclusion that Theorem 2 yields a good characterization which problems can be solved well in practice and which cannot.

How accurately do we need to calculate? In order to prove Theorem 2, we first show how to transform a pseudo-polynomial time algorithm into an algorithm with polynomial smoothed running time. Later we discuss the other direction. A well-known approach that transforms a pseudo-polynomial time algorithm into a fully polynomial time approximation schemes is to round the coefficients in the objective function after a logarithmic number of bits and to use the pseudo-polynomial time algorithm to compute an optimal solution with respect to the rounded coefficients in polynomial time. In general, this solution is not an optimal solution with respect to the original, non-rounded coefficients since, in the worst case, even the smallest rounding can change the optimal solution. However, we will show that instances which are obtained by our probabilistic input model are robust against small roundings of the coefficients. That is, rounding the coefficients slightly does not change the optimal solution with high probability. The main tool for showing this is a surprising fact from probability theory, the so-called *Isolating Lemma*.

Let an arbitrary perturbed instance $\mathrm{per}_\sigma(I)$ of a linear binary optimization problem be given. Let $\mathcal{S} \subseteq \{0,1\}^n$ denote the feasible region and assume that the goal is to maximize the linear function $c^T x$ with respect to $x \in \mathcal{S}$. The coefficients $c_1, \ldots, c_n$ are independent Gaussian random variables with standard deviation σ whose means are specified by an adversary in the interval $[-1, 1]$. In this setting, the event that there exist two solutions with the same objective value can be neglected as it has probability 0. Let $x^* \in \mathcal{S}$ denote the optimal solution, i.e., $x^* = \mathrm{argmax}\{c^T x \mid x \in \mathcal{S}\}$, and let x^{**} denote the second best solution, i. e., $x^{**} = \mathrm{argmax}\{c^T x \mid x \in \mathcal{S}, x \neq x^*\}$. The *winner gap* Δ denotes the difference of the objective values of x^* and x^{**}, i. e., $\Delta = c^T x^* - c^T x^{**}$ (see Figure 4.2). Intuitively, one might think that Δ is typically very small. Assume for example that $\sigma = 1/n$ and that $\mathcal{S}$ contains exponentially many solutions. Then with high probability every coefficient c_i lies in the interval $[-2, 2]$ and there are exponentially many solutions whose objective values lie all in the interval $[-2n, 2n]$. Hence, if one sorts the solutions according to their objective values, then the average distance between the objective values of neighboring solutions is exponentially small. Surprisingly, for random coefficients the distance Δ is nonetheless polynomially large with high probability. This was first observed by Mulmuley, Vazirani, and Vazirani [599], who used this observation to design a randomized parallel algorithm for finding maximum matchings.

Lemma 1 (Isolating Lemma). *Let $\mathcal{S} \subseteq \{0,1\}^n$ denote an arbitrary feasible region and let $c_1, \ldots, c_n$ be independent Gaussian random variables with standard deviation σ and arbitrary means. Then for every $\varepsilon \geq 0$,*

$$\Pr[\Delta \leq \varepsilon] < \frac{n\varepsilon}{\sigma} \ .$$

Proof. In the following, we denote by $[n]$, for $n \in \mathbb{N}$, the set $\{1, \ldots, n\}$ of natural numbers between 1 and n. If there is a variable x_i that takes on the same value in all feasible solutions, then this variable does not affect the winner gap and can be ignored. Thus, without loss of generality, we can assume that for every $i \in [n]$, there exist two feasible solutions that differ in the i-th variable. Under this assumption, we can define the winner gap Δ_i with respect to position $i \in [n]$ by

$$\Delta_i = c^T x^* - c^T y \ , \tag{4}$$

where x^* denotes the optimal solution, i. e., $x^* = \mathrm{argmax}\{c^T x \mid x \in \mathcal{S}\}$, and y denotes the best solution differing from x^* in the i-th position, that is, $y = \mathrm{argmax}\{c^T x \mid x \in \mathcal{S}, x_i \neq x_i^*\}$.

Clearly, the best solution x^* and the second best solution x^{**} differ in at least one position, that is, there exists an $i \in [n]$ with $x_i^* \neq x_i^{**}$. If x^* and x^{**} differ in the i-th position, then $\Delta = \Delta_i$. Thus, Δ is guaranteed to take a value also taken by at least one of the variables $\Delta_1, \ldots, \Delta_n$. In the following, we prove $\Pr[\Delta_i \leq \varepsilon] \leq \sqrt{2/\pi} \cdot \varepsilon/\sigma$, for $1 \leq i \leq n$, which implies

$$\Pr[\Delta \leq \varepsilon] \leq \Pr[\exists i \in [n] : \Delta_i \leq \varepsilon] \leq \sum_{i \in [n]} \Pr[\Delta_i \leq \varepsilon] \leq \sqrt{\frac{2}{\pi}} \cdot \frac{n\varepsilon}{\sigma} < \frac{n\varepsilon}{\sigma} \ .$$

Let us fix an index $i \in [n]$. We partition the set $\mathcal{S}$ of feasible solutions into two disjoint subsets $\mathcal{S}_0 = \{x \in \mathcal{S} \mid x_i = 0\}$ and $\mathcal{S}_1 = \{x \in \mathcal{S} \mid x_i = 1\}$. Now suppose that all random variables c_k with $k \neq i$ are fixed arbitrarily. Under this assumption, we can identify an optimal solution among the solutions in $\mathcal{S}_0$ as the objective values of the solutions in $\mathcal{S}_0$ do not depend on c_i. Although the objective values of the solutions in $\mathcal{S}_1$ are not fixed, we can nevertheless identify

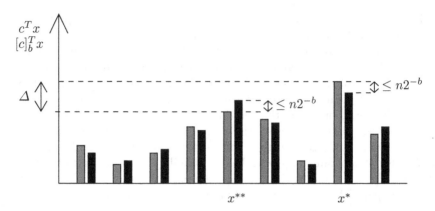

Fig. 4.3. The gray bars depict the objective values of the solutions from $\mathcal{S}$ w.r.t. the original coefficients c. The black bars depict the objective values of the solutions from $\mathcal{S}$ w.r.t. the rounded coefficients $[c]_b$.

an optimal solution in $\mathcal{S}_1$ because the unknown outcome of the random variable c_i does not affect the order among the solutions in $\mathcal{S}_1$. For $j \in \{0,1\}$, let $x^{(j)}$ denote an optimal solution among the solutions in $\mathcal{S}_j$. We observe $\Delta_i = |c^T x^{(1)} - c^T x^{(0)}|$ because the solutions x^* and y as defined in (4) cannot be contained in the same set $\mathcal{S}_j$, $j \in \{0,1\}$. We have shown $\Delta_i = |Z|$ for the random variable $Z = c^T x^{(1)} - c^T x^{(0)}$. Observe that the random variable c_i appears as additive term in Z. Hence, for fixed c_k with $k \neq i$ the density function of Z is a shifted variant of the density function of c_i. Since c_i is a Gaussian random variable with standard deviation σ, the suprema of the densities of c_i and Z can be bounded by $1/(\sqrt{2\pi}\sigma)$. Hence, $\Pr[\Delta_i \leq \varepsilon] = \Pr[Z \in [-\varepsilon,\varepsilon]] \leq \sqrt{2/\pi} \cdot \varepsilon/\sigma$. This completes the proof of the Isolating Lemma. $\qquad\square$

Let $\lfloor c_i \rfloor_b$ denote the coefficient c_i rounded down after the b-th bit after the binary point, let $\lceil c_i \rceil_b$ denote c_i rounded up after the b-th bit, and let $[c]_b$ denote either $\lfloor c_i \rfloor_b$ or $\lceil c_i \rceil_b$. We write $\lfloor c \rfloor_b$ and $\lceil c \rceil_b$ to denote the vectors obtained from c by rounding each coefficient down and up after the b-th bit after the binary point, respectively. We use $[c]_b$ to denote an arbitrary vector obtained from c by rounding each coefficient either down or up after the b-th bit, where different coefficients may be rounded differently. For every $i \in [n]$, c_i and $[c_i]_b$ differ by at most 2^{-b}. Hence, for every $x \in \mathcal{S}$ and every vector $[c]_b$, we have $|c^T x - [c]_b^T x| \in [0, n2^{-b}]$. If $\Delta > n2^{-b+1}$, then rounding every coefficient after its b-th bit does not change the optimal solution because for $x \neq x^*$ we conclude (see also Figure 4.3)

$$[c]_b^T x^* \geq c^T x^* - n2^{-b} \geq c^T x + \Delta - n2^{-b} > c^T x + n2^{-b} \geq [c]_b^T x .$$

This yields the following corollary.

Corollary 2. *Let an arbitrary instance of a linear binary optimization problem with n variables be given and let σ denote the standard deviation of the pertur- bation. For every $p \in (0,1]$ and every $b > \log(n^2/(p\sigma)) + 1$, the probability that rounding every coefficient after its b-th bit after the binary point changes the optimal solution is bounded from above by*

$$\Pr\left[\Delta \leq n2^{-b+1}\right] < \frac{n^2 2^{-b+1}}{\sigma} \leq p .$$

Hence, for every $p > 0$, rounding each coefficient after a logarithmic number of bits preserves the optimal solution with probability at least $1 - p$. In other words, if one rounds the coefficients after a logarithmic number of bits, then the optimal solution x' with respect to the rounded coefficients, which can be computed by the pseudo-polynomial algorithm in polynomial time, is also the optimal solution x^* of the original instance with constant probability.

The Adaptive Rounding Procedure. We prove that the existence of a ran- domized pseudo-polynomial time algorithm for a binary optimization problem Π implies polynomial smoothed complexity for Π. We design an algorithm with polynomial smoothed complexity calling the pseudo-polynomial algorithm with higher and higher precision until the solution found is certified to be optimal. We describe a verifier, that, based on the first b bits after the binary point of each coefficient, either certifies optimality or reports FAILURE, stating that it has not sufficient information to ensure optimality.

Certifying Optimality. Let x' denote an optimal solution with respect to the rounded coefficients $\lfloor c \rfloor_b$. To check whether x' is also optimal with respect to the original coefficients c, we generate another rounded vector $[c]_b$. This time the rounding depends on the computed solution x'. For all i with $x'_i = 1$, we set $[c_i]_b = \lfloor c_i \rfloor_b$ and for all i with $x'_i = 0$, we set $[c_i]_b = \lceil c_i \rceil_b$. Observe that the function $\delta(x) = c^T x - [c]_b^T x$ is maximal for $x = x'$. Next we compute an optimal solution x'' for the problem with the vector $[c]_b$. If $x' = x''$, then x' simultaneously maximizes $\delta(x)$ and $[c]_b^T x$. Consequently, it maximizes the sum $\delta(x) + [c]_b^T x = c^T x$ as well and, hence, x' must be the true optimal solution x^*. Thus, the algorithm outputs x' as a certified optimal solution if $x' = x''$ and reports FAILURE otherwise.

In the previous section we have seen that the optimal solution with respect to coefficients that are rounded after the b-th bit can only deviate from x^* if the winner gap Δ does not exceed $n2^{-b+1}$. Hence, if $\Delta > n2^{-b+1}$, then x' can be certified to be the optimal solution with respect to the non-rounded coefficients because then $x' = x^*$ and $x'' = x^*$.

Analysis of the Adaptive Rounding Procedure. The Isolating Lemma can be exploited to transform a pseudo-polynomial time algorithm into an algorithm with polynomial smoothed complexity by an adaptive rounding approach: First every coefficient is rounded down after one bit after the binary point. Then the pseudo-polynomial time algorithm is used to compute an optimal solution x' with respect to the rounded coefficients, and the verifier is called to check if x' is also optimal with respect to the original coefficients, i.e., if $x' = x^*$. In the affirmative case, the algorithm can output x', otherwise the precision b is increased by one, that is, one more bit of every coefficient is taken into account, and the steps are repeated with the more accurately rounded coefficients until x' can be certified to be the optimal solution. We prove the following lemma on the running time of this adaptive rounding procedure.

Lemma 2. *The adaptive rounding procedure has polynomial smoothed running time.*

Proof. We show that a polynomial P with the same properties as in (3) exists. Let $\mathcal{A}$ denote the randomized pseudo-polynomial time algorithm for the linear binary optimization problem Π. If we consider only instances of Π in which all coefficients in the objective function are integers, then the expected running time of $\mathcal{A}$ is bounded by some polynomial P' in W and $N \geq n$, where W denotes the largest absolute value of any of the coefficients, N denotes the input size, and n denotes the number of binary variables. For each precision b, algorithm $\mathcal{A}$ is called twice in the adaptive rounding procedure; once to find a solution x' with respect to the coefficients $\lfloor c \rfloor_b$ and once by the verifier for finding the solution x'' with respect to the coefficients $\lceil c \rceil_b$. Hence, the expected running time of each iteration of the adaptive rounding is bounded by $2 \cdot P'(N, W) + \mathrm{poly}(n) \leq c_1(NW)^{c_2}$ for sufficiently large constants c_1 and c_2.

To analyze the running time of the adaptive rounding, we need to estimate W, the largest absolute value of any integer coefficient that results from rounding combined with the omission of the binary point. W is the product of two factors: The first factor, $W_1 = 2^b$, is due to the scaling and depends on the number of revealed bits after the binary point of each coefficient. The second factor W_2 corresponds to the integer part of the largest absolute value of any coefficient. This way, $W = W_1 W_2 = 2^b W_2$. Let b_0 denote the precision for which the verifier concludes optimality. For given b_0 and W_2, we can estimate the expected running time of the adaptive rounding by

$$\mathrm{E}\left[\mathcal{C}_{\mathrm{AR}}(\mathrm{per}_\sigma(I))\right] = \sum_{b=1}^{b_0} c_1(N2^b W_2)^{c_2} \leq c_1'(N2^{b_0} W_2)^{c_2'} , \qquad (5)$$

for sufficiently large constants c_1' and c_2'.

Hence, we have to estimate how large the values of b_0 and W_2 typically are. The expected absolute value of every coefficient is at most 1. We can use Markov's inequality and a union bound to obtain $\Pr[W_2 > 3n/p] \leq p/3$, for every $p \in (0, 1]$. In Corollary 2, we have seen that the probability that the certifier fails after b bits after the binary point of each coefficient have been revealed can be bounded by $n^2 2^{-b+1}/\sigma$. Thus $\Pr\left[b_0 > \log(3n^2/(\sigma p)) + 1\right] \leq p/3$.

In (5), we substitute b_0 by $\log(3n^2/(\sigma p)) + 1$, W_2 by $3n/p$, and multiply the resulting polynomial by $3/p$. We denote the polynomial obtained this way by P.

There are three reasons for which the running time of the adaptive rounding can exceed the polynomial P: b_0 can exceed $\log(3n^2/(\sigma p)) + 1$, W_2 can exceed $3n/p$, and the total running time T_A of all executions of A can exceed its expected value by a factor of $3/p$. Hence, for all $N \in \mathbb{N}$, $\sigma \in (0,1]$, $p \in (0,1]$, and for all $I \in \mathcal{I}_N$ we have

$$\Pr\left[\mathcal{C}_{\mathrm{AR}}(\mathrm{per}_\sigma(I)) \geq P\left(N, \frac{1}{\sigma}, \frac{1}{p}\right)\right]$$
$$\leq \Pr\left[b_0 > \log\left(\frac{3n^2}{\sigma p}\right) + 1\right] + \Pr\left[W_2 > \frac{3n}{p}\right] + \Pr\left[T_A > \frac{3}{p}\mathrm{E}\left[T_A\right]\right]$$
$$\leq \frac{p}{3} + \frac{p}{3} + \frac{p}{3} = p \ .$$

This shows that the polynomial P has the desired property.   □

From Polynomial Smoothed Complexity to Pseudo-Polynomial Running Time. In order to prove Theorem 2, it only remains to show how an algorithm with polynomial smoothed running time can be transformed into a randomized algorithm with expected pseudo-polynomial running time. Since we are aiming for a pseudo-polynomial time algorithm, we can assume that all coefficients in the objective function are integers. Let M denote the largest absolute value of these numbers. The idea is to perturb all numbers only slightly such that the perturbation changes the value of each coefficient by at most $1/(2n)$ and, hence, the objective value of any solution by at most $\frac{1}{2}$ with high probability. In order to achieve this, the reciprocal of the standard deviation σ has to depend polynomially on M and n. We then use an algorithm with polynomial smoothed complexity to compute an optimal solution x^* for the perturbed problem. We bound the error that is due to the random perturbation and use this bound to show that x^* is also optimal for the original problem. For more details, we refer the reader to [86].

Extensions. As mentioned above, Beier and Vöcking's result is more general than the one we presented. They consider linear binary optimization problems in which also the set of feasible solutions is randomly perturbed. First of all, observe that typical optimization problems have a combinatorial structure that should not be touched by the randomization. Consider for example the traveling salesman problem. In most applications it makes sense to assume that the distances are perturbed as they are subject to small random influences. However, it does not make sense to perturb the combinatorial structure, i. e., the property that every feasible solution is a Hamiltonian cycle in the graph. Hence, one has to be careful when perturbing the set of feasible solutions. In [86] problems are considered for which the set of feasible solutions is given as intersection of an arbitrary fixed ground set $\mathcal{S} \subseteq \{0,1\}^n$ and sets of solutions $x \in \{0,1\}^n$ that satisfy linear constraints of the form $w^T x \leq t$ or $w^T x \geq t$. To be more precise, the set of feasible solutions is $\mathcal{S} \cap \mathcal{B}_1 \cap \ldots \cap \mathcal{B}_k$, where k denotes the number of linear constraints and each $\mathcal{B}_i \subseteq \{0,1\}^n$ denotes the set of solutions satisfying the i-th linear constraint. Consider for instance the *constrained shortest path problem* in which a graph $G = (V, E)$ with distances $d : E \rightarrow \mathbb{R}_{\geq 0}$ and weights $w : E \rightarrow \mathbb{R}_{\geq 0}$ is given, and the goal is to find the shortest path from a given source s to a given sink s' whose weight does not exceed a given threshold t. This problem is NP-hard, and it does not make sense to perturb the combinatorial structure, i.e., the property that every feasible solution is a path from s to s'. In many applications, one can argue, however, that the weights are subject to random influences, and hence, it makes sense to assume that the weights are perturbed numbers. In [86] it is shown that Theorem 2 also applies to linear binary optimization problems with perturbed linear constraints. When a linear binary optimization problem is given, one can decide which expressions shall be perturbed (either only the objective function, or only the linear constraints, or both) and one obtains the following result.

Theorem 3 (Beier, Vöcking [86]). *A linear binary optimization problem Π has polynomial smoothed complexity if and only if there exists a randomized algorithm for solving Π whose expected worst-case running time is pseudo-polynomial with respect to the perturbed coefficients.*

The main idea for proving Theorem 3 is again an adaptive rounding procedure as in the case of perturbed objective functions. In the proof of Theorem 2, we argued that rounding the coefficients in the objective function after a logarithmic number of bits does not change the optimal solution with high probability by exploiting the winner gap. If we do not round the coefficients in the objective function but the coefficients in the constraints, then it can happen that the optimal solution x^* becomes infeasible due to the rounding or that an infeasible solution with higher objective value than x^* becomes feasible due to the rounding. Again, one needs to show that solutions obtained by the semi-random input model are robust against small roundings of the coefficients with high probability.

For the sake of simplicity assume that we have one perturbed constraint $w^T x \leq t$. Two structural properties are defined, namely the *loser gap* and the *feasibility gap*. The feasibility gap Γ measures the distance of the optimal solution x^* to the threshold t, that is $\Gamma = t - w^T x^*$. A solution $x \in \mathcal{S}$ is called a *loser* if it has a higher objective value than the optimal solution x^* but does not satisfy the constraint $w^T x \leq t$. Let $\mathcal{L} \subseteq \mathcal{S}$ denote the set of losers. The loser gap Λ describes the distance of $\mathcal{L}$ to the threshold t, that is, $\Lambda = \min_{x \in \mathcal{L}} w^T x - t$. These definitions are illustrated in Figure 4.4. If the feasibility gap is large enough, then rounding the coefficients in the constraint cannot make the optimal solution infeasible. If the loser gap is large enough, then no solution with higher objective value than x^* can become feasible due to the rounding. Beier and Vöcking show that, similar to the winner gap, also loser and feasibility gap are polynomially large with high probability which implies, similar to the case of perturbed objective functions, that the adaptive rounding procedure has polynomial smoothed running time.

Additionally, also the perturbation model considered in [86] is more general. One drawback of the Gaussian model that we describe above is that one cannot

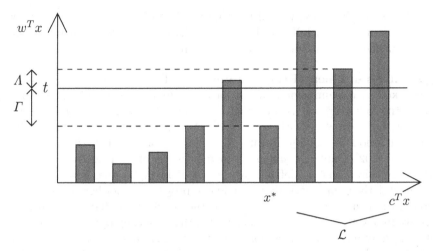

Fig. 4.4. Illustration of the definitions of $\mathcal{L}$, loser gap Λ, and feasibility gap Γ. The horizontal axis ranges over all solutions from $\mathcal{S}$ sorted by their objective values.

guarantee that after the perturbation all coefficients are positive, which is essential to many problems. In the model in [86] the perturbation is not restricted to the addition of Gaussian random variables. Basically, one can define for each coefficient an arbitrary density function which is bounded by ϕ. Analogously to the parameter σ, the supremum of the density ϕ can be seen as a measure for the concentration of the random variables and hence as a measure how close the analysis is to a worst-case analysis. Observe that for Gaussian random variables $\phi \sim 1/\sigma$. In order to obtain a non-negative domain, one could, for example, perturb the adversarial number by adding uniform random variables from the interval $[0, 1/\phi]$.

In [679] Theorem 3 is generalized from binary optimization problems to integer optimization problems in which the range of the integer variables is polynomially bounded. The main difficulty of this generalization is to bound the sizes of loser and feasibility gap in the case of integer variables.

4.4.2 Smoothed Analysis of the Simplex Algorithm

Linear programming is one of the most important problems in mathematical optimization and operations research. It is interesting from a theoretical point of view because many problems are shown to be polynomial-time solvable by reducing them to a linear programming problem. Moreover, linear programming arises in numerous industrial applications. The importance of linear programming in industrial applications stems in part from the existence of fast and reliable algorithms for finding optimal solutions. In this section, we survey recent results on the smoothed complexity of the simplex algorithm for solving linear programs.

Since the probabilistic analyses of the simplex algorithm are quite complex, we cannot present them in full detail here. We merely state the main results and roughly outline the main ideas for proving them.

Algorithms for Linear Programming. In a linear programming problem, one is asked to maximize or minimize a linear function over a polyhedral region. In the following, we assume that the goal is to maximize $z^T x$ subject to the constraints $Ax \leq y$ with $x, z \in \mathbb{R}^d$, $A \in \mathbb{R}^{n \times d}$ and $y \in \mathbb{R}^n$. The first practical method for solving linear programs was proposed in the late 1940's by Dantzig [202]. Dantzig's *simplex algorithm* walks along neighboring vertices of the polyhedron that is defined by the set of linear inequalities $Ax \leq y$. A fundamental theorem states that if a linear program is neither infeasible nor unbounded, then there exists a vertex of the polyhedron that maximizes the objective function. Additionally, every vertex that is locally optimal in the sense that there does not exist a neighboring vertex with larger objective value can be shown to be also globally optimal. For a given initial vertex of the polyhedron, the simplex algorithm picks in each step a neighboring vertex with better objective value until either a locally optimal solution is found or unboundedness is detected. The initial feasible solution is found by the application of the simplex method to a different linear program for which an initial vertex is known and whose optimal solution corresponds either to a vertex of the original polyhedron defined by $Ax \leq y$ or shows that the linear program is infeasible.

The simplex method as described above leaves open the question of which step is made when there is more than one neighboring vertex on the polyhedron with larger objective value. The policy according to which this decision is made is called the *pivot rule*. For most deterministic pivot rules that have been suggested, examples are known showing that in the worst case the simplex algorithm can take an exponential number of steps (see, e. g., [27]). For some random pivot rules, the complexity is still open. For example, the best known upper bound for the *random facet rule* is $n^{\mathcal{O}(d)}$ [449, 541], whereas the best known lower bound is only $\Omega\left(n^2\right)$ [318]. Despite many attempts, it is still unclear whether there exists a pivot rule with polynomial worst-case complexity.

Another related open question concerns the diameter of polytopes. The *Hirsch conjecture* states that there should always be a walk of length at most $n - d$. Kalai and Kleitman proved that there is always a path of length at most $n^{\log_2 d + 2}$ [450]. This, however, does not imply that the simplex method will find this path.

The observations made in practice tell a different story. The simplex algorithm is still one of the most competitive algorithms for solving linear programs that occur in practical applications. It is fast and reliable even for large-scale instances and for the pivot rules that have been shown to require an exponential number of iterations in the worst case. Examples on which the simplex algorithm needs many iterations occur only very rarely in practice.

The question whether optimal solutions of linear programs can be found in polynomial time has been answered in 1979 by Khachian [472]. He applied the *ellipsoid method*, originally developed for solving non-linear optimization problems, to linear programming and proved that it converges polynomial time with respect to d, n, and L, where L denotes the number of bits needed to represent the linear program. Though from a theoretical point of view a breakthrough, the ellipsoid method is drastically outperformed by the simplex algorithm in practice.

The *interior-point method*, another method for solving linear programs with polynomial worst-case complexity, was introduced in 1984 by Karmarkar [463]. In contrast to the ellipsoid method, the interior-point method is competitive with and occasionally superior to the simplex algorithm in practice. However, one advantage of the ellipsoid method is that it can be applied in a more general setting. For applying the ellipsoid method one does not need to know the constraints explicitly; it is enough to know a *separation oracle*, that is, an efficient algorithm that for a given point $x \in \mathbb{R}^d$ decides whether this point is a feasible solution or not, and computes a *separating hyperplane* in the latter case. A separating hyperplane is a hyperplane such that x lies on one side of this hyperplane and the set of feasible solutions on the other side. Hence, the ellipsoid method can also be used for solving linear programs with exponentially many constraints in polynomial time if the constraints are described implicitly by a separation oracle.

In order to narrow the gap between the observations made in practice and the exponential lower bounds for many pivot rules, many average-case analyses of the simplex algorithm have been performed. Borgwardt showed that the expected running time of the *shadow vertex pivot rule*, which we describe in detail later, is polynomially bounded for linear programs in which the constraints are drawn independently from spherically symmetric distributions [124]. Independently, Smale proved bounds on the expected running time of Lemke's *self-dual parametric simplex algorithm* on linear programs from spherically symmetric distributions [745]. His analysis was substantially improved by Megiddo [552].

Geometry of Linear Programs. In this section, we briefly review some facts about the geometry of linear programs. The set $\mathcal{P}$ of feasible solutions of a linear program is defined by a set of linear inequalities, i.e., $\mathcal{P} = \{x \in \mathbb{R}^d \mid Ax \leq y\}$. Let $a_1, \ldots, a_n$ denote the rows of A, and let $y_1, \ldots, y_n$ denote the entries of the vector y, the so-called *right-hand sides*. The set of points from $\mathbb{R}^d$ that satisfy a linear equation $a_i x = y_i$ is called a *hyperplane*. It is a $(d-1)$-dimensional *subspace* of $\mathbb{R}^d$. The set of points from $\mathbb{R}^d$ that satisfy a linear inequality $a_i x \leq y_i$ is called a *halfspace*. Observe that the set of feasible solutions $\mathcal{P}$ is the intersection of n halfspaces, a so-called *polyhedron*. Let $\mathcal{HS}$ be a halfspace defined by a hyperplane $\mathcal{H}$. If the intersection $f = \mathcal{P} \cap \mathcal{HS}$ is a subset of $\mathcal{H}$, then f is called a *face* of $\mathcal{P}$. Intuitively this means that $\mathcal{P}$ and $\mathcal{HS}$ just touch each other and have no common interior points. In the following, we use the term *vertex* to denote a face of dimension zero, that is, a point, and we use the term *edge* to denote a face of dimension one, that is, a line segment.

In the following, we assume that the linear programs we consider are *nondegenerate*, that is, there do not exist $d + 1$ hyperplanes of the form $a_i x = y_i$

that intersect in one point. This assumption is satisfied with probability 1 in the probabilistic model that we introduce below. Under this assumption, every vertex of the polyhedron of feasible solutions is the intersection of exactly d hyperplanes $a_i x = y_i$. Hence, every vertex can be described by specifying the d constraints that are satisfied with equality.

Smoothed Linear Programs. The main point of criticism against the average-case analyses of the simplex algorithm is that *random* linear programs do not reflect *typical* linear programs that occur in practice. In order to bypass this problem, Spielman and Teng invented the model of smoothed analysis [749]. Spielman and Teng consider linear programs of the form

$$\text{maximize} \quad z^T x$$
$$\text{subject to} \quad (\overline{A} + G)x \leq (\overline{y} + h) \ ,$$

where $\overline{A} \in \mathbb{R}^{n \times d}$ and $\overline{y} \in \mathbb{R}^n$ are chosen arbitrarily by an adversary and the entries of the matrix $G \in \mathbb{R}^{n \times d}$ and the vector $h \in \mathbb{R}^n$ are independent Gaussian random variables that represent the perturbation. These Gaussian random variables have mean 0 and standard deviation $\sigma \cdot (\max_i |(\overline{y}_i, \overline{a}_i)|)$, where the vector $(\overline{y}_i, \overline{a}_i) \in \mathbb{R}^{d+1}$ consists of the i-th component of $\overline{y}$ and the i-th row of $\overline{A}$ and $|\cdot|$ denotes the Euclidean norm, that is, for a vector $c = (c_1, \ldots, c_l)$, $|c| = \sqrt{c_1^2 + \cdots + c_l^2}$. Without loss of generality, we can scale the linear program specified by the adversary and assume that $\max_i |(\overline{y}_i, \overline{a}_i)| = 1$. Then the perturbation consists of adding an independent Gaussian random variable with standard deviation σ to each entry of $\overline{A}$ and $\overline{y}$. Observe that we can replace this two-step model by a one-step model in which each entry is an independent Gaussian random variable and an adversary is allowed to choose the means of these random variables.

The Shadow Vertex Pivot Rule. Spielman and Teng analyze the smoothed running time of the simplex algorithm using the *shadow vertex pivot rule*. This pivot rule has been considered before by Borgwardt in his average-case analysis [124]. It has been proposed by Gass and Saaty [319] and it has a simple and intuitive geometric description which makes probabilistic analyses feasible. Let x_0 denote the given initial vertex of the polyhedron $\mathcal{P}$ of feasible solutions. Since x_0 is a vertex of the polyhedron, there exists an objective function $t^T x$ which is maximized by x_0 subject to the constraint $x \in \mathcal{P}$. In the first step, the shadow vertex pivot rule computes an objective function $t^T x$ with this property. Using standard arguments from analytic geometry, one can show that such an objective function can be found efficiently. If x_0 is not the optimal solution of the linear program, then the vectors z and t are linearly independent and span a plane. The shadow vertex method projects the polyhedron $\mathcal{P}$ onto this plane. The *shadow*, that is, the projection, of $\mathcal{P}$ onto this plane is

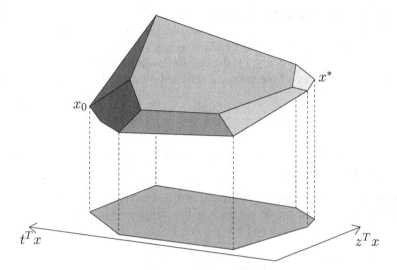

Fig. 4.5. The polyhedron is projected onto the two-dimensional plane spanned by the vectors z and t

a possibly unbounded polygon (see Figure 4.5). This polygon has a few useful properties:

- The vertex x_0 is projected onto a vertex of the polygon.
- The optimal solution x^* is projected onto a vertex of the polygon.
- Each vertex of the polygon is the image of a vertex of the polyhedron.
- Each edge of the polygon is the image of an edge between two adjacent vertices of the polyhedron.

Observe that the simplex algorithm in dimension two is very easy; it just follows the edges of the polygon. Due to the aforementioned properties, we can apply the two-dimensional simplex algorithm to the polygon obtained by the projection, and the walk along the edges of the polygon corresponds to a walk along the edges of the original polyhedron. Furthermore, once the optimal solution on the polygon is found, we can compute its pre-image on the polyhedron, which is an optimal solution of the linear program.

The number of steps performed by the simplex algorithm with shadow vertex pivot rule is upper bounded by the number of vertices of the two-dimensional projection of the polyhedron. Hence, bounding the expected number of vertices on the polygon is the crucial step for bounding the expected running time of the simplex algorithm with shadow vertex pivot rule. Actually, all probabilistic analyses make use of a dual interpretation of the shadow vertex pivot rule, which we do not present here because it is not essential for understanding the results. Spielman and Teng consider first the case that the polyhedron $\mathcal{P}$ is projected onto a fixed plane specified by two fixed vectors z and t. They show the following result on the expected *shadow size*, that is, the number of vertices of the polygon.

Theorem 4 (Spielman, Teng [749]). *Let $z \in \mathbb{R}^d$ and $t \in \mathbb{R}^d$ be independent vectors, and let $a_1, \ldots, a_n \in \mathbb{R}^d$ be independent Gaussian random vectors of standard deviation σ centered at points each of norm at most 1. Let $\mathcal{P} = \left\{ x \in \mathbb{R}^d \mid \forall i \in [n] : a_i x \leq 1 \right\}$ denote the polyhedron of feasible solutions. The number of vertices of the polygon obtained by projecting $\mathcal{P}$ onto the plane spanned by z and t is*

$$O \left(\frac{nd^3}{\min(\sigma, 1/\sqrt{d \ln n})^6} \right) .$$

Later this result was improved and the proof was substantially simplified by Deshpande and Spielman.

Theorem 5 (Deshpande, Spielman [240]). *Under the same assumptions as in Theorem 4, the number of vertices of the polygon obtained by projecting $\mathcal{P}$ onto the plane spanned by z and t is*

$$O \left(\frac{n^2 d \ln n}{\min(\sigma, 1/\sqrt{d \ln n})^2} \right) .$$

Two-Phase Simplex Method. Though the main ingredients of the analysis, Theorems 4 and 5 alone do not yield a polynomial bound on the smoothed running time of the simplex algorithm. There are three main obstacles that one has to overcome. First, we have not yet described how the initial feasible solution is found. By a binary search approach one can show that testing feasibility of a linear program and finding an arbitrary feasible solution are computationally as hard as solving a linear program to optimality (see, e. g., [628]). Hence, the question how the initial solution is found cannot be neglected. The last two problems that have to be addressed concern the assumptions in Theorems 4 and 5. It is assumed that the right-hand sides in the constraints are all 1 and furthermore, it is assumed that the vector t is fixed independently of the constraints. Both assumptions are not satisfied in the probabilistic model we consider but we will later describe how Theorems 4 and 5 can be applied nevertheless.

As we have briefly mentioned above, the problem of finding an initial feasible solution can be solved by a two-phase simplex method. In the first phase, a linear program with a known feasible solution is solved. The solution of this linear program is then used as initial feasible solution of a second linear program whose optimal solution corresponds to the optimal solution of the original linear program. If one assumes that no degeneracies occur, which happens with probability 1 in the probabilistic input model, then for every vertex of the polyhedron of feasible solutions exactly d constraints are satisfied with equality. Spielman and Teng propose to choose a random subset I of the given constraints of size d and to ensure that the intersection of these d constraints becomes a vertex x_I of the polyhedron by adapting the right-hand sides appropriately. This way a linear program LP' is obtained from the original linear program LP. The shadow vertex simplex method can be used to find an optimal solution of LP', starting at vertex x_I, which is a vertex of the polyhedron due to the modified constraints.

Then a linear program LP^+ is defined that interpolates between LP' and LP. Starting with the optimal solution of LP', which is a feasible solution of LP^+, the shadow vertex method finds an optimal solution of LP^+, which corresponds to an optimal solution of the original linear program LP.

It remains to show that for both phases of the above described simplex algorithm the expected number of steps is polynomially bounded. Therefore, in the analysis in [749], Theorem 4 is used as a black box. However, the analysis is not immediate from this bound due to the aforementioned problems. The dominant complication when analyzing the first phase is that the plane onto which the polyhedron is projected is not independent of the polyhedron. Very roughly stated, the idea of how to resolve this issue is to consider the projection of the polyhedron onto a plane that is fixed in a special way. For this fixed plane, one can apply Theorem 4. Then it is shown that the expected number of shadow vertices on this fixed plane is close to the expected number of shadow vertices on the plane we are actually interested in. The main obstacle for analyzing the number of shadow vertices in the second phase is that the right-hand sides of the constraints are not 1. Instead, the constraints are of the form $a_{i,1}x_1 + \cdots + a_{i,d}x_d \leq y_i$, where the $a_{i,j}$ and y_i are Gaussian random variables. The constraints can be brought into the form $(a_{i,1}/y_i)x_1 + \cdots + (a_{i,d}/y_i)x_d \leq 1$. The vector $(a_{i,1}/y_i, \ldots, a_{i,d}/y_i)$, however, is no Gaussian random vector anymore. Spielman and Teng show that typically a family of Gaussian random vectors can be constructed whose distributions are similar to the distribution of $(a_{i,1}/y_i, \ldots, a_{i,d}/y_i)$. Based on this observation, they apply Theorem 4 to bound the expected number of shadow vertices in the second phase. Altogether, the following theorem is proven.

Theorem 6 (Spielman, Teng [749]). *Let $z \in \mathbb{R}^d$ be chosen arbitrarily, let $a_1, \ldots, a_n \in \mathbb{R}^d$ be independent Gaussian random vectors centered at $\bar{a}_1, \ldots, \bar{a}_n$ and $y_1, \ldots, y_n$ be independent Gaussian random variables centered at $\bar{y}_1, \ldots, \bar{y}_n$. Furthermore, let the standard deviation of the Gaussian vectors and variables be $\sigma \cdot \max_i |(\bar{y}_i, \bar{a}_i)|$. Then there exists a polynomial P and a constant σ_0 such that for all $\sigma < \sigma_0$, $z \in \mathbb{R}^d$, $\bar{a}_1, \ldots, \bar{a}_n \in \mathbb{R}^d$, and $\bar{y} \in \mathbb{R}^n$, the expected running time of the two-phase shadow vertex simplex method on the linear program $\max z^T x$ subject to $Ax \leq y$ is at most $P(n, d, 1/\sigma)$.*

Beyond Hirsch Conjecture. Recently, the smoothed analysis of the simplex algorithm was substantially improved by Vershynin [804]. His contributions are twofold. On the one hand he proposes a different solution for finding an initial vertex of the polyhedron of feasible solutions. On the other hand, he improves the bound on the expected number of shadow vertices. In [749], the intersection of d randomly chosen constraints becomes a vertex of the polyhedron by modifying the right-hand sides. Vershynin suggests to add d constraints whose intersection is a vertex of the polyhedron at random. He shows that with constant probability adding the constraints does not change the optimal solution. Hence, in expectation after a constant number of independent trials, d constraints are found whose addition to the linear program does not change the optimal solution. The advantage of this method is that the initial vertex is now independent of the original linear program and, hence, also the plane onto which the polyhedron is projected is independent of the original polyhedron. Furthermore, Vershynin obtains the following improved bound on the expected number of shadow vertices.

Theorem 7 (Vershynin [804]). *Under the same assumptions as in Theorem 4, the number of vertices of the polygon obtained by projecting $\mathcal{P}$ onto the plane spanned by z and t is*

$$O\left(\frac{d^3}{\sigma^4}\right) .$$

Combining both improvements yields the following remarkable result.

Theorem 8 (Vershynin [804]). *Under the same assumptions as in Theorem 6, the expected number of pivot steps in Vershynin's two-phase shadow vertex simplex method is at most*

$$O\left(\max\left(d^5\log^2 n, d^9\log^4 d, d^3\sigma^{-4}\right)\right) .$$

Observe that the expected number of pivot steps is only polylogarithmic in the number of constraints n while the previous bound was polynomial in n.

A Randomized Polynomial-Time Simplex Algorithm. In this section, we briefly mention a recent result on the simplex algorithm. Kelner and Spielman derived the first randomized variant of the simplex algorithm that provably runs in expected polynomial time [469]. Though their algorithm uses a perturbation and is based on ideas from the smoothed analysis in [749], the expectation is only taken over the random decisions of the algorithm. In particular, even for worst-case inputs the expected running time is polynomially bounded.

The proposed simplex variant does not walk along vertices of the polyhedron of feasible solutions. The problem of finding an optimal solution is reduced to the problem of testing boundedness of another linear program. Since boundedness does not depend on the right-hand sides, they can be randomly perturbed. This way a perturbed polyhedron is obtained. The shadow vertex method is then run on the perturbed polyhedron for a polynomial number of steps. Either it finds a certificate for boundedness or unboundedness or the distribution of the perturbation is adjusted and the shadow vertex method is started again with differently perturbed right-hand sides. The details of this approach are beyond the scope of this exposition.

4.4.3   Conclusions and Open Questions

There is still a variety of open questions about the smoothed analysis of algorithms. It would be of great interest to show that the simplex algorithm has polynomial smoothed running time not only for the shadow vertex pivot rule but also for other pivot rules that are commonly used in practice. In [749], Spielman and Teng conjecture that the expected diameter of perturbed polytopes is polynomially bounded in n, d, and $1/\sigma$. A proof of this conjecture or a counterexample is still missing.

Furthermore, it would be interesting to study other perturbation models for linear programs as well as for discrete problems. One drawback of the perturbation models that have been analyzed so far is that the magnitude of the perturbation depends on the largest number in the input. This means that the relative perturbation of small numbers is quite large. In fact, after the perturbation the largest quotient between different numbers is only polynomially large with high probability which is much smaller than in typical worst-case instances. Hence, for some problems it might be more realistic to study *relative perturbations* instead, that is, perturbations where each number is perturbed with a magnitude depending on its value. Another criticism of smoothed analysis is that it destroys the *zero-structure* and replaces zeros with small values. Theorem 3 is still true when zeros are not perturbed. Whether Theorem 6 still holds for *zero-preserving perturbations* is not yet known.

Last but not least, let us discuss the relevance and the practicality of probabilistic analyses for Algorithm Engineering. At first glance one might think that the relevance is limited since probabilistic analyses tend to be more involved than worst-case analyses and hence they are not suitable if one just wants to get a brief impression on the performance of an algorithm. Moreover, the smoothed analysis of the simplex algorithm did not (yet) help to improve the performance of the simplex algorithm; it merely explained observations that have been made in practical applications. Furthermore, the degree of the polynomial that appeared in Spielman and Teng's original analysis is quite large. However, their result should be seen as a first step that initiated further studies like the one of Vershynin who proved that the expected number of steps depends only polylogarithmically on the number of constraints, which is interesting from a practical as well as from a theoretical point of view. An example for which probabilistic analyses already led to algorithms with better performance on practical inputs is the knapsack problem. Beier and Vöcking analyzed two different heuristics for the knapsack problem [84, 83]. Using observations obtained from their analyses, they proposed a new heuristic for the knapsack problem that combines different concepts of the previous heuristics and outperforms classical heuristics on typical inputs [85]. Hence, we believe that probabilistic analyses can help to gain more insights into problems and algorithms and can help to find better heuristics.

4.5   Realistic Input Models

Most of the problems studied in combinatorial optimization come from real world applications. In order to study these real world applications, one has to find an appropriate abstract model. The choice of this model is often crucial as it determines whether theoretical results have meaningful consequences in practice. Essentially, there are two reasons for which a model can fail to yield meaningful consequences. If the model does not capture the complexity of the real world application, then the theoretical results might be too optimistic. If, on the other hand, the considered model is too general, then algorithms for solving the abstract problem get needlessly complicated or the problem might even become intractable, even though it might be tractable in practice. A model can be too general because useful properties of real world inputs are not taken into account during the process of abstraction.

A good example to illustrate the effects of a model that is too general is the TSP. As we have already mentioned in the beginning of this section, a very abstract model for the TSP is to assume that the input consists of an arbitrary complete graph with a distance for each edge. In this case, it is NP-hard to compute any constant factor approximation. However, TSP instances that arise from real world applications often satisfy the triangle inequality. For these instances a 3/2-approximation can be found in polynomial time. If the distances satisfy not only the triangle inequality but are induced by points in the Euclidean space, then even a PTAS exists. Hence, the most general model for the TSP leads to complexity results that are too pessimistic for most real world applications.

Other examples where additional assumptions on the inputs dramatically reduce the complexity of finding optimal solutions are problems that can be solved in pseudo-polynomial time, like, e. g., the *constrained shortest path problem* and the *knapsack problem*. Both problems are NP-hard but there exist pseudo-polynomial time algorithms for solving them [383, 419]. Thus, inputs which satisfy the *similarity assumption*, that is, all numbers (like distances, weights, profits, etc.) are polynomially bounded in the input size, can be solved in polynomial time.

The examples presented so far show that models that are too general can lead to wrong conclusions about the complexity of a problem. They also motivate the search for properties that typical real world inputs satisfy in order to obtain more realistic input models. In the following, we focus our discussion on geometric problems. For these problems there exist already several well studied input models which are claimed to be realistic for different real world applications. In the following sections, we present some of these models and discuss their relationships. Finally, we consider the problem of finding *binary space partitions* (BSP) and analyze how the different input models influence the complexity of this problem.

4.5.1   Computational Geometry

We start the discussion of input models for geometric problems with an example. Assume that we are given a set S of n triangles in the plane, and the goal is to describe the shape of the union of these triangles by a set of straight line segments. The number of line segments needed is called the *union size* of the triangles. If we allow arbitrarily shaped triangles, one can easily generalize the example in Figure 4.6 with eight triangles to an arbitrary number n of triangles for which $\Omega(n^2)$ line segments are needed.

However, in the canonical generalization of the example in Figure 4.6 for n triangles, the acute angle of the triangles is $\Theta(1/n)$ and therefore becomes very

Fig. 4.6. The union size of triangles: A bad example

small with increasing number of triangles. Matoušek et al. [540] show that such worst-case examples do not exist if every angle is larger than a constant δ. To be more precise, they show that $O(n \log \log n)$ segments suffice to describe the boundary of the union of such triangles.

Besides the aforementioned model in which the angles are bounded from below there exist other restricted input models for geometric problems. These input models are (1) *fatness*, (2) *low density*, (3) *unclutteredness*, and (4) *small simple cover complexity*. Each of these models assigns one or two parameters to the objects of a scene. In the following, we give some intuition about the models. A scene is *fat* if all its objects are *fat*. An object is *fat* if it is not long and skinny. A scene has *low density* if no ball B is intersected by many objects whose minimum enclosing ball has a radius which is at least as large as the radius of B. A scene is *uncluttered* if any hypercube that does not contain a vertex of one of the bounding boxes of the objects is not intersected by many objects. Finally, a scene has *small simple cover complexity* if the objects in the scene can be covered with few balls such that each ball is intersected by only a few objects.

De Berg et al. [207] investigate the relationships between these models and raise the question whether the parameter(s) of a given scene with respect to one of the above-mentioned models can be computed efficiently. This is of special interest as there are data structures which require the values of the model's parameter(s) as input in order to work correctly. An example of such a data structure is a *range searching data structure* developed by Overmars and van der Stappen [623]. Examples of data structures that show better behavior for inputs that belong to one of the above-mentioned input models than for general inputs are data structures for *point location* and *binary space partition*.

The rest of this section is organized as follows. First we introduce some basic definitions and notations. Then we introduce the aforementioned input models formally, investigate their relationships, and shortly discuss algorithms for computing the parameter(s) of the models for a given scene. Finally, we analyze *binary space partitions* for uncluttered scenes.

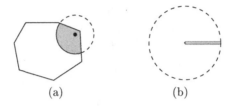

(a)   (b)

Fig. 4.7. For computing the fatness, one has to measure the ratio of the size of the shaded region and the area of the complete circle. (a) A fat object. (b) An object with small fatness.

4.5.2   Definitions and Notations

We refer to the *d-dimensional Euclidean space* as $\mathbb{E}^d$. A *scene* is a collection of n constant complexity objects $\mathbb{O}_i \subseteq \mathbb{E}^d$. Sometimes we will assume that the objects are non intersecting, that is, their interiors are pairwise disjoint. Given an object $\mathbb{O}$ we refer to the radius of its minimum enclosing ball as radius($\mathbb{O}$), and to its *bounding box* as bb($\mathbb{O}$). We will usually assume that bb($\mathbb{O}$) is axis-parallel and that it is of minimum volume among all axis-parallel boxes that contain $\mathbb{O}$. Sometimes, we shall additionally require that bb($\mathbb{O}$) is not an arbitrary box but a cube. We refer to this cube as mec($\mathbb{O}$), the *minimum enclosing hypercube* of $\mathbb{O}$. Finally, we refer to the bounding box of a scene as bb(S), and to its minimum enclosing hypercube as mec(S).

4.5.3   Geometric Input Models

In this section we formally define the aforementioned geometric input models and comment on algorithms for computing the parameter(s) of the models for a given scene.

Definition 7 (Fatness). *Let $\mathbb{O} \subseteq \mathbb{E}^d$ be an object and let β be a constant with $0 \leq \beta \leq 1$. Define $U(\mathbb{O})$ as the set of balls centered inside $\mathbb{O}$ whose boundary intersects $\mathbb{O}$. We call the object $\mathbb{O}$ β-fat if for all balls $B \in U(\mathbb{O})$: vol($\mathbb{O} \cap B$) $\geq$ $\beta \cdot$ vol(B). The fatness of $\mathbb{O}$ is defined as the maximal β for which $\mathbb{O}$ is β-fat.*

Figure 4.7 illustrates the notion of fatness. The fatness of a scene is defined as the maximal β for which every individual object is β-fat. Vleugels [812] shows that the fatness of an object $\mathbb{O}$ equals vol($\mathbb{O}$)/($\omega_d \cdot$ diam($\mathbb{O}$)^2) if $\mathbb{O}$ is convex, where diam($\mathbb{O}$) denotes the diameter of $\mathbb{O}$ and ω_d denotes the volume of the d-dimensional unit ball. Computing the fatness of a non-convex object is more difficult; for deeper insights into this topic we refer the reader to [812].

Definition 8 (Low Density). *Let $S = \{\mathbb{O}_1, \ldots, \mathbb{O}_n\}$ be a d-dimensional scene, and let $\lambda \geq 1$ be a parameter. We call S a λ-low-density scene if for any ball B, the number of objects $\mathbb{O}_i \in S$ with radius($\mathbb{O}_i$) > radius(B) that intersect B is at most λ. The density of S is the smallest λ for which S is a λ-low-density scene.*

De Berg et al. [207] show how to compute the density of a planar scene $\mathcal{S}$ consisting of n polygonal objects in time $O(n \log^3 n + \lambda n \log^2 n + \lambda^2 n)$, where λ is the density of the scene.

Definition 9 (Clutteredness). *Let $\mathcal{S}$ be a d-dimensional scene, and let $\kappa \geq 1$ be a parameter. We call $\mathcal{S}$ κ-cluttered if any hypercube whose interior does not contain a vertex of one of the bounding boxes of the objects in $\mathcal{S}$ intersects at most κ objects in $\mathcal{S}$. The clutter factor of a scene is the smallest κ for which it is κ-cluttered. A scene is called uncluttered if its clutter factor is constant.*

The clutter factor of a planar scene $\mathcal{S}$ consisting of n polygonal objects can be computed in time $O(n \log n + n\kappa \log \kappa)$, where κ is the clutter factor. Again, this was shown by de Berg et al. [207].

In order to define the notion of simple cover complexity, we call a ball δ-*simple* if it intersects at most δ objects in a given scene $\mathcal{S}$.

Definition 10 (Simple Cover Complexity). *Let $\mathcal{S}$ be a d-dimensional scene, and let $\delta > 0$ be a parameter. A δ-simple cover for $\mathcal{S}$ is a collection of δ-simple balls whose union covers $\mathrm{bb}(\mathcal{S})$. We say that $\mathcal{S}$ has (σ, δ)-simple cover complexity if there is a δ-simple cover for $\mathcal{S}$ of cardinality σn. The δ-simple cover complexity of $\mathcal{S}$ is the smallest σ for which $\mathcal{S}$ has (σ, δ)-simple cover complexity.*

The complexity of computing the δ-simple cover complexity of a given scene and a given δ is still open. However, de Berg et al. [207] conjecture that this problem is NP-hard.

4.5.4 Relationships between the Models

De Berg et al. [207] investigate relationships between the models. In this section we summarize their results. The relationships between the models are depicted in Figure 4.8. A directed arrow between two models M_1 and M_2 indicates that every instance that satisfies the properties of M_1 also satisfies the properties of M_2. Note that the reverse direction is not true.

Formally, the hierarchy is proven by the following theorem. For its proofs we refer the reader to [207].

Theorem 9. *1. Any d-dimensional scene consisting of β-fat objects has density at most $2^d \beta$.*
  2. For any parameters λ, β with $\lambda \geq 1$ and $\beta > 0$, there is a two-dimensional λ-low density scene that is not β-fat.
  3. Any d-dimensional λ-low-density scene has a clutter factor of at most $\lceil \sqrt{d} \rceil^d \cdot \lambda$.
  4. For any parameters κ, λ with $\kappa \geq 1$ and $\lambda \geq 1$, there is a two-dimensional κ-cluttered scene that is not a λ-low density scene.
  5. There are constants $\sigma = O(2^{4d} d(\sqrt{d})^{d-1})$ and $c = O(10^d \kappa)$ such that any d-dimensional κ-cluttered scene has $(\sigma, c\kappa)$-simple cover complexity.
  6. For any parameters σ, δ, κ with $\sigma \geq 2$, $\delta \geq 1$, and $\kappa \geq 1$, there are scenes with (σ, δ)-simple cover complexity that are not κ-cluttered.

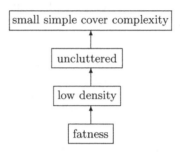

Fig. 4.8. Relations between the models

4.5.5 Applications

In this section, we discuss several applications of the input models we introduced in the previous sections. There are a lot of applications where the assumption that the inputs come from one of the presented input models dramatically reduces the computational complexity.

Consider for instance the *motion planning problem for a robot* with f degrees of freedom in a scene of n disjoint objects. The degree of freedom of a robot corresponds to the number of its joints. In this case, one seeks for a collision-free motion of the robot in the scene. Typically, this problem is transferred to the problem of finding a continuous curve in the free-space. The free-space consists of all placements of the robot in the scene such that the robot does not collide with one of the obstacles. Van der Stappen [793] argues that the complexity of this approach heavily depends on the complexity of the free-space which may be as bad as $\Theta(n^f)$. Furthermore, he shows that the complexity reduces to $O(n)$ if a constant complexity robot moves amidst constant complexity fat objects.

Another example comes from ray tracing. Given a scene and a query ray one has to determine the first object in the scene that is hit by the query ray. In many real world applications octrees perform very well. However, the worst-case analysis of the query time does not predict this, as it is $\Omega(n)$.

Mitchell [578] considers the *Euclidean TSP with neighborhoods (TSPN)*: We are given a collection of regions (neighborhoods) in the plane, and the goal is to find a shortest tour that visits each region. The problem is motivated by the fact that a salesperson wants to visit potential buyers who are willing to meet the salesperson within certain neighborhoods. If the regions are points, then we have the standard Euclidean TSP which admits a PTAS. However, in the case of arbitrarily shaped regions the problem is APX-hard. Mitchell introduces a weaker notion of fatness in which it is only assumed that for every region the radius of the smallest circumscribing circle to the radius of the largest inscribed circle is bounded by some constant. Based on this definition, he shows that TSPN with fat neighborhoods admits a PTAS.

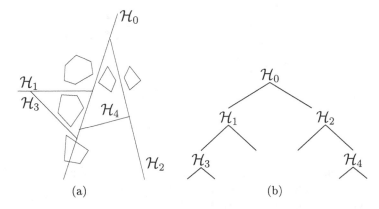

Fig. 4.9. An example of a binary space partition with its corresponding tree

In many geometric applications one likes to partition the space recursively until a termination criterion is satisfied. One such approach are *binary space partitions* BSPs. In the following, we introduce BSPs formally, discuss their applications, and finally analyze their size if an uncluttered scene is to be partitioned.

Binary Space Partitions. Given a set of non-intersecting objects, some geometric problems can be solved using the following preprocessing steps: Recursively partition the space by oriented hyperplanes into halfspaces until all subspaces satisfy some termination condition. As the space partition may also split objects we would like to choose the hyperplanes in such a way that the fragmentation of the objects is small.

In this section we consider a special kind of space partitions namely *binary space partitions* BSPs. Given a set of objects we want to partition the objects by hyperplanes until all objects are separated from each other, that is, until every subspace is either empty or contains only a fragment of a single object. An example is depicted in Figure 4.9.

A natural representation for a BSP is a binary tree, where each internal node corresponds to a division induced by a hyperplane. BSPs can be used to detect objects that are hidden by other objects. Detecting such objects is important for generating images from changing positions in a 3d-scene quickly. Therefore one traverses the BSP tree in a symmetric order relative to the viewing point which generates a correct priority order of (the fragments) of the objects. Paterson and Yao [630] discuss other applications of BSPs and show how to construct a BSP of size $O(n^{d-1})$ for n non-intersecting objects in $\mathbb{R}^d$ and $d \geq 3$, where the size of a BSP is the number of leaves of the BSP tree. For $d = 2$ they show how to construct BSPs of size $O(n \log n)$. Moreover, they show that their construction is best possible, that is, they construct 3-dimensional scenes for which every BSP has size $\Omega(n^2)$. However, since these scenes are rather unrealistic and since

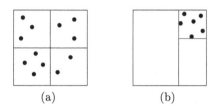

Fig. 4.10. (a) An octree split, (b) a kd-split

BSPs are efficient for many real world scenes, de Berg [205] considers BSPs in the case of uncluttered scenes, that is, for scenes whose clutter factor is constant. In this case, he shows how to construct BSPs of linear size.

In the following we will present and analyze this approach in detail: Given n non-intersecting, polygonal objects in $\mathbb{R}^d$ with constant complexity we present an algorithm that constructs a BSP tree of linear size. The algorithm has two stages and can be implemented to run in time $O(n \log^2 n)$. In the first stage cubes are recursively split guided by the vertices of the bounding boxes of the objects, whereas in the second stage the standard BSP approach is applied to the cubes generated in first stage.

First Stage: We consider the set of bounding boxes of the scene's objects of the scene, and refer to the set of their vertices as V. Given an arbitrary cube C we refer to the subset of all vertices of V lying in the interior of C as $V_C \subseteq V$.

In the first stage only cubes with $V_C \neq \emptyset$ are split recursively. Empty cubes are not split. An *octree split* of a cube C splits C into 2^d equally sized subcubes $C_1, \ldots, C_{2^d}$. We call an octree split useless if all points of V_C are in the interior of one subcube. In this case we do not perform an octree split but a *kd-split*. To define a kd-split, let C_j be the subcube containing all vertices of V_C if we would perform an octree split, and let v be a vertex of the cube C that is also a vertex of C_j. Additionally, let C_j' be the smallest cube with v as one of its vertices that contains all points from V_C in its closure. Now, C is split using planes through the facets of the cube C_j'. The notions of an octree and kd-split are depicted in Figure 4.10.

Observe now that a kd-split does not necessarily produce cubes but arbitrary cells. However, the only cell on which we recurse after performing a kd-split is the cube C_j'. Finally, we have to describe how the initial cube is chosen. We choose the minimum enclosing cube of all objects of the scene as the initial cube.

In order to describe the second stage of the algorithm we have to prove the following lemma.

Lemma 3. *The first stage of the algorithm results in an intermediate BSP consisting of $O(n)$ cells that are boxes and do not contain a vertex from the set V in their interior.*

Proof. The second part of the lemma is clearly true, as the recursive construction only terminates when a cell is empty. Thus, it remains to prove the first part.

Observe that each split increases the number of cells by a constant. To be precise, an octree split increases the number of cells by $2^d - 1$, a kd-split by d. Furthermore, when a cell is split at least one point from the current subset V_C lies on the splitting planes, or V_C is partitioned into at least two subsets. Now observe that the first case can occur at most $|V|$ times, and the second case at most $|V|-1$ times. Hence, the total number of cells is at most $|V|(2^d - 1) + (|V| - 1)d + 1 = O(n)$.   □

Second Stage: The second stage of the algorithm is rather simple. We recursively partition the cells of the intermediate partition until each cell in the final BSP is intersected by only one object. We do this in the following way. For a cell C let S_C be the set of object fragments inside of C. We recursively partition C by taking planes through the facets of the objects.

Now, in order to show that the final BSP has only linear size we prove the following lemma.

Lemma 4. *Let S be an uncluttered scene. Then any cell in the intermediate partition is intersected by $O(1)$ objects.*

Proof. Consider a cell C of the intermediate partition. By construction, C does not contain a vertex of one of the bounding boxes of the objects in its interior. Thus, if C is a cube, the lemma follows immediately by our assumption that the scene is uncluttered.

If C is not a cube, then it was created by a kd-split and does not contain a vertex from one of the bounding boxes of the objects. Observe now that we can cover the cell C with a constant number of cubes that are contained in the union of all empty cells that are created by this kd-split. Again, since every such cube does not contain a vertex of one of the bounding boxes and due to our assumption that the scene is uncluttered every such cell is intersected by $O(1)$ objects. Thus, the lemma follows.   □

We are now ready to prove the following theorem.

Theorem 10 (de Berg [205]). *Let S be an uncluttered scene in $\mathbb{R}^d$ consisting of non-intersecting, polygonal objects. Then there exists a linear size binary space partition for the objects in S.*

Proof. The theorem follows due to Lemma 4 since in the intermediate BSP every cell is intersected by $O(1)$ objects. Thus the second stage is performed on a constant number of objects in each recursive call and therefore does not increase the asymptotic size of the final BSP.   □

Finally, we would like to comment on the running time to build the BSP and on the assumption that the objects are polygonal. De Berg [205] shows how to construct the data structure in time $O(n \log^2 n)$. The main difficulty is how to find the splitting planes of a cell efficiently. De Berg shows how to find them efficiently with the help of a technique called *tandem search technique* which we will not present here. The assumption that the objects are polygonal is important in the second stage of the algorithm since in this stage hyperplanes through the facets of the objects are chosen. In the case of curved objects one would need a different approach. However, if every pair of objects could be separated by a constant number of hyperplanes then the approach would still be applicable. That is, for any uncluttered scene of convex objects BSPs of linear size exist.

4.6   Computational Testing

Many optimization problems arising from real-world applications (e. g., the *Steiner tree problem*, the *traveling salesman problem* or different kinds of *packing problems*) are known to be computationally hard; that is, no polynomial time algorithms are known for them so far. Nevertheless, one is interested in solving concrete instances optimally in "reasonable" time, e. g., within 1 hour or 1 day, as this might be satisfactory in practical settings. And this can surely be possible even though the algorithms in question may not have a polynomial worst-case bound. Then, a worst-case analysis might be too pessimistic and might prevent us from applying the developed algorithm, although it meets our demands.

Furthermore, if a problem admits a polynomial time algorithm, e. g., with running time $O(n^3)$, this does not directly imply its practical usefulness. For instance, large constants may be hidden by the O-notation or complex data structures may be needed to reach the running-time bound.

Therefore, it is important to not only consider *theoretical* but also *experimental* measures of performance. Two such experimental measures and techniques of analysis will be presented and discussed in Sections 4.6 and 4.7, respectively. Finally, Section 4.8 deals with the question of how we can learn something about the *asymptotic* performance of an algorithm, if solely experimental data is given. All these techniques require an implementation as well as a carefully chosen set of test instances. As Chapter 6 points out what has to be taken into consideration when implementing an algorithm, and Chapter 8 gives hints on how a set of test instances should be chosen, the following sections are based on the assumption that these two phases have already been accomplished, i. e., an implementation and a set of test instances exist.

An obvious *experimental* measure for the performance of an algorithm is the time a computer needs to solve a set of test instances or a set of instances which are required to be solved in practical settings. In the rest of this section we formalize this concept and discuss its advantages and disadvantages.

Evaluating different algorithms under the criterion of *computational running time* means to measure the *CPU time* each algorithm needs to solve a set of test instances and to choose the fastest one. Modern operating systems can output the consumed CPU time after solving an instance.

Definition 11. *The* CPU time *a computer C needs to solve an instance I using algorithm A is the actual time (measured by a stop clock) C needs to solve I if 100% of the CPU power can be used to run algorithm A.*

Usually some percentage of the CPU power is consumed by the operating system or other programs. These effects are eliminated by the CPU time. To compare two or more algorithms using the measure of CPU time the following three steps have to be performed:

(1) Implementation of each algorithm using the same programming language.
(2) Creation of instances, e. g., using randomization.
(3) Running each algorithm (on the same computer) on the created instances while measuring the CPU time.

In practical settings when dealing with concrete instances computational testing clearly has respectable merits and is a reasonable way to analyze an algorithm – as discussed above. But in particular when different researchers want to compare their algorithms some problems arise naturally. The first problem is that the CPU time depends greatly on the computational environment such as the computer and the chosen programming language. Even though researchers may agree on using the same programming language and the same computer the programming skills and the programming style of the researcher still play an important role. This can be overcome by distinguishing not only between the different algorithms but also between the different implementations of them. Hence, an algorithm can have different running times just because of its implementation. From a theoretical point of view this extension may not seem to be convenient because it is always assumed that the implementation is done best possible. But it would emphasize the necessity of developing algorithms that are not only as fast as possible from a theoretical point of view but also allow efficient implementations. Especially in practical settings the last property should not be undervalued.

A disadvantage of computational testing is that it requires an implementation of the algorithm which may cause a lot of work. For a theoretic analysis only the pseudocode of an algorithm is needed. Therefore, if an algorithm seems to be inferior to other algorithms after a theoretic analysis there is no need to apply the method of computational testing additionally.

4.7   Representative Operation Counts

The idea of *counting representative operations* for measuring the performance of an algorithm was, e. g., used in [92,598]. Ahuja and Orlin formalized the concept in [17, 15] and applied it for instance to the *network simplex algorithm*. This chapter uses in particular the description they give.

The main idea of this technique is to identify operations that *dominate* the running time of an algorithm and to specify the amount of CPU time in O-notation by only considering these operations. We refer to the dominating operations also as *bottleneck operations* or simply *bottlenecks*. In contrast to the worst-case analysis the method of counting representative operations does not provide a theoretical upper bound on the number of executions of the bottleneck operations. Instead, it experimentally counts the number of executions of the bottleneck operations for every instance that was solved by the algorithm.

In Section 4.7.1 we formalize and discuss the technique of counting representative operations. In Section 4.7.2 further applications of this method are presented. In particular we discuss the concept of *virtual running time* and how to compare algorithms using representative operations.

4.7.1 Identifying Representative Operations

In this section we formalize the concept of counting representative operations. Let A be the code of a computer program (the implementation of an algorithm). Then A consists of a constant number of lines $a_1, \ldots, a_K$ of code. We assume that the execution of any line consumes at least one and at most a constant number of time units, i. e., the time for executing a line in A is assumed to be $\Theta(1)$. We write $\alpha_k(I)$, $k = 1, \ldots, K$, to denote the number of times line a_k is executed while running A on instance I. Under the given assumptions the CPU time $CPU(I)$ algorithm A takes to solve instance I lies within a constant factor of the number of times each line of code is executed.

Lemma 5.

$$CPU(I) = \Theta \left(\sum_{k=1}^{K} \alpha_k(I) \right) .$$

This implies that we have to keep track of α_i for every line $a_1, \ldots, a_K$. In the program code of an algorithm there are usually lines which are executed if and only if some other line is executed. Consider, for example, the following small piece of code with $n \in \mathbb{N}$ being a problem parameter:

Algorithm 2. Summation and Multiplication

```
1: sum ← 0
2: prod ← 1
3: i ← 1
4: while i ≤ n do
5:     sum ← sum + i
6:     prod ← prod · i
7:     i ← i + 1
```

Instead of counting the number of executions for each of the lines from 4 to 7 it suffices to count the number of times line 5 is executed. In this case line 5 is called a representative operation. In fact, every other line from 4 to 7 can be chosen as a representative line for the whole piece of code; but none of the lines from 1 to 3 can. To formalize the concept of representative operations Ahuja and Orlin introduced the following definition:

Definition 12. *Let $S \subseteq \{1, \ldots, K\}$ and $a_S = \{a_k : k \in S\}$. Then a_S is called a* representative set *of lines of a program code if there exists a $c \in \mathbb{R}$ such that*

$$\alpha_i(I) \leq c \cdot \sum_{k \in S} \alpha_k(I) \ .$$

for every instance I and for every line a_i, $i = 1, \ldots, K$.

Hence, the number of times line a_i is executed is bounded or dominated up to a constant factor by the number of times the lines from S are executed. The following corollary of Lemma 5 relates the representative set a_S to the CPU time [17].

Corollary 3. *Let a_s be a representative set of lines of a program code. Then*

$$CPU(I) = \Theta \left(\sum_{k \in S} \alpha_k(I) \right) \ .$$

4.7.2   Applications of Representative Operation Counts

The idea of identifying a representative set of operations can be used for further analysis of an algorithm. It can be used to identify operations that asymptotically have a strong influence on the running time of an algorithm. These operations are called *asymptotic bottleneck operations*. Furthermore, representative operations can be used to compare algorithms and to define *virtual running time*, a tool for estimating the CPU time. We give a short overview of all these topics in the next paragraphs and compare each concept with computational testing and worst-case analysis.

Asymptotic Bottleneck Operations. Let a_S be a set of representative operations of some program code, and $\alpha_S = \sum_{k \in S} \alpha_k$. Then some of the representative operations may consume more execution time than others do if the problem size grows. For some operations the percentage of time they gain (from $CPU(I) = \Theta(\sum_{k \in S} \alpha_k(I))$) may even approach zero for an increasing problem size. This leads to the following definition [17]:

Definition 13. *An operation is called an asymptotic non-bottleneck operation if its share in the computational time becomes smaller and approaches zero as the problem size increases. Otherwise, the operation is called an asymptotic bottleneck operation.*

One way to find asymptotic bottleneck operations is to plot the curves $\frac{\alpha_k}{\alpha_S}$ for all $k \in S$ over increasing instance size. All fractions are bounded by 1 but some of them may have a non-decreasing trend for growing problem sizes and these are exactly the asymptotic bottleneck operations.

Asymptotic bottlenecks can give deeper insights into the behavior of an algorithm, but the results have to be interpreted carefully. The first point we have to take into consideration is that we assumed that each operation can be performed in time $\Theta(1)$; therefore, constants are hidden in this analysis. In particular in practical settings an improvement of a constant factor can make an algorithm applicable.

Counting representative operations has its advantage in identifying bottleneck operations. This is crucial for improving the running time of an algorithm; CPU time hides bottlenecks. Furthermore, counting representative operations does not provide a theoretical upper bound on the number of performed operations as a worst-case analysis does.

Comparing Algorithms Using Representative Operations. Suppose we are given two algorithms A_1 and A_2. Then representative operation counts can be used to identify the one that asymptotically performs better using a quite intuitive approach. Let a_{S_1} and a_{S_2} be a set of representative operations for algorithm A_1 and A_2, respectively. We say that algorithm A_1 is asymptotically superior to algorithm A_2 if and only if

$$\lim_{|I| \to \infty} \frac{\sum_{k \in S_1} \alpha_k(I)}{\sum_{k \in S_2} \alpha_k(I)} = 0 \ .$$

This concept may be misleading since we do not care about the instances themselves but only about their size. As the comparison requires an implementation of both algorithms as well as running them on many instances the same result could be obtained using CPU time which would be less work.

Virtual Running Time. Virtual running time makes use of representative operation counts to estimate the actual CPU time. It is an approach towards a machine independent measure just as worst-case and average-case running time are. The virtual running time $V_A(I)$ of an algorithm A on instance I with representative operations $a_1, \ldots, a_K$ is defined as

$$V_A(I) = c_1 \cdot \alpha_1(I) + \cdots + c_K \cdot \alpha_K(I) \text{ with } c_1, c_2, \ldots, c_K \in \mathbb{R}_{\geq 0} \ .$$

The constants $c_1, \ldots, c_K$ can be computed, for instance, using the least squares method for the points $(CPU(I), \alpha_1(I), \ldots, \alpha_K(I))$, where $CPU(I)$ is the CPU time of algorithm A on instance I. The least squares method minimizes the function $\sum_{I \in \mathcal{I}} (\text{CPU}(I) - V_A(I))^2$, for $\mathcal{I}$ being a set of instances.

Ahuja and Orlin computed the virtual running time for the network simplex algorithm and obtained the following expression:

$$V_A(I) = \frac{\alpha_1(I) + 2\alpha_2(I) + \alpha_3(I)}{69000} \ .$$

After computing the constants $c_1, c_2,$ and c_3 they compared the actual running time for 25 instances with their estimation V_A and found out that the error is at most 7%.

Virtual running time as a performance measure has to be used carefully because the instances chosen for the linear regression may have special properties that can lead to an under- or overestimation. Furthermore, one has to take into consideration that a misestimation is likely if the representative operations are correlated.

An advantage of this concept is that it points out the percentage of the CPU time a representative operation consumes; e. g., the representative operation a_2 in the network simplex algorithm consumes twice as much running time as every other representative operation does. Note that this does not identify the second operation as an asymptotic bottleneck operation but as a bottleneck for the size of the chosen instances.

Another advantage is that the virtual running time can easily be transferred from one computer to another. Let $\bar{\mathcal{I}}$ be the set of instances that were used to compute the constants $c_1, \ldots, c_K$ for a computer C_1 and $\mathcal{H}$ the set of all instances evaluated on this computer. If the implementation is moved to another computer C_2 then only the instances from $\bar{\mathcal{I}}$ have to be run again to obtain the c_is for C_2. As all $\alpha_k(I)$ for $I \in \mathcal{H}$ are known, the virtual running time can be obtained without further evaluations.

Ahuja and Orlin [17] state the elimination of effects such as *paging* and *caching* as a third advantage of virtual running time. These effects arise when an instance does not fit completely in the fast memory of the computer. Then time is spent on transferring data from the slower memory to the CPU. During that time no operations are performed and therefore large instances may need significantly more time. These effects can be eliminated if only instances that fit completely into the fast memory are chosen for computing the c_is. Modern operating systems eliminate these effects also in the CPU time they output (compare Section 4.6). In a worst-case analysis or an average-case analysis these effects are also not considered.

Furthermore, virtual running time can even be used to detect paging and caching effects by computing the c_is for small instances and comparing the virtual running time to the actual running time for large instances.

4.8   Experimental Study of Asymptotic Performance

This section deals with the question, how and in how far finite experiments can or cannot support studies of asymptotic performance. We will discuss some so-called *curve bounding rules* by means of which one hopes to derive asymptotic trends of an algorithm's (average case) performance from pure data analysis. All approaches and techniques presented in this section have their origin in an article by McGeoch et al. [551].

Asymptotic analysis of an algorithm's performance, as discussed in the whole chapter, is one of the main issues computer scientists—especially theoretical computer scientists—are concerned with. To repeat it in a nutshell: The ultimate goal in a performance analysis is in many cases to find a closed-form expression for the running time with respect to some input parameters such as the input size. Unfortunately, it is often far too difficult to derive a closed-form expression, i. e., a formula that can be evaluated in a finite number of "standard operations", for the running time. In this case, one might try to find an asymptotic upper and/or lower bound on either the worst case or the average case running time, or both. But even the task of finding such bounds might eventually turn out to be too complex to be done by means of a pure theoretical analysis—given that one is not happy with trivial bounds, and with large gaps between the best known upper and lower bound.

If a rigorous mathematical analysis of the asymptotic performance fails or is incomplete, as a result of enormous mathematical difficulties to overcome, then it can be helpful to perform problem specific experiments and to carefully analyze their results, in order to find out the truth about the asymptotic performance.

This section describes and discusses two different approaches to experimental analysis of asymptotic performance. The first approach is based on the so-called scientific method, which is successfully applied in the natural sciences. The second approach is a *heuristic method* which is based on so-called *curve bounding rules* for the derivation of hopefully correct and close upper or lower bounds from pure data analysis.

The idea behind the scientific method, which has been sketched in Chapter 1, is a core idea with respect to Algorithm Engineering. Section 4.8.1 gives hints on how this idea can be applied to performance analysis.

Section 4.8.2 presents and "justifies" different curve bounding rules. A preliminary evaluation of each rule will be given with respect to the experimental results that are described in [551]. But a detailed description of the experiments containing all of the data will not be given.

Finally, Section 4.8.3 summarizes the main results of Section 4.8.2, and draws some preliminary conclusions.

Difficulties with Experimentation. Asymptotic analysis via experimentation presents fundamental problems to the researcher:

Unbounded Input Size. In some sense asymptotic analysis via pure experimentation is inherent impossible. For the sake of seeing this clearly, recall the definition of the *asymptotic growth of functions* (Definition 1), and consider the following.

Assume that we want to study the performance of an algorithm $\mathcal{A}$ on input instances x of size $|x| \in \mathbb{N}$, denoted by n. Furthermore, assume that we have defined how to measure $|x|$ and how to measure the running time of $\mathcal{A}$ on x in a machine independent way. Then, an asymptotic performance analysis aims at finding functions $g_l, g_u \in \mathcal{F}^{\oplus}$ such that, e. g., the worst case or the average case running time $T_{\mathcal{A}}(n)$ of $\mathcal{A}$ on inputs of size n can be classified as $T_{\mathcal{A}}(n) \in O(g_u(n))$ (*asymptotic upper bound*) or as $T_{\mathcal{A}}(n) \in \Omega(g_l(n))$ (*asymptotic lower bound*).

As can be seen from Definition 1, $T_{\mathcal{A}}(n) \in O(g_u(n))$ and $T_{\mathcal{A}}(n) \in \Omega(g_l(n))$ are statements about inputs x of *all* sizes $n \in \mathbb{N}$. In contrast to this, experiments can only test *some* inputs of *finite* sizes $n < N$ for a given constant $N \in \mathbb{N}$, as any experiment—unless one is not interested in its outcome—must be limited in time and space. Therefore, the outcome of an experiment can never be a *proof* of an asymptotic bound.

Too Many Inputs. Even if we bound the input size by some constant $N \in \mathbb{N}$ it is most likely that only a relatively small fraction of the input instances of a given size $n < N$ can be tested in the course of an experiment, because in most cases the number of distinct input instances of size n grows exponentially with n or is infinite. This means that even for bounded input sizes, a worst case analysis via pure experimentation will fail as a result of limited resources—unless we know the worst case instances.

Fortunately, the worst-case performance of a given algorithm is not always the most interesting measure of performance. We might be far more interested in its average case performance. In such a case, experimentation combined with statistical knowledge and infallible power to interpret the outcome of experiments enables us to find almost arbitrarily reliable *hypotheses* on the average-case performance, by means of random sampling of input instances. The degree of the hypotheses' reliability—given the above-mentioned infallibility—depends upon the relative number of random samples that we are willing and able to test for each considered input size n. Similarly, experimentation can help us to find hypotheses on the *expected* performance of a *randomized* algorithm by building the average of the results of repeated runs for each considered input x.

4.8.1   Performance Analysis Inspired by the Scientific Method

Experiments can be used to formulate hypotheses on the average case performance $T_{\mathcal{A}}(n)$ of an algorithm $\mathcal{A}$ on inputs of size n. Apart from this, it seems to be intuitively clear that experimentation with algorithms can be used in a way which is suggested by the scientific method.

In the following, some suggestions on how the scientific method can be applied in the context of performance analysis will be made. But first, let us think about some general difficulties that are faced, when we use experiments to formulate a hypothesis on the performance of an algorithm.

$O(\cdot)$'s are not Falsifiable. Not only can experiments never be used as a *proof* of a theorem on the asymptotic performance of an algorithm, but also can we in no way formulate a *hypothesis* on an algorithm's asymptotic performance by means of O-notation, because this would not be scientifically sound: A statement like $T_{\mathcal{A}}(n) \in O(n \log n)$ cannot be falsified by a finite experiment, for even if someone presents a set of data that clearly indicates a quadratic behavior of $\mathcal{A}$, we can always claim that this strange behavior will stop for large enough inputs.

So, one has to be careful when formulating hypotheses on the asymptotic performance. In the given example, it would for instance be scientifically sound to state that $T_{\mathcal{A}}(n) \leq 3n \log n$ for $n > 7$—as this can be falsified experimentally by presenting a constant input size $n' > 7$ such that $T_{\mathcal{A}}(n') > 3n \log n$ holds.

However, not every sound hypothesis is automatically a good hypothesis: The statement $T_{\mathcal{A}}(n) \leq n \log n$ for all $n > 10^{999}$ may be scientifically sound, but it is at least unfair, as from a practical viewpoint it can hardly be falsified experimentally—due to natural resource limitations.

How to Find Good Hypotheses? Unless one roughly knows about the performance of an algorithm in advance, it is almost impossible to guess a good hypothesis on its performance from the analysis of experimental data alone. This is again partly due to the fact that only bounded input sizes can be tested, as for relatively small inputs, the influence of second order terms with large coefficients can prevent us from finding a higher order term which bounds the performance asymptotically. Another profound difficulty is faced, when we decide to measure running time in terms of the machine's actual execution time. Then, our interpretation of the experimental results have to take a complex model of the underlying machine into account. Therefore, if we are not explicitly interested in an algorithm's performance on a specific machine, then we might be better off deciding for a *machine independent* performance measure, like the number of comparisons between input elements for a comparison based sorting algorithm.

The curve bounding rules presented in Section 4.8.2 are intended to yield good hypotheses on functions $g(n)$ that bound sets of data derived from performance measurements of algorithms. Not surprisingly, the curve bounding rules have a tendency to fail in the above-mentioned scenario, where the true bound $f(n)$ of the data curve contains a second order term that has a strong influence for "small" inputs.

The following paragraphs shed some light on how the scientific method can be applied to performance analyses.

Building a Useful Hypothesis. Sometimes, the performance of an algorithm that we are most interested in is too difficult to analyze theoretically for us. Nevertheless, we might be able to learn something about its performance via experimentation. This paragraph gives a detailed example, based on [696], of how the scientific method can be applied for building a *useful hypothesis* on the performance of such an algorithm $\mathcal{A}$. The idea behind this example is as follows: Even if we are not able to theoretically analyze $\mathcal{A}$, this may not hold for a simpler variant $\mathcal{B}$ of $\mathcal{A}$, and it may be possible to draw a hypothetical conclusion on $\mathcal{A}$'s performance from the results of the theoretical analysis of $\mathcal{B}$. If so, then this hypothesis can be validated with experiments—hopefully in a successful way.

Before describing a detailed example which uses the above-mentioned methodology, some notions have to be introduced.

Consider the following *parallel disk model*: A processor with M words of *internal memory*, $M \in \mathbb{N}$ large enough, is connected to D parallel disks (*external memory*), $D \in \mathbb{N}$. For each disk D_i, $i = 1, \ldots, D$, a queue Q_i that buffers *blocks* to be written onto D_i resides in the internal memory. In one *I/O step*, every disk potentially can read or write one block of B words.

Now, let W denote an upper bound for the tolerated total number of blocks currently stored in all queues, and $W \in O(D)$, let $|Q_i|$ denote the number of blocks currently stored in queue Q_i, and assume that whenever a set of new blocks is appended to the queues $Q_1, \ldots, Q_D$, the destination queue is chosen independently and uniformly at random for each of the blocks. Consider the following procedure WRITE that uses a subroutine WRITE-TO-DISKS($Q_1, \ldots, Q_D$)

which writes one block of each non-empty queue Q_i to the corresponding disk D_i concurrently:

```
1: procedure WRITE((1 − ε)D blocks)
2:     append blocks to Q₁,...,Q_D
3:     WRITE-TO-DISKS(Q₁,...,Q_D)
4:     while |Q₁| + ··· + |Q_D| > W do
5:         WRITE-TO-DISKS(Q₁,...,Q_D)
```

Now we have all prerequisites to describe algorithm $\mathcal{B}$, which is called THROTTLE by the authors of [551], as being a sequence of N invocations of WRITE$((1 − \varepsilon)D$ blocks) which starts with empty queues Q_i and has fixed but arbitrary parameters $W, N \in \mathbb{N}$ and $\varepsilon \in (0,1)$. For *positive* ε writing $(1 − \varepsilon)D$ blocks is a reduction of the theoretical peak bandwidth of D blocks per time step. This may serve as an explanation of the name THROTTLE.

Experimentation revealed to the authors of [696] that another algorithm $\mathcal{A}$ (called EAGER by the authors of [551]), which admits D instead of only $(1 − \varepsilon)D$ blocks in each invocation of WRITE, has a better performance than THROTTLE with respect to *average throughput per invocation of* WRITE. Thus, Sanders et al. [696] were most interested in proving a theorem on the average throughput of EAGER, but—they failed. Therefore, they decided to analyze THROTTLE and thereby hoped to learn something about EAGER too.

One of the results of this analysis is that—under the assumption of an extremely large (but still finite) threshold value W such that the while-loop is never entered during an invocation of WRITE—the expected sum of queue lengths $|Q|$ at any invocation of WRITE$((1 − \varepsilon)D$ blocks) is bounded from above by $D/(2\varepsilon)$ and that the probability of $|Q|$ exceeding qD for any $q > 0$ is less than $\exp(-\Omega(D))$. Hence, setting $W = c \cdot D/(2\varepsilon)$ for some constant $c > 1$ reduces the probability of *waiting steps* between two subsequent invocations of WRITE$((1 − \varepsilon)D$ blocks) considerably (which implies that THROTTLE may be a good choice for *real time applications*). Furthermore, setting ε to $D/(2W)$ yields an expected overall buffer requirement of no more than W.

This inspired Sanders et al. [696] to formulate the *hypothesis* that EAGER (THROTTLE with $\varepsilon = 0$) has an average throughput of about $(1 − D/2W) \cdot D$ blocks per time step. The hypothesis was supported by the result of an experiment which measured the average throughput of EAGER with respect to different ratios $W/D \in \{0, 1, 2, 4, 6, 8, 10, 12\}$ for two settings of D, namely $D \in \{8, 256\}$, respectively.

Validating a Theory. Instead of analyzing a simpler variant $\mathcal{B}$ of the algorithm $\mathcal{A}$ we are interested in, and then using the results of this analysis to formulate a hypothesis on $\mathcal{A}$'s performance, it may as well be possible to turn the theoretical analysis of $\mathcal{A}$ into a feasible task by making some simplifying *assumption*, like, for instance, the assumption of *independence* of some random variables that are obviously *not* independent from one another. The result of the analysis under this assumption can be viewed as a *theory* in the sense of the scientific method. Experimental validation of this theory is of course necessary.

Supporting the Improvement of a Theoretical Analysis. Our last suggestion on how to apply the scientific method to performance analysis is perhaps the most obvious one: Experimentation can be used to get a hint on whether some theoretically proven asymptotic bound is sharp or is not sharp. In the latter case one might be inspired to prove a better bound—and possibly succeed.

4.8.2   Empirical Curve Bounding Rules

In this main part of Section 4.8, the curve bounding rules which have been introduced by [551] will be described and discussed. These rules are intended to reveal asymptotic trends of an algorithm's performance—given experimental data alone. Recall that we can never *prove* an *asymptotic* bound by means of the analysis of *finite* experimental data and that whatever trend we find is in no way reliable. However, sometimes an *unreliable trend* is better than nothing.

Notations. The input size of an algorithm $\mathcal{A}$ will be denoted with x rather than n to get some notational compatibility with related literature about data analysis. The *performance* of $\mathcal{A}$ on inputs of size x—given some fixed and reasonable performance *measure*—is denoted with a function $f(x)$. In the following, f measures the *expected cost* of $\mathcal{A}$ with respect to randomly chosen inputs, according to a uniform distribution. In case of $\mathcal{A}$ being a randomized algorithm, the expected cost $f(x)$ also takes the random experiments of $\mathcal{A}$ into account.

We only consider *experiments* which are intended to reveal a trend of the asymptotic performance of a given algorithm $\mathcal{A}$, and produce a pair of vectors (X, Y) such that $X[i] \in \mathbb{N}$ is an input size and $Y[i] \in \mathbb{R}^+$ is a result of the experiment's performance measurements for inputs of size $X[i]$, $i = 1, \ldots, k$ for some $k \in \mathbb{N}$. By convention, the vector X is assumed to contain *pairwise distinct* values, arranged in *increasing order*.

Throughout the rest of this section, $f(x)$ and $\bar{f}(x)$ will denote arbitrary functions whereas $g(x)$ and $\bar{g}(x)$ will denote *simple* functions in the sense that they are free from lower order terms which asymptotically have no influence on the growth rate of a function. The bar notation denotes functions that are *estimates*.

Now assume that $O(\bar{g}(x))$ is an asymptotic upper bound estimate of a function $f(x)$. Then we say that $O(\bar{g}(x))$ is *correct* if in fact $f(x) \in O(\bar{g}(x))$. A correct asymptotic upper bound estimate $O(\bar{g}(x))$ is called *exact* if there does not exist a *simple* function $g(x) \neq \bar{g}(x)$ such that $f(x) \in O(g(x))$ and $O(g(x)) \subset O(\bar{g}(x))$ holds. Analogous notations are defined for *lower* bound estimates.

Definition of the Curve Bounding Problem. Given an algorithm $\mathcal{A}$ and a pair of vectors $(X, Y) \in \mathbb{N} \times \mathbb{R}^+$ that results from experimental measurements of $\mathcal{A}$'s performance in the above-mentioned sense, determine an asymptotic *trend* of f—the function which measures the true (and unknown) performance of $\mathcal{A}$—by purely analyzing the experimental data (X, Y).

The word "trend" instead of "bound" is used consciously in order to indicate that every *asymptotic* bound derived from pure data analysis is *unreliable*—as long as we have no theoretical proof of this bound. So, whenever we will use the term *curve bounding* in order to refer to solving the curve bounding problem, this detail of the definition has to be kept in mind.

Note that curve *bounding* is by far not the same as curve *fitting*. For example, a polynomial of degree three may exactly fit (interpolate) four data points, but may at the same time define a quite bad bound of the data curve, if this curve actually represents a linear behavior.

The Rules and Their Description. A curve bounding rule analyzes the pair of vectors (X, Y) and then reports an estimator $\bar{g}(x)$ of a complexity class together with a bound type which is either *upper*, *lower* or *close*. *Upper* signifies a claim that $f(x)$ is in $O(\bar{g}(x))$, and *lower* signifies a claim that $f(x)$ belongs to $\Omega(\bar{g}(x))$. A rule will report a bound type *close* if the class estimator $\bar{g}(x)$ seems to be too close to the data curve to call it an upper or a lower bound—according to the criteria being used to distinguish between upper and lower bounds.

The five main strategies for bounding curves that are suggested by the authors of [551] can be outlined as follows:

- The *Guess-Ratio* (GR) rule "guesses" a function $\bar{f}(x)$ and evaluates it according to the apparent convergence of the sequence of ratios

$$\left(\frac{Y[1]}{\bar{f}(X[1])}, \dots, \frac{Y[k]}{\bar{f}(X[k])} \right) =: \frac{Y}{\bar{f}(X)}.$$

- The *Guess-Difference* (GD) rule also guesses a function $\bar{f}(x)$, but evaluates the sequence of differences

$$(\bar{f}(X[1]) - Y[1], \dots, \bar{f}(X[k]) - Y[k]) =: \bar{f}(X) - Y$$

  rather than the sequence of ratios.
- The *Power* (PW) rule combines log-log transformation of X and Y, linear regression on the transformed data, and residual analysis.
- The *Box Cox* (BC) rule combines a parametric transformation of Y values with linear regression and residual analysis.
- The *Difference* (DF) rule generalizes Newton's divided difference method for polynomial interpolation in such a way that it is defined and terminates for any of the considered data sets (X, Y).

All these rules can be viewed either as *interactive tools* or as *offline algorithms*. Therefore, it makes sense to describe them with a small set of simple *oracle functions*. If a rule is used as an interactive tool, then a human provides the values of the oracle functions. Otherwise, the oracles are implemented. The following list contains these oracle functions together with suggestions for their implementation. In contrast to [551], our description of the oracles distinguishes clearly between their pure functionality and suggestions for their implementation.

- The TREND-oracle TREND(X, Y) decides whether Y appears to be *increasing* with X, *decreasing* or *neither*.

  An implementation may take another input $c_r \in (0, 1)$ and compare the *sample correlation coefficient* r, computed on X and Y, to a cutoff parameter which is set to c_r.

- The CONCAVITY-oracle CONCAVITY(X, Y) decides whether the data curve Y appears to be *convex*, *concave* or *neither*.

  An implementation may perform a linear regression on X and Y, followed by an examination of the sequence S of the residual's signs. The return value may be "convex" (or "concave upward"), if S obeys the regular expression $(+)^+(-)^+(+)^+$, "concave" (or "concave downward"), if S obeys the expression $(-)^+(+)^+(-)^+$, and "neither" in any other case. As *outliers* may prevent the oracle from finding a given tendency of the data curve to be convex or concave, it makes sense to apply some kind of *smoothing* to the residuals before the sequence S is analyzed.

- The DOWN-UP-oracle DOWN-UP(X, Y) decides whether the sequence of Y-values appears to be first decreasing and then increasing, which essentially is the same as to decide whether the data curve Y appears to be *convex*. Anyway, the DOWN-UP-oracle is used only to distinguish between *convexity* and *non convexity* and thus does not have to be as powerful as the CONCAVITY-oracle. An implementation may smooth the Y-values and then compute the sequence

$$D := (Y[2] - Y[1], \ldots, Y[k] - Y[k-1])$$

of differences between successive smoothed Y-values. If the signs of D obey the regular expression $(-)^+(+)^+$ then it may return *true*, otherwise *false*. In order to adjust the smoothing operation, another input parameter s may be taken and used in the same way as for an implementation of the CONCAVITY-oracle suggested.

- The NEXT-ORDER- and the NEXT-COEF-oracle take a function $f(x) = a \cdot x^b$, a flag bit d and a positive constant c as input, and then change the function's exponent b and coefficient a, respectively, according to the direction d (+ or −) and to the step size c. For the sake of simplifying our description of the curve bounding rules, we will assume that the step size c is set to a default value, like 0.01, rather than being an input parameter.

  In order to deal with the situation where a decrement of size c would yield a negative coefficient a or a negative exponent b, an implementation of the subroutines may reset c to $c/10$ as often as necessary for a decrementation to yield a positive result.

The following five paragraphs will justify each of the above-mentioned rules by respectively presenting a class of functions F_R for which rule R is *guaranteed* to report a *correct* asymptotic bound estimate $O(\bar{g}(x))$ or $\Omega(\bar{g}(x))$. This *guarantee of correctness* for a rule R and a given class F_R of functions is defined as follows:

Definition 14. *We say that a curve bounding rule R is* guaranteed correct *for a class of functions F_R, if there exists a k_0 such that for all $k \geq k_0$, all* *k-dimensional vectors X of positive input sizes and all functions $f \in F_R$ the following implication is true: If*

$$Y = f(X) := (f(X[1]), \ldots, f(X[k]))$$

holds, then the application of R on (X, Y) always yields a correct *asymptotic bound estimate for $f(x)$.*

The Guess Ratio Rule. The *Guess Ratio* rule (GR) iterates over guess functions $\bar{f}(x) = x^b$, evaluating each one of them according to the apparent convergence of the ratios $Y/\bar{f}(X)$, where the TREND-oracle is used to determine whether the current ratio appears to converge to zero. The following pseudocode describes GR:

```
1: procedure GUESS-RATIO(X, Y)
2:     f̄(x) ← x⁰
3:     trend ← TREND(X, Y/f̄(X))
4:     while trend is increasing do
5:         ḡ(x) ← f̄(x)
6:         NEXT-ORDER(f̄, +)
7:         trend ← TREND(X, Y/f̄(X))
8:     return (ḡ(x), lower)
```

Let $\mathbb{Q}^+$ and $\mathbb{N}^+$ denote the set of positive rational and positive natural numbers respectively. Then, a class of functions which justifies the GR rule in the sense of Definition 14 can be described as

$$F_{GR} := \left\{ f \colon \mathbb{N}^+ \to \mathbb{Q}^+ \mid f(x) = a_1 x^{b_1} + \cdots + a_t x^{b_t}, t \in \mathbb{N}^+ \right\}$$

for $a_1, \ldots, a_t \in \mathbb{Q}^+$ and $b_1, \ldots, b_t \in \mathbb{Q}$ with $b_1 > 0$ and $b_1 > \cdots > b_t \geq 0$.

In order to believe the *guarantee of correctness* of GR for any $f \in F_{GR}$ and $Y = f(X)$, consider an arbitrary *guess function* $\bar{f}(x) = x^b$ that is generated during the course of GUESS-RATIO(X, Y). The following observation is crucial:

$$f(x) \in \omega(\bar{f}(x)) \overset{f \in F_{GR}}{\Leftrightarrow} f/\bar{f} \text{ is asymptotically strictly increasing, i.e. there exists}$$
an $N \in \mathbb{N}$ such that $(f/\bar{f})(x)$ is strictly increasing for all $x \geq N$.

For $k \geq 2$ and TREND(X, Y) always reporting an *increasing* trend if for some $i \in \{1, \ldots, k-1\}$ the values $Y[i], \ldots, Y[k]$ are strictly increasing, the guarantee of correctness now follows inductively: As $b_1 > 0$ holds, $f/\bar{f}$ is strictly increasing for the initial guess $\bar{f}(x) = x^0$ such that the while-loop is entered and the estimate $\bar{g}(x)$ is initialized correctly, i.e. $f(x) \in \Omega(\bar{g}(x))$ holds. Assume that the current asymptotic lower bound estimate $\bar{g}(x)$ is correct and the while-loop condition is tested for a new guess function $\bar{f}(x)$ derived from an invocation of the NEXT-ORDER-oracle. If TREND$(X, Y/\bar{f}(X))$ returns *increasing*, the while-loop is entered and $\bar{g}(x)$ is set to $\bar{f}(x)$, which is correct by our observation (see above). Otherwise, if TREND$(X, Y/\bar{f}(X))$ does not return *increasing*, then GUESS-RATIO(X, Y) simply returns the current estimate $\bar{g}(x)$ together with the bound type *lower*, which is correct by our assumption.

The Guess Difference Rule. The *Guess Difference* (GD) rule also iterates over several guess functions $\bar{f}(x)$, but evaluates differences $\bar{f}(X) - Y$ rather than ratios and reports a bound type *upper* rather than *lower*. The guess functions are of the form $\bar{f}(x) = a \cdot x^b$ for $a, b \in \mathbb{Q}^+$. The initial guess function has to be defined by the user as well as a *limit* for the number of tolerated iterations of an inner while-loop, which is used to find out, whether $f(x) \in O(x^b)$ for the current guess function $\bar{f}(x) = ax^b$:

```
1: procedure GUESS-DIFFERENCE((X, Y), a, b, limit)
2:     f̄(x) ← ax^b
3:     ḡ(x) ← x^b
4:     downup ← true
5:     while downup do
6:         downup ← DOWN-UP(X, f̄(X) − Y)
7:         l ← 1
8:         while not downup and l < limit do
9:             NEXT-COEF(f̄, −)
10:            downup ← DOWN-UP(X, f̄(X) − Y)
11:            l ← l + 1
12:        if downup then
13:            ḡ(x) ← x^{b'}, where currently f̄(x) = a'x^{b'}
14:            f̄(x) ← ax^{b'}
15:            NEXT-ORDER(f̄, −)
16:    return (ḡ(x), upper)
```

Under the condition that the initial guess function $\bar{f}(x) = ax^b$ is a correct upper bound estimate for $f(x)$, the Guess Difference rule is guaranteed correct for all functions $f(x)$ of the class

$$F_{GD} := \{f \colon \mathbb{N}^+ \to \mathbb{Q}^+ \mid f(x) = a_1 x^{b_1} + a_2\},$$

where a_1, b_1 and a_2 are *positive* rationals. This is due to the following observation for an arbitrary guess function $\bar{f}(x) = ax^b$ and $f \in F_{GD}$, $f(x) = a_1 x^{b_1} + a_2$:

(1) If $f(x) \in o(\bar{f}(x))$ holds, then $b > b_1$ follows and the difference $\bar{f}(x) - f(x)$ must eventually—for "large" x—increase.

Investigation of the difference's derivative reveals, that the difference has a unique minimum at $x_0 = (a_1 b_1/(ab))^{1/(b-b_1)}$ in $\mathbb{R}^+$. Note that x_0 is inversely related to the guess function's coefficient a. Therefore, $\bar{f}(x) - f(x)$ strictly increases on $\mathbb{N}^+$, if a is comparably large, whereas for small values of a, an *initial* decrease can be observed on $\mathbb{N}^+$. In the latter case, we say that $\bar{f} - f$ has the *down-up property*.

(2) Otherwise, if $f(x) \notin o(\bar{f}(x))$ holds, then $b \leq b_1$ follows and the difference curve can never have the down-up property, which again is revealed by an investigation of its derivative (distinguishing the two cases $b = b_1$ and $b < b_1$).

So, if for the given $\bar{f}(x) = ax^b$ and $f(x) \in F_{GD}$ the curve $\bar{f} - f$ has the down-up property, then we know that $f(x) \in o(\bar{f}(x))$ holds. What GD actually does is adjusting the coefficient a of the guess function in a way which makes the position x_0 of the difference curve's minimum—if existent—move to larger values. This increases the chance to detect the down-up property. Now, let the dimension k of the data vectors X and Y be at least 4, such that a DOWN-UP-oracle has a chance to discover the down-up property for a suitably chosen vector X. Furthermore, let f belong to F_{GD} with $f(x) = a_1 x^{b_1} + a_2$, let Y be equal to $f(X)$, and assume that the initial guess function $\bar{f}(x) = ax^b$ labels a correct asymptotic upper bound estimate of f. Then, it can be shown inductively that GD is guaranteed correct for F_{GD}: The initial upper bound estimate $\bar{g}(x) = x^b$ is correct by our precondition. Then, assume that the current estimate $\bar{g}$ is correct and the outer while-loop is entered for a new guess function $\bar{f}(x) = ax^{b'}$. Two cases have to be distinguished:

(a) If the inner while-loop is left because the DOWN-UP-oracle has answered *true*, then the difference curve has the down-up property—given that the oracle does not fail. Hence, $f(x) \in O(\bar{f}(x))$ by our observation (see above) and the subsequent assignment of $x^{b'}$ to $\bar{g}$ yields a correct upper bound estimate $\bar{g}$.

(b) Otherwise, if the DOWN-UP-oracle never answers *true*, then GD leaves the outer while-loop without changing the current estimate $\bar{g}$ and returns it— which is correct by our assumption.

The Power Rule. The *Power* (PW) rule is based on a standard technique for fitting curves to data, namely *linear regression*. A linear regression on a data set (X, Y) computes the parameters of a linear function $\bar{f}(x) = m \cdot x + b$ such that the *residual sum of squares* (RSS) is minimized, i. e. m and b are chosen such that

$$\sum_{i=1}^{k} (Y[i] - \bar{f}(X[i]))^2 = \min \left\{ \sum_{i=1}^{k} (Y[i] - (m' \cdot X[i] + b'))^2 \mid m', b' \in \mathbb{Q} \right\}$$

holds. Let LINEAR-REGRESSION(X, Y) be a procedure that performs a linear regression on (X, Y) and returns the slope m of the linear regression fit $\bar{f}$ together with the residuals vector $R((X, Y), \bar{f}) := (Y[1] - \bar{f}(X[1]), \ldots, Y[k] - \bar{f}(X[k]))$. Then, PW can be described in pseudocode as follows:

```
 1: procedure POWER-RULE(X, Y)
 2:     X' ← log X := (log X[1], . . . , log X[k])
 3:     Y' ← log Y
 4:     (m, R) ← LINEAR-REGRESSION(X', Y')
 5:     ḡ(x) ← x^m
 6:     residuals-curve ← CONCAVITY(X', R)
 7:     if residuals-curve is convex then
 8:         return (ḡ, lower)
 9:     else if residuals-curve is concave then
10:         return (ḡ, upper)
11:     else
12:         return (ḡ, close)
```

The class of functions for which PW is guaranteed correct is

$$F_{PW} := \{f \colon \mathbb{N}^+ \to \mathbb{Q}^+ \mid f(x) = bx^m\},$$

where b and m are arbitrary positive rationals: Let k be at least 3 (for smaller values of k the application of the CONCAVITY -oracle does not make sense) and Y be $f(X)$ for any $f(x) = bx^m \in F_{PW}$. Application of the log-log transformation in the first two lines of PW yields $Y' = m \cdot X' + \log b$ which is a linear relationship. Hence, the result of the linear regression on (X', Y') is $(m, (0, \ldots, 0))$, and PW returns $\bar{g}(x) = x^m$ together with the bound type *close*, as the residuals curve is neither *convex* nor *concave*. Obviously, this result is correct.

You may wonder whether the PW can also be justified by a class of functions that allows lower order terms like the class F_{GD}, which contains functions $f(x) = bx^m + c$ for positive rationals b, c and m. The answer is "no!", as in this case the log-log transformed data does not lie on a straight line. Up to now, two variations of PW have been suggested in order to deal with lower order terms:

- The *High-End Power Rule* (PW3) applies PW only to the three highest data points, i. e. to the data points that belong to the indices $k - 2, k - 1$ and k. It can at least be *motivated* by F_{GD}.
- The *Power Rule with Differences* (PWD) applies PW to *differences* of successive Y-values rather than to pure Y-values and can be *justified* with F_{GD}, but—it only works if the X-values are chosen such that $X[i] = \Delta \cdot X[i - 1]$ for a constant $\Delta > 1$ and all $i \in \{2, \ldots, k\}$.

The intuition behind PW3 is as follows: If Y is $f(X)$ for some $f \in F_{GD}$, $f(x) = bx^m + c$, then the log-log transformed data *approaches* a straight line for growing input sizes X_i:

$$\log(bx^m + c) = m \log x + \log(b + c/x^m) \overset{x \to \infty}{\longrightarrow} m \log x + \log b = \log(bx^m)$$

Therefore, PW is the more likely to find the correct slope m of the data curve $f(X)$ the higher the data points are, to which it is applied.

In order to prove that PWD is guaranteed correct for the class F_{GD} we first describe it properly:

```
1: procedure PWD(X, Y)
2:     X' ← (X[1], ..., X[k − 1])
3:     Y' ← (Y[2] − Y[1], ..., Y[k] − Y[k − 1])
4:     return POWER-RULE(X', Y')
```

Let k be at least 4, let $X[i]$ be equal to $\Delta \cdot X[i - 1]$ for a constant $\Delta > 1$ and all $i \in \{2, \ldots, k\}$, and let Y be $f(X)$ for any function $f(x) = bx^m + c \in F_{GD}$. It suffices to show that $Y' = c'(X')^m$ holds for some positive rational c', as we have already shown that in this case an invocation of POWER-RULE(X', Y') yields the correct result $(x^m, close)$. It is

$$
\begin{aligned}
Y'[i] &= f(X[i+1]) - f(X[i]) \\
&= bX[i+1]^m + c - bX[i]^m - c \\
&= b(\Delta X[i])^m - bX[i]^m \\
&= c'X'[i]^m
\end{aligned}
$$

for the positive constant $c' = b(\Delta^m - 1)$ and all $i \in \{1, \ldots, k-1\}$—as desired.

The Box Cox Rule. A generalization of PW would be to apply any transformation on X, or on Y or on both X and Y, that produces a straight line in the transformed scale, and then to invert this transformation suitably in order to obtain a bound estimate for the original data curve—if it was a transformation on Y, or on both X and Y. For example, if $Y = X^2$, then the transformation $Y' = \sqrt{Y}$ would yield a linear dependency of Y' on X, as well as the transformation $X' = X^2$ would result in a linear connection between X' and Y. Obviously, only in the former case an inversion of the transformation is necessary to get a bound for Y.

Yet, the difficulty with this approach is that the quality of different transformations can hardly be compared in most cases, because every transformation changes the scale of the data points such that the *straightness* (as our measure of quality) of the transformed data curve has to be determined relative to the change of the scale.

Nevertheless, the *Box Cox* (BC) rule *does* perform a transformation of the data which is based on the Box Cox curve-fitting method (see [50] e.g.). This method applies a transformation on Y that is parameterized by λ, $\lambda \in \mathbb{R}$, and defines a measure of straightness that *does* permit the comparison of transformations for different values of λ. The transformation on Y that depends upon λ is defined as follows:

$$
Y^{(\lambda)} = \begin{cases} \frac{Y^\lambda - 1}{\lambda Y_{\text{geo}}^{\lambda-1}} & \text{if } \lambda \neq 0 \\ Y_{\text{geo}} \ln(Y) & \text{if } \lambda = 0 \end{cases}
$$

where all operations on vector Y are to be understood componentwise, and where Y_{geo} denotes the geometric mean of the Y-values, i.e.

$$
Y_{\text{geo}} = \left(\prod_{i=1}^{k} Y[i] \right)^{1/k} .
$$

The quality or straightness of a transformation $Y^{(\lambda)}$ is defined as the *residual sum of squares* (RSS) that results from a linear regression on X and $Y^{(\lambda)}$. Hence, the Box-Cox curve-fitting method computes the inverse of a transformation $Y^{(\lambda)}$ that minimizes the RSS.

Due to the high level of abstraction of [551] with respect to the description of BC, we feel free to add some details that may not have been intended by the authors of [551]—but appear to be reasonable to us. So, the following description of BC is to be understood as our suggestion on a possible implementation:

Let $b_{\min}$, $b_{\max}$, and δ be in $\mathbb{Q}^+$ with $b_{\min} \leq b_{\max}$ and $\delta \leq b_{\max} - b_{\min}$. The BC iterates over guess functions x^b, where the range $[b_{\min}, b_{\max}]$ of b has to be defined by the user. It can be implemented such that the guess function's exponent b is initialized with $b_{\min}$ and increased by the additive constant δ in each iteration—until $b_{\max}$ is exceeded. (This is mainly what we added to the description of BC by [551].) During each iteration, the transformation parameter λ is set to $1/b$ and the corresponding transformation $Y^{(\lambda)}$ is evaluated with the help of a linear regression on X and $Y^{(\lambda)}$ which returns the RSS together with the residuals vector. Finally, a guess function $x^{b'}$ that produced the minimum RSS is returned as bound estimate $\bar{g}$ together with a bound type that is determined with the help of the CONCAVITY-oracle applied to X and R', where R' may denote the residuals vector that belongs to $\bar{g}$.

For the sake of precision, a description of BC in pseudocode follows:

```
1:  procedure BOX-COX((X, Y), b_min, b_max)
2:      b ← b_min
3:      rss-min ← ∞
4:      while b ≤ b_max do
5:          λ ← 1/b
6:          (rss, R) ← LINEAR-REGRESSION(X, Y^(λ))
7:          if rss < rss-min then
8:              rss-min ← rss
9:              R-min ← R
10:             b' ← b
11:         b ← b + δ
12:     ḡ(x) ← x^b'
13:     residuals-curve ← CONCAVITY(X, R-min)
14:     if residuals-curve is convex then
15:         return (ḡ, lower)
16:     else if residuals-curve is concave then
17:         return (ḡ, upper)
18:     else
19:         return (ḡ, close)
```

Assume that $Y = f(X)$ holds for some $f(x) \in F_{PW}$, $f(x) = ax^b$. Then, $Y^{(\lambda)}$ is a linear function of X *if and only if* λ is equal to $1/b$. Therefore, if the guess function x^b is tested during the iteration of BC and $k \geq 3$ holds (such that the CONCAVITY-oracle is not fooled by its input), then BC is guaranteed to yield the correct result $(x^b, close)$. In this very restricted sense, BC is guaranteed correct for the class F_{PW}.

The Difference Rule. The *Difference Rule* (DR) is based on Newton's polynomial interpolation formula: Let $x_0, \ldots, x_n$, $n \in \mathbb{N}$, be strictly increasing real numbers and $y_0, \ldots, y_n \in \mathbb{R}$ be the values of an unknown function f at $x_0, \ldots, x_n$.

Then the corresponding *unique* interpolation polynomial I_n of degree at most n—a polynomial satisfying the *interpolation constraints* $I_n(x_i) = y_i$ for $i = 0, \ldots, n$—can be represented via the $n + 1$ *Newton polynomials*

$$N_0(x) := 1, \quad N_i(x) := \prod_{j=0}^{i-1}(x - x_j) \quad (i = 1, \ldots, n),$$

where N_i is a product of i linear factors and thus is of degree i, as follows:

$$I_n(x) = \sum_{i=0}^{n} c_i N_i(x)$$

The coefficients c_i are the i-th *divided differences* $[x_0, \ldots, x_i] = [x_i, \ldots, x_0]$ which are defined recursively and induced by the interpolation constraints:

$$[x_i] := y_i \text{ for } i = 0, \ldots, n \text{ and } [x_{j_0}, \ldots, x_{j_l}] := \frac{[x_{j_1}, \ldots, x_{j_l}] - [x_{j_0}, \ldots, x_{j_{l-1}}]}{x_{j_l} - x_{j_0}}$$

for each sequence $j_0, \ldots, j_l$ of successive indices in $\{0, 1, \ldots, n\}$.

Now, what DR actually does—given the data (X, Y)—is based on a well known scheme for iteratively computing the coefficients of the corresponding interpolation polynomial. In accordance to that scheme, DR iteratively computes vectors $Y_0, Y_1 \ldots, Y_{k-1}$ of divided differences whose first component $Y_i[1]$, respectively, is the i-th divided difference c_i:

$$Y_0 := Y, Y_i := ([X[1], \ldots, X[i+1]], \ldots, [X[k-i], \ldots, X[k]]) \quad (i = 1, \ldots, k-1),$$

where Y_i, $i = 1, \ldots, k-1$, can be built efficiently from Y_{i-1} and X as follows:

$$Y_i := (Y_i[1], \ldots, Y_i[k-i]), \quad Y_i[j] := \frac{Y_{i-1}[j+1] - Y_{i-1}[j]}{X[j+i] - X[j]} \quad (j = 1, \ldots, k-i)$$

The following observation is crucial with respect to the idea behind DR: If $Y = f(X)$ for a polynomial f of degree $d < k$, then I_{k-1} is equal to f, the divided differences $c_{d+1} = Y_{d+1}[1], \ldots, c_{k-1} = Y_{k-1}[1]$ are equal to zero, and the components of Y_d must be equal. Furthermore, if f has *nonnegative* coefficients, then the sequence of components of vector $Y_0, \ldots, Y_{d-1}$ respectively must be strictly increasing.

If DR knew in advance that Y is equal to $f(X)$ for a polynomial f of degree $d < k$, then it could stop on finding a first Y_i whose components are all equal and return $(x^i, \textit{close})$—which would be a correct result. But—unfortunately—DR does not know anything about f in advance, and therefore needs a heuristic stopping criterion: It seems to be a reasonable heuristic to stop for the first Y_i that does not appear to be increasing and then to return the *upper* bound estimate $\bar{g}(x) = x^i$. We sum up the description of DR by means of pseudocode:

```
1:  procedure DIFFERENCE-RULE(X, Y)
2:      i ← 0
3:      Y₀ ← Y
4:      X₀ ← X
5:      trend ← TREND(X₀, Y₀)
6:      while trend is increasing and i < k − 1 do
7:          i ← i + 1
8:          compute Yᵢ from Yᵢ₋₁ and X (see above)
9:          Xᵢ ← X[1..k − i] := (X[1], ..., X[k − i])
10:         trend ← TREND(Xᵢ, Yᵢ)
11:     ḡ(x) ← xⁱ
12:     return (ḡ, upper)
```

Given that the TREND-oracle does not fail, the preceding paragraphs directly imply that DR is guaranteed correct for all polynomials with nonnegative coefficients and degree less than k, i. e. for the class

$$F_{DF} = \{f \colon \mathbb{N}^+ \to \mathbb{Q}^+ \mid f(x) = a_{k-1}x^{k-1} + \cdots + a_1 x + a_0\},$$

where $a_0, a_1, \ldots, a_{k-1} \in \mathbb{Q}_0^+ := \mathbb{Q}^+ \cup \{0\}$.

Some Experimental Results. The authors of [551] performed several experiments in order to validate the curve bounding rules. Without going too much into detail (for details see the aforesaid paper), the main observations concerning these experiments will be given in the following:

The first experiment used a small input vector X containing only powers of two ranging from 16 to 128, i. e. $X = (16, 32, 64, 128)$, and constructed measurement vectors $Y = f(X)$ (mainly) for parameterized functions $f(x) = ax^b + cx^d$, where the parameters and the small input sizes were chosen such that the rules got "stressed" and the limits of their successful applicability could be found. In this context, different combinations of $b \in \{0.2, 0.8, 1.2\}$ and $d \in \{0, 0.2, b - 0.2\}$—respecting the constraint $b > d$—as well as $a = 3$ and $c \in \{1, -1, 10^4\}$, where c was always set to 10^4 in case of a constant second order term ($d = 0$), turned out to be a good choice, as they shed some light on the rule's behavior in situations where large second order terms ($c \gg a$ or $b \approx d$) or even negative second order terms ($c = -1$) dominate Y for small input sizes.

Generally, one could see that the rules do not work well on functions that are decreasing or—to speak more clearly—decreasing for the tested input sizes. This was most obvious for GR, which always failed on functions with *negative second order terms*. A reason for this behavior may be, that a function f, with a negative second order term, approaches its true asymptote g from below in the sense that the ratio $Y/\bar{f}(X)$ still has a tendency to *increase* if $\bar{f}$ is already equal to g or if $\bar{f}$ is only slightly larger than g. This fools the TREND-oracle. As an example, you may take $f(x) = n^2 - n$, its true asymptote $g(x) = n^2$, and the guess function $\bar{f}(x) = n^{2.01}$: If you plot the ratio $f(x)/\bar{f}(x)$ for $n \in [1, 100]$, you will observe an increasing trend although $f(x) \notin \Omega(\bar{f}(x))$ holds.

In contrast to GR, PW and its variations worked quite well on those functions with negative second order terms. Furthermore (—but not surprisingly), PWD and DF successfully managed to eliminate *large constant second order terms*, whereas the opposite is true for BC. The latter may be due to an intrinsic property of the λ transformations $Y^{(\lambda)}$ on which BC is based—as well as on the way it *may* have been implemented and used: The authors of [551] report that BC often produced a numerical error in those situations, because it happened to try assigning $1/0$ to λ. How could that have happened?—If Y contains the values of a constant function or appears to contain the values of a constant function, because of f containing a very large constant second order term, then the constant estimate $\bar{g}(x) = x^b = x^0$ either *is* or *falsely seems* to be the true asymptote g of f and the straightest λ transformation will be found for $b \approx 0$. Now, assume an implementation of BC that initializes b with $b_{\max}$, produces the next guess via a call to NEXT-ORDER(x^b, −), and stops the iteration no earlier than on finding a first transformation that does not decrease the current minimal RSS value. Then, according to the implementation suggested by [551], BC will iteratively decrease b by some constant δ until this would yield a negative value, and then it will go on decreasing b by division through 10 in each step. Clearly, this results in a numeric error for the computation of the transformation parameter $\lambda = 1/b$.

However, our suggestion for the implementation of BC (see above) is not likely to produce a numerical error, as it restricts b to values in $[b_{\min}, b_{\max}]$, where $b_{\min} > 0$ holds. But, nevertheless, it may yield false bound estimates for data that appears to be constant.

Obviously, second order terms—especially large or negative ones—have influence on the performance of the rules. But it is clear that their influence weakens with increasing input sizes. Therefore, a second experiment repeated the first one for *larger input sizes*, namely with X extended by another power of two: $X = (8, 16, 32, 64, 128, 256)$. The main observation concerning this experiment is that the rules in general seem to be quite unresponsive with respect to changes of the largest input size—except GD: Now, in contrast to the first experiment, GD was much more often able to find an initial *downup* curve and thus to report a bound that was tighter than the user supplied initial guess.

A third experiment added *random noise* to some of the functions that seemed to be easy to bound for all rules during the first two experiments. To each of these functions $f(x)$ different random variates ε_i were added for $i = 1, 2, 3$. The random variates ε_i were drawn independently from a normal distribution with mean 0 and standard deviation set to the constants 1 ($i = 1$), 10 ($i = 2$), and to the arithmetic mean of the function values $f(X[j]), j = 1, \ldots, k, (i = 3)$. For each i, two independent trials were run, in order to check for spurious positive and negative results.

Not surprisingly, the third experiment showed that the quality of the bounds returned by any rule degrades as dramatically as random noise increases.

As a forth experiment, the rules were tested for *algorithmic data sets* derived from experimental performance analyses that had been performed earlier and whose data sets had not been intended to serve for testing the curve bounding rules. The result of these tests seems to yield not much new insight in the performance of the curve bounding rules: All rules managed to get at least within a linear factor and sometimes within a $\sqrt{x}$ factor of the true bound. But in some cases, it was even hard to distinguish the quality of the bounds, as the true bound was not known exactly. Of course, none of the rules will ever be able to distinguish between logarithmic terms and low order exponents like $x^{0.2}$, as long as logarithmic factors are not produced by the NEXT-ORDER-oracle. But, the authors of [551] report that even including logarithmic terms as guess functions does not help the rules to find logarithmic terms as being part of the true asymptotic bound with any reliability.

Some Remarks. One of the most direct approaches to the curve bounding problem appears to be the application of some general (nonlinear) regression method to the data, followed by a residuals analysis in order to determine the bound type. Surprisingly, the authors of [551] report that an application of this approach to a given data set led to contradictory results for *different* general regression methods. The adaptability of this approach to the curve bounding problem might be an interesting question for future research.

An approach based on Tukey's [785] "ladder of transformation", which seems to be reasonable at first glance, was abandoned by the authors of [551], as it turned out to yield contradictory bound claims like $\Omega(x^{2.2})$ and $O(x^{1.8})$ for the same data set depending on whether the transformations were applied to X or to Y.

The fact that most of the rules fail in the presence of large second order terms inspired the authors of [551] to design a hybrid method especially for bounding functions $f(x) = ax^b + cx^d$ with rational exponents $b > d \geq 0$ and positive real coefficients $a \ll c$. This rule incorporates an iterative diagnosis and repair technique that combines the existing heuristics, and is designed to find upper bounds on the input data. The result of an experimental validation of the rule by the aforesaid authors was a complete success, with respect to functions $f(x) = ax^b + cx^d$ with large second order terms. However, the behavior in all other cases—e. g. for functions with negative second order terms—was either not better or even worse than that of the existing rules described above.

The rules, as they are described above, cannot find exponential bounds, because of their guess functions $\bar{f}$ and bound estimates $\bar{g}$ being polynomials. But, a simple modification turns each rule $R \in \{\text{GR, GD, PW, PWD, BC, DF}\}$ that is guaranteed correct for F_R into a rule R' that is "guaranteed correct" for $F_{R'} := a^{F_R} := \{a^f \mid f \in F_R\}$, where a is any constant greater than 1—in the sense that the exponent f is bounded correctly: Let f be in one of the above defined classes F_R and $Y = a^{f(X)}$. Then, a logarithmic transformation $\hat{Y} \leftarrow \log Y$ yields $\hat{Y} = \hat{f}(X)$, for some member $\hat{f}$ of F_R which differs from f only by a *positive constant factor*. Therefore, a subsequent application of R to $(X, \hat{Y})$ will result in a correct bound for the exponent f.

Furthermore, we can easily invent a rule that is guaranteed correct for all exponential functions $f(x) = a^x, a > 1$: Simply iterating over guess functions $\bar{f}(x) = b^x$ for a certain range of $b > 1$, choosing the guess function that minimizes, e.g., the RSS, and determining the bound type by means of residual analysis, will do. But the performance of this rule for any data that represents some non exponential behavior can be considered as highly unreliable.

4.8.3 Conclusions on the Experimental Study of Asymptotic Performance

This section was dedicated to the question of how to use finite experiments in order to study the asymptotic performance of algorithms. The content is thereby mainly based on [551], i.e., all approaches and techniques presented here are taken from the aforesaid paper. Our only contribution in this context may be a new and sometimes perhaps a little more detailed description of the curve bounding rules, as well as our own preliminary view on the general topic and on some aspects of the presented techniques and approaches.

We have shown some of the difficulties that are faced when experiments are used for studying asymptotic performance. In fact, experiments can never be used to *prove a theorem* on the asymptotic performance, as they can only test inputs of limited size. Nevertheless, they can be used to support asymptotic analysis in a way that is suggested by the so-called *scientific method* which has its origin in the natural sciences, where it is applied with utmost success. This method views science as a cycle between theory and experimentation: Theory can inductively and partially deductively (by means of *theories* that are based on specific *assumptions*) formulate *experimentally falsifiable hypotheses*. These hypotheses can be validated with experiments, which in turn may lead to new or refined hypotheses and theories, and so on. In Section 4.8.1 we have presented some suggestions on how to apply the scientific method to performance analysis and have given a few hints on what difficulties have to be overcome.

The curve bounding rules presented in Section 4.8.2 are intended to yield asymptotic *trends* by pure analysis of experimental data. Applying the terminology of the scientific method, their results can be viewed as theories—based on the assumption of *guaranteed correctness*. However, preliminary experimental investigations revealed that this assumption is false in most cases. But let us be more precise about the results of these experimental investigations: They showed clearly that the rule's performance depends strongly on the quality of the input data (X, Y). The reliability of each rule's output grows, if the range of tested input sizes grows and if the amount of random noise in the data is reduced. For the data that was tested, the rules could in most cases get within a linear factor or even a $\sqrt{x}$ factor of the true asymptotic bound. In situations where we do not know anything about the true asymptotic performance bound of some algorithm, this might help us to roughly know the true bound's order of magnitude, and inspire us to go for a proof of this bound. But if we are interested in fine distinctions between performance bounds of no more than a logarithmic factor, e.g. between $O(n)$ and $O(n \log n)$, then the rules fail. The authors of [551] report that even including logarithmic terms as guess functions does not help the rules to find logarithmic terms as being part of the true asymptotic bound with any reliability.

We reach the conclusion that the scientific method is a promising approach to performance analysis: It intends to combine theory and experimentation in a way that leads to the best possible overall result. Our recommendation concerning the curve bounding rules is to use them in a careful way: You should be aware of their limited reliability. Up to now, it seems that the use of a curve bounding rule R is most reasonable, if it is known in advance that the true bound of the data curve belongs to the class F_R of functions for which R is guaranteed correct in the sense of Definition 14. From this viewpoint, it appears to be an intriguing task for future research to find sophisticated curve bounding rules that are guaranteed correct for classes of functions that differ considerably from F_{GR}, F_{GD}, F_{PW} and F_{DF}. Furthermore, it may be worthwhile to find out whether there are *more* classes of functions for which the existing rules are guaranteed correct or not. Finally, there are many algorithms (e. g., graph algorithms) whose running time depends on more than one input parameter (e. g., on the number of vertices as well as on the number of edges), and it is not clear up to now how a curve bounding rule that returns an asymptotic trend depending on more than one input parameter might look like.

4.9   Conclusions

We have presented several techniques for analyzing the behavior of algorithms. The most classical measure is to consider the behavior in the worst case. The advantage of this kind of analysis is that it is robust and that it can give very strong positive results. If the worst-case behavior of an algorithm is good, then the algorithm performs well on every possible input. On the other hand, this is a very restrictive requirement which is not met for many algorithms. Nonetheless, some of these algorithms perform very well on typical inputs that arise in industrial applications.

In order to narrow the gap between the theoretical results and the observations made in practice, one has to find a way of modeling typical inputs, rather than just to consider the worst case. One possible solution might be to analyze the behavior on random inputs. The main disadvantage of such an average-case analysis is that its outcome depends heavily on the chosen probability distribution on the set of inputs. In most applications it is not clear how to choose a probability distribution that reflects typical instances, and hence average-case analyses are often of limited relevance for practical considerations. A more promising approach is to consider the behavior on semi-random inputs that have a certain adversarial structure which is only slightly perturbed at random. Such a hybrid between worst-case and average-case analysis is formulated in the model of smoothed analysis. This relatively new kind of analysis has already led to some interesting insights into the behavior of certain algorithms and heuristics.

Another possibility of modeling typical inputs is to consider the worst-case behavior on a restricted set of inputs. Therefore, one has to identify and formalize properties of typical inputs. In particular for geometric problems, there exists a hierarchy of different natural properties and restrictions and there are numerous problems whose complexity decreases significantly if one considers only inputs that satisfy one of these properties.

There are, of course, also a lot of methods for evaluating the performance of an algorithm experimentally. We presented the method of counting representative operations which uses statistical methods to predict the running time of an algorithm. One advantage of this method is that it can help to identify bottleneck operations. The major disadvantage is that no theoretical bounds are obtained. Anyhow, an experimental analysis may lead to the formulation of a *falsifiable* hypothesis. As a means for obtaining a falsifiable hypothesis on the asymptotic performance of an algorithm, given solely experimental data, we discussed some so-called *curve bounding rules*.

Let us conclude that in our opinion analyzing the behavior of an algorithm is essential for gaining new insights that lead to a better understanding and might help to improve the algorithm. There are several different ways and techniques how such an analysis can be performed, and we tried to point out the advantages and disadvantages of each of these, but we cannot give a general advice which technique and measure should be used. The "right" choice depends on many different factors, like how much effort one is willing to invest and which goal is to be achieved.

Chapter 5. Realistic Computer Models

Deepak Ajwani* and Henning Meyerhenke**

5.1 Introduction

Many real-world applications involve storing and processing large amounts of data. These data sets need to be either stored over the memory hierarchy of one computer or distributed and processed over many parallel computing devices or both. In fact, in many such applications, choosing a realistic computation model proves to be a critical factor in obtaining practically acceptable solutions. In this chapter, we focus on realistic computation models that capture the running time of algorithms involving large data sets on modern computers better than the traditional RAM (and its parallel counterpart PRAM) model.

5.1.1 Large Data Sets

Large data sets arise naturally in many applications. We consider a few examples here.

- GIS terrain data: Remote sensing [435] has made massive amounts of high resolution terrain data readily available. NASA already measures the data volumes from satellite images in petabytes (10^{15} bytes). With the emergence of new terrain mapping technologies such as laser altimetry, this data is likely to grow much further. Terrain analysis is central to a range of important geographic information systems (GIS) applications concerned with the effects of topography.
- Data warehouses of companies that keep track of every single transaction on spatial/temporal databases. Typical examples include the financial sector companies, telecommunication companies and online businesses. Many data warehouse appliances already scale to one petabyte and beyond [428].
- The World Wide Web (WWW) can be looked upon as a massive graph where each web-page is a node and the hyperlink from one page to another is a directed edge between the nodes corresponding to those pages. As of August 2008, it is estimated that the indexed web contains at least 27 billion webpages [208].

    Typical problems in the analysis (e.g., [129,509]) of WWW graphs include computing the diameter of the graph, computing the diameter of the core

---

* Supported by German Science Foundation (DFG) grant ME 3250/1-1, DFG grant ME 2088/1-3, and by MADALGO - Center for Massive Data Algorithmics, a Center of the Danish National Research Foundation.
** Partially supported by German Science Foundation (DFG) Research Training Group GK-693 of the Paderborn Institute for Scientific Computation (PaSCo) and by DFG Priority Programme 1307 *Algorithm Engineering*.

M. Müller-Hannemann and S. Schirra (Eds.): Algorithm Engineering, LNCS 5971, pp. 194–236, 2010.

of the graph, computing connected and strongly connected components and other structural properties such as computing the correct parameters for the power law modeling of WWW graphs. There has also been a lot of work on understanding the evolution of such graphs.

Internet search giants and portals work on very large datasets. For example, Yahoo!, a major Internet portal, maintains (as of 2008) a database of more than a petabyte [426].

– Social networks: Social networks provide yet another example of naturally evolving massive graphs [55]. One application area is citation graphs, in which nodes represent the papers and an edge from one paper to another shows the citation. Other examples include networks of friends, where nodes denote individuals and edges show the acquaintance, and telephone graphs, where nodes represent phone numbers and edges represent phone call in the last few days. Typical problems in social networks include finding local communities, e. g., people working on similar problems in citation graphs.

– Artificial Intelligence and Robotics: In applications like single-agent search, game playing and action planning, even if the input data is small, intermediate data can be huge. For instance, the state descriptors of explicit state model checking softwares are often so large that main memory is not sufficient for the lossless storage of reachable states during the exploration [267].

– Scientific modeling and simulation (e. g., particle physics, molecular dynamics), engineering (e. g., CAD), medical computing, astronomy and numerical computing.

– Network logs such as fault alarms, CPU usage at routers and flow logs. Typical problems on network logs include finding the number of distinct IP addresses using a given link to send their traffic or how much traffic in two routers is common.

– Ad hoc network of sensors monitoring continuous physical observations – temperature, pressure, EMG/ECG/EEG signals from humans, humidity etc.

– Weather prediction centers collect a massive amount of weather, hydrological, radar, satellite and weather balloon data and integrate it into a variety of computer models for improving the accuracy of weather forecasts.

– Genomics, where the sequence data can be as large as a few terabytes [111].

– Graphics and animations [281].

Note that the term "large" as used in this chapter is in comparison with the memory capacity and it depends not only on the level of memory hierarchy but also the computational device in use. For instance, road network of a small city may fit in the main memory of modern computers, but still be considered "large" for route planning applications involving a flash memory card on a small mobile device like Pocket PC [342, 699] or in the context of cache misses.

Next, we consider the traditional RAM model of computation and the reasons for its inadequacy for applications involving large data sets.

5.1.2   RAM Model

The running time of an algorithm is traditionally analyzed by counting the number of executed primitive operations or "instructions" as a function of the input size n (cf. Chapter 4). The implicit underlying model of computation is the one-processor, *random-access machine (RAM)* model. The RAM model or the "von Neumann model of computation" consists of a computing device attached to a storage device (or "memory"). The following are the key assumptions of this model:

- Instructions are executed one after another, with no concurrent operations.
- Every instruction takes the same amount of time, at least up to small constant factors.
- Unbounded amount of available memory.
- Memory stores words of size $O(\log n)$ bits where n is the input size.
- Any desired memory location can be accessed in unit time.
- For numerical and geometric algorithms, it is sometimes also assumed that words can represent real numbers accurately.
- Exact arithmetic on arbitrary real numbers can be done in constant time.

The above assumptions greatly simplify the analysis of algorithms and allow for expressive asymptotic analysis.

5.1.3   Real Architecture

Unfortunately, modern computer architecture is not as simple. Rather than having an unbounded amount of unit-cost access memory, we have a hierarchy of storage devices (Figure 5.1) with very different access times and storage capacities. Modern computers have a microprocessor attached to a file of *registers*. The *first level (L1) cache* is usually only a few kilobytes large and incurs a delay of a few clock cycles. Often there are separate L1 caches for instructions and data. Nowadays, typical *second level (L2) cache* has a size of about 32-512 KB and access latencies around ten clock cycles. Some processors also have a rather expensive *third level (L3) cache* of up to 256 MB made of fast static random access memory cells. A cache consists of *cache lines* that each store a number of memory words. If an accessed item is not in the cache, it and its neighbor entries are fetched from the main memory and put into a cache line. These caches usually have limited associativity, i. e., an element brought from the main memory can be placed only in a restricted set of cache lines. In a *direct-mapped* cache the target cache line is fixed and only based on the memory address, whereas in a *full-associative* cache the item can be placed anywhere. Since the former is too restrictive and the latter is expensive to build and manage, a compromise often used is a *set-associative* cache. There, the item's memory address determines a fixed set of cache lines into which the data can be mapped, though within each set, any cache line can be used. The typical size of such a set of cache lines is a power of 2 in the range from 2 to 16. For more details about the structure of caches the interested reader is referred to [631] (in particular its Chapter 7).

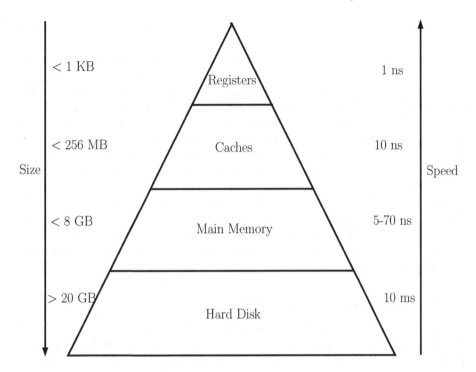

Fig. 5.1. Memory hierarchy in modern computer architecture

The *main memory* is made of dynamic random access memory cells. These cells store a bit of data as a charge in a capacitor rather than storing it as the state of a flip-flop which is the case for most static random access memory cells. It requires practically the same amount of time to access any piece of data stored in the main memory, irrespective of its location, as there is no physical movement (e. g., of a reading head) involved in the process of retrieving data. Main memory is usually volatile, which means that it loses all data when the computer is powered down. At the time of the writing, the main memory size of a PC is usually between 512 MB and 32 GB and a typical RAM memory has an access time of 5 to 70 nanoseconds.

Magnetic *hard disks* offer cheap non-volatile memory with an access time of 10 ms, which is 10^6 times slower than a register access. This is because it takes very long to move the access head to a particular track of the disk and wait until the disk rotates into the seeked position. However, once the head starts reading or writing, data can be transferred at the rate of 35-125 MB/s. Hence, reading or writing a contiguous block of hundreds of KB takes only about twice as long as accessing a single byte, thereby making it imperative to process data in large chunks.

Apart from the above mentioned levels of a memory hierarchy, there are instruction pipelines, an instruction cache, logical/physical pages, the translation lookaside buffer (TLB), magnetic tapes, optical disks and the network, which further complicate the architecture.

The reasons for such a memory hierarchy are mainly economical. The faster memory technologies are costlier and, as a result, fast memories with large capacities are economically prohibitive. The memory hierarchy emerges as a reasonable compromise between the performance and the cost of a machine.

Microprocessors like Intel Xeon have multiple register sets and are able to execute a corresponding number of threads of activity in parallel, even as they share the same execution pipeline. The accumulated performance is higher, as a thread can use the processor while another thread is waiting for a memory access to finish.

Explicit parallel processing takes the computer architecture further away from the RAM model. On parallel machines, some levels of the memory hierarchy may be shared whereas others are distributed between the processors. The communication cost between different machines is often the bottleneck for algorithms on parallel architectures.

5.1.4   Disadvantages of the RAM Model

The beauty of the RAM model lies in the fact that it hides all the 'messy' details of computer architecture from the algorithm designer. At the same time, it encapsulates the comparative performance of algorithms remarkably well. It strikes a fine balance by capturing the essential behavior of computers while being simple to work with. The performance guarantees in the RAM model are not architecture-specific and therefore robust. However, this is also the limiting factor for the success of this model. In particular, it fails significantly when the input data or the intermediate data structure is too large to reside completely within the internal memory. This failure can be observed between any two levels of the memory hierarchy.

For most problems on large data sets, the dominant part of the running time of algorithms is not the number of "instructions", but the time these algorithms spend waiting for the data to be brought from the hard disk to internal memory. The I/Os or the movement of data between the memory hierarchies (and in particular between the main memory and the disk) are not captured by the RAM model and hence, as shown in Figure 5.2, the predicted performance on the RAM model increasingly deviates from the actual performance. As we will see in Section 5.5.2, the running times of even elementary graph problems like breadth-first search become I/O-dominant as the input graph is just twice as large as the available internal memory. While the RAM model predicts running time in *minutes*, it takes *hours* in practice.

Since the time required by algorithms for large data sets in the sequential setting can be impractical, a larger number of processors are sometimes used to compute the solution in parallel. On parallel architectures, one is often interested in the parallel time, work, communication costs etc. of an algorithm. These performance parameters are simply beyond the scope of the traditional one-processor RAM model. Even the parallel extension of the RAM model, the

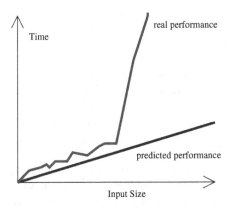

Fig. 5.2. Predicted performance of RAM model versus its real performance

PRAM model, fails to capture the running time of algorithms on real parallel architectures as it ignores the communication cost between the processors.

5.1.5   Future Trends

The problem is likely to aggravate in the future. According to Moore's law, the number of transistors double every 18 months. As a result, the CPU speed continued to improve at nearly the same pace until recently, i.e., an average performance improvement of 1% per week. Meanwhile, due to heat problems caused by even higher clock speeds, processor architects have passed into increasing the number of computing entities (*cores*) per processor instead. The usage of parallel processors and multi-cores makes the computations even faster. On the other hand, random access memory speeds and hard drive seek times improve at best a few percentages per year. Although the capacity of the random access memory doubles about every two years, users double their data storage every 5 months. Multimedia (pictures, music and movies) usage in digital form is growing and the same holds true for the content in WWW. For example, the number of articles in the online encyclopedia Wikipedia has been doubling every 339 days [830] and the online photo sharing network Flickr that started in 2004 had more than three billion pictures as of November 2008 [289] and claims that three to five million photos are updated daily on its network. Consequently, the problem sizes are increasing and the I/O-bottleneck is worsening.

5.1.6   Realistic Computer Models

Since the RAM model fails to capture the running time of algorithms for problems involving large data sets and the I/O bottleneck is likely to worsen in future, there is clearly a need for realistic computer models – models taking explicit care of memory hierarchy, parallelism or other aspects of modern architectures. These models should be simple enough for algorithm design and analysis, yet they should be able to capture the intricacies of the underlying architecture. Their performance metric can be very different from the traditional "counting the instructions" approach of the RAM model and algorithm design on these models may need fundamentally different techniques. This chapter introduces some of the popular realistic computation models – external memory model, parallel disk model, cache-oblivious model, and parallel bridging models like BSP, LogP, CGM, QSM etc. – and provides the basic techniques for designing algorithms on most of these models.

In Section 5.2, many techniques for exploiting the memory hierarchy are introduced. This includes different memory hierarchy models, algorithm design techniques and data structures as well as several optimization techniques specific to caches. After the introduction of various parallel computing models in Section 5.3, Section 5.4 shows the relationship between the algorithms designed in memory hierarchy and parallel models. In Section 5.5, we discuss success stories of Algorithm Engineering on large data sets using the introduced computer models from various domains of computer science.

5.2   Exploiting the Memory Hierarchy

5.2.1   Memory Hierarchy Models

In this section, we introduce some of the memory hierarchy models that have led to successful Algorithm Engineering on large data sets.

External Memory Model. The I/O model or the external memory (*EM*) model (depicted in Figure 5.3) as introduced by Aggarwal and Vitter [11] assumes a single central processing unit and two levels of memory hierarchy. The internal memory is fast, but has a limited size of M words. In addition, we have an external memory which can only be accessed using I/Os that move B contiguous words between internal and external memory. For some problems, the notation is slightly abused and we assume that the internal memory can have up to M *data items of a constant size* (e. g., vertices/edges/characters/segments etc.) and in one I/O operation, B contiguous data items move between the two memories. At any particular timestamp, the computation can only use the data already present in the internal memory. The measure of performance of an algorithm is the number of I/Os it performs. An algorithm A has lower I/O-complexity than another algorithm A' if A requires less I/Os than A'.

Although we mostly use the sequential variant of the external memory model, it also has an option to express disk parallelism. There can be D parallel disks and in one I/O, D arbitrary blocks can be accessed in parallel from the disks. The usage of parallel disks helps us alleviate the I/O bottleneck.

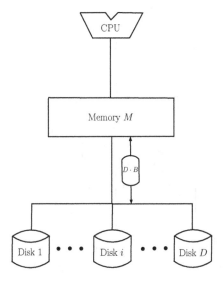

Fig. 5.3. The external memory model

Parallel Disk Model. The parallel disk model (depicted in Figure 5.4) by Vitter and Shriver [810] is similar to the external memory model, except that it adds a realistic restriction that only one block can be accessed per disk during an I/O, rather than allowing D *arbitrary* blocks to be accessed in parallel. The parallel disk model can also be extended to allow parallel processing by allowing P parallel identical processors each with M/P internal memory and equipped with D/P disks.

Sanders et al. [696] gave efficient randomized algorithms for emulating the external memory model of Aggarwal and Vitter [11] on the parallel disk model.

Ideal Cache Model. In the external memory model we are free to choose any two levels of the memory hierarchy as internal and external memory. For this reason, external memory algorithms are sometimes also referred to as *cache-aware* algorithms ("aware" as opposed to "oblivious"). There are two main problems with extending this model to caches: limited associativity and automated replacement. As shown by Sen and Chatterjee [724], the problem of limited associativity in caches can be circumvented at the cost of constant factors. Frigo et al. [308] showed that a regular algorithm causes asymptotically the same number of cache misses with LRU (least recently used) or FIFO (first-in first-out) replacement policy as with optimal off-line replacement strategy. Intuitively, an algorithm is called *regular* if the number of incurred cache misses (with an optimal off-line replacement) increase by a constant factor when the cache size is reduced to half.

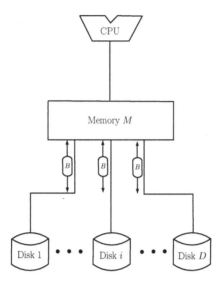

Fig. 5.4. The parallel disk model

Similar to the external memory model, the ideal cache model [308] assumes a two level memory hierarchy, with the faster level having a capacity of storing at most M elements and data transfers in chunks of B elements. In addition, it also assumes that the memory is managed automatically by an optimal offline cache-replacement strategy, and that the cache is fully associative.

Cache-Oblivious Model. In practice, the model parameters B and M need to be finely tuned for an optimal performance. For different architectures and memory hierarchies, these values can be very different. This fine-tuning can be at times quite cumbersome. Besides, we can optimize only one memory hierarchy level at a time. Ideally, we would like a model that would capture the essence of the memory hierarchy without knowing its specifics, i.e., values of B and M, and at the same time is efficient on all hierarchy levels simultaneously. Yet, it should be simple enough for a feasible algorithm analysis. The cache-oblivious model introduced by Frigo et al. [308] promises all of the above. In fact, the immense popularity of this model lies in its innate simplicity and its ability to abstract away the hardware parameters.

The cache-oblivious model also assumes a two level memory hierarchy with an internal memory of size M and block transfers of B elements in one I/O. The performance measure is the number of I/Os incurred by the algorithm. However, the algorithm does not have any knowledge of the values of M and B. Consequently, the guarantees on I/O-efficient algorithms in the cache-oblivious model hold not only on any machine with multi-level memory hierarchy but also on all levels of the memory hierarchy at the same time. In principle, these algorithms are expected to perform well on different architectures without the need of any machine-specific optimization.

The cache-oblivious model assumes full associativity and optimal replacement policy. However, as we argued for the ideal cache model, these assumptions do not affect the asymptotics on realistic caches.

However, note that cache-oblivious algorithms are usually more complicated than their cache-aware I/O-efficient counterparts. As a result, the constant factors hidden in the complexity of cache-oblivious algorithms are usually higher and on large external memory inputs, they are slower in practice.

Various Streaming Models. In the data stream model [603], input data can only be accessed sequentially in the form of a data stream, and needs to be processed using a working memory that is small compared to the length of the stream. The main parameters of the model are the number p of sequential passes over the data and the size s of the working memory (in bits). Since the classical data stream model is too restrictive for graph algorithms and even the undirected connectivity problem requires $s \times p = \Omega(n)$ [387] (where n is the number of nodes in a graph), less restrictive variants of streaming models have also been studied. These include the stream-sort model [12] where sorting is also allowed, the W-stream model [232] where one can use intermediate temporary streams, and the semi-streaming model [284], where the available memory is $O(n \cdot polylog(n))$ bits.

There are still a number of issues not addressed by these models that can be critical for performance in practical settings, e. g., branch mispredictions [451], TLB misses etc. For other models on memory hierarchies, we refer to [53, 658, 505, 569].

5.2.2 Fundamental Techniques

The key principles in designing I/O-efficient algorithms are the exploitation of locality and the batching of operations. In a general context, *spatial locality* denotes that data close in address space to the currently accessed item is likely to be accessed soon whereas *temporal locality* refers to the fact that an instruction issued or a data item accessed during the current clock cycle is likely to be issued/accessed in the near future as well. The third concept is *batching*, which basically means to wait before issuing an operation until enough data needs to be processed such that the operation's cost is worthwhile. Let us see in more detail what this means for the design of I/O-efficient algorithms.

- **Exploiting spatial locality:** Since the data transfer in the external memory model (as well as the cache-oblivious model) happens in terms of block of elements rather than a single element at a time, the entire block when accessed should contain as much useful information as possible. This concept is referred to as "exploiting spatial locality". The fan-out of B in a B-tree exploiting the entire information accessible in one I/O to reduce the height of the tree (and therefore the worst-case complexity of various operations) is a typical example of "exploiting spatial locality".

Spatial locality is sometimes also used to represent the fact that the likelihood of referencing a resource is higher if a resource near it (with an appropriate measure of "nearness") has just been referenced. Graph clustering and partitioning techniques are examples for exploiting "nearness".

- **Exploiting temporal locality:** The concept of using the data in the internal memory for as much useful work as possible before it is written back to the external memory is called "exploiting temporal locality". The divide and conquer paradigm in the external memory can be considered as an example of this principle. The data is divided into chunks small enough to fit into the internal memory and then the subproblem fitting internally is solved completely before reverting back to the original problem.
- **Batching the operations:** In many applications, performing one operation is nearly as costly as performing multiple operations of the same kind. In such scenarios, we can do lazy processing of operations, i. e., we first batch a large number of operations to be done and then perform them "in parallel" (altogether as one meta operation). A typical example of this approach is the buffer tree data structure described in more detail in Section 5.2.3. Many variants of external priority queue also do lazy processing of decrease-key operations after collecting them in a batch.

The following tools using the above principles have been used extensively in designing external memory algorithms:

Sorting and Scanning. Many external memory and cache-oblivious algorithms can be assembled using two fundamental ingredients: scanning and sorting. Fortunately, there are matching upper and lower bounds for the I/O complexity of these operations [11]. The number of I/Os required for scanning n data items is denoted by $\text{scan}(n) = \Theta(n/B)$ and the I/O complexity of sorting n elements is $\text{sort}(n) = \Theta(\frac{n}{B} \log_{M/B} \frac{n}{B})$ I/Os. For all practical values of B, M and n on large data sets, $\text{scan}(n) < \text{sort}(n) \ll n$. Intuitively, this means that reading and writing data in sequential order or sorting the data to obtain a requisite layout on the disk is less expensive than accessing data at random.

The $O(n/B)$ upper bound for scanning can easily be obtained by the following simple modification: Instead of accessing one element at a time (incurring one I/O for the access), bring B contiguous elements in internal memory using a single I/O. Thus for the remaining $B - 1$ elements, one can do a simple memory access, rather than an expensive disk I/O.

Although a large number of I/O-efficient sorting algorithms have been proposed, we discuss two categories of existing algorithms - merge sort and distribution sort. Algorithms based on the *merging paradigm* proceed in two phases: In the *run formation phase*, the input data is partitioned into sorted sequences, called "runs". In the second phase, the *merging phase*, these runs are merged until only one sorted run remains, where merging k runs $S_1, \ldots, S_k$ means that a single sorted run S' is produced that contains all elements of runs $S_1, \ldots, S_k$. In the external memory sorting algorithm of Aggarwal and Vitter [11], the first phase produces sorted runs of M elements and the second phase does a $\frac{M}{B}$-way merge, leading to $O(\frac{n}{B} \log_{M/B} \frac{n}{B})$ I/Os. In the cache-oblivious setting, funnel-sort [308] and lazy funnelsort [131], also based on the merging framework, lead to sorting algorithms with a similar I/O complexity. Algorithms based on the *distribution paradigm* compute a set of splitters $x_1 \leq x_2 \leq \ldots \leq x_k$ from the given data set S in order to partition it into subsets $S_0, S_1, \ldots, S_k$ so that for all $0 \leq i \leq k$ and $x \in S_i$, $x_i \leq x \leq x_{i+1}$, where $x_0 = -\infty$ and $x_{k+1} = \infty$. Given this partition, a sorted sequence of elements in S is produced by recursively sorting the sets $S_0, \ldots, S_k$ and concatenating the resulting sorted sequences. Examples of this approach include BalanceSort [616], sorting using the buffer tree [35], randomized online splitters [810], and algorithms obtained by simulating bulk-synchronous parallel sorting algorithms [215].

Simulation of Parallel Algorithms. A large number of algorithms for parallel computing models can be simulated to give I/O-efficient algorithms and some-times even I/O-optimal algorithms. The relationship between the algorithms designed in the two paradigms of parallel and external computing is discussed in detail in Section 5.4.

Graph Decomposition and Clustering. A large number of external memory graph algorithms involve decomposing the graphs into smaller subgraphs. Planar graph separator [528] and its external memory algorithm [535] are a basis for almost all I/O-efficient planar graph algorithms [45, 40, 46]. Similarly, the tree-decomposition of a graph leads to external algorithms for bounded treewidth graphs [534]. For general graphs, the I/O-efficient undirected BFS algorithm of Mehlhorn and Meyer [555] relies on clustering of the input graph as an important subroutine. These separators, decompositions and clusterings can be used to divide the problem into smaller subproblems that fit into the internal memory [46] or to improve the layout of the graph on the disk [555].

Time Forward Processing. Time forward processing [35] is an elegant tech-nique for solving problems that can be expressed as a traversal of a directed acyclic graph (DAG) from its sources to its sinks. Given the vertices of a DAG G in topologically sorted order and a labelling ϕ on the nodes of G, the prob-lem is to compute another labelling ψ on the nodes such that label $\psi(v)$ for a node v can be computed from labels $\phi(v)$ and the labels $\psi(u_1), \ldots, \psi(u_k)$ of v's in-neighbors $u_1, \ldots, u_k$ in $O(sort(k))$ I/Os. This problem can be solved in $O(sort(m))$ I/Os, where m is the number of edges in the DAG. The idea [35] is to process the nodes in G by increasing topological number and use an external priority queue (Section 5.2.3) to realize the "sending" of information along the edges of G. When a node u_i wants to send its output $\psi(u_i)$ to another node v, it inserts $\psi(u_i)$ into priority queue Q and gives it priority v. When the node v is be-ing evaluated, it removes all entries with priority v from Q. As every in-neighbor of v sends its output to v by queuing it with priority v, this provides v with the required labels and it can then compute its new label $\psi(v)$ in $O(sort(k))$ I/Os.

Many problems on undirected graphs can be expressed as evaluation problems of DAGs derived from these graphs. Applications of this technique for the construction of I/O-efficient data structures are also known.

Distribution Sweeping. Goodrich et al. [349] introduced distribution sweeping as a general approach for developing external memory algorithms for problems which in internal memory can be solved by a divide-and-conquer algorithm based on a plane sweep. This method has been successfully used in developing I/O-efficient algorithms for orthogonal line segment intersection reporting, all nearest neighbors problem, the 3D maxima problem, computing the measure (area) of a set of axis-parallel rectangles, computing the visibility of a set of line segments from a point, batched orthogonal range queries, and reporting pairwise intersections of axis-parallel rectangles. Brodal et al. [131] generalized the technique for the cache-oblivious model.

Full-Text Indexes. A full-text index is a data structure storing a text (a string or a set of strings) and supporting string matching queries: Given a pattern string P, find all occurrences of P in the text. Due to their fast construction and the wealth of combinatorial information they reveal, full-text indexes are often used in databases and genomics applications. The external memory suffix tree and suffix array can serve as full-text indexes. For a text T, they can be constructed in $O(sort(n))$ I/Os [280], where n is the number of characters in T. Other external full text indexing schemes use a hierarchy of indexes [58], compact Pat trees [176] and string B-trees [285].

There are many other tools for designing external memory algorithms. For instance, list ranking [733, 168], batch filtering [349], Euler tour computation [168], graph blocking techniques [10, 615] etc. Together with external memory data structures, these tools and algorithms alleviate the I/O bottleneck of many problems significantly.

5.2.3   External Memory Data Structures

In this section, we consider basic data structures used to design worst-case efficient algorithms in the external memory model. Most of these data structures are simple enough to be of practical interest.

An I/O-efficient storage of a set of elements under updates and query operations is possible under the following circumstances:

- Updates and queries are localized. For instance, querying for the most recently inserted element in case of a stack and least recently inserted element in case of a queue.
- We can afford to wait for an answer of a query to arrive, i.e., we can batch the queries (as in the case of a buffer tree).

– We can wait for the updates to take place, even if we want an online answer for the query. Many priority queue applications in graph algorithms are examples of this.

For online updates and queries on arbitrary locations, the B-tree is the most popular data structure supporting insertion, deletion and query operations in $O(\log_B n)$ I/Os.

Stacks and Queues. Stacks and queues are two of the most basic data structures used in RAM model algorithms to represent dynamic sets of elements and support deletion of elements in (last-in-first-out) LIFO and (first-in-first-out) FIFO order, respectively. While in internal memory, we can implement these data structures using an array of length n and a few pointers, it can lead to one I/O per insert and delete in the worst case. For the case of a stack, we can avoid this by keeping a buffer of $2B$ elements in the internal memory that at any time contains k most recently added set elements, where $k \leq 2B$. Removing an element needs no I/Os, except for the case when the buffer is empty. In this case, a single I/O is used to retrieve the block of B elements most recently written to external memory. Similarly, inserting an element uses no I/Os, except when the buffer runs full. In this case, a single I/O is used to write the B least recent elements to a block in external memory. It is not difficult to see that for any sequence of B insert or delete operations, we will need at most one I/O. Since at most B elements can be read or written in one I/O, the amortized cost of $1/B$ I/Os is the best one can hope for storing or retrieving a sequence of data items much larger than internal memory.

Analogously, we keep two buffers for queues: a read buffer and a write buffer of size B consisting of least and most recently inserted elements, respectively. Remove operations work on the read buffer and delete the least recent element without any I/O until the buffer is empty, in which case the appropriate external memory block is read into it. Insertions are done to the write buffer which when full is written to external memory. Similar to the case of stacks, we get an amortized complexity of $1/B$ I/Os per operation.

Linked Lists. Linked lists provide an efficient implementation of ordered lists of elements, supporting sequential search, deletion and insertion in arbitrary locations of the list. Traversing a pointer based linked list implementation used commonly in an internal memory algorithm may need to perform one I/O every time a pointer is followed. For an I/O-efficient implementation of linked lists, we keep the elements in blocks and maintain the invariant that there are more than $\frac{2}{3}B$ elements in every pair of consecutive blocks. Inserting an element can be done in a single I/O if the appropriate block is not full. If it is full but any of its two neighbors has spare capacity, we can push an element to that block. Otherwise, we split the block into two equally sized blocks. Similarly for deletion, we check if the delete operation results in violating the invariant and if so, we merge the two violating blocks. Split and merge can also be supported in $O(1)$ I/Os similarly.

To summarize, such an implementation of linked lists in external memory supports $O(1)$ I/O insert, delete, merge and split operations while supporting $O(i/B)$ I/O access to the ith element in the list.

B-tree. The B-tree [77, 182, 416] is a generalization of balanced binary search trees to a balanced tree of degree $\Theta(B)$. Increasing the degree of the nodes helps us exploit the information provided by one I/O block to guide the search better and thereby reducing the height of the tree to $O(\log_B n)$. This in turn allows $O(\log_B n)$ I/O insert, delete and search operations. In external memory, a search tree like the B-tree or its variants can be used as the basis for a wide range of efficient queries on sets.

The degree of a node in a B-tree is $\Theta(B)$ with the root possibly having smaller degree. Normally, the n data items are stored in the $\Theta(n/B)$ leaves (in sorted order) of a B-tree, with each leaf storing $\Theta(B)$ elements. All leaves are on the same level and the tree has height $O(\log_B n)$. Searching an element in a B-tree can be done by traversing down the tree from the root to the appropriate leaf in $O(\log_B n)$ I/Os. One dimensional range queries can similarly be answered in $O(\log_B n + T/B)$ I/Os, where T is the output size. Insertion can be performed by first searching the relevant leaf l and if it is not full, inserting the new element there. If not, we split l into two leaves l' and l'' of approximately the same size and insert the new element in the relevant leaf. The split of l results in the insertion of a new routing element in the parent of l, and thus the need for a split may propagate up the tree. A new root (of degree 2) is produced when the root splits and the height of the tree grows by one. The total complexity of inserting a new element is thus $O(\log_B n)$ I/Os. Deletion is performed similarly in $O(\log_B n)$ I/Os by searching the appropriate leaf and removing the element to be deleted. If this results in too few elements in the leaf, we can fuse it with one of its siblings. Similar to the case of splits in insertion, fuse operations may propagate up the tree and eventually result in the height of the tree decreasing by one. The following are some of the important variants of a B-tree:

- Weight balanced B-tree [47]: Instead of a degree constraint (that the degree of a node v should be $\Theta(B)$ in a normal B-tree), in this variant, we require the weight of a node v to be $\Theta(B^h)$ if v is the root of a subtree of height h. The weight of v is defined as the number of elements in the leaves of the subtree rooted in v.

- Level balanced B-tree: Apart from the insert, delete and search operations, we sometimes need to be able to perform divide and merge operations on a B-tree. A divide operation at element x constructs two trees containing all elements less than and greater than x, respectively. A merge operation performs the inverse operation. This variant of B-tree supports both these operations in $O(\log_B n)$ I/Os.

- Partially persistent B-tree: This variant of the B-tree supports querying not only on the current version, but also on the earlier versions of the data structure. All elements are stored in a slightly modified B-tree where we also associate a node existence interval with each node. Apart from the normal B-tree constraint on the number of elements in a node, we also maintain that a node contains $\Theta(B)$ alive elements in its existence interval. This means that for a given time t, the nodes with existence intervals containing t make up a B-tree on the elements alive at that time.

– String B-tree: Strings of characters can often be arbitrarily long and different strings can be of different length. The string B-tree of Ferragina and Grossi [285] uses a blind trie data structure to route a query string q. A blind trie is a variant of the compacted trie [482, 588], which fits in one disk block. A query can thus be answered in $O(\log_B n + |q|/B)$ I/Os.

Cache-oblivious variants of B-trees will be discussed later in Section 5.2.6.

Buffer Tree. A buffer tree [35] is a data structure that supports an arbitrary sequence of n operations (inserts, delete, query) in $O(\frac{n}{B} \log_{\frac{M}{B}} \frac{n}{B})$ I/Os. It is similar to a B-tree, but has degree $\Theta(M/B)$ and each internal node has an associated buffer which is a queue that contains a sequence of up to M updates and queries to be performed in the subtree where the node is root. New update and query operations are "lazily" written to the root buffer (whose write buffer is kept in the internal memory), while non-root buffers reside entirely in external memory. When the buffer gets full, these operations are flushed down to the subtree where they need to be performed. When an operation reaches the appropriate node, it is executed.

Priority Queue. The priority queue is an abstract data structure of fundamental importance in graph algorithms. It supports insert, delete-min and decrease-key operations in $O(\frac{1}{B} \log_{\frac{M}{B}} \frac{n}{B})$ I/Os amortized, while keeping the minimum element in the internal memory. The key technique behind the priority queue is again the buffering of operations. The following invariants added to the buffer tree provide an implementation of the priority queue:

– The buffer of the root node is always kept in the internal memory.
– The $O(M/B)$ leftmost leaves, i. e., the leaves of the leftmost internal node, are also always kept in the internal memory.
– All buffers on the path from the root to the leftmost leaf are empty.

The decrease-key operation in external memory is usually implemented by inserting the element with the new key and "lazily" deleting the old key.

There are many other external memory data structures, like interval tree [47], priority search tree, range tree, Bkd-tree [649], O-tree [453], PR-tree [42] etc. For a survey on I/O-efficient data structures, refer to [808, 37, 36, 809].

5.2.4   Cache-Aware Optimization

In this section we present some important techniques for an efficient use of caches. Recall that caches are part of the memory hierarchy between processor registers and the main memory. They can make up several levels themselves and exploit the common observation that computations are local. If the code does not respect the locality properties (temporal and spatial), a required data item is likely to be not in the cache. Then, a *cache miss* occurs and several contiguous data words have to be loaded from memory into the cache.

Some techniques to avoid these expensive cache misses are presented in this section. Although these concepts are mainly designed for caches in the original sense, some of them might also give insights for the optimization of any level of the memory hierarchy. We consider two computationally intense areas, namely numerical linear algebra and computer graphics. In particular for numerical applications it is well-known that on many machine types the theoretical peak performance is rarely reached due to memory hierarchy related issues (e. g., [335]). Typically, the codes in both fields perform most work in small computational kernels based on loop nests. Therefore, while instruction cache misses are no problem, the exploitation of locality for efficient reuse of already cached data must be of concern in order to obtain satisfactory performance results.

Detecting Poor Cache Performance. The typical way in practice to analyze the performance of a program, and in particular its performance bottlenecks, is to use profiling tools. One freely available set of tools for profiling Linux or Unix programs comprises gprof [351] and the Valgrind tool suite [613], which includes the cache simulator cachegrind. While gprof determines how much CPU time is spent in which program function, cachegrind performs simulations of the L1 and L2 cache in order to determine the origins of cache misses in the profiled code. These results can also be displayed graphically with kprof [498] and kcachegrind [825], respectively.

Some tools provide access to certain registers of modern microprocessors called *performance counters*. These accesses provide information about certain performance-related events such as cache misses without affecting the program's execution time. Note that a variety of free and commercial profiling and performance tuning tools exists. An extensive list of tools and techniques is outside the scope of this work. The interested reader is referred to Kowarschik and Weiß [497] and Goedecker and Hoisie [335] for more details and references.

Fundamental Cache-Aware Techniques. In general, it is only worthwhile to optimize code portions that contribute significantly to the runtime because improvements on small contributors have only a small speedup effect on the whole program (cf. Amdahl's law in Chapter 6, Section 6.3).

In cases where the profiling information shows that severe bottlenecks are caused by frequent cache misses, one should analyze the reasons for this behavior and try to identify the particular class of cache-miss responsible for the problem. A cache miss can be categorized as *cold miss* (or *compulsory miss*), *capacity miss*, or *conflict miss* [395]. While a cold miss occurs when an item is accessed for the first time, a capacity miss happens when an item has been in the cache before the current access, but has already been evicted due to the cache's limited size. Conflict misses arise when an accessed item has been replaced because another one is mapped to its cache line. The following selection of basic and simple-to-implement techniques can often help to reduce the number of these misses and thus improve the program performance. They fall into the categories data access and data layout optimizations. The former consists mostly of loop transformations, the latter mainly of modifications in array layouts.

Loop Interchange and Array Transpose. Since data is fetched blockwise into the cache, it is essential to access contiguous data consecutively, for example multidimensional arrays. These arrays must be mapped onto a one-dimensional memory index space, which is done in a *row-major* fashion in C, C++, and Java and in a *column-major* fashion in Fortran. In the former the rightmost index increases the fastest as one moves through consecutive memory locations, where in the latter this holds for the leftmost index.

The access of data stored in a multidimensional array often occurs in a loop nest with a fixed distance of indices (*stride*) between consecutive iterations. If this data access does not respect the data layout, memory references are not performed on contiguous data (those with stride 1), which usually leads to cache misses. Therefore, whenever possible, the order in which the array is laid out in memory should be the same as in the program execution, i. e., if i is the index of the outer loop and j of the inner one, then the access $A[i][j]$ is accordant to row-major and $A[j][i]$ to column-major layout. The correct access can be accomplished by either exchanging the loop order (*loop interchange*) or the array dimensions in the declaration (*array transpose*).

Loop Fusion and Array Merging. The *loop fusion* technique combines two loops that are executed directly after another with the same iteration space into one single loop. Roughly speaking, this transformation is legal unless there are dependencies from the first loop to the second one (cf. [497] for more details). It results in a higher instruction level parallelism, reduces the loop overhead, and may also improve data locality. This locality improvement can be highlighted by another technique, the *array merging*. Instead of declaring two arrays with the same dimension and type (e. g., `double a[n], b[n]`), these arrays are combined to one multidimensional array (`double ab[n][2]`) or as an array of a structure comprised of `a` and `b` and length `n`. If the elements of `a` and `b` are typically accessed together, this ensures the access of contiguous memory locations.

Array Padding. In direct-mapped caches or caches with small associativity the entries at some index i of two different arrays might be mapped to the same cache line. Alternating accesses to these elements therefore cause a large number of conflict misses. This can be avoided by inserting a *pad*, i. e., an allocated, but unused array of suitable size to change the offset of the second array, between the two conflicting arrays (*inter-array padding*). The same idea applies to multidimensional arrays, where the leading dimension (the one with stride-1 access) is padded with unused memory locations (*intra-array padding*) if two elements of the same column are referenced shortly after another.

For additional cache-aware optimization techniques the interested reader is again referred to Kowarschik and Weiß [497] and Goedecker and Hoisie [335].

Cache-Aware Numerical Linear Algebra. The need for computational kernels in linear algebra that achieve a high cache performance is addressed for instance by the freely available implementations of the library interfaces *Basic Linear Algebra Subprograms* (BLAS) [105] and *Linear Algebra Package* (LAPACK) [30]. While BLAS provides basic vector and matrix operations of three different categories (level 1: vector-vector, level 2: matrix-vector, level 3: matrix-matrix), LAPACK uses these subroutines to provide algorithms such as solvers for linear equations, linear least-square and eigenvalue problems, to name a few. There are also vendor-specific implementations of these libraries, which are tuned to specific hardware, and the freely available *Automatically Tuned Linear Algebra Software* (ATLAS) library [829]. The latter determines the hardware parameters during its installation and adapts its parameters accordingly to achieve a high cache efficiency on a variety of platforms. In general it is advantageous to use one of these highly-tuned implementations instead of implementing the provided algorithms oneself, unless one is willing to carry out involved low-level optimizations for a specific machine [829].

One very important technique that is used to improve the cache efficiency of numerical algorithms is *loop blocking*, which is also known as *loop tiling*. The way it can be applied to such algorithms is illustrated by an example after giving a very brief background on sparse iterative linear equation solvers. In many numerical simulation problems in science and engineering one has to solve large systems of linear equations $\mathbf{A}x = b$ for x, where x and b are vectors of length n and the matrix $\mathbf{A} \in \mathbb{R}^{n \times n}$ is sparse, i.e., it contains only $O(n)$ non-zero entries. These systems may stem from the discretization of a partial differential equation. As these linear systems cannot be solved by direct methods due to the large runtime and space consumption this would cause, iterative algorithms that approximate the linear system solution are applied. They may range from the basic splitting methods of Jacobi and Gauß-Seidel over their successive over-relaxation counterparts to Krylov subspace and multigrid methods [686]. The latter two are hard to optimize for cache data reuse [781] due to global operations in the first case and the traversal of a hierarchical data structure in the second one.

Since Krylov subspace and multigrid methods are much more efficient in the RAM model than the basic splitting algorithms, some work to address these issues has been done. Three general concepts can be identified to overcome most of the problems. The first aims at reducing the number of iterations by performing more work per iteration to speed up convergence, the second concept performs algebraic transformations to improve data reuse, and the third one removes data dependencies, e. g., by avoiding global sums and inner products. See Toledo's survey [781] for more details and references.

For multigrid methods in particular, one can optimize the part responsible for eliminating the high error frequencies. This *smoothing* is typically performed by a small number of Jacobi or Gauß-Seidel iterations. If the variables of the matrix

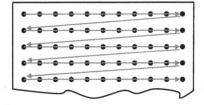 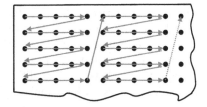

Fig. 5.5. Rather than iterating over one complete matrix row (left), the loop blocking techniques iterates over small submatrices that fit completely into the cache (right)

correspond to graph nodes and the non-zero off-diagonal entries to graph edges, one can say that these algorithms update a node's approximated solution value by a certain edge-weighted combination of the approximated solution values at neighboring nodes. More precisely, the iteration formula of Gauß-Seidel iterations for computing a new approximation $x^{(k+1)}$ given an initial guess $x^{(0)}$ is

$$x_i^{(k+1)} = a_{i,i}^{-1}\left(b_i - \sum_{j<i} a_{i,j}x_j^{(k+1)} - \sum_{j>i} a_{i,j}x_j^{(k)}\right), 1 \le i \le n.$$

Some of the previously presented data layout and access optimizations can be applied to enhance the cache performance of the Gauß-Seidel algorithm [497]. Data layout optimizations include array padding to reduce possible conflict misses and array merging to improve the spatial locality of the entries in row i of $\mathbf{A}$ and b_i. As indicated above, a very effective and widely used technique for the improvement of data access and therefore temporal locality in loop nests is loop blocking. This technique changes the way in which the elements of objects, in our case this would be $\mathbf{A}$ and also the corresponding vector elements, are accessed. Rather than iterating over one row after the other, the matrix is divided into small block matrices that fit into the cache. New inner loops that iterate within the blocks are introduced into the original loop nest. The bounds of the outer loops are then changed to access each such block after the other. An example of this process assuming the traversal of a dense matrix is shown in Figure 5.5.

For simple problems such as matrix transposition or multiplication this is rather straightforward (a more advanced cache-oblivious blocking scheme for matrix multiplication is described in Section 5.2.5). However, loop blocking and performing several Gauß-Seidel steps one after another on the same block appears to be a little more complicated due to the data dependencies involved. When iterating over blocks tailored to the cache, this results in the computation of parts of $x^{(k')}, k' > k+1$, before $x^{(k+1)}$ has been calculated completely. However, if these blocks have an overlap of size $k' - (k+1)$ and this number is small (as is the case for multigrid smoothers), the overhead for ensuring that each block has to be brought into the cache only once is small [723]. This blocking scheme eliminates conflict misses and does not change the order of calculations (and thus the numerical result of the calculation). Hence, it is used in other iterative algorithms, too, where it is also called *covering* [781].

The case of unstructured grids, which is much more difficult in terms of cache analysis and optimization, has also been addressed in the literature [254]. The issues mainly arise here due to different local structures of the nodes (e. g., varying node degrees), which make indirect addressing necessary. In general, indirect addressing deteriorates cache performance because the addresses stored in two adjacent memory locations may be far away from each other. In order to increase the cache performance of the smoother in this setting, one can use graph partitioning methods to divide the grid into small blocks of nodes that fit into the cache. Thus, after a reordering of the matrix and the operators, the smoother can perform as much work as possible on such a small block, which requires the simultaneous use of one cache block only.

The speedups achievable by codes using the presented optimization techniques depend on the problem and on the actual machine characteristics. Kowarschik and Weiß [497] summarize experimental results in the area of multigrid methods by stating that an optimized code can run up to five times faster than an unoptimized one.

5.2.5   Cache-Oblivious Algorithms

As indicated above, cache-aware optimization methods can improve the runtime of a program significantly. Yet, the portability of this performance speedup from one machine to another is often difficult. That is why one is interested in algorithms that do not require specific hardware parameters.

One algorithmic technique to derive such *cache-oblivious* algorithms is the use of space-filling curves [687]. These bijective mappings from a line to a higher-dimensional space date back to the end of the 19th century [635, 390]. They have been successfully applied in a variety of computer science fields, e. g., management of multimedia databases and image processing as well as load balancing of parallel computations (see Mokbel et al. [583]). When applied to objects with a regular structure, for instance structured or semi-structured grids, space-filling curves often produce high-quality solutions, e. g., partitionings of these graphs with high locality [862]. Here we present how this concept can be used to derive a cache-oblivious matrix multiplication algorithm. However, in case of unstructured grids or meshes that contain holes, space-filling curves usually work not as well as other approaches. The way to deal with these issues is shown afterwards by means of the cache-oblivious reordering of unstructured geometric meshes.

Matrix Multiplication. Multiplying two matrices is part of many numerical applications. Since we use it as a reference algorithm throughout this chapter, we define it formally.

Problem 1. Let $\mathbf{A}$ and $\mathbf{B}$ be two $n \times n$ matrices stored in the memory mainly intended for the computational model. Compute the matrix product $\mathbf{C} := \mathbf{AB}$

Algorithm 3. Naive matrix multiplication

1: **for** $i = 1$ to n **do**
2:     **for** $j = 1$ to n **do**
3:         $C[i,j] = 0.0$;
4:         **for** $k = 1$ to n **do**
5:             $C[i,j] = C[i,j] + A[i,k] \cdot B[k,j]$;

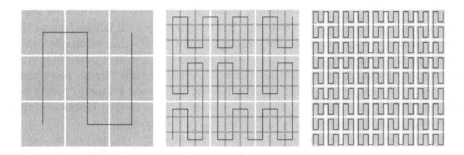

Fig. 5.6. Recursive construction of the Peano curve

and store it in the same type of memory using an algorithm resembling the naive one (cf. Algorithm 3).

Algorithm 3 is called standard or naive[1] and requires $O(n^3)$ operations. It contains a loop nest where two arrays of length n are accessed at the same time, one with stride 1, the other one with stride n. A loop interchange would not change the stride-n issue, but by applying the loop blocking technique, cached entries of all matrices can be reused. An automatic and therefore cache-oblivious blocking of the main loop in matrix multiplication can be achieved by recursive block building [369]. Several techniques have been suggested how to guide this recursion by space-filling curves. A method based on the Peano curve [635] (see Figure 5.6, courtesy of Wikipedia [634]) seems to be very promising, because it increases both spatial and temporal locality. We therefore illustrate its main ideas, the complete presentation can be found in Bader and Zenger [57].

Again, the key idea for a cache-efficient computation of $\mathbf{C} := \mathbf{AB}$ is the processing of matrix blocks. Each matrix is subdivided recursively into $n_x \times n_y$ block matrices until all of them are small, e. g., some fraction of the cache size. To simplify the presentation, we use nine recursive blocks (as in Figure 5.6) and the recursion stops with submatrices that have three rows and three columns. Note that, according to its authors [57], the algorithm works with any block

---

[1] *Naive* refers to the fact that asymptotically faster, but more complicated algorithms exist [758,186].

size $n_x \times n_y$ if n_x and n_y are odd. Each submatrix of size 3×3 is stored in a Peano-like ordering, as indicated by the indices:

$$\begin{pmatrix} a_0 \ a_5 \ a_6 \\ a_1 \ a_4 \ a_7 \\ a_2 \ a_3 \ a_8 \end{pmatrix} \cdot \begin{pmatrix} b_0 \ b_5 \ b_6 \\ b_1 \ b_4 \ b_7 \\ b_2 \ b_3 \ b_8 \end{pmatrix} = \begin{pmatrix} c_0 \ c_5 \ c_6 \\ c_1 \ c_4 \ c_7 \\ c_2 \ c_3 \ c_8 \end{pmatrix}$$

The multiplication of each block is done in the standard way, for example, $c_7 := a_1 b_6 + a_4 b_7 + a_7 b_8$. In general, an element c_r can be written as the sum of three products $c_r = \sum_{(p,q) \in I_r} a_p b_q$, where I_r contains the three respective index pairs. Hence, after initializing all c_r to 0, one has to execute for all triples (r, p, q) the instruction $c_r \leftarrow c_r + a_p b_q$ in an arbitrary order. To do this cache-efficiently, jumps in the indices r, p, and q have to be avoided. It is in fact possible to find such an operation order where two consecutive triples differ by no more than 1 in each element, so that optimal spatial and very good temporal locality is obtained. The same holds for the outer iteration, because the blocks are also accessed in the Peano order due to the recursive construction.

The analysis of this scheme for the 3×3 example in the ideal cache model with cache size M shows that the spatial locality of the elements is at most a factor of 3 away from the theoretical optimum. Moreover, the number of cache line transfers $T(n)$ for the whole algorithm with n a power of 3 is given by the recursion $T(n) = 27T(n/3)$. For blocks of size $k \times k$ each block admits $T(k) = 2 \cdot \lceil k^2/B \rceil$, where B is the size of a cache line. Altogether this leads to the transfer of $O(n^3/\sqrt{M})$ data items (or $O(n^3/B\sqrt{M})$ cache lines) into the cache, which is asymptotically optimal [781] and improves the naive algorithm by a factor of $\sqrt{M}$. The Peano curve ordering plays also a major role in a cache-oblivious self-adaptive full multigrid method [553].

Mesh Layout. Large geometric meshes may contain hundreds of millions of objects. Their efficient processing for interactive visualization and geometric applications requires an optimized usage of the CPU, the GPU (*graphics processing unit*), and their memory hierarchies. Considering the vast amount of different hardware combinations possible, a cache-oblivious scheme seems most promising. Yoon and Lindstrom [853] have developed metrics to predict the number of cache misses during the processing of a given mesh layout, i. e., the order in which the mesh objects are laid out on disk or in memory. On this basis a heuristic is described which computes a layout attempting to minimize the number of cache misses of typical applications. Note that similar algorithmic approaches have been used previously for unstructured multigrid (see Section 5.2.4) and for computing a linear ordering in implicit graph partitioning called graph-filling curves [702].

For the heuristic one needs to specify a directed graph $G = (V, E)$ that represents an anticipated runtime access pattern [853]. Each node $v_i \in V$ corresponds to a mesh object (e. g., a vertex or a triangle) and a directed arc (v_i, v_j) is inserted into E if it is likely that the object corresponding to v_j is accessed directly after the object represented by v_i at runtime. Given this graph and some probability measures derived from random walk theory, the task is to find a one-to-one mapping of nodes to layout indices, $\varphi : V \rightarrow \{1, \dots, |V|\}$, that reduces the expected number of cache misses. Assuming that the cache holds only a single block whose size is a power of two, a cache-oblivious metric based on the *arc length* $l_{ij} = |\varphi(v_i) - \varphi(v_j)|$ is derived, which is proportional to the expected number of cache misses:

$$COM_g(\varphi) = \frac{1}{|E|} \sum_{(v_i, v_j) \in E} \log(l_{ij}) = \log\left(\left(\prod_{(v_i, v_j) \in E} l_{ij}\right)^{\frac{1}{|E|}}\right),$$

where the rightmost expression is the logarithm of the geometric mean of the arc lengths. The proposed minimization algorithm for this metric is related to multilevel graph partitioning [386], but the new algorithm's refinement steps proceed top-down rather than bottom-up. First, the original mesh is partitioned into k (e.g., $k = 4$) sets using a graph partitioning tool like METIS [468], which produces a low number of edges between nodes of different partitions. Then, among the $k!$ orders of these sets the one is chosen that minimizes $COM_g(\varphi)$. This partitioning and ordering process is recursively continued on each set until all sets contain only one vertex. Experiments show that the layout computed that way (which can be further improved by cache-awareness) accelerates several geometric applications significantly compared to other common layouts.

Other Cache-Oblivious Algorithms. Efficient cache-oblivious algorithms are also known for many fundamental problems such as sorting [308], distribution sweeping [131], BFS and shortest-paths [134], and 3D convex hulls [158]. For more details on cache-oblivious algorithms, the reader is referred to the survey paper by Brodal [130].

5.2.6   Cache-Oblivious Data Structures

Many cache-oblivious data structures like static [650] and dynamic B-trees [90, 88,133], priority queue [132,38], kd-tree [9], with I/O complexity similar to their I/O-efficient counterparts have been developed in recent years. A basic building block of most cache-oblivious data structures (e.g., [9,90,88,133,657,89]) is a recursively defined layout called the *van Emde Boas layout* closely related to the definition of a van Emde Boas tree [794]. For the sake of simplicity, we only describe here the van Emde Boas layout of a complete binary tree T. If T has only one node, it is simply laid out as a single node in memory. Otherwise, let h be the height of T. We define the top tree T_0 to be the subtree consisting of the nodes in the topmost $\lfloor h/2 \rfloor$ levels of T, and the bottom trees $T_1, \dots, T_k$ to be the $2^{\lfloor h/2-1 \rfloor}$ subtrees of size $2^{\lceil h/2 \rceil} - 1$ each, rooted in the nodes on level $\lceil h/2 \rceil$ of T. The van Emde Boas layout of T consists of the van Emde Boas layout of T_0 followed by the van Emde Boas layouts of $T_1, \dots, T_k$.

A binary tree with a van Emde Boas layout can be directly used as a static cache-oblivious B-tree [650]. The number of I/Os needed to perform a search in

T, i. e., traversing a root-to-leaf path, can be analyzed by considering the first recursive level of the van Emde Boas layout when the subtrees are smaller than B. The size of such a *base tree* is between $\Theta(\sqrt{B})$ and $\Theta(B)$ and therefore, the height of a base tree is $\Omega(\log B)$. By the definition of the layout, each base tree is stored in $O(B)$ contiguous memory locations and can thus be accessed in $O(1)$ I/Os. As the search path traverses $O(\log n / \log B) = O(\log_B n)$ different base trees (where n is the number of elements in the B-tree), the I/O complexity of a search operation is $O(\log_B n)$ I/Os.

For more details on cache-oblivious data structures, the reader is referred to a book chapter by Arge et al. [39].

5.3   Parallel Computing Models

So far, we have seen how the speed of computations can be optimized on a serial computer by considering the presence of a memory hierarchy. In many fields, however, typical problems are highly complex and may require the processing of very large amounts of intermediate data in main memory. These problems often arise in scientific modeling and simulation, engineering, geosciences, computational biology, and medical computing [108, 147, 388, 494, 660] for more applications). Usually, their solutions must be available within a given timeframe to be of any value. Take for instance the weather forecast for the next three days: If a sequential processor requires weeks for a sufficiently accurate computation, its solution will obviously be worthless. A natural solution to this issue is the division of the problem into several smaller subproblems that are solved concurrently. This concurrent solution process is performed by a larger number of processors which can communicate with each other to share intermediate results where necessary. That way the two most important computing resources, computational power and memory size, are increased so that larger problems can be solved in shorter time.

Yet, a runtime reduction occurs only if the system software and the application program are implemented for the efficient use of the given parallel computing architecture, often measured by their *speed-up* and *efficiency* [503]. The *absolute speedup*, i. e., the running time of the best sequential algorithm divided by the running time of the parallel algorithm, measures how much faster the problem can be solved by parallel processing. Efficiency is then defined as the absolute speedup divided by the number of processors used.[2] In contrast to its absolute counterpart, *relative speedup* measures the inherent parallelism of the considered algorithm. It is defined as the ratio of the parallel algorithm's running times on one processor and on p processors [767].

To obtain a high efficiency, the application programmer might not want to concentrate on the specifics of one architecture, because it distracts from the actual problem and also limits portability of both the code and its execution

---

[2] On a more technical level efficiency can also be defined as the ratio of real program performance and theoretical peak performance.

speed. Therefore, it is essential to devise an algorithm design model that abstracts away unnecessary details, but simultaneously retains the characteristics of the underlying hardware in order to predict algorithm performance realistically [379]. For sequential computing the random access machine (RAM) has served as the widely accepted model of computation (if EM issues can be neglected), promoting "consistency and coordination among algorithm developers, computer architects and language experts" [533, p. 1]. Unfortunately, there has been no equivalent with similar success in the area of parallel computing.

One reason for this issue is the diversity of parallel architectures. To name only a few distinctions, which can also be found in Kumar et al. [503, Chapter 2], parallel machines differ in the control mechanism (SIMD vs. MIMD), address-space organization (message passing vs. shared memory), the interconnection networks (dynamic vs. static with different topologies), and processor granularity (computation-communication speed ratio). This granularity is referred to as *fine-grained* for machines with a low computation-communication speed ratio and as *coarse-grained* for machines with a high ratio. As a consequence of this diversity, it is considered rather natural that a number of different parallel computing models have emerged over time (cf. [379, 533, 539, 743]).

While shared-memory and network models, presented in Sections 5.3.1 and 5.3.2, dominated the design of parallel algorithms in the 1980's [798, Chapters 17 and 18], their shortcomings regarding performance prediction or portability have led to new developments. Valiant's seminal work on bulk-synchronous parallel processing [789], introduced in 1990, spawned a large number of works on parallel models trying to bridge the gap between simplicity and realism. These bridging models are explained in Section 5.3.3.

In Section 5.3.5 we present an algorithmic example and comparisons for the most relevant models and argue why some of them are favored over others today. Yet, considering recent works on different models, it is not totally clear even today which model is the best one. In particular because the field of parallel computing experiences a dramatic change: Besides traditional dedicated supercomputers with hundreds or thousands of processors, standard desktop processors with multiple cores and specialized multicore accelerators play an ever increasing role.

Note that this chapter focuses on parallel *models* rather than the complete process of parallel Algorithm Engineering; for many important aspects of the latter, the reader is referred to Bader et al. [56].

5.3.1 PRAM

The parallel random access machine (PRAM) was introduced in the late 1970s and is a straightforward extension of the sequential RAM model [300]. It consists of p processors that operate synchronously under the control of a common clock. They have each a private memory unit, but also access to a single global (or shared) memory for interprocessor communication (see [432, p. 9ff.]). Two measures determine the quality of a PRAM algorithm, the *time* and the *work*. Time denotes the number of parallel time steps an algorithm requires, work the product of time and the number of processors employed. Alternatively, work can be seen as the total number of operations executed by all processors. Three basic models are usually distinguished based on the shared memory access, more precisely if a cell may be read or written by more than one processor within the same timestep. Since there exist efficient simulations between these models, concurrent access does not increase the algorithmic power of the corresponding models dramatically [432, p. 496ff.].

The PRAM model enables the algorithm designer to identify the inherent parallelism in a problem and therefore allows the development of architecture-independent parallel algorithms [379]. However, it does not take the cost of interprocessor communication into account. Since the model assumes that global memory accesses are not more expensive than local ones, which is far from reality, its speedup prediction is typically inconsistent with the speedups observed on real parallel machines. This limitation has been addressed by tailor-made hardware [632, 806] and a number of extensions (cf. [23, 533] and the references therein). It can also be overcome by using models that reflect the underlying hardware more accurately, which leads us to the so-called network models.

5.3.2   Network Models

In a network model the processors are represented by nodes of an undirected graph whose edges stand for communication links between the processors. Since each processor has its own local memory and no global shared memory is present, these links are used to send communication messages between processors. During each algorithm step every node can perform local computations and communication with its neighbor nodes. If the algorithm designer uses a network model with the same topology as the actual machine architecture that is supposed to run the algorithm, the performance inconsistencies of the PRAM can be removed. However, porting an algorithm from one platform to another without a severe performance loss is often not easy. This portability issue is the reason why the use of network models is discouraged today for the development of parallel algorithms (see, e. g., [198]). For more results on these models we refer the interested reader to the textbooks of Akl [22] and Leighton [514], who present extensive discussions and many algorithms for various representatives of networks, e. g., arrays, meshes, hypercubes, and butterflies.

5.3.3   Bridging Models

The issues mentioned before and the convergence in parallel computer architectures towards commodity processors with large memory have led to the development of bridging models [198, 199]. They attempt to span the range between algorithm design and parallel computer architecture [332] by addressing the issues experienced with previous models, in particular by accounting for interprocessor communication costs and by making only very general assumptions about

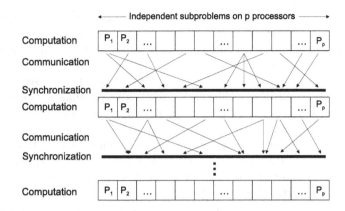

Fig. 5.7. Schematic view of a sequence of supersteps in a BSP computation

the underlying hardware. The presentation in this section is mainly in historical order, mentioning only the most relevant bridging models and important variations.

Bulk-Synchronous Parallel Model and its Variants. The bulk-synchronous parallel (BSP) model [789] consists of a number of sequential processors with local memory, a network router that delivers messages directly between any pair of processors for interprocessor communication, and a mechanism for global synchronization at regular intervals. A BSP algorithm is divided into so-called *supersteps*, each of which consists of local computations on already present data, message transmissions and receptions. Between each superstep a synchronization takes place, as illustrated in Figure 5.7. This decoupling of computation and communication simplifies the algorithm design to reduce the likelihood of errors.

For the analysis of such an algorithm three parameters besides the input size n are used: the number of processors p, the minimum superstep duration l arising from communication latency and synchronization (compare [329]), and finally the gap g, which denotes the ratio between computation and communication speed of the whole system. The model assumes that delivering messages of maximum size h (so-called *h-relations*) within one superstep requires $gh + l$ machine cycles. This accounts for the cost of communication by integrating memory speed and bandwidth into the model. Hence, the cost of a superstep is $w + gh + l$, where w denotes the maximum number of machine cycles over all processors required for local computation in this superstep. The cost of the complete algorithm is the sum of all supersteps' costs. Another measure sometimes used is called *slackness* or *slack*. It refers to the lower bound of n/p from which on the algorithm's runtime achieves an asymptotically optimal, i. e., linear, speedup.

On some parallel machines very small messages exhibit significant overhead due to message startup costs and/or latency. This can lead to a severe misestimation of an algorithm's performance [444]. Therefore, one variation of Valiant's original model called BSP* [76] addresses the granularity of messages by introducing a parameter B, the "optimum" message size to fully exploit the bandwidth of the router. Messages smaller than B generate the same costs as messages of size B, thus enforcing their algorithmic grouping to achieve higher communication granularity.

Many parallel machines can be partitioned into smaller subsets of processors where communication within each subset is faster than between different ones (consider, e. g., the BlueGene/L supercomputer architecture [778], a cluster of symmetric multiprocessors, or grid computing with parallel machines at different sites). This fact is incorporated in the decomposable BSP model [209], abbreviated D-BSP. Here the set of processors can be recursively decomposed into independent subsets. For each level i of this decomposition hierarchy, the p processors are partitioned into 2^i fixed and disjoint groups called i-clusters ($p = 2^k$, $k \in \mathbb{N}$, $0 \leq i \leq \log p$). A D-BSP program proceeds then as a sequence of labeled supersteps, where in an i-superstep, $0 \leq i < \log p$, communication and synchronization takes place only within the current i-clusters. Messages are of constant size and each level i of the decomposition hierarchy has its own gap g_i, where it is natural to assume that the gap increases when one moves towards level 0 of the hierarchy, thereby rewarding locality of computation. According to Bilardi et al. [99], D-BSP models real parallel architectures more effectively than BSP. As usual, this comes along with a more complicated model.

Coarse-Grained Multicomputer. Observed speedups of BSP algorithms may be significantly lower than expected if the parameter g and the communication overhead are high, which is true for many loosely-coupled systems like clusters. This is mainly due to the impact of small messages and has led to the coarse-grained multicomputer (CGM) model [216]. CGM enforces coarse-grained communication by message grouping, a similar idea as in the BSP* model, but without using an additional model parameter. It consists of p processors with $O(\frac{n}{p})$ local memory each, which are connected by an arbitrary connection network (even shared memory is allowed).

Analogous to BSP, an algorithm consists of supersteps that decouple computation and communication. The main difference is that during each communication round every processor groups all the messages for one target into a single message and sends and receives in total $O(\frac{n}{p})$ data items with high probability. Furthermore, communication calls can be seen as variations of global sorting operations on the input data, which facilitates a simple estimation of communication costs. Typically, the total running time is given as the sum of computation and communication costs, where the number of communication rounds (and therefore supersteps) is desired to be constant. Coarse-grained parallel algorithms based on the CGM model have become quite popular, e. g., see two special issues of Algorithmica on coarse-grained parallel computing [212, 213].

QSM. The authors of the Queuing Shared Memory (QSM) model advocate a shared-memory model enriched by some important architectural characteristics such as bandwidth constraints [332]. Their main argument is that a shared-memory model allows for a smooth transition from sequential algorithm design to symmetric multiprocessors and, ultimately, massively parallel systems. Consequently, the QSM model consists of a number of homogeneous processors with local memory that communicate by reading from and writing to shared memory. Like BSP this model assumes program execution in phases between which synchronization is performed. Within each phase one is free to interleave the possible operations shared-memory read, shared-memory write, and local computation arbitrarily. The only parameters used are the number of processors p and the computation-communication gap g.

Shared-memory accesses during a phase may access the same location either reading or writing (but not both) and complete by the end of that phase. For the cost analysis one determines the cost of a single phase, which is the maximum of the costs for the three following operations: maximum number of local operations, gap g times the maximum number of shared-memory reads or writes, and the maximum shared-memory contention. The cost of the complete algorithm is again the sum of all phase costs.

5.3.4   Recent Work

Bridging Models. To cover follow-up research, we first turn our attention to heterogeneous parallel computing, where one uses a heterogeneous multicomputer by combining different types of machines over different types of network. This can be viewed as a precursor to grid computing. Hence, the two extensions of CGM and BSP that incorporate heterogeneity, HCGM [587] and HBSP [836], might be of interest there. Both models account for differing processor speeds, but possible network differences are not distinguished. This issue and limited success of heterogeneous high performance computing may prevent a wide applicability of these models without modifications.

A more recent bridging model is PRO [322], a restriction of BSP and CGM whose main characteristic is the comparison of all metrics to a specific sequential algorithm A_{seq} with time and space complexity $T(n)$ and $S(n)$, respectively. Similar to CGM, the underlying machine consists of p processors having $M = O(S(n)/p)$ local memory each, where a coarseness of $M \geq p$ is assumed. The execution proceeds in supersteps of separated computation and communication. The latter is performed with grouped messages and costs one time unit per word sent or received. Interestingly, the quality measure of PRO is not the time (which is enforced to be in $O(T(n)/p)$), but the range of values for p that facilitate a linear speedup w.r.t. A_{seq}. This measure is called Grain(n) and shown to be in $O(\sqrt{S(n)})$ due to the coarseness assumed in the model. The better of two PRO algorithms solving the same problem with the same underlying sequential algorithm is therefore the one with higher grain.

As noted before, there are a large number of other parallel computing models, mostly modifications of the presented ones, dealing with some of their issues. Yet, since they have not gained considerable importance and an exhaustive presentation of this vast topic is outside the scope of this work, we refer the interested reader to the books [22,192,193,503,514,660], the surveys [190,379,465,533,539, 743], and [332,353,790].

Multicore Computing: Algorithmic Models and Programming Frameworks. Most models that have been successful in the 1990s do not assume shared memory but incorporate some form of explicit inter-processor communication. This is due to the widespread emergence of cluster computers and other machines with distributed memory and message passing communication during that time. Meanwhile nearly all standard CPUs built today are already parallel processors because they contain multiple computing cores. The idiosyncracies of this architectural change need to be reflected in the computational model if algorithms are to be transformed into efficient programs for multicore processors or parallel machines of a large number of multicore CPUs.

One particular issue, which combines the topics hierarchical memory and parallel computing, is the *sharing* of caches. In modern multicore processors it is common that the smallest cache levels are private to a core. However, usually the larger the cache level is, the more cores share the same cache. Savage and Zubair [701] address cache sharing with the universal multicore model (UMM). They introduce the Multicore Memory Hierarchy Game (MMHG), a pebbling game on a DAG that models the computations. By means of the MMHG Savage and Zubair derive general lower bounds on the communication complexity between different hierarchy levels and apply these bounds to scientific and financial applications.

With the prevalence of multicore chips with shared memory the PRAM model seems to experience a renaissance. While it is still regarded as hardly realistic, it recently serves as a basis for more practical approaches. Dorrigiv et al. [253] suggest the LoPRAM (low degree parallelism PRAM) model. Besides having two different thread types, the model assumes that an algorithm with input size n is executed on at most $\mathcal{O}(\log n)$ processors – instead of $\mathcal{O}(n)$ as in the PRAM model. Dorrigiv et al. show that for a wide range of divide-and-conquer algorithms optimal speedup can be obtained. Vishkin et al. [806] propose a methodology for converting PRAM algorithms into explicit multi-threading (XMT) programs. The XMT framework includes a programming model that resembles the PRAM, but relaxes the synchronous processing of individual steps. Moreover, the framework includes a compiler of XMTC (an extension of the C language) to a PRAM-on-chip hardware architecture. Recent studies suggest that XMT allows for an easier implementation of parallel programs than MPI [399] and that important parallel algorithms perform faster on the XMT PRAM-on-chip processor than on a standard dual-core CPU [150].

Valiant extends his BSP model to hierarchical multicore machines [791]. This extension is done by assuming d hierarchy levels with four BSP parameters each, i. e., level i has parameters (p_i, g_i, L_i, m_i), where p_i denotes the number of subcomponents in level i, g_i their bandwidth, L_i the cost of synchronizing them, and m_i the memory/cache size of level i. For the problems of associative composition, matrix multiplication, fast Fourier transform, and sorting, lower bounds on the communication and synchronization complexity are given. Also, for the problems stated above, algorithms are described that are optimal w. r. t. to communication and synchronization up to constant factors.

A more practical approach to map BSP algorithms to modern multicore hardware is undertaken by Hou et al. [413]. They extend C by a few parallel constructs to obtain the new programming language BSGP. Programs written in BSGP are compiled into GPU kernel programs that are executable by a wide range of modern graphics processors.

The trend to general purpose computations on GPUs can be explained by the much higher peak performance of these highly parallel systems compared to standard CPUs. Govindaraju et al. [350] try to capture the most important properties of GPU architectures in a cache-aware model. They then develop cache-efficient scientific algorithms for the GPU. In experiments these new algorithms clearly outperform their optimized CPU counterparts.

The technological change to multicore processors requires not only algorithmic models for the design of theoretically efficient algorithms, but also suitable programming frameworks that allow for an efficient implementation. Among these frameworks are:

- OpenMP [161], Cilk++ [174], and Threading Building Blocks [667] are APIs or runtime environments for which the programmer identifies independent tasks. When the compiled application program is executed, the runtime environment takes care of technical details such as thread creation and deletion and thus relieves the programmer from this burden.
- Chapel [155], Fortress [24], Unified Parallel C (UPC) [95], Sequoia [282], and X10 [162] are parallel programming languages, whose breakthrough for commercial purposes has yet to come.
- CUDA [617], Stream [8], and OpenCL [473] are intended for a simplified programming of heterogeneous systems with CPUs and GPUs, in case of OpenCL also with other accelerators instead of GPUs.

A further explanation of these works is outside the scope of this chapter since their main objective is implementation rather than algorithm design.

5.3.5   Application and Comparison

In this section, we indicate how to develop and analyze parallel algorithms in some of the models presented above. The naive matrix multiplication algorithm serves here again as an example. Note that we do not intend to teach the development of parallel algorithms in detail, for this we refer to the textbooks stated in the previous section. Instead, we wish to use the insights gained from the example problem as well as from other results to compare these models and argue why some are more relevant than others for today's parallel algorithm engineering.

Algorithm 4. PRAM algorithm for standard matrix multiplication

---

The processors are labelled as $P(i,j,k), 0 \le i,j,k < p^{1/3}$.

1: $P(i,j,k)$ computes $C'(i,j,k) = A(i,k) \cdot B(k,j)$
2: **for** $h := 1$ **to** $\log n$ **do**
3:    **if** $(k \le \frac{n}{2^h})$ **then**
4:       $P(i,j,k)$ sets $C'(i,j,k) := C'(i,j,2k-1) + C'(i,j,2k)$
5: **if** $(k = 1)$ **then**
6:    $P(i,j,k)$ sets $C(i,j) := C'(i,j,1)$

Algorithm 5. BSP algorithm for standard matrix multiplication

---

Let **A** and **B** be distributed uniformly, but arbitrarily, across the p processors denoted by $P(i,j,k)$, $0 \le i,j,k < p^{1/3}$. Moreover, let $\mathbf{A}[i,j]$ denote the $s \times s$ submatrix of **A** with $s := n/p^{1/3}$. Define $\mathbf{B}[i,j]$ and $\mathbf{C}[i,j]$ analogously.

1: $P(i,j,k)$ acquires the elements of $\mathbf{A}[i,j]$ and $\mathbf{B}[j,k]$.
2: $P(i,j,k)$ computes $\mathbf{A}[i,j] \cdot \mathbf{B}[j,k]$ and sends each resulting value to the processor responsible for computing the corresponding entry in **C**.
3: $P(i,j,k)$ computes each of its final n^2/p elements of **C** by adding the values received for these elements.

Algorithm Design Example. Algorithm 4 [432, p. 15f.] performs matrix multiplication on a PRAM with concurrent read access to the shared memory. Here and in the following two examples we assume that the algorithm (or program) is run by all processors in parallel, which are distinguished by their unique label. The algorithm's idea is to perform all necessary multiplications in $\log n$ parallel steps with $n^3/\log n$ processors (Step 1) and to compute the sums of these products in $\log n$ parallel steps (Steps 4 and 6). The latter can be done by means of a binary tree-like algorithm which sums n numbers in the following way: Sum the index pair $2i-1$ and $2i, 1 \le i \le n/2$ in parallel to obtain $n/2$ numbers and proceed recursively. Hence, for the second step $O(n^3)$ processors require $O(\log n)$ steps. This would lead to a time complexity of $O(\log n)$ and a suboptimal work complexity, because the processor-time product would be $O(n^3 \log n)$. However, it is not difficult to see that Step 4 can be scheduled such that $O(n^3/\log n)$ processors suffice to finish the computation in $O(\log n)$ timesteps, resulting in the optimal work complexity for this algorithm of $O(n^3)$.

This algorithm illustrates both the strength and the weakness of the PRAM model. While it makes the inherent parallelism in the problem visible, the assumption to have $p = n^3/\log n$ processors to solve a problem of size $n \times n$ is totally unrealistic today. On the other hand we can use the idea of emulating the algorithm with only $p' < p$ processors. If each of the p' processors operates on a block of the matrix instead of a single element, we already have an idea how a coarse-grained algorithm might work.

Indeed, Algorithm 5, due to McColl and Valiant [543], performs matrix multiplication in the BSP model by working on matrix blocks. Its cost analysis

Algorithm 6. CGM and PRO algorithm for standard matrix multiplication

Let the matrices $\mathbf{A}$ and $\mathbf{B}$ be distributed onto the processors blockwise such that processor $P(i,j)$ stores $\mathbf{A}[i,j]$, the $s \times s$ ($s = n/p^{1/2}$) submatrix of $\mathbf{A}$, and $\mathbf{B}[i,j]$, $0 \le i,j < p^{1/2}$.

1: $P(i,j)$ computes $\mathbf{C}[i,j] := \mathbf{A}[i,j] \cdot \mathbf{B}[i,j]$.
2: **for** superstep $i := 1$ to $p^{1/2}$ **do**
3:     $P(i,j)$ sends the block of $\mathbf{A}$ processed in the previous step to $P(i,(j+1)$ mod $p^{1/2})$ and receives the new block from $P(i,(j-1)$ mod $p^{1/2})$.
4:     $P(i,j)$ sends the block of $\mathbf{B}$ processed in the previous step to $P((i+1)$ mod $p^{1/2},j)$ and receives the new block from $P((i-1)$ mod $p^{1/2},j)$.
5:     $P(i,j)$ determines the product of the current submatrices of $\mathbf{A}$ and $\mathbf{B}$ and adds the result to $\mathbf{C}[i,j]$.

proceeds as follows: the first superstep requires the communication of $n^2/p^{2/3}$ values, resulting in $O(g \cdot n^2/p^{2/3} + l)$ time steps. Computation and communication of Superstep 2 account together for $O(n^3/p + g \cdot n^2/p^{2/3} + l)$ time steps and the final superstep requires costs of $O(n^2/p^{2/3} + l)$. This yields a total runtime of $O(n^3/p + g \cdot n^2/p^{2/3} + l)$, which is optimal in terms of communication costs for any BSP implementation of standard matrix multiplication [543]. Algorithm 5 is therefore best possible in the sense that it achieves all lower bounds for computation, communication, and synchronization costs. Note that the memory consumption can be reduced at the expense of increased communication costs [544], a basic variant of which is presented in the following paragraph.

Recall that the CGM model requires that communication is grouped and may not to exceed $O(n^2/p)$ values per round (note that the input size of the considered problem is n^2 instead of n). Hence, the blocking and communication scheme of the algorithm above has to be adapted. First, this is done by setting $s := n/p^{1/2}$. Then, using the definitions from Algorithm 5 and assuming for simplicity that s and $p^{1/2}$ are integers, we obtain Algorithm 6, which is briefly mentioned by McColl [543].

It is easy to verify that the computation costs account for $O(n^3/p)$ and the communication costs for $O(n^2/p^{1/2})$ cycles. Thus, it becomes a valid CGM algorithm with $O(p^{1/2})$ communication rounds and can also be used in the PRO model with the desired speedup property. To compute the quality measure Grain(n), observe that the communication within the loop must not be more expensive than the computation. This is fulfilled whenever $n^3/p^{3/2} \ge n^2/p \Leftrightarrow p \le n^2$ and we obtain with the coarseness assumption the optimal grain of $O(n)$.

The examples for the more realistic bridging models show that blocking and grouping of data is not only essential in the external memory setting but also for parallel algorithms. It is sometimes even better to perform more internal work than necessary if thereby the communication volume can be reduced. Note that this connection between the two computational models is no coincidence since both aim at the minimization of communication. For the I/O model communication means data transfers to/from the external disk, for parallel models it refers to inter-processor communication. Before we investigate this connection in more detail in Section 5.4, the bridging models discussed above are compared.

Further Model Comparison. The reasons for discouraging the sole use of PRAM and network models for parallel algorithm development have already been discussed before. In this brief comparison we therefore focus on the major bridging models.

The main aim of another bridging model, called LogP [198], is to capture machine characteristics for appropriate performance prediction. This burdens the algorithm designer with the issue of stalling due to network contention and nondeterminism within the communication. Since it has been shown that stall-free LogP programs can be efficiently emulated on a BSP machine (and vice versa) [100], this has led to the conclusion that BSP offers basically the same opportunities as LogP while being easier to deal with. Consequently, apart from a number of basic algorithms for LogP, there seems to be little interest in further results on design and analysis of LogP algorithms (compare [661] and [187]).

A similar argument applies to QSM, because it can also be emulated efficiently on a BSP machine (and vice versa) [332, 661]. Although QSM can be used to estimate the practical performance of PRAM algorithms and it requires only two parameters, it seems that it has had only limited success compared to BSP related models based on point-to-point messages. This might be due to the fact that it does not reward large messages and that more focus was put on massively parallel systems rather than shared-memory machines. It remains to be seen if some QSM ideas might experience a revival with the ubiquity of multicore CPUs.

One restriction of the coarse-grained models BSP, CGM (and also PRO, which has yet to prove its broad applicability) is their disregard of actual communication patterns. Although some patterns are more expensive than others, this is not incorporated into the models and can show large differences between estimated and actual performance [353, 444]. Nevertheless, for many algorithms and applications these models and their extensions provide a reasonably accurate performance and efficiency estimate. Their design capabilities capture the most important aspects of parallel computers. Moreover, the analysis can be performed with a small set of parameters for many parallel architectures that are in use today and in the near future. Another reason for the wide acceptance of BSP and CGM might be their support of message passing. This type of interprocessor communication has been standardized by the Message Passing Interface Forum[3] as the MPI library [747], whose implementations are now probably the most widely used communication tools in distributed-memory parallel computers.

All this has led to the fact that BSP and CGM have been used more extensively than other models to design parallel algorithms in recent years [187]. Even libraries that allow for an easy implementation of BSP and CGM algorithms have been developed. Their implementations are topics of a success story on parallel computing models in Section 5.6.

---

[3] See http://www.mpi-forum.org/

Given the convergence of parallel machines and networking hardware to commodity computing and the prevalence of multicore CPUs with shared memory and deep memory hierarchies, a model that combines these features in a both realistic and simple way would certainly be valuable, as Cormen and Goodrich already expressed in 1996 [190]. Recently, Arge et al. [43] have proposed the Parallel External-Memory model as a natural parallel extension of the external-memory model of Aggarwal and Vitter [11], to private-cache chip multiprocessors.

On the other hand, the connection between parallel and external memory algorithms has been investigated by stating efficient simulations of parallel algorithms in external memory. These results are presented in the upcoming section.

5.4   Simulating Parallel Algorithms for I/O-Efficiency

Previously in this chapter we have presented several models and various techniques for I/O-efficiency, cache optimization, and parallel computing. Generally speaking, I/O-efficient algorithms are employed to deal with massive data sets in the presence of a memory hierarchy, while parallel computing is more concerned with the acceleration of the actual on-chip computations by dividing the work between several processors. It might not be a surprise that there are some similarities between the models and techniques. In cases where one needs to process extremely large data sets with high computational power, methods from both fields need to be combined. Unfortunately, there is no model that incorporates all the necessary characteristics.

In this section we show the connection of the concepts presented previously and indicate how to derive sequential and parallel external memory algorithms by simulation. Generally speaking, simulations transform known parallel algorithms for a given problem P into an external memory algorithm solving P. The key idea is to model inter-processor communication as external memory accesses. Since efficient parallel algorithms aim at the minimization of communication, one can often derive I/O-efficient algorithms this way. Note, however, that the simulation concept should be thought of as a guide for designing algorithms, rather than for implementing them.

First, we explain a simulation of PRAM algorithms in Section 5.4.1. Since there exists an obvious similarity between bulkwise inter-processor communication and blockwise access to external memory, one would also expect I/O-efficient simulation results of coarse-grained parallel algorithms. Indeed, a number of such simulations have been proposed; they are discussed in Section 5.4.2.

5.4.1   PRAM Simulation

The first simulation we describe obtains I/O-efficient algorithms from simulating PRAM algorithms [168]. Its value stems from the fact that it enables the efficient transfer of the vast amount of PRAM algorithms into the external memory setting. The key idea is to show that a single step of a PRAM algorithm processing n data items can be simulated in $O(sort(n))$ I/Os. For this consider a PRAM algorithm A that utilizes n processors and $O(n)$ space and runs in time $O(T(n))$. Let each processor perform w.l.o.g. within a single PRAM step $O(1)$ shared-memory (SM) reads, followed by $O(1)$ steps for local computation and $O(1)$ shared-memory writes. We now simulate A on an external memory machine with one processor. For this assume that the state information of the PRAM processors and the SM content are stored on disk in a suitable format.

The desired transformation of an arbitrary single step of A starts by simulating the SM read accesses that provide the operands for the computation. This requires a scan of the processor contexts to store the read accesses and their memory locations. These values are then sorted according to the indices of the SM locations. Then, this sorted list of read requests is scanned and the contents of the corresponding SM locations are retrieved and stored with their requests. These combined values are again sorted, this time according to the ID of the processor performing the request. By scanning this sorted copy, the operands can be transferred to the respective processor. After that, we perform the computations on each simulated processor and write the results to disk. These results are sorted according to the memory address to which the processors would store them. The sorted list and a reserved copy of memory are finally scanned and merged to obtain the previous order with the updated entries. This can all be done with $O(1)$ scans and $O(1)$ sorts for n entries, so that simulating all steps of A requires $O(T(n) \cdot sort(n))$ I/Os in total.

This simulation has a noteworthy property in case of PRAM algorithms where the number of active processors decreases geometrically with the number of steps. By this, we mean that after a constant number of steps, the number of active processors (those that actually perform operations instead of being idle) and the number of memory cells used afterwards has decreased by a constant factor. Typically, the work performed by these algorithms, i.e., their processor-time product, is not optimal due to the high number of inactive processors. These inactive processors, however, do not need to be simulated in the external memory setting. One can therefore show that such a non-optimal PRAM algorithm leads to the same simulation time of $O(T(n) \cdot sort(n))$ I/Os as above, which means that the non-optimal work property of the simulated algorithm does not transfer to the algorithm obtained by simulation.

5.4.2 Coarse-Grained Parallel Simulation Results

The simulations of coarse-grained parallel algorithms shown in this section resemble the PRAM simulation. They also assume that the state information of the simulated processors are stored on disk, and they simulate one superstep after the other. This means that one reads the processor *context* (memory image and message buffers) from disk first and then simulates incoming communication, computation, and outgoing communication, before the updated context is written back to disk. However, the actual implementations need to consider the idiosyncrasies of the different coarse-grained parallel models.

Note that the virtual processors of the parallel algorithm are simulated by a possibly smaller number p of processors in the external memory model. Then, the simulation starts with processors $0, \ldots, p - 1$, proceeds with the next p processors, and so on. This serialization of the parallel program is valid due to the independence of processors within the same superstep. Recall that M denotes the size of the internal memory and B the block size in the EM model.

Single-processor Simulations. Since it is based on a simple framework, we proceed our explanation with the sequential simulation of *BSP-like* algorithms [734]. A BSP-like algorithm assumes the memory space to be partitioned into p blocks of suitable size. It proceeds in discrete supersteps, is executed on a virtual machine with p processors, and satisfies the following conditions (cmp. [734, Definition 1]):

- In superstep $s, s \geq 1$, processor $p_i, 0 \leq i < p$, operates only on the data in block $\mathcal{B}_i$ and on the messages $Mes(j, i, s), 0 \leq j < p$.
- In superstep $s, s \geq 1$, processor $p_i, 0 \leq i < p$, generates messages $Mes(i, j, s+ 1)$ to be 'sent' to $p_j, 0 \leq j < p$. The size of each message is at most $M/3p$. The initial messages of timestep 1 are void.

Then, the simulation can proceed for each superstep as described at the beginning of this section. In each superstep processor $p_i, 0 \leq i < p$, fetches $\mathcal{B}_i$ and its respective message buffers $Mes(j, i, s), 0 \leq j < p$, from disk, simulates the computations of the superstep, and stores the updated block $\mathcal{B}_i$ as well as new message buffers to disk in suitable locations.

For these BSP-like algorithms new parameters $P = \lceil 3 \cdot n/M \rceil, G$, and L are introduced to relate coarse-grained models to the EM model. The I/O transfer gap G denotes the ratio of the number of local computation operations and the number of words that can be transferred between memory and disks per unit time, while L denotes the synchronization time of the simulation. They measure the quality of their simulation by the notion of c-optimality [329], which is transferred to the I/O setting. An EM algorithm is called c-*optimal* if its execution time is at most c times larger than that of a sequential computer with infinite memory. The main result states that if the BSP parameters (p, g, l) coincide with the new parameters (P, G, L) and there is a c-optimal BSP algorithm for the same problem, then the corresponding BSP-like algorithm in external memory is also c-optimal [734, Theorem 3].

If one accepts that the external memory size is bounded from above by M^2 (which is a reasonable assumption), the simulation of PRO algorithms in external memory is another option [370]. It introduces the notion of RAM-*awareness*, which provides a measure for the number of random memory accesses that might correspond to page faults. If this measure of a PRO algorithm A on $p = \text{Grain}(n)$ processors does not exceed the sequential runtime of the underlying algorithm and A requires $T(n)$ time and $S(n)$ space over all processors, A can be simulated in $O(T(n))$ computation time with $O(S(n)/\operatorname{Grain}(n) + \operatorname{Grain}(n))$ internal and $O(S(n))$ external memory.

Multiple-processor Simulations.   Dehne et al. [215, 214] show how to simulate algorithms for the models BSP, BSP*, and CGM on sequential and parallel machines with parallel disks. These combined models are then called EM-BSP, EM-BSP*, and EM-CGM, respectively, and extend the parameter set of their underlying parallel models by M (local memory size for each processor), D (number of parallel disks connected to each processor), B (transfer block size), and G (I/O transfer gap in terms of memory block transfer). More precisely, the simulation costs are the same as for the simulated program plus the costs induced by I/O, which is taken as the maximum over all processors.

As above, the simulation of the v virtual processors is performed in supersteps. During each such superstep every simulating processor loads the context of the virtual processors for which it is responsible from the disk. Whenever virtual communication is replaced by parallel disk I/O, care is taken that irregular routing schemes are mapped to disks in a balanced way to obtain optimal I/O costs. Amongst others, this is done by setting the total communication amount of each processor to $\Theta(n/v)$ and by fixing the message size to $c \cdot B$ for some $c \geq 1$, which resembles the idea of BSP*.

The c-optimality notion [329] is extended from local computation to cover also communication and I/O. Using this, one can show that a work-optimal, communication-efficient, and I/O-efficient algorithm can be simulated with a small overhead by an algorithm that is also work-optimal, communication-efficient, and I/O-efficient for a wide range of parameters by using the techniques of Dehne et al. [215]. There, it is also shown that these methods have led to improved parallel EM algorithms.

Cache-Oblivious Simulation of D-BSP.   For the final topic of this section, our simulation target is one level higher in the memory hierarchy. More precisely, we simulate D-BSP programs to achieve sequential cache-oblivious algorithms [636]. (Related simulation results are also presented by Bilardi et al. [99].) The technique exploits that the D-BSP model assumes a hierarchical decomposition of a BSP computer in processor groups to capture submachine locality. Recall that the cache in the Ideal Cache Model (ICM) contains M words organized into lines of B words each. It is fully associative and assumes the optimal offline strategy for cache-line replacement. To simulate a D-BSP program in the ICM in a cache-oblivious manner, the simulation algorithm for improving locality in a multilevel memory hierarchy [279] is adapted. First of all, the slower memory of the ICM hierarchy is divided into p blocks of size $\Theta(\mu)$, where μ is the size of one D-BSP processor context. Each block contains one processor context and some extra space for bookkeeping purposes.

Recall that each processor group on level i of the D-BSP hierarchy is called an i-cluster. Its processors collaborate with each other in an i-superstep. Therefore, the simulation proceeds in rounds, where each round simulates one i-superstep for a certain i-cluster in two phases (local computation and communication) and determines the cluster for the next round. Message distribution for intra-cluster communication is simulated by sorting the contexts of the processors involved, similar to the method proposed by Fantozzi et al. [279]. In particular by simulating the same cluster in consecutive supersteps, this simulation strategy is able to improve the locality of reference, because the necessary processor contexts are already cached. If sorting the processors' contexts for simulating communication is done in a cache-oblivious manner, the whole algorithm is cache-oblivious since it does not make use of the parameters M and B.

5.5 Success Stories of Algorithms for Memory Hierarchies

In this section we describe some implementations of algorithms for memory hierarchies that have improved the running time on very large inputs considerably in practice.

5.5.1 Cache-Oblivious Sorting

Brodal et al. [135] show that a careful implementation of a cache-oblivious lazy funnelsort algorithm [131] outperforms several widely used library implementations of quicksort on uniformly distributed data. For the largest instances in the RAM, this implementation outperforms its nearest rival std::sort from the STL library included in GCC 3.2 by 10-40% on many different architectures like Pentium III, Athlon and Itanium 2. Compared to cache-aware sorting implementations exploiting L1 and L2 caches, TLBs and registers [41, 504, 843, 782], the cache-oblivious implementation is not only more robust – it exploits several levels of memory hierarchy simultaneously – but also faster. Overall, the results of Brodal et al. [135] show that for sorting, the overhead involved in being cache-oblivious can be small enough in order to allow nice theoretical properties to actually transfer into practical advantages.

5.5.2 External Memory BFS

The implementation of the external memory BFS algorithms [600, 555] exploiting disk parallelism on a low cost machine makes BFS viable for massive graphs [19, 20]. On many different classes of graphs, this implementation computes BFS level decomposition of around billion-edge graphs in few *hours* which would have taken the traditional RAM model BFS algorithm [191] several *months*. In fact, the difference between the RAM model algorithm and the external memory algorithms is clearly visible even when more than half of the graph fits in the internal memory. As shown in Figure 5.8, the running time of the traditional BFS algorithm significantly deviates from the predicted RAM performance taking *hours*, rather than *minutes* for random graphs less than double the size of the internal memory. On the other hand, the external BFS implementations referred to as MR_BFS and MM_BFS in the plot, compute the BFS level decomposition in a few *minutes*.

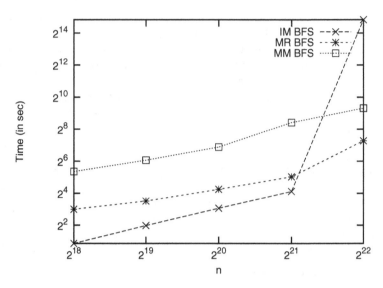

Fig. 5.8. Running time of the RAM model BFS algorithm IM_BFS [191] and the external memory BFS algorithms MR_BFS [600] and MM_BFS [555] with respect to the number of nodes (n) of a random graph. The number of edges is always kept at $4n$.

5.5.3 External Suffix Array Construction

The suffix array, a lexicographically sorted array of the suffixes of a string, has received considerable attention lately because of its applications in string matching, genome analysis and text compression. However, most known implementations of suffix array construction could not handle inputs larger than 2 GB. Dementiev et al. [229] show that external memory computation of suffix arrays is feasible. They provide a EM implementation that can process much larger character strings in hours on low cost hardware. In fact, the running time of their implementation is significantly faster than previous external memory implementations.

5.5.4 External A*-Search

In many application domains like model checking and route planning, the state space often grows beyond the available internal memory. Edelkamp et al. [267] propose and implement an external version of A* to search in such state spaces. Embedding their approach in the model checking software SPIN, they can detect deadlocks in an optical telegraph protocol for 20 stations, with an intermediate data requirement of 1.1 Terabytes on hard disk (with only 2.5 GB of available main memory).

5.6   Parallel Bridging Model Libraries

The number of publications on parallel algorithms developed for one of the major bridging models, in particular BSP and CGM, shows their success in the academic world. Moreover, following the Algorithm Engineering paradigm and for an easier use of these models in practice, library standards have been developed. The older one is the BSPlib standard [393], whose corresponding library implementations shall provide methods for the direct transformation of BSP algorithms into parallel applications. According to Bisseling [102], two efficient implementations exist, the Oxford BSP toolset [625] and the Paderborn University BSP library (PUB) [119]. A more recent implementation [766] has been developed, which facilitates the use of BSPlib on all platforms with the message-passing interface MPI. Its objective is to provide BSPlib on top of MPI, making the library portable to most parallel computers. CGMlib is a library following the same ideas for the coarse-grained multicomputer model. So far, there exists only one implementation known to the authors [157]. Although a widespread use of these libraries outside the academic world is not apparent, their influence should not be underestimated. They can, for instance, be used for a gentle introduction to parallel programming [102] and as a basis for distributed web/grid computing [344, 118].

Note that there exist many more languages, libraries, and tools for parallel programming, as well as applications, of course. Even an approximate description of these works would be outside the scope of this chapter. Since they are also not as close to the original models, we instead refer the interested reader to Fox et al. [305] and various handbooks on parallel computing [108, 147, 388, 494, 660]. They cover many aspects of parallel computing from the late 1980s until today.

5.7   Conclusion

The simple models RAM and PRAM have been of great use to designers of both sequential and parallel algorithms. However, they show severe deficiencies as well. The RAM model fails to capture the idiosyncrasies of large data sets that do not fit into main memory, the PRAM does not model the costs arising by inter-processor communication. Since both, parallel computation and the processing of very large data sets, have become more and more important in practice, this has led to the development of more realistic models of computation. The external memory (EM) model has proved to be quite successful in algorithm engineering on problems involving large data sets that do not fit in the main memory and thus, reside on the hard disk. In the parallel setting the bulk-synchronous approach (BSP) is very important, which models inter-processor communication explicitly. Several variants of both have been developed, e. g., to include the specifics of caches (ICM) or of coarse-grained communication (CGM). Although developed for different purposes, all these models have several strategies in common on how to avoid I/O transfer and communication, respectively, in particular the exploitation of locality and the grouping of data before their transmission.

Fundamental techniques for an efficient use of the memory hierarchy or of parallel computers have been illustrated by means of different external memory data structures, cache-aware, cache-oblivious, and parallel algorithms. This has been supplemented by a description of successful implementations of external memory algorithms that facilitate the efficient processing of very large data sets. Also, libraries for an easy implementation of parallel algorithms developed in one of the models mentioned above have been presented. These examples show the impact of realistic computational models on the design and practical implementation of algorithms for these purposes. Moreover, one can say that for very large data sets and complex parallel computations it is hardly possible nowadays to obtain efficient programs without using the techniques and ideas of the models presented in this chapter.

Despite these successes it should be noted that models necessarily have their disadvantages because they are only abstractions and simplifications of the real world. While the interest in new parallel models seemed to be decreasing until the mid 2000s, the general breakthrough of multicore processors has produced a number of new models and in particular practical programming frameworks (parallel languages, runtime environments, etc.). A rather simple model combining parallelism and memory hierarchy issues, in particular with automated optimizations in a hardware-oblivious way, would certainly be a step forward towards even more realistic performance prediction. The very recent proposals on multicore models have yet to prove their suitability in this regard. From a practical perspective it will be very interesting to see which developments in languages and runtime environments will experience widespread adoption both in academia *and* in industry. We believe that a mostly seamless transition from a realistic model to the actual implementation – as previously in the sequential case – will be the key to success.

Chapter 6. Implementation Aspects

Marc Mörig, Sven Scholz, Tobias Tscheuschner, and Eric Berberich

6.1 Introduction

The implementation of complex algorithms is a highly demanding task. Therefore, best practice rules and principles from software engineering should be applied whenever possible. The interested reader is referred to the multitude of textbooks in this field, for example [748, 568]. In this chapter, we focus only on selected issues which are particularly relevant to achieve the goals of Algorithm Engineering.

Papers are written for human readers, not machines. The description of an algorithm is typically written in a way that allows the reader to easily understand the algorithm and its key properties. This is achieved by focusing on the big picture, or in other words, omitting details, referencing to other papers for subtasks, and describing algorithms in pseudocode or totally verbal. Sometimes omitted details are highly nontrivial as in the case of geometric algorithms, where the description and correctness proof of an algorithm usually assume the Real RAM machine model. This model allows to store real numbers in $O(1)$ space and perform arithmetical operations in $O(1)$ time with them. In other cases the description contains errors. Mehlhorn and Mutzel [557] describe how an algorithm for recognizing planar graphs [412] can be augmented to construct a combinatorial planar embedding. They note that the original paper only stated that this could be done and later attempts to describe the needed modifications in detail contained errors. The authors found the errors only when trying to implement the modifications. The task of the implementer is to fill in details and "translate" the description into a programming language, until a variant of the algorithm has been created that can be processed reasonably fast by a computer. Experienced implementers essentially agree what constitutes a good implementation [561, Section 1.5], [278, 770, 246]. We have grouped these goals into four groups: an implementation should be correct, efficient, flexible and easy to use.

Correctness. Implementations must be correct. Having an incorrect implementation that may compute garbage without the user noticing it, is unacceptable. An implementation of an algorithm is correct if it performs according to the algorithm's specification. Correctness is therefore a matter of assuring that description and implementation coincide and may well be achieved by changing the specification. Often algorithms are sophisticated enough to be hard to implement correctly and programmers will make mistakes even in simple programs. Since proving the correctness of an implementation has been found to be very hard, techniques which increase our confidence in the correctness of an implementation are important.

M. Müller-Hannemann and S. Schirra (Eds.): Algorithm Engineering, LNCS 5971, pp. 237–289, 2010.

Efficiency. Implementations should be efficient. Efficiency will not only allow the user to solve small problems fast, but will also enable him to solve large problems in a reasonable time. In contrary to asymptotic running time, which is the common theoretical efficiency measure, for an implementation what matters is the running time for the input it is actually used for. This means that also constant factors must be tuned. Tuning can be guided by analysis (Chapter 4) and heuristic arguments, but mostly calls for experimentation (Chapter 8). Small changes in a critical part of the algorithm may well have a large impact on the running time. Efficiency and flexibility are competing goals. An algorithm in a library cannot be expected to perform as well as an implementation specialized for a certain application, but it should be more flexible and easy to use.

Flexibility. An implementation, especially in a library, should be flexible. Under flexibility, we cover several goals: modularity, reusability, extensibility, and adaptability. An implementation is modularized if it is separated into several parts, called modules, which interact only through well specified interfaces. Modularity supports correctness in the sense that the correctness of an implementation is reduced to the correctness of the modules and their interaction. Reusability and extensibility mean that it should be possible to easily develop further algorithms on top of the existing modules. All of the implemented functionality should be made available through a well-structured and well-specified interface. Adaptability asks for similar properties just from a different viewpoint. It should be possible to easily exchange modules of the implementation with modules from other implementations or libraries providing the same functionality. Last not least, a library could provide several modules with the same interface and identical or similar functionality. Flexibility, i.e., the ability to easily exchange data structures and subalgorithms and the availability of choices is a central goal of Algorithm Engineering. It enables the user to provide his own subalgorithms and data structures best fitting his problem, or choose the best combination from the available choices.

Ease of Use. An implementation should be easy to use. It must enable a new user to understand the interface and design quickly, so he can integrate the provided code into his own code easily. The main points that must be considered when trying to reach good usability are interface design and documentation. The interfaces should exhibit the complete functionality, without being too large. Common conventions for interfaces to different modules support usability as well, as consistently chosen names. The implementation should be accompanied by documentation that covers both the usage and the source code of the implementation. We view maintenance of an algorithmic software library also in connection with ease of use. Maintainability is supported by modularity and good documentation.

These are important goals, and pursuing all of them is a hard task. Some of them support each other but especially efficiency is hard to achieve while maintaining the other properties. It is therefore desirable to keep the implementation process itself efficient. There are tools and strategies supporting the implementer to this end. We have dedicated a section of this chapter to each of the central goals and to the implementation process itself.

The last section is devoted to geometric algorithms. These algorithms are described and proven to be correct under the assumption of exact real arithmetic. First attempts to implement these algorithm using hardware floating-point arithmetic failed. Straightforward implementations of exact number-types are however much slower than hardware floating-point numbers. It is an achievement of Algorithm Engineering that convenient to use, general and moderately efficient exact number-types are as well available as specialized highly efficient solutions to the exactness problem. We describe approaches for these number-types and answer the question, how geometric algorithms can be implemented both correctly and efficiently.

6.2 Correctness

6.2.1 Motivation and Description

Programs are written by human beings. Human beings sometimes make mistakes. Thus, programs sometimes contain mistakes. This section addresses the problem that programs might not always fulfill the job they are written for.

But what does it mean "(not) to fulfill the job?"

Definition 1. *[112] Let f be a function, P be a deterministic program that (seemingly) computes f and I be the set of all feasible inputs for f (resp. P). For $x \in I$ we call $f(x)$ (resp. $P(x)$) the output of f (resp. P) on the input x. P is called "correct" if $P(x) = f(x)$ for all $x \in I$, otherwise P is called "buggy".*

We will look at several methods, namely "testing", "checking", and "verifying" that detect — with different reliability — whether an implemented program satisfies its specification, i. e., the program is correct. And finally we have a look at methods that help us to debug the program if we found a bug: "Debugging".

6.2.2 Testing

In order to achieve correctness one should try to design for testing right from the beginning. Good programmers test early and often. Thinking about testing also helps to avoid errors and to clarify interfaces. In order to ease testing one should try to minimize dependencies. Checking assumptions and invariants helps a lot. Design for testing is of course closely related to designing for program checking.

Program testing is the process of executing a given program P on a subset T of I and verifying whether $P(x) = f(x)$ for all $x \in T$. If $P(x) \neq f(x)$ for any element $x \in T$, then we know that P is buggy, but we do not know whether the program is correct if $P(x) = f(x)$ for all $x \in T$ (except $T = I$). Thus, testing is rather the process of finding errors than of increasing the reliability of the program. Nevertheless, testing can provide some confidence in the correctness of a program.

Because in general the set of feasible inputs is too large, the central job in testing is to find a test set T for which it is likely to find an error. In the following, we will have a look at two of the common methods [236].

Random Data Generation. This is perhaps the easiest and weakest way to design test data. The data is randomly chosen from the set of possible inputs I.

A great advantage of this method is that it is applicable to all programs, and therefore a random testing procedure is easily reused. Furthermore, this method probably uncovers mistakes which occur in many instances. If, in addition, an "actual probability distribution on the input sequences" is given or a sampling procedure that reflects it, then one can estimate the "operational reliability" [264] of the program.

If there is no such distribution given, the random process naturally ignores possible structures in the input domain. Thus, important classes of test sets (e. g., classes of inputs which are often used in the lifetime of the program) may be left unexecuted. Moreover, independently from the question whether there is a probability distribution given on the input, the random data generation ignores any structure of the code itself (it is a so-called "black box method"). The following technique does consider the code (it is a "white box method").

Input Space Partitioning. As we have already seen, the main task of Program Testing is to find test data that is likely to reveal errors. In fact, it is hard to measure the probability of finding an error for a given test set.

The input space partitioning method — as the name says — partitions the input space into classes and executes P on one or more representative elements of each class. The goal is to identify classes for which the execution of elements leads to similar errors. Therefore, the selection of representatives of many different such classes should reveal many different errors.

For example the *statement coverage* demands on the test set that every statement of the code is executed at least once. In this case, the different classes are formed by the inputs that execute specific statements. It can easily be seen that these classes are not necessarily disjoint. Thus, the partition of the input space is not a partition in the common mathematical sense. Unfortunately the Statement Coverage may ignore specific classes of mistakes as we will see soon. Hence there are other input space partitioning methods, which we consider below. But first we have to state a definition:

Definition 2. *The* control flow graph *[331] is constructed from the code by means of some exemplary basic programming structures in the following way (see Fig. 6.1).*

- *Graph (a) represents an I/O, an assignment or a procedure call statement.*
- *(b) is an* if-then-else *statement,*
- *(c) is a* while *loop and*
- *(d) constitutes the graph of two sequential statements.*

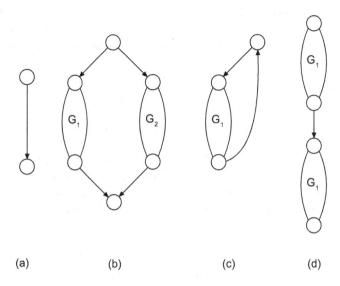

(a)   (b)   (c)   (d)

Fig. 6.1. Constructing the control-flow graph from the code

If the code contains an if-then block (without an else-branch) the graph (b) is taken whereby G_2 is empty.

There are different approaches of generating test data on the basis of the control flow graph. The *edge coverage*, for example, demands on a test set for which each edge of the control flow graph is executed at least once. The number of paths needed in this case is linear in the number of edges. Thus, this approach is applicable if there are no non-reachable edges in the graph. Moreover the edge coverage is finer than the statement coverage because a non-existing else branch of an if-then statement is covered at least once by the edge coverage.

Another approach is the *path coverage*. It demands on the test set that each possible path in the control graph is traversed at least once. This does obviously fulfill the edge coverage condition, too. On the other hand the path coverage may discover mistakes that are possibly overlooked by the edge coverage: There may be errors in the code that only occur under specific preconditions of a statement. If the statement is executed just once (like in an edge covering test set), the preconditions may not be complied. Such mistakes are more likely to be revealed by the path coverage. Hence, the path coverage reveals more errors in general. Unfortunately, the control flow graph contains an infinite number of different paths if there are while loops in the program code. But even if there are no while loops in the code, the if-then-else statements let the number of different paths increase exponentially in the number of statements. Thus, a coverage of all possible paths cannot be guaranteed for all programs. Nevertheless, it may be helpful to design test data that executes many paths.

Drawbacks of Testing. Testing only provides correctness statements for the executed inputs. This may be a very small part of the set of all possible inputs. Therefore the confidence in the correctness of the program may be small. Edsger Dijkstra resumes [200]:

> *"Program testing can be used to show the presence of bugs,*
> *but never to show their absence!"*

But there is also another drawback of Program Testing. It concerns the question how the correct output for a given input for the specified function f is maintained. Usually the programmer does not have a second program that provides this information (and who knows whether this program isn't buggy). Altogether, the precondition for the application of Testing is the existence of an oracle that provides certain information on the outcome of the desired inputs.

6.2.3   Checking

In the previous section we have seen that testing neither provides general mathematical statements for programs that pass a test nor a method is given that generally states whether $P(x) = f(x)$ or $P(x) \neq f(x)$. Both characteristics are supplied by program checkers.

The definition of program checkers was given in [112]. We will modify it for our purposes.

Definition 3. *A program checker C_f for a computational decision or search problem f is defined as follows: $C_f^P(x)$ is a program that satisfies the following conditions for any program P (supposedly for f) and all inputs $x \in I$ (the instances of the problem f):*

1. *If P is correct, then $C_f^P(x) = CORRECT$ (i. e., $P(x)$ is correct)*
2. *If $P(x) \neq f(x)$, then $C_f^P(x) = BUGGY$ (i. e., P is buggy)*

The definition allows the checker to run the program P on any input of its choice. If the checker outputs CORRECT, then it has verified that the program works correctly on the given input. On the other hand, if the checker outputs BUGGY, then the program is verified to contain a bug. Notice that the output BUGGY does not necessarily mean that the program gives an incorrect answer for the given input. If the program is faulty but gives a correct answer on the given input, the checker may output CORRECT or BUGGY. This makes sense especially in the following case: a program outputs the same answer on all inputs and the answer is correct for the given input. In this case it is desirable that the checker outputs BUGGY although the answer is correct for the given input.

Notice furthermore that the checker does not verify that the output of P is correct for *all* inputs but just for the *given* input. In program verification (see Section 6.2.4) it is proven that the program is correct for all inputs. Thus, checking is some kind of a mixture of testing and verification. It does not handle all inputs (like testing), but the treated inputs are verified (like in program verification). This unites two benefits: It is easier than program verification, because a lower number of inputs is verified, and it is more often applicable than testing, because no oracle is needed to check the correctness of a specific output (in fact, the oracle is simulated by program checking).

Now we have a look at a simple checker introduced by [112] for the following problem related to the greatest common divisor (gcd).

ExtendedGCD

Input: Positive integers a, b

Output: Positive integers d, s, t such that $d = gcd(a, b)$
and $a \cdot s + b \cdot t = d$

To check the output of this algorithm one must obviously verify that $d \mid a$ (d divides a without remainder), $d \mid b$ and $a \cdot s + b \cdot t = d$. But this is also sufficient, because this representation is unique: there cannot be an integer $d' < d$ for which there are $s', t' \in \mathbb{Z}$ with $a \cdot s' + b \cdot t' = d'$: Because $d|a$ and $d|b$ we have $d|(a \cdot s' + b \cdot t')$ and thus $d|d'$ which is a contradiction. Hence, we have a deterministic algorithm that checks the correctness of the *ExtendedGCD* algorithm by performing two divisions, two multiplications and one addition.

Certifying Algorithms. Program checking uses a given program as a black box, i. e., it gives the black box some inputs, checks whether the output is correct, and then it makes a statement about the correctness of the program. Certifying algorithms request extra services from the program code. It strengthens the requirements made on the output of a program. The goal is to simplify the construction of checkers. A certifying algorithm does not only compute the output it is supposed to, it also computes a certificate that makes it easy for a checker to prove that the computed answer is correct.

Consider the problem of deciding whether a given graph $G = (V, E)$ is bipartite, i. e., whether there are two disjoint subsets V_0 and V_1 of V with $V_0 \cup V_1 = V$ such that for all $\{u, v\} \in E$ we have either $u \in V_0$ and $v \in V_1$ or reversely $u \in V_1$ and $v \in V_0$.

Let P be a program that supposedly decides this question. How can one check whether a given answer YES or NO is correct? In most cases the bare answer does not help very much. But what could be a useful answer? Mehlhorn et al. [560] stated

> "a program should justify (prove) its answer in a way
> that is easily checked by the user of the program."

In order to find the justification in our problem, we consider the following lemma. For a proof see e. g., [851].

Lemma 1. *A graph $G = (V, E)$ is bipartite if and only if it contains no cycle with odd length.*   □

A certifying algorithm for our problem could provide the following extra information assisting the binary answer. If the answer is YES, the program outputs YES and two sets of nodes V_0 and V_1 that indicate the partitioning of V. This output makes it easy to check the correctness of the answer. If the answer is instead NO, then the algorithm outputs NO and a cycle of odd length. This output is also easily checked. Hence, we know what a good certificate for our problem could be. Now we have to construct it.

A certifying bipartiteness checker

(1) Find a spanning tree T in G. Put the vertices with even depth into V_0 and the vertices with odd depth into V_1.
(2) Check for all edges in $G \setminus T$ whether the adjacent nodes are both in V_0 or both in V_1.
(3) If there is such an edge (u, v), output NO and the path between u and v in T together with the edge (u, v). If there is no such edge, output YES together with V_0 and V_1.

Before we show the correctness we state the following lemma.

Lemma 2. *In T, the length of a path connecting two vertices of V_0 (resp. V_1) in T is even, and the length of a path connecting two vertices between V_0 and V_1 in T is odd.*   □

According to Lemma 1, trees are bipartite, because they contain no cycles at all. Thus, T is bipartite. If G itself is bipartite, then in step (2) no edge can be found which fulfills the condition. Hence, the output is correct. Otherwise, if G is not bipartite, then there is an odd cycle C in G. But T does not contain cycles. Hence, an odd cycle must have at least one edge from $G \setminus T$. If there is an edge in $C \setminus T$ that connects vertices within V_0 (resp. V_1), we have a path of even length between them, which is a contradiction to Lemma 2. If we do not have a path of even length between them, then all edges in C connect vertices between V_0 and V_1. This means that the cycle itself is bipartite, and therefore it must have even length, because of Lemma 2. But this is a contradiction to the assumption that C has odd length.

We summarize: There is a certifying algorithm for testing whether a given graph is bipartite, and it is easy to find a checker that proves the correctness of the output based on the witness provided by the certifying algorithm. In general, constructing checkers is not an easy task. Therefore, the time needed to do this may be greater than the expected gain of a greater confidence in the correctness of the program.

On the other hand the checker itself may be buggy. One approach to tackle this problem is to verify the checker. This may be easier than the verification of the checked program (e. g., consider again the gcd-checker from [112]).

A drawback of the concept of certifying algorithms is that for some problems it may be difficult to say what a certificate could actually look like, and for some problems it may be hard to compute a certificate according to a given description. For example, let n be a given integer, an answer for the question what a certificate for the statement "YES, n is prime" could look like is not obvious (although an answer was given in [646]). On the other hand detecting a certificate for the answer "NO, n is not prime", i. e., finding a non-trivial factor of n, is difficult in general. Thus, the task of designing certifying algorithms may be tough and the time needed to do it may in some cases be too large. Nevertheless, we heavily advise the reader to try it!

6.2.4 Verification

The strongest way of showing the correctness of a program is to verify it, i. e., to prove that the program fulfills the specification it was written for. The fundamental aid for the verification of programs was introduced by C.A.R. Hoare [397].

The calculus of Hoare is a formal logic system which provides a set of logical rules that allow the derivation of statements. The central element of Hoare's logic is the Hoare triple

$$\{P\}\ S\ \{Q\},$$

which consists of the assertion P that is true before the program S is executed and the assertion Q that is true after the completion of S.

Several axioms and rules form the logic: the assertion axiom, the rules of consequence (if-then-else), the composition rule (considering the logical AND), and the rule of iteration (while-loops). These axioms and rules handle the basic elements of procedural programs. We will have an exemplary look at one of them, the assertion axiom:

$$\{P[E/x]\}\ x := E\ \{P\}$$

The assertion $\{P[E/x]\}$ arises from the assertion P by substituting E for all occurrences of x, where x is a variable and E is an expression. A concrete example for a triple described by the assertion axiom:

$$\{x+1=0\}\ y := x+1\ \{y=0\}$$

The Hoare logic as described in [397] is only suitable for the verification of partial correctness. This is enough for our definition of programs because we assumed that they halt on every input. If this is not guaranteed one might desire a proof of total correctness. For this purpose the iteration rule of Hoare was extended (see e. g., [777]).

An interesting aspect of verification is that several steps can be automated. Hence, there are theorem prover tools. PVS [624], for example, was used to validate the algorithms of an implementation of an exact arithmetic [518].

Proving the correctness of a program can be very hard and therefore infeasible from a certain length of the program code on. Furthermore, the proofs themselves may contain mistakes as they are written by humans, too. Moreover, the verification of a program does not enclose any statements concerning compiler or hardware mistakes.

6.2.5   Debugging

In the sections above, we discussed methods how to find out, whether a program contains an error or how to indicate the absence of errors. But what if we actually found an error in the behavior of the program? In this section, we handle methods of fixing such errors. The main reference for this section is Andreas Zeller's book "Why Programs Fail" [858], which we recommend to the reader for further inspection.

Terms and Definitions. Assume that we found an instance $x \in I$ for which $f(x) \neq P(x)$. This discrepancy we call a *failure*. The failure became apparent by the execution of the program code. Thus, there must be a part of the code that is responsible for the existence of the failure. This part of the code we call a *defect*. The defect itself causes a state of the program execution that does not fit to the specification. Such a state we call *infected*. An infected state may cause another infected state, so that the infection propagates through the states. A state that is not infected is called *sane*. A transition from a sane state to an infected state we call an *infection*.

The definitions together with our interest in the infection define what debugging in fact is: Debugging is a search problem. We are searching that part of the code that is responsible for the infection.

Causes and Relevance. If our programs fail we usually ask ourselves "Why?". This question asks for *a* or maybe even for *the* cause of the failure. But what precisely is a cause?

Definition 4. *A* cause *of a failure is an event preceding the failure, without which the failure would not occur.*

This definition of a cause is necessary but not sufficient for a successful search of the defect, because according to this definition the existence of the program itself is also a cause of the failure. But this is a cause we are obviously not interested in. Thus, we are not only searching a cause, but a cause with a specific property. We are searching for a minimum cause.

Definition 5. *A* minimum cause *is an event for which one cannot subtract any non-empty subset of the circumstances of the event such that the failure still occurs.*

This definition finally describes what exactly we are searching for. Moreover it describes what we have to do: we must separate the relevant from the irrelevant.

Observation. At the beginning of the execution we have a sane state. At the end of the execution we have an infected state. If we want to find out which part of the code is responsible for the existence of the infected state at the end we have to inspect the states in between and decide whether they are already infected.

The problem with the observation of the states is that execution of the program goes in a forward manner, but reasoning about the existence of an infected state usually goes backward. For example, if you use a debugger and set a breakpoint at a position in the program for which you are sure that the program state is still sane, then you step forward, and step forward, ... and then you've gone too far. At this point you would like to go backward and see where the infected state comes from. This feature was not supported by debuggers for a long time.

But there is a tool called "*omniscient debugger*" [521] for Java, which simply records all program states. In this tool, you have the feature of stepping backward in time while observing the current state. Thus, you can begin at the failure and step backward — or forward, if desirable — until you reach the infection.

The obvious drawback is that the set of data that must be recorded is very large: about 100 MB per second. Furthermore, the program execution may slow down by a factor of 10 or more. But there is an option of setting a point in time from which the omniscient debugger begins the record. Moreover, one may record just a specific subset of the system.

Although the omniscient debugger is very useful to observe the states, the question for the cause of the values of certain variables is not answered automatically. There may be a lot of dependencies between the values of the variables. Thus, we still have to separate relevant from irrelevant to find the origin of a value of a variable. For this purpose we introduce dynamic backward slices.

A *dynamic backward slice* for a writing operation to a variable v is the subset of the program code that influenced the value of v for the given execution. The dynamic backward slice is dynamic, because it only considers the actual execution instead of all possible executions as for a static slice. And it is backward, because it does not consider parts of the code that are influenced by the value of the given variable. These would be contained in a forward slice. We now describe the dynamic backward slice more formally and concurrently give a method how to compute it.

Definition 6. *Let w be a writing operation to variable v, let r_i be the variables read in the statement of w, and assume that $line(r_i)$ returns the line of code in which variable r_i was written the last time. Then we define*

$$DynBackSlice(w) := \bigcup_i (DynBackSlice(r_i) \cup \{line(r_i)\}).$$

The knowledge about the dynamic backward slices separates relevant from irrelevant. If you know that v has an incorrect value in a given state, you immediately know which statements, respectively which other variables had influence on v in the given execution and — sometimes also important — which not.

Another helpful possibility to automate the search for an infection is to determine conditions, which are necessary for the sanity of a state. The check of these conditions can be done by the program. Such extensions of the code are called *assertions* and generally have the following structure.

if (condition) then printf(); and halt();

The condition usually determines whether the given state is still sane. If the state is not sane, then an arbitrary part of the data may be printed and the program is halted. At this point we want to refer to Section 6.2.3 where we discussed how to check data invariants and preconditions respectively postconditions of parts of the code. These methods may help to find the conditions of an assertion. As you can see in this context: it is helpful to have attended on modularity in the design phase (Section 3.5.1), because it is easier to check invariants for short modules than for long functions.

As stated in the last subsection, debugging is a search problem, and we have to separate relevant from irrelevant. Let us assume that we executed the code on many inputs — some failing and some passing runs. Then there may be parts of the code that were executed *only* in passing runs. These parts cannot contain the defect. Parts that were executed in passing and in failing runs are ambiguous and parts that were executed *only* in failing are highly suspect. The tool "Tarantula" written in Java [442] highlights the code according to this differentiation. As input, it takes arbitrary software system's source code and the results of the execution of a set of test inputs. It accelerates the searching process very much, because you only have to look at the code and can easily identify those parts of the code that contain the defect with a high probability.

The superficial effect of debugging tools is, of course, that the task of searching the defects is supported. But on the other hand, a debugging tool that helps searching the error very much, may also be counterproductive in the sense that the programmer is seduced to trust on the debugger and neglect accuracy in the design.

6.3   Efficiency

Next to correctness, efficiency is a major requirement for an algorithm to be applicable. An efficient implementation will enable the user to solve small problems more quickly, solve more or larger problems in a fixed time frame and solve very large problems at all. Textbooks [191, 742] stress the importance of asymptotic running time and selecting an algorithm with a good asymptotic running time is usually the first step towards an efficient implementation. But what really matters is the actual running time when the implementation is being used. The description of an algorithm in a textbook or paper usually does not tell you how to implement it with small constant factors. When refining the description to an implementation, the implementer therefore has to look carefully where he can improve the running time.

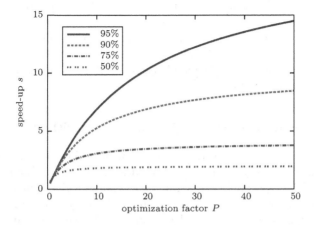

Fig. 6.2. Speed-ups by optimization for $r_p \in \{95\%, 90\%, 75\%, 50\%\}$

However in almost all cases it is only worth the effort to optimize code portions which contribute significantly to the runtime. Large improvements on small
contributors have only little effect as expressed by Amdahl's law [26]. If r_p (resp.
$r_s = 100\% - r_p$) denotes the ratio of the program's execution time spent in
optimized (resp. unoptimized) code portions and P the factor by which the optimized code is accelerated, then the total speedup s achieved by optimization
is given by

$$s = \frac{1}{r_s + r_p/P}.$$

Figure 6.2 shows the total speedup values for different r_p, illustrating the fact
that s is rather limited whenever r_p is not large. By understanding the bottlenecks of the algorithm and profiling the first implementation, the implementer
can find out quickly which code sections contribute largely to the running time
and then concentrate on optimizing these parts. Fine-tuning the remaining parts
will probably take longer than the gain in running time is worth. Profiling can
be done by instrumenting the code with timers or using profiling tools such as
gprof [351]. Chapter 8 contains rules and hints how profiling and other experiments should be performed.

Optimizing an algorithm for a library or for a special problem at hand is
a different task. For a library, the implementer does not know what kind of
input the user will provide. He must therefore provide an implementation that
is efficient on all possible inputs. In many cases, there will not be an optimal
solution. The implementer can then make several algorithms available to the user
or let the user take certain decisions. This is only possible through a flexible
design. When implementing for a certain problem, there is usually additional
information about the input available. The implementer should try to exploit
this information as much as possible to speed up the algorithm.

There is no such thing as a "theory of efficient implementations" and it is hard to find programming language independent advice on how to create efficient implementations in the literature, due to the nature of the problem. There are, however, books, e. g., [93,570,571] full of speed-up tricks or examples of efficient solutions for certain problems. We have tried to collect the more general tips in the remainder of this section.

6.3.1 Implementation Tricks – Tuning the Algorithms

The description of many algorithms leaves open several parameters from which the implementer can choose freely without destroying important properties of the algorithm. These parameters can range from numerical parameters (e. g., the size of some buffer) over data structures (balanced binary trees, priority queues) and sub-algorithms (sorting) to the algorithm itself. While these parameters may not affect the asymptotic running time, they will affect the actual running time of the implementation. The task of the implementer is to carefully investigate the possibilities and choose a solution best suiting his needs. This investigation will be supported best by a flexible design allowing to exchange parts of the implementation easily.

When implementing algorithms for efficiency, Mehlhorn and Näher [561] recommend to *"concentrate on the best and average case after getting the worst case 'right.'"* They name algorithms for computing a maximum cardinality matching in bipartite graphs as one of their best examples for tuning parameters. We like to mention it as a good example of Algorithm Engineering: The authors form hypotheses how various variants of the algorithm behave, based on heuristic arguments and then perform experiments to confirm or disprove the hypotheses. Their first algorithm for maximum cardinality matching in bipartite graphs is due to Ford and Fulkerson [293]. Although it does not have an optimal worst case running time, it is in the end competitive for some inputs. It proceeds as follows:

1: **procedure** FORDFULKERSON(Graph G)
2:     Matching $M \leftarrow$ some matching in G
3:     **for all** nodes v in G **do**
4:         **if** there is an M-augmenting path p starting in v **then**
5:             augment M by p
6:     **return** M

Apart from using different data structures, the authors explore two parameters in this algorithm, namely how to find the initial matching and how to compute the augmenting path. For the first choice, the proposed possibilities are starting from the empty matching or constructing a matching using a greedy heuristic. They argue that the heuristic, while having a short running time, will already match a large number of nodes in random graphs and confirm this by experiments. They *"recommend exploring the use of a heuristic always,"* but also note that the effects of a heuristic will be small for good algorithms. This is later confirmed when applying the heuristic to the best algorithm. To find an augmenting path, they propose using a breadth-first search (bfs) or a depth-first search (dfs). The bfs will find the shortest augmenting path, while the dfs may explore the entire graph although an augmenting path of length 1 exists. For this reason, bfs performs better on average, which the authors again confirm by experiments. From their implementation of the bfs and dfs the authors derive another principle. To implement the bfs and the dfs, certain nodes must be marked during the algorithm. Clearing the marking for all nodes after each augmentation step takes $\Theta(n)$ time, such that the runtime of the algorithm is $\Omega(n^2)$. If each node when being marked is also put on an additional stack, then after the augmentation only the markings of nodes actually touched must be cleared. The authors call this the principle of *"paying only for what we actually have touched and not for what we could have conceivably touched."* Elaborating further on this idea, they achieve that n^2 is no longer a lower bound for the asymptotic runtime of the algorithm. Note that a lower bound only tells how bad an algorithm performs. To claim that an algorithm performs good in the best case, a small upper bound on the family of all lower bounds must be given. The authors show that each lower bound of the algorithm is $O(m)$, improving the best case.

In a divide-and-conquer algorithm $\mathcal{A}$, one of the open parameters is the minimum size M at which a problem will still be divided into subproblems. No matter how large or small M is chosen, as long as it is fixed and does not depend on the input, the asymptotic running time of $\mathcal{A}$ will not change. Typically, in the description of the algorithm, M is chosen such that the problem becomes trivial. There may however exist another algorithm $\mathcal{B}$ solving the same problem which has a worse running time on large instances but is faster in solving small problems. The implementer can then determine at which problem size M algorithm $\mathcal{B}$ is the better choice, stop dividing if the subproblem becomes smaller than M and use $\mathcal{B}$ to solve it. This principle could be called *stop dividing early*. Sedgewick [717] applied it to the quicksort algorithm, sorting sub-arrays of length smaller M using insertion sort. Musser [602] proposed a different criterion to stop dividing in a quicksort algorithm. If at some point in the algorithm the recursion depth is larger than some bound in $O(\log n)$, the sub-array is not divided further but sorted using heapsort. This results in an algorithm with running time in $O(n \log n)$ but preserves the practical performance of quicksort for uniformly distributed input.

Reference Counting. Reference counting is a technique that allows several equivalent objects to share representations with automatic resource management. It has been described frequently in various versions [561, 570, 759]. In reference counting several handles point to a representation. The handles act as proxies [313], interaction with the representation is only possible through the handles. The representation to be reference counted contains a counter `ref_count` knowing how many handles currently point to it. When a new handle points to the representation, `ref_count` will be increased, when a handle is removed `ref_count` will be decreased, allowing to automatically release the resources used by the representation once no more handles point to it. Copying a reference counted object only creates a new handle. Changing an object will change

Fig. 6.3. Invasive reference counting layout

the representation and therefore all objects it currently represents. Sometimes this may be undesirable for the type being shared. Then a copy-on-write strategy avoids changing other objects. Before the modification takes place an actual copy of the representation is made and the handle through which the modification takes place is redirected.

Whether to share representations of equivalent objects can be decided on the type level, but also for individual objects. When the decision to share representations is made on the type level, it can be completely hidden from the user. Strings are usually reference counted and feature a copy-on-write strategy. This pays off since strings require dynamic memory, are copied often and modified rarely. Another example where sharing representations can be useful is software number types. Unlike the number types available from hardware, software number types allow to compute with arbitrary precision, e.g., in the field of rational numbers. Consider an algorithm which is generic in the number type it uses. Passing function arguments by value will be inefficient for software number types, while passing a pointer will be inefficient for the hardware number types. If the software number type is however reference counted, passing by value will only create a new handle at a moderate cost.

Sometimes one also has the ability to identify individual objects as being equivalent. This allows to speed up a program by preventing that already known results, like comparisons, are computed again. First equivalent objects must be identified. This is most easily done when constructing them. Consider for example the construction of two segments bounding a triangle, where a segment is represented through its endpoints. These two segments will have a common end point and thus may share this point in their representation. The sharing can for example be implemented through simple pointers or by having the points reference counted. Sometimes objects are recognized to be equivalent somewhere in the course of an algorithm. Then their representations may be unified by redirecting all references to the first representation to the second one and deleting the first. If it is not required by the algorithm, it is rarely advisable to enforce a single representation for equivalent objects but the chance for identification should be taken whenever possible. Kettner [470] has designed and implemented a reference counting scheme which allows to unify representations using a union-find data structure, which allows to filter comparison tests very efficiently. First, pointers to the representation can be checked to detect identity before another, presumably less efficient, algorithm is run to compare the underlying representations. In case of equality, one representation can be discarded, while pointers to it are moved to the remaining representation. Different policies are possible.

Full details are given in Kettner's paper. Furthermore, in the case of the two segments, an affine transformation on the segments must be applied to only three instead of four end points. Here actually care must be taken, not to apply the transformation twice to the shared endpoint. Sharing representations as described here, will definitely increase the complexity of the implementation, impairing readability and maintainability. It will have a positive impact on the running time only, if the operations which are avoided by sharing representations are more expensive than the overhead for managing shared representations.

Sentinels. Algorithms that are traversing some data structure usually need to test whether they have reached the end of the data structure. These end-of-data-structure tests can be removed from an algorithm using a so-called *sentinel*, e. g., in a linear search [93]. When searching in a list, the element searched for will be placed as a sentinel right at the end of the list in a new node before the search is performed. This assures that the element will be found before the end of the list is reached. The element then is in the list if it was found in some node before the sentinel node. Finally the sentinel must be removed again. This trades the time for an end-of-list test within the search loop to time for inserting and removing the sentinel node and an additional test after the search. In the case of an array, this can only be done if the array has been allocated with additional space to hold the sentinel. Here the sentinel should rather be swapped with the element at the end of the array, to avoid overwriting data. The data structures and algorithms in the C++ standard template library [727, 755] are generic in the types on which they work. This makes the use of sentinels in the library implementation unattractive as it would impose unnecessary restrictions on the types that can be handled and therefore sentinels are completely avoided. The user is however free to place his own sentinels inside the data structures.

Lazy Evaluation. From the perspective of efficiency, the best computations are those never performed at all. This may sound a little bit strange, but in the context of so-called *lazy evaluation* the statement perfectly makes sense. The word "lazy" means that computations (or other operations) are not performed before their result is really *used.* When dealing with matrices (of size n times n, say) the statement:

```
matrix3 = matrix1 * matrix2;
```

usually means that after the assignment `matrix3` holds all the n^2 values of the product that has been computed. If in an extremal case e. g., only the top left entry is used afterwards, that means that all the $n^2 - 1$ values have been computed for nothing. If however the object `matrix3` holds the information that it has to behave like the product of `matrix1` and `matrix2`, but no computation and no copying takes place until the top left entry is requested, the extra computations can be avoided. This only works as long as `matrix1` and `matrix2` are not changed in the meantime, but we already learned about reference counting and how to deal with such cases. Not only time consuming calculations may be avoided, but also e. g., database operations. Why construct a large object from a database completely when only few fields are read afterwards?

Over-Eager Evaluation. A concept that seems to be diametrically opposed is *over-eager evaluation*: values are computed just in case they might be used sometimes later. Consider for instance a class for linked lists. Computing the length of such a list takes time linear in the number of list entries. On the other hand such an object could also hold the redundant information about the length in an extra field and whenever the length is requested, just return the content of that field. There are mainly two ways of doing that: first, every time the list is modified, the length is updated, or second, when the length is requested for the first time, it is computed and cached for the next time. In both cases time is saved whenever the length is requested more than once. Another type of over-eager evaluation namely *prefetching* becomes interesting when one has to consider different levels of memory. In terms of main memory, fetching data from hard disc with random access is extremely slow: every time the head has to be moved to the correct position before a block can be read. Normally such a block contains more data that is actually demanded. According to the principle of locality, data that is demanded shortly after is often saved nearby. So it is a good idea not to forget the block that has just been read and to cache it. Moreover, prefetching means that the neighboring blocks are also read (best in a sequential manner instead of multiple random accesses) and cached since the likelihood of needing data from some of these blocks is high. This example was taken from the domain of hardware and most algorithm engineers might just want to use hardware as a necessary means, but do not want to implement the drivers. So let us have a look at another example: dynamic arrays. Almost every implementation of dynamic arrays uses prefetching. The data is normally stored in a fixed size array and if the size of that array is insufficient, a larger array has to be allocated and the data has to be copied. If the size was always increased by just the amount currently needed, a sequence of n append operations would cause n such allocation and data copy procedures which implies an $\Theta(n^2)$ time bound for the n append operations. With prefetching on the other hand the effort can be reduced to $O(n)$ amortized time by doubling the size of the underlying array every time it gets too small.

6.3.2   Implementation Tricks – Tuning the Code

Apart from such high level tricks, there are many ways to help a computer to run a program faster. Most of them are specific to the hardware, to the operating system, or to the programming language. There are way to many to know them all (the AIX performance tuning guide [18] alone lists 63 system parameters that *can* affect performance) and modern compilers do a lot of performance optimization themselves, but keeping some of these low level reliefs in mind when coding may help improving efficiency. Collections of recommendations that are intended for, but not all limited to C++ can be found e. g., in [570,571].

Temporary Objects. Using object oriented programming languages, many programmers are not aware of the huge number of objects that have to be created and destroyed when their program runs. For Java programs an example that is often mentioned in connection with object creations is the use of strings: Every operation modifying an object of type String causes the creation of a new String object. Moreover the concatenation via the += operator is realized by using a temporary object of type StringBuffer. Writing string1 += string2 results in virtually the same code as writing

```
string1 = (new Stringbuffer(string1)).append(string2).toString().
```

For C++ programs one of the most obvious source of temporary objects being created and destroyed shortly after, is the use of an object as return value of a function. The object is created inside the function and returning it means, that this newly created object is copied and destroyed afterwards. There are several possibilities to avoid this behavior. First, returning pointers to objects created with new instead of returning objects. But the price one has to pay for reducing the number of object creations is, that the programmer has to take care of all these pointers and has to assure that the objects are properly deleted to avoid memory leaks. So this way should only be used in certain cases where the correct usage can be assured. Second, one can use non-const references instead of returning objects. A reference to the object that is to contain the result of some function is passed to the function as a parameter. Inside the function the object is modified and nothing has to be copied and returned. The third possibility is to make use of the optimizations that modern compilers provide: Objects may be optimized out of existence. But the programmer has to offer the chance of applying this optimization to the compiler. In [570] an example is given, that nicely illustrates such a situation. Imagine a class Rational that represents rational numbers and that has a constructor which takes the numerator and the denominator as parameters. Without optimization in a function call like the following

```
const Rational
operator * ( const Rational& lhs, const Rational& rhs) {
  return Rational( lhs.numerator()   * rhs.numerator(),
                   lhs.denominator() * rhs.denominator() );
}
...
Rational r1, r2, r3;
...
r3 = r1 * r2;
```

an object of type Rational would be created inside the function and copied to r3. But compilers supporting so-called *return value optimization* can directly write the values to r3 without creating a temporary object. The specification of C++ makes it easier for compilers to optimize unnamed objects out of existence than named objects [570]. Only some recent compilers do support the so called *named return value optimization (NRVO)*, but most do support the return value optimization for unnamed objects. So when there is the choice, an unnamed object should be preferred over a named object to help the compilers to produce fast programs.

Built-In Data Types. Depending on the machine a program is running on, the choice which built-in data types are used can also affect the running time. Because of the development of faster and faster hardware for floating-point operations the old truism that using integers is faster than using floating-point numbers has become less important. However there are still differences. The AIX performance tuning guide [18] lists several examples for C++. Loading an `unsigned char` into a register takes two instructions less than loading a `signed char` and in most cases it takes less instructions to manipulate an `int` than a `char` or `short`. Unless there are large arrays of these types, the increase of required storage space is more than annihilated by the decrease of the compiled code's size.

Conditional Branches. Modern processors gain speedup from not processing instruction after instruction, instead via pipelining they begin to process operations before the preceding operations are totally completed. Due to that fact every conditional branching may slow down the computation: Which operations are to be loaded into the pipeline depends on the result of a preceding operation. Filling the pipeline could be suspended until the result is available or the pipeline can be filled with the operations of one of the paths. In the latter case, the pipeline has to be stopped, emptied and refilled if actually another path has to be executed. Improvements such as branch prediction help to reduce the slow down, but – unless the prediction is always perfect – can not avert it. Therefore, avoiding conditional branches, especially inside loops, should always be worth a thought. Imagine e. g., a routine counting the occurrences of upper case letters, lower case letters and digits in an ASCII text string. A naive implementation of the classification could look like this:

```
if ((character >= '0') and ((character <= '9')) {
    characterType = DIGIT;
} else if ((character >= 'A') and ((character <= 'Z')) {
    characterType = UPPERCASE;
} else if ((character >= 'a') and ((character <= 'z')) {
    characterType = LOWERCASE;
} else {
    characterType = OTHERS;
}
count[characterType]++;
```

This piece of code contains 6 comparisons and 3 conditional branches. If the strings to process are sufficiently long, using an array that holds the type for every of the 256 characters may drastically decrease the running time of the classification, although the time complexity stays the same:

```
characterType = typeTable[character];
count[characterType]++;
```

In this example avoiding the branches will probably yield the major speedup, but there is still room for improvements. The code above uses two indirections. By counting characters and collecting the numbers afterwards only one indirection is needed in the main loop:

```
int count[256];
forall (character in word) {
    count[character]++;
}

int digits = 0;
for (int i = '0'; i <= '9'; i++) digits += count[i];
...
```

In the last example the speedup was mainly gained for the price of increased memory usage. Replacing **short** by **int** means that more memory is used to store the data and storing precomputed values when using over-eager-evaluation of course also increases memory usage. As long as memory is not the limiting factor, this time-space trade-off seems to be not a problem, but one should always be aware of it.

Memory Hierarchy. Modern computers not only consist of a CPU and main memory, but also have one or more memory caches in between. Roughly speaking, the cache contains copies of several regions of the main memory that were recently accessed. Accessing an address that is currently cached is much faster than accessing an address that is not currently cached. The latter case is called a cache miss. Because of the existence of caches, the running time of an algorithm is influenced by its memory access pattern. *Cache aware* techniques are modifications to the memory layout of a data structure or the way an algorithm accesses memory, which try to minimize the number of cache misses but without giving a performance guarantee. Section 5.2.4 has a collection of these techniques. Some are performed by compilers, others must be done by the implementer.

Inlining. We would also like to mention function inlining as a possibility for optimization. A function call incurs a certain overhead, that can be avoided by inlining the function. This basically consists of copying the function body to the place where the function is called. Many programming languages have support for some kind of automatic inlining, e. g., through the **inline** keyword in C and C++. Function inlining not only removes the overhead of the function call but also allows the compiler to perform its optimizations over a larger part of code, reducing the computation time further. Together with the **template** feature in C++ automatic inlining allows to write code that is general and does not have any or very little overhead compared to a special version. We will look at an example in the next section. Too much inlining will however lead to an increased compilation time and also to larger executables. It may then slow down the computation because of more cache misses in the instruction cache.

Argument Passing to Functions. Objects can be passed to a function *by value* or *by reference*, where in some programming languages, passing a pointer to an object by value must be used to work around a missing call by reference mechanism. Passing by value involves copying. For all but very small objects this is a source of inefficiency and should be avoided whenever possible. Imagine you perform a binary search function where the sorted array is passed by value to recursive calls. Argument passing is discussed in Section 6.4 of Leiss' programmers companion to algorithm analysis [515].

Often objects are passed by value in order to ensure that the calling function does not modify them. Programming languages like C++, however, offer a better alternative: const references. On an object passed by const reference the compiler allows only for operations that claim not to modify the object, for example, functions that use a const reference as well or member functions declared as const. For the latter the compiler checks that they do not modify an object. Basically, this constness mechanism ensures that objects passed by const reference are not modified. Since it is a call by reference, they are not copied either, i.e., expensive copying is saved. However, C++ allows you to sabotage the constness mechanism by casting constness away. This is a relict from the pre-standard times of C++ when it was not possible to distinguish logical constness from physical constness. The former allows for special changes in the internal representation of an object as long as these changes do not affect the objects state and behavior as seen from an outside perspective. Physical constness means changing the bits of the actual representation of an object is not allowed. Nowadays, programmers can declare members of a class to be *mutable* to permit modifications despite formal constness. Sometimes, getting constness to work correctly is a fairly non-trivial task.

Squeezing Space to Improve Locality. Often, reducing space complexity also reduces time complexity, simply because more smaller objects fit into faster memory, thereby making I/O transfer less likely. Often there is also an involved trade-off between time and space. For example, packed data structures like bit vectors or bit arrays use less space while accessing the individual elements becomes more complicated and more expensive.

Sometimes, however, it is very easy to save space. In many programming languages, especially C and C++, the order of member declarations in a class definition can be crucial because of alignment restrictions. For example, usually int must be aligned at a four byte boundary, while a short must be aligned on a two byte boundary. Regarding char, there are usually no restrictions. So lets assume we have to declare one short, two char, and three int in a class. If we use declaration sequence char, int, char, int, short, int, the class will take six bytes, while it takes only four bytes using the sequence char, char, short, int, int, int. Thus, by such a simple rearrangement we save one third of the space. Novice programmers are often not aware of this.

Exploiting Algebraic Identities. For an arithmetic expression one might consider replacing it with an algebraically equivalent expression that is cheaper to evaluate [93]. Horner's rule for polynomial evaluation is an illustrative example. On some platforms, we might save time by replacing multiplications and divisions by powers of two by left and right shift operations. However, there is a caveat regarding floating-point operations. With floating-point arithmetic, some algebraic identities do not hold anymore. While floating-point addition is still commutative with IEEE 754, it is not associative due to rounding errors: The results of the summation of more than two floating-point values might depend on the summation order. Thus, when rearranging arithmetic expressions for floating-point evaluation, one should keep rounding errors in mind. Fortunately, exploiting algebraic identities sometimes both saves time and gives more accurate results: Consider comparison of Euclidean distances. The Euclidean distance of two points p and q is the square root of the sum of the absolute differences of the Cartesian coordinates of p and q. However, in order to compare two such distances it is not necessary to take square roots. Comparison of the squared distances saves the square root operations and is more accurate.

Exploiting Word Parallelism. To evaluate certain expensive expressions, it can be very helpful to use the full word width of the underlying computer architecture. For example, using logical bitwise OR on two 64-bit sets, we are performing 64 operations in parallel. An instructive collection of bitwise tricks and techniques can be found in Knuth's Fascicle 1 of Volume 4 of The Art of Computer Programming [483]. *Broadword computing* refers to efficient n-bit computations for fairly large values of n. Some very recent studies have demonstrated the speed-up potential of broadword computing [805, 337].

6.3.3 Code Generation

Sometimes it is conceptually clear how the most efficient code will look like, but writing it down may be tedious and hence will be error prone. Or the most efficient code is undesirable from the readability and maintainability point of view. In these cases, we may want some tool to generate the code for us. Some programming languages come with features that allow to generate code in some way, but most times the tool will be some external program. This has the negative side effect that our software is now written in two languages, the input language for our code generator and the programming language we are using.

A typical example is the implementation of mathematical operations on objects of fixed and small size, e. g., the inversion of a regular 4×4 matrix. A nice and clean way to do this would be to implement the Gauss-Jordan elimination or Cramer's rule for arbitrary n and use it with $n = 4$. Much more efficient is it to write down an algorithm for $n = 4$, unroll all the loops and eliminate common subexpressions. Modern compilers perform loop unrolling and common subexpression elimination, however only to some extend. Loop unrolling may be hindered by the growth in code size or when the compiler cannot determine that $n = 4$ holds, common subexpressions will rarely be eliminated due to the fact that certain algebraic identities of the real numbers do not hold for floating point numbers. Computer algebra systems are environments which can handle mathematical objects well, having various functions to manipulate them in certain ways. Major computer algebra systems have support for the generation of code in various languages, either build in or as expansion package. Therefore, they have long been and still are a natural choice to automatically perform the optimizations described above and generate efficient code [797, 201].

Fortune and van Wyk [298, 299] developed a compiler for exact geometric predicates on integers, called LN. It takes as input a multivariate polynomial whose sign must be computed and bounds on the bit-length of each of the operands. It uses this information to compute bounds on the bit-length of all intermediate and output values, to compute an a priori error bound and to produce exact evaluation code. In the generated code the expression is first evaluated using floating-point arithmetic and only if the sign of the result cannot be verified by the error bound, the exact evaluation is triggered. The exact evaluation code stores large integers as tuples of floating-point numbers and each arithmetic operation is tailored to the bit-length of its operands. The code generated by LN is faster than code using arbitrary precision integer arithmetic due to the filter and because the exact evaluation code avoids most of the overhead needed when dealing with variable bit-length integers. The downside is, that code generated by LN is inefficient for input of smaller bit-length, both in the error bound and in the number of variables and operations it uses for the exact evaluation. Furthermore, once generated, the code cannot reliably be used with input of larger bit-length, limiting flexibility. Similar approaches to automatically generate efficient exact predicates are due to Burnikel et al. [144] and Nanevski et al. [608].

The `template` feature of C++ is mostly used to implement generic data structures and algorithms, see Section 6.4.1. It can however also be used to write more efficient code. Reis et al. [669] have used templates in their library SYNAPS to implement efficient linear algebra operations. The technique is already presented by Veldhuizen [109, 801, 802] and Stroustrup [759, Section 22.4.7]. Consider a vector class `Vector` holding n numbers and having an `operator[]`, allowing to access the elements. The fastest way of getting the sum of three vectors x,y,z into another vector `sum` would be the instruction

```
for(int i=0;i<n;i++) sum[i] = x[i] + y[i] + z[i];
```

For the sake of shortness and readability one would however like to write `sum = x + y + z;`. This requires the implementation of an `operator+` and an `operator=`. A naive implementation of these operators could look like

```
inline Vector operator+(const Vector& s,const Vector& t){
  Vector tmp;
  for(int i=0;i<n;i++) tmp[i] = s[i] + t[i];
  return tmp;
}
```

```
inline Vector& operator=(const Vector& s){
  for(int i=0;i<size;i++) v[i] = s[i];
  return *this;
}
```

The execution of sum = x + y + z; now will allocate two temporary vectors
tmp1 and tmp2 with tmp1 holding the result of y+z and tmp2 holding the result
of x+tmp1. This allocation is very time consuming and accounts for most of the
overhead in this solution. More overhead comes from the fact that the two addi-
tions and the assignment will be performed in separate loops. Using templates
and inlining and relying on the optimization of the compiler, more efficient code
can be generated. First it can be observed that no computation must be performed until an assignment is done. The trick is now to let operator+ return a
proxy object of type Vsum which holds references to the addends and models the
addition.

```
template<class S,class T>
struct Vsum{
  const S& s; const T& t;
  Vsum(const S& ss,const T& tt):s(ss),t(tt){}
  double inline operator[](const int i)const{return s[i]+t[i];}
};
```

```
template<class S,class T>
inline Vsum<S,T> operator+(const S& s,const T& t){
  return Vsum<S,T>(s,t);
}
```

When more than one addition is performed, as in the case of sum = x + y +
z;, in the second addition one of the addends is no longer of type Vector but
of type Vsum<Vector,Vector>. Hence, the operator+ and Vsum are generic in
which kind of addends they accept, and the C++ compiler will automatically
generate the right code. In the operator+ above, there is almost no requirement
on the type of the addend. The assignment operator however only accepts types
which have an operator[] returning a number.

```
template<class S>
inline Vector& operator=(const S& s){
  for(int i=0;i<n;i++) v[i] = s[i];
  return *this;
}
```

This holds for other vectors as well as for Vsum<S,T> which now recursively
requires the same from S and T. The instruction s[i] will call the inline
operator[] of a Vsum object, which will recursively call other inline functions
until actually a value is reached. The compiler may now eliminate these function

calls, resulting in code equivalent to the first approach. But even if no optimization is performed, the new approach may be faster because it only requires the allocation of small objects of type Vsum instead of temporary vectors.

It is clear that this approach can be extended to further arithmetical operations by introducing operators and proxy classes which model these operations. It allows to use vectors efficiently through a simple and clean interface. The drawbacks are an increased compilation time and a larger executable due to the inlining, slightly more complicated code on the implementation side and as always with templates, very hard to decipher error messages. Reis et al. [669] have not measured the runtime differences between the three versions of vector arithmetic.

6.4   Flexibility

Flexibility of an implementation is the the ability to (re)use an algorithm or a data structure in changing environments. The environment consists of the input we have to handle, other software that interacts with our implementation and the hardware our implementation is running on. Here are some examples:

- **input:** When computing the Delaunay triangulation of a set of points in the plane, the input points may have hardware integer coordinates or bigfloat coordinates. In both cases we want a correct and efficient solution. This requires to replace the predicates or the number type used in the predicates in the Delaunay triangulation algorithm.
- **other software:** We need containers for storing objects. A container should not be rewritten for every type, instead it should be flexible in the type it can hold. An algorithm for selecting a maximal object from a container should work for types we do not know yet, stored in containers we do not know yet.
- **hardware:** The TwoProduct algorithm from Section 6.7.2 can be implemented with only two floating-point operations on hardware with a fused-multiply-add instruction. Thus we will want to replace the algorithm when compiling for such hardware.

We can see that flexibility requires the ability to easily exchange subalgorithms and data structures. This further requires, that modules performing equal or similar tasks have identical interfaces. There are syntactical and semantical requirements on modules that can be exchanged. A flexible sorting algorithm must e. g., be supplied with code performing a comparison of two objects. A syntactical requirement is that this code exists and is supplied to the sorting algorithm. A semantic requirement may be that the comparison code implements a total order on the type that is to be sorted, as this may be needed by the correctness proof of our sorting algorithm. Syntactical requirements can be checked by a compiler, semantical requirements usually can not be checked automatically.

In Algorithm Engineering flexibility is not only desirable to ease reuse, but it also allows to perform experiments more easily, cf. Chapter 8. Which of the many implementations of an abstract data type is best in a certain algorithm applied to certain input can often only be decided by experiments. Two algorithms for the same purpose and using equal subalgorithms can be compared more meaningful if both use the same implementation of the subalgorithms. Performing such experiments efficiently and without code duplication requires a flexible design.

Which part of an algorithm should be exchangeable must be decided by the implementer. Sometimes suggestions are given in the description of an algorithm, i. e., when an abstract data type is used. Then the implementer must not only choose at least one specific implementation of the abstract data type, he can also decide to make that part easily exchangeable. Aside from such obvious decisions the implementer has to decide with the anticipated usage in mind. Flexibility requirements may also only be discovered by going through the Algorithm Engineering cycle or when an actual reuse scenario arises. Then a refactorization may be necessary.

6.4.1   Achieving Flexibility

Design patterns describe general, mostly simple and elegant solutions to software engineering problems which arise time and again. To achieve flexibility, our software prototype should be designed for change. To this end, design patterns like *Strategy, Visitor, Iterator, Abstract Factory, Observer*, and several others are helpful. For details we recommend the by now classic book on design patterns by Gamma et al. [313].

First of all, we would like to have (sub)algorithms exchangeable. To decouple algorithms and data structures, each algorithm should come with its own class. Instead of implementing algorithms just for one specific data structure, they should be designed to work for a whole bunch of data structures which have to satisfy a minimal set of requirements.

Different variants of an algorithm can be made exchangeable using the Strategy pattern. It declares an interface common to all supported algorithms. Depending on the context, this interface can be used to call the algorithm defined by a concrete strategy. If the concrete strategy can be selected at compile-time and does not have to be changed at run-time, C++ templates can be used to configure a class with a strategy.

Let us exemplify some of these aspects using the problem of sorting. The question arises which language features of C/C++ can be used to facilitate the exchange. We shall now briefly discuss some of the language features and compare their weaknesses and strengths. What parts in sorting should be exchangeable? First of course the type to sort. Next comes the order on the type, represented by some code comparing two objects. We want that order to be independent of the type, i. e., we want to be able to sort ints non-increasing or non-decreasing or we may want to sort some type according to its semantic or just by its address in memory, when any order suffices. And finally we want the container that holds the objects to be sorted to be exchangeable.

Our first solution is based on *weak typing* and *function pointers*. For a lack of alternatives, this choice has been made in the quicksort implementation of the C standard library. The qsort function is given a pointer to the first object, the number of objects and the physical size of the objects to be sorted, it assumes the objects are stored in a C style array. The last argument is a function pointer to a function performing a comparison of two objects.

```
void qsort( void *buf,
            size_t num,
            size_t size,
            int (*compare)(const void *, const void *) );
```

Therefore, the `qsort` function is flexible in the type it can sort and the comparison operator for that type. Allowing both parameters to be exchangeable and independent of each other requires to weaken type safety. The compiler will accept the code even if `size, compare` and the type to sort do not match as they should. An advantage of supplying functionality to an algorithm through a function pointer is, that the algorithm must be compiled only once. Old code can call new code, which is provided through the function pointer, without recompilation. A disadvantage is, that one may need to weaken type safety to achieve true flexibility, as in the `qsort` example above. Another issue is, that the call to the function supplied as function pointer can not be inlined in the typical scenario. When the function is called very often and has a short running time, e. g., when sorting `ints` with `qsort`, the function call will be a serious run-time overhead.

Another way to achieve flexibility is to use *object-oriented* programming techniques, more precisely *polymorphism*. Here we present an example inspired by a solution in the Java language. The syntactic requirements of the code to be exchanged are captured in one or more base classes.

```
class Comparable{
public:
  virtual bool lessThan(Comparable *C) = 0;
};
```

Any type that is to be sorted can now inherit from `Comparable` and is then forced to implement the `lessThan()` function. When the `lessThan()` function is called through a `Comparable` pointer, at runtime the actual type of the object pointed to is determined and the corresponding `lessThan()` function is called. This allows us to implement a sorting function that sorts a C style array of `Comparable` pointers.

```
void sort(Comparable ** buf, size_t num);
```

The advantages of polymorphism are again the ability to let old code call new code and the ability to establish type safety at runtime. The syntactical requirements are visible in one place, namely the base class and the semantical requirements can be documented next to it. Note that our solution here actually introduces an inflexibility, as the order given by the `lessThan()` function is tied to the type, sorting with respect to a different order requires to create a new type. Polymorphism is however a good choice when a whole set of actually different types can be handled equally in our code. The major downside of polymorphism is the cost of virtual function calls. They are quite expensive compared to regular function calls, since first the function to be called must be determined.

C++ provides the features of *templates* [800]. Using templates to achieve flexibility is called *generic programming*, sometimes when a lot of computations are deferred to compile time also *template metaprogramming*. A function (or class) template is a regular function, parameterized by one or more types. The parameter may be used in the implementation of the function as if it was a real type having the necessary functionality. To use the function template, the parameters must be fixed, at compile time. This is called *instantiating* the template. Then the compiler checks if all the functionality required from a parameter is actually available. Here is an interface to the sort function from the C++ standard library. Note that the type to be sorted is not visible in the interface, instead two arguments of a type parameterized as RandomAccessIterator must be given. These arguments describe a range or sequence of the objects to be sorted.

```
template <class RandomAccessIterator>
void sort(RandomAccessIterator first, RandomAccessIterator last);
```

The implementation of sort assumes among other things, that the type inserted for RandomAccessIterator has a dereference operator *, such that e.g., the expression *first gives access to the first of the objects to be sorted. It is further assumed that the type of these objects has a comparison operator < and some other functionality. A type and associated types that fulfill all the requirements imposed by the function template on the template parameter is called a *model* for this parameter. An example for a model of the RandomAccessIterator is a simple pointer to an int, so one can use sort to sort a simple C style array of ints.

```
int intarr[5] = {1, 5, 3, 4, 2};
std::sort(intarr,intarr+5);
```

Note that sort is our first example, where the container storing the objects can be exchanged, although in this interface again the order is tied to the type. The syntactical requirements made by a function template are scattered throughout its implementation. It is therefore considered good practice to collect the syntactic requirements in a single place e.g., by providing a dummy model, and furnish them with a documentation of the semantical requirements. Examples for this are the famous documentation of SGI's STL implementation [727] and the CGAL manual [152].

The dependency of a template on a type parameter is resolved at compile time, giving static type safety. Resolving this dependency early, allows functions used in the template to be inlined at the place where they are called. In the sort template an example for such a function would be the comparison operator, there will be no function call overhead when comparing build in types and it can be avoided for custom types. Even when no inlining occurs, using generic programming to achieve flexibility incurs no runtime overhead compared to an inflexible solution where the types are fixed a priori. When inlining occurs, not only the function call overhead is removed, the compiler is also given the chance to optimize over a larger section of code which may result in more efficient code. In Section 6.3.3, we give an example where efficient linear algebra operations with a nice call syntax are implemented. The technique relies on the ability of the compiler to inline functions and then fold constant intermediate objects. In case that a better implementation is possible if a template parameter is of a certain type, i.e., a (any) pointer, or an `int`, *specialization* allows to specify a different version of the template just for this type or value of the parameter.

The focus on runtime efficiency for templates comes at a price, which is code duplication. For each instantiation of a template with different parameters, the compiler will generate new code. This leads to larger executables and also longer compile times. Since with most current compilers the definition of a template must be completely visible at the point of instantiation, in projects which heavily rely on templates, even a small change in the code my require to rebuild the complete project. This aggravates the problem with long compile times and may be a serious issue in the development process. Code duplication will occur even when the parameter types are, if not identical, similar enough to share an implementation. Stroustrup [759, Section 13.5] shows how specialization can be used to avoid code duplication for the `std::vector` template and other containers. Using his technique, each instantiation of a `std::vector` with a pointer type uses the same (compiled) code.

A template is not a type, only an instantiation of a template is. The name of the type then consists of the name of the template and its parameters, i.e., `std::vector<int>`. As there may be multiple parameters and they themselves may be template instances, type names tend to become large. Large type names make code hard to write and hard to read. The `typedef` keyword allows to introduce aliases for type names, reducing this problem a bit. We mentioned already, that the syntactical requirements of a template on its parameters are not easily visible. This problem is aggravated by the fact that error messages from code involving templates are usually much harder to decipher than other error messages.

Overall however, the good runtime performance and great flexibility achievable with templates easily make up for the shortcomings. To let users take full advantage of these benefits, it is however necessary to distribute the source code. This may be an issue in commercial projects. In open source projects where this is a non-issue by definition and in academic projects, generic programming has been used widely and successfully ever since it has been supported adequately by compilers.

Iterators are the mechanism that makes it possible to decouple algorithms from containers. They should be used to access an aggregate object's contents without exposing its internal representation. A container class need only provide a way to access its elements by iterators. This allows to implement a generic algorithm that can operate on many different kind of containers. In the standard template library (STL) of C++, algorithms are templates, and are parameterized by the type of iterator. Five different categories are defined for iterators: input, output, forward, bidirectional, and random-access iterators.

The observer pattern can be used to separate the pure purpose of algorithms from extensions. For example, in Algorithm Engineering operation counts are very useful for the performance analysis but do not contribute to the functionality. Likewise, visualization and animation of data structures and algorithms can greatly help to understand the algorithm's behavior.

6.5   Ease of Use

Ease of use for a software component means that a user can easily operate it without having a steep learning curve. For a non-experienced user it should be intuitive to work with the compiled program or the methods provided by a library. As for products for the world-wide market, implementations in Algorithm Engineering should address as much users as possible. Scientists in Algorithm Engineering are encouraged to publish their software to increase comparability and reproducibility of their work, so that additional users come up quite quickly or others continue to develop this piece of software. These people reject to use or develop software if they fail to install, execute, include, or understand it. The ease of use of an implementation can mainly be increased by two goals: A well-chosen interface and a well-written documentation.

6.5.1   Interface Design

"A user interface is well-designed when the program behaves exactly how the user thought it would." [752]. This implies that an implementer has to figure out what is expected from his software. In Algorithm Engineering this means to design an interface that is closely related to the algorithm, providing easy access to it, while also maintaining handles to all the detailed options. This task is like a tightrope walk. On the one hand the interface should be as easy as possible, such that users can quickly start to use the software. Names should be intuitive, while signatures of functions and command line options keep clear. On the other hand, an advanced user wishes for a more powerful interface that offers all the tools for more complex scenarios, which allows to have hands on very specific parts of the algorithm (or data structures).

Note that the term of a well-designed interface applies to two ends of the software development process: Compiled programs and software libraries: For programs the command line options (the graphical user interface) require a basic set of options that are easy to access, while more complex tasks can be hidden in advanced options (or menus). In library development, the task is even more critical. One often deals with a lot of objects that interact. Each single one aims for a simple but powerful interface. On top of this, the communication between entities is another task that needs to be designed to be simple without losing functionality. It is best to support very simple methods with intuitive names. More advanced accessing and modifying methods should also be implemented, while declaring them in the *documentation* as (more) advanced. See Section 6.5.2 for further details.

A high "ease of use" often comes along with high modularity. In analogy to the real world, an implementation should decompose the problem into entities of smaller size, such that one has very basic building blocks. These can be combined successfully to bigger items, while maintaining the invariant of simplicity for each composed object, i. e., to keep the interface and perceivability as simple as intended. The topmost layer is obviously expected to fulfill this condition, too. This way the implementer also ensures the easy rearrangement of parts. For more details, we refer to Section 6.4.

6.5.2   Documentation and Readability

Any code, software, or program only makes sense if one is able to understand what it is good for. Documentation is the way to reach this goal. Note that software always also addresses human beings, not only computers. Without documentation a user or developer quickly fails to use it and in the consequence capitulates. Therefore, extensive documentation is encouraged, although it requires a remarkable amount of time: Either one pays to create the documentation in the beginning, or one pays a terrible price if one has no documentation at all. Most programmers see the documentation task as a necessary evil, if they see it at all. They simply do not believe that this work can be useful [629], i. e., that documentation is the only way to report in a natural language what the software is capable of and to serve as a knowledge base for future maintainers of the code. A very desirable resolution is "to keep all program design documentation complete, precise, and up to to date" [65].

Unfortunately, if done at all, most documentation is incomplete and inaccurate. The main problems are of an organizational kind [629]:

- Documentation can be written as the documenter becomes conscious of facts, or as the program executes parts. Both approaches lack an easy method to find out what is missing and maintaining such documentation is also a horrible task.
- Boring Prose: Too many words are used to describe a single feature, or same things are repeated in different sections. Both leads to inattentive reading and undiscovered errors. A solution is to document by concerns, i. e., at some unique place that only covers a certain concern about the software and nothing else.
- Confusing and Inconsistent Terminology: Documenters name same things differently or similar things same. This results in a mixture of terms that no one can ever understand.
- Involvement: Documentation is often written near the end of a project. All people involved already know a lot about the software, but forget at the same time to mention basic things within the documentation. This way, newcomers

fail to enter the usage of the system. Advice: Give documentation for proof-reading (understanding) to someone outside the project.

Is it important that readers feel natural to follow the documentation. It should be as hierarchical as the modular design. Each new step is introduced with general information while adding simple things first and concluding with the more advanced stuff. This way, it is convenient to learn how to use or maintain the unknown software.

Documentation can be distinguished with respect to the addressed readers and its intended function. Several structures are possible. We refer to the one given by [691, 16] which consists of three main parts.

User Documentation. This part addresses users of a software (component). Users require different kinds of information and even different types of users must be addressed. The success of a software depends highly on the quality of the documentation without additional assistance. In large software systems some parts can be kept internal. It is an option whether to provide user documentation for these parts, but it is encouraged to do so, since it also supports other developers as reusers.

User documentation for a software, or a even single component, consists of up to five parts, depending on its size [748]. The *functional description* introduces provided services and requirements to present the global picture. It is followed by an *installation manual* to advise system administrators with detailed information how to install the system. An *introductory manual* (*tutorial*) leads novices in an informal way through the main parts and the standard features. This way, unexperienced users get in touch with the new piece of software [362]. The full detailed description of all features and error messages is contained in the *reference manual*. These texts can be extended with a *system administrator manual*. User documentation is also known as *external* documentation.

Concerning the reference manual, there are tools available that help to write the corresponding documentation next to the implementation. Here we just name two of them without going into detail what they accomplish in full finery.

- *Doxygen* [796] is a documentation system for C, C++, and IDL. It can generate an online class browser (in HTML) and/or an off-line reference manual (in LaTeX) from a set of documented source code files. Doxygen can also be configured to extract the structure from undocumented source files. This can be very useful for quickly finding your way in large source distributions.
- *DOC++* [252] is a documentation system for C/C++ and Java generating both LaTeX output for high quality hard-copies and HTML output for sophisticated online browsing of your documentation. The documentation is extracted directly from the C++ header or Java class files.
- *Javadoc* has been develop by Sun Microsystems to generate API documentation in HTML for Java source code. It uses tags within a Java block comment to collect appropriate data for classes and methods.

System Documentation. This part collects information that are relevant for the development of a software. New developers should be lead into the internals of the project. Maintainer must be enabled to apply later modification without additional assistance. In particular, [748] speaks about the following parts. The *requirements* define the contract between a user (end user or reuser) and the developer. The *overall design and structure* lists all available components and their relations. Internal algorithmic details are explained in *implementation details*.

In addition, source documentation helps developers and maintainers to "read" the code [861], which is more than analyzing, debugging, or developing it. Usually several programmers work on the same program and have to read and understand each others code. Even for a single programmer it is sometimes hard to read his own code after a few weeks if some basic rules have been disregarded.

Note that each source code is possibly reused in the future and, with the help of a detailed maintenance and documentation of source code, no one is forced to choose one of the unacceptable methods: Making dangerous assumptions, scrutinizing the implementation or interrogating the author. Source code conventions and documentation are therefore an irreplaceable necessity, as well as an important discipline to increase development efficiency and quality [495].

Source code documentation mainly reflects the decisions that have been made while writing the code ensures that the experiences that led to these decisions do not have to be made once more. Users and maintainers will also be happy if they read why a certain decision has not been taken [629]. Comments for single lines or small blocks support the understanding why the implementer has chosen this particular set of instructions. Even explaining the include statement for a particular header file may make sense [861]. The overall goal is to find a balance, describing all salient program features comprehensively but concisely. The comments should cover all parts of the code, but a too exhaustive usage might on the other hand reduce the readability of the code. The advice is to document reasonably enough.

Forgetting to document the code itself should not be forgiven [854]. As we also do not forgive coders when they forget to document the interface. But projects often lack of time and omit to document the system sufficiently. Section 6.5.3 introduces literate programming that can improve the situation.

Finally, the system documentation may also contain information about *test plans and reports.*

Process Documentation. User and system documentation describe the current state of a software. Process documentation concentrates on the dynamics during the development. It supports effective management and allows to control the progress of the project and its quality in relation to the spent efforts. The process documentation mainly comprises the following parts: The *project plan* defines schedules and goals. The *organization and resource plans* describe personnel and non-personnel allocations. The management might set up *project standards* that all members must follow. Important technical details are collected in *working papers.* In particular, developers use these documents to record certain design rationales. All these items should be extended by a *log book* to store inter-member communications and also by *reading aids*, such as indices, or table of contents.

As one can see, documentation is a non-trivial very important task. The mentioned parts only give a brief overview of the key ingredients. There are much more details that should be considered when documenting software, as for example known bugs, upcoming support questions, limitations, or existing test cases.

Coding Conventions. As already mentioned, software projects are strongly encouraged to set up *coding conventions*, i. e., rules that are intended to improve the readability of code. Such collections reflect the good practice gained from many people over a long time. They cover subject areas such as *naming, formatting*, and also *programming practices*. Some of these rules are arbitrary fixings, but complying with them makes the code consistent and thus more easy to read.

Different coding conventions may contradict each other, e. g., the usage of the underscore '_' which is commonly used for `composed_variable_names` in C code, vs. the "camel case" which is used for `composedVariableNames` in some C++ libraries such as QT and in Java. Which rule to apply depends on the individual taste, and that question can usually not be definitely answered. But again: sticking to a certain set of rules improves the readability conspicuously, especially if several persons work on the same code. If the usage of capital letters in names and the usage of white space is consistent within the whole code, it is much easier to grasp the meaning of distinct parts. The rules concerning the naming of identifiers do not only address syntactical issues. The meaning of an identifier should be reflected by its name. Coders sticking to such conventions will quickly experience the advantages of them. For example, it can be very helpful to know from the notation whether an identifier represents a variable, a method, a type, a class, a concept, or a constant. Let us mention, that bigger software projects often setup their own coding conventions.

Sometimes the readability is improved by breaking a rule, which should be allowed in some special cases. We give an example. For people that are familiar with matrices it might be easier to detect the error in a fragment like this

```
m[0][0] = v00;    m[0][1] = v01;    m[0][2] = v02;
m[1][0] = v10;    m[1][1] = v11;    m[1][2] = v12;
m[1][0] = v20;    m[1][1] = v21;    m[1][2] = v22;
```

than if it was spread over 9 lines. So everybody should feel free to consider to break the otherwise very helpful rule "*Each line should contain at most one statement*".

6.5.3 Literate Programming

Literate programming [480] changes the view for system documentation, i.e., if reusers benefit from documented internals of the system. In some settings it can also be applied to document interface descriptions for reused components.

So far, the programmer's primary goal was to produce source code that can be read by a computer. Literate programming focuses on the humans reading the programmer's work. Source and documentation are contained in the same file. Even more special: The source code is just the add-on to the textual description that the computer understands better. Special tools help to extract the two ingredients efficiently. In contrast to embedded documentation tools like Doxygen [796], literate programming is more powerful. It supports a full-fledged typesetting tool like TEX. This allows the "programmer" to write the "program" in a way that is best for human understanding. If you write for someone else, you automatically care more about identifier names and the structure, for example. The programmer even gets support by tools that enhance the programming language to rearrange the chosen order when the code is processed by the compiler or interpreter. This enables to choose the order in a way that optimizes exposition [799].

Programming under the literate programming paradigm should support other intelligent beings with the meaning of the program instead of only convincing a machine to act in a certain way [835]. It increases the quality of the result, since software developers have to examine and explain the code block by block — in a convenient manner. Literate programming helps to highlight subtleties of an algorithm, since the documentation and the code are written next to each other. In addition, the typesetting system out-of-the-box enables the programmer to be more powerful. Literate programming systems allow to use tables, figures, lists, special indentation. Code can be automatically emphasized — italic font for identifiers or bold face for reserved words.

There is a big list of literate programming systems. We only collect a selected set taken from [530]. Many other tools are available on the Internet.

- The original *WEB* system was developed by Knuth [479]. It combined Pascal source code with TeX typesetting.
- The *CWEB* System of Structured Documentation [484] is a version of *WEB* for documenting C, C++, and Java programs.
- *FunnelWeb* [835] is a powerful literate-programming macro preprocessor that enables you to weave programs and documentation together. It is a production quality tool that was specifically engineered for practical everyday use.
- *noweb* [662] is designed to meet the needs of literate programmers while remaining as simple as possible. Its primary advantages are simplicity, extensibility, and language-independence. *Noweb* uses 5 control sequences in comparison to *WEB*'s 27. The *noweb* manual is only 3 pages long; an additional page explains how to customize its LaTeX output.

There are famous examples [481, 561, 792] using literate programming. On the other hand Sametinger [691, 18.3] points out, that its widespread acceptance is still lacking. Tool support and tool integration was missing in the past years. A complex software system requires an informative and easy visualization of all relation of its components. Integrated development tools that combine literate programming and browsing software components have not been available. The acceptance may increase if development environments include better literate programming support. Another reason might be that people think of literate programming producing "monolithic" output, unlike to the well-known hyperlinked documentation techniques.

6.6   Implementing Efficiently

6.6.1   Reuse

Probably the most powerful way to make implementing more efficiently is reuse: If the program we aim for has been written before, we are done! Within the scope of Algorithm Engineering the algorithms are usually new ones so it will be quite unlikely to find an existing implementation of it. However the idea remains important: "Do not re-reinvent the wheel all the time"! In most cases subalgorithms, data structures or code fragments do exist. Reuse occurs on different levels. Sometimes code fragments are reused in a different place of the same program (copy and paste). Or, sometimes the code of complete methods or classes is available (e. g., on the web) and is reused. There also exist libraries of data structures and algorithms which allow systematic reuse (see Chapter 7).

But not only code, also knowledge can be reused when writing new code. In the field of software engineering so called *design patterns* were devised [313]. These patterns give generic solutions to commonly occurring design and implementation problems (see Section 6.4). Applying these patterns does not imply a reuse of existing code but a reuse of knowledge which also helps to obtain a stable implementation in less time.

By using existing code and ideas, the effort is reduced because things do not have to be done over and over again. In addition the quality is improved, because the existing code is already reviewed and tested and the existing ideas have been surveyed by many other programmers.

6.6.2   Programming Language

The question which programming language is the best cannot be generally answered. Sometimes the problem that is to be solved encourages certain choices, e. g., *Fortran* is considered to be specialized on numeric computations whereas *PERL* concentrates on string manipulation.

There is also an interaction of the programming language and the reuse issue. Sometimes the language determines which libraries can be used for a project. Often it is the other way around and the libraries or other existing code determines which programming language is used.

If the programmer has the choice between several nearly equally appropriate programming languages, his own abilities and preferences play also a major role.

The following paragraphs are not meant for ranking one language over the other, but for denoting some issues that might be part of the responsibility of the implementer and therefore may have influence on the choice of the appropriate programming language for a particular project.

According to Zeller [858], some languages are more prone to certain kind of bugs than others – in particular, languages, where *undefined behavior* is part of the semantics, which means that for some constructs the semantics is deliberately not specified. To name just two examples, Zeller specifically refers to the *char* type whose value range is not explicitly specified in C and to the problems stemming from uninitialized variables (or rather general: memory that is read before written) in C++ and other languages. More recent languages, such as Java and C#, feature almost every single aspect of the program execution to be well defined, including forced initialization.

One quite powerful feature of the new generation languages is automatic memory management, coupled with a garbage collector. This frees the programmer from performing manual memory management or reference counting. If this feature is not available in the chosen language, dynamic allocation and deallocation of memory has to be carefully crafted and should, in the best case, already be integrated into the design phase. In fact, it must be ensured for instance, that no premature return statement may entail a manually allocated chunk of memory to remain unreleased, as otherwise a memory leak would be the consequence. Altogether, automatic memory management eliminates an entire category of robustness problems due to errors, such as circular references, dangling pointers, and, as already mentioned, memory leaks.

However, premature returns may not only result in memory leaks. Instead, there are a couple of resources that must explicitly be released when no longer in use, e. g., (I/O-)streams, locks, sockets, devices and so on [858]. In opposite to memory blocks, these resources are usually not audited by a special runtime mechanism. However, Zeller notes that advanced compilers as well as external tools are quite capable of detecting most of such "code smells" of resources potentially not being released properly. Nevertheless, it seems to be most appropriate not to rely too much on such tools, but consider the allocation and deallocation of resources already in the course of designing the program flow based on the control structures.

Last, but not least, the *type-system* of a language may support robustness. The task of a type-system is to assign to a memory block a semantical meaning and, in doing so, prevent certain forms of erroneous or undesirable program behavior (called type errors). Depending on how strong this enforcement takes place, one distinguishes between *weakly typed* and *strongly typed* languages. Weakly typed languages permit to (more or less easily) change or re-interpret the meaning of such an assigned memory block, usually on the basis of coercions (implicit conversions) and castings (explicit conversions). Strongly typed languages provide an increased type-safety, i. e., only operations defined by the associated type can be performed on an object. Type-safety eliminates an entire category of errors, stemming from invalid casts, bad pointer arithmetic, and to some extend even malicious code [255]. A lack of type-safety demands the implementer to add this problem to his considerations.

Apart from the strength of a type-system, it may also play a role at which point of time this enforcement takes place. *Static typing* requires the variables to be bound to types at compile time – either by explicitly declaring the binding (*declarative* or *manifest typing*) or by letting it get inferred based on the context (*inferred typing*). *Dynamic typing* enforces this binding at runtime. Static and dynamic typing are not mutually exclusive – a combination of both is also possible. Altogether, the benefit of static typing is that it allows (however not *implies*) the types to be checked at compile-time, whereas dynamic typing allows this check to be performed not earlier than at run time. In regard to this, Bloch [110] argues that it is always beneficial to detect programming errors as quickly as possible, in particular before the program is run. He concludes that "to get the most robust programs, you want to do as much static type checking as possible" [803]. In fact, if static type checking is not provided, it is strongly advisable, not to say essential, to carefully design a mechanism for handling exceptional situations of failing checks raising at runtime.

Note that several of these nice features of programming languages may be partially in conflict with efficiency.

6.6.3 Development Environment

Depending on the programming language, there exists a variety of *integrated development environments* (*IDEs*) that make programming easier and more efficient. They manage complete projects, help with compiling and debugging the programs, and support the writing. Some of the features most IDEs have, are

Editor: An editor that is tailored to the specific programming language. It marks special code fragments such as keywords, identifiers, or comments (*syntax highlighting*) to improve the readability. It generates code fragments and makes suggestions on how to finish a prefix (*code completion*) to avoid slips and to quicken typing. It ensures formatting according to some coding conventions. It marks syntactical errors as well as some semantical errors such as unreachable code.

Compiler / Interpreter: The code can be compiled and/or executed directly from within the IDE. The process of compiling, linking etc. is managed by the IDE (build-automation).

Debugger: The code can be run step by step to be able to trace the states of the program.

Class Browser: For object oriented languages the IDE's offer the possibility to browse the hierarchical class structure. Documentation automatically generated from the source code is displayed to enable orientation in complex projects and the IDE finds declarations and references to identifiers.

Refactoring: Tools help the programmer to consistently rename identifiers, to inline method invocations, or to change the structure of the code.

6.6.4 Avoiding Errors

Implementing does not mean to write code only. It involves also that the program has to be executable and that obvious defects are fixed. There is no clear border between writing code and fixing errors. Defects in the code can be detected by running and debugging the program. The costs for the detection and the removal varies but the cheapest errors are the ones never made. Some categories of errors can easily be avoided.

- Slips can be reduced by using a better development environment. Syntax errors due to mistakes in writing are avoided by choosing the correct identifier from a list of all possible ones. If syntax errors that occurred never the less are highlighted by the editor, they can easily be removed while writing. Runtime errors due to uninitialized variables can also be avoided using an appropriate development environment that checks for initialization.
- Apart from the slips which a programmer could detect on his own by rereading his code, there are falsities the programmer would do repeatedly. That may be errors only he would do or errors that would also happen to other people. The programmer should note a defect and its correction if the search for it took long, if the costs caused by it were high, and if it kept undiscovered for a long time. By writing it down not only the search for subsequently occurring defects becomes faster but the awareness of them also may help to avoid similar errors in the future.

Since the old lore that a program either is trivial or it contains defects is corroborated over and over again, the programmer should use all the help he can get. There is a variety of tools that perform a static code analysis and report on code fragments that possibly contain a defect or in some cases try to verify properties of the program. Probably one of the most commonly known is *lint* [441] for C-code with its followers *lclint* and *splint* [751].

6.6.5 Versioning

Since programming is not a trivial process, usually decisions have to be amended with hindsight. A versioning system helps the programmer to handle several versions of the code and to go back to a prior version. Although tools like *cvs (Concurrent Versions System)* and *svn (SubVersioN)* are mostly applied in projects that several people work on, such a versioning system could also be applied in single-programmer projects. Since the results of experiments performed have to be reproducible, it is important to be able to associate the results to the version of the program the results were produced with. Using a versioning system, a single note (version number or date respectively) is sufficient to easily reconstruct the corresponding program version.

6.7 Geometric Algorithms

Correctly implementing geometric algorithms is a special problem which arises from the delicate interaction of combinatorial and numerical data. Geometric algorithms are described using predicates. A predicate is a black box that answers questions about certain geometric constellations, like "Is point p inside circle c?" or "Do two segments s_1, s_2 intersect?" How to implement these predicates is rarely discussed in a paper describing a specific algorithm because a correct implementation in the real RAM model is easy and takes constant time. But the real RAM does not exist, so in practice one has to sacrifice either correctness or constant time. The classic approach has been to sacrifice correctness and use hardware floating-point arithmetic in the implementation, believing that the rounding error introduced by this will be small and will not affect the algorithm. Experience has proven this to be wrong; any kind of conceivable error may happen. Programs crash, loop forever or in the worst case compute garbage without the user noticing. Several such errors have been reported in the literature, e. g., [731] and [561, Section 9.6]. Kettner et al. [471] describe simple cases where an algorithm for computing the convex hull of a set of points in the plane fails and examine the bizarre "geometry" of the planar floating-point orientation predicate.

The planar orientation predicate, used in many geometric algorithms, determines for three points $p = (p_x, p_y), q = (q_x, q_y)$ and $r = (r_x, r_y) \in \mathbb{R}^2$ the position of r to the oriented line through p and q. The predicate can be computed by evaluating the sign of a determinant:

$$D = \begin{vmatrix} p_x & p_y & 1 \\ q_x & q_y & 1 \\ r_x & r_y & 1 \end{vmatrix} = (q_x - p_x)(r_y - p_y) - (q_y - p_y)(r_x - p_x) \ .$$

The point r is on the line, if D is zero and it is to the left (right) of the line, if D is greater (smaller) than zero. Thus only the sign of D is of interest. In an implementation, the mathematical operations $+, -, \cdot, /$ may simply be replaced by their floating-point counterparts $\oplus, \ominus, \odot, \oslash$. We will continue to use this notation for floating-point operations later on.

$$D = (q_x \ominus p_x) \odot (r_y \ominus p_y) \ominus (q_y \ominus p_y) \odot (r_x \ominus p_x) \ .$$

Floating-point operations do not always deliver the mathematically correct result but the correct result rounded to a representable floating-point number. Thus with floating-point arithmetic, only an approximation of D is computed which may have the wrong sign in certain cases. In a plane sweep algorithm for computing the convex hull of a set of points in the plane, points outside of the current hull are added and the hull is updated appropriately. With a floating-point predicate it will in certain cases happen, that the predicate reports that the point is on the "outside" of all lines supporting convex hull edges. This is however geometrically impossible and will most likely result in the algorithm crashing or looping infinitely.

The problem with inexact arithmetic is that it makes decisions that are inconsistent with each other or Euclidean geometry in general. To overcome this problem, it may be possible to redesign an algorithm in a way that it can cope with the inaccuracy, however this has been done successfully only for a small number of problems. Section 3.5.3 contains more information on this approach.

The second possibility is to implement the predicates correctly using some exact arithmetic. This principle emerged as the Exact Geometric Computation Paradigm [846] and has been very successful because it does not require any change in the algorithm. We will therefore first look at exact software number types. As the usage of these types typically is much more expensive than hardware floating-point arithmetic we will further look at techniques that reduce the cost of exact arithmetic. A large part will be dedicated to the number type leda::real which combines several techniques into a highly general, easy to use and moderately efficient solution.

6.7.1   Correctness: Exact Number Types

We can assume that a predicate consists of computing a number from input values using a given formula and then return true or false based on the sign of the computed number. The requirements for a number type used in a geometric algorithm are therefore clear. It must be possible to represent all input numbers in the number type. The number type must support all needed arithmetical operations and functions and finally it must be possible to compute the sign of a number from its representation. We will now mention a few of the available exact number types, roughly ordered by capabilities.

The simplest case for exact arithmetic arises when all the numerical input data to an algorithm is integral and only the operations $\pm, \cdot$ are used, i.e., all computations are in the ring $\mathbb{Z}$. The binary representation of an integer is finite; algorithms for adding and multiplying these representations are taught in primary school. An integer α is represented as $\alpha = s \cdot \sum_{i=0}^{k-1} a_i \cdot 2^{i \cdot b}$, where $k = \lceil \lceil \log_2 |\alpha| \rceil / b \rceil$ and $s \in \{-1, 1\}$. The a_i are unsigned integers with b bits, called words, and all k of them are actually saved to memory. For example with $b = 3$:

$$-117 = -1110101_2 = -1 \cdot (001_2 \cdot 2^{2 \cdot 3} + 110_2 \cdot 2^3 + 101_2) .$$

Implementations typically not only support the standard operations $\pm, \cdot$, but also div, mod giving the quotient and remainder of integer division and gcd for computing the greatest common divisor. Assuming that all operands have at most k words, addition can be done in $O(k)$; multiplication algorithms range from $O(k^2)$ to $O(k \cdot \log k \cdot \log \log k)$. Quotient and remainder can simultaneously be computed in $O(M(k))$ time; computing the greatest common divisor of two numbers takes $O(M(k) \log k)$ time, where $M(k)$ is the time for one multiplication [814]. All other types of "high accuracy" arithmetic are somehow reduced to arithmetic over integers.

Bigfloat software floating-point numbers are somewhere in between integer and rational number types. A bigfloat α is represented by an integer mantissa m and an integer exponent e with $\alpha = m \cdot 2^e$. In some implementations the exponent is not arbitrary in size, but some hardware supported type with a limited range. This is done because it is efficient and the exponent rarely becomes very large or small, but it may lead to overflow or underflow. The mantissa is typically an arbitrary precision integer. Then the operations $\pm, \cdot$ can be performed exactly by adapting the length of the mantissa with each operation. Bigfloats are a superset of hardware floating-point numbers and support the same set of operations. They can also be used with a fixed mantissa length if the needed length for an operation to be exact is known, or to compute approximations.

When the division operation / is needed as well, one has to switch to rational arithmetic. A rational number α can be represented as $\alpha = a/b$, where a and $b > 0$ are relatively prime integers. All operations can be reduced to operations over integers with an additional renormalization step to make the numerator and denominator relatively prime again. The requirement of a and b being relatively prime can be dropped to avoid an expensive renormalization step. This may however lead to a and b becoming unnecessarily large in a cascaded computation.

Another operation one would like to have is $\beta = \sqrt[k]{\alpha}$, where $\alpha \geq 0$ and β is the unique non-negative real number with $\beta^k = \alpha$. The natural environment for this operation is the field of real algebraic numbers $\mathbb{A}$ because it is closed under the $\sqrt[k]{\ }$ operation.

Definition 7 (Real Algebraic Number). *A real number α is called* algebraic *if there is a polynomial $p = \sum_{i=0}^{n} a_i x^i \in \mathbb{Z}[X]$ with $p(\alpha) = 0$. If there is such a p with $a_n = 1$, α is called an* algebraic integer. *The polynomial p is called* a minimal polynomial *of α if its degree is minimal among all $q \in \mathbb{Z}[x]$ with $q(\alpha) = 0$. It is called* the minimal polynomial *if additionally $a_n > 0$ and $\gcd(a_n, \ldots, a_0) = 1$. The roots of the minimal polynomial p of α are called the* conjugates *of α and the* degree *of α is the degree of p.*

Real algebraic numbers are a superset of integer and rational numbers. It follows directly from the definition that a real algebraic number α can be represented as $\alpha = (p, [a_1, a_2])$ where $p \in \mathbb{Z}[x]$ is a polynomial, $a_1, a_2 \in \mathbb{Q}$ and $[a_1, a_2]$ is an isolating interval for α, i.e., α is the only root of p in $[a_1, a_2]$. In some applications real algebraic numbers arise quite naturally in this representation [94]. Note that not all real algebraic numbers can be expressed using integers and the operations $\pm, \cdot, /, \sqrt[k]{\ }$. Still those and other operations, like taking a real root of a polynomial with real algebraic coefficients, can be performed using the representation as polynomial and isolating interval. It is further possible to compute arbitrarily good rational or floating-point approximations and also the sign of a number [576, 847]. Computing with algebraic numbers is however expensive in comparison to other arbitrary precision number types. In Section 6.7.3 we will have a closer look at an implementation of real algebraic numbers using a different technique.

Beyond real algebraic numbers, not much is known. While Chang et al. [160] show that a special geometric problem involving transcendental numbers can be solved exactly, it is in general unknown whether the sign of a number can be computed if the functions exp or log are admitted [672]. On the other hand, for geometric algorithms it often suffices to increase the available precision just a little. The techniques for computing with expansions do exactly this and deserve attention. We believe there is still room for improvement using these and similar approaches. For example an algorithm equivalent to TwoProduct can be implemented with only two floating-point operations on hardware with a fused-multiply-add instruction. Most of the mentioned number types have been implemented and are available in several libraries. An overview can be found in Section 7.6.

6.7.2 Efficiency: Floating-Point Filters and Other Techniques

We have now seen some exact number types that allow us to correctly implement predicates for geometric algorithms. The first experiments with this approach showed that exact arithmetic is slower than hardware arithmetic by several magnitudes. Karasick et al. [458] report a slowdown factor of up to 10000 when replacing hardware arithmetic with off-the-shelf arbitrary-precision rational arithmetic in an algorithm for computing Delaunay triangulations. Fortune and van Wyk [298, 299] report a slowdown of 40 to 140 when computing 2D and 3D incircle tests with arbitrary precision integer arithmetic instead of hardware arithmetic. In both cases the authors were able to significantly reduce this slowdown.

Floating-point filters are the most common technique to reduce the cost of exact arithmetic, by avoiding the use of exact arithmetic whenever possible. The key observation is, that approximate computations with floating-point arithmetic are fast and compute the correct result most of the time. Assume a predicate depends on the sign of a number γ which has to be computed from some input values. Using hardware floating-point arithmetic, an approximation $\hat{\gamma}$ to γ and an error e_γ are computed, guaranteeing $|\gamma - \hat{\gamma}| \le e_\gamma$. Then the sign of γ is equal to the sign of $\hat{\gamma}$, if $|\hat{\gamma}| > e_\gamma$. This case is called a filter success, since the sign of γ is known. The case $|\hat{\gamma}| \le e_\gamma$ is called a filter failure, in this case something else must be done to compute the sign of γ. If a bound on all input numbers is known, the error bound e_γ may be computed a priory, resulting in a so called *static filter*. The requirement to know a bound on all input numbers is sometimes impractical, therefore *almost static filters* update the error bound whenever new data is added to the set of all input values. In case of a success, the overhead of a static filter consists only of comparing the approximation with the error bound. Since the error bound is however not based on the actual values used to compute $\hat{\gamma}$, static filters tend to fail often. A *dynamic filter* computes the error bound along with the approximation. This gives a tight bound and therefore fewer filter failures, but computing the bound is usually at least as expensive as computing the approximation. Another way to implement a dynamic filter is to compute γ using hardware floating-point interval arithmetic [136]. Interval arithmetic is discussed below. With respect to the characteristics of different filter types, efficient predicates typically *cascade* filters. That is, first a computationally inexpensive filter is used which may however have a high failure rate. If it fails, the approximation or the error bound or both are improved, using a more expensive filter with lower failure rate. This may be repeated several times, with an exact evaluation at the last stage only.

Fortune and van Wyk [298] described one of the first floating-point filters. It applies to integer input and the operations $\pm, \cdot$. The LEDA book [561, section 9.7] discusses several aspects of floating-point filters and gives further references.

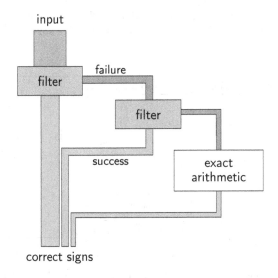

Fig. 6.4. Sign computation using cascaded floating-point filters

Burnikel et al. [144] describe a floating-point filter which applies to all numbers and the operations $\pm, \cdot, /, \sqrt{}$ when performed in floating-point arithmetic with a p-bit mantissa. Together with the approximation $\hat{\gamma}$ of γ an upper bound $\hat{\gamma}_{\mathrm{sup}}$ on the absolute value of $\hat{\gamma}$ and an index ind_γ are computed, following Table 6.1. The approximation then fulfills

$$|\gamma - \hat{\gamma}| \le \hat{\gamma}_{\mathrm{sup}} \cdot \mathrm{ind}_\gamma \cdot 2^{-p}$$

so the error is given by $e_\gamma = \hat{\gamma}_{\mathrm{sup}} \cdot \mathrm{ind}_\gamma \cdot 2^{-p}$. The filter by Burnikel et al. is semi-static; for a predicate of fixed size the value $\mathrm{ind}_\gamma \cdot 2^{-p}$ is known a priory while the value $\hat{\gamma}_{\mathrm{sup}}$ must be computed along with the approximation. If only the operations $\pm, \cdot$ are involved, the filter can be made static if an upper bound on the absolute value of all input numbers is known. Using a floating-point filter before resorting to exact arithmetic speeds up the easy cases, where the result of the computation is far from zero, while slowing down the hard cases only a little. Section 7.9 reports on a case study [703] that compares different ways to implement the orientation predicate used in a convex hull algorithm. The approaches using floating-point filters outperform all the approaches directly using exact arithmetic, showing the advantage of using filtering.

Interval arithmetic is a generalization of real arithmetic from numbers to intervals. Here a number x is represented by an interval $[a, b]$ and the only information known is $x \in [a, b]$. In the optimal case, x is represented by $[x, x]$. Let $f : \mathbb{R}^n \to \mathbb{R}$ be a continuous function and $C = [a_1, b_1] \times \cdots \times [a_n, b_n]$. Then f is extended to intervals through $f(C) = \{f(x) \mid x \in C\}$. Since f is continuous, $f(C)$ is again an interval. The basic property of interval arithmetic holds:

$$c \in C \Rightarrow f(c) \in f(C). \tag{1}$$

Table 6.1. Rules for computing parameters for the floating-point filter by Burnikel et al. [144]. round gives the nearest floating-point value and sqrt is the floating-point implementation of the square root.

expression γ	approximation $\hat{\gamma}$	supremum $\hat{\gamma}_{\text{sup}}$	index ind_γ
p-bit γ	γ	$\|\gamma\|$	0
$\gamma \in \mathbb{R}$	$\texttt{round}(\gamma)$	$\|\hat{\gamma}\|$	1
$\alpha + \beta$	$\hat{\alpha} \oplus \hat{\beta}$	$\hat{\alpha}_{\text{sup}} \oplus \hat{\beta}_{\text{sup}}$	$1 + \max\{\text{ind}_\alpha, \text{ind}_\beta\}$
$\alpha - \beta$	$\hat{\alpha} \ominus \hat{\beta}$	$\hat{\alpha}_{\text{sup}} \oplus \hat{\beta}_{\text{sup}}$	$1 + \max\{\text{ind}_\alpha, \text{ind}_\beta\}$
$\alpha \cdot \beta$	$\hat{\alpha} \odot \hat{\beta}$	$\hat{\alpha}_{\text{sup}} \odot \hat{\beta}_{\text{sup}}$	$1 + \text{ind}_\alpha + \text{ind}_\beta$
α/β	$\hat{\alpha} \oslash \hat{\beta}$	$\dfrac{(\|\hat{\alpha}\|\oslash\|\hat{\beta}\|\oplus\hat{\alpha}_{\text{sup}}\oslash\hat{\beta}_{\text{sup}})\oslash}{(\|\hat{\beta}\|\oslash\hat{\beta}_{\text{sup}}\ominus(\text{ind}_\beta+1)\cdot2^{-p})}$	$1 + \max\{\text{ind}_\alpha, \text{ind}_\beta + 1\}$
$\sqrt{\alpha}$	$\texttt{sqrt}(\hat{\alpha})$	$\begin{cases}\texttt{sqrt}(\hat{\alpha}_{\text{sup}})\odot2^{\lceil p/2\rceil} & \text{if } \hat{\alpha}=0 \\ (\hat{\alpha}_{\text{sup}}\oslash\hat{\alpha})\odot\texttt{sqrt}(\hat{\alpha}) & \text{if } \hat{\alpha}>0\end{cases}$	$1 + \text{ind}_\alpha$

The problem in interval arithmetic is how to compute $f(C)$ or some small interval $[a, b]$ that contains $f(C)$. For the standard arithmetic operations optimal results are:

$$
\begin{aligned}
[a, b] + [c, d] &= [a + c, b + d] \\
[a, b] - [c, d] &= [a - d, b - c] \\
[a, b] \cdot [c, d] &= [\min\{ac, ad, bc, bd\}, \max\{ac, ad, bc, bd\}] \\
\frac{[a, b]}{[c, d]} &= [\min\{\tfrac{a}{c}, \tfrac{a}{d}, \tfrac{b}{c}, \tfrac{b}{d}\}, \max\{\tfrac{a}{c}, \tfrac{a}{d}, \tfrac{b}{c}, \tfrac{b}{d}\}] \quad \text{for } 0 \notin [c, d] \\
\sqrt[k]{[a, b]} &= [\sqrt[k]{a}, \sqrt[k]{b}] \quad \text{for } a \geq 0.
\end{aligned}
\tag{2}
$$

Reducing an expression to these basic operations may however give pessimistic results. Consider for example the function $f : \mathbb{R} \to \mathbb{R}$, $f(x) = x^2$. Then $f([-1, 2]) = \{x^2 \mid x \in [-1, 2]\} = [0, 4]$. Computing an interval containing $f([-1, 2])$ using the rule for multiplication however gives $[-1, 2] \cdot [-1, 2] = [-2, 4]$, which includes negative numbers as the result of a square. The endpoints of intervals may be represented using e. g., hardware floating-point numbers or bigfloats. When a newly computed endpoint cannot be represented in the number type chosen, left endpoints must be rounded towards $-\infty$ and right endpoints must be rounded toward $+\infty$ to ensure that Equation (1) still holds. The IEEE 754 floating-point standard [420] and most bigfloat implementations support the necessary rounding modes. When it is known that a number x is in an interval $[a, b]$ then the sign of x is known if $0 \notin [a, b]$. Approximating x by interval arithmetic may therefore reveal the sign if x is not close to 0.

When computing in the affine vector space $\mathbb{R}^d$, the division operation / may be avoided by using homogeneous coordinates. Each Cartesian point $(x_1, \ldots, x_d)$ is mapped to the homogeneous point $(h_1, \ldots, h_d, h_{d+1})$, where $x_i = h_i/h_{d+1}$. Therefore, if the Cartesian points are rational, the h_j can all be chosen to be integral and relatively prime. The $d + 1$ th coordinate in the homogeneous point acts as a common denominator to all the other coordinates, so homogeneous coordinates are a generalization of the reduction of rational arithmetic to integer arithmetic. Other geometric objects may also be translated to homogeneous coordinates, e. g., the line $aX + bY + c = 0$ transforms to $aX + bY + cZ = 0$. Observe that the homogeneous variant of each point on the Cartesian line is on the homogeneous line. When working with rational input data or on a problem requiring division it is often much more efficient to use a homogeneous representation.

The d-dimensional projective space consists of all homogeneous points $h \in \mathbb{R}^{d+1}\backslash\{0\}$, where two points g and h are considered to be equal if and only if $g = \lambda \cdot h$ for some $\lambda \neq 0$. The $d + 1$ th coordinate does not have a special role and $h_{d+1} = 0$ is explicitly allowed. In the projective space, objects are not orientable any more, e. g., lines have only one side. For this reason care is required when performing sideness tests using a homogeneous representation of Cartesian coordinates, one way is to require $h_{d+1} > 0$. On the other hand, geometric constellations that require special treatment in affine space, are handled easily in projective space,e. g., parallel lines. The intersection point of the two lines in projective space always exists. Even if this point does not have a Cartesian preimage, it may be used in further computations and a result meaningful in affine space may be computed from it. The projective space may therefore be used to simplify code performing computations in the affine space.

Modular arithmetic [814] is an approach to integer arithmetic, hence it can be used to implement predicates using the operations $\pm, \cdot$ for integer input [137,627]. It is based on the following theorem.

Theorem 1 (Chinese Remainder Theorem). *Let $m_1, m_2, \ldots, m_k$ be pairwise relatively prime and $m = m_1 \cdot m_2 \cdot \ldots \cdot m_k$. Then*

$$f : \mathbb{Z} \to \mathbb{Z}/m_1\mathbb{Z} \times \mathbb{Z}/m_2\mathbb{Z} \times \ldots \times \mathbb{Z}/m_k\mathbb{Z}$$
$$f(\alpha) = (\alpha \bmod m_1, \alpha \bmod m_2, \ldots, \alpha \bmod m_k)$$

is a surjective ring homomorphism with kernel $m\mathbb{Z}$.   □

If the result γ of a computation is known to be in the range $-n < \gamma < n$, one chooses distinct prime numbers $p_1, \ldots, p_k$ such that $p_1 \cdot \ldots \cdot p_k > 2n$, computes $\gamma_j = \gamma \bmod p_j$ by performing the computation modulo each p_j, and then reconstructs γ. Here the reconstruction is the most expensive part. By Theorem 1 $\gamma = 0$ if and only if $\gamma_j = 0$ for all j. Modular arithmetic can therefore also be used to filter if a result is zero. This is contrary to floating-point filters which can only filter results far away from zero. One way to obtain a bound n would be to approximate γ by $\hat{\gamma}$ with an error of e_γ. If $|\hat{\gamma}| > e_\gamma$ the sign of γ is known. Otherwise $|\gamma| \leq |\hat{\gamma}| + e_\gamma \leq 2e_\gamma$ gives a bound that can be used for modular arithmetic. Choosing the p_j smaller than, but close to half the biggest representable integer on a machine allows the compute the γ_j and to reconstruct the sign of γ with hardware arithmetic. The reconstruction of γ itself however may require higher precision arithmetic. Using the prime number theorem it can be shown, that there are sufficiently many primes of this size for any conceivable task [814, exercise 18.19]. Modular arithmetic is particularly useful if intermediate numbers in the computation are known to be considerably larger than the final result.

A way to account for the rounding error in hardware floating-point arithmetic is to use so-called error-free transformations. Error-free transformations allow to transform an expression involving floating-point numbers into a mathematically equivalent expression more suited for a particular purpose, e.g., sign computation. We will give the details of three algorithms, FASTTWOSUM, TWOSUM and TWOPRODUCT for transforming the sum and the product of two floating-point numbers into the sum of two floating-point numbers. Paying attention to the details is central to Algorithm Engineering and these error-free transformations are basic building blocks of many other algorithms. They work correctly in IEEE 754 [420] arithmetic in the round-to-nearest rounding mode. Given two floating-point numbers a and b, FASTTWOSUM and TWOSUM compute floating-point numbers x and y with $a + b = x + y$ and $a \oplus b = x$, unless overflow occurs. FASTTWOSUM requires that $|a| \geq |b|$.

1: **procedure** FASTTWOSUM(a, b)	1: **procedure** TWOSUM(a, b)
2: $\quad x \leftarrow a \oplus b$	2: $\quad x \leftarrow a \oplus b$
3: $\quad b_{\text{virtual}} \leftarrow x \ominus a$	3: $\quad b_{\text{virtual}} \leftarrow x \ominus a$
4: $\quad y \leftarrow b \ominus b_{\text{virtual}}$	4: $\quad a_{\text{virtual}} \leftarrow x \ominus b_{\text{virtual}}$
5: $\quad$ **return** (x, y)	5: $\quad b_{\text{roundoff}} \leftarrow b \ominus b_{\text{virtual}}$
	6: $\quad a_{\text{roundoff}} \leftarrow a \ominus a_{\text{virtual}}$
	7: $\quad y \leftarrow a_{\text{roundoff}} \oplus b_{\text{roundoff}}$
	8: $\quad$ **return** (x, y)

FASTTWOSUM is due to Dekker [217], TWOSUM is due to Knuth [477]. Using TWOSUM, the exact rounding error y of a floating-point addition can be computed at the cost of five additional floating-point operations. The cost reduces to two operations if it is known in advance whether a or b has larger absolute value. Shewchuk [731] notes that using TWOSUM is "usually empirically faster" than first comparing $|a|$ and $|b|$, and then using FASTTWOSUM. This may be different with other architectures and compilers and should be tested before selecting one of the possibilities. Given two floating-point numbers a and b, TWOPRODUCT computes floating-point numbers x and y with $ab = x + y$ and $a \odot b = x$, unless overflow or underflow occurs.

1: **procedure** TWOPRODUCT(a, b)	1: **procedure** SPLIT(a)
2: $\quad x \leftarrow a \odot b$	2: $\quad c \leftarrow (2^{\lceil p/2 \rceil} + 1) \odot a$
3: $\quad (a_{\text{hi}}, a_{\text{lo}}) \leftarrow$ SPLIT(a)	3: $\quad a_{\text{big}} \leftarrow c \ominus a$
4: $\quad (b_{\text{hi}}, b_{\text{lo}}) \leftarrow$ SPLIT(b)	4: $\quad a_{\text{hi}} \leftarrow c \ominus a_{\text{big}}$
5: $\quad e_1 \leftarrow x \ominus (a_{\text{hi}} \odot b_{\text{hi}})$	5: $\quad a_{\text{lo}} \leftarrow a \ominus a_{\text{hi}}$
6: $\quad e_2 \leftarrow e_1 \ominus (a_{\text{lo}} \odot b_{\text{hi}})$	6: $\quad$ **return** $(a_{\text{hi}}, a_{\text{lo}})$
7: $\quad e_3 \leftarrow e_2 \ominus (a_{\text{hi}} \odot b_{\text{lo}})$	
8: $\quad y \leftarrow (a_{\text{lo}} \odot b_{\text{lo}}) \ominus e_3$	
9: $\quad$ **return** (x, y)	

TwoProduct is due to Dekker [217] who attributes Split to Veltkamp. The Split algorithm produces two non-overlapping floating-point values a_{hi} and a_{lo} such that $|a_{hi}| \geq |a_{lo}|$ and $a = a_{hi} + a_{lo}$. Furthermore for floating-point numbers with a p-bit mantissa both a_{hi} and a_{lo} will use at most $\lfloor p/2 \rfloor$ consecutive bits of their mantissa. Therefore the products $a_{hi} \odot b_{hi}$ etc. in TwoProduct are computed without rounding error. On an architecture with a fused-multiply-add instruction an equivalent to TwoProduct may be implemented using only two floating-point operations.

Other error-free transformations are known, e. g., for splitting floating-point numbers, allowing to perform later computations exactly [684, 685], or explicitly accessing the mantissa and exponent of a floating-point number [665].

Many geometric predicates may be implemented as computing the sign of a polynomial expression. Using TwoProduct any polynomial expression on floating-point numbers may be transformed into a sum. Ratschek and Rokne [665] present an algorithm, which they call ESSA for exact sign of a sum algorithm, to compute the sign of the sum of floating-point numbers. ESSA iteratively performs error-free transformations on the largest positive and the smallest negative number in the current sum, thereby decreasing the sum of the absolute values of the summands. The iteration continues until the sum vanishes, or the largest positive number clearly dominates the sum of negative ones, or vice versa. The algorithm is not affected by overflow or underflow. Other algorithms for summing up floating-point numbers, have appeared recently. They are also based on error-free transformations [684, 685] or use a wider accumulator [237] to compute approximations of the sum with a small relative error, allowing us to conclude the sign of the sum.

Based on work by Priest [648], Shewchuk [731] developed techniques to achieve exact arithmetic by extending hardware floating-point arithmetic. He calls two floating-point numbers x and y with $|x| < |y|$ *non-overlapping* if there are integers r, s with $y = r2^s$ and $|x| < 2^s$. Less formally, x and y again with $|x| < |y|$ are non-overlapping if the least significant nonzero bit of y is more significant than the most significant nonzero bit of x. For example -10.1_2 and 1100_2 are non-overlapping while 101_2 and 10_2 do overlap. A number is represented as the sum of non-overlapping floating-point numbers, ordered by absolute value. Such a sum is called an *expansion*. Clearly expansions are a superset of the floating-point numbers they are based on. Note that the output of FastTwoSum, TwoSum and TwoProduct is an expansion. Shewchuk further presents algorithms to add and multiply expansions, again using the error-free transformations FastTwoSum, TwoSum and TwoProduct.

Then, based on expansions, Shewchuk [731] develops 2D and 3D orientation and incircle tests. The sign of an expansion is the sign of the summand with largest absolute value so it suffices to transform the polynomial expression of the predicate into an expansion. Instead of doing this straightforwardly, he computes several approximations and uses error bounds to check whether the approximation already suffices to decide the sign of the number to be computed. A key feature of the predicates is, that when a filter fails, some intermediate results are reused to compute better approximations until the exact result has been reached. This is contrary to the usual application of floating-point filters, where the approximation and error bound are thrown away when switching to an exact arithmetic. Therefore his predicates are very efficient, their runtime is only a small multiple of inexact evaluation, except for almost degenerate input. They are considered state-of-the-art for robust predicates on floating-point input. Shewchuk notes that neither overflow nor underflow will occur if the exponent of the input numbers is in the range $[-142, 201]$, so for these numbers the predicates are truly exact. An implementation of Shewchuks algorithms for expansions and his predicates are available from [730].

6.7.3 Easy to Use: The Number Types CORE::Expr and leda::real

One way to represent a number is to record its creation history. This approach has been taken in the implementation of the number types CORE::Expr [457] and leda::real [141]. A CORE::Expr or a leda::real may be created from an integer, a bigfloat, a rational number or more generally as a real root of a polynomial with integer coefficients. Therefore both number types span the set of real algebraic numbers. Supported operations are $\pm, \cdot, /, \sqrt[k]{\ }$ and taking a real root of a polynomial whose coefficients are itself a CORE::Expr or leda::real. It is possible to compute an arbitrarily accurate rational or bigfloat approximations and to compute the sign of a CORE::Expr or leda::real. As with the functionality, the implementations of both types are quite analogous. Here we will concentrate on the leda::real number type. We will ignore the operation of taking a root of a polynomial for simplicity reasons, instead we only discuss creation from integers and the operations $\pm, \cdot, /, \sqrt[k]{\ }$.

A leda::real is represented as a node in a directed acyclic graph (DAG), cf. Figure 6.5. Each sink of this graph contains an integer, that it represents. An intermediate node is labeled with an operation $\circ \in \{\pm, \cdot, /, \sqrt[k]{\ }\}$. It represents the number α resulting from the operation applied to the numbers represented by its children. Further, each node contains an approximation $\hat{\alpha}$ of α and an error $e_\alpha \geq 0$ guaranteeing $|\alpha - \hat{\alpha}| \leq e_\alpha$. Both $\hat{\alpha}$ and e_α are bigfloats. An arithmetic operation $\gamma = \alpha \circ \beta$ with this representation is simple. A new node corresponding to γ is created, labeled with $\circ$ and having the nodes corresponding to α and β as children. Approximation and error $\hat{\gamma}$ and e_γ are computed from $\hat{\alpha}, e_\alpha, \hat{\beta}, e_\beta$ using for example bigfloat interval arithmetic.

Representing a number γ as a DAG allows to increase the accuracy of the approximation $\hat{\gamma}$ by increasing the mantissa length of the bigfloat numbers and recomputing all approximations from the leaves upwards to the root. In this approach the error is reported bottom-up. The approach does however not allow simple conclusions on how much the accuracy of $\hat{\gamma}$ will increase before the computation is started.

A different approach is the paradigm of precision driven arithmetic. Here accuracy is requested top down. An approximation $\hat{\gamma}$ of γ can be requested,

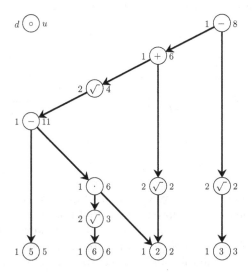

Fig. 6.5. A DAG representing the expression $\sqrt{5 - 2 \cdot \sqrt{6}} + \sqrt{2} - \sqrt{3}$. The parameters u and d are used for the BFMSS separation bound, discussed later in this section.

where e_γ is given in advance. This is possible for the leafs of a DAG since they represent integers which are explicitly known. Let $\gamma = \alpha \circ \beta$, then e_α, e_β and a mantissa length L are determined such that the final $\hat{\gamma}$ will have the requested accuracy. Then $\hat{\alpha}, \hat{\beta}$ are computed recursively, requesting an accuracy of e_α, e_β. Finally $\hat{\gamma} = \hat{\alpha} \odot \hat{\beta}$ is computed using bigfloat arithmetic with mantissa length L. To illustrate this principle, let $\gamma = \alpha \cdot \beta$. It is requested that $|\hat{\gamma} - \gamma| \le e_\gamma$. Choose

$$e_\alpha \le \frac{e_\gamma}{4(|\hat{\beta}| + |e_\beta|)},$$

using the *current* values of $\hat{\beta}$ and e_β. Compute $\hat{\alpha}$ requesting an accuracy of e_α. Then choose

$$e_\beta \le \frac{e_\gamma}{4|\hat{\alpha}|}$$

and compute $\hat{\beta}$ requesting an accuracy of e_β. Finally choose

$$\varepsilon \le \frac{e_\gamma}{2M} \quad \text{where } |\hat{\gamma}| \le M.$$

M can be computed as $M = 2^{\lceil \log_2 |\hat{\alpha}| \rceil + \lceil \log_2 |\hat{\beta}| \rceil}$. Set $L = -\lfloor \log_2 \varepsilon \rfloor$ such that the relative error in the bigfloat multiplication is at most ε. Compute $\hat{\gamma} = \hat{\alpha} \odot \hat{\beta}$

using bigfloat arithmetic with mantissa length L. Then

$$
\begin{aligned}
|\hat{\gamma} - \gamma| &= |\hat{\gamma} - \hat{\alpha} \cdot \hat{\beta} + \hat{\alpha} \cdot \hat{\beta} - \hat{\alpha} \cdot \beta + \beta \cdot \hat{\alpha} - \beta \cdot \alpha| \\
&\leq |\hat{\gamma} - \hat{\alpha} \cdot \hat{\beta}| + |\hat{\alpha}| \cdot |\hat{\beta} - \beta| + |\beta| \cdot |\hat{\alpha} - \alpha| \\
&\leq |\hat{\gamma}| \cdot \varepsilon + |\hat{\alpha}| \cdot e_\beta + |\beta| \cdot e_\alpha \\
&\leq |\hat{\gamma}| \cdot \frac{e_\gamma}{2M} + |\hat{\alpha}| \cdot \frac{e_\gamma}{4|\hat{\alpha}|} + |\beta| \cdot \frac{e_\gamma}{4(|\hat{\beta}| + |e_\beta|)} \\
&\leq |\hat{\gamma}| \cdot \frac{e_\gamma}{2|\hat{\gamma}|} + \frac{e_\gamma}{4} + |\beta| \cdot \frac{e_\gamma}{4|\beta|} \\
&\leq \frac{e_\gamma}{2} + \frac{e_\gamma}{4} + \frac{e_\gamma}{4} = e_\gamma.
\end{aligned}
$$

Using separation bounds, which we will discuss next, precision driven arithmetic allows to directly compute an approximation that is accurate enough to conclude the sign of γ. Iteratively increasing the accuracy is however preferable because often the sign can be concluded from an approximation with lower accuracy. Precision driven arithmetic then allows to control how often an expression must be reevaluated. In the implementation of `leda::real` the number of provably correct binary digits in $\hat{\gamma}$ doubles with each iteration.

A number γ that is actually zero can only be recognized to be zero from an approximation when the approximation is error-free. This is, however, not possible if some intermediate number in the computation does not have a finite floating-point representation. In the presence of $/, \sqrt[k]{\ }$ this is almost always the case. Therefore, the need for separation bounds arises.

Definition 8 (Separation Bound). *A number $\zeta > 0$ is called a separation bound for α if $\alpha \neq 0$ implies $|\alpha| \geq \zeta$.*

The sign of α is known once the error of the approximation is smaller than $\frac{1}{2}\zeta$: either $|\hat{\alpha}| > e_\alpha$ or $|\alpha| \leq |\hat{\alpha}| + e_\alpha \leq 2e_\alpha < \zeta$ and therefore $\alpha = 0$. To be practical, a separation bound should also be *constructive* i.e. easily computable. The bounds which are used for algebraic numbers represented by a DAG, maintain for each intermediate number, that is for each node in the DAG, a set of parameters from which a separation bound for the number can be computed. The parameters for a node are computed from the parameters of its children and further predecessors. Here the so called BFMSS bound [142,143] will be described. The BFMSS bound conceptually represents an algebraic number as $\gamma = \gamma_u/\gamma_l$, where γ_u and γ_l are algebraic integers, and then maintains upper bounds $u(\gamma)$ and $l(\gamma)$ on the absolute value of the conjugates of γ_u and γ_l as depicted in Table 6.2.

Theorem 2 (BFMSS Separation Bound). *Let γ be given as a DAG and $u(\gamma), l(\gamma), D(\gamma)$ as given in Table 6.2. Then $\gamma = 0$ or $|\gamma| \geq u(\gamma)^{1-D(\gamma)} l(\gamma)^{-1} > 0$.*

$\square$

The parameters u and d are also attached to each node of the DAG in Figure 6.5 for $\gamma = \sqrt{5 - 2 \cdot \sqrt{6}} + \sqrt{2} - \sqrt{3}$. Note that $l = 1$ for each node. We have $D(\gamma) = 16$ and $u(\gamma) = 8$, resulting in $\zeta = 8^{-15} = 2^{-45}$. Hence, it suffices to evaluate γ to 46 binary digits to conclude $\gamma = 0$.

Table 6.2. Parameters for the BFMSS bound

γ	$u(\gamma)$	$l(\gamma)$	$d(\gamma)$
$\gamma \in \mathbb{Z}$	$\lvert\gamma\rvert$	1	1
$\alpha \pm \beta$	$u(\alpha)l(\beta) + u(\beta)l(\alpha)$	$l(\alpha)l(\beta)$	1
$\alpha \cdot \beta$	$u(\alpha)u(\beta)$	$l(\alpha)l(\beta)$	1
α/β	$u(\alpha)l(\beta)$	$l(\alpha)u(\beta)$	1
$\sqrt[k]{\alpha}$ and $u(\alpha) \geq l(\alpha)$	$\sqrt[k]{u(\alpha)l(\alpha)^{k-1}}$	$l(\alpha)$	k
$\sqrt[k]{\alpha}$ and $u(\alpha) < l(\alpha)$	$u(\alpha)$	$\sqrt[k]{u(\alpha)^{k-1}l(\alpha)}$	k

$$D(\gamma) = \prod_{\alpha \in \mathrm{DAG}(\gamma)} d(\alpha)$$

A separation bound dominates another separation bound if it always gives a better, i.e., higher bound. Among the currently known constructive separation bounds, the BFMSS bound, the Li-Yap bound and an improved degree-measure bound are not dominated by other bounds. It has further been shown that there are expressions where either the BFMSS or the Li-Yap bound is better [142,143,523]. An orthogonal approach is that of p-ary bounds. It amounts to factoring powers of a prime p out of the numbers, maintaining them separately. The idea was successfully applied to the BFMSS and the degree-measure bound, resulting in bounds dominating the original BFMSS and the degree-measure bound [637].

Despite these sophisticated internals the two number types `CORE::Expr` and `leda::real` are designed for ease of use. The internals are completely hidden from the user. All supported operations are available to the user in the same fashion they are available for, e.g., the C++ `double` type. The number types are reference counted, so passing arguments by value does not incur overhead and the memory management is done automatically. This allows to easily replace an inexact number type in an existing program. To allow for a reasonable speed, both number types have a built-in dynamic floating-point filter. `CORE::Expr` and `leda::real` provide highly general, easy to use and reasonably efficient number types. They are however inferior to solutions to the exactness problem specifically tuned to an application. Designing and implementing such a solution will however take much more time from the implementer. A bottleneck in the approach of `CORE::Expr` and `leda::real` are good separation bounds. Examination of the actual size of non-zero numbers and the computed separation bound suggests that the currently known bounds are overly pessimistic. Finding better bounds, especially bounds where the impact of the algebraic degree of a number is small would result in a great speed-up.

Chapter 7. Libraries

Roman Dementiev and Johannes Singler

7.1 Introduction

There are many definitions for the term *software library* in computer science,
e. g., "a collection of program components that can be used in many programs"
by Plauger [640]. However, we should regard the term "component" here in a
most general way, without the special meanings it is associated with in software
engineering. Also, being a loose collection is not enough. The parts of the library
should seamlessly work together and complement each other in a reasonable way,
addressing related tasks. "Using a program element" is not necessarily limited
to calling a function or a method, it includes executing a whole program, for
example.

So, at first sight, it is related rather to Software Engineering than to Algorithm
Engineering. However, as we will show in this chapter, libraries, in particular
algorithm libraries, are a very useful concept in Algorithm Engineering as well.
Actually, developing them is a "major goal" of Algorithm Engineering [234].

From the highest abstraction level, we must discriminate software libraries
and *software systems*. Software systems also provide functionality that facilitates
developing software. There is a difference in level between the system and the
program that runs on the system, though. The software system might have
capabilities that are not directly accessible to the program. Examples for software
systems are computer algebra systems and numerical computation systems like
MATLAB. Programs running on a software system have only indirect access
to assets like the screen, computer memory and computing power. Having said
that, the contrary applies to software libraries. They are usually based on the
same foundation as the actual program. Both approaches share the fact that
they foster the reuse of already implemented functionality.

The definition that a software library helps in implementing software is not
sufficient, of course. Taking just some foreign source code that implements a
complex algorithm might help as well. The difference is that libraries are particularly built for the sole purpose of being used by other programs. Thus, they
usually provide better quality than "some already-written code". This includes
features like ease of use, flexibility and extensibility, correctness and robustness,
not to forget efficiency.

Libraries for the most different kinds of applications exist. There are libraries
which are supposed to facilitate GUI programming, others simplify the access to
hardware or certain subsystems, yet others implement data structures and corresponding algorithms. The development of libraries was started in the numerical algorithms community. Key players were the *Numerical Algorithms Group
(NAG)* and the Bell Research Laboratories [374]. The reason for this is that in
the beginning, computers were mainly used to solve numerical problems.

M. Müller-Hannemann and S. Schirra (Eds.): Algorithm Engineering, LNCS 5971, pp. 290–324, 2010.

There are numerous subtypes of software libraries, including *function libraries*, *class libraries* and *component libraries*. This distinction comes from a Software Engineering point of view, and is based on the programming paradigm the library is obeying. In Algorithm Engineering, we are of course most interested in *algorithm libraries*, which is a distinction in terms of functionality. The programming paradigm—as mentioned above—is subordinate.

Nevertheless, we describe some of the paradigms here. Function libraries offer a number of ordinary function calls. Those might be grouped semantically, i. e., a subset of them should be called in a certain order, with certain dependent arguments, to achieve the desired result. No syntactic coherence is given, though, except maybe naming conventions. In contrast to that, *class libraries* provide encapsulation of functions that belong together by means of classes. Instantiating objects avoids the necessity of holding global state in some background memory. Class invariants can be put up this way, which helps in creating correct programs and avoiding unwanted side-effects. Still, the number of methods associated with a class is usually quite limited. This is why class libraries are an example of "reuse at small scale" [59]. In contrast to this, a *component library* provides items of greater functionality. Components are designed to be both self-contained and easily interchangeable. They are usually able to give information about themselves, both at development time and runtime. They can still be implemented using classes, but the abstraction is on a higher level.

After this discussion, we have to clarify that from our point of view, algorithm libraries can include necessary data structures, of course, since data structures and algorithms are always deeply intertwined.

Algorithm Engineering tangles software libraries from both sides. Utilizing existing libraries simplifies the implementation of new or improved algorithms. This is often accompanied by increased performance and stability, since the building blocks taken are usually already well-tested and tuned. On the other hand, library implementations of algorithms are developed by applying Algorithm Engineering to given problems.

This leads us to the two major questions of this chapter:

– Why is library XY useful for us in Algorithm Engineering?
– What was the role of Algorithm Engineering in developing of library XY?

Organization of the Chapter. In Section 7.2, we will briefly introduce many established libraries while Section 7.3 will give further motivation for the use of libraries in Algorithm Engineering. Starting off with the design goals and paradigms in Section 7.4, we will investigate more deeply the functionality and Algorithm Engineering aspects of selected libraries, grouped by functionality domain. Those five domains are *fundamental operations* (Section 7.5), *advanced number types* (Section 7.6), *basic data structures and algorithms* (Section 7.7), *graphs* (Section 7.8), and finally, *computational geometry* (Section 7.9). We will conclude in Section 7.10.

7.2   Library Overview

In this section, we enumerate and briefly introduce many algorithm libraries, coarsely grouped by functionality. Some libraries are very specific to an application area, while others are of general use. It is well possible that a library relies on other libraries. Usually, more specific libraries use more general ones, e. g., some library specialized on external memory computation might be based on another that provides basic I/O-routines.

Of course, we cannot discuss all possible candidates of libraries here. We will restrict ourselves to deeply investigate only libraries that are based on the C++ programming language [759]. This is because C++ is the most widely accepted programming language in the Algorithm Engineering community [741,148], and also widely used in industry. It offers both syntactic wealth and excellent performance, and supports both the object-oriented and the generic programming paradigm. C++ also obeys the so-called *zero-overhead rule*, i. e., if one does not actually use some part of the functionality, one also does not have to pay for it by a performance or space penalty. For example, the overhead for runtime polymorphism is only introduced when declaring functions explicitly virtual. Since C++ is usually compiled to binary code, its execution speed is excellent. The user has complete control over the data, since the memory management is explicit and interchangeable. The use of platform-specific processors is possible without overhead through intrinsics or embedded assembler code. Highly optimizing compilers are available on most platforms. The ISO standardized C++ in 1998 and approved a technical corrigendum in [429], so there must be no patents or copyrights restricting the use of this language. There are some drawbacks as well, though. The representation of number types is not completely specified, so the casting of types is dangerous. Those issues can usually be solved by providing a small platform- and/or compiler-specific part. No self-inspection at runtime of the interface is supported, i. e., enlisting the classes and their public methods and properties offered by the library. This could be useful for dynamically choosing and exchanging algorithms. Also, due to the lack of a binary intermediate format without functional restrictions, much code must be compiled over and over again, which can lead to lengthy compile times, in particular when using generics extensively.

An extensive comparison of many modern programming languages can be found in [647], whereby C# [266] is still missing there. Fortran might also be an option, however, it is considered to be specialized on numeric computations by most computer scientists. The most recent programming languages like Java and C# concentrate on making programming easier and less error-prone for algorithmically simple applications, sacrificing other qualities for that. They are usually not compiled to binary code, but to some intermediate language. A just-in-time-compiler (JIT) transforms the intermediate code to a binary one just before execution, sometimes after some part of the program has already been run. This makes the code platform-independent and therefore easily portable. Due to time constraints and because semantic information might have gone lost through the intermediate representation, the JIT usually cannot optimize the code as well as

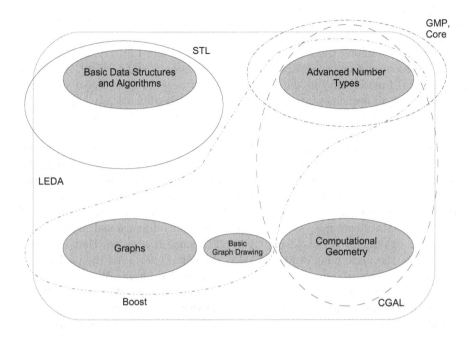

Fig. 7.1. The functionality of selected libraries

a native compiler could. Also, both platforms count on automatic memory management based on garbage collection, which can introduce memory organization phases of unpredictable length at unsuitable points in time. Hence, the resulting programs usually run slower and use more memory, which is particularly bad in Algorithm Engineering, since one wants to make the program performance the best possible.

In the following paragraphs, we list libraries grouped by functionality. An overview of the most important ones' functionalities and the resulting overlap is visualized in Figure 7.1.

Basic Algorithms and Data Structures. From an algorithmic point of view, the most elementary libraries are those which provide basic data structures and algorithms which in turn are part of many other algorithms. This functionality usually includes container types like linked lists, stacks, queues, dictionaries and priority queues. A *container type* keeps a (possibly huge) number of elements of a certain type in a more structured way, e. g., arranged in one or multiple dimensions, in a certain order. It is accompanied by suitable basic algorithms, e. g., sorting, searching, and enumeration patterns like iterators. Of course, there are many libraries that do not only provide this functionality, but offer much more. Nevertheless, we include such libraries in our discussion.

Modern programming languages come as programming platforms with a library that is more or less part of the language specification. Most of these libraries also comprise the addressed basic data structures and algorithms. The most renowned among them is probably the C++ standard library, in particular its most essential part, the *Standard Template Library (STL)* [640]. The STL has minimal functionality in the terms described here. In fact, it is a specification only, not an implementation. Since its standardization already happened in 1998, many implementations are available today. Usually, they belong to a C++ compiler; in principle, they are interchangeable.

To collect valuable extensions to the STL in a common place, and also to prepare the next version of the C++ standard [760], the *Boost* library [462, 120] was launched in 1998. It is developed by an open source community project and consists itself of many different sublibraries. As a small part, it adds to the basic data structures and algorithms of the STL. Specialized variants are provided for certain data structures, e. g., wrappers for multi-dimensional arrays. It is not useful to employ Boost without the STL, since it assumes that the STL will provide the underlying stuff. Actually, the correct term for the packages is Boost libraries (*plural*), since each part is in turn called *library*. We will consider all Boost libraries as a single library which is reasonable, although the Boost libraries indeed have greater independence between each other.

A library that comes downright from the Algorithm Engineering community is the *Library of Efficient Data Structures and Algorithms (LEDA)* [559, 513]. Its development was started in 1988 at the Max Planck Institut für Informatik in Saarbrücken. Nowadays, it is distributed commercially, but there also exists a free version with reduced functionality. LEDA[1] offers very broad functionality, naturally including basic data structures and algorithms. In contrast to the libraries mentioned so far, it usually provides multiple variants for abstract data types. Users can choose the one fitting their needs best, e. g., in terms of space and time complexity, tailored to the specific application. A lot of experience in algorithm design and engineering has been incorporated into LEDA[2], it forms a prototype of an algorithmic library.

Graphs. The most natural extension to the basic data structures are graph data structures and algorithms. Hence, the libraries mentioned in the last sections are usual suspects for also supporting this functionality. This field is beyond the scope of the STL, though. Boost must pitch in for this insufficiency with the *Boost Graph Library (BGL)* [736], a major sublibrary of Boost. LEDA has extensive graph support as well, as discussed later on. There also is a code repository from Donald Knuth, called *Stanford Graph Base (SGB)*. The author

---

[1] There is some disagreement about grammar and library names. The names STL and BGL are most often prefixed by the article "the", while LEDA is not. We are not aware of any grammatical rule that decides this, and stick to the tradition.

[2] The term LEDA also names a queen of Sparta from Greek mythology. There is a myth about "Leda and the swan", which gives some background on the cover page of the LEDA Book [561]. Also, do not mix up the library with the multi-paradigm programming language of the same name.

announced that the fourth volume of his famous series "The Art of Computer Programming" will be largely based on this C code. The coherence is rather loose, thus the code cannot be termed a library.

Geometry. Algorithms in Computational Geometry are notorious for being very hard to implement [206, Chapter "Introduction"] [471]. Numerical instabilities can lead to crashing programs while most algorithms are described for the theoretical *general position* assumption, i.e., no three points of the input lie on a straight line, no four points lie on a circle, etc. LEDA is the pioneering library that supports robust geometric computing for arbitrary inputs. It provides many algorithm implementations for two-dimensional geometry and some implementations for three-dimensional case. d-dimensional geometry exists as an extension package. Based on the LEDA experience, the *Computational Geometry Algorithms Library (CGAL)* project [151] was started some years later by a large academic consortium [278]. It has enjoyed the improved template support of C++ compilers that had evolved in the meantime. CGAL follows the generic programming paradigm to allow for great flexibility and modularity of its geometric components. As LEDA, it supports 2-, 3- and d-dimensional robust geometry. The EXACUS library [94, 276] aims for systematic support of *non-linear* geometry. The current version of EXACUS can compute exact arrangements of curves and curve arcs of arbitrary algebraic degree in the plane and quadrics in space, and perform Boolean operations on polygons bounded by such segments. The computations are mathematically correct for arbitrary position input. In the meantime, many packages of EXACUS have been integrated into CGAL.

Graph Drawing. Graph Drawing is a relatively new field in Computer Science. Its goal is to develop algorithms that embed graphs into two or three dimensions. Criteria are applied to measure the "prettiness" of the result. One tries to minimize the number of crossing edges in non-planar graphs, for example. Since many problems are computationally hard, and also, there are not always sharp criteria for the quality of the drawing, heuristic methods are applied very often. Several libraries have evolved from the academic community, e.g., the *Open Graph Drawing Framework (OGDF)* [618], and *Visone* [807], specialized in visualizing social networks. *GraphViz* [315, 356] is a graph drawing application, its algorithms are also available in a library. The field has many commercial applications, because the programs can visualize complex facts for human analysis. Hence, two commercial libraries are on the market: *Tom Sawyer Visualization*, and *yFiles*. In addition to many graph drawing solutions, they include basic graph algorithms as well. It stands out that both commercial libraries are available for both the .NET and the Java platform, Tom Sawyer also for C++.

Numerics. The libraries mentioned so far are designed to work on instances of encapsulated data types, i.e., they provide functionality to work on mostly discrete, combinatorial objects, while numerical problems are continuous. Here, trade-offs between accuracy and processing speed are of crucial importance. The applied number types are usually quite simple. Rounding errors and approximate results are tolerated. Still, a major goal of these libraries is to sustain numerical precision to the furthest extent reasonable. We will not discuss them here in detail, but mention some of them with references for further reading.

Numerical libraries usually provide functionality like basic linear algebra, random numbers, statistics, and so on. The GNU Scientific Library [82,363] is written in Fortran, also usable from other languages. Closely related to this library is the package LAPACK [30,507], supporting linear equations, least-square optimization, singular-value decomposition, and eigenvalue/eigenvector solution. LAPACK is written in Fortran language and has been converted to the C package CLAPACK [175]. Blitz++ [802,109] makes extensive use of generic programming through C++ templates to achieve best computation performance. It offers dense arrays and vectors, random number generators, and small vectors and matrices. However, the GNU scientific library has a richer functionality than Blitz++. The *Matrix Template Library* [737,593] actually uses template metaprogramming to generate performance-critical code for linear algebra for a wide variety of matrix formats. All libraries mentioned here are provided as open-source.

Advanced Number Types. Some applications require exactness in computations involving numbers, for example geometric theorem proving (see also Sections 3.5 and 6.2). Libraries like the *GNU Multiple Precision Arithmetic Library (GMP)* [355,334], the *Core library* [457,189], MPFR [592], LEDA and Boost provide number types for such demands. They implement integers, rationals, algebraic numbers and floating points numbers with arbitrary length/precision.

Particular Machine Models. There are lots of libraries which specialize in supporting particular machine models, which are described in detail in Chapter 5.

The most common models are for parallel computation and external memory computation. The specialization on such a model is in general orthogonal to the functionality of the library. Most such libraries provide only basic equipment since more complex algorithms can then be built on top of them. Sometimes, an ordinary implementation can be recycled by just redirecting calls to low-level functions to the library for the particular machine model.

For libraries concerned with parallel computation, one must distinguish two aspects. A library can provide basic platform functionality only, which usually includes communication, locking and maybe load-balancing. Examples are the BSPlib [393,625] for the Bulk Synchronous Parallel model [789] and the *CGMlib* [156,153] for the Coarse-Grained Multicomputer model. Some of them are integrated into the language through the compiler, OpenMP [159] and ClusterOpenMP being examples. Concurrency libraries like the *POSIX threads* [146] might be considered a part of the operating system. On the other hand, there are libraries that provide algorithmic functionality like STAPL [29] with multiple backends. The STL implementation of GCC, libstdc++, features a so-called parallel mode, based on the MCSTL [740] for shared-memory systems. The CGMlib also includes basic algorithms, in particular with its counterpart *CGMgraph* for graph algorithms. There also exists a parallelized version of the BGL [360,633] for shared-memory systems. Gustedt et al. [371] present with parXXL an integrated environment for scalable fine-grained development on large coarse-grained platforms. SWARM (SoftWare and Algorithms for Running on Multi-core) is another recent portable open-source parallel library of basic primitives that fully exploit multicore processors [54]. The Intel Threading Building Blocks [427] are somewhat a hybrid. It provides concurrent data structures and a parallelization framework, and a sorter in addition.

The *external memory model* [811,569] makes the assumption that the data to be processed does not fit into the main memory of the executing computer (also see Chapter 5, Section 5.2.1). Many algorithms have already been developed for this model in theory. Much less had been done for evaluating their practical fitness. The problem here, as in other areas, was the large layer of non-existing implementations of basic external memory (I/O-efficient) algorithms and data structures. TPIE [44,782] and LEDA-SM [195] (both discontinued) have been started to reduce this gap. The STXXL library [231,761] implements interfaces of the STL; its containers and data structures handle very large data sets I/O-efficiently. Besides the compatibility with the STL, another aim of the STXXL is high performance: it supports parallel disks and optimally overlaps I/O and computation. Recent versions [81] add support for parallel internal computation, covering both the shared-memory parallel and the external memory model.

7.3   Libraries as Building Blocks

When a new problem in algorithmics arises, a first, simple algorithm is usually given. Then, other researchers try to improve the quality of this algorithm, which often results in a better, but more complicated one. It may use complex data structures and algorithms which are already well-known, but not implemented. Hence, although the proposed algorithm might look simple at first glance, intricacies in the utilized parts may keep one from actually implementing and testing it. This is why many algorithms never have been used in production systems, although being more efficient than already available solutions. In this section, we show how libraries can help in writing competitive implementations of sophisticated algorithms, which is particularly important in Algorithm Engineering. Thus, libraries can be seen as *building blocks* for complex algorithms.

Aiming this high, libraries in particular should strive for the goals described in Chapters 3 and 6. The quality of robustness is very important. Also, the implementation aspects *correctness*, *flexibility*, and *ease of use* need to be considered to the greatest extent possible. These demands are accompanied by the desire for good efficiency and extensive functionality. The better these criteria are met, the more benefit comes from using a library. In the following, we will illustrate this in more detail.

Libraries are usually exactly specified and well-tested. Hence, the implementer can concentrate on the parts of the algorithm that are actually new, which might enable her to actually succeed in implementing the algorithm [234]. This avoids errors in low-level parts which can be very hard to find. The authors of LEDA argue that "Algorithm + LEDA = Program". This means that all complex parts in an algorithm description, e. g., complex data structure operations in a pseudo-code, can be written down easily using LEDA.

Often, only some specified functionality and asymptotic bounds are required for a data structure or an algorithm, no concrete implementation is requested. For real-world performance, however, the constant factors are also important, they can make a huge difference. Since algorithm libraries often provide multiple versions of some functionality or data structure, the implementer can easily exchange those components and compare their effects on running time and memory footprint. Too much effort would have to be invested into those parts to make them competitive, otherwise.

Also, a library implementation sets a benchmark on the performance for the solution of a problem, because it is typically more general than any self-made implementation. Often, comparison are done against library implementations, e. g., in [283, 306]. Taking the advantages of robustness and generality of the library implementation into account, another implementation must achieve much better performance, to be taken into consideration.

Altogether, algorithms that are implemented as part of a library are used more often by practitioners and therefore have more impact in the according area. Non-experts in the algorithmic field can also directly benefit from the developments in theory. Also, more feedback from users to the developers can be expected. This helps to mitigate the often-cited "gap between theory and practice".

There is other functionality in libraries to improve an implementation besides algorithms. Tools like the Boost Template Metaprogramming Library in fact enhance the language the code is written in, C++ in this case. Through its use, certain computations can be moved to compile time, which allows for a better optimization by the compiler in many cases. Also, invariants and static post-/pre-conditions can be verified at compile time to make an algorithm implementation more robust. Also, data type traits [605] can be used for the selection of the best algorithm to use. Another example of this kind is concept checking, which is used in STL implementations, for example. The use of expression templates (see Subsection 7.7.2) simplifies the customization of generic algorithms and therefore fosters their utilization.

If libraries want to have great impact, they must be well-documented. This does not only include the description of the functionality and the corresponding API, but also the behavior and expected performance for different kinds of input.

We do not want to conceal here that using libraries might have disadvantages in certain cases. For instance, libraries must usually make compromises in terms of running time and memory usage. In principle, a tailor-made implementation can always be as least as efficient as a library implementation. Often, it will be *more* efficient. However, in most cases, this drawback incurs only small constant factors and does not outweigh the additional time spent in developing and testing the code thoroughly.

Library code is supposed to be a "black box". This is particularly true if the source code is not available. This lack of insight might be a problem for analyzing and debugging a program that uses a library.

Major problems can occur if the user employs multiple libraries that are incompatible with each other. This incompatibility most often stems from data types contained in those libraries. The algorithms of one library can usually not be applied to data that is held in another library's data structures, specific compatibility layers being an exception. In general, the only solutions is to convert from one data type to the other or to abandon some libraries completely.

Although libraries should be easy to use, they still demand some effort in learning how to use them. And after all, many libraries are not gratuitous, which also biases the consideration between library usage and proprietary development.

The last argument against the usage of libraries is that responsibility is given to some "external force". As recent history shows, this problem particularly arises in the context of security holes. The whole program can be compromised if there is a flaw in one of the used libraries. Legal issues might be touched in this case.

7.4 Basic Design Goals and Paradigms of Combinatorial and Geometric Libraries

In this section, we introduce the design goals of the major libraries. This helps to understand the decisions made in the development of those libraries which are then documented in the following sections.

LEDA is supposed to provide "algorithmic intelligence" [561, Preface] to the user. Its usefulness extends to a broad range of applications because it consists of a huge collection of algorithms from very different parts of computer science. One could term this the *horizontal dimension*. On the other hand, LEDA claims to contain everything that is needed to develop an algorithmically challenging application. Thus, it also contains very low-end input/output operations like file stream, and provides GUI support as well. This could be characterized as the *vertical dimension* of LEDA. In consequence, LEDA is probably the library with the broadest functionality. The tall vertical range can partly be explained by the lack of appropriate libraries that support the according functionality at the time its development was started. This makes parts of the library platform-dependent, in contrast to the other libraries, which only depend on the standardized language features.

According to LEDA's research leaders, Kurt Mehlhorn and Stefan Näher, there were four principal design goals in the development of LEDA [561, Chapter "Introduction"], in the order of importance: ease of use, extensibility, correctness, efficiency. It sounds surprising that efficiency is stated last, as it is actually included in the name of the library. However, the authors claim that efficiency is worthless without the remaining three goals fulfilled. This reminds one of the famous phrase [478]: "Premature optimization is the root of all evil in programming." We will look at the experimental performance of LEDA in the subsequent sections. Still, the library always promises best *asymptotic* running time, at least with high probability. As already mentioned, it provides multiple variants of many of its data types and algorithms, to match specific needs. Therefore, it is very well suited for doing Algorithm Engineering by testing many alternatives. Also, there is a lot of formalized documentation, including support tools for generating different output format from in-source-code documentation.

Since 1995, there is a commercial version available, the freely available academic license was discontinued at version 4.2.1 in 2001. Unfortunately, this old version is not quite usable any longer since most modern compilers are not compatible with its code any more. At least, there exists a free version with reduced functionality. There are several LEDA extension packages available, e. g., a package for d-dimensional geometry, and one for dynamic graphs, which emphasizes the extensibility.

Although being inferior in terms of functionality broadness, the Standard Template Library came only later than LEDA. Its development started at the Hewlett-Packard Labs before 1995, led by Alexander Stepanov and Meng Lee [755]. In 1998, it was incorporated in the ISO C++ standard at a late stage. It only *specifies* the functionality an *implementation* must provide. Hence, there is not *the one* STL. This makes it hard to compare the practical efficiency of the STL to other libraries. A very wide-spread implementation licensed under the LGPL is the one by the GNU project [321]. It is based on the implementation by SGI [727], which is particularly renowned for its documentation. In turn, the SGI code is based on the exemplary implementation by Hewlett-Packard. Another implementation is STLport [756], free and claimed to be highly portable. Dinkumware [250] offers a commercial implementation which claims to be very efficient.

The goal of the STL is to provide "a core of the most widely used facilities" [640], not everything a programmer might need. To make this comparatively small core applicable to all sorts of data, the generic programming paradigm is used extensively. Actually, the library was designed for the Ada programming language in the first place, since C++ had not yet supported genericity through templates. Compared to LEDA, the STL exploits the language features of C++ to a much larger extent. Since it came later and was designed along with the language standard, the compilers had already evolved to some kind of stability and supported most features of the standard. In contrast, for example, LEDA uses exceptions only little.

The Boost library was initiated to provide a collection of extensions to the STL. While the STL only wants to provide a common core functionality, Boost's approach is to provide everything a reasonably large number of programmers might like to use. Therefore, its functionality extends greatly beyond that of the STL. Many new areas are touched, like graphs and parsers. A huge part is devoted to extending the language with syntactic sugar, to name the lambda expression library and the smart pointer library. A considerable part of the Boost libraries has been accepted for inclusion into the upcoming C++ standard, the current draft is called TR1. Thus, parts of Boost might be genuine parts of the STL in a few years. Its general paradigms are similar to the ones of the

STL: Provide robust and generally efficient implementations. There are rarely multiple variants of a data type or an algorithm. Hence, each implementation must remain a compromise between generality and optimization to a specific application.

In contrast to this, LEDA has platform-specific parts. This is a negative consequence of supporting features like file system access and graphics. Also, there is some assembler for basic operations on number types integrated. Boost and the STL only require a standard-compliant C++ compiler, and use its C library for the backend.

The driving goal of the CGAL project stems from Algorithm Engineering: it is to "make the large body of geometric algorithms developed in the field of computational geometry available for industrial application" [278]. CGAL and EX-ACUS strive for correctness, flexibility, efficiency and ease of use. The flexibility is achieved by the generic programming paradigm in the style of STL. Another goal is adaptability: e. g., library implementations must work with any existing user code satisfying certain interface requirements. One of CGAL's guideline is a high degree of flexibility for experts; however, there is also a rule to provide default shortcuts for novices who appreciate the ease of use in the first place. CGAL always leaves the decision which underlying basic types (like number types) and algorithms should be used, to the user, who can choose the most efficient and sufficiently exact alternatives for her application. The library aims for a good quality code with documentation following the style of LEDA manuals. A large distributed developer community reviews and tests new CGAL submissions.

As we argued earlier, it is most important that algorithms supplied by a library work correctly. None of the libraries mentioned here uses formal verification to prove the correctness of its algorithms. They provide testing measures to give some assurance, though. LEDA, in particular, includes many algorithms that return a result which is easily checkable. For complex problems, this can include additional information, such as witnesses, for a particular result. An example case is the test of a graph for bipartiteness. When the algorithm gives a positive result, it also returns the partition of the graph. The two sets of nodes can then be checked for the absence of edges between nodes of the same set (see also Section 6.2.3). The GCC implementation of the STL comes with a testsuite that checks very many use cases. Most Boost libraries come with test cases, as does CGAL.

There is also the aspect of licence fees. LEDA was started as an academic project, and turned into a commercial product later. On one hand, this means that the library is actively supported and maintained. On the other hand, one must pay for a license, at least for full functionality.

The STL is standardized by the ISO, which means that there may be no patents or copyrights associated with it. There are free implementations available, as listed before, so it should be available to everyone at no charge.

7.5   Fundamental Operations

Each program contains operations that programmers consider as atomic, fundamental parts of the programming language, but in fact, complex runtime mechanisms are hidden behind those, which can influence running time and memory footprint significantly. This includes memory management, access to data structures, and calling subroutines. They are usually not mentioned in a theoretical description of an algorithm, because they do not influence the asymptotic running time. However, the constant factors they introduce can be critical in practice. Thus, there is a lot of potential to improve performance here.

7.5.1   Memory Management

Every C/C++ compiler comes with a built-in memory manager for dynamic memory allocation. Memory is usually allocated from the operating system in large chunks, and redistributed to the application in smaller blocks. This avoids the overhead of calling the operating system every time. Thus, there is usually a trade-off between time and space efficiency. There are many ways to get a good compromise, this is a complex topic [837]. For example, *free lists* can save freed memory blocks of a certain size for future use, but this space might be lost if blocks of that size are not requested again. On the other hand, fragmenting the memory might result in complex data structures for maintenance and thus slow down execution.

The STL therefore allows the user to specify a custom memory manager for containers, called an allocator. This is mainly an interface, nothing more than an arbitrary default implementation is requested.

Boost comes with the Pool library, which provides efficient managing of blocks of one certain size. In particular, it features bulk deallocation, if desired without calling the destructor. LEDA provides its own memory manager [779], which is mandatorily used for its own data types. Both memory managers provide free lists, without inducing any space overhead. This allows for efficient reuse of objects.

The types that benefit most from such a memory manager are small types which are created and destroyed frequently. While the size of a type can be determined at compile time, its number of (de)allocations cannot be predicted. Thus, the choice which type in general, and which specific allocation is done by which memory manager, must be left to the library user. With the STL, the user can *and* must choose the type for every allocation (sequence) or container instantiation. With LEDA, the user can choose per type, or allocate a number of bytes manually. No parameterization of containers is possible, in this sense. There might be a workaround through deriving differently allocated variants of the element class from a base type, though. The developers of LEDA report great speed improvement by using the LEDA memory manager for small types such as graph nodes and edges. However, no comparison to recent implementations of the memory allocators are given. The results obtained in [561, Chapter "On the Implementation of LEDA"] might be outdated.

This is an example that shows where gaps between theoretical algorithms and a practical implementation can be wide. The difficulties of dynamic memory allocation are mostly ignored by theoretical algorithms. Usually, it is assumed that allocating memory costs only constant and actually negligible time. It is an achievement of Algorithm Engineering to call attention to this important functionality, and to optimize it. In this case, Algorithm Engineering was not used for a particular algorithm, but rather something more fundamental.

7.5.2   Iterators versus Items

The possibility to address elements as members of a data structure can speedup programs considerably. For example, searching a tree for an element and inserting it, if not yet contained, only takes one tree search. The element can be inserted just where the search had to stop. In case we cannot remember this location between the two operations, two searches would have to be performed.

Another example is search for related elements. The program can help the library in finding an element by giving some position close by that might have been determined by an earlier search. This kind of searching is known as *finger search*. Such operations often need to know about internal data organization which goes beyond the plain specification of the abstract data type. This is dangerous because of being prone to incompatibilities. However, some algorithms from theory often need a pointer to a particle deep down in a data structure to achieve good asymptotic complexity.

This functionality usually does not degrade performance, but greatly improves it for some applications, a discovery made in experimental evaluation in the context of Algorithm Engineering. There are different ways to achieve this functionality. The STL and Boost implement the *iterator concept*, while LEDA features the *item concept*[3]. Both allow the access to an element in the context of the container. However, there are fundamental differences.

The STL iterator concept is an implementation of the iterator design pattern [313], which defines an iterator to "provide a way to access the elements of an aggregate object sequentially without exposing its underlying representation". Thus, an iterator usually allow access to the "current element" in an iteration over the sequence of elements. But there is additional functionality in the STL. There exist iterators that also allow jumps to distant elements, deletion of the element referenced by the iterator, and insertions before or after the referenced element. This adds some kind of "location" property to the iterator.

Since the iterator concept implicates a linear order between the elements, it is unclear how to apply the concept to data types like priority queues or two-dimensional search data structures. In fact, the STL does not provide an addressable priority queue.

An item is a pointer to an element contained in a data structure, thereby giving explicitly a location in the structure. The only operation items can execute

---

[3] Here, we refer to only what is called *dependent item* in [561]. *Independent items* are not implicitly related to any container. Those rather resemble handles or smart pointers, examples being points and segments in geometry.

self-contained is testing for equality to another item, testing for being nil, and assignment. All other operations are methods of the container class. The iteration pattern can be implemented using an item as the resulting reference to the current element, but this item is not an iterator itself.

Iterators can be manipulated and dereferenced autonomically, as they implicitly know the associated container, while for accessing the information contained in an item, a method of the container must be called. Therefore, iterators are "heavier" than items.

Iterators are vulnerable to intermediate changes to the container, in some cases, while items are usually not. A delete or insert instruction potentially invalidates all iterators associated with the container, i. e., their behavior is undefined afterward. Of course, both iterators and items are invalidated when the corresponding element is deleted.

An interesting hybrid approach is presented in [347], where the iterator concept is split. A *position* allows one to access the element directly, but is invalidated when making a change to the container. In contrast to this, a *locator* adds a level of indirection, but stays valid despite modifications.

7.5.3   Parameterization of Data Types

The most important decision in designing a library which provides container types, is the following: How do we combine the meta data needed for each element of the *container type* with the actual *data type*, to form an *element type*? That is, how do we provide parameterized containers?

The best compromise has to be found considering compatibility (compilers), efficiency (running time), and ease-of-use (compile time, code size). Therefore, this is an Algorithm Engineering task.

There are two extreme solutions for the problem and hybrid variants of them. The first solution is to generate a new type for each combination of container type and data type, ideally using generic programming. The second solution is to have only one element type for each container type, and to keep a weakly typed reference to the actual data.

The STL and Boost employ the first solution, in this case supported by the C++ template mechanism. LEDA uses a hybrid approach, called the "LEDA solution" [517]. There is only one element type per container type, containing a so-called *generic pointer (GenPtr)*. This pointer establishes the connection to the actual data. To avoid the necessity of excessive casting on the user's side, a shallow wrapper class is provided by means of generic programming. This wrapper just transcribes all method calls to the actual data structure class. Since there is no real functionality, all calls can be inlined and therefore, no performance penalty is incurred when using an optimizing compiler. However, there is one more indirection in accessing the data. This implies two disadvantages: Two objects instead of only one must be allocated and freed each time an item is added or removed, respectively. In particular for small data types, the incurred overhead might not be negligible. Also, item and data object will probably lie quite far apart in address space. Thus, the cache efficiency is at risk due to worse locality. At least, there is an optimization for small data types. If the size of the data type is less or equal the size of a GenPtr—nowadays usually 32 or 64 bits—the data will be stored directly instead of the GenPtr. This approach avoids most disadvantages of the second solution, still wasting some memory if the data type is actually *smaller* than a pointer. However, it will keep compilers from applying advanced optimization and inlining [558] for complex types.

One advantage of using the second solution is that library code can be distributed in binary form and therefore be kept secret, while if using C++ templates to the full extent, all source code must be provided. Also, code size and compile time decrease when not using generics, because they can lead to code duplication. There are countermeasures for that supported by C++ templates, e. g., partial specialization. Instantiating a container for one pointer type suffices for all pointer types since a pointer has usually the same size for all types pointed to. There is no difference in treating it, either, inside the container functionality. Precompiled header files can speed up compilation, since they avoid multiple parsing of the same file. Actually, the `export` keyword described in the C++ standard should make it possible to distribute generic code in object files. However, no well-established compiler supports this feature so far, although having been introduced years ago.

At the time when the LEDA development was started, the template support of the compilers was admittedly quite limited. Thus, the decision to not fully exploit generics was the right one. Nevertheless, the LEDA developers go astray their paradigm with the latest innovation. The LEDA static graphs use generics extensively to provide excellent performance.

7.5.4 Callbacks and Functors

Generic algorithms are only useful if they can be customized by the user to serve a specialized purpose. Also, comparison and hash functions for user-defined types are needed for certain containers. Algorithm Engineering requires to provide a solution that is both time- and space-efficient as well as flexible.

The easiest solution to parameterize an algorithm is to pass some callback function pointer, which is plain C style. However, this incurs a performance penalty since a branch to a non-constant address usually cannot be predicted by the processor. Also, no inlining of the function to be called can happen, in general. There will be a branch, and therefore probably also an instruction cache fault. The advantage of a function pointer is its flexibility at runtime, since one can exchange the called function at runtime.

The STL introduced functor classes, i. e., classes which provide certain methods to be called back. Since the functor is a template parameter of the algorithm, the actual call is already known at compile time and the compiler is able to generate specific code for this call. Thus, an optimizing compiler can inline the call and achieve unimpaired performance. Another benefit is that both the functionality and additional data can be passed in one parameter. This helps

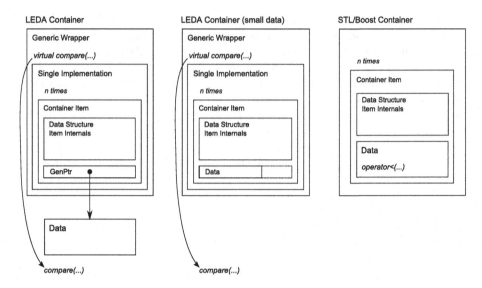

Fig. 7.2. Different ways of parameterizing containers

to avoid complicated and type-unsafe casting from and to some pointer of type void* which is usually the only additional information possible to pass. Boost uses the same mechanism as the STL.

LEDA has to rely on virtual function calls, though. As mentioned above, only the wrapper classes are parameterized. Inner functions which are compiled to a binary library, must call user-defined functions. There is no other way to achieve this than a virtual function call. In terms of performance, this corresponds to a call of a function pointer. At least, LEDA contains some optimizations that avoid this penalty for small and built-in data types. These were incorporated after experiments showed that there was too much overhead in space and time, in particular for those small types.

The different approaches in parameterizing containers are summarized in Figure 7.2. Section 7.7.2 concretizes the options described here, and gives code examples and performance numbers.

7.6 Advanced Number Types

In this section we will overview the advanced number types available in libraries. See Chapter 6 for their theoretical background and specific implementation details of these types.

Theoretical algorithms work in the real RAM model of computation with precise numbers of unlimited accuracy. However, most programming languages, including C++, do not provide a number type which meets all demands of the mathematical abstraction. C++ models integer numbers by the types short, int, long and long long with fixed precision of p bits, where $p \leq 64$. Therefore, numbers, whose absolute value is greater or equal 2^p, can not be represented, and all arithmetic operations on C++ built-in integers are computed modulo 2^p. Floating point numbers, as compatible with the IEEE floating-point standard [420], are implemented in all modern processors. They are represented by a triple (s, m, e), where s is the sign bit of the number, m and e are the fixed-size mantissa and exponent of the number, respectively. The value[4] of the triple is of the following form: $(-1)^s \cdot m \cdot 2^e$. In many C++ compilers, the processor's floating point numbers are mapped to **float** and **double** types having single and double accuracy. Since C++ built-in number types have only a limited accuracy, they can only *approximate* the mathematical numbers.

Integer numbers. If a programmer neglects the limitations of C++ built-in number types and operations on them, the implementations produce incorrect results and may crash [471] [860, Chapter "Number types"]. To avoid these problems, libraries provide special number types which have a higher degree of exactness. LEDA's type **integer** realizes the mathematical type integer using a dynamic array of unsigned **longs**. This way the degree of precision is only limited by the capacity of main memory. It supports all operations of ordinary C++ built-in integers like $+,-,*,/,\%, ++$, etc. Despite the fact that the implementation of **leda::integer** is highly optimized, even using assembler for critical code sections [561, Chapter "Numbers and Matrices"], the speed of these operations is about 30-50 times slower than the speed of C++ **ints** [860]. The GNU Multiple Precision Arithmetic Library (GMP) [355], written in C, has a similar type called **mpz_t**. The library is highly optimized for speed: As the LEDA library it uses sophisticated numerical algorithms. Most inner loops are written in assembler language for a wealth of different processors. The simplicity and elegance in GMP are sacrificed for the sake of performance. However, the user-friendliness of the original C interface is improved in the C++ class interface of the GMP library and third-party wrappers (e. g., **CGAL::Gmpz**). The C++ class interface applies the expression template technique described in detail in Chapter 6 to avoid the costs of constructing temporary number objects. For example, an expression like **a=b+c** results in a single call to the underlying GMP C library that adds numbers **b** and **c**, and assigns the result to **a**. Other tricks, contributing to the low-level efficiency of GMP, can be found in [355]. A study in [703] showed that **leda::integer** could be up to several times faster than the GMP **mpz_t**, wrapped into **CGAL::Gmpz**, in convex hull algorithms for values of medium size. However, since the library implementations have been revised since 1998 the speedup factors are probably out-of-date. The **BigInt** number type of the Core library [457] is a wrapper of the GMP's **mpz_t**.

Rational Numbers. If an algorithm requires exact computation involving division of two integers then the result cannot be represented as an integer without loss of precision. For such a scenario, LEDA provides a **rational** type which keeps

---

[4] According to the IEEE floating-point standard 754 [420], the actual value is computed slightly differently and relies on a tricky encoding of the triple components.

the numerator and denominator as `leda::integer` members. The mathematical operations on `leda::rationals` are 30-100 times slower than the operations on the built-in `double` [860]. GMP also has a rational type (`mpq_t`). The difference between `leda::rational` and GMP `mpq_t` is that the former does not automatically normalize the quotient in the arithmetic operations if the numerator and denominator have a common factor, since this is an expensive operation. The latter also requires that the operands of arithmetic operations are normalized and the operation implementations normalize the result(s) as well. The Boost type `rational` does not stick to a fixed type to represent the numerator and denominator; instead, the user is free to choose the underlying type. This type must obviously provide the basic arithmetic operations. The rational number `BigRat` of the Core library is a wrapper of the GMP's `mpq_t`. CGAL's rational type `Quotient` is similar to the `leda::rational`, but allows the user to choose the underlying integer type.

Floating-Point Numbers. GMP provides a floating number type `mpf_t`, where the number of bits to represent the mantissa are defined by the user, the exponent size depends on the size of the machine word. In calculations, GMP uses fewer mantissa bits if it suffices to represent the number value. The `mpf_t` type is not compatible to the IEEE standard: The results of computations may differ on different computers. LEDA's `bigfloat` type extends the built-in floating point types. In contrast to GMP, it stores the mantissa and the exponent as arbitrary precision `leda::integers`. In arithmetic operations, the mantissas of `leda::bigfloat` are rounded to a value given by the user bit length. The rounding mode is also chosen by the user. The software floating-point number of the MPFR library [592] has similar features. The Core library implements a floating point number type name `BigFloat` with the mantissa, represented as the `BigInt` data type, and the exponent is stored as a C++ `unsigned int`. The accuracy to be maintained in arithmetic operations is user-defined. Additionally, the `BigFloat` tracks the error bound of the number's value using the interval arithmetic. The error intervals are automatically maintained when performing arithmetic with `BigFloats`.

Interval Arithmetic. Interval arithmetic is ubiquitous in reliable scientific computing, in particular, it is heavily used in computer graphics and computational geometry. Interval arithmetic allows one to quantify the propagation of rounding errors if one has to live with floating point numbers (e.g., for speed reasons). LEDA contains an implementation of interval arithmetic using `double` as basic type to represent the interval borders. MPFI [591] is an implementation of interval arithmetic based on the MPFR's floating point number. A generic type that supports interval arithmetic is included in Boost. The user can choose the basic type. It already works out-of-the-box for the built-in C++ types and can be adapted to other base types if one provides functions that define rounding rules and the handling of exceptional cases. The support library of `boost::interval` helps to generate various commonly needed policies for user types.

Algebraic Numbers. Many kinds of problems require exact computation involving roots of a polynomial with rational coefficients also known as *algebraic numbers.* To carry out computations with real algebraic numbers, LEDA provides the type `real`, which supports exact computations with k^{th} roots for an arbitrary integer k, the rational operators $+,-,^*$, and $/$, and comparison operators [561, Chapter "Numbers and Matrices"]. LEDA `real` is a sophisticated type: It stores the complete expression as a directed acyclic graph (DAG) defining the value, i. e., every operation on reals adds a node to the graph and records the operation to be performed at the node and the inputs to the node. When the sign of a `leda::real` instance needs to be computed, the DAG is traversed computing the required precision adaptively (see Section 6.2). In this case the computations are performed using `leda::bigfloats`. The Core library offers an algebraic number type, called `Expr`, too. Its internal architecture and functionality are very similar to those of `leda::reals`. Algebraic number implementations also support exact zero-testing. Despite of the internal complexity, the real algebraic types are designed to be very easy to use and provide reasonable speed while being the most general number type available.

7.7 Basic Data Structures and Algorithms

In the following section, we will describe the features of several libraries, restricted to a certain functionality. This section is about elementary data structures and algorithms, supported by the STL, Boost and LEDA. Iterators and basic algorithms provide access to the items in the containers in certain ways. Again, we will treat Boost along the lines of STL, and will only mention whether the functionality is an extension to the STL provided by Boost, or genuine.

7.7.1 Data Structures

STL and LEDA both offer linear lists, stacks, queues, and arrays of dynamic size with constant amortized random access time, namely `array` and `vector`, respectively. Additionally, LEDA provides more efficient variants for stacks and queues of bounded size. Note that the latter is a small example of applied Algorithm Engineering, since it allows for exploiting special cases for better performance.

Also, numerous variants of dictionary types are offered, i. e., (multi)maps and (multi)sets. There are many little and intricate semantic differences between LEDA and the STL.

Again, LEDA has specializations for sets of C++ built-in integers, for limited or unlimited range. At least the latter one could also be integrated transparently by template specialization into an STL implementation. LEDA and Boost offer *union-find data structures.* They are particularly useful for graph algorithms like minimum spanning tree, and collections of trees, which in turn is useful for priority queue implementations.

Hash maps and hash sets are not included in the standardized version of the STL; however, they usually come as vendor extensions. They are also suggested for the upcoming C++ standard under the names `unordered_map` and unordered_set, respectively. There is no implementation yet for this interface in Boost, but there are hashed indices available as a part of the much more complex sub-library MultiIndex. Also, the Hash sub-library provides hash functions per se. LEDA supports hashes in several variants.

Priority queues are a very delicate ingredient and advanced versions are quite difficult to implement. The STL only offers one parameterized data type priority_queue, which is usually based on the heap operations provided by the algorithm part. In contrast to this, LEDA offers five different implementations, including Fibonacci heaps, pairing heaps, d–heaps, monotonic heaps, and Van Emde-Boas trees, the latter for supporting C++ built-in integer keys only. For a complete list including references, see the LEDA online documentation [512, "List of data structures"].

The wide variety of implementation options is the greatest advantage of LEDA when it comes to basic data structures. It allows the algorithm engineer to exchange semantically equivalent algorithms easily, by just changing one token and recompiling. Also, it provides some advanced containers that allow one to sustain a good asymptotic running time for special cases, e. g., containers designed for C++ built-in integer elements.

A lot of Algorithm Engineering was done while developing the LEDA container types. There is an extensive comparison about the performance of the different implementations of priority queues [561, Chapter "Advanced Data Types"], for example. Many combinations of algorithms, problem size, and input were analyzed for this problem. This helps the user to find the best-suiting implementation she needs without testing all of them herself. This comparison is limited to the LEDA platform itself, with its intrinsic drawbacks mentioned above.

7.7.2   Algorithms

The algorithms provided by the STL are very basic. They are separated from the data structures as far as possible, having a very thin interface only, namely the different iterator types. The functionality includes mapping, i. e., executing a function for each element of a sequence (see next subsection), finding elements fulfilling a criterion, string search, partitioning a sequences, merging two sorted sequences into one, sorting, and random shuffling. Boolean operations on sets are supported as well rather numerical stuff like accumulation (also usually called reduction) and prefix sum.

Many of these functions are one-liners, so they are probably considered "to easy" by LEDA and thus not included, but sort of course is.

Parameterizing Enumeration. Enumerating a set of items is probably the most basic and frequently used "algorithm." For this task, the STL provides the generic algorithm for_each and miscellaneous variants. Unfortunately, C++ does yet not provide closures[5], therefore a functor object is needed to perform the work. A class must be defined, because the algorithm implementation cannot see

---

[5] A *closure* is a function that refers to free variables in its lexical context.

that class, otherwise. Hence, the code to be executed tends to be placed quite far from the location it is called from. Also, the code does not have access to local variables at the call spot. The advantage of being able to reuse those functors easily usually does not make up for this. We illustrate this in Figure 7.3.

Luckily, Boost produces some relief in this case. The Boost Lambda library and its *expression templates* allow the user to construct functors in place, by applying usual function calls and operators to variable placeholders (e. g., _1). However, adding a second variable to the output call could already complicate the code a lot, since the template metaprogramming involved in the library is kind of fragile.

In the upcoming C++ standard (C++ 0x), closures will be added to the language syntax under the name *lambda expressions*. This simplifies parameterization a lot, and also allows references to the lexical context.

LEDA solves this problem in yet another way. It provides C style macros to assign each item, one after the other, to a local variable. This is very easy to use, but not very flexible.

Performance. Sorting functionality is of course provided by both the STL and LEDA. Particularly the LEDA sorting algorithms suffer from the slow callback mechanism for custom comparators. Each time a comparison must be performed, a virtual function call is needed. Again, there are optimizations for built-in types. However, the performance is still bad when the items are large structures with a simple key.

The most interesting question is on the practical performance of LEDA, compared to both STL and Boost as well as to custom hand-tuned implementations. Unfortunately, there has not been any recent publication comparing their performance.

A study in [230] measures the performance of different library search trees: LEDA (a, b)-tree (with $a = 2$ and $b = 16$), STL map (red-black tree), and LEDA van Emde Boas (vEB) tree. Up to certain input size STL map performs better as it executes less CPU instructions. For larger inputs, not fitting into the cache, cache-efficiency plays a greater role and $(2, 16)$-trees win. LEDA's vEB tree is the slowest, despite of a better asymptotic complexity for integer keys of bounded range. A re-engineered vEB implementation presented in [230] outperforms all considered library implementations. The experiments also confirm the importance of memory management in Algorithm Engineering: A specialized LEDA allocator gives the best performance.

The authors of [306] develop cache-conscious STL-compatible lists. As a byproduct they present results of a test that traverses a doubly-linked lists with *randomly shuffled* elements, comparing GCC STL [321] and LEDA. LEDA's running times are slightly better than the times of STL [306, Figure 5(d)], which could be explained by the use of a customized memory allocator of LEDA that uses a smaller number of memory chunks to allocate list items. Therefore, the traversal incurs less cache faults.

STL (C++2003)

```
class print_int
{
public:
  void operator()(const int& i)
  {
    std::cout << (i + 1);
  }
};

void print_vector_stl_2003()
{
  std::vector<int> v(10);
  for_each(v.begin(), v.end(), print_int());
}
```

STL (C++0x)

```
void print_vector_stl_0x()
{
  std::vector<int> v(10);
  for_each(v.begin(), v.end(), [] (int i) { std::cout << (i + 1); } );
}
```

Boost Lambda

```
using namespace boost::lambda;

void print_vector_boost()
{
  std::vector<int> v(10);
  for_each(v.begin(), v.end(), std::cout << (_1 + 1));
}
```

LEDA

```
void print_vector_leda()
{
  leda::array<int> v(10);
  int i;
  forall(i, v)
    std::cout << (i + 1);
}
```

Fig. 7.3. Calling an operation for each element of a container

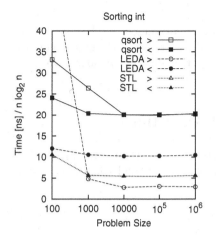 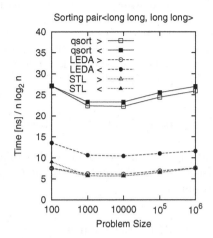

Fig. 7.4. A benchmark on sorting, comparing LEDA, the STL, and qsort

To support our predictions on performance basing to the different item access costs, we ran a little benchmark on sorting, comparing LEDA 6.2, the STL, and the qsort function (the two latter in the GCC implementation). The test machine was an AMD Athlon X2 with 2.0 GHz clock rate and 512 KB L2 cache, the code was compiled using GCC 4.3.2 with full optimization. We sorted sequences of 32-bit C++ integers, representing a small type, and pairs of 64-bit C++ integers, representing a larger, user-defined type. We sorted both in ascending and descending order, where the latter requires to provide the sorting algorithm with a user-defined comparator. The results are presented in Figure 7.4, the x-axis is logarithmic, and the y-axis shows the time divided by $n \log_2 n$, i.e., by the comparison-based lower bound for sorting.

LEDA performs exceptionally well for ascending order, beating the STL by a factor of two for large inputs, but being very slow for small inputs. This suggest that the library switches to integer sorting for this particular case. For the pair case, this margin vanishes. Sorting *descending* makes passing a user-defined comparator necessary, the default **compare** function cannot be used any longer. In this case, LEDA is about half as fast as the STL, for a wide range of input size. For the STL, ascending or descending makes hardly any difference, as expected. The qsort function from the C library, using callback functions for both comparators, performs much worse than both STL and LEDA, in all usual cases.

In general, i.e., for user-defined item types and comparators, the STL seems to be faster than LEDA, as expected. However, it is hard to generalize this finding to other algorithms, since the algorithmic intelligence is usually greater in most other cases, and low-level issues lose importance when compared to careful algorithm design.

7.7.3 Summary and Comparison

LEDA has a greater algorithmic variety in the area of elementary data structures than the STL and Boost. On the down hand side, there is a performance penalty due to inefficiencies on a lower level. In cases, the algorithmic advantage may outweigh this penalty.

7.8 Graph Data Structures and Algorithms

In this section, we compare the functionality and the Algorithm Engineering aspects of LEDA and the *Boost Graph Library (BGL)* [736] when it comes to graphs.

7.8.1 Data Structures

First of all, both LEDA and the BGL provide graph data structures. The algorithms are then applied to those.

The BGL defines multiple graph concepts, i. e., requirements a graph data structure must fulfill to be qualified for particular algorithms. Two classical exemplary implementations for graph data structures, adjacency matrix and adjacency list, are included. The latter can be parameterized on their part with container types for the node sequence and for the edge sequences of each node. This is the easiest possibility to customize such a graph data structure. Additionally, the user is downright invited to implement custom graph data structures on which the algorithms can be executed as well. This might be particularly useful for graphs that are given implicitly, e. g., grid graphs, or for graphs with certain restrictions, e. g., graphs with bounded or fixed degree. *Static graphs* are graphs that do not change any more after having been constructed. They could also be implemented more (space-)efficient on a custom basis, cooperating with the BGL.

LEDA basically has two graph data structure families, dynamic graphs and static graphs. All algorithms work on these two types only. It is not possible for the user to come up with custom ones, she can only parameterize the existing ones. For the dynamic case, there is only one underlying type that comes in slight variations, `leda::graph`. There is a directed and an undirected version as well as one specialized for planar maps, i. e., a graph with a planar geometric embedding. However, the underlying type itself is already full-fledged and has a "fat interface" [512, "Static Graphs"]. It is based on an adjacency list model and supports both primal and dual combinatorial embeddings. Therefore, it has a quite large overhead when not all of its functionality is actually used. Its space requirement is $11n + 12m$ machine words, where n denotes the number of nodes, and m denotes the number of edges as usual. A machine word can be 64 bits on a modern computer, so an edge takes up to 96 bytes, which is very much.

The `static_graph` type provided by LEDA is much more space efficient and also faster than the regular graph type. It comes in different flavors, which differ in the interface they offer. Depending on the type, one can only iterate over incoming *and* outgoing edges or over the outgoing edges of a node only, respectively. Also, for a given edge, only source *or* target might be accessible by the user. In the extreme case `opposite_graph`, one can only determine one end of the edge if the other one is known. Common to all of the types is that the graph must not be changed after the construction phase which is put off through a specific method call. Also, the insertion of nodes and edges must follow a certain order. All variants use some kind of edge array which make iteration over nodes and edges very fast, improved by higher cache-efficiency due to better locality. The more restrictions are accepted on the functionality, the better the performance is.

In both libraries, manipulations to nodes and edges are performed by means of handles to those objects, called node item and edge item in LEDA, and node descriptor and edge descriptor in the BGL. They are related to iterators, but not quite the same. We will see later why.

7.8.2   Node and Edge Data

The major issue in the design of graph data structures is how to associate information with nodes and edges. Most graph algorithms need such additional information like e. g., node color, visited-flags, or edge weights, either as input, output, or as temporary values. The BGL terms this additional information *properties*. Of course, one could just add all needed fields to the node and edge record, respectively. However, this can be inefficient in both time *and* space, in particular, if one wants to run a sequence of graph algorithms on a certain graph. One algorithm might need other data fields for nodes and edges to hold its current state than some other. Adding all those fields together is also a bad idea since it takes all space, although not all fields are used at the same time. Some fields may be used by many algorithms in the very same way, others might be used by only one. Having too much slack between important data fields hurts the performance due to less cache locality. The strongest argument against the integration of the data fields right into the structure is that it might be just impossible with language means, because the user has passed a graph data structure to the algorithm that cannot be changed any more.

As a conclusion, there must be a way to add additional information dynamically, after the graph data structure is already set up. Both LEDA and the BGL provide many ways to achieve this, which differ in time and space efficiency. Again, the Algorithm Engineer can choose and test the different variants, since the syntax to access the data is usually the same.

For both LEDA graph families, one can reserve memory for additional data beforehand, so-called slots. They will be used later on when a `node_array` or an `edge_array` is associated with the graph. The assignment of arrays to slots can be made statically or dynamically. If there is no empty slot, the appropriate constructor will allocate new memory. Also, both graph families can be parameterized with additional node and edge data directly, accepting the disadvantages mentioned above. However, this data cannot be used by algorithms from the

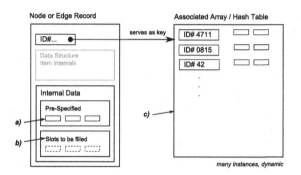

Fig. 7.5. All methods to associate data with nodes and edges combined. a) shows static internal data. b) labels slots that can be filled dynamically. c) points to an exemplary associated data structure.

library since they do not know the names of the variables. The most flexible, but also slowest solution, is to use `node_maps` and `edge_maps`, respectively. They associate data with the according node or edge handle, using a hash. Thus, they allow the graph to change while still remaining valid. Figure 7.5 presents the different possibilities in combination.

Boost supports a mechanism for integrating properties into the graph structure directly, with an interface that allows generic algorithms to access those properties by tag names, e. g., vertex name and edge weight. This is termed *internal properties* in BGL. External properties are also supported by BGL, i. e., dynamically added information that cannot be accessed by name. No matter whether internal or external, the desired property map can be accessed by a given name transparently. This is very convenient for implementing generic algorithms.

Both libraries can be used together. Since the Boost graph type is easily exchangeable, there is also one that wraps a LEDA graph. This should make performance comparisons easier, which is good for Algorithm Engineering.

7.8.3   Algorithms

LEDA and the BGL provide the basic graph algorithms depth-first-search and breadth-first-search. While the BGL allows the user to customize them widely by a callback mechanism, the LEDA versions only return lists of the visited nodes in the appropriate order. Later, we will see how to work-around that problem in LEDA. Both libraries provide measures to generate random graphs of different properties. The more advanced graph problems covered by both libraries include topological sorting, shortest path in all important variants, minimum-spanning trees, transitive closure, detection of (strongly/bi-connected) connected components, maximum flow in a network, basic graph drawing algorithms (circle layout, force-based, planar layout), and graph isomorphism.

BGL

```
add_edge(A, B, g);

std::vector<vertex_t> topo_order(num_vertices(g));
topological_sort(g, topo_order.rbegin(), color_map);
```

LEDA

```
g.new_edge(A, B);

list<node> ts;
bool acyclic = TOPSORT(g, ts);
```

Fig. 7.6. Calling topological sorting using BGL and LEDA, respectively

The BGL also offers some very special algorithms like reverse Cuthill-McKee ordering for matrix computations, smallest last vertex ordering, Sloan ordering, and sequential vertex coloring. Presumably designed for implicit graphs is its A* search implementation.

LEDA features other algorithms on graphs, namely minimum-cost flow, many variants for the matching problem, and Euler tours. It also has algorithms for embedding/embedded graphs, e. g., checking for planarity, planar layout, s-t-numbering, triangulation, etc., which mostly belong to computational geometry (see Section 7.9).

The short example in Figure 7.6 shows how those algorithms are called in each respective library. The flexibility of Boost allows the user to come up with custom graph data structures that only provide a minimalistic set of methods. On the down side, this requires a syntax which sometimes is counter-intuitive, already for simple operations like adding a node or an edge, which are not methods of the graph class, but just functions in the namespace. The libraries converge to the same kind of syntax when it comes to calling algorithms.

While the BGL only provides iterators on the sequences of all nodes or edges in their canonical order, LEDA offers graph iterators which are actually backed by graph algorithms, e. g., depth- or breadth-first-search. This is desperately needed because the usual LEDA graph algorithms allow only for little parameterization in terms of functionality, as mentioned above. So, while the BGL has the approach to supply customizable algorithms through callbacks at many interesting points (visitor pattern [313]), LEDA provides iterators that keep the state of the traversal and allow for the manipulation of the interesting objects by means of a loop.

A good overview on the problem of decoupling algorithms from data structures is given in [501]. The concept explained there uses an additional indirection, anticipating the concept applied by the BGL. In fact, it augments the LEDA library to introduce more flexibility to its graph algorithms.

The authors of [639] propose an extension to the C++ programming language to support better flexibility in graph algorithms. Their main concern is the classification of graphs. Every algorithm works on graphs of a certain class, e. g., planar and/or directed. Because all possible combinations of properties lead to an exponential explosion, a language extension is suggested to bypass this problem. Again, this is what the BGL does using template specialization.

A good example for Algorithm Engineering is the introduction of static graphs into LEDA. They were passed to an already existing and unchanged version of a maximum-flow algorithm [607]. In fact, the maximum-flow problem appears to be an exemplary problem in Algorithm Engineering. There have been many improvements over time [234]. The authors show that a more specialized, yet still sufficiently general implementation of graphs yields much better performance than a general one. The speedup is not due to an improvement of the asymptotic worst case running time, but because of a reduction of the constant factors. Since the memory consumption also drops, the result is a complete success. All known implementations that are based on the same preflow-push algorithm by Goldberg and Tarjan, are superseded. The one provided by the BGL is in fact beaten by an order of magnitude. The result also shows a nice comparison in performance between the different methods to associate node and edge data. External storage is slower than using a dynamically assigned slot, which is in turn slower than a statically assigned slot. Using hash maps for external data is even slower, as was already stated in [561, Chapter "Graphs and their Data Structures"].

Another class of graph algorithms is the detection of graph isomorphisms [485, 792] of different kinds. The *VFlib* [188, 291] specializes on this field. Boost only provides very basic functionality, testing for an isomorphism and the construction of a 1-to-1 mapping if existent. The LEDA implementation is much more advanced. It also supports subgraph isomorphism and graph monomorphism, and can enumerate all possible mappings or at least calculate their number, in certain cases also for a combinatorial explosion of possible mappings. For the actual isomorphism problem, there are two algorithms implemented, which perform differently well depending on the graph structure. One of them is a back-tracking algorithm which supports all three kinds of problems. It has been implemented using advanced data structures [739] that allow for a running time that is in average four times faster than the VFlib implementation, the maximum speedup being around 20.

7.8.4 Summary and Comparison

When using LEDA, one must choose between two extremes. Either take the standard LEDA graph type supporting every functionality, having much overhead. Or take the LEDA static graph type which provides excellent performance, restricting its interface to a very minimum. Restricting the algorithms to those two types allows for a nice call syntax.

On the other side, calling the BGL sometimes requires a weird syntax for executing algorithms. The syntactical elegance is sacrificed for more extensibility with respect to graph data structures.

7.9 Computational Geometry

In this section, we consider LEDA, CGAL and EXACUS with respect to Algorithm Engineering in computational geometry. We will also mention the main geometric functionality of these libraries briefly.

Geometric algorithms operate on primitive objects like points, segments, lines, rays, planes, etc. Primitive functions on a few geometric objects returning a bit or two bits of information, e. g. if two segments intersect, or the sign of the triangle defined by three points, are called *predicates*. Another kind of primitive functions *construct* and return new geometric objects: e. g., the intersection point of two lines. The classes implementing the basic geometric objects and the primitive functions operating on these geometric objects are usually encapsulated in a separate software layer called *geometric kernel*. LEDA and CGAL offer geometric kernels for 2D (plane), 3D (space) and higher dimensional geometry.

As it was mentioned before, *robust* geometric algorithms, coping with any kind of inputs, are one of the primary goals of Algorithm Engineering in computational geometry (see Sections 3.5 and 6.2). Handling degenerate cases counts on the implementation of the algorithms: The code must produce correct output on all possible inputs. The problem of imprecise arithmetic can be both tackled in the algorithm implementation and in the underlying geometric kernel. The latter solution is much easier with respect to the implementation efforts: one only has to use objects and functions from an exact kernel without changing the implementation code. Many variants of kernels are offered by LEDA and CGAL, having different degrees of accuracy and computational overhead.

7.9.1 Kernels and Exact Number Types

LEDA Kernels. The development of LEDA has outlived many pitfalls known in geometric computing [561, Chapter "The Geometry Kernels"]. In 1991, the first geometric LEDA implementations assumed non-degenerate inputs and relied on a kernel based on the imprecise floating point arithmetic. As a consequence, programs delivered wrong results or even crashed. This experience drove the authors of LEDA and other researchers to revise the foundations and develop theoretical backgrounds of exact geometric computation. Three years later, LEDA had a new *rational* kernel with exact predicates and constructions, and new robust implementations of many geometric algorithms without need for the non-degeneracy assumption. This achievement can be considered as a success example of Algorithm Engineering, where practical experience has pushed the developers to revise the theory, fitting it to real-world requirements.

The Role of Advanced Number Types in Geometry Libraries. Exact kernels of
LEDA and CGAL rely on advanced number types implementing exact arithmetic. The LEDA rational kernel uses `integer` homogeneous coordinates to
offer correctness. Another option would be to use Cartesian coordinates where
each component is represented by a LEDA `rational`, keeping the numerator
and denominator as `integer` members. Obviously, the solution with rationals
is less space efficient and also needs more arithmetic operations. Exact *curved*
geometry requires an even more advanced coordinate type. It must implement a
real algebraic number, i. e., a real number which is a root of a polynomial with
rational or integer coordinates.

Furthermore, LEDA has a *real number kernel* that allows one to make computations with objects having `leda::real` coordinates. As discussed in Chapter 6,
geometric computations with advanced number types can be very slow, therefore
the exact LEDA kernels use them only in a small number of cases, when it is
really needed for the exactness. One tries to compute the correct result using
plain floating point numbers, if this fails the exact arithmetic is used. This technique is called *floating-point filtering* and is used by the LEDA exact kernels by
default. EXACUS follows a similar filtering strategy for exact *non-linear* geometry, computing arrangements of curves and surfaces. For performance reasons, it
always employs the simplest possible number type, i. e., integers where possible,
rather than rationals, and algebraic numbers the last [94].

CGAL Kernels. The geometric kernels of CGAL are highly configurable. One
can choose the number type to represent coordinates and coefficients: The user
can provide any number type like the powerful LEDA `real`, the built-in C++ `int`
or a user type. The extent of CGAL's requirements of a number type is small. A
type can be made compliant to CGAL very easily. The coordinate representation
is also up to the user: One can choose Cartesian or homogeneous representation,
however, the requirements on the underlying number type are slightly different.
CGAL is very flexible with respect to the floating filtering support, as well. Given
any Cartesian kernel K, one can easily construct a `CGAL::Filtered_kernel<K>`
with *exact* and *fast* predicates that employ filtering. The predicates will first
try to make exact decisions using a fast inexact kernel, based on floating point
arithmetic. Only if they fail in doing so, they call predicates from much slower
exact kernel. There are also other ways to achieve filtering in CGAL, see [152].

Floating-Point Kernels. One might ask why the floating-point kernels are still
useful at all: programs based on them may produce incorrect results or even
crash. However, their inimitable advantage is their speed, which is most critical
in applications like visualization and computer graphics working in real-time.
For algorithms which do not insert the constructed data into predicates, fast
kernels with exact filtered predicates and inexact constructions would suffice to
avoid crashes, since the control flow will be correct then. The `CGAL::Exact_`
`predicates_inexact_constructions_kernel` is an example of such a kernel.

7.9.2   Low-Level Issues in Geometric Kernels

Both CGAL and LEDA define the geometric objects in the kernel non-modifiable. For example, there is no method to set the Cartesian coordinates of a point. The idea behind this decision is the following: Geometric implementations should not assume anything about the representation of the primitive objects. In order to translate a point by a vector, one has to call a method of the point that returns a new point object representing the translated position. Such patterns of use cause many copy and assignment operations, which might be expensive if a "fat" underlying kernel number type is used, e. g., LEDA `bigfloat`. To reduce copying overhead, some kernels can use reference counting techniques: kernel objects point to a shared representation using the reference counting technique (see Chapter 6). All LEDA's kernels are reference counted. The implementation of reference counting is simplified in LEDA and CGAL, because the kernel objects are immutable.

Originally, all CGAL kernels were reference counted only. However, after the study [703] has shown that non-reference kernels can be faster, CGAL has integrated 2D and 3D kernels in both variants, with reference counting and without. The superiority of kernels without reference counting can be explained by the fact that for simple and small number types like C++ `int` and `double`, the overhead of reference counting will outweigh the costs of copying. This is one of the examples of Algorithm Engineering's impact on CGAL. The higher dimensional CGAL kernels are reference counted, which is quite reasonable, because one single Cartesian point must already hold at least 4 coordinate components.

Differences between LEDA and CGAL. We should underline some crucial differences between the LEDA and CGAL kernels. CGAL kernels can be instantiated with any number type. LEDA has a set of predefined kernels based on floating point, rational and real types. In CGAL, geometric algorithms are decoupled from the kernels. The algorithm implementations can work with any given kernel; the kernel is given as a template parameter. There are quite large requirements on the kernel, however, algorithms in CGAL actually need only a few of them. The flexibility of CGAL contributes to a better tuning of real applications. One can configure a kernel that provides just the required degree of accuracy but not more, keeping efficiency the best possible. For example, if only exact predicates are needed, but no exact construction, then one chooses the predefined `CGAL::Exact_predicates_inexact_constructions_kernel` based on floating point filters. If one knows the input range values, and a certain knowledge of the computations carried out is available, then one can find out that floating point numbers with a *high fixed precision* will suffice for successful computation. In this case, a CGAL kernel instantiated with a floating point number having the given precision (e. g., LEDA `bigfloat`) will do the job.

Another powerful option, available only in CGAL, are user kernels. The user can define her own implementation of geometric objects like points, providing the point class itself and geometric primitives (predicates) on the objects. A much easier way to define a custom kernel is to define only the predicates but reuse the existing CGAL implementations of geometric objects.

Memory Management. As mentioned in Section 7.5, memory allocation issues are important in Algorithm Engineering. Geometric algorithms have a specific pattern of requests to the memory allocator. They usually ask for many small objects of fixed size, i.e., points, segments, circles, etc., which is particularly true for low-dimensional geometry. In particular, the speed of object allocation/deallocation plays a great role for CGAL and LEDA because the kernel objects are *non-modifiable* and thus programs might create even more kernel object instances. Therefore, LEDA and CGAL have optimized memory allocators which can satisfy such requests very quickly. For the allocation pattern of geometric algorithms the free list allocator (Section 7.5) has good performance. The allocator must maintain only a small number of lists of free chunks, each for a certain kernel object type. This approach is concretely used by the so-called `Compact_container` in CGAL. It consists of a list of blocks of linearly growing size in combination with a free list. It features very fast (de-)allocation at moderate space overhead, but does not support efficient enumeration of the contained elements.

Polymorphism in CGAL. Virtual member functions can result in a noticeable performance degradation (Section 7.5). Therefore, CGAL avoids the run-time polymorphism based on virtual functions. However, some CGAL functions like `intersection` of two segments need to return a polymorphic value: It could be a point, a segment (e.g., in case the input segments overlap), or empty. The standard solution would be to derive all geometric objects from one generic object. This approach has a space penalty of storing a pointer to virtual function table with each (potentially small) object. C++ compilers keep only a single copy of a virtual function table per type. This implies another call indirection that might cost additional running time. Instead, CGAL code uses the Runtime Type Information (RTTI) mechanism of C++ in order to determine the type of the returned object and to proceed accordingly. For compilers which do not yet support RTTI, CGAL relies on its own methods which can check whether two types match.

7.9.3   Functionality

LEDA and CGAL have a overwhelming wealth of high-level geometric data structures. Among them are two- and higher-dimensional search data structures: range, segment, and interval trees, as well as skip lists. Point set data structures, based on dynamic Delaunay triangulations, exist in both libraries. They support efficient update, search, closest point queries, and different types of range query operations. Polygon and polyhedron structures are supported as well. LEDA also offers polygons where some bounding edges can be circular arcs. LEDA and CGAL own many geometric algorithm implementations: 2/3/dD convex hull algorithms, Boolean operations on polygons and polyhedra, segment and curve intersection, computing arrangements, different kinds of triangulations, Voronoi diagrams, etc. Many of the LEDA algorithm implementations exist both in the form of a function call and as a dynamic data structure supporting on-line update operations. Since for many problems there is no universally best algorithm for all types of inputs, the libraries offer implementations of several algorithms. Geometric algorithms of LEDA usually return a LEDA list of objects. CGAL follows the approach of the STL and stores the result in a user output iterator given by a template parameter. For a complete list of existing implementations of geometric algorithms and data structures refer to the original manuals [152, 512]. Future versions of CGAL are expected to exploit parallelism in the algorithms [69].

In 2D the EXACUS library can compute predicates on conics and cubic curves and their intersections. Boolean operations on polygons with curve-segment edges can be performed using a generic implementation of a sweep-line algorithm. Computing the arrangements of cubic curves in the plain is available as well. EXACUS offers computations with quadrics in space that includes predicates on quadrics, their intersection curves and points, and arrangements of quadrics.

All CGAL, EXACUS and LEDA implementations of geometric algorithms do not assume that the input is in "general position", i. e., they handle all degenerate cases. Both CGAL and LEDA implement the exact geometric computation paradigm.

7.9.4 Performance

Performance of Geometric Libraries and Their Kernels. Apparently, a lot of engineering effort was invested during the development of LEDA, CGAL and EXACUS. It is very interesting to compare the performance of the library implementations, since a great part of the functionality is common. Such comparisons would reveal advantages and disadvantages of decisions taken in the library design. The study by Schirra [703] mentioned above presents many interesting results concerning the performance comparison of libraries. According to the experiments the template-based CGAL implementations have outperformed LEDA implementations. Despite the fact that these were implementations of the same algorithm and the predicates in both kernels are very similar, CGAL was faster. The reason is that some of the predicates in LEDA are not inlined by the compiler. A Java-style kernel, with a design where all access member functions are virtual, has been also tested against CGAL kernels. Because of the virtual function calls, the implementations with Java-style kernels are 4–6 times slower than the corresponding CGAL kernel implementations. There exists a web page [606] with results of some benchmarks comparing LEDA 4.4 and CGAL 2.4 implementations. The numbers show that Delaunay triangulation of LEDA (Dwyer algorithm) is faster than the CGAL implementation, both for inexact and exact computations. An explanation could be that the CGAL's Delaunay triangulation is only available as a dynamic data structure whereas LEDA's solution is offline. In a benchmark testing 2D convex hull algorithm implementations on floating point kernels, CGAL and LEDA perform equally well. The tests also include 3D convex hull algorithms with exact and inexact kernels, see [606] for details.

7.10   Conclusion

Algorithm libraries are an integral part of Algorithm Engineering. They absorb the best practices and make the engineering achievements easily available for a wide user base. The high availability of fast and robust implementations in software libraries accelerates Algorithm Engineering itself since new computational results can be obtained with less effort due to code reuse.

To be successful, libraries need to be robust, correct, flexible, extensible, and easy to use. By obeying to these requirements, they set high standards on the quality of other implementations.

Algorithm libraries fasten the transfer of theoretical results into industry applications. Implementing number types that work fast and correct for all inputs is an extremely difficult job. Fortunately, libraries can help by providing unlimited length integers, floating-point numbers of arbitrary precision, interval arithmetic, real algebraic numbers, etc. The successful LEDA, CGAL and STL/Boost libraries are widely used in both commercial products and academia. They provide well-engineered easy-to-use implementations of many very useful algorithms and data structures for the most fundamental combinatorial and geometric problems. Robust geometrical implementations that can cope with any possible input are highly demanded by industry. This wish is gradually coming true thanks to LEDA, CGAL and EXACUS.

Chapter 8. Experiments

Eric Berberich, Matthias Hagen*, Benjamin Hiller**, and Hannes Moser***

8.1 Introduction

Experimentation plays an important role in the Algorithm Engineering cycle. It is a powerful tool that amends the traditional and established theoretical methods of algorithm research. Instead of just analyzing the theoretical properties, experiments allow for estimating the practical performance of algorithms in more realistic settings. In other fields related to Computer Science, like for instance Mathematical Programming or Operations Research, experiments have been an indispensable method from the very beginning. Moreover, the results of systematic experimentation may yield new theoretical insights that can be used as a starting point for the next iteration of the whole Algorithm Engineering cycle.

Thereby, a successful experiment is based on extensive planning, an accurate selection of test instances, a careful setup and execution of the experiment, and finally a rigorous analysis and concise presentation of the results. We discuss these issues in this chapter.

8.1.1 Example Scenarios

In the Algorithm Engineering cycle, experimentation is one of the four main steps besides design, theoretical analysis, and implementation. There are many reasons why experiments are that important. We give a few examples here.

1. The analysis shows a bad worst-case behavior, but the algorithm is much better in practice: The worst-case behavior may be restricted to a small subset of problem instances. Thus, the algorithm runs faster in (almost) all practically relevant cases.
2. A theoretically good algorithm is practically irrelevant due to huge constants hidden in the "big Oh" notation.
3. A promising analysis is invalidated by experiments that show that the theoretically good behavior does not apply to practically relevant problem instances.
4. A specific algorithm is hard to analyze theoretically. Experimental analysis might provide important insights into the structure and properties of the algorithm.

* Supported in part by a Landesgraduiertenstipendium Thüringen.
** Supported by the DFG research group "Algorithms, Structure, Randomness" (Grant number GR 883/10-3, GR 883/10-4).
*** Supported by the Deutsche Forschungsgemeinschaft, project ITKO (iterative compression for solving hard network problems), NI 369/5.

M. Müller-Hannemann and S. Schirra (Eds.): Algorithm Engineering, LNCS 5971, pp. 325–388, 2010.

5. Experiments lead to new insights that can be used in the next cycle of the Algorithm Engineering process.

In the following, we discuss an example for each of these situations in more detail.

Example 1: Quite often experimenters observe a considerably better running time behavior of an algorithm than predicted by theory. Thus, the worst-case behavior is restricted to a very small subset of problem instances. A classic example is the simplex method for linear programming, whose running time is exponential in the worst case. However, its practical running time is typically bounded by a low-degree polynomial [15].

Example 2: In algorithm theory, an algorithm is called efficient if the asymptotical running time is small. However, in many cases there exists a hidden constant factor that makes the algorithm practically useless. An extreme example in graph theory is Robertson and Seymour's algorithm for testing whether a given graph is a minor of another [675, 676]. This algorithm runs in cubic time, however, the hidden constant is in the order of 10^{150}, making the algorithm completely impractical. Another example of this kind is Bodlaender's linear-time algorithm which determines for a given graph and a fixed k whether the graph has treewidth at most k [113]. Unfortunately, even for very small values of k, the implemented algorithm would not run in reasonable time. The "big Oh" notation facilitates the design of algorithms that will never get implemented, and the actual performance of an algorithm is concealed. Moreover, algorithms often rely on other algorithms in several layers, with the effect that an implementation would require an enormous effort. Thus, the "big Oh" is in some sense widening the gap between theory and practice.

Example 3: Moret and Shapiro tested several algorithms for the minimum spanning tree problem (MINIMUM SPANNING TREE) using advanced Algorithm Engineering methods [586]. They analyzed the following algorithms: Kruskal's, Prim's, Cheriton and Tarjan's, Fredman and Tarjan's, and Gabow et al.'s. They tried several different data structures (i. e., different kinds of heaps) and several variants of each algorithm. Moret gives a concise survey of this work [584]. The interesting result is that the simplest algorithm (Prim's) was also the fastest in their experiments, although it does not have the best running time in theory. The other algorithms are more sophisticated and have better worst-case asymptotic running time bounds. However, the sophistication does not pay off for reasonable instance sizes. Moret also stresses the value of Algorithm Engineering: By studying the details of data structures and algorithms one can refine the implementation up to the point of drawing entirely new conclusions, which is a key aspect of Algorithm Engineering. With this methodology, Moret and Shapiro's fastest implementation of Prim's algorithm got nearly ten times faster than their first implementation.

Example 4: This example is about algorithms whose theoretical analysis is extremely difficult, like for instance Simulated Annealing, Genetic Algorithms, and union-find with path compression. Both the analysis of the running time and of the solution quality is very difficult using existing methods. For instance, union-find with path compression is relatively easy to describe and was known to yield very efficient behavior. However, its exact characterization took many years till Tarjan achieved a proof of tight bounds [771]. In such cases, experimental analysis can be a fruitful alternative that yields interesting results more efficiently.

Example 5: As a last example we want to mention the Traveling Salesman Problem. In an incremental process, the methods to solve that problem (exactly or approximately) became more and more sophisticated over the years. Beginning with a few hundred cities, researchers are now able to solve instances of more than ten thousand cities [33]. In Section 8.6.1, the Traveling Salesman Problem is also used as an example of how to analyze results of experiments graphically.

8.1.2 The Importance of Experiments

The examples of the last section showed the importance of experimentation in the Algorithm Engineering cycle for just a few situations. This section is dedicated to describe more generally the motivation to conduct experiments. It is based mainly on several articles and surveys [408, 437, 548, 584].

For the analysis step of the Algorithm Engineering process, there exist usually three different methods, namely worst-case analysis, average-case analysis and experimental analysis. The theoretical methods are more sophisticated than experimental analysis. Since the early days of Computer Science theoretical analysis and experiments have been used. Computing pioneers such as Floyd and Knuth combined theoretical analysis and experiments. They used machine-dependent fine-tuning to derive efficient algorithms that performed well both in theory and practice. However, later on the focus has lain on theoretical analysis, whereas experiments were mainly used in other fields. From the two ways of analyzing algorithms, only theoretical analysis developed into a science. Since there is still missing a well-established methodology for experimentation, the quality of works in this discipline varies strongly, and the results are difficult to compare and to reproduce. This disequilibrium has to be balanced by deliberate experimental analysis.

Recently, the interest in experimental analysis has grown. There are various reasons for this newly arisen interest. One might be that computer scientists become aware that theoretical analysis cannot reveal all facets of algorithmic behavior, especially when concerning real-world applications. Of course many other reasons, for instance the fact that computational experiments are much cheaper these days, might have helped too.

This newly arisen interest is also reflected in an increasing number of publications in the field. Some major contributors are:

- Jon Bentley's *Programming pearls* columns in *Communications of the ACM* and his *Software Exploration* columns in *UNIX Review.*
- David Johnson initiated the Annual ACM/SIAM Symposium on Discrete Algorithms (SODA), which also invites a few experimental studies.

- The *ACM Journal of Experimental Algorithmics* (ACM JEA) was initiated to give a proper outlet for publications in the field of computational experiments.
- The *Engineering and Applications Track* at the *European Symposium on Algorithms* (ESA), which was formerly known as *Workshop on Algorithm Engineering* (WAE).
- The *Workshop on Algorithm Engineering and Experiments* (ALENEX).
- The *International Symposium on Experimental Algorithms* (SEA), which was formerly known as *Workshop on Experimental Algorithms* (WEA).

Compared to theoretical analysis, experimentation in Computer Science is still in the "fledgling stages." In other (natural) sciences, like for instance physics, theories are completely based on experiments. Scientists have developed mature methods to derive meaningful results out of experimentation (mature in the sense that they have been revised and approved many times). Computer science lacks such well-established methods, which are generally accepted as a standard for empirical studies by the community. Obviously, Computer Science differs in many ways from other natural sciences. For instance, on the one hand in natural science the results of theories are compared to a golden standard (the nature). On the other hand, in Computer Science we just report results or compare them with another experiment of the same type. Moreover, Computer Science is much easier to understand: In principle, we could derive nearly any information about a given program by profound analysis. In Computer Science, unlike other natural sciences, we know — at least in principle — the underlying mechanisms, like for instance source code, compilers, and computer architecture, that yield our results. But unfortunately, the processes we observe are by far too complex to be understood easily.

Therefore, like in other sciences, we need an empirical science of algorithms to be able to invent evidence-based explanatory theories. Certainly, this does not mean that theoretical Computer Science will become obsolete. There is absolutely no reason to abandon theoretical analysis, as it has proved to serve perfectly to draw many important conclusions, to gain a deeper insight into problems and to help to design new data structures and algorithms. However, theoretical analysis should be supplemented with experimentation, which is exactly the goal of the whole cyclic process of Algorithm Engineering.

With this approach, we would hopefully narrow the big gap between theory and practice, helping people to benefit more directly from the deep understanding of problems and algorithms gained by theory. Since experimental work is often considered not worthwhile and rejected by theorists, it is important to stress that empirical science is not the opposite of theory (e. g., quantum electrodynamics shows that an empirical science can be rather theoretical), at least when it would be evolving to a real science. We think that mainly the deficiency of unassailable and clean scientific experimental work and research principles are the cause for the lack of major success of experiments in algorithmics. In this chapter we give an overview of approaches that aim to resolve these problems.

8.1.3   The Experimentation Process

The task of experimentation is to answer a formulated hypothesis or a question using meaningful test data that has been obtained by some reproducible process, the experiment. Reproducibility here means that the experiment can be repeated, yielding qualitatively the same results and conclusions. A research experiment should have a purpose, be stated and defined clearly prior to the actual testing, and, of course, it is important to state the reason why experimentation is required.

The experimenter has great latitude in selecting the problems and algorithms. He has to decide how to implement the algorithm (see Chapter 6), to choose the computing environment, to select the performance measures, and he has to set the algorithm options. Furthermore, he is responsible for generating a good report which presents the results in an appropriate way. These choices can have a significant effect on the results, the quality, and the usefulness of the experiment as a whole. Therefore, the experimenter has to plan his experiments with care. He should document all decisions such that the experiment can be reproduced at any time. In order to improve the quality of experiments, the planning should be done following some systematics.

In the literature (i. e., [60,584]), experimentation is a process whose steps can be described as follows.

1. Define the goals of the experiment (Section 8.2).
2. Choose the measures of performance and factors to explore (Section 8.2).
3. Choose a good set of test instances (Sections 8.3 and 8.4).
4. Implement and execute the experiment (Section 8.5).
5. Analyze the data and draw conclusions (Section 8.6, see also Chapter 4).
6. Report the experiment's results (Section 8.7).

Note that this process is in almost every case an iterative process, meaning that it might be necessary to go back to some earlier step to revise some of the decisions made earlier. The process is often also incremental in the sense that the results motivate further experiments to answer new questions. In the following we shortly describe what an experimenter should consider in each step. Then, each step will be described in more detail in the corresponding sections of this chapter.

Define the goals of the experiment. There are manifold types of experiments, having its seeds in different motivations. At first, the researcher has to find out which type of experiment is needed. Depending on that type, the experiment and the presentation of the results have to be adapted properly. For that reason it is always helpful to define primary goals for the experiment. These goals should always be kept in mind during the whole experimentation process. Another important question in the first step is the newsworthiness of the experiment, that is, whether the results are interesting and whether they have the potential to lead to new valuable insights. We discuss these issues briefly in Section 8.2.1, where we also shortly subsume literature we consider worth reading.

Choose measures of performance and factors to explore. Depending on the problem and the type of experiment, the experimenter has to select the *measures* (e. g., running time) that are suited for a good understanding of underlying processes of the algorithm and that describe its performance at its best. We discuss how to find good measures, and we present some standard measures as well as other important alternatives in Section 8.2.2. With the measures we are also facing the task of obtaining their values. Several techniques exist to improve *data quality* as well as the *speed* of the experiment, which we discuss in Section 8.2.4.

Another important question of the second step is the choice of the *factors*, that is, choosing the properties of the *experimental environment* or setup that influence the result of the experiment (e. g., the input size). Some factors have a major influence on the measures, others are less important. The experimenter's task is to choose the factors that permit to analyze the algorithm as good as possible. This task is described in Section 8.2.3.

Choose a good set of test instances. The test instances used in algorithmic experiments directly affect the observed behavior of the tested algorithms. After characterizing some *fundamental properties* that should influence the choice of test instances in Section 8.3.1 we identify *three different types* of test instances used in most experiments. We analyze their respective strengths and weaknesses in Section 8.3.2 before giving some final suggestions on how to choose good test instances in Section 8.3.3.

For many problems collections of test instances are already available on the Internet. We call such collections *test data libraries* and describe properties of a perfect library in Section 8.4.1. The issues arising in the context of creating and maintaining a library are discussed in Sections 8.4.2 and 8.4.3. A brief compendium of existing libraries follows in Section 8.4.4.

Implement and execute the experiment. Executing the experiments seems to be a trivial task, since the computer actually *does the job*. If done without care, the obtained results are just useless.

Section 8.5.1 explains what to consider when setting-up the *laboratory*, so that the experimenter can work in a nice and clean environment that eliminates systematic errors. The actual work in experimentation is done by the computer. It runs all experiments, but the human operator has also some tasks. Section 8.5.2 gives advice on how to make the running phase simple without losing information or introducing new errors.

Analyze the data and draw conclusions. The data generated by the experiment needs to be analyzed carefully in order to draw sound conclusions. In Section 8.6.1 we give advice on how to employ graphical methods to analyze the data. The focus is on using diagrams to reveal information that might not be obvious.

Section 8.6.2 complements this rather informal approach with an overview on using statistical methods for data analysis. We start giving a brief overview on the basic concept of a *hypothesis test* as a major statistical tool. Instead of going into further details of statistical analysis, we rather try to capture general ideas of using it in the context of algorithm analysis by describing studies and results found in the literature. The goal is to provide an overview and to somehow give the flavor of the methods.

For the more general question of how to use experiments in order to analyze the *asymptotic* running time of algorithms we refer to Chapter 4, especially to Section 4.8. One general suggestion (made in Section 4.8.1) is to make use of the scientific method (known from the natural sciences), that is, to combine theoretical deductive reasoning and experimental analysis to reach the best possible overall result. But apart from that, Section 4.8.2 describes and assesses a specific approach to finding *hypotheses* on the asymptotic running time of algorithms *by pure analysis of experimental data*.

Report the experiment's results. Proper reporting of the results and the details of the experiment is very important for a good experimental study. Too many papers reporting experimental results have failed to achieve the main requirement for a good experiment: Being reproducible for doing further research. Section 8.7 deals with good practices for proper reporting and mentions pitfalls and problems to watch out for. We also give some hints on how to make the best out of diagrams and tables, in order to substantiate the claims and findings of the experiment.

Here we give some publications we consider worth and important to read before getting started.

Moret's paper [584] is a good starting point. It generally describes existing experimental work and briefly sketches the whole experimentation process from the planning to the presentation of the results. A more comprehensive work is Johnson's paper, which principally addresses theorists [437]. It describes how to write good papers on experiments, and it includes many recommendations, examples, and common mistakes in the experimentation process. Another recommendable paper from Hooker motivates experimentation in general [408]. It highlights the advantages of experimentation, states with which kind of prejudice it is often confronted. Furthermore, Hooker gives a nice comparison with natural sciences, and he presents some examples where experimentation is successfully applied. The paper by Barr et al. focuses on experiments with heuristic methods [60]. However, people from other areas might also find some interesting aspects and observations in this paper. McGeoch's paper [545] mainly concerns the questions of how to obtain good data from experimentation and how to accelerate experiments significantly. She proposes the use of *variance reduction techniques* and *simulation speed-ups*.

Each of these publications describes experimental work from a slightly different point of view, however, the authors basically agree in their description of the experimentation process in general.

8.2 Planning Experiments

This section describes the test planning, what an experimenter should think about *before* implementing the algorithm and starting to collect data. The planning of an experiment is a challenging process that takes a considerable amount of time. However, a careful plan of the experiment prevents many types of severe problems in later steps of the experiment. Planning is a necessary requirement in order to do high quality experimental research.

8.2.1   Introduction

First of all, we have to think about the motivation to perform an experiment. There are many reasons to conduct experimental research. In the literature we can find many different types of experiments with diverse motivations [437, 584, 60]. Depending on what an experimenter is trying to show, the corresponding experiment and the report of its results have to be adapted properly. There is a wide range of possible goals of an experiment, the following list states a few.

- Show the superiority of an algorithm compared with the existing ones.
- Show the relevance of an algorithm for a specific application.
- Compare the performance of competing algorithms.
- Improve existing algorithms.
- Show that an existing algorithm performs surprisingly bad.
- Analyze an algorithm/problem to better understand it (experimental analysis).
- Support/reject/refine conjectures on problems and algorithms.
- Checking for correctness, quality, and robustness of an algorithm.
- Develop refined models and optimization criteria.

In the planning step we have to define a clear set of objectives, like questions we are asking and statements we want to verify.

Another important part of that planning step is to verify the newsworthiness of the experiment. That is, whether the experiment would actually give us interesting new insights. One way to achieve newsworthiness is to answer interesting questions on a sound basis, going beyond pure running time comparison. We give a few examples:

- Does the performance of several algorithms for the same problem differ and do some of the algorithms clearly dominate the others? (Statistics can help here.)
- Does dominance hold for all instances or only for some subset? If so, what are the structural properties of this subset?
- What are the reasons for dominance (e. g., structural properties of inputs, comparison of operation counts for critical operations)?
- How much does each phase of the algorithm contribute to the running time/performance of the algorithm?

These questions cannot be answered quickly. They have to be considered in the whole experimentation process.

8.2.2 Measures

By a *measure* of performance we generally mean quantities related to the algorithm and obtained by the execution of the experiment. There are several widely used measures that are quasi standard. However, each measure has its advantages and disadvantages. Thus, the correct choice of an appropriate measure can be crucial for a good understanding and analysis of the experiment.

In the first part of this section, we describe several well-known as well as some more exotic measures that appeared in literature. Then, we briefly describe how to generally find good measures.

Three measures are used in almost any publication about experimental algorithms:

- running time,
- space consumption, and
- value/quality of the solution (heuristics and approximation algorithms).

Depending on the type of experiment, at least one of these measures is a must-have. However, these popular measures should not be used solely. The first two measures highly depend on the chosen programming language, compiler, and computer (processor, cache, memory, ...), and therefore the results are very difficult to generalize and to compare. Furthermore, they depend on the implementation style and the skill of the programmer. Therefore, some investigators therefore assure that all crucial parts are implemented by the same programmer, e. g., as described in [584]. Running times in particular are problematic when they are very small. Because the system clock's granularity cannot be chosen arbitrarily, we get distorted results. However, this can be resolved by several runs with the same input data set. The choice of the test instances, as described in Section 8.3, also has a strong influence, especially on the value/quality of the solution in the case of heuristics.

Most notably, it is very unlikely that a good understanding of the problem and the algorithm emerges from these measures. They are aggregate measures that do not reveal much about the algorithm's behavior (for instance, we cannot discover *bottleneck operations*, which are fundamental operations that are performed repeatedly by the algorithm and influence the running time at most).

We need other measures in order to gain a deeper understanding of the algorithms to test. Moret recommends to "always look beyond the obvious measures" [584]. In the following we describe some other measures that appear in literature (see, e. g., [15, 60, 584]).

Extensions of running time. First of all, it is sometimes useful to extend the notion of running time. For instance, in the case of heuristics, we might measure the time to find the best-found solution, that is, the time required to find the solution that is used to analyze the quality of the heuristics. Moreover, there exists a difference between the time that is required to produce the best-found solution and the total time of the run that produced it. In the case of heuristics that are multi-phase or composite (i. e., initial solution, improved solution, final solution), the time and the improvement of quality in each phase [60] should be measured, too.

Structural measures. For a good understanding of the algorithm we need structural measures of various kinds (e. g., number of iterations, number of calls to a crucial subroutine, memory references, number of comparisons, data moves, the number of nodes in a search tree). Several publications recommend the use of memory references (mems) as a structural substitute for running time [15, 481, 584]. But other measures, like for instance the number of comparisons, the number of data moves (e. g., for sorting algorithms), and the number of assignments, should be considered as well, depending on the algorithm to be analyzed.

Bottleneck operation counts. The idea of counting the number of calls to a crucial subroutine, or to count the number of executions of a major subtask, leads to the general concept of *asymptotic bottleneck operation*. We call an operation an *asymptotic nonbottleneck operation* if its fraction in the computation time becomes smaller and approaches zero as the problem size increases. Otherwise, we call the operation an *asymptotic bottleneck operation*. In general, there exists no formal method for determining asymptotic bottleneck operations, since an algorithm might behave completely different for small instances than for sufficiently large instances. However, it seems to be a quite useful approach in practice [15]. Bottleneck Operation Counts are also often used when comparing heuristic optimization algorithms. In this case, the evaluation of the fitness function is often the bottleneck when running the algorithm on real-world problems. For a more detailed description we refer to Chapter 4.

Virtual running time. Ahuja et al. [15] advocate the use of *virtual running time*. The virtual running time is an estimate of the running time under the assumption that the running time depends linearly on "representative operations" (potential bottleneck operations). The loss of accuracy, that is, the estimate of the running time compared with the actual running time, can be remarkably small. Ahuja et al. present case studies with a difference of at most 7%, in many cases below 3%. Virtual running time can be used to detect asymptotic bottleneck operations, it is particularly well-suited for tests on various systems, and it permits us to eliminate the effects of paging and caching in determining the running times. We refer the reader to Chapter 4 for a more detailed description of this notion.

Finally, we want to describe some notions that are not measures in the strong sense, but considered as such in some publications since their impact is generally underestimated by many experimenters.

The first "measure" of this kind is robustness. If an algorithm performs well or the computed solution has a good quality only for a few problem instances it is evidently not very interesting in a general setting. Therefore, an algorithm should perform well over a wide range of test instances. For instance, one could measure the number of solved instances of a benchmark library of hard instances in order to estimate the robustness of an algorithm. The second "measure" we want to mention is the ease of implementation. There are many examples of algorithms that have been selected for use in practice just because they are easy to implement and understand, although better (but more complicated) alternatives exist. Not only the running time is important, but also the time needed for the implementation of the algorithm. Especially if the running time is not a crucial factor, the ease of implementation (e. g., expressed in lines of code, or by estimating the man-months needed for an implementation) can be an important argument in favor of some algorithm. Note that the ease of implementation depends highly on the underlying programming language, programming tools, and the style of the programmer, among many other influences. The third "measure" to mention is scalability, which basically means that algorithms can deal with small as well as large data sets. Obviously, these "measures" cannot be determined very exactly, but even a very rough estimate can help to better classify the algorithm in question. However, it is important to stress that these "measures" are limited and therefore they should be applied with care. Note that these "measures" are also presented as design goals in Chapter 3.

As stated before, good measures that help understanding an algorithm are usually not the most obvious ones. Therefore, we briefly discuss how to find such good measures in practice. Several authors give various hints on this issue, for instance, Johnson states a nice list of questions to ask in order to find the right measures [437]. At the beginning, it is recommended to do research subsumed as *exploratory experimentation*. One of the first experiments could be to observe how the running time of the algorithm is affected by implementation details, parameter settings, heuristics, data structure choices, instance size, instance structure, and so forth. Furthermore, we might check if a correlation between running time and the count of some operations exists. Then, we try to find out the bottlenecks of the algorithm. It is also interesting to see how the running time depends on the machine architecture (processor, cache, memory, ...), and how the algorithm performs compared with its competitors. Obviously, these experiments should be conducted with other (standard) measures as well (e. g., replace "running time" with "space consumption" in the above description). Profilers can and should be used to quickly find good structural measures.

In general, a look should be taken at data representing differences as well as ratios. Furthermore, one should use measures that have small variance within a sampling point (which will be defined in the following section) as compared to the variance observed between different sampling points [60].

8.2.3 Factors and Sampling Points

The *factors* of an experiment comprise every property of the experimental environment or setup that influences the result of the experiment (i. e., the measures) [60]. The most obvious factors are the parameters of the algorithm, but we also consider other influences as, for instance, the computing environment. The experimenter has to find out which factors have a major influence on the measures. He has to define what to do with other factors that are not important or cannot be controlled. Factors generally can be expressed by some value, for instance the processor speed, the memory usage, or the value of some configuration variable for an algorithm. We refer to such values as a *level* of a factor [60]. For a run of an algorithm we have to define a *sampling point*, that is, we have to fix the factors at some level. The experimenter has to define which sampling points will be considered in the experiment, and how many runs should be performed for each sampling point.

By applying some preliminary tests, we can find out which factors actually do have a major influence, as for instance the input size, the number of iterations for an approximation algorithm, threshold levels, algorithms to solve subproblems (e. g., sorting and data structures), characteristics of the test instances, and the machine architecture. Among these, the experimenter has to pick out the ones he is interested in. These factors will possibly be altered during the experimental analysis to set up new experiments. For such factors, we have to decide which levels should be selected. This decision depends highly on the purpose of the experiment and the questions that are asked. The levels are the specific types or amounts that will be used in each run. For instance, if the factor is quantitative, then we have to choose the values we consider and how they are spaced (e. g., the selected levels of the factor "input size" could be $10, 10^2, 10^3, 10^4, \dots$). Note that qualitative factors make sense as well. For instance, to classify test instances as small, medium size, or big, or to choose a certain type of data structure (e. g., binary tree, hash), or looking at boolean values (e. g., optimization on or off).

Other factors might not be interesting for the experimenter. In this case, he has to fix them on a certain level for all runs. Obviously, a good reason for choosing a certain level must exist. For instance, the factor "main memory" could be fixed at 1024 MB, but this is only reasonable if there is evidence that the memory usage of the tested algorithm will never even get close to that amount.

Finally, some factors might exist that are ignored, because we assume them not to influence the outcome or having a sufficiently low influence. Of course, there must be evidence for this assumption. For instance, if we measure the running time by looking at the processor time of the algorithm, and if one factor is the "user load" of the machine on which we perform the experiment, then we might ignore the user load because we trust in the operating system that the measured processor time is computed correctly. Other factors that have to be ignored out of necessity are factors that we do not understand or cannot control. For instance, such a factor could be the total load of the machine where the experiment is performed. Even if we assure that no other important processes are running, the necessary operating system's processes themselves cannot be controlled that easily. Especially for such factors, it is recommended to randomize them if possible, in order to keep an undesired influence as low as possible [547]. The process of finding good factors can take quite some time, and it is important to document the whole process. The finding of good factors is also part of the running phase of the experiment, which is described in more detail in Section 8.5.2.

For each run of the experiment a sampling point has to be chosen. With the number of factors that have to be altered the number of possible sampling points increases, since in theory we could try all possible combinations of factor levels. In most settings, this number is by far too high in order to perform an experiment for every possible sampling point. Therefore, the experimenter has to select a reasonable number of sampling points that reflect the overall behavior of the tested algorithm as good as possible. In order to decrease the variance of the test data, the experimenter also has to consider that the experiment should possibly be run several times for the same sampling point (see also Sections 8.2.4 and 8.6.2). With a good and elaborated prior selection of sampling points (by always having the primary goals of the experiment in mind), the experimenter can avoid many useless experiments that use up expensive resources. Furthermore, it can be avoided to have experiments run again in a later step, because it became clear in the analysis that the used sampling points were not adequate or sufficient.

Finally, we want to mention a comprehensive approach for experimental design called DOE (Design Of Experiments), which especially deals with the careful design of experiments and the choice of factors and sampling points in order to allow a sound subsequent statistical analysis [60, p. 20]. For more information about DOE we refer to Section 8.6.2.

8.2.4   Advanced Techniques

In this section we briefly explain advanced methods that should be considered when planning an experiment, like for instance simulation [511,545,547,546,622], simulation speedup as well as variance reduction techniques [545]. They have the goal to improve the process of obtaining experimental data. In a nutshell, simulation speed-up deals with the question of how to speed up the process of obtaining data, i. e., how to make the test runs faster. With faster test runs, we can obtain more data in less time, helping us to decrease the variance notably. However, not only simulation speedup can reduce variance, but other more sophisticated techniques for this purpose exist. Conversely, a reduced variance admits fewer test runs, thus, speeding up the entire process of gathering data. Note that these techniques are not a luxury additive in test design. Often, much improvement may be needed for the data to be useful.

A common paradigm in simulation research is to differentiate between a real-world process (e. g., an economic system, weather, public transport) and a mathematical model of such a process, to predict its future behavior in reality. For the purposes of algorithm design, the real-world process is an application program running in a particular computing environment, whereas the mathematical model is the underlying algorithm. If the algorithm cannot be analyzed sufficiently, then a simulation program is developed, which may be identical with the application program. Not all researchers make this distinction, as well as we did not mention it before this point. However, this point of view is useful to explain the following techniques.

Usually, we have to deal with measures that are influenced by random noise. Thus, we get different numerical values for each test run. In order to get a reliable value for the measure, we repeat the test run several times and compute the mean value over all test runs. However, for measures with high variance (or "spread"), we need a high number of runs in order to get a reliable mean value with low deviation. In the following we outline several known approaches to reduce variance, where only the intuitive idea behind each technique is described. More exact mathematical descriptions of these techniques can be found in the literature (e. g., [545]).

Common Random Numbers. This technique should be considered when we want to compare two algorithms on randomly generated instances and we expect that the compared measure is positively related with respect to the input instances. The idea is to use the same random instance for each test run of the two algorithms, which is equivalent to generate the instance from the same random numbers, hence the name. Since the measure is assumed to be positively related, the variance of the difference of the measures of the two test runs for each random instance is expected to be lower than the variance of the measure of each algorithm separately. A positive side effect of this technique is that we have to compute only half the number of test instances compared to the situation where we generate a random instance for each algorithm separately.

Control Variates. If there are two measures of the same algorithm that are positively correlated, then we can make use of this technique to decrease the variance of one such measure. Suppose that the running time and the memory usage of an algorithm correlate positively, i. e., the algorithm needs more memory if it is running for a longer time. For each test run, we compute the difference between the mean value of the memory usage and the memory usage observed in that run. Due to the positive correlation, we can use this difference to "correct" the value of the running time for that test run. This method provably reduces the variance of the running time values.

Antithetic Variates. The idea behind this technique is simple: If we have two measures that have the same distribution, but are negatively correlated, then the sum of these two measures has a lower variance. Namely, if the difference between the first measure and its mean is positive, then the difference between the second measure and its mean is likely to be negative. Thus the sum of both measures compensates the deviation of each measure, and therefore the "sum measure" has a reduced variance.

Conditional Expectation. This technique is sometimes also called "Conditional Monte Carlo" or "Conditional Mean". Suppose we have two measures, for which we know that the mean of the first measure is a function of the mean of the second measure. For each test run, rather than obtaining the first measure directly, we can also take the second measure and then compute the corresponding value of the first using the known function. This method works if the variance of the second measure is smaller than the variance of the first measure.

These were just four important techniques that are most likely to be generally applicable. In literature, many other techniques of this type can be found.

Next, we address simulation speedup. Until now, the idea was to implement an algorithm and then perform the tests directly on it. The key idea of simulation speedup is to partially simulate the algorithm. Because sometimes it is not necessary to implement it as a whole, we might skip parts of the implementation and replace them by a simulation. This is more efficient due to knowledge which the implemented algorithm would not have.

Variance reduction and simulation speed-up are closely related. With simulation speed-up, we are automatically able to reduce variance, as the improved efficiency permits us to take more trials within the same amount of time. Conversely, a smaller variance implies that less trials are needed. Thus, the overall running time decreases. McGeoch [545] gives several examples of algorithms to which these techniques have been successfully applied.

8.3 Test Data Generation

When evaluating algorithms experimentally, the experimenter usually runs the algorithms on several test instances while measuring interesting values. Obviously, the used test instances may substantially affect the observed behavior of the algorithms. Only a good choice of test instances can result in meaningful conclusions drawn from the respective algorithmic experiment. Hence, the decision what test instances to use is one of the crucial points in test design (cf. Section 8.1.3). Due to its importance we address the problem in more detail here.

The outline of this section is as follows. Section 8.3.1 contains basic properties that every experimenter should try to accomplish when choosing test instances. We introduce three different types of test instances in Section 8.3.2 and analyze their respective strengths and weaknesses. Section 8.3.3 contains some final suggestions for test data generation.

8.3.1 Properties to Have in Mind

There is a wide agreement in the literature that choosing test instances is a difficult task since any choice of test instances allows for criticism. But there is also a wide agreement on some basic, potentially overlapping, properties that an experimenter should have in mind while selecting test instances. Note that the properties are not only important for the test instance selection, but for the whole experimental process in general. If the selection of test instances helps to achieve the properties, the result is most likely a good set of test instances. We compiled the following list using the corresponding discussions in several articles [60, 196, 197, 375, 408, 409, 430, 437, 526, 546, 584, 585, 663].

Comparability. The results of algorithmic experiments should be comparable to other experiments. While this should be taken for granted, there are lots of algorithmic experiments ignoring it.

If different tests in a paper use test instances with different characteristics, it is mostly not valid to compare the measurements. There may be some occasional exceptions, but more often the comparisons are meaningless and cannot reveal anything. However, *Comparability* should not only hold in one paper, it is also desirable for experiments from different authors.

Today, the standard solution to assure *Comparability* is to make the instances or their generator programs available on the Internet. To ensure that other researchers can use the instances it is advisable to use a widely accepted format to store them. If the publicly available instances are included in new experiments, they ensure comparability to already published studies using the same instances. The potential abuse that other researchers might optimize their algorithms exactly for these instances is made harder if the experiments include lots of varied enough instances (cf. *Quantity* and *Variety* below).

In the phase of test design, *Comparability* means to be aware of standard test data libraries (cf. Section 8.4) and instances used in former experiments on similar algorithms.

Measurability. For heuristics it is often tested how far from an optimal solution the heuristic's solution of a test instance is. Hence, it is desirable to be able to measure the optimal solution in advance.

Unfortunately, nontrivial instances with known solutions are often very small or too much effort must be spent on measuring an optimal solution, e. g., for NP-hard problems. However, problem generators can construct artificial instances with a built-in optimal solution that is known in advance [499]. But one has to be aware that such a generation process may yield quite unrealistic problem instances (cf. the discussion on artificial instances in Section 8.3.2).

Furthermore, for NP-hard problems it is very unlikely to be able to efficiently generate meaningful instances with known solutions [692].

Portability. In the early days of algorithmic experiments the large and bulky data of some non-trivial examples caused *Portability* problems. Such instances were too large to be published in journals. Researchers could only obtain them by depending on the cooperation of others that had previously used the same instances.

Today, with the availability of many instances on the Internet there are two main sources of *Portability* problems. One arises when proprietary considerations preclude the supply of the test instances. One should try to exclude such proprietary test instances from experiments since they clearly degrade the above mentioned *Comparability*. However, there are also circumstances, e. g., in VLSI-design, where it is impossible not to use proprietary instances in the experiment.

Another possible source of *Portability* problems is the format in which the instances are stored. Using a widely accepted or some standard format helps to exchange instances with other researchers. The main reason is that such a standard usually is well-documented and everyone knows how to decode it. There already exist common standards for some areas, like the cnf-format for SAT-instances (cf. Section 8.4.4). These standards are mostly a special ASCII or even binary encoding of the instances.

If there is no common format at hand, the experimenter has to choose one considering some important points. First, the instances have to be stored in a way such that everyone can convert them quite simply to another format. This means that the format itself has to be documented by the inventor. Furthermore, the format should avoid redundancies, it should be extensible, there should be an efficient decoding routine, and storing the instances should not need too much memory. In some situations (cf. the CSPLib in Section 8.4.4), even a human readable format may have advantages. Another option is to use XML. But keep in mind that XML is not designed for the purpose of storing test instances. Hence, usage of XML as an instance format is really rare up to now.

Purpose. Some studies do not explicitly consider the *Purpose* of the experiment when choosing test instances. An example would be to keep in mind whether the experiment should show the potential of an algorithm (where lots of different instances are needed) or just the practicality of an algorithm in specific situations (where more restricted instances have to be chosen). The used test instances should always match the *Purpose* of the experiment.

Quantity. The number of test instances to use depends on the goals of the experiment. Preliminary testing to show feasibility requires only a small number of instances. However, the experiments we have in mind are of another kind. To assess strengths and weaknesses of an algorithm or to compare it against other approaches requires large-scale testing in terms of the number of instances used. Choosing many instances helps to protect being fooled by peculiar experiences with few instances and yields more informative studies. Unfortunately, in many studies the set of test instances is too small compared to the total range of potential instances. Hence, the drawn conclusions tend to be meaningless.

Reproducibility. When experiments are reported, the test instances have to be given in enough detail that another researcher could at least in principle reproduce the results. If the instances were obtained by using a generator, it usually suffices to give the settings of the important parameters of the generator and the seed of a potentially used random number generator. Nevertheless, generated instances with unique properties that are difficult to reproduce should be given as precise instances. This corresponds with *Comparability* from above since making the instances publicly available also supports *Reproducibility*.

Although *Reproducibility* is widely acknowledged to be important, a lot of published experiments are not really reproducible. One of the main reasons, besides the ignorance of some experimenters, might be the problem of proprietary test instances not available to the public.

Significance. To ensure *Significance* of an experiment, instances from widely accepted test data libraries should be included, which also corresponds to *Comparability*. Of further interest are instances that test the limits of the algorithm or even cause it to fail. Too easy instances reveal little on an algorithms behavior on hard instances. Hence, one key to ensure *Significance* is the *Quantity* and *Variety* of the test instances. However, it is a challenge to generate meaningful test instances, especially for the assessment of heuristics. The experimenter often has to trade off the need for the sample of instances to be representative and the cost of obtaining the instances.

Unbiasedness. Unintended biases should not be introduced into the test instances used. One such example would be to use only instances that the tested algorithm can easily solve. The potential conclusion that the algorithm solves all instances very fast is heavily biased by the choice of instances. Hence, observance of *Quantity*, *Significance* and *Variety* helps to be unbiased in the problem selection.

Another source of biases can be encountered in the generation process of potentially used artificial instances (cf. Section 8.3.2).

Variety. The test instances used in an experiment should have different characteristics to show how algorithmic performance is affected. But in many studies the instances have been too simple and too limited in scope, e.g., when only few instances of small size are used to demonstrate sometimes pathological algorithmic behavior. Instances that are too easy do not allow for good conclusions. Large-scale testing, in terms of the range of the instance sizes and the variety of instance properties, is required since this is the only way to reflect the diversity of factors that could be encountered. Demonstrating the potential and the usefulness of an algorithm also requires a wide *Variety* of test instances since otherwise the strengths and weaknesses cannot be assessed accordingly. However, if the scope is to show practicality in specific situations, much more restrictive sets are allowed. Again, the above mentioned *Purpose* of the experiment is crucial for the decision.

8.3.2   Three Types of Test Instances

Roughly, there are three different types of test instances an experimenter could use. Namely, these are real-world instances, artificial instances, and perturbed real-world instances. In this section we assess their respective strengths and weaknesses according to the properties discussed in Section 8.3.1.

Real-World Instances. Real-world instances originate from real applications. They therefore reflect the ultimate *Purpose* of any tested algorithm. Several authors have already discussed the usage of real-world instances [60, 196, 197, 341, 400, 375, 430, 437, 584, 663]. In the following, we give a brief survey of their observations.

The property of being representative for real-world behavior is one of the main reasons that real-world instances should be used in algorithmic experiments whenever possible. Very often, the goal of an algorithmic experiment is to evaluate practical usefulness. Then, real-world instances cannot be excluded from the experiment since they allow an accurate assessment of the practical usefulness of any tested algorithm.

However, in the early days of algorithmic experiments real-world instances usually where handpicked. Hence, the collection and documentation was quite expensive. Today these problems do not carry that much weight since most test data libraries (cf. Section 8.4) already include real-world instances and are easily available on the Internet. Real-world instances that are used in well-documented experiments usually make their way into such a library. Nevertheless, real-world instances may have a proprietary nature and thus may not be available for public use. This causes *Comparability* problems.

Another more serious problem with the usage of real-world instances is that it is often difficult or even impossible to obtain a sufficient number of large enough instances. Small instances can be solved too fast on current machines such that the running times shrink to negligibility. Hence, there often are troubles in achieving *Quantity* and *Variety* just using real-world instances. But even if real-world instances would be available in large enough *Quantity* and *Variety* they usually to not allow to draw general conclusions about how an algorithm operates. The main reason is that typically instance properties cannot be isolated in real-world instances. However, this is necessary to show how changing several properties affects the performance. Before we describe a possible way to overcome these issues by using artificial instances, we close with a short summary of the main advantages and disadvantages of real-world instances.

Advantages	**Disadvantages**
– representative of real-world behavior (*Purpose*)	– only of bounded size (*Variety*)
	– only few available (*Quantity*)
– allow assessment of practical usefulness	– sometimes proprietary (*Comparability*)
	– lack of control of characteristics

Artificial Instances. Usually, artificial instances are randomly generated by a generator program given a list of parameters. One of the earliest examples is NETGEN which generates network problem instances [476]. Using artificial instances is a possibility to overcome the main disadvantages of real-world instances. Hence, they were already studied by other authors [60, 196, 197, 357, 375, 400, 409, 430, 437, 526, 584, 621, 663]. We compiled our following discussion from these papers.

The usage of generator programs ensures the fast and cheap availability of a very large *Quantity* of instances. If the generator program is well-written, one key property is that it can provide arbitrarily large instances which assists *Variety*. This allows the experimenter to determine the size of a biggest instance that can be solved in reasonable time. If the generator program is written for machine independence and the parameters affecting the generation process are well-documented, they provide an effective means to ensure *Reproducibility* and *Comparability*. Good generator code often becomes a standard and can be found in existing test data libraries (cf. Section 8.4). Generators usually are not proprietary.

A good generator program allows the experimenter to control instance characteristics through adjusting parameters that affect the generation process. Thus, instance properties can be isolated and their effect on the algorithm's performance can be estimated. However, generator programs may be biased in the way that unintended correlations are built into the instances or that only instances with particular characteristics are produced. Hall and Poser analyze existing generation processes for machine scheduling problems and state that some widely used approaches actually are biased in such a way [375]. Further resources of biases may be rounding problems in the generation process or the used random number generator, e. g., when only the last bits are examined [325]. L'Ecuyer gives some useful hints on the usage of random number generators [511].

When evaluating heuristics or approximation algorithms for intractable problems, an important value is the quality of the found solution (cf. Section 8.2.2). It would be nice to know the value of an optimal solution in advance. Such a feature is offered by some generators. They are able to produce instances with a known optimal solution that is concealed from the tested algorithms. However, restricting the tests only to instances with known solutions is likely to yield unconvincing results. One reason is that instances with a built-in solution often have a narrow and very artificial nature and thus are not representative. Furthermore, instances with known solutions do not constitute the primary goal of heuristics or approximation algorithms that are designed to handle cases where an optimum is unknown and too hard to find.

Being not representative for real-world behavior is one of the main points artificial instances are often criticized for. The argument is that artificial instances can only be meaningful if there is some evidence that they can predict the algorithm's behavior on real-world instances. In fact, very often artificial instances do not resemble real-world behavior and thus drawn conclusions may not be valid for real-world instances. An example is the frequent assumption of a uniform distribution to select artificial instances from an instance population. Of course, there are studies where it can be well justified to generate the instances uniformly at random, e. g., when comparing sorting algorithms on integer sequences [504]. But in most cases real-world instances are not distributed uniformly. Real-world instances include structure, and it is certainly true that unstructured artificial instances tell us little about real-world performance. As an example Johnson states that asymmetric TSP-instances, with independently chosen distance matrix entries from small ranges, often are particularly easy to solve [437]. Algorithms succeeding on them may dramatically fail on more realistic instances. However, there are also examples where it seems impossible to build realistic models. For example, McGeoch points out that network flow problems occur in so many areas that it is very difficult to cover all of them in a generator program [546].

Nevertheless, there are some definitive advantages when using artificial instances. A careful design of the generator program can guarantee that at least some properties of realistic instances are met. And very often this is the best one can hope for since there is one main difficulty when trying to generate perfectly realistic artificial instances. It requires very sophisticated analyzes to identify appropriate parameters and corresponding values that would lead to realistic artificial instances. In fact, hardly any generator really can produce realistic data. But the ability to control the instance characteristics should not be underestimated when considering the main advantages and disadvantages of artificial instances.

Advantages	Disadvantages
– arbitrary size available (*Variety*) – arbitrary number available (*Quantity*) – rarely proprietary (*Comparability*) – ability to control characteristics	– lack of realism (*Purpose*) – difficult to assess real-world performance (*Purpose*) – susceptible to unintended correlations and biases (*Unbiasedness*)

Perturbed Real-World Instances. When comparing the lists of advantages and disadvantages of real-world and artificial instances the observation is that they are inversions of each other. Several researchers suggest a way to try to combine the advantages of both real-world and artificial instances [357, 400, 621, 663, 732]. The following discussion is based on these papers.

Starting from real-world instances, a controlled variation by a generator program yields perturbed real-world instances. Such instances are a compromise of real-world and artificial instances.

Due to the number of perturbed real-world instances that can be obtained from one real-world instance, their available *Quantity* is better than for real-world instances. However, the size of the perturbed instances may not differ dramatically from the size of the original real-world instance, and the inherent structure of the real-world instances nearly stays the same. Hence, perturbed real-world instances cannot support *Variety* in the way artificial instances can.

Another problem is the ability to resemble real-world behavior. On the one hand, perturbed real-world instances cannot be seen as actual real-world instances due to the perturbation. But on the other hand, they retain much of the inherent structure. This causes their degree of realism to fall somewhere in between real-world and artificial instances.

However, the most serious problem with perturbed real-world instances is that it is often very hard to identify interesting parameters that have to be changed to obtain useful perturbed real-world instances from given real-world instances. This difficulty cuts back the benefits perturbed real-world instances have. For this reason, Shier suggests to use a meta-algorithm that, given an algorithm and a test instance, would generate interesting perturbed instances [732]. But this still seems to be dreams of the future.

We conclude with a short summary of the advantages and disadvantages of perturbed real-world instances.

Advantages	Disadvantages
– better *Quantity* than real-world instances	– *Variety* comparable to real-world instances
– more realistic than artificial instances	– less realistic than real-world instances
	– often hard to identify meaningful perturbation

8.3.3   What Instances to Use

There is no proven right way for the choice of good test instances, and the debate which instances to use continues. Since the choice of test instances usually is limited by time and space restrictions, some tradeoff will always have to be made. We can derive some helpful suggestions from our above discussion and the references therein.

To ensure the *Comparability* with previous studies standard test sets and generators should be used whenever possible. Proprietary instances should only be used under special circumstances and with adequate justification. There may be scenarios where it is impossible not to use proprietary instances, but in most cases the lack of *Comparability* is too large compared to their usefulness.

We have seen that real-world instances and artificial instances are quite contrary in their advantages and disadvantages. The inclusion of real-world instances enables the assessment of the practical usefulness of any tested algorithm. However, since another goal should be to test against a *Variety* of instances, the only way is to additionally include artificial instances. They may rarely be realistic enough to completely substitute the real-world instances, but their most important advantages are their nearly infinite variety, and that the experimenter may isolate special instance properties that directly affect performance. Very often structures can be found in the artificial instances that allow a careful comparison to the real-world instances and thus enable the experimenter to evaluate the predictive quality of the random results.

Very often instances are chosen on which the tested algorithm performs well or it is easy to demonstrate improvement over previous algorithms. But additionally, there should be always included test instances where the tested algorithm is likely to perform poorly. This enables the judgment of potential weaknesses which indicates *Significance* and *Unbiasedness*.

Altogether, our suggestion is to use at least real-world *and* artificial instances. Finding meaningful perturbed real-world instances often is too hard compared to their benefits. It mostly suffices to use artificial instances in addition to real-world instances. Before choosing instances the experimenter should be aware of the practice in the corresponding field to know which instances were used in past experiments. However, the *Purpose* of the experiment should determine the final choice of instances.

As a last remark, we point out that regardless which instances are used in an experiment, they have to be conscientiously documented and made available to the public to ensure *Comparability* and *Reproducibility*. Furthermore, a good talk on algorithmic experiments states what instances were used [550].

8.4   Test Data Libraries

In Section 8.3.1 we have seen that, in order to ensure *Comparability* and *Reproducibility* of algorithmic experiments, it is essential to make the test instances or their generator programs with the corresponding parameter settings publicly available. A convenient way is the usage of test data libraries. These are collections of test instances and generators focused more on a single problem, like the library for the satisfiability problem (cf. Section 8.4.4), or on a set of related problems, like the libraries for constraint solving or theorem proving (cf. Section 8.4.4).

The outline of this section is as follows. Section 8.4.1 contains properties of a perfect library. In Section 8.4.2 we focus on issues relating to the creation of a library, whereas Section 8.4.3 discusses challenges of an already established library. Section 8.4.4 closes with a brief compendium of existing test data libraries that again highlights some of the most important library issues.

8.4.1   Properties of a Perfect Library

Today, very often the test instances used in algorithmic experiments are obtained from test data libraries. Thus, it is important to be able to identify good libraries. We provide some properties that are characteristic for the quality of test data libraries. Our following alphabetical list is based on discussions by several authors [60, 341, 357, 327, 328, 409, 375, 410, 668, 768].

Accuracy. A library should be as error-free as possible. This applies to the contained instances or generator programs and as well to their documentations or any other included data. An example would be that the instances should have unambiguous names in the library.

> Any error found has to be corrected immediately and documented in a kind of "history of changes".

Availability. In the days before the Internet came up, the test data libraries were books or available on magnetic tapes that had to be ordered from the maintainers [290, 668]. Nowadays, lots of libraries for nearly any problem are freely available on the Internet. Thus, they are easy to find and accessible for any experimenter.

Completeness. A library should be as comprehensive as possible. On the one hand, this means that libraries should contain all test instances or generators known for the respective problems. Ideally, an experimenter should not need to look elsewhere to find appropriate test instances. Newly occurring test instances should be included immediately.

> But on the other hand, this also means that additional information on the test instances should be included. Such further information might be the

best known solution, performance data of algorithms solving the instances, references to studies where the instances were used, pointers to state-of-the-art algorithms, or any useful statistic.

Coverage. A library should contain all meaningful instances of the respective problems. Hence, it should be as large as possible. New instances have to be included whenever available (cf. *Extensibility*). However, very large libraries require a sophisticated design to guarantee the *Ease of Use*.

Difficulty. There should be contained neither just hard nor just easy problems in a library. Practical problems often differ very much in their difficulty, and this mix should be reflected in the library. Even very easy problems may be useful for first expositions on a newly developed algorithm. For a newcomer difficulty ratings for the instances would ease the choice of appropriate instances.

Note that even for established libraries there may be doubts concerning the *Difficulty*. For example, Holte showed that for the UCI Machine Learning Repository the accuracy of some very simple classification rules compared very favorably with much more complex rules [403]. However, the practical significance of this result depends on whether or not the UCI instances are representative for real-world instances. On the one hand, many UCI instances were drawn from applications and thus should be representative. But on the other hand, many of the instances were taken from studies of machine learning algorithms. Hence, they might be biased since often experimenters only include instances that their algorithms can solve. The conclusion is that only a careful analysis and selection of instances ensures a wide range of *Difficulty* in a library.

Diversity. The instances contained in a library should be as diverse as possible. There should be real-world instances from applications, as well as artificial instances that allow the evaluation of the influence of special instance properties on algorithmic performance.

Unfortunately, very often instances from certain applications are favored while others are neglected. The instances in a library should represent instances from all applications where the respective problem might occur.

The more diverse the instances in a library, the easier it is to choose a varied set of instances. This helps to prevent an experimenter from over-fitting algorithms, testing them only on a few instances with similar structure.

Ease of Use. A library should be easy to use. This includes obtaining instances from the library but also reporting errors or suggesting new instances. Ideally, there are software tools that might help to convert instances from the library to another format or that support the submission of new instances.

Also the navigation in the library is a crucial point. An experimenter should have no problems finding the instances that match his purpose or realizing that such instances are not contained in the library.

Extensibility. Although desirable, it is very unlikely that a library contains all meaningful instances of a problem (*Completeness*). Hence, a library should be extensible, and the addition of new instances should be as easy as possible (cf. *Ease of Use*).

Another aspect of *Extensibility* is not only the inclusion of new instances of the original problem but the addition of related problems, e. g., including SAT-instances in a 3SAT-library.

Independence. A library should be as independent as possible from any algorithm solving the corresponding problems. This means that the instances included in the library should be chosen as unbiased as possible, not preferring only instances where solely one algorithm succeeds.

Furthermore, this means that the format in which the instances are represented in the library should not be proprietary to only a few algorithms.

Topicality. A library should be as up-to-date as possible. If, for example, the best known solution to an instance or the rating of an instance changes due to new studies, the respective information in the library has to be updated to prevent duplication of results.

8.4.2   The Creation of a Library

The creation of a library involves very different aspects. First of all, a choice of the data format to represent the instances has to be made. For the main points considering the data format, we refer to the corresponding discussion in the *Portability* part of Section 8.3.1.

Ideally, the decision what format to use in a library should not be done by a single person, but rather by the research community. For example, the DIMACS Implementation Challenges [248] have served to establish common data formats for several problems, like the cnf-format for SAT-instances. Nevertheless, even if there is already a commonly accepted format, there might be some arguments for modifying it, e. g., if it does not allow for future extensions, like including new properties. Hence, as early as in the choice of the data format, future *Extensibility* can be assisted.

But *Extensibility* is not the only property from our above list (cf. Section 8.4.1) that has to be considered already in the creation process. Another one is *Completeness*. Ideally, a new library should include all instances that are known to the community so far. This often simultaneously supports *Difficulty* and *Diversity*. But to collect all the known instances the support of the community is essential. Hence, the library project should be advertised as soon as possible to find lots of contributors that provide test instances. The resulting benefit for the community is one single place where all instances can be found. This should attract researchers to cooperate if they get to know the project through formal and informal advertisements in mailing-lists, on conferences, or in journals. But not only active researchers should be encouraged to provide instances. Also industry should be asked to support applications data—possibly breaking their proprietary nature.

Through the collection of the known instances some problems might arise. The library creator must ensure that the instances are as unbiased as possible. Including only instances from published algorithmic studies might favor feasible instances since most studies only include data that shows how well the studied algorithm performs. Unfortunately, such instances that have already been solved by some algorithm have a selective advantage in a couple of libraries. To protect against such a narrow selection that would influence *Independence*, also existing generator programs have to be included. They can provide lots of instances that are new to almost every algorithm.

The collected instances have to be carefully transformed to the data format of the library to prevent from errors (*Accuracy*). This could be the birth of a tool that is able to convert the instances from one format to another. Such a tool should be included in the library as well (*Ease of Use*).

And last but not least, the *Availability* of the finished library is a crucial point. Today there is a very convenient solution—the Internet. Creating a website for the library not only enables almost everyone to access the library, but also allows to use the features of the Internet, like creating hyperlinks to papers that use the instances from the library. A welcome page of the library could, for example, contain links to the instance and generator program pages, links to descriptions of the problems, and a link to a technical manual describing the library and its data format. All the individual pages of the library should have a common layout to support a consistent representation and the *Ease of Use*.

However, with using the Internet there might occur a problem when having the library at only one server. As Johnson pointed out: "Never trust a website to remain readable indefinitely" [437]. For the library creator, this means that at least one mirror-site of the library on a different server should be created to protect against unavailability.

8.4.3   Maintenance and Update of a Library

After the creation of a library the work is in no way finished. We might just as well argue that it even has started.

Hardware and algorithms become faster, and thus instances might become too easy. For future generations of hardware and algorithms, the typical and demanding problem instances change. This means that a static library would quickly become obsolete since it cannot represent such changes. But besides the major changes, like including new useful instances (*Extensibility*) or revising the data format, there are still other minor activities for a created library. Based on our list of properties from Section 8.4.1, reported errors have to be corrected (*Accuracy*) and new results for the library instances or pointers to new studies should be included (*Topicality*). Hence, a good library has to be continuously maintained and updated. A history of the changes to the library may support the *Ease of Use*.

The responsibility for all that work should be shared by several persons. We refer to them as maintainers of the library. Ideally, the maintainers themselves are active researchers in the library's field. This allows them to assess the significance of submitted instances and to keep track of current trends in the community. However, this also means that there has to be sufficient financial support enabling the maintainers to spend part of their time on the library. Maintaining a library should also be credited by the community, like being on the editorial board of a journal.

Table 8.1. Examples of established test data libraries

Library	Short Description
CATS	combinatorial optimization and discrete algorithms
CSPLib	constraint satisfaction problems
FAP web	frequency assignment problems
GraphDB	exchange and archive system for graphs
MIPLIB	real-world mixed integer programs
OR-Library	operations research problems
PackLib^2	packing problems
PSPLIB	project scheduling problems
QAPLIB	quadratic assignment problem
QBFLIB	satisfiability of quantified Boolean formulas
SATLIB	satisfiability of Boolean formulas
SNDlib	survivable fixed telecommunication network design
SteinLib	Steiner tree problems in graphs
TPTP	thousands of problems for theorem provers
TSPLIB	traveling salesman and related problems

Nevertheless, the work should not only be done by a few maintainers. The community as a whole is asked to provide new useful instances, point to new interesting results, and report errors. Contributing researchers should be acknowledged for their suggestions in the library. If the support of the community is missing, a library project might even fail. Lots of researchers should be encouraged to use the library. Thereby, they will most likely become active contributors. This again emphasizes that the role of a broad advertisement of the library cannot be overestimated.

Altogether, a library can be seen as kind of an ongoing open source software project. New stable versions have to be provided in regular intervals by some responsible maintainers, assisted by a community of volunteers.

8.4.4 Examples of Existing Libraries

There is a wide variety of existing test data libraries. Table 8.1 lists some of them, but is by far not meant to be complete. All of these libraries may be easily found on the Internet by using any search engine. We close our discussion of test data libraries with a more detailed view on four example libraries. Thereby, we summarize the most important issues from the previous sections.

CATS. The ambitious library CATS was announced in 1998 [341]. Different pages, each devoted to a specific problem, with a unified layout should be maintained by volunteers using contributions from researchers. Unfortunately, it seems that the community did not use and support the CATS library as it would have deserved. But as we pointed out in Sections 8.4.2 and 8.4.3, the support of the community is crucial for the success of a library.

CSPLib. The first release of CSPLib stems from March 1999 [327, 328]. It contained 14 problems in 5 overlapping areas. Today there are 46 problems from 7 areas. Hence, at first glance the library is not very large—although 46 is only the problem not the instance count.

Since very often the solvability of a constraint satisfaction problem depends on data representation, the library creators decided to be as unprescriptive as possible. The only requirement is that the problems are described using natural language. The main point is that no instances have to be given. Thus, the CSPLib is rather a problem than an instance library, which somehow qualifies our above remark on the library size. On the one hand, using natural language description eases the input of new problems which might encourage researchers to contribute. But on the other hand, the derivation of concrete instances from the specification might be quite cumbersome. Both factors influence the *Ease of Use*, which is an important property for every library.

SATLIB. It was established in June 1998 [410]. Different from the above described CSP-situation, there is a widely used and accepted data format for SAT-instances—the cnf format from the Second DIMACS Implementation Challenge. As we pointed out in Section 8.4.2 such a widely accepted data format is the basis for a wide usage of the library.

Unfortunately, the current stable version 1.4.4 of SATLIB is still from 2001. The SATLIB-page announces an update since 2003, but as we pointed out in Section 8.4.3 this includes lots of work. This is a downside of maintainers being active researchers. Since they also have to do non-library work, necessary activities concerning the library may take a while. A possible way out might be the engagement of some assistants, when major changes are due. But this would require a broad financial support of the library.

TPTP. The library containing instances for evaluating automated theorem provers started in 1993 [768]. It has become a nearly perfect library.

Again, different to the situation for constraint satisfaction problems, widely accepted data formats exist, which are used to represent the instances. Over the years, TPTP continuously grew from 2295 instances from 23 domains in release v1.0.0 to currently 8894 instances from 35 domains in release v3.2.0. Instance files include ratings denoting their difficulty.

The library not only includes many of the instances known to the community, but also generator programs for artificial instances. Thus, it is as comprehensive and diverse as it could be. Due to its *Completeness* and *Diversity*, TPTP served as a basis for lots of CADE ATP System Competitions in the last years.

Concluding, we can state that TPTP is a highly successful and influential library for the field of automated theorem proving. Such an impact should be the main purpose of any library.

8.5   Setting-Up and Running the Experiment

The setup of experiments and their execution require a precise plan that describes the steps to be taken, in every science. These phase is located between the design idea, its implementation, and the evaluation of results together with insights gained during one run through the cycle of Algorithm Engineering. First, you have to think about what you want to report on, to find falsifiable hypotheses that should be supported or rejected by experiments. Section 8.2 covers this part. If not yet done, you should then implement the algorithm. For details see Chapter 6. How to come up with a meaningful, big amount of input instances has been discussed in Section 8.3. Before we can evaluate results in Section 8.6 it is needed to set up a well-suited *test-bed* and run the algorithms on the data, a non-trivial task. This section focusses on the difficulties that arise in Algorithm Engineering, that mainly consist of two areas of interest. First, experiments in computer science have been ignored for quite a long time. Only in the recent years, researchers rediscover their strength and possibilities. Some of the hints given in this section address in general computer scientist and aim to encourage them to run experiments. The goal is lead the community to good experimental work, as it is the case in other sciences. Thus, the hints mainly adapt state-of-the-art rules, applied in e. g., in natural sciences, and turns them towards computer science. Second, the cycle of Algorithm Engineering naturally forces experimenters to run similar experiments over and over again. Thus, further remarks recommend how to ease this process, while still being accurate as an experimental science demands. For the sake of better distinction, the *setup-phase* is elaborated first in Section 8.5.1, followed by hints applicable in the *running-phase* mentioned in Section 8.5.2. It is useful to learn about pitfalls of both phases before running any experiment. Section 8.5.3 gives additional advice for approximation algorithms and collaborative experiments.

Most pieces of advice originate from the recommended overview paper written by Johnson [437] and a crisp collection of "DOs" and "DON'Ts" stated by Gent et al. [325]. We extend them by hints presented in a paper of Moret [584]. Given suggestions and motivations are also influenced by personal experiences. These are gained by experimenting in the area of computational geometry done in the past yeast and those planned for the future. Some analogies to natural sciences are taken into account from personal communications.[1] Most of the given hints and suggestions are not problem-specific, since they can be applied to almost any experiment one can think of. Otherwise, special cases are pointed out. This section mainly collects an important set of high-level hints for an experimenter. For problem-specific experiments, possibly proper and case-specific extensions have to be done. Furthermore, as "DON'Ts" describe prohibitions all pieces of advice are stated in a positive, constructive manner. Several ones might overlap with others, which is due to the complexity of the whole area. Thus, the reader should not be bothered, when reading some statements twice. In contrast, this emphasizes the argument's importance and points out existing correlations.

---

[1] With Peter Leibenguth.

8.5.1   Setup-Phase

A well-organized laboratory is essential for a successful experiment in natural sciences. Often, scientists, in these areas, have to deal with a lot of restrictions or have to experiment outside of the laboratory. Unlike finding their laboratory somewhere, algorithmic scientists have to use computers. The experimenter is faced with the possibility to adjust a huge bunch of parameters. Algorithm Engineering aims for a best choice. Experiments serve to support the chosen decisions or falsify some considered hypothesis. Otherwise, if experiments are set up arbitrarily, their results may loose every meaning. In the following, we collect advice, such that an experimenter can avoid some pitfalls that might occur during the setup of an algorithm experiment.

Use available material! When reinventing the wheel, an experimenter may loose huge amounts of his limited time to finish the experiment. Public repositories or selected requests to other researchers should help to save time. To use available material is suggested. Two reasons exist to do so. First, experiments should be finished as soon as possible, which does not mean to carelessly execute them. Second, results need to be related to exiting set-ups and experiments. For the sake of reusability, the focus lies on available test instances and implementations.

Test sets may be obtainable from internet repositories as presented in Section 8.4 or from the authors' homepages. Some journals support publishing of additional material, so this is another place to look. If there is a standard library of instances, you are always supposed to use this instance library. In case the original test set is not available, but was generated artificially in some way, you should regenerate instances with the same parameters as the original one. This requires a detailed description of the generation process and the parameters used in the original paper.

The same holds for the implementation. Sometimes the source code is publicly available. In other cases the authors may be willing to provide it for further experiments. If you do not have access to the source code, you should implement the algorithm yourself, taking into account the implementation details that were reported. A new implementation in your computing environment or recompiling available source code is clearly preferable to make the old results comparable to yours [60]. However, a new implementation may be infeasible, for instance, because the algorithm is too complex or important details of it are unknown (e. g., of a commercial implementation). In this case you have to stick to some reasonably good implementation.

Once an implementation and the original or similar test sets are available, it is a good idea to try to reproduce the original results qualitatively. In particular, this is running the experiments on the test set, measuring the necessary quantities and checking whether the data is consistent with the claims in the original publication. A discrepancy should be pursued, as it is usually indicating a flaw in the implementation or test setup.

To enable other researchers to participate in the process of Algorithm Engineering, is is recommended to publish as many details as possible to ensure reproducibility. At its best, it is advised to provide source code and full data sets.

Ensure you use reasonably efficient implementations! An efficient implementation is the most fundamental part for the experimentation procedure. Johnson [437] states three major advantages.

- Allow to support claims of practicality and competitiveness.
- Results of inefficient implementations are useless, since they most probably change the picture one would actually expect from implementation in practice.
- Allow to perform experiments on more and respectively larger instances, or to finish the study more quickly.

Chapter 6 already discusses the implementation task with all its aspects. A main source of information how to reach efficient code is contained in Section 6.3.1 that describes tuning techniques. Often it is impossible to implement all known speed-up techniques (it would take too many resources and too much time). But then one has to be careful with claims such that the resulting implementation equipped with these tricks would be competitive to the ones using speed-ups. Such an argument lacks plausibility. It is completely unknown whether certain tricks make sense for any other algorithm, and if so, in how far they actually improve the running time. Similar arguments hold for other performance measures.

Compilation. In order to get efficient code, it is important to choose the right combination given by the platform. Note that the programming language matters as much as the compiler and its options. In general, you should take a comparable environment. If you only benchmark your algorithm, then the programming language is quite unimportant, but in case you compare with others, even if only copying their running times, it is advised to use roughly the same technology for the implementation. If existing experiments are implemented using C++, coding your algorithm in **Java** will make a comparison very difficult.

To avoid unnecessary slowdowns, you should always run compiled code instead of interpreted code. For sure, compiling code is a science in itself, but basic rules can be stated here, too. When you compile code for experiments which include timing, switch off all debugging and sanity checks in your code. A print-statement usually takes a huge amount of time, and pre-, post- and assert-conditions also only slow down the computation time. They only aim for the correctness of your code during runtime, while especially for non-trivial routines, they might influence the worst-case running time. Therefore, failures in these conditions on your test data indicate bugs. Testing your code on the data with active conditions is required, but for generating publishable performance measures and also to distribute your software, remember to deactivate them. If now new errors or crashes appear, you can be quite sure, that a sanity check contains a side-effect which should be definitely avoided.

Deactivating debug code and compiling in optimized fashion also holds for supporting libraries used in the implementation of your algorithm(s). Commonly, these supporting libraries are used for subroutines or atomic functionality. Usually, they are called quite often and you have to ensure you select the right implementation. An infamous example is using a $\Theta(n^2)$ sorting routine. Especially when you use experiments to approximate the asymptotic running time of a theoretically unanalyzed algorithm, such an influence is without doubt. Even if it is the case that you have chosen the theoretical best-known algorithm for a subroutine, big constant factors, that play an important role in implementations, will influence the algorithms performances dramatically and may destroy competitiveness of the implementation of your algorithm. Note that in experiments we always compare implementations of algorithms only and not their theoretical behavior.

Coding. Section 6.3 already suggests not to spent too much time for fine-tuning. The bottom-line is to produce reasonable efficient code in a reasonable amount of time. Code documentation as explained in Section 6.5 is also demanded. It serves to remember details of the implementation and helps others to understand your software, especially when published under an open source licence. Published software enables other researchers to run your experiments on their own machine, maybe slightly modified due to new algorithmic ideas. Furthermore, they possibly submit bugs to you.

Section 6.2 has covered techniques to avoid bugs. Some bugs should be fixed when entering the experimental phase. Namely, the bugs that make the software crash, and bugs that lead to a wrong output. But there are also bugs that negatively influence the performance of the algorithm. To find such bugs bears out as a non-trivial task and experiments seem to be the main technique to detect such hidden errors. They will never show up voluntarily, you have to search for them, which needs some indication. Otherwise, you just believe that the performances are already optimal. The only chance to find them is some deviation in the results. Profiling your code gives a very good overview which subroutines are called very often, and which consume a lot of time. Unfortunately, some bugs cannot be detected by a profiler, e. g., filter failures as mentioned in Section 6.3.1. Either you design and prove theoretically the lack of such failures, or you have to implement a testing layer in between the high-level parts of the algorithm and its subroutines, to see whether equal objects are not identified. Both methods are rather disappointing and success is not guaranteed. If you do not believe in bugs that destroy the performance of an algorithm look at this example. Consider an implementation of quicksort whose choice of the pivot element is *not random* due to some wrong variable usage, e. g., by accident. Whenever your algorithm needs to sort some *structured* containers, quicksort suddenly performs at its worst-case running time of $O(n^2)$.

Systematic Errors. It seems that systematic errors during experiments on algorithms can be avoided from scratch, while, for example, physicists face uncertainties in there measurement devices or are unable to measure at the actual point of interest. Unfortunately, these appearances are deceptive. At a first glance, nearly everything seems to be under control, but you have to make sure that you have control of the right points. A wrong position of a timer, e. g., in the innermost loop, changes the whole performance of an algorithm dramatically. This example comes along with having too many timers in the code. You should always scrutinize whether your decisions make sense in your setting and whether your measuring methods keep the experiment free of bad influences.

Check your input data! Before running the actual experiments ensure you use correct input data. In general, if your input data set covers a significant part of the allowed input space for your algorithm, you are doing the right thing. Section 8.3.1 discusses in detail what needs to be considered to find a set of instances with enough variety, and Section 8.3.2 deals with advantages and disadvantages of artificial and real-world data. A useful set of instances contains a balanced mixture of both.

Your data sets might be corrupted or faulty generated. Real-world data are often corrupted or need special preprocessing. Buggy generators may create artificial data that do not produce the desired sets. Careful experimentation checks the appropriateness of such data before running time-consuming algorithms. As explained in Section 8.3.2 non-random numbers might also bias the data generated sets. In general, each single data instance should be free of redundancies, for example, the same points twice when computing the convex hull of points. Otherwise, you only check the caching strategy rather than running the algorithm on a bigger instance. Of course, it is useful to see whether an implementation handles redundancies optimally, but better check this performance with its own experiment.

Data sets might also be to simple. This mainly addresses input data that are processed within a fraction of a second. Instances should be chosen in a way that measurement's noise does not affect the results. Hereby, noise denotes points which affect running time in general independent of the specific algorithm which should be tested. Today's computers consists of several units, e. g., pipeline, register, memory hierarchy. Hence, it takes some setup time until all operational units of the computer fully work on executing an algorithm. This is denoted by measurements noise, which barely can be ignored if your input instance runs only for some milliseconds. On current machines, a good advice is to use input data that run at least a second. The situation might be different, when aiming for counts only or when dealing with real-time computations.

Use different platforms! The best implementation is only as good as the supporting environment. This means that the environment plays an important role in setting up an experiment. In computer science, the performance of an implemented algorithm crucially depends on the used hard- and software. The following questions need to be answered. Which processor is used? How much memory is available? How is the memory hierarchy organized? How many registers are available? What is the underlying operating system? Which compiler was used, additionally given chosen compiler options? Which supporting libraries are utilized? Obviously, you cannot test your algorithm for all possible combinations of hard- and software, but restricting yourself to implement it only in one specific environment may change the picture. Beyond, it may lead to hypothesizing non-existing conclusions of the data due to specific behavior in the external environment, e. g., a special caching strategy of the operating system which influences the movement of data.

It is strongly recommended to test algorithms at least on a small set of different architectures and with different compilers. A good balance between different environments and fine-tuning of code for each one should be found. Running the same experiments on different platforms helps to avoid to draw the wrong conclusions. Whenever these implementations show surprising differences in their performance measure, it is a must to ask why and to find the answer. These differences show whether the implementation in the environments are free of dependencies to the setup and therefore allow to draw setup-independent conclusions.

Aiming for comparability of experiments, the calibration of the machine(s) is a lot more useful than just stating the architecture and the speed of your processor. Architectures change within a couple of years dramatically, which makes it difficult to relate new results to old ones then. Calibrating the machine means to compile and run in your setup a small piece of code that is publicly available and known as well as accepted in the community. Its output states more about the problem-specific performance of the machine than the CPU speed does. Future researchers can then adapt their machines the same way which enables them to normalize the old results to their own new results. There is a chance that this normalization fails. But in most cases it is much more valuable than normalizing to the pure CPU speed and obviously better than forgetting about it.

Use appropriate formats! Section 8.3.1 already discusses the need to carefully select the format for input instances. On the output side of the algorithm we will see a bunch of results, at least the measures selected during the design of the experiment, e. g., running time. See Section 8.2.2 for more details. If we are purely interested in the primary measure(s), we can just print this information to the console. But thinking a little bit further, it can be seen that it is really useful to have self-documenting programs. Consider a question of a reviewer that comes months after you actually run the experiments or you want to do a follow-up study. In both cases you have to remember most of the old results, and expect that your personal memory might forget most of these things. Therefore, it is strongly recommended to create some self-explaining output format for each run that collects all relevant data, which, for example, consists of the following list.

- Main measures, like CPU time, solution quality, and memory usage.
- Algorithm data, like the name and version of the algorithm, its parameter settings.
- Meta data, like the date, the name of the instance.
- Setup data describing the used machine, memory hierarchy, used compiler and its flags.
- Supplemental measures that can be useful when evaluating the data in the future, like intermediate values, operation times or simple counts of operation calls.

Especially, when computing the additional data, one should avoid to harm the overall performance of the algorithm. If an additional value can be stated without extra costs, it would be careless to omit it, since otherwise, you need to rerun the experiment to get its data, which would be really expensive. A sophisticated design of the experiment that checks which data should be outputted before starting the actual running phase is strongly advised.

The used output format should be of clear and effective syntax. Furthermore, avoid using abbreviations, since every value that cannot be interpreted correctly in the future is useless. XML might be a good candidate as format choice, but one should definitively check whether it fits all needs while staying simple enough.

We want to go even further and enforce every setup to combine input instances, implementations, and results into a common framework.

Do use version control! So far, we have learned that the setup for an empirical study is far away from naively implementing some small environment. In contrast, most experiments start with some initial setup and are constantly evolving. They become larger and more complex, e. g., new algorithms are being added, methods are changing, additional instances should be tested and bugs will be fixed. In summary, this is a perfect setting for a version control system like *Concurrent Version System (cvs)* or *Subversion (svn)* that have already been recommended for the implementation of an algorithm in Section 6.6.5. A version control system allows to store snapshots of the current system in a common repository, which can be also accessed and fed by a group of developers.

Putting all changes of your setup constantly on a repository provides several advantages:

- It allows you to go back in time by checking out old versions, it *ensures reproducibility*. You are able to rerun all your experiments.
- It also provides tools to compare two versions, which offers the possibility to check which changes result in better or worse algorithmic performance.
- Not using a version control system is a quick way to loose control over different versions of your environment. You may store your files within time-stamped directories. But then, fixing a bug in one version, while improving a heuristic in another one will quite surely lead to a third version, which contains the bug again. Version control cares for these changes. Thus, a fixed bug cannot appear again in the future as it might happen when human beings maintain different copies of a file.

– Storing subsidiary data close to the executables of the experiment is much better than maintaining a bunch of files, or even to use your personal memory that might be more forgetful than everyone hopes for.

Obviously, the version control on a central server only makes sense, when the repository is under control of a reliable backup system. Otherwise, you may lose your complete work which contradicts the aim of reproducibility. Assuming that version control systems are error free may lead to useless experiments, too. Although version control systems like cvs and svn are quite matured, having an eye on its operation, e. g., whether diff works fine and versions are properly stored, is good advice.

Use scripting! As we know, Algorithm Engineering, and especially experimentation, consists of an iterative procedure to progress and to reach publishable results. Several tasks have to be performed a repeated number of times or similar jobs should be controlled over and over again. Instead of starting each single run manually, it is advised to analyze the structure of the experimentation in detail. Its evaluation will lead to a bunch of scripts and proper pipelining. At its best, it suffices to only press *the red button*. In the end, processed data are collected and may be already presented in figures which are a fundamental help in data evaluation. Scripting and version control are fundamental partners. With such a setup, the researcher can concentrate on developing algorithms and selecting or generating instances while the actual experiments run automatically, maybe scheduled at regular times on your machine or during night.

With ExpLab [389] a set of tools is provided that collect the mentioned parts out-of-the-box. It offers scripts that allow to set up and run computational experiments, while also automatically documenting the environment in which an experiment is run. Assuming that the same environment is still available, it allows to easily rerun the experiments and to have a more accurate comparison of computational results. Finally, ExpLab provides text output processing tools that help dramatically to eliminate some tasks needed for collecting and analyzing the output. Its overall goal is to augment existing tools to reach a comfortable experimentation environment. Unfortunately, its development has been stopped and it is built on top of cvs instead of svn.

8.5.2   Running-Phase

Once the laboratory is prepared and set up, it is time to start the experiment. During setup you tried to exclude all environmental errors for the experiment. But obviously, while running an experiment further errors can be made. In a natural science experiment, wrong timing may destroy the whole result. Furthermore, forgetting to write down parameters disposes you of the possibility to publish any valid result. In some way, these strict rules seem to be forgotten when publishing experimental results in computer science, especially performance measures of algorithms. In contrast, reviewers would be very happy to get informed about the main facts the experiment was run with. Therefore, applying adapted methodology from natural science to your experimental running phase prevents you from having no answer to questions asked by colleagues or, even worse, reviewers. It is recommended to check in how far the following hints should already be considered during the setup, although they address directly the running-phase.

Keep notes! Each experiment in natural sciences is only valid, if any other similarly equipped laboratory can reproduce the same result. That requires a detailed description of what you did and what you found out. In computer science this should also apply.

During setup you already decided, which data will be collected and how to store them. The claimed hypotheses also prompt you to combine algorithms with data instances. A script lets them run and produces a vast amount of output. Ensure that this output is also accessible in the future, which means to put them under version control, too. In case you get asked you can present all details, or you can also test other instances in the future and relate them quite accurately to your original results.

Additionally, you should remember to write down and store all good and bad conditions of your algorithm. You might rely on your personal memory, but to be sure, it is a better idea to store them explicitly. Furthermore, consider the possibility of handing over the laboratory to a colleague. He can only build on the content stored in the repository since he has no direct access to your memory.

Change of Factors! Some algorithms can be fine-tuned by one or several external parameters, also known as *factors* as explained in Section 8.2.3. The actual behavior of a heuristic or the overall algorithm can be influenced. For an experimental setup it is necessary that the parameters are either completely fixed and reported or they purely depend on the data given in the instances to be computed. In the first case, reproducibility forces to assign some values. Usually, it would be very interesting to know how the algorithm behaves with other settings. If not fixing parameters, most people experiment with the settings to find out which combination leads to the best algorithm's performance. Due to this fact, before determining the parameters, an algorithm is actually not properly specified. Only by searching for the proper values experimentally, the algorithm will be finally determined. But this may result in having different algorithms for different instances. In contrast, we also want to encourage you to experiment in certain boundaries with the parameters, since these might lead to unexpectedly good performances.

To sum up, if you use different parameter settings, where each applies to a set of different instances, the choices must be well-defined or should be determined algorithmically from the instances. You also need to report and describe the adjustments in all details, as well as the running times spent to find the optimal parameter settings in your publication.

Change only one thing at a time! This advice is closely related to the preceding one, as well to the planning phase of the experimental work. While the first one deals with the parameter settings of an algorithm, the latter one must be considered when testing different instances. Thus, to reach reliable results it forbids to vary more than one parameter from one run to the next. In the example of different instances this means that you either change the size of the input, its complexity, or you chose another type of variation. If you need to change parameters of your algorithm, also make sure that you only tune one parameter at the same time.

This rule originates from natural sciences, where you also change, for instance, either temperature or pressure, but never both at the same time. Obviously, it forbids changing the type of the instance in combination with tuning some parameters. Especially in this case you get performance values that never mark valuable comparison results.

Run it often enough and with appropriate data sets! Once everything is set up, relying on a single run may lead to conclusions without value. Each proposed claim should be supported by a set of independent runs. You also need a significant amount of runs to reduce the influence of external factors, i. e., to average and probably get rid of the noise. Especially randomly generated data might have a big variety, even when they originate from the same generator. If you want to check the performance of several algorithms on randomly generated data, it is a good choice to use the same set of instances for all algorithms instead of generating them independently for each run.

It is recommended [437, 325] to look at as large instances as possible. First, this gives a better indication of the asymptotic behavior of the running time or the approximation gap of your algorithms. Second, important aspects and effects may only occur at large instance sizes due to some boundary conditions, e. g., cache effects. Looking at huge instance sizes also strengthens your claims, especially when the instances are bigger than the ones you expect in practical environments.

If you are using scripts or the tools proposed in Section 8.5.1 it should be easy to set up a powerful and automatic schedule which can run during the night and present you a list of results the next morning, depending on the algorithm(s) and data sets.

Look at the results! This sounds like an obvious piece of advice, but it is a crucial one. First of all, check whether the actual output, the result the algorithm is implemented for, is correct. If not, you have to search for bugs. If the results are correct, check whether the global picture is consistent. If you are in the lucky position, that your scripts have produced some plots automatically, these pictures help to find out whether the algorithm(s) on the checked instances behave smoothly. Either you will see a picture, as you might have expected, which then supports your claimed hypotheses, or, in contrast, some anomalies occur, e. g., exceptional high or low running time for a specific instance or family of data sets. Have a closer look at them and explain why they behave differently. An origin might be a bug. Or you will detect that this behavior is intrinsic to the algorithm, because this certain family of data always forces the algorithm to compute it that special way.

In Section 8.6 we explain how to evaluate the performance values in more detail. The now following tools already have to be considered during the running phase of the experiment.

– Be sure that all important and interesting subsidiary values are contained in the output of every run. You may have identified them in advance. Now, they help to understand the runs with more insight and maybe they give the right hint why certain data forces the algorithm to work differently.
– Much more insight to the algorithmic operations can be gained from the results of a profiler, a tool that collects run time information of a program, i. e., it measures the frequency and duration of function calls. Well-known profilers are `gprof`[2] and more recently `callgrind/KCachegrind`.[3] Analyzing such gathered information presents quite exactly and itemized where runtime is spent, how often functions are called, where the algorithm behaves as expected and where not. In general it helps to optimize the code. Here, the number of function calls define a very good picture on the topological structure of the algorithm. In a sense, it gives a function to each called subroutine in the input size. Computed ratios of used time and number of function calls, i. e., normalization, show which subroutines take longer than others. By having a close look at the profiled runs, you can also find out why a worst-case algorithm of $O(n^2)$ behaves in most cases similar to $O(n \log n)$ or why a quite complicated algorithm outperforms a simple one.

   Unfortunately, it depends on the specific algorithm how to analyze all this information and what can be derived from it. Note that you have to check whether the output of the profiler really makes sense. In most combinations, it is necessary that every involved code is compiled for profiling. Otherwise, durations of subroutine calls, say of external libraries, are assigned uniformly instead of assigning them to the actual calling functions. Let us consider the example, where fast integer multiplication is provided by an external library. The algorithm has two fine-tuned subroutines, one that needs to multiply quite small integers (< 50 bits), another one is multiplying quite long integers (> 200 bits). If both subroutines are roughly called the same number of times, then a wrong configuration, where functions cannot be profiled in detail, will present you that both roughly need the same amount of time, since it just averages over all calls to integer multiplication. But actually, the second routine takes much more time than the first one. The bottom-line is to be careful when interpreting presented data of a profiler.

Do unusual things! At a first glance, this final suggestion sounds spooky. Do not get it wrong. Obviously, you should avoid following futile ideas all the time.

---

[2] http://www.gnu.org
[3] http://kcachegrind.sourceforge.net

But in some situations, it might be helpful to vary an implementation a little bit. In most cases, it will be only justified, that you bark up the wrong tree. But maybe your algorithm turns out to behave better. An example can be a randomized choice of pivot versus a deterministic choice. Bearing away can help to understand better what your algorithm does. Sometimes, you should allow yourself to open your mind to crazy ideas. It helps to be more creative. A lot of serendipities in other sciences originate from doing crazy things rather than following the rules, or, as you might know from famous examples, they happen by accident. In software experiments this may relate to an implementation that is actually buggy, but has a better performance.

8.5.3   Supplementary Advice

The last parts listed in detail how to setup the environment for good experimentation and how to run them with care, based on the assumptions that you know what you want to see. But experimentation is more than just executing algorithms and evaluating the results that support or disprove some hypotheses. Note that experimentation actually consists of more than the setup-phase and a single round of the running-phase. Only a cycle of testing and refinement, supported by profilers, measurement and evaluation of data, allows to identify bottlenecks, to reduce the usage of the memory, or to find out, which intermediate values should be cached and many more. All these efforts may lead to a speed-up in running time, sometimes by an order of magnitude, or even several orders of magnitude.

In case you started with some open research questions, the first results of a running-phase may quickly lead to new questions. It is a law by itself, that good experiments constitute a rich source of new conjectures and hypotheses. Actually, some exploratory experiments, without going too much into details, help to find good initial questions. These may show whether an algorithm is competitive or not. We propose, you spent the first half of your time to generate lots of data and search for patterns and anomalies. Based on this, you can finalize the implementation while you consider the advice mentioned before. Namely, design the important questions and then, perform trustworthy experiments to support your claims. Evaluation may already lead to newsworthy results, or you iterate. Experimenting is a dynamic process, but ensure to fix a point where you stop it.

The end of this section covers two additional subjects. First, we give hints when dealing with approximation algorithms, and second, we outline some details, when jointly experimenting within a group of researchers and sites, respectively.

Approximation or Heuristic Algorithms. Up to now, we mainly focused on the running time as the main performance measure of an algorithm. In contrast, an approximation algorithm needs to be handled differently. Its main performance measure consists of the solution quality. Approximation algorithms usually deal with NP–hard problems, where one obviates handling the exponential number of possibilities, or in problem areas where running time is crucial, whereas the result does not need to be optimal. In most cases, approximation algorithms compute better solutions the longer they run. So running time and approximation value may be related. However, researchers often choose the wrong stopping criterion, since otherwise their algorithms would run very long.

Choose the right stopping criterion! There are two critical stopping criteria for an approximation algorithm, namely running time and a known optimal value. For the latter one there is an exception: When an algorithm can prove the found solution to be optimal it is admissible to stop immediately. Unfortunately, most algorithms fail to designate such a proof. But taking a known optimal solution as an a-priori stopping value raises the question why to run the approximation algorithm at all. In practical settings this criterion is purely without any sense, since for any interesting input the optimal solution is surely unknown. Usually, one seeks for near optimal performance values in relation to some other quantity. For example, a good travelling salesman tour with respect to low query times. But, tests with only these special data sets omit to reflect performance in practice and fail to be reproducible. You will see dramatically different running times for similar instances, depending on whether the optimal solution is known or not.

Fixing a certain amount of time as the running time of an approximation algorithms also contradicts the need of reproducibility. Note that "run-the-algorithm-for-an-hour" is, in some sense, an undefined algorithm. Changes in the setup, e. g., all factors described in Section 8.2.3 that define the experiment like machine, operating system, or implementation, lead easily to results of another quality. In some settings this idea looks like the perfect choice to compare the quality of algorithms, but if you run the same tests on a machine which is much faster, all algorithms will, hopefully, perform better, which is less critical, while a change in the relative ranking is more substantially.

Much better than time bounds are structural measures such as number of branching steps, number of comparisons, or maximal depth of tree as introduced in Section 8.2.2. Using such measures enables us to have a well-defined algorithm, whose running time and quality of solution is expressible as a function of this combinatorial count. At least the latter should be reproducible now. It is possible to combine the solutions with the running time in relation to the combinatorial count. Listings of these relation allows future researchers to compare their solutions to yours and to detect the influences two different environments have. When switching machines, one has to apply benchmarking and normalization as explained in Section 8.5.1.

Another possibility of a stopping criterion may be a result that is close to a bound. Such a bound must be easy to compute while *close* means to differ from it only by a small factor, like 0.01. Consider, for example, a minimization problem with an optimal value OPT for a certain instance and for which we know a lower bound LB. The current approximation of a algorithm is given by APP. If $APP < 1.01LB$ we know that $APP < 1.01OPT$, since $LB < OPT$, and the algorithm decides to stop in this case. Note that this requires that the approximation algorithm is able to improve its result with more invested time.

Joint Work. Especially when comparing different algorithms one might expect that common work is undesired by competitors. Obviously, no one is interested in losing a game. But at the same time, you might spent more time on other tasks than on implementing someone else's algorithm as enthusiastically as your algorithm, with the goal of an efficient implementation.

What prevents researchers from working together more closely? It is not as worse as it seems. Indeed first steps are already done, e. g., by maintaining common databases for instances. Of course, there are already collaborations when running experiments, but too few at the large scale. If we assume for now, that people of a community are willing to and decide to set up a common laboratory, then we have to check what else needs to be considered in addition to the previous suggestion.

Split the work! As said, no one has the time to do the whole job. One solution is that everyone who wants to participate in the common laboratory has to concentrate only on his small specific task. In terms of algorithmic experiments this equals to provide an efficient implementation of an algorithm. Using version control, it is quite easy to commit new software to a common repository that is set up following the general rules mentioned earlier. Of course, a single site or person has to install the environment, but compared to implementing several efficient algorithms, this is quite an easy task. A discerning reader may come up with the question of how to ensure the same quality for all implementations such as using the same new speed-up tricks. This is indeed a problem, the community has to deal with. We propose to publish the results on a website.[4] Significant changes in the performance values are immediately visible to everyone involved, which results in asking questions and starting discussions, why some algorithm performs much better than others. In general, implementing an algorithm needs to follow some common guidelines to be constituted when starting the collaboration. All questions related to this should be covered in Chapter 6.

Generating the actual results requires two following steps. First, one has to select on which instance sets the algorithms should be tested. Second, one has to run the experiments. Instances that should obviously use the same common format, either come from an instance database, or researchers can put their own generated data sets also under version control and then combine it with algorithms. In some cases, the group may agree to have a committee to decide which combinations make sense. For the second task, the group may rely on some scripts to be written. Actually, the whole procedure especially makes sense when running the experiments regularly, while algorithms, or at least their implementations, are still under development, which means that there are still untested ideas.

---

[4] The community has to decide whether the site is publicly available or closed to members.

Finally, everyone profits from the collaboration since progress in some algorithm is visible to all, and people start to discuss and to improve their own implementation based on this knowledge. Additionally, a regular execution of the committed experiments makes it easy to check out, how a new heuristic and algorithmic idea performs. Since the work assigned to an individual is quite small, while constantly comparing with others, the idea of a common laboratory as presented here, seems to be a fruitful environment for experimental research in algorithmics, and we encourage communities to install corporate laboratories.

8.6   Evaluating Your Data

After you have run your experimental setup you are left with a bunch of data. The next task is to figure out whether this data supports your working hypothesis and what else may be deduced from it.

The first thing to keep in mind is to look at the data without being biased by your working hypothesis. Of course, the working hypothesis provides a starting point for the investigations.

In general, it is important to observe patterns in the data and to try to explain them. This explanation step may involve a more detailed analysis and also new experiments. For example, you might discover that a branch-and-bound algorithm using your new pruning rule performs worse than using the old one. The reason for this might be either poor pruning or too much time spent for the pruning so that in total it does not pay off. To investigate this question you would need to look at the number of nodes visited by the algorithm and the fraction of the time spent for pruning. Depending on your experimental setup, you may be able to derive this additional data from the results you already have. Otherwise you would need to rerun your experiments.

It usually pays off to let your experimental setup generate "raw" data, i. e., instead of averages and maybe minimum and maximum record all values, as well as related quantities which might be of interest. Although this may create large amounts of data it saves you from running your probably time-consuming experiments often. Nevertheless you should always think about whether the data you have is really sufficient to provide support for your hypothesis. If this is not the case you need to gather more data.

The significance of your findings is increased if you can provide explanations or more detailed accounts. For instance, it is not only interesting which algorithm runs faster, but also where the respective running times come from, i. e., which parts of the algorithm contribute to the running time. Sometimes it is possible to look at more machine-independent running time measures, for example nodes evaluated in a branch-and-bound algorithm, improvement steps taken in a local search heuristic, or simply the number of iterations. It may be worthwhile to investigate how these measures depend on instance size, since the machine-independence of these measures gives better insights in the algorithm rather than the computing environment.

So far we have only talked about the general evaluation philosophy. In the following, we describe two ways of actually deriving something interesting from your data. The first method is *graphical analysis*, which uses diagrams and plots to discover patterns. Although this sounds simple, it is indeed a standard tool of statisticians for arriving at good hypotheses. Graphical analysis provides key insights and can also give some evidence for conclusions.

Then we give an overview of *statistical analysis*, which provides numerical methods that can be used to check hypotheses, e. g., those obtained via graphical analysis. Statistical analysis is a tool that is widely used in other experimental areas, but has rarely been applied to experiments on algorithms. However, Barr et al. [60, p. 22] recommend to employ statistical analysis wherever possible.

A drawback of statistical analysis is that it assumes certain experimental setups which sometimes cannot be achieved. In this case, statistical analysis is not applicable; but graphical analysis always is.

8.6.1   Graphical Analysis

Pictures and diagrams can be of great help to realize what is going on, since they can represent vast amounts of data in a succinct way, at least if done properly. This makes it easy to spot patterns which otherwise would be lost in a pile of numbers or in large tables. The main issue here is to find the "right" diagram that reveals the things we are interested in. This diagram serves two purposes: First, it gives you some insight you did not have before and thus guides your investigations. On the other hand, it may be useful to communicate your results to other people. Further hints on this use will be given in Section 8.7.2.

There are some guidelines on using diagrams for analyzing numerical data in the statistics literature. Other sources of inspiration on how to employ diagrams can be found in the literature on experimental algorithms. The paper of Sanders [693] gives extensive advice on how to use diagrams to report experimental results in algorithmics and has been a major source for this section. Most of this advice is helpful for analysis too, so we present it here. As examples, we will just name a few types of diagrams commonly used in the experimental literature and highlight their uses.

The diagram type most often encountered in the experimental literature on algorithms plots some metric (e. g., running time) as a function of some parameter (e. g., input size of instance). The usual interpretation is that the variable on the x-axis is "independent", whereas the variable on the y-axis is "dependent", i. e., there is a functional relation between the two. This relation is most often interpreted to imply causality, so this diagram type is most suited for settings where assuming this causality is reasonable. In the example, this causality is given: an increase in input size causes an increase in running time. We will call this diagram type *functional plot*.

Figure 8.1 gives an example of a functional plot, which is in fact a special case, namely a time series, where time is shown on the x-axis. Time is not given explicitly here, but the number of nodes explored so far is of course some sort of time-scale. Time series are often used to show the convergence of algorithms.

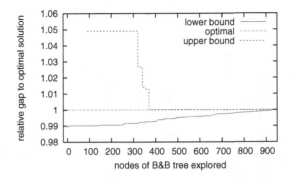

Fig. 8.1. A functional plot showing the typical behavior of branch-and-bound algorithms. Displayed are the upper and lower bounds relative to the optimal value evolving with the number of nodes of the tree that have been explored so far. Every time an improved solution is found, the upper bound drops and remains on this level for some time. Note that an optimal solution has been found after about 370 nodes, but it takes another 550 nodes to raise the lower bound such that optimality can be proven.

If functional plots are used to give average values, they should be augmented to depict more information of the range of the data. One way to do this is to provide error bars which indicate the standard deviation of the data. Even more information is contained in box plots which characterize the underlying distribution by five values and are explained in more detail later.

A diagram type often used to investigate the relationship of two variables is the *scatter plot*. The graph of the scatter plot is just the set of points corresponding to the measurements, see the example in Figure 8.2. It is adequate if it is unclear which of the variables is "independent" or "dependent". A scatter plot can be applied if the data are not ordered quantities and thus cannot be associated to points on the axes. For instance, it is not clear in which order to put the instances you measured solution quality for in order to come up with a suitable functional diagram. Instead, you can use use a scatter plot relating instance size to solution quality. A scatter plot can also be used to compare many different measurements, e. g., the performance of many TSP heuristics in Figure 8.2.

Other famous diagram types are the *bar chart* and the *histogram*. The bar chart consists of bars, whose heights represent numerical quantities and are scaled proportionally. Thus they ease visual comparison and are appropriate in situations where multiple quantities need to be compared. Figure 8.3 gives an example of a bar chart used for assessing the usual tradeoff on a branch-and-bound algorithm.

A special kind of a bar chart with a different purpose is the histogram. Histograms are used to analyze distributions of some quantity. To this end, the range of the quantity is divided in so-called buckets, i. e., intervals of equal size, and for each bucket the percentage of values lying in this interval gives the height

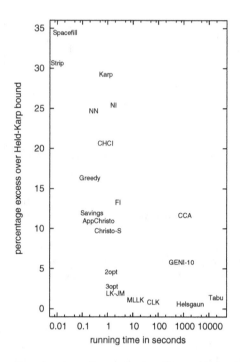

Fig. 8.2. A scatter plot showing the approximation ratio and the running time of some heuristics for the symmetric TSP from the report of Johnson and McGeoch [439], p. 382. The data represents averages over a set of 10,000-city random Euclidean instances. Each heuristic's label depicts its average excess over the Held-Karp lower bound, which is a well-known and rather good lower bound for TSP problems. In this special case of a scatter plot the data points are marked with the name of the heuristic they arise from.

of the bar in a bar chart. Figure 8.4(a) shows a variant of a histogram known as *frequency polygon* [506], where the data points of the histogram are connected by lines instead of being represented by bars. This type of diagram is better suited to comparing a set of distributions.

In statistics, distributions are often compared using the already mentioned box plots, also known as box-and-whisker diagram. Box plots are based on quartiles, which are special quantiles. The (empirical) p-quantile a_p for $0 \leq p \leq 1$ of a sample of n numbers $x_1, \ldots, x_n$ is defined as

$$a_p := x_{\lceil pn \rceil}$$

i.e., a_p is the smallest value such that at least pn values of the sample are less than a_p. The box plot uses quartiles, i.e., the quantiles $a_0, a_{0.25}, a_{0.5}, a_{0.75}, a_1$. Notice that a_0 is the minimum, $a_{0.5}$ the median and a_1 the maximum of the distribution. A box plot of a distribution consists of a line ranging from a_0 to

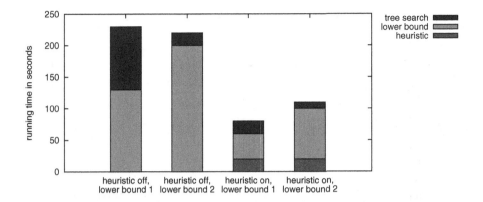

Fig. 8.3. A bar chart showing hypothetical data for a branch-and-bound algorithm. The diagram shows running time data for four different settings used to solve the same instance. An initial heuristic can be used or not and there is a choice between two kinds of lower bounds. Lower bound 1 runs fast and gives weak lower bounds, whereas lower bound 2 runs longer and gives stronger bounds.

Obviously, the better quality of the lower bounds provided by method 2 significantly decreases the time spent for searching the tree, since fewer nodes need to be visited. However, it only pays off to use lower bound 2 if the heuristic is not used, since the total time is lowest if the heuristic and lower bound 1 are used.

a_1, where the interval $(a_{0.25}, a_{0.75})$ is drawn as a larger box, which contains an extra line indicating $a_{0.5}$. See Figure 8.4(b) for an example that gives the same data as the frequency polygon diagram in Figure 8.4(a).

Of course, sometimes these diagram types do not fit the purpose or the data to analyze. In this case you should try to make up your own kind of visualization for your data or look into one of the many sources on statistical graphics and exploratory data analysis, e. g., [785, 784, 277].

Apart from choosing a suitable type of diagram there is a lot to be gained by using appropriate scales on the axes and focusing on the most interesting part of the diagram. Most common are linear and logarithmic scales, where the first is appropriate if the numbers are in a relatively small range whereas the latter is useful if the numbers are of different orders of magnitude. For instance, if one is interested in the asymptotic behavior of the running times of some algorithms as a function of the instance size, instance sizes usually grow by a constant factor in order to cover instances sizes of different magnitudes with few instances. In that case, both axes should be logarithmic, since instance sizes grow exponentially by setup, and running times are exponential too if they are at least linear in the input size. Similarly, if instance sizes grow additively by a constant but the

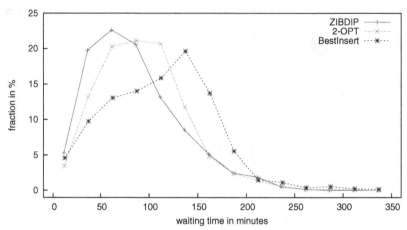

(a) A frequency polygon plot of the waiting time distributions.

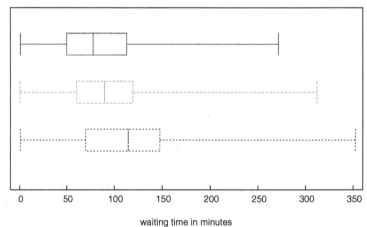

waiting time in minutes

(b) A box plot of the waiting time distributions.

Fig. 8.4. Comparison of waiting time distributions achieved by some vehicle dispatching algorithms. The data is taken from a computational study that compares algorithms for dispatching service vehicles, where the customers' waiting times are the major quality of service criterion [396]. BestInsert and 2-OPT are heuristics based on local search, whereas ZIBDIP is an exact algorithm based on Integer Programming techniques.

Both diagrams indicate that optimization algorithms achieve a much better waiting time distribution than simple heuristics. In the frequency polygon plot the distribution of ZIBDIP is the one that is farthest left, indicating short waiting times for many customers. In the box plot, all quartiles of ZIBDIP's distribution are smaller than the respective quartiles of the heuristics' distributions, giving the same conclusion.

Table 8.2. Running time data of Johnson's example [437]

instance size	100	316	1000	3162	10000	31623	100000	316227	1000000
Algorithm A	0.00	0.02	0.08	0.29	1.05	5.46	23.0	89.6	377
Algorithm B	0.00	0.03	0.11	0.35	1.38	6.50	30.6	173.3	669
Algorithm C	0.01	0.06	0.21	0.71	2.79	10.98	42.7	329.5	1253
Algorithm D	0.02	0.09	0.43	1.64	6.98	37.51	192.4	789.7	5465
Algorithm E	0.03	0.14	0.57	2.14	10.42	55.36	369.4	5775.0	33414

running times of the considered algorithms are known to be roughly exponential, it is a good idea to use a logarithmic y-axis scale.

Sometimes the problem itself suggests a suitable unit for one of the axes, which may even allow to get rid of one degree of freedom [693].

It may pay off to invest problem-specific knowledge to find an interesting view on the data. Normalization, as suggested by Johnson [437], is an example. Suppose you know a lower bound for a set of functions you want to compare, e. g., $f_1(n), f_2(n) \in \Omega(n)$. Then it may be helpful to look at $f_1'(n) := f_1(n)/n, f_2'(n) = f_2(n)/n$ instead of f_1, f_2, since the "common part" is factored out and thus differences become more visible. Although you lose the possibility to directly read off the values from the normalized diagram, it is still possible to get a good intuition. As Sanders [693] points out it is usually possible to find intuitive names for this new quantity.

A simpler "close-up" effect can be gained by adjusting the plotted range $[y_{\min}, y_{\max}]$ of the y-axis. However, this has the disadvantage that relative comparisons are no longer possible visually. The y-range can also be narrowed down by clipping extreme values of clearly dominated algorithms.

To give an impression on what a good diagram can achieve, we cite the following example from Johnson [437, p. 26]. Consider the data in Table 8.2, which gives running time in seconds for five different algorithms, depending on the input size. From the way the data is arranged it is obvious that the running times of different algorithms are ranked in a consistent way over all instance sizes.

In order to learn more about the data we generate a diagram. The first shot is diagram 8.5(a) in Figure 8.5, which depicts just the data as-is on a linear scale. Algorithms E and D seem to be much worse than the other three on large instances. However, there is no clear picture for smaller instances, since the plots essentially coincide. Furthermore, almost all data points are in the left half of the diagram. Changing to a logarithmic x-scale (diagram 8.5(b)) fixes this, but still there is much coincidence of the plots. If both axes are logarithmic (diagram 8.5(c)), the consistent ranking of the running times becomes apparent. Now all five plots seem to have approximately the same slope, which would indicate the same asymptotic behavior. We know from the first diagram that this is not quite true. Let us now put some more knowledge in the game. Johnson states that there is a lower bound of $\Theta(n \log n)$ for all algorithms. We can use this to normalize the running time of the algorithms and still keep the logarithmic

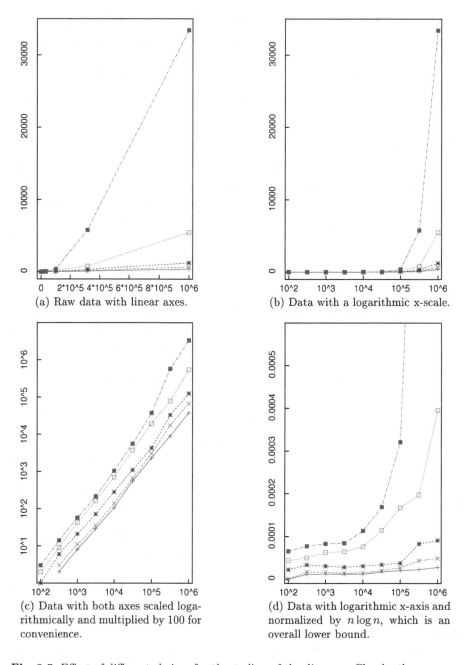

(a) Raw data with linear axes.

(b) Data with a logarithmic x-scale.

(c) Data with both axes scaled logarithmically and multiplied by 100 for
convenience.

(d) Data with logarithmic x-axis and
normalized by $n \log n$, which is an
overall lower bound.

Fig. 8.5. Effect of different choices for the scaling of the diagram. Clearly, the amount
of information discernible from the diagram increases: In diagrams 8.5(c) and 8.5(d) it is
evident that the ordering of the algorithms is consistent. However, only diagram 8.5(d)
reveals that the performance of algorithms D and E are asymptotically much worse
than the lower bound, a fact that cannot be seen directly from the table.

x-axis to obtain diagram 8.5(d). This diagram is really revealing: It shows the consistent ranking, brings out the asymptotically worse running times of algorithms E and D, and indicates that the other three algorithms are asymptotically optimal (up to a constant).

Some of the suggestions involved a lot of work, e. g., playing around with different types of diagrams, transformation of the data, looking at different combinations of measures and so on. However, much of this work can be automated using scripting languages, which even makes it fun to do these things. For example, languages like Perl and Python can be used to extract exactly those numbers you are currently interested in and to convert them in a format suitable for further processing. This processing can be done by a spreadsheet application or a graph-drawing scripting language such as `gnuplot`.

You should also keep in mind that your data has only a limited precision, which is usually smaller than the number of digits available. This is especially true for running times, which often vary much depending on factors you cannot control. This variance can be reduced by producing multiple measurements and using the average or more sophisticated variance reduction methods mentioned in Section 8.2.4. The danger in pretending too much precision is to end up analyzing the noise of the measurements.

8.6.2 Statistical Analysis

The purpose of this subsection is to give an impression of how statistical analysis works and how it can be applied to analyzing data describing the performance of algorithms. We will review the basic concepts and main ideas and give specific examples from the literature.

Why should one be willing to use statistical analysis when the kind of ad-hoc numerical data analysis used before seemed appropriate? One reason is that statistical analysis, applied properly, can give much stronger support for claims or indicate that claims are not justified by the data. It is a tool for assessing the explanatory power and significance of your data. Moreover, you can gain a deeper understanding of the data, for instance, it is possible to analyze the impact of parameter choices on the performance of the algorithm and to distinguish between significant and insignificant parameters. An example will be discussed later in this section. Finally, a statistical analysis of your data may suggest directions for further experiments.

A key ingredient for a proper and successful statistical analysis is a carefully designed experiment. In fact, there is a whole branch in statistics concerned with this, naturally it is called *Design of Experiments (DOE)*. Barret al. [60, p. 20] suggest that "all doctoral students of operations research should receive training in DOE". Even if you do not use its methods, knowing the methodology leads to clearer thinking about experiments and their pitfalls.

DOE methodology is widely used in other experimental fields, such as psychology, the social sciences or industrial product development. It provides methods for designing experiments such that certain systematic errors can be eliminated or at least reduced and the influence of nuisance factors can be controlled.

Furthermore, there are some well-established so-called *experimental designs*, which describe how to carry out the experiment. For these designs, DOE provides analysis methods as well as methods to check the model assumptions a posteriori.

The general tool to analyze the data is *hypothesis testing*. A statistical test is characterized by a so-called *null hypothesis*, assumptions on the experiment, i. e., how the data is generated, and a *test statistic*, which is a number computed from the data. The purpose of the test is to check whether some data is consistent with the null hypothesis or not. The null hypothesis is the converse of the research hypothesis of the experimenter, and the research hypothesis makes up the alternative hypothesis. If the null hypothesis is not consistent with the data, it is rejected and there is some evidence that the research hypothesis is true.

Before doing the test, you need to choose a number $0 < \alpha < 1$, the *significance level*, which is something like the confidence you want to achieve. For example, $\alpha = 0.05$ tells you that you are ready to accept 5% error, i. e., when doing the test very often (of course with different data), the result may be wrong for 5% of the trials. Then you just compute the test statistic for your data, compute or look up the so-called p-value of the statistic. If the p-value is smaller than the chosen significance level, the null hypothesis is rejected.

The formal background of hypothesis testing is the following. It is assumed that the assumptions and the null hypothesis hold. One can then compute the probability that the realization of the test statistic is obtained under these assumptions; this is exactly the p-value. If this probability is very low, in particular smaller than the confidence level, this result is rather unlikely and thus provides evidence against the null hypothesis, leading to its rejection.

As an example, we will describe the famous sign test (see [735]). It works on a sample $(x_1, \ldots, x_n)$ of n real numbers. The assumptions are that all the x_i are drawn independently from the same distribution. The null hypothesis is that 0 is the median of the distribution. To compute the test statistic S, remove all x_i that are 0 and decrease n accordingly. Now define S by

$$S := |\{i \mid x_i > 0\}| .$$

Notice that only the sign of x_i matters, hence the name of the test. If the null hypothesis is true, the probability that x_i is greater than zero is the same as that it is smaller than zero, i. e., this probability is $1/2$. Therefore, S is distributed according to a binomial distribution with parameters $1/2$ and n. Suppose the observed value of S is k, w. l. o. g. $k \geq n/2$. Now the p-value is easy to compute: It is just the probability that S is *at least* k, that is $1/2^n \sum_{i=k}^{n} \binom{n}{i}$. For example, if $n = 15$ and $k = 12$ we get a p-value of 0.018, leading to a rejection of the null hypothesis at a significance level of $\alpha = 0.05$. Instead, we have some evidence that the real median is *greater than* 0. Note that we could not conclude this if we selected a significance level of $\alpha = 0.01$.

A standard application of the sign test is to compare pairwise samples from two different distributions. For comparing two algorithms, suppose there are two samples $(x_1, \ldots, x_n)$ and $(y_1, \ldots, y_n)$ where x_i and y_i are performance measures of both algorithms on the same instance i. The question is: Is it true that the first algorithm is better than the second? To answer this question, consider the sequence of *differences*, given by $d_i = y_i - x_i$ and do the sign test on this sample. The null hypothesis is that the medians of the performance distribution are equal, i.e., the performance of both algorithms is the same. If sufficiently many d_i are positive, this null hypothesis is rejected and there is evidence that the first algorithm is better. Notice, however, that the null hypothesis is also rejected if there are *too few* positive d_i, which would indicate that the second algorithm is better.

One final note about the assumptions of the sign test in this application. These were that the differences are drawn independently and from the same distribution. Clearly, the assumption "same distribution" is no problem, since we look at the distribution of running times difference on all possible instances. If the instances are generated independently at random, the independence assumption is obviously fulfilled. However, this is not true if we look at selected (real-world) instances. Applying the sign test in such a setting is only valid if we can be sure that the selected instances are reasonably representative and diverse or we restrict ourselves to instances that "look like these sample instances".

Let us now turn to some example applications of statistical analysis from the literature.

The Sign Test and Heuristics for the TSP. This example is taken from Golden and Stewart [345], who compare a new heuristic for the Euclidean Traveling Salesman Problem (TSP). They also give some introduction to the statistical methods used.

Golden and Stewart introduce the new algorithm $CCAO$ which combines four techniques. It starts constructing a partial tour from the convex hull of the cities, includes remaining cities via criterions known as cheapest insertion, angle selection and finally improve this solution via a postprocessor known as Or-opt. Other successful postprocessors are 2-opt and 3-opt, which try to find better tours by exchanging 2 or 3 edges of the current tour until no further improvement is possible. It is known that solutions produced by 3-opt are usually a bit better than those of Or-opt, which in turn are much better than those of 2-opt. Unluckily, the gain in solution quality comes at the price of substantially longer running time.

The study is based on only eight instances, which seem to be among the largest ones that have been published at that time (1985). It is not clear that this selection of instances is representative as required for a good test set as explained in Section 8.4. Moreover, usually a larger number of samples is required in order to draw statistical significant conclusions. In fact, Design of Experiments theory provides methods to compute in advance how many samples are necessary to reach a given significance level. However, the main purpose of the paper is to promote the use of statistical methods for assessing algorithms.

In a first experiment the authors compare CCAO to other heuristics. Applying the sign test to assess solution quality indicates that CCAO is better than heuristics with a weak postprocessor, i. e., 2-opt. They also realize that CCAO is as good as those with a strong postprocessor, i. e., Or-opt or 3-opt.

In their second experiment they evaluate the influence of accuracy and efficiency of the postprocessor. This is done by combining the first three ingredients of their algorithm ("CCA") with each of the three postprocessor and the value without postprocessing. Applying the sign test again, they are able to verify the following:

- The running time of 2-opt is smaller than that of Or-opt which is smaller than 3-opt on all 8 instances.
- The solution quality of 2-opt is worse than both Or-opt and 3-opt.
- The solution quality of Or-opt and 3-opt is statistically indistinguishable.

They also did further experiments to assess the contribution of the algorithm's ingredients.

There is an extension to the sign test, namely the Wilcoxon test, which takes the value of the differences into account and allows stronger conclusions at the price of stricter assumptions. Although applicable, Golden and Stewart did not apply the Wilcoxon test for their worked-out analyzes, but encourage the reader to do so.

Using Design of Experiments Methods to Assess Network Algorithms. Amini and Barr [28] conducted an elaborate study regarding the performance of network algorithms for reoptimization, as it often arises e. g., in branch-and-bound algorithms. Their goal is to find out which of the three algorithms PROPT, DROPT and KROPT is best suited for reoptimization.

To this end, they want to perform the following kind of experiment. Starting from a base instance they generate a series of sub-instances, which are randomly modified versions of the base instance, with only small changes between them. This is typical for reoptimization-based algorithms.

Amini and Barr study the following five factors:

Factor	Levels
class of network problem	transportation, transshipment
problem size	small, medium, large
type of change	cost, bound, RHS
percentage change	5%, 20%
type of reoptimizer	PROPT, DROPT, KROPT

Two other factors, the number of sub-instances per series and the number of changes, are fixed to 200 and 20, respectively, after some pilot experiments (which are evaluated by statistical analysis). All in all there are 108 experimental conditions to be studied.

The analysis is based on a *split plot design*, which is an advanced design from the theory of Design of Experiments, see e. g., [210]). A main feature of the split plot design is that the influence of a subset of the factors is better estimated than the influence of combinations of the remaining factors, which are called blocked factors. However, a split plot design enables good statements about the influence of non-blocked factors for a *fixed* combination of the blocked factors. In this case, the blocked factors are problem class and size. This means that the experiment yields insight about how the non-blocked factors (type of change, percentage change, and reoptimizer) should be combined for each problem class / problem size combination, which is really interesting.

The actual experiment is run as follows: In advance, four base instances per problem class and problem size combination have been fixed. Now one out of the 108 conditions is selected at random, the base instance is chosen randomly and 200 sub-instances according to the remaining parameters are generated randomly. Finally, all three reoptimizers are run on them and the total CPU time is recorded. All in all, 86,400 sub-instances are solved.

The authors report the following results obtained by using Tukey's HSD (Honestly Significant Difference) Test [729,210]. This test yielded detailed information on the influence of combinations of factors. For example, considering the two factors type of change and reoptimizer, the HSD test indicates that it is best to choose PROPT if cost coefficients have changed, whereas DROPT deals best with changes to the bounds or the RHS. Looking at the four factors problem class, type of change, problem size and reoptimizer, the TSD results were (cf. Table 8.3):

- transportation problems:
  - PROPT performs best for medium and large problems with cost changes
  - DROPT performs best for bound changes on large problems and for RHS changes on medium and large problems
  - on all other combinations, PROPT and DROPT are indistinguishable, but better than KROPT
- transshipment problems:
  - PROPT performs again best for medium and large problems with cost changes
  - all three algorithms are indistinguishable for bound and cost changes on small problems
  - in the remaining cases, PROPT and DROPT are indistinguishable, but better than KROPT

All of these results were obtained using a significance level of 5%.

It is important to note that the careful design of the experiment allowed the application of HSD test, which in turn provided very detailed information on when to choose which algorithm.

Linear Regression for Comparing Linear Programming (LP) Algorithms. In their overview paper on statistical analysis of algorithms Coffin and Saltzmann [181] propose a method for comparing algorithms they call head-to-head comparison. They illustrate this method on data from the literature, which evaluates the interior-point LP solver OB1 to the simplex-algorithm-based LP solver MINOS.

Table 8.3. Dominance relations between PROPT, DROPT, and KROPT for the 4-factor combination (problem class, problem size, type of change, reoptimizer) extracted from the experimental data of Amini and Barr [28]. A "•" indicates that this algorithm dominates the others, whereas a "o" indicates algorithms that could not be distinguished from each other, but dominated the remaining algorithms. Finally, situations in which no results could be obtained are marked "–".

(a) Results for transportation problems

type of change	problem size	KROPT	PROPT	DROPT
cost	small		o	o
	medium		•	
	large		•	
bound	small		o	o
	medium		o	o
	large			•
RHS	small		o	o
	medium			•
	large			•

(b) Results for transshipment problems

type of change	problem size	KROPT	PROPT	DROPT
cost	small	o	o	o
	medium		•	
	large		•	
bound	small	o	o	o
	medium		o	o
	large		•	
RHS	small	–	–	–
	medium		o	o
	large		o	o

The fundamental idea of head-to-head comparison is to express the running time of one algorithm depending on the running of the other, allowing a direct comparison. Coffin and Saltzmann propose the following dependence

$$y = \beta_0 x^{\beta_1} \epsilon,$$

where x and y denote the running time of MINOS and OB1, respectively, ϵ is a (random) error and β_0, β_1 are unknown constants. This relation has interesting desired properties. First, if the running time for MINOS is 0, the running time for OB1 is 0, too. Second, assuming $\beta_0, \beta_1 > 0$ we have that if the running of MINOS increases, those of OB1 does also. Notice that this need not hold for particular instances (differences there go in the error ϵ), but describes a general trend. Finally, $\beta_1 = 1$ indicates that the running times are proportional. A drawback of this model is that as the running time of MINOS increases, so does the variance of OB1's running time, which is undesired since it hinders using tests and regression methods.

This drawback can be alleviated if using a log-transformation, yielding

$$\log y = \log \beta_0 + \beta_1 \log x + \log \epsilon.$$

This transformation has two positive aspects. Once, it reduces variance. Second, we now have essentially a linear model. Thus linear regression can be used, giving $\beta_0 = 1.18$ and $\beta_1 = 0.7198$ as estimates. Furthermore, a hypothesis test for the null hypothesis $\beta_1 = 1$ can be done, yielding to reject this hypothesis at a p-value of 10^{-4}. Thus it is reasonable to assume that OB1 is asymptotically faster than MINOS.

Apart from this case study, Coffin and Saltzmann give many more case studies and lots of hints for statistical analysis of experiments on algorithms. The examples presented here are supposed to give a flavor of how statistical analysis can be applied to experimental analysis of algorithms. It has to be stressed, however, that the methods of statistical analysis have to be applied with great care to get meaningful results. We will say a little bit more on this in the next section.

8.6.3   Pitfalls for Data Analysis

So far we introduced some methods to analyze experimental data. We want to conclude this section by mentioning common pitfalls to watch out for.

Graphical Analysis. As mentioned in the section on graphical analysis, on the one hand a good diagram can greatly contribute to the analysis. On the other hand, using a bad diagram can be misleading. Therefore it is important to use a diagram type that is suitable for the type of analysis done. For instance, it may happen that due to a logarithmic scale a small absolute difference seems to be substantial and thus leads to wrong conclusions.

As Bast and Weber [68] point out, one has to be careful when dealing with averages, especially if different performance measures are involved. In particular, if algorithm A is better on average than algorithm B with respect to one performance measure, this does not say anything about the relation with respect to another performance measure, even if there is a monotone transformation between the performance measures. To see this, just suppose that algorithm A is good on average for the first performance measure, but is very bad on some instances, whereas algorithm B is not as good, but never very bad. If the other performance measure now penalizes bad behavior more strongly, algorithm B may become better than algorithm A. Bast and Weber emphasize that even if the standard deviation intervals that are usually indicated by error bars are disjoint, it is possible that the order of the averages reverses.

The solution to this issue is of course to evaluate each performance measure on the raw data and only average afterwards. This is another reason for collecting raw data instead of averaged or aggregated data.

Statistical Analysis. Every statistical test requires some assumptions on the stochastic nature of the data. A statistical test is invalid if these assumptions are violated and therefore conclusions drawn from them may not be trustworthy. Therefore, it has to be checked and possibly discussed whether the assumptions are reasonable. If some of them are not, it is often possible to resort to some weaker test. Furthermore, some tests are more robust than others. The literature on non-parametric statistics usually contains hints on the robustness of tests and the assumptions required, see e. g., [753, 183, 735].

A similar problem may arise when analyzing data from a designed experiment. One usually uses some kind of probabilistic model for the data. For any analysis to make sense, the model should be appropriate in the sense that it "fits" the data (or vice versa). There are some ways to test the "fit" and the fulfillment of the assumptions which are discussed in the DOE literature ([210]). These tests should always be done *before* any analysis is carried out. Furthermore, the type of analysis done has to be applicable to the design and model used.

8.7   Reporting Your Results

When reporting your results you usually want to convince the reader of the scientific merit of the work. An important requirement for this is that you raise and answer interesting questions. However, for experimental work it is equally important that the results are reproducible. When talking about reproducibility, we do not mean that an experiment can be redone exactly as it was, since this is unachievable, given the rapid development of computing equipment. Instead, we think of a weaker form of reproducibility: An experiment is reproducible, if a very similar experiment can be set up which gives the same quantitative results and conclusions.

These requirements lead to some principles for reporting which are considered to be good practice [437, 60]) and will be discussed in detail here. Finally, we provide hints on good use of tables and diagrams for reporting experimental data and conclusions from it.

8.7.1   Principles for Reporting

This section is organized around the following principles for good reporting, which are slightly adapted from the list of principles given in Johnson [437].

- Ensure newsworthiness of results.
- Indicate relation to earlier work.
- Ensure reproducibility and comparability,
- Report the full story.
- Draw well-justified conclusions and look for explanations.
- Present your data in informative ways.

Ensure Newsworthiness of Results. This principle directly relates to the scientific merit of your experimental work. Clearly, it is necessary to deal with interesting questions on a sound basis, regarding your experimental methodology. As mentioned earlier, it is often more appealing to go beyond pure running time comparison. These questions were explained in more detail in Section 8.2 and others.

A good report states clearly the motivation for the work and describes the context of it, explaining the specific contribution of this work. The motivation may come from e. g., questions raised in earlier experimental papers, assessing the "practical" performance of algorithms studied only theoretically, and from real-world applications.

Indicate Relation to Earlier Work. Of course, you should have read the relevant literature to know what already has been done.

You should compare your results to those from the literature. This comparison can be a hard task for a number of reasons. First of all, you will most likely be using different computing hardware and software. Since running times are influenced by many factors, e. g., machine speed and architecture, compiler, and sophistication of implementation, a direct comparison is not very meaningful. Another obstacle is that earlier publications may not focus on aspects you are interested in, use other performance measures and so on.

A part of this difficulty can be overcome if it is possible to use the test set and the implementation of the original work. If available, you should use these. How to proceed when they are not available has been discussed in Section 8.5.1. The main benefit of using the original implementation is that you get the best comparability possible, since you can run the original algorithm and your new one on the same equipment.

A fall-back method to make running times of earlier papers roughly comparable to your measurements is to estimate the relative speed difference of the machines. This can be done using benchmark values obtainable for both machines. Sometimes problem-specific benchmarks are available. For instance, the DIMACS Implementation Challenge on the Traveling Salesman Problem [439, 249] employed a benchmark implementation to normalize the running times across a wide range of different platforms. To this end, every participant had to run this benchmark implementation on his machine and to report the running time, which in turn was used for normalization. Johnson and McGeoch [439] report that accuracy was about a factor of 2, which was sufficient for the running time differences that occurred.

In any case you should clearly report on how you tried to make these values comparable.

Ensuring Reproducibility and Comparability. This principle is in some sense the counterpart of the preceding one. The goal is to make life of future researchers who want to build on your work easier, which essentially means providing enough detail to allow qualitative reproduction of your results.

To this end, you should give a detailed description of the experimental setup. This encompasses information such as machine type, processor number and processor speed, operating system, implementation language and compiler used, but also experimental conditions like run time or space limits. If you used a generator to create test instances you need to describe the generator and the parameters used for test set creation, too.

Of course it is necessary to describe the implementation of your algorithm detailed enough to facilitate reproduction. This implies that you mention and describe all non-straightforward implementation details which have a significant impact on your results. For complex heuristics, this includes the stopping rule used (if the heuristic has no natural way to terminate) and the values of potential parameters used to achieve your results. These parameters must not be set on a per-instance basis, since this is not generalizable. However, you may use some kind of rule to determine parameters from instance parameters which then needs to be described as well.

The best way to ensure reproducibility is to publish both the instances used for the experiment and the source code of your implementation. Some journals already support and even encourage this. For example, the ACM Journal on Experimental Algorithmics (JEA) invites submitters to also publish supplementary files, which can be source code or data files. Publishing the source code requires a certain level of documentation to make it useful for other people. You also have to make sure that the data you publish is actually consistent with the source code, i. e., binaries will produce essentially this data.

Instances should be made available in a machine-readable, well-known and well-documented format, cf. Section 8.4. If there is already an instance library for this specific problem, it may be possible to extend the library by some of your instances, since instance libraries are often maintained to reflect progress. Although it would suffice to publish the instance generator used, it is usually better to make the actually used instances available.

It is a good idea to archive the raw data of your experiments (not just the "processed" data used and given in the report) at a safe place so you can later access it. This can be useful if you or somebody else is interested in doing further research. Again, version control systems can be useful here.

Report the Full Story. It is good scientific practice to report results (i. e., data) as they are. This also implies that anomalous results contradicting your conclusions must not be omitted. Instead, it is worthwhile to investigate their origin and, if no explanation can be found, to state this clearly. Any anomalies in the data, e. g., those contradicting your or other's results, should be noted in the paper. It is then clear that their occurrence is not due to typographical or other error.

When reporting running times for heuristics without stopping criterion (such as local search) do report the total running time used by the heuristic, not just the time until the best solution was found. As Johnson [437] points out, considering only the time for the best solutions essentially means pretending clairvoyance of the heuristic, since it has no way to decide that no better solution will be found. The running time should also include time spent for preprocessing and setup, which should be given separately. Reporting the total running time of the heuristic gives a clear indication of the effort needed to get this solution and allows better comparison to competing methods.

For similar reasons, it is also desirable to report the total running time invested in your computational study, since omitting this time can give a distorted picture. For instance, if it took some time to find the parameters that make a heuristic perform well the real effort to get good solutions with this heuristic is much larger than just running the heuristic once with those parameters. A similar effort might be necessary to suit the heuristic to differently structured instances. It is also interesting to know how much you gained by tuning the parameters, i.e., you should indicate the typical solution quality before and after tuning. You should try to look at more machine-independent running time measures, as suggested in Section 8.6 and account on these findings in detail.

When evaluating heuristics it is important to assess the quality of solutions, since this allows quantifying the time / quality tradeoff when using this heuristic. Preferably, you should compare the heuristic to exact solution values. If exact solutions turn out to be too expensive to compute, you may resort to good lower bounds which can be obtained by e. g., Linear Programming or Lagrangian relaxations. As a last resort, you can compare solution values to best-known ones or to those of other heuristics.

The purpose of heuristics is to produce hopefully good solutions in much shorter time than exact methods can. Complex heuristics may produce a sequence of improving best solutions. For these you should indicate how solution quality evolves in time. This can be done using diagrams, showing solution quality as a time series. Another possibility suggested by Barr et al. [60] is to use derived descriptive measures. They suggest the ratio

$$r_{0.05} = \frac{\text{time to within 5\% of best}}{\text{time to best found}},$$

which measures how fast the heuristic converges to its best attainable value. This metric is not suitable for comparing different algorithms, since the value of the best solution found may differ significantly.

Another interesting point to investigate is how solution quality changes with growing instance size. In fact, this is just a special case of *robustness*, which is discussed in Section 3.5: An algorithm should perform well on a large set of instances. Similarly, if the behavior of a heuristic depends on some parameters, its solution quality should not deteriorate with small changes of "good" parameter settings. The robustness of an algorithm should be addressed and reported, for example by giving standard deviations for the quality in a quality-time graph [60], indicating the spread of quality after a fixed computation time for the whole instance set studied.

To get a better understanding of a complex algorithm and its specific features, the contribution of each strategy or phase should be assessed and reported on.

It is also worthwhile to mention unsuccessful algorithmic ideas that you tried. This may save other researchers from spending further effort on them. For instance, if your heuristic was not able to find a feasible solution on a certain class of instances, this is something to report.

Draw Well-justified Conclusions and Look for Explanations. Reporting on an experimental study requires interpreting the data. It is clearly not sufficient to just describe the algorithm and to give a table of numbers. The data you provide in your report needs to be explained in a convincing and consistent way by suitable claims. Be sure to support your claims with convincing diagrams and tables. These must not hide any contradicting data; instead, you need to argue why they can be neglected for your claims. Of course your claims need to be supported by the data.

In order to support or challenge your claims, it may be worthwhile to employ statistical analysis (see Section 8.6.2). This can provide additional evidence and confidence or rejection for your claims.

As mentioned several times before and recommended in the literature [437, 325], you should look at and report on as large instances as possible. Looking at huge instance sizes provides stronger support for claims, especially on asymptotic behavior. Moreover, the reader gets an impression on how the algorithms scale with problem size.

Present Data in Informative Ways. Large amounts of numbers are usually considered to be rather dull and boring. This need not be the case, however, it is necessary to present the data in interesting and revealing ways. Using appropriate diagrams and clearly-structured tables can help a lot here. See Section 8.7.2 for more detailed hints.

Statistical methods to support your claims are best used for general conclusions, such as recovering trends and correlations between variables. Usually, it is not interesting to do lots of experimental runs just to get tight confidence intervals, since these apply only to the specific setting.

You should also avoid reporting too much data (within the paper!). If you generated much data for many instances you should try to cluster similar instances and report representative results for each cluster. It is also possible to report averages and similar summary statistics (e. g., minimum and maximum, medians, quartiles) to get an impression of the results. The full data could be put into the appendix or made available electronically via the Internet. You can safely omit the results for dominated algorithms, but you should indicate in the paper that they are dominated and therefore dropped.

8.7.2   Presenting Data in Diagrams and Tables

Experimental studies usually yield large amounts of data which are in a sense the result of the study and thus need to be reported on in some sensible way. There are two ways to present that data: pictures (i. e., diagrams) and tables. Both have their advantages and drawbacks which will be discussed here. We also give advice on how to make best use out of them.

Diagrams are useful for recognizing patterns, trends, etc.; their use for analyzing data has already been discussed. They give a quick impression and quick overview and can make vast amounts of data comprehensible and ease comparison of different data sets. However, they tend to hide details (which is an advantage, too) and make it hard to figure out exact values. Tables, on the other hand, reporting the data as it is, although this might be hard to interpret.

The natural conclusion is to use tables for small amounts of data. Tufte [784, p. 56] recommends using tables for sets of 20 numbers or less. Tables may also be useful to report exact values for larger data sets in addition to some diagram. Larger tables are particularly out of place at oral presentations [550].

Tables. When using tables (especially larger ones) it is important to structure them in order to highlight important information and aspects of the data [437]. Tables can often be made more accessible by choosing a sensible ordering of rows and columns. The sorting should reflect properties of the data. For instance, the rows in Table 8.2 on page 373 have been ordered according to the running time of the algorithms, which makes the the consistent ranking of the algorithms apparent. Similarly, it is better to sort instances by their size than their names.

Tables should not only give the data as measured, but also provide interesting related information contributing to the interpretation of the data. The obvious example is when you give a solution value and a lower bound, then you should include a column indicating the resulting optimality gap.

Of course, tables and the reported data need to be labeled properly. This encompasses stating the exact meaning of the rows and the columns and the units of quantities as well as further details important for interpretation. If you include numbers from different sources, try to make them comparable and indicate their origin.

Diagrams. Most fundamental things for creating good diagrams have already been discussed in Section 8.6.1 since they are useful both for data analysis and presentation. We therefore focus on more detailed hints which become more important for reporting.

The general advice is to avoid too much information in one diagram. Although you as the expert for your experimental setup and analysis can probably cope with more information in one diagram, this same diagram may be too complicated for your audience. One issue might be too many data sets in a diagram, e. g., too many curves. The number of curves which can be displayed in a reasonable way depends on their overall complexity or information density. If the curves lie close together or you cannot tell on first sight which is above or below these are indications that you should think about improving the diagram.

The following hints on how to cope with too many curves have been collected by Sanders [693]. A first possibility is to consider different scaling of the axes as explained in Section 8.6.1 in order to find a better view on the data. It may be possible to remove dominated curves and to indicate that removal. In some cases, similar curves can be combined to a single one. For example, to show that an algorithm is always better than some other ones it suffices to plot the best result of all the other algorithms. Finally, you should consider decomposing a diagram into different ones with differing y-scales, both showing only a subset of the original plots.

Consistency in the diagram is important, since inconsistency is confusing and tends to distract the reader's attention to resolving that discrepancy. Consistency is reflected in many details. For example, if results for one algorithm are presented in several diagrams, be sure to use the same line and point styles and color for plots of that algorithm. Similarly, algorithm labels for corresponding plots should be in the top-down order of the plots.

The design of the diagram should be as clean as possible. You should use marks for data points which are clearly distinguishable, but not too large. Data points belonging to the same data set can be connected to better indicate that they belong together. However, as Johnson [437] points out, such lines implicitly suggest a trend and/or that interpolation between the data points is possible or sensible. Connecting the points should therefore be avoided if possible. If necessary, you should use unobtrusive (e. g., thin gray) straight lines to do this – splines are a no-no since they amplify the implicit "interpolation" claim.

There are some books on diagram design, e. g., the book of Tufte [784]. He introduces the principle of data-ink maximization which essentially requires to make best use of the ink used to draw the diagram. For example, he suggests to avoid grids since they usually interfere too much with the data drawn. He also gives hints and examples on how to improve existing diagrams as well as inspiration to design new ones.

Finally, your diagrams need to be labelled clearly and completely. Ideally, they are understandable on their own, without having to read the corresponding text passages. To achieve this, you should try to succinctly provide all information needed for interpretation. At the least, you should explain or mention unusual axis scales (e. g., log, normalized), what has been measured and is displayed. You should highlight important features and any specialty of your diagram.

Chapter 9. Case Studies

Daniel Delling, Roberto Hoffmann, Maria Kandyba, and Anna Schulze

9.1 Introduction

In this chapter we outline success stories of Algorithm Engineering on three well-known problems: *Shortest paths, Steiner trees*, and the construction of *Voronoi diagrams*. All these topics have real-world applications of particular importance, and therefore received a lot of attention by various research groups in the last decades.

The analysis of these three problems and the design of first algorithms date back already to the middle of the 20th century. While for the shortest paths problem and Voronoi diagrams polynomial algorithms were found quite early, the Steiner tree problem was shown to be NP-hard. For this problem, exact algorithms, which have exponential worst-case running times, and fast approximation methods were proposed. The first exact approaches for Steiner trees could not deal with the instances, coming up from the real-world applications. Therefore, more efficient methods and implementations which fit much better to the requirements stemming from practice were required. In the last ten years, a significant progress was achieved. Thereby, not only approximation methods, but also exact exponential algorithms for NP-hard problems were tuned and optimized, making some of them praxis-relevant for the first time.

The research on these problems gives a deeper insight into the current methods and ideas of Algorithm Engineering. Each of them has its own history of development which we now briefly outline.

The *shortest path problem* is one of the fundamental and therefore well-studied problems of combinatorial network optimization. Given two vertices in a network, it looks for a shortest path between these vertices in the network (provided that the vertices are connected). Without additional constraints it is solvable in polynomial time and there exist various long-known classical efficient algorithms. However, for huge problem instances stemming from real-world applications these algorithms are too slow in practice. Therefore, to obtain quick answers to their problems, many practitioners preferred fast heuristics over exact methods. Since 1999, a great amount of research has been done to develop *exact* shortest path algorithms which base on the traditional ones, but are much more efficient when applied to large real-world datasets.

The *Steiner tree problem* comes in different versions. In a geometric setting, we are given a set of points in the plane and look for a shortest interconnection which spans all given points. In a more abstract setting, we are given an undirected graph $G = (V, E)$ and a subset of its vertices $T \subseteq V$ and look for a connected subgraph of G spanning all vertices in T.

The problem has also many important applications ranging from VLSI-design to the study of phylogenetic trees. With the first exact algorithms one could

M. Müller-Hannemann and S. Schirra (Eds.): Algorithm Engineering, LNCS 5971, pp. 389–445, 2010.

only solve very small instances of the Steiner tree problem to optimality. For quite some time no significant improvements have been achieved. The situation changed quite dramatically when several research groups started to exploit a couple of new structural insights into the problem. With these improvements the benchmark instances from SteinLib [491] can now be solved to optimality within admissible computation times. Indeed, only recently it has become possible to compute optimal solutions for many of these benchmark problems at all. Beside exact approaches several powerful heuristics exist which can be used to solve even huge instances of about 100,000 given points within few percent of optimality. Theoretical research has also led to the development of approximation algorithms. Those approximation algorithms which provide the best proven approximation guarantees, however, turn out to be rather impractical and have never been implemented.

The last section of this chapter deals with the computation of *Voronoi diagrams*, which deliver the partition of space into regions by given sites in a way, that the region for a site contains all points that are closer to this site than to any other. We introduce the Voronoi diagrams and present their applications to different areas of science (e. g., geographical information services, convex hull calculation, for preventing moving robots from hit-and-run) as well as the challenge of their computation and different algorithmic approaches.

For all these problems, we are not concerned with describing all recently proposed algorithms in detail, nor will we give proofs of their correctness. We focus on the main ideas motivating these algorithms and showcase the successful application of Algorithm Engineering principles.

9.2   Shortest Paths

In this section, we first introduce the shortest path problem and outline the traditional approaches that have been used to solve it. We then discuss the engineering of tailored route planning algorithms in transportation networks. It turns out that this development splits into four phases, in which we explain most of the techniques developed within the last 50 years.

Shortest Path Problems. An instance of a shortest path problem is a graph $G = (V, E)$ and a length function on the edges $l : E \rightarrow \mathbb{R}$. Additionally, there may be a *source* $s \in V$ and a *sink* $t \in V$, collectively called *terminal nodes*. Let $n := |V|$ and $m := |E|$.

The *point-to-point shortest path problem* (P2P) consists of connecting s and t in G in a shortest possible way, e.g. finding a path P with s and t as start and end points respectively, so that the length $l(P) = \sum_{e \in P} l(e)$ is minimized. Such a path P is then called a *shortest (s, t)-path*. An extension of this problem is the *single-source shortest path problem* (SSSP), in which the shortest paths from s to all other nodes $v \in V \setminus \{s\}$ has to be computed. If we ask for shortest paths between all possible pairs of nodes, the problem is called all-pairs shortest paths (APSP).

These problems have been extensively studied in the past. The algorithms for SSSP turned out to be fundamental for the solution of other variants of shortest path problems. In the following, we will discuss the solution methods for SSSP and their application for P2P. For APSP see, e.g., [235].

The mainly used algorithms for the SSSP problem are *labeling algorithms*, which can be classified into the two groups of *label-setting* and *label-correcting* methods. These algorithms iteratively assign *distance labels* to each node, such that after the final iteration a distance label at node v represents the length of a shortest (s, v)-path, which we denote as dist(s, v). Label-setting methods determine an exact (permanent) distance label of one node per iteration. Unfortunately, they can handle only a restricted set of instances, for example, acyclic graphs with arbitrary edge lengths or arbitrary graphs with nonnegative edge lengths. The label-correcting methods are more flexible and, in general, do not have such restrictions regarding its input. Such an algorithm may change all distance labels multiple times and only after the final step they all become permanent. However, the label-correcting algorithms are in general less efficient with respect to worst-case running time compared to label-setting ones. A good overview and discussion on both groups of labeling algorithms can be found in [15].

Dijkstra's Algorithm. In general, a labeling method for SSSP stores label distances $d(v)$, parent nodes $p(v)$ and a status $\sigma(v) \in \{$unreached, labeled, settled$\}$ for every node v. Initially, the only labeled node is s with $d(s) = 0$. All other nodes v are unreached with $d(v) = \infty$. In each iteration, one of the labeled nodes u will become settled and all of its unreached neighbors become labeled. For a neighbor v of u, the distance label $d(v)$ and the parent node $p(v)$ are updated if $d(u) + l(u, v) < d(v)$. We call this *relaxing* the edge (u, v). The method terminates when no labeled nodes exist. Finally, the resulting shortest paths can be reconstructed using the parent nodes.

The main question in developing or engineering an efficient SSSP algorithm is how to store and manage the set of labeled nodes and the order in which they are processed. E.g., the Bellman-Ford-Moore algorithm uses a FIFO queue to process the labeled nodes. This algorithm is label-correcting and runs in $O(nm)$ time. Even though this is the best known worst-case bound for general graphs, experiments show that this algorithm is often slower than other methods in practice. One of the reasons is that most SSSP instances do have nonnegative edge functions; for this special case, Dijkstra [244] suggested a label-setting algorithm in 1959, on which most algorithms discussed in this paper are based.

Dijkstra's algorithm (cf. Algorithm 7) uses a priority queue to hold the labeled nodes. In each iteration, it selects a node which has the smallest distance label. It can be easily shown that if the length function is nonnegative, this algorithm settles each node exactly once; otherwise the number of settles may be exponential. Once a node u gets settled, its label distance – and hence the currently shortest (s, u)-path – will never be changed again. Hence, the running time of Algorithm 7 is given be Equation (1).

Algorithm 7. Dijkstra's algorithm using a priority queue Q.

1: **for all** $u \in V$ **do** $d(u) = \infty$	▷ initializing distance labels
2: $Q.\text{insert}(s, 0)$	
3: $d(s) = 0$	
4: **while** $!Q.\text{empty}()$ **do**	
5: $\quad u = Q.\text{deleteMin}()$	▷ settling u
6: $\quad$ **for all** $(u, v) \in E$ **do**	▷ relaxing edges
7: $\quad\quad$ **if** $d(u) + l(u, v) < d(v)$ **then**	
8: $\quad\quad\quad d(v) = d(u) + l(u, v)$	▷ found shorter path to v
9: $\quad\quad\quad$ **if** $v \notin Q$ **then**	
10: $\quad\quad\quad\quad Q.\text{insert}(v, d(v))$	
11: $\quad\quad\quad$ **else**	
12: $\quad\quad\quad\quad Q.\text{decreaseKey}(v, d(v))$	

$$T_{\text{Dijkstra}} = T_{\text{init}} + n \cdot T_{\text{deleteMin}} + m \cdot T_{\text{decreaseKey}} + n \cdot T_{\text{insert}} \qquad (1)$$

So, the running time of this algorithm depends on the implementation of the priority queue, in particular, on the choice of its corresponding data structure.

The output of Dijkstra's algorithm is a *shortest path tree* rooted at s. However, Dijkstra's algorithm can easily be adapted to solve the P2P problem with non-negative length function for given terminal nodes s and t: the algorithm starts computing the shortest path tree for s and terminates as soon as t is settled.

Speed-Up Techniques. After its publication in 1959, several approaches on improving the running time of Dijkstra's algorithm have been proposed. On the one hand, researches tried to reduce the worst-case running time by introducing different types of priority queues or gave better bounds for specific graph classes. On the other hand, researches introduced *speed-up techniques* for specific inputs, in particular for transportation networks. Roughly speaking, Dijkstra computes the distance to all possible locations in the network being closer than the target we are interested in. Clearly, it does not make sense to compute all these distances if we are only interested in the path between two points. Moreover, transportation networks hardly change between two queries. Starting from this observation, speed-up techniques split the work into two parts. During an *offline* phase, called preprocessing, additional data is computed that accelerates point-to-point queries during the *online* phase. In the following, we explain most of those techniques developed since 1959. It turns out that the research splits into four phases which we explain in the following.

9.2.1   Phase I: "Theory" (1959 – 1999)

The first phase starts directly after Dijkstra's publication in 1959 and reached a time window of about 40 years. Most of the research during these years concentrated on improving the theoretical worst-case running time by introducing better data structures. Note that within these years several approaches have been proposed which we only scratch here. Some basic speed-up techniques, i.e., A* and bidirectional search, have been introduced in this phase as well. Since later techniques use them as ingredients, we present them in more detail.

Priority Queues. In its original form [244], Dijkstra uses a list to maintain the distance labels. This results in a $O(1)$ running time for each `insert` and `decreaseKey` operation, while `deleteMin` takes $O(n)$ time in the worst case. This yields an overall running time of $O(n^2)$. This bound has been improved several times by using more sophisticated priority queues. For example, a binary heap yields a running time of $O(m \log n)$. The best bound for general (positive) edge weights is $O(m + n \log n)$ and is achieved by applying a Fibonacci heap. If edge weights are given by integers, a bound of $O(m + n \log \log n)$ is given in [780]. Dial [241] achieves a worst-case bound of $O(m + nC)$ if the integers are in a range from 0 to C. This bound can be improved to $O(m \log \log C)$ [795], $O(+n\sqrt{\log C})$ [16], and $O(m + n \log \log C)$ [780]. Note that improving the worst-case running time still is focus of *theoretical* research on shortest paths. An extensive computational study on different variants of Dijkstra's algorithm (as well as several label-correcting algorithms) has been conducted by Cherkassky, Goldberg, and Radzig [167]. Their work (with first drafts appearing in 1993) can now be classified as pioneering for Algorithm Engineering. They demonstrated how fruitful the interaction between experimental evaluation of algorithm behavior and the theoretical analysis of algorithm performance can be.

Bidirectional Search. The idea of bidirectional search is to accelerate P2P-queries by starting a second simultaneous search from the target t. The so-called *backward* search operates on the *reverse graph*, where the direction of each edge is reversed. Such an idea arose already in the 60's [202], offering the advantage that no implicit information on the given graph is required. Using some alternation strategy between forward and backward search, one can define a bidirectional search algorithm: it maintains the sets of forward and reverse distance labels (d_f and d_r, respectively) as well as an upper bound μ, i. e., the shortest (s, t)-path seen so far. This upper bound is computed in the following way: whenever one of the search directions (w. l. o. g. the forward search) relaxes an edge (v, w) and w has already been settled by the opposite direction, $d_f(v) + l(v, w) + d_r(w)$ is computed. The first time such a situation occurs, this bound is stored and will be updated when necessary. Note that the edge (v, w) must be stored as well if the path realizing μ shall be reconstructed. The algorithm terminates as soon as $k_f + k_r \geq \mu$, where k_f depicts the minimum key of the forward priority queue, and k_r the one of the backward queue.

Euclidean A*-search [382]. The main idea of the goal-directed version of Dijkstra's algorithm, called A^*, is to manipulate the settling order of labeled nodes by redefining the given length function. By this, the sink t is settled earlier than it would be settled by traditional Dijkstra.

Suppose that the shortest path distance $\pi_t^*(v)$ to the sink is known for every v. Then the priorities in the queue can be change in a beneficial way, based on the following idea: instead of distance label $d(v)$, the value $k(v) = d(v) + \pi_t^*(v)$ is used as the priority for any labeled node v. Note that as v is to be settled $d(v) = \text{dist}(s, v)$ and $k(v)$ is the length of the shortest (s, t)-path. Therefore, only the nodes on the shortest (s, t)-path will be settled, each of which exactly once. Moreover, it can easily be shown that this algorithm is equivalent to Dijkstra's algorithm performed on the same input graph when using the alternative nonnegative length function:

$$l_{\pi_t^*}(v, w) := l(v, w) - \pi_t^*(v) + \pi_t^*(w). \tag{2}$$

Of course, the exact values $\pi_t^*(v)$ will be unknown in general. So, one has to settle for an approximation of π^*. A function $\pi_t : V \to \mathbb{R}$ is called a *feasible potential function* if:

$$\pi_t(t) = 0 \text{ and } 0 \le l_{\pi_t}(v, w) := l(v, w) - \pi_t(v) + \pi_t(w) \; \forall (v, w) \in E. \tag{3}$$

It turns out that condition (3) implies that the approximations $\pi_t(v)$ must be lower bounds for the length of a shortest path from v to t. So, the performance of an A^* algorithm is highly dependent on the feasible potential function used: If $\pi_t \equiv 0$, the A^*-search is equivalent to the original version of Dijkstra's algorithm. In contrast, knowledge of exact distances would indeed result in a perfect reduction of search space. In general, tighter lower bounds lead to a smaller number of settled nodes. Therefore, it is crucial to find a good compromise between the quality of the lower bounds and the associated cost for obtaining them. The classic approach works for embedded graphs in the plane and uses Euclidean bounds in order to obtain feasible potentials.

Bidirectional A^*. Note that A^*-search can also be used within the bidirectional search framework. The drawback of such an approach is that, in general, the termination criterion of the bidirectional search — i. e., to stop on the first node which is settled from both directions – becomes invalid. One possibility to overcome this drawback is to redefine the termination condition [641]. Algorithms of this type are called *symmetric*. They are based on the following termination condition: the algorithm terminates either if the priority queues of both search direction are empty or one of the searches has already reached the sink t. An alternative is to use the same length function for both the forward and reverse search routines, requiring $\pi_t(v) + \pi_s(v) = c$, for all $v \in V$ and some constant c. Such algorithms are called *consistent*. See [421] for details.

9.2.2 Phase II: Speed-Up Techniques for P2P (1999 – 2005)

In 1999, Schulz et al. initiated the search for new speed-up techniques for Dijkstra's algorithm on large-scale real networks [714]. In their work, the authors introduced two general approaches for speed-up techniques: exploit a natural hierarchy within the network, or make the search goal-directed. The former approach tries to identify unimportant parts of the graph that can be *skipped* as soon as one is sufficiently far away from source and target of the query, while the latter tries to prune edges directing "away" from the target.

Goal-Directed Search. For goal-directed search, two approaches have been proved useful: either change the ordering the nodes are visited or prune edges directing in to the "wrong" direction. A* is a representative of the former, while Geometric Containers and Arc-Flags are examples for the latter. Note that A* has been significantly enhanced during phase II by the introduction of landmarks which we explain in the following.

Landmark-A* (ALT). As already discussed in Section 9.2.1, the success of A*-search depends on the quality of the potentials. In [338], Goldberg et al. suggest a new lower-bounding technique with preprocessing based on *landmarks*. It can be applied to all problem instances whose length function satisfy the triangle inequality. The main idea is to choose landmarks $L \subset V$ as a small subset ($\approx$ 16) of all graph nodes; for each such landmark $\ell \in L$ a complete shortest path tree to (and from) all other nodes is computed during the preprocessing.

Computing lower bounds using this precomputed information is then part of the query algorithm. As, by assumption, the triangle inequality is satisfied, the distances from each node $v \in V$ to a landmark ℓ lead to a feasible potential function $\pi_t^{(\ell)}(v) := \max\{\text{dist}(v, \ell) - \text{dist}(t, \ell), \text{dist}(\ell, t) - \text{dist}(\ell, v)\}$. To achieve better bounds the maximum over all landmarks will be chosen, as the maximum function over feasible potentials is also a feasible potential: $\pi_t(v) := \max_{\ell \in L} \pi_t^{(\ell)}$.

Obviously, the quality of the lower bounds heavily depends on the choice and number of landmarks. Although several algorithms were proposed for landmark selection [338, 342], their qualities relative to each other are highly dependent on the specific problem instances and there is no single best selection scheme. Note that Landmark-A* is often also called the ALT-algorithm (**A***, **L**andmarks, and the **T**riangle inequality).

Geometric Containers. The idea of geometric containers is to precompute a set $M(e)$ of nodes for each edge of the graph. This container includes a superset of all nodes that lie on a shortest path starting with e. Then, in an s–t query, an edge e needs not be relaxed if $t \notin M(e)$. In [714], $M(e)$ is specified by an *angular range*. Better results can be achieved with other *geometric containers* [816, 818], the best trade-off in search space reduction and query performance is achieved for axis parallel rectangles.

Arc-Flags. A crucial problem of geometric containers is that preprocessing is based on solving APSP. Arc-Flags, introduced in [510, 493], improve on this by reversing the idea of geometric containers. Instead of storing a container for each edge, the graph is partitioned in k cells. Then, each edge gets assigned a k-bit flag, where the i-th bit is set to true if at least one node in cell i lies on a shortest path starting with e.

Preprocessing of Arc-Flags is split into two parts: partitioning the graph and computing arc-flags. In [582], several approaches for partitioning have been evaluated. It turns out that the best results are achieved for k-way arc-separator algorithms, e.g., METIS [467]. The obtained partitions fulfill most requirements of a useful partition: balanced cell-sizes, connected, and a small number of edges connecting two regions. Setting arc-flags can be done by constructing a shortest path tree from each *boundary node* (a node adjacent to a node of a different cell) on the reverse graph. An edge gets a flag for a cell i set to `true` as soon as it is a tree-edge for at least one of those trees grown. In [392], Hilger et al. show how to accelerate preprocessing further by growing a single *centralized* shortest path tree from each cell.

Arc-Flags can be made bidirectional in a straightforward manner: Compute a second set of flags for each edge of the reverse graph and use them to prune the backward search. The stopping criterion is the standard one from bidirectional Dijkstra.

Hierarchical Approaches. Roughly speaking, hierarchical approaches try to prune unimportant nodes or edges as soon as the search is sufficiently far away from source and target. This can either be achieved by "skipping" unimportant parts of the graph or by some kind of centrality measure indicating the importance of a node. In the following, we explain a representative for both approaches.

Multi-Level Techniques. In [716, 404, 405], Schulz et al. designed and empirically investigated the following multi-level approach for timetable queries in public transportation. Their work is based on previous results, published in [714, 715].

To construct the graph G_{i+1} from G_i they choose a subset $V_{i+1} \subseteq V_i$. For each shortest path connecting two nodes $u, v \in V_{i+1}$ in G_i which does not contain any other node of V_{i+1} there is an an edge $(u, v) \in E_{i+1}$ with according weight. Analogously, there are edges — connecting G_i and G_{i+1} — representing shortest paths between any two nodes $w \in V_i \setminus V_{i+1}$ and $v \in V_{i+1}$ as long as these paths do not contain any other node from V_{i+1}. Note that this implicitly partitions the nodes V_i with respect to their incidence with G_{i+1}. This yields a *hierarchy* on which a so-called *multi-level graph* $\mathcal{M}$ is based; a graph G_i is called the *i-th level* of $\mathcal{M}$.

An (s, t)-query algorithm applies a search algorithm to a subgraph S of $\mathcal{M}$, exploiting the above partitioning property. Such subgraph S, which is substantially smaller than G_0, depends on the specific query and is therefore determined on the fly.

Reach. Another hierarchical approach was introduced by Gutman [372] and involves the notion of *reach*: Let P be a s–t path in G, and let v be a node on P. The *reach* $r_P(v)$ of v w.r.t. P is defined as $\min\{\text{dist}_P(u, v), \text{dist}_P(v, w)\}$, with dist_P denoting the length of the subpath of P between the two specified nodes. The *reach of* v is now defined as

$$r(v) := \max\{r_P(v) \mid P \text{ is a shortest path in } G \text{ containing } v\} \ .$$

Intuitively, if the reach of a node v is high, we know that v lies in the middle of a "long" shortest path. Now, we can make up the following pruning condition: When settling a node v, we can *prune*, i.e., not relax any edge $(v, u) \in E$, if $r(v) < \min\{\text{dist}(s, v), \text{dist}(v, t)\}$ holds. While $\text{dist}(s, v)$ is given by the key of v in the priority queue, $\text{dist}(v, t)$ is not known in general. However, using some lower bounds $\underline{\text{dist}}(v, t)$ does not violate correctness of the pruning condition.

The computation of the exact reaches could be done by computing APSP. But even specialized, more efficient algorithms, as presented in [339], are too expensive for large graphs. Fortunately, we can use upper bounds $\bar{r}$ for the reaches instead. Since the reaches are completely independent of the query algorithm, the upper bounds for the reaches can be computed in advance. In [372], an efficient algorithm is suggested to compute the upper bounds. The main idea is to iteratively construct partial shortest path trees for each node. These are then used for finding the nodes with a low reach and temporarily removing them from G (redefining the costs on the edges in the remaining graph appropriately). This step is then iteratively performed on smaller graphs until we have some $\bar{r}(v)$ for all nodes v. Note that some nodes u might have $\bar{r}(u) = \infty$ if we decide to terminate this process early, in order to save computation time.

To render the pruning condition as effective as possible, good lower bounds on the distances are needed. Originally (in [372]), Euclidean distances were used to compute these bounds. This resulted in such algorithms to be only applicable to graphs with given layout information. An alternative method that avoids this restriction was suggested in [339], where a bidirectional version of reach-based pruning was introduced. More precisely, when settling a node u in the forward direction, we already know the exact $\text{dist}(s, u)$. The distance from u to t can be estimated as the distance already covered by the reverse search. Hence, we do not require any layout information and virtually no additional effort for computing the lower bounds on distances.

Combinations. The interested reader may have noticed that goal-directed and hierarchical search exploit different facts for accelerating the query algorithm. Hence, it seems promising to combine speed-up techniques among each other. In [714], the authors combine their goal-directed and hierarchical approach with each other. The experimental evaluation confirms that combinations indeed further reduces query times: a speed-up of 62 is reported for timetable information in railway networks. In [407, 406], all pre 2004 techniques are systematically combined among each other. It turns out that depending on the graph type, different combinations perform best. For the real-world graph examined, a combination of bidirectional search and geometric containers leads to the best running times.

Final Remarks on Phase II. The main contribution in phase II was the introduction of the most fundamental concepts for accelerating P2P-queries: hierarchical and goal-directed speed-up techniques. It turns out that both approaches are the fundament of most of the techniques developed during the following phase III.

However, a crucial problem during phase II was the unavailability of *public* data sets. Each group working on route planning algorithms had his own (classified) data set for testing their developed speed-up technique. This made the comparison of the techniques almost impossible. Moreover, the networks used for evaluation still were quite small. As a result, a preprocessing based on APSP was still feasible.

9.2.3   Phase III: Road Networks (2005 – 2008)

A second turning point in research on P2P was the publication of large continental-sized road networks, namely of Europe and the USA. The resulting graphs, made available in 2005, have up to 24 million nodes and 58 million edges. For the first time, it was possible to compare different approaches on a challenging input. Immediately after the publication of these data sets, a kind of "horse race" for the fastest technique on this input started. Inspired by the DIMACS implementation challenge on shortest paths [233], many techniques were developed. Especially the hierarchical approaches surged a high interest since road networks seem to inherit a natural hierarchy due to different road categories, i.e., motorways, national roads, urban streets, and rural roads. In the following, we discuss how to compare speed-up techniques among each other, present the developed hierarchical approaches and their impact on combinations with goal-directed techniques.

Note that some cited papers in this subsection have been published after 2008. The reason for this is that we refer to the later published journal version of this paper. The first publication however, *always* falls within the given years between 2005 and 2008.

Methodology of Comparison. The quality of speed-up technique can be evaluated by three criteria: preprocessing time, preprocessing space, and the resulting speed-up over Dijkstra' algorithm. In general, preprocessing time should be within some hours, even for huge inputs, the additional space should be *linear* in the number of nodes, while query times should be as low as possible.

Engineering Hierarchical Approaches. As already mentioned, the hierarchical approach seems most promising for route planning in road networks: the resulting graphs are sparse, i.e., $m \in O(n)$, and some roads are more important for quickest paths than others. Hierarchical approaches try to exploit this natural hierarchy.

Highway Hierarchies (HH). The first hierarchical speed-up technique capable of preprocessing the European road network was Highway Hierarchies, introduced by Sanders and Schultes in [697] and significantly enhanced in [698]. Preprocessing times are below one hour for Europe and the US while random queries, i.e., source and target are picked uniformly at random, on these inputs take 1 ms on average.

Basically, preprocessing conducts two phases: a node-reduction routine followed by identifying so-called highway-edges. The node-reduction iteratively removes low-degree nodes and introduces additional edges, so called *shortcuts*, in order to preserve distances between non-removed nodes. While this procedure adds only a few edges at the beginning of the preprocessing, more and more edges are added at later iteration steps. Hence, an edge reduction scheme is applied by classifying edges as *highway* edges or not. Therefore, a local neighborhood $N_h(v)$ for each node v is defined. The neighborhood $N_h(v)$ (for some predefined constant h) consists of the h closest nodes to v. An edge $(u, v) \in E_H$ then is a *highway edge* if there exists some shortest path $P = \langle u', \ldots, u, v, \ldots v' \rangle$ with $v \notin N_h(u')$ and $u \notin N_h(v')$. It turns out that non-highway edges can be removed.

Summarizing, the preprocessing adds shortcuts to the graph and assigns a level information to each node, i.e., the iteration step it was removed by node-reduction. The query algorithm is basically a slight modification of a bidirectional Dijkstra algorithm. [698] is a very good example of Algorithm Engineering. It showcases the main engineering principles and aspects which are crucial for a better performance of an algorithm.

The RE algorithm. Inspired by Highway Hierarchies, Goldberg et al. [339] introduces the concept of shortcuts to reach. The key observation is that the reach value of a removed node can be bounded directly during removal. Moreover, Goldberg et al. improve the iterative computation of reaches over [372] by removing all nodes from the graph that have their final reach value assigned. In combination with a similar node-reduction scheme as presented in [698], reach values can be computed for continental-sized road networks within 1 to 2 hours. It turns out that shortcuts make queries more effective by reducing the number of nodes traversed and by reducing the reach-values of the nodes bypassed by shortcuts. The query performance, however, cannot compete with Highway Hierarchies. However, the RE algorithms harmonizes perfectly with the ALT-algorithm (cf. *Combinations* at the end of this subsection).

Transit-Node Routing. In [66], Bast et al. improved the average running times by another two orders of magnitude. The key observation is that if you drive somewhere "far away", you pass by a very few spots, no matter where you go. In a city for example, these important spots are the ramps to the motorway. It turns out that the number of those spots in a continental-sized road network is only about 10 000. So, it is feasible to precompute all distances between those so-called *transit* nodes and from every node to its *relevant* transit nodes, called *access* nodes. With this information at hand, a long- and mid-range query can be reduced to 3 table-lookups yielding query times of below 4 μs for random queries. The final ingredient of Transit-Node Routing is a locality filter in order to decide whether a path is local or not. If the path is local, another speed-up technique, i.e., Highway Hierarchies, is used for determining the quickest path. More layers of transit nodes are introduced for improving the running times of local queries as well. A remarkable fact about Transit Node Routing is that a brief abstract has been published in Science [67].

Highway-Node Routing. Although Transit-Node Routing was the fastest technique by the beginning of 2007, its space consumption is quite high and both the preprocessing and query algorithm are complicated. Highway-Node Routing [712] improves on this by engineering the multi-level method due to [715,716,404,405]. Again, for a given sequence of node sets $V =: V_0 \supseteq V_1 \supseteq \ldots \supseteq V_L$ a hierarchy of *overlay graphs* is constructed: The level-ℓ overlay graph consists of the node set V_ℓ and an edge set E_ℓ that ensures the property that all distances between nodes in V_ℓ are equal to the corresponding distances in the underlying graph $G_{\ell-1}$. A bidirectional query algorithm takes advantage of the multi-level overlay graph by never moving downwards in the hierarchy — by that means, the search space size is greatly reduced. The node classification of HNR is given by a precomputed HH. The advantage of HNR over HH is its easier search algorithm and a simple way to update the preprocessed data in case edge weights change due to delays or traffic jams. The preprocessing effort is less than for Highway Hierarchies, while query times are slightly higher for Highway-Node Routing.

Contraction Hierarchies. The main disadvantage of Highway-Node Routing is that the node classification stems from the complicated Highway Hierarchies preprocessing. [323] improves on this by obtaining a node classification by iteratively contracting the 'least important' node, i.e., the node is removed and shortcuts are added for preserving distances between remaining nodes. This yields a hierarchy with up to $|V|$ levels. Here, importance of a node u is given by several properties such as the degree of node u, the number of already contracted neighbors, and others.

By this procedure, the input graph G is transferred to a search graph G' by storing only edges leading from unimportant to important nodes. As a remarkable result, G' is *smaller* (at least in road networks) than G yielding a *negative* overhead per node. Finally, by this transformation, the query is simply a plain bidirectional Dijkstra search operating on G'. Although the concept of Contraction Hierarchies is much simpler than the one of Reach or Highway Hierarchies, query performance of Contraction Hierarchies is up to 5 times better.

Combinations with Goal-Directed Techniques. Naturally, all hierarchical techniques engineered during the third phase can again be combined with goal-directed techniques. Two candidates proved useful for combinations: the ALT-algorithm and Arc-Flags. In the following, we report on these combinations.

REAL. Goldberg et al. [339, 340] have successfully combined their advanced version of REach with landmark-based A* search (the ALt algorithm), obtaining the REAL algorithm. As already mentioned, reach based pruning requires a lower bound to the target. When this is provided via landmark information, query performance increases over reach-based pruning based on implicit bounds. Moreover, it turns out that running A* instead of Dijkstra harmonizes well with reach. The resulting query performance is comparable to Highway Hierarchies. In the most recent version [340], the authors introduce a variant where landmark distances are stored only with the more important nodes, i.e., nodes with high reach values. By this means, the memory consumption can be reduced significantly.

HH*. [225] combines highway hierarchies [698] (HH) with landmark-based A*search. Similar to [340], the landmarks are not chosen from the original graph, but for some level k of the highway hierarchy, which reduces the preprocessing time and memory consumption. As a result, the query works in two phases: In an initial phase, a plain highway query is performed until the search reaches level where landmark information is available. So, for the remaining search, the landmark distances are available: a combined (goal-directed) algorithm can be used.

SHARC. [71, 72] integrates contraction into Arc-Flags. The key observation is that arc-flags of removed edges during contraction can be set automatically *without* costly computations. Although such computed flags are suboptimal, they can be refined as very last step of the preprocessing. A remarkable fact about SHARC is that Arc-Flags are set in such a way that long shortcuts are preferred over other edges as long as the target is "far away". As soon as the search approaches the target, unneeded (long) shortcuts are pruned. This can be achieved *without* any modification to the query algorithm of Arc-Flags. In other words, SHARC is a unidirectional goal-directed approach that encodes hierarchical properties via the Arc-Flags. The advantage of this approach is its easy usage in scenarios where bidirectional search is prohibitive (cf. Section 9.2.4).

Hierarchical Arc-Flags. In [73], Arc-Flags are combined with Contraction Hierarchies and Transit-Node Routing yielding the fastest known route planning algorithms for (static) road networks. The key observation of both approaches is that the costly preprocessing of Arc-Flags can be restricted to the "upper" part of the hierarchy constructed by the hierarchical ingredient. By this, the search is additionally made goal-directed, improving query performance between a factor of 2 and 10. Since arc-flags are only computed for the "important" part of the graph, the additional preprocessing effort stays limited.

Results. As already mentioned, most of the research during phase III was driven by the available road networks. Since this benchmark data set was used in almost all publications on route planning since 2005, Table 9.1 reports the results of all above mentioned speed-up techniques on the European road network. We report the preprocessing effort in time and *additional* bytes per node. Query performance is evaluated by running random queries, i.e., source and target are picked uniformly at random, and by reporting the average number of settled nodes and the resulting average query times. Note that all experiments were conducted on comparable machines. Also note that preprocessing space does *not* include path unpacking information which in practice needs about 4-8 additional bytes per node.

Table 9.1. Overview of the performance of various speed-up techniques, grouped goal-directed, hierarchical, and combined techniques on the European road network benchmark data set. Column *data from* indicates from which paper the figures where taken from, while *speed-up* refers to the (rough) speed-up over unidirectional Dijkstra. The preprocessing effort is given in hours and minutes and *additional* bytes per node.

		PREPRO.		QUERIES		
		time	space	#settled	time	speed
technique	data from	[h:m]	[bytes/n]	nodes	[ms]	up ($\approx$)
Dijkstra	[74]	0:00	0	9 114 385	5 592	1
Bidir. Dijkstra	[74]	0:00	1	4 764 110	2 713	2
ALT	[226]	0:13	128	74 669	53.6	100
Arc-Flags	[392]	35:56	25	1 593	1.1	5 000
Highway Hierarchies	[711]	0:13	48	709	0.61	9 000
RE	[340]	1:23	17	4 643	3.47	1 600
Transit-Node Routing	[711]	1:52	204	N/A	0.0034	1.6 mio.
Highway-Node Routing	[711]	0:15	2.4	981	0.85	6 500
Contraction Hierarchies	[323]	0:25	-2.7	355	0.16	35 000
REAL	[340]	2:21	36	679	1.11	5 000
HH*	[711]	0:14	72	511	0.49	11 000
SHARC	[72]	1:21	14.5	654	0.29	19 000
CH+AF	[73]	1:39	12	45	0.017	330 000
TNR+AF	[73]	3:49	321	N/A	0.0019	3 mio.

We observe that purely goal-directed techniques either suffer from long pre-processing times (Arc-Flags) or rather low speed-ups combined with a high space consumption (ALT). Hierarchical approaches perform much better: Contraction Hierarchies has a very low preprocessing effort combined with a speed-up of up to 35 000 over Dijkstra's algorithm. If a user is willing to accept a higher pre-processing effort (both space and time), Transit-Node Routing achieves average query times of below 4 μs. These values can be further improved by a combination of Arc-Flags: Contraction Hierarchies with Arc-Flags score query times of below 20 μs, while the goal-directed variant of Transit-Node Routing even has a query performance of below 2 μs.

Final Remarks on Phase III. The most remarkable fact about phase III is the concept of shortcuts. Introduced as (minor) ingredient for Highway Hierarchies, it turned out that shortcuts are *the* solution to route planning in road networks. Any other technique from phase II can be made efficient by a combination with shortcuts reducing preprocessing effort *and* improving query performance significantly. Finally, it even turned out that shortcuts on their own are a very potent and easy speed-up technique, i.e., Contraction Hierarchies.

With the end of phase III in 2008, route planning in static road networks can be considered as "solved". The developed route planning algorithms provide a wide spectrum for the user's needs: the fastest technique, Transit-Node Routing combined with Arc-Flags computes quickest paths in a few microseconds, Contraction Hierarchies combined with Arc-Flags needs less than 50 microseconds with much less space consumption, while preprocessing times of all techniques are within a few hours.

9.2.4 Phase IV: New Challenges on P2P (Since 2008)

While the route planning problem on static road networks was considered as solved, a lot of other problems remained open, e.g., timetable information in public transportation networks, time-dependent (road) networks, handling graph updates due to traffic jams or delays, or finding better routes via multi-criteria optimization. In this last subsection, we discuss very recent developments and open problems for route planning in transportation networks.

Closing the Circle: Back to Theory. A challenging task is to *understand* why speed-up techniques perform so remarkably well on road networks. These networks are almost planar and have small separators. These properties may help to explain the remarkably good practical performance. However, many researchers believe that this is due to the hidden hierarchy in the networks such that only very few edges, i.e., the motorways, are important for long-range queries. Very recently, Abraham et al. [1] provided the first rigorous proofs of efficiency for several heuristics. They introduced the notion of *highway dimension*. Roughly speaking, a graph has small highway dimension if for every $r > 0$ there is a sparse set of vertices S_r such that every shortest path of length greater than r hits a vertex from S_r. Sparse here means that every ball of radius $O(r)$ contains a small number of elements of S_r. The authors succeeded to show that graphs with low highway dimension have provable guarantees of efficiency for several of the methods discussed in this chapter (sometimes with small modifications): Reach (RE), Contraction Hierarchies, Highway Hierarchies (HH), Transit-Node Routing, and SHARC. They also introduced a simple generative model for road networks, and show that the resulting networks have low highway dimension. Future work will show whether enhanced generative models may lead to even tighter bounds.

Another interesting question is whether the problem of determining the preprocessing that minimizes the average search space of a speed-up technique is NP-hard or not.

Network Analysis. Closely related to the just mentioned problem is the question whether we can somehow *predict* the performance of a speed-up technique on a given network. Although some work on such indices has already been done in [75], it seems as if this preliminary study is more a starting than an end point for network analysis with respect to the performance of speed-up techniques.

Augmented Scenarios. Besides giving a theoretical foundation of the achieved results, research moved on to the adaption of the route planning algorithms to augmented scenarios, e.g., dynamic or time-dependent graphs, multi-criteria optimization, other networks, etc. The main challenge here is to preserve correctness of the adapted techniques and to keep the loss in query performance limited.

Dynamic Scenarios. Most of the speed-up techniques discussed so far require the graph to be *static*, i.e., neither the topology nor the edge weights change between two queries. However, *updates* to a transportation network appear quite frequently in practice, i.e., traffic jams or delays of trains. In order to keep the queries correct, the preprocessed data needs to be updated. The most straight forward way would be to recompute the preprocessing from scratch after an update. However, this is infeasible since even the fastest methods need more than 10 minutes for preprocessing. The solution is to identify the invalid parts of the preprocessing and recompute only the affected parts.

Geometric Containers was the first technique studied in such a *dynamic* scenario [817]. The key idea is to allow suboptimal containers after a few updates. However, this approach yields quite a loss in query performance. The same holds for the dynamic variant of Arc-Flags [97]: after a number of updates, the quality of the flags gets worse yielding only low speed-ups over Dijkstra' algorithm. The ALT algorithm, however, works in a dynamic graphs as long as the edge weights do not drop below their initial value. This is a reasonable assumption because in most times, delays or traffic jams only increase the overall travel times. Still, query performance decreases if too many edges are perturbed [226]. The only hierarchical techniques working in a dynamic scenario are Highway-Node Routing and its successor, Contraction Hierarchies. Since edges contribute to shortcuts, they also need to be updated as soon as the original edge is updated. This is achieved by storing sets of nodes from which the preprocessing needs to be repeated if an edge is updated [712, 221].

Summarizing, all above techniques work in a dynamic scenario as long as the number of updates is small. As soon as a major breakdown of the system occurs, it is most often better to repeat the complete preprocessing.

Time-Dependency. In practice, travel duration in a transportation network often depends on the departure time. It turns out that efficient models for routing in almost all transportation systems, e.g., timetable information for railways or scheduling for airplanes, are based on *time-dependent* networks. Moreover, road networks are not static either: there is a growing body of data on travel times of important road segments stemming from road-side sensors, GPS systems inside cars, traffic simulations, etc. Using this data, we can assign *speed profiles* to roads. This yields a time-dependent road network.

Switching from a static to a time-dependent scenario is more challenging than one might expect: The input size increases drastically as travel times on congested motorways change during the day. On the technical side, most static techniques rely on bidirectional search, this concept is complicated in time-dependent scenarios since the arrival time would have to be known in advance for such an approach. Moreover, possible problem statements for shortest paths become even more complex in such networks. A user could ask at what time she should depart in order to spend as little time traveling as possible. As a result, none of the existing high-performance techniques can be adapted to this realistic scenario easily.

The key idea for adapting speed-up techniques to this challenging scenario was the concept of ingredients [219]: identify very basic ingredients of route planning, i.e., bidirectional search, landmarks, Arc-Flags, and contraction, and check which ingredients contribute to which technique. By augmenting the ingredients such that correctness can still be guaranteed, the following speed-up techniques work in time-dependent networks: ALT [609, 222], SHARC [218, 220], and Contraction Hierarchies [70]. One of the most remarkable facts about time-dependent route planning is that the concept of shortcuts gets quite space consuming: the travel time function assigned to the shortcut is as complex as all edge functions the shortcut represents. The reason for this is that we need to *link* the travel time functions (cf. [220] for details). For example, Contraction Hierarchies which relies solely on shortcuts yields an overhead of $\approx 1\,000$ bytes per node [70] in a time-dependent scenario whereas the overhead in a time-independent scenario is almost negligible (cf. Table 9.1). Very recently, first results on how to reduce the memory consumption of time-dependent SHARC have been published [140]. The key idea is not to store the travel time function for shortcuts: instead, it is evaluated on-the-fly. It turns out that the performance penalty is quite low.

For a more detailed overview over time-dependent route planning, we direct the interested reader to [228].

Multi-Criteria. In transportation networks, the quickest connection often is not the "best" one. Especially in railway networks, a user is willing to travel slightly longer if the number of transfers is less. A common approach to cope with such a situation is to find *Pareto-optimal* (concerning other metrics than travel times) routes. Such routes have the property that each route is better than any other route with respect to at least one metric under consideration, e.g., travel costs or number of train changes.

The straightforward approach to find all Pareto-optimal paths is the generalization [381, 538, 579] of Dijkstra's algorithm: Each node $v \in V$ gets a number of multi-dimensional labels assigned, representing all Pareto paths to v. By this generalization, Dijkstra loses the label-setting property, i.e., now a node may be visited more than once. It turns out that a crucial problem for multi-criteria routing is the number of labels assigned to the nodes. The more labels are created, the more nodes are reinserted in the priority queue yielding considerably slow-downs compared to the single-criteria setup. In the worst case, the number of labels can be exponential in $|V|$ yielding impractical running times [381]. In railway networks, however, [595] observed that in such networks, the number of labels is limited such that the brute force approach for finding *all* Pareto paths is often feasible. Experimental studies finding all Pareto-optimal solution vectors (and sometimes also all corresponding Pareto-optimal paths) in timetable graphs can be found in [651, 652, 713, 653, 594, 365, 251]. In most cases a special version of A* is adapted to this scenario. The only speed-up technique developed during phase III that has successfully adapted to a multi-criteria scenario is SHARC [227]. The idea for augmentation is the same as for adaption to time-dependent networks: augment the basic ingredients and leave the basic concept untouched.

Multi-Modal. The interested reader may have noticed that all techniques discussed so far only work in *one* transportation network at a time. On the long run, however, we are interested in *multi-modal* queries where we change the type of transportation along our journey. Unfortunately, it is not sufficient to merge all networks and compute quickest paths in the resulting bigger network: The quickest path may force us to change the type of transportation too frequently. A possible approach to this problem is the LABEL CONSTRAINED SHORTEST PATH PROBLEM. The idea is as follows. Each edge gets a label assigned depicting the type of transportation network it represents. Then, only a path between s and t is valid if certain constraints are fulfilled by the labels along the path.

Up to the beginning of phase IV, only theoretical results [565, 63] or evaluation of basic techniques [62, 61] for the LABEL CONSTRAINED SHORTEST PATH PROBLEM have been published. The only attempt for using insights gained during phase III for multi-modal route planning can be found in [223], which adapts ideas from Transit-Node Routing to the multi-modal scenario. The main idea is to preprocess, for each node of a road network, all relevant *access-nodes* to the public transportation network. Then, the query algorithm can skip the road network which makes up most of the combined network under consideration. The authors report average query times of below 5 ms on a network with 50 million nodes and 125 million edges, a speed-up of more than 30 000 over a label constrained variant of Dijkstra's algorithm.

Flash Memory. As soon as a speed-up technique should be used on a mobile device, space consumption plays a crucial role. Moreover, the data needs to be ordered in such a way that the number of accesses to the flash memory stays as small as possible. Goldberg and Werneck were the first who implemented their goal-directed ALT technique on a mobile device [342]. The results, however, are not very good since query times decrease significantly over the implementation of a server. Keeping the requirement of few flash memory accesses in mind, a hierarchical speed-up technique seems more promising for implementation on a mobile device: most of the query is carried out on a small subgraph. Indeed, Contraction Hierarchies also works in such a scenario [699]. The authors report query times of less than 100 ms on a mobile device. Moreover, they were able to reduce the space consumption *including* the graph from ≈ 20 bytes per node to ≈ 8 bytes per node (all values refer to the European road network).

Remarks on Phase IV. It should be noted that phase IV is not finished yet, for most of the above mentioned problems, only first results have been published. Even for the time-dependent scenario, space consumption is the main issue to

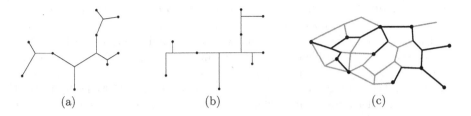

Fig. 9.1. (a) Euclidean Steiner tree, (b) rectilinear Steiner tree on the same terminal set as in (a), (c) Steiner tree in a network with the black dots being the terminals

deal with in the near future. In the field of multi-modal route planning, the ultimate goal would be to have a graph modeling the world-wide transportation network. Computations of best connections (by multi-criteria optimization) in such a huge graph will definitely be challenging, even with the insights gained in phase III. The main academic challenge, however, is the theoretical analysis of the techniques developed so far.

9.2.5 Conclusions

In this section, we presented a review of the research on point-to-point shortest paths along its historical lines. It turns out that we can make up four phases of development. The first phase starts directly after Dijkstra's publication in 1959. During this phase, researchers tried to improve the worst-case running times by the introduction of clever data structures. Moreover, first basic speed-up techniques, i.e., bidirectional search and A*, were developed. The phase ends in 1999 with the publication of Schulz et al. on speed-up techniques [714] leading to a number of follow-up studies and the development of new speed-up techniques. The third phase starts by the introduction of publicly available continental-sized road networks. These challenging huge inputs directly lead to a kind of "horse race" for the fastest technique on this input. The climax of this race was surely the DIMACS implementation challenge on shortest path in 2006 [233]. At the end of the third phase, i.e., in 2008, the route planning problem on static road networks was considered as solved. Hence, in phase IV, researches focused on new challenges in the field of route planning. While some of them are already solved, a lot of open problems still persist.

9.3 Steiner Trees

Given a set of cities we search for a shortest interconnection of these. This problem is one of the variants of the Steiner tree problem which asks for a connection of a set of points (so-called *terminals*) with lines of shortest total length. See Figure 9.1 for different examples of Steiner trees. Historically, the first who considered a Steiner tree problem was Fermat (1601–1665). He posed the following question: *"Given three points in the plane, find a fourth point such that the sum of its distances to the three given points is minimum."* Torricelli found a solution for Fermat's problem with circle and ruler before 1640. The generalization of the problem to n given points for which we search for a point which minimizes the sum of the distances to the n points was considered by many researchers; also by the mathematician Jacob Steiner (1796–1863). In 1934 Jarník and Kössler were the first who investigated the problem to find a shortest interconnection for n given points which interconnects them [433]. Courant and Robbins referred to Steiner in their popular book *"What is Mathematics?"* [194], establishing the notion "Steiner tree problem".

Variants of the Problem. There are two main variants of the Steiner tree problem, the Steiner tree problem in networks and the geometric Steiner tree problem. Given a graph $G = (V, E)$, a subset $T \subseteq V$ called *terminals*, and a length function $l : E \to \mathbb{R}_{\geq 0}$, a *Steiner tree* is a connected subgraph of G spanning all terminals. The Steiner tree problem in networks asks for a Steiner tree with minimum length for the given instance. Such a tree is called *Steiner minimum tree*.

For the *geometric Steiner tree problem* we get as input a set of points (also called terminals) in the plane and a distance function. A Steiner tree is a set of line segments interconnecting all terminals. Moreover, it is allowed to introduce auxiliary points (so-called *Steiner points*) to shorten the overall length of the Steiner tree. A Steiner tree with minimum total length is called Steiner minimum tree.

The Euclidean and the rectilinear versions are the most studied geometric Steiner tree problems. These types of geometric Steiner tree problems only differ by their distance functions which are defined as follows: The Euclidean and rectilinear distance between two points $u = (u_x, u_y)$ and $v = (v_x, v_y)$ are $\|uv\|_2 = \sqrt{|u_x - v_x|^2 + |u_y - v_y|^2}$ and $\|uv\|_1 = |u_x - v_x| + |u_y - v_y|$, respectively. See also Figure 9.1 for examples of Steiner trees. An instance of the rectilinear Steiner tree problem can be transformed into an instance of the Steiner tree problem in graphs. Hanan [380] observed that there is a Steiner minimum tree which includes only edges from the grid induced by vertical and horizontal lines through all terminals. Thus, the constructed graph instance has quadratic size in the number of terminals.

Further variants of the Steiner tree problem are, e.g., the node weighted Steiner tree problem and the group Steiner tree problem. In the *node weighted Steiner tree* problem, besides the edges also the nodes have assigned weights and one wants to find a Steiner tree with minimum total weight. In the *group Steiner tree* problem, the set of terminals is partitioned into groups and we search for a Steiner tree which contains at least one terminal of each group.

All typical variants of the Steiner tree problem are NP–hard, as has been shown for networks [464], for the Euclidean [316] and for the rectilinear Steiner tree problem [317]. Therefore, besides exact algorithms approximation algorithms have been considered. But due to recently developed algorithmic techniques, exact algorithms can now even solve problem instances with several thousands of terminals to optimality. These approaches use powerful combinatorial insights and linear programming based formulations.

Overview. In the following we give a survey on the design and implementation of algorithms for the Steiner tree problem and their development over the years. After describing one key application, we start with a presentation of the progress for exact algorithms in Section 9.3.1. The most interesting fact in this regard is that for almost twenty years there was no substantial improvement. Then two approaches have been developed which we will investigate in Section 9.3.1. The first one mainly based on combinatorics and the second one being a linear programming approach. In Section 9.3.2, we turn to approximation algorithms and heuristics: First, we present a general greedy framework for which many different variants exist. Afterwards, we discuss two heuristics which deliver quite good empirical results.

Applications and Modeling. The Steiner tree problem models several real-world problems. As an example we discuss the physical design of VLSI chips where in the placement and routing process Steiner trees are used. After a very rough overview of the main phases of VLSI design in which Steiner trees are used, we point out different requirements of the chip design and the appropriate Steiner tree models.

In the logical design phase it has been specified which elementary logical units (*circuits*) are to be used and which of the chosen circuits must be connected by wires so that the chip performs in the way it should. Each circuit is characterized by its width, its height, its contact points (so-called *pins*) and its electric properties. A *net* is a set of circuits that must be connected by a wire (as specified in the logical design phase). The list of circuits and the list of nets are the input of the physical design phase. Here, the task is to assign the cells to a certain rectangular area (placement) and connect (route) the nets by wires.

The physical design is a highly demanding process. In a first step, the circuits are embedded on the placement area. In the placement process, each circuit receives its exact position.

If we consider each circuit of a net as a terminal, a Steiner tree is a solution of the required interlinkage of a net. The exact positions of the wires are established in the routing phase. To process the routing in appropriate time, it is divided into global and local routing. In the global routing phase, the topology of the wires is determined. Afterwards, the wires get their exact positions in the local routing phase. For the global design very fast algorithms are needed. Here an inaccuracy up to a certain degree is tolerable. Once a rough layout structure is fixed more accurate models and solutions are required. To work towards a feasible routing, one objective is to minimize the length of the interlinkages of a net. This can be modeled by classical Steiner trees [173]. But in VLSI design many more constraints have to be considered. E. g., the wires can be placed on a number of different routing layers. Each layer prefers one of usually two approved perpendicular directions. To connect adjacent layers so-called *vias* are used. The layers may have varying cost depending on the material and the available routing space. If we want to model these constraints, we search for a *minimum cost Steiner tree* which take via costs and layer costs into account [852].

Other constraints are preplaced macros or other circuits. Wires may run over obstacles but are not allowed to exceed a given length on top of an obstacle. This requirement can be modeled by *length restricted Steiner trees*: A length restricted Steiner tree is allowed to run over obstacles; however, if we intersect the Steiner tree with some obstacle, then no connected component of the induced subtree may be longer than a given fixed length [415, 597].

In the detailed routing phase, we are faced with the group Steiner tree problem, since the logical units typically allow the nets to connect to several electrically equivalent pins [856]. Nowadays, a chip consists of millions of nets and for each net we must solve a Steiner tree problem. The different Steiner trees have to be edge disjoint. This is modeled by the *Steiner tree packing problem*: We simultaneously search for a set of Steiner trees in a given graph where each edge is allowed to be used at most once [361].

Here we see a relevant challenge of Algorithm Engineering because in the placement as well as in the two phases of the routing process we must solve different Steiner tree problems. For a more detailed description of application of Steiner trees in VLSI design, see [516, 257]. On account of these applications we need good and fast algorithms for the problem. It is important to design algorithms which are efficient on real world instances and not only to judge an algorithm by its worst case running time. Even if in early design stages inaccurate solutions are admissible, approximations and heuristics can be in the later design process insufficient. So, also for an NP-hard problem as the Steiner tree problem it makes sense to search for exact algorithms. And as we see in the following section the area of exactly solvable instances could be highly expanded. Another aspect is that we need exact algorithms to determine the empirical performance of heuristics. A benefit of the many applications of the Steiner tree problem is that they provide numerous test instances to measure the performance of implemented algorithms.

Structural properties. The graph of a Steiner tree without an embedding in the plane is called a *topology*. A Steiner tree is called *full* if each of its terminals has degree one. Each Steiner tree is the concatenation of sets of full components. That is, it is either a full Steiner tree or splits into two or more full Steiner trees at terminals of degree greater than one. See Figure 9.2 for an example.

9.3.1   Progress with Exact Algorithms

In 1961, Melzak established the first finite algorithm for the Euclidean Steiner tree problem. His approach is to first construct a minimal tree for every full topology. Then one selects the shortest tree composed of a subset of these generated full trees [564]. Regarding the network Steiner tree problem, a new approach

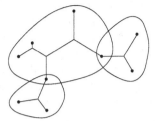

Fig. 9.2. Full components of a Euclidean Steiner tree

was introduced by Dreyfus and Wagner in 1971, which was based on dynamic programming [256]. Here the Steiner minimum tree for a given terminal set is recursively computed by Steiner trees for all proper subsets of the terminals. Both approaches were varied and advanced by multiple researchers, e. g., Smith, Ganley and Cohoon, and Fößmeier and Kaufmann [746, 314, 302]. Comparing these three algorithms points out the gap between theory and practice. The algorithm of Ganley and Cohoon has a worst case running time of $O(k^2 \cdot 2.38^k)$ for instances with k terminals [302]. This bound has recently been improved to $O((2+\delta)^k n^{12/\sqrt{\delta/\ln(1/\delta)}})$ for sufficiently small δ by Fuchs et al. [309]. Björklund et al. [104], in turn, achieved the first $\tilde{O}(2^k n^2 + nm)$ algorithm for the Steiner tree problem in graphs with n vertices, k terminals, and m edges with bounded integer weights. However, these improvements seem to be only of theoretical value, given the progress by other methods. To the best of our knowledge, only problems with no more than 50 terminals could be solved. This opened a huge field for Algorithm Engineering to improve also the practical running times.

In 1998, a breakthrough was established by Nielsen, Warme, Winter and Zachariasen who developed the program GeoSteiner and continuously improved it in the following years [823, 614, 824]. GeoSteiner was developed for solving instances of the Euclidean and rectilinear Steiner tree problems. In 2002 it was generalized to the so-called *uniform orientation metrics (λ-metrics)* where one can use orientations building consecutive angles of π/λ [614]. For the Steiner tree in networks an algorithm and implementation was introduced by Daneshmand and Polzin in 2001 and improved until today [644, 645]. Their implementation is currently the most efficient for the network Steiner tree problem. Measured by the number of terminals it can compute larger instances than the GeoSteiner program. Nevertheless, also the GeoSteiner approach can solve instances with more than a thousand terminals. It is also worth noting that for the GeoSteiner algorithm the problem is modeled as a combinatorial problem, whereas Daneshmand and Polzin use integer linear programming. This emphasizes that it is also important for the design of efficient algorithms and implementations to look for an appropriate modeling of the problem. Due to the impressive performance of these two algorithms we illustrate them in the course of the following two sections.

Combinatorial Approach to the Geometric Steiner Tree Problem. First we present the above-mentioned combinatorial algorithm for the geometric Steiner tree problem introduced by Nielsen, Warme, Winter and Zachariasen. The basic idea is to compute full Steiner minimum trees for subsets of the terminals and subsequently combine them to a tree for all terminals. This approach can be seen as the top-down pendant of the bottom-up method due to Melzak: All topologies are enumerated and Steiner minimum trees are computed by partitioning into full subtopologies.

The rough course of the algorithm can be described as follows: In a first step full Steiner trees are generated and powerful pruning techniques are used to reduce the number of full Steiner trees. Then a subset of the remaining full Steiner trees has to be extracted whose full components can be concatenated to obtain a Steiner tree spanning all terminals.

Up to this new approach the bottleneck was the computation of full Steiner trees. But as a result of the speed-up in generating full Steiner trees, the bottleneck moved to the concatenation of trees. In consequence, researchers started focusing on developing better techniques for this subproblem. One example of this kind is due to Warme who improved the concatenation dramatically [821]. He formulated the concatenation of full Steiner trees as a problem of finding a minimum spanning tree in a hypergraph. In this hypergraph the vertices are the terminals and the hyperedges are the generated full Steiner trees. In previous algorithms, concatenation was always done by enumerating all possible combinations of full components which is apparently not all too efficient. Notwithstanding Warme's approach, the concatenation is up to now still the bottleneck.

The GeoSteiner algorithm was first developed for Euclidean and rectilinear geometries, but later has been adapted also to other geometries. However, the general framework is similar in all cases. In the following sections we describe the two phases of the GeoSteiner algorithm in more detail. We mainly focus on the mechanisms which are responsible for improving the empirical running time.

Generating Full Steiner Trees. Instead of enumerating all topologies for all subsets of terminals, GeoSteiner confines itself to construct only full components without enumerating all subsets. It starts with a selected terminal, designated as a root. Then it grows this component by adding further terminals one by one. Successively each terminal is chosen as the root. Tests are applied to each single tree to determine its possible optimality. We discuss such pruning tests in the next paragraph. Only relatively few subsets of terminals actually survive these tests.

In empirical tests it was observed that approximately less than $4n$ full Steiner trees were to be generated. All other possible Steiner trees could successfully be excluded by the tests. This is a main advantage compared to the approaches developed until then. However, in theory the number of full Steiner trees can

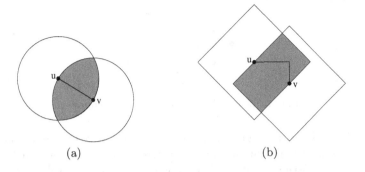

Fig. 9.3. (a) Euclidean lune, (b) rectilinear lune

be exponential in the number of terminals. To illustrate this, the number of full topologies considered by Melzak's approach is

$$f(n) = \sum_{k=2}^{n} \binom{n}{k} \cdot g(k), \quad \text{with} \quad g(k) = \frac{(2k-4)!}{2^{k-2}(k-2)!}.$$

The function g is super-exponential in k, i.e., it increases faster than every exponential function (e.g., $g(4) = 3$, $g(6) = 105$ and $g(8) = 10395$).

Pruning Techniques. A vast set of tests to prune the set of feasible Steiner trees has been developed. We only introduce three of them in the next part to illustrate the structure of these tests. These tests were not only introduced and used by the developers of GeoSteiner but also by other researchers as e.g., Daneshmand and Polzin for the network Steiner tree problem (see Section 9.3.1).

Bottleneck Steiner Distances. Consider a minimum spanning tree on the terminals for the Steiner tree problem. For each pair of terminals memorize the length of a longest edge of the path in this tree connecting them. This length is called *bottleneck Steiner distance*. It is easy to see that no edge on the path of a minimum Steiner tree between two terminals can be longer than the associated bottleneck Steiner distance. So, if during the construction of some full Steiner tree we get an edge longer than the associated bottleneck Steiner distance, this tree can be pruned away.

Lune Property. Another useful pruning technique depends on how close other terminals are to an edge. A *lune* of a line segment uv is the intersection of two cycles both with radius $l(u,v)$ measured in the corresponding metric. The cycles are centered at u and v, respectively (see Figure 9.3). It is straightforward to see that in a Steiner minimum tree no lune may contain terminals. Otherwise, we can construct a shorter tree. Therefore, we check for all edges added during the construction of full Steiner trees whether the associated lune is empty.

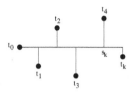

Fig. 9.4. Intermediate rectilinear full component

Upper Bounds. Several good heuristics for Steiner trees are available. They imply upper bounds for the full Steiner trees constructed by the algorithm.

During the construction of a full component F we successively add terminals and Steiner points to the current component. Assume $t_1, \ldots, t_k$ are the terminals and s_k the most recent Steiner point added to F (see Figure 9.4). Use one of the heuristics to determine a Steiner tree S, for $t_1, \ldots, t_k$ and s_k as terminals. This means we force the tree to contain s_k. If S is shorter than the constructed component F then F cannot be contained in a Steiner minimum tree. A simple heuristic is to compute the minimum spanning tree of the terminals. For this and further heuristics see Section 9.3.2.

Concatenating Full Steiner Trees. The concatenation of full Steiner trees is metric-independent in contrast to their generation. In the preceding steps, we have computed a set $\mathcal{F} = \{F_1, F_2, \ldots, F_m\}$ of full Steiner trees. Since $\mathcal{F}$ is the result of the enumeration of all those full Steiner trees that may possibly be part of the solution, some subset of $\mathcal{F}$ constitutes the full components of a Steiner minimum tree for all terminals. Thus, the concatenation problem is to find such a subset of minimum total length.

This problem can be solved using dynamic programming or backtrack search. The first has better asymptotic running time than backtrack search but in common practical scenarios it showed less efficiency. After developing the framework of generating the set of possible full Steiner trees and pruning most of them away, the concatenation phase becomes the bottleneck [823]. On account of this, Warme proved that the concatenation problem is equivalent to finding a minimum spanning tree in a hypergraph with the terminals being the vertices and the computed full Steiner trees being the edges of the hypergraph. Furthermore, he developed an algorithm to solve it [822]. This idea, which will be discussed later, has been a breakthrough and led to excellent practical results. In the next part we give a brief overview on the progress concerning the concatenation of full Steiner trees.

Dynamic Programming. The algorithm of Ganley and Cohoon [314] which is an enhancement of the algorithm of Dreyfus and Wagner [256] is based on full Steiner trees. It uses the fact that a Steiner tree is either a full Steiner tree or splits into two or more full Steiner trees. The algorithm considers subsets of terminals with increasing cardinality and computes a Steiner minimum tree either as a full Steiner tree or composed of full Steiner trees with smaller cardinality.

The running time of this algorithm for the rectilinear Steiner tree problem is $O(n^2 \cdot 2.62^n)$. This approach has been further improved by Fößmeier and Kaufmann to a running time upper bounded by $O(n^2 \cdot 2.38^n)$ [302]. Recently, the worst case running time of this algorithm was shown to be $O(n^2 \cdot 2.357^n)$ [310].

These approaches give the best asymptotic worst case running time for the concatenation problem. However, in practice only sets of about up to 40 terminals can be computed because of the huge memory requirements [301]. It will turn out that *backtrack search* yields better results. We also note that the asymptotic worst case running times of the dynamic programming approach cannot be transferred to the Euclidean case because in contrast to rectilinear Steiner trees no better upper bound than $O(2^n)$ for the number of full Steiner trees is known. The number of needed full rectilinear Steiner minimum trees can be bounded by $O(n \cdot 1.357^n)$ [310].

Backtrack Search. The backtrack search algorithm starts with a single full Steiner tree $F \in \mathcal{F}$ and seeks a tree of shortest length interconnecting all terminals and containing F. More precisely, full Steiner trees are added recursively until all terminals are interconnected or it can be concluded that the constructed tree or subtree cannot be optimal. In the latter case the search backtracks and tries to add another full Steiner tree.

It is essential to apply cut-off tests because otherwise the running time would amount to $\Theta(2^m)$, for m being the number of constructed full Steiner trees, and the algorithm would become impractical. The first who introduced such tests was Winter [838]. He considered only relatively simple cut-off tests such that the concatenation still dominates the generation already for $n \approx 15$. More tests were performed during the next years by Cockayne and Hewgill [179, 180]. They applied *problem decomposition, full Steiner tree compatibility* and *full Steiner tree pruning* to the concatenation phase. Problem decomposition splits the initial concatenation problem into several subproblems. This approach, however, did not stand the test for larger problem instances.

Full Steiner tree compatibility and other pruning tests are significantly better approaches. Two full Steiner trees are incompatible if they cannot appear simultaneously in any Steiner minimum tree. For example they are incompatible if they span two or more common terminals. There is a series of compatibility tests which can be applied without much computational effort while still significantly reducing the number of Steiner trees to be considered.

One good pruning technique is to examine a full Steiner tree F and its set of compatible full Steiner trees. If the union of these is disconnected, e. g., they do not span all terminals, then F can be pruned away.

A real improvement was given by Winter and Zachariasen in 1997 [839]. They managed to solve instances of up to 140 terminals which was a striking progress compared to the dynamic programming methods. However, the latest approach of Warme brought an even more drastic rise concerning the size of instances that could be solved [822].

Hypergraphs. The approach of Warme models the concatenation problem as a minimum spanning tree problem in hypergraphs [822]. The vertices of the hypergraph $H = (V, E)$ are simply the terminals of the Steiner tree problem and the edges reflect the computed full Steiner trees, i.e., each edge is a set of vertices which corresponds to the terminals spanned by the full tree. A *chain* in H from $v_0 \in V$ to $v_k \in V$ is a sequence of vertices and hyperedges $(v_0, e_0, v_1, e_1, v_2, \ldots, e_{k-1}, v_k)$. All vertices and hyperedges have to be distinct and $v_i, v_{i+1} \in e_i$ for $i = 0, 1, \ldots, k - 1$. A spanning tree in H is a subset of hyperedges $E' \subseteq E$ such that there exists a unique chain between any pair of vertices $v_i, v_j \in V$. The uniqueness implies that the spanning tree in H constitutes a Steiner tree in the original instance.

The minimum spanning tree problem is known to be NP–hard for hypergraphs containing edges of cardinality four or more [822]. Warme developed an integer programming formulation that can be solved via branch-and-cut. Let $c \in \mathbb{R}^{|E|}$ be a vector denoting the costs of the edges and $x \in \{0, 1\}^{|E|}$ a vector indicating whether an edge is chosen for the minimum spanning tree or not. For $e \in E$ we denote by $|e|$ the cardinality of the hyperedge e. The linear program is given by:

$$\min c^T x$$

$$s.t. \qquad \sum_{e \in E} (|e| - 1)x_e = |V| - 1 \qquad (4)$$

$$\sum_{e \in E: |e \cap S| \geq 1} (|e \cap S| - 1)x_e \leq |S| - 1, \quad \forall S \subset V, |S| \geq 2 \qquad (5)$$

$$x_e \in \{0, 1\} \qquad \forall e \in E$$

Equation (4) forces the exact number of edges of a minimum spanning tree. Constraint (5) corresponds to the well-known subtour elimination constraints which guarantee that there do not appear any cycles.

This integer program is solved via branch-and-cut. Lower bounds are provided by the linear programming relaxation. The problem of this formulation is the exponential number of subtour elimination constraints given by the inequalities (5). Therefore, we add these constraints by separation methods. More precisely, we first add the constraints for $|S| = 2$. Then we solve the LP and get a solution which possibly violates some not considered constraints. To find violated constraints, one possible approach is to solve a series of max-flow problems.

Experimental Results. All approaches and ideas discussed so far were combined and implemented in a program package called GeoSteiner [824]. Test beds for the implementation are VLSI-instances, instances of the OR-library, TSPLIB instances and randomly generated instances [79, 668]. Instances for 1000 terminals can be solved in less than 4 minutes for both, the Euclidean and rectilinear case[1]. Also for other geometries like the octilinear geometry, where four

---

[1] Computed on a 930 Pentium III Linux machine with 1 GB of memory.

directions differing by 45 degrees are allowed, the largest instance of the OR-library (containing 10000 terminals) can be solved in less than two days [614][1].

In 1998 Warme, Winter and Zachariasen published a comprehensive experimental study of their program [823]. In the following we resume their conclusions. The power of the pruning techniques becomes apparent by the small number of full Steiner trees which are generated. Approximately $4n$ full Steiner trees remain in the rectilinear and $2n$ in the Euclidean case (for n being the number of terminals). An interesting phenomenon detected during tests of the algorithm is that it is not necessarily an advantage to prune away as many Steiner trees as possible. In fact, it was empirically observed that if fewer full Steiner trees are constructed, e. g., more full Steiner trees are pruned away, the branch-and-cut algorithm requires more separation iterations and branch-and-bound nodes [823]. Due to the sophisticated approach for concatenating full Steiner trees, most of the running time for the considered problem instances was spent in the generation phase [614].

On randomly generated instances full rectilinear Steiner trees span on average 2.95 terminals, and full Euclidean 2.70, respectively. For $n = 500$, the largest rectilinear (resp. Euclidean) full Steiner tree of a Steiner minimum tree computed by the program spans 7 (resp. 6) terminals. Once again we observe the importance of the pruning tests. Plenty of full Steiner trees with many terminals can be pruned away once they turn out to be of no importance for the Steiner minimum tree.

However, there is one disadvantage, though. Fößmeier and Kaufmann developed seemingly "difficult" instances for which the number of full Steiner trees fulfilling a so-called *tree star condition* is exponential [301]. These instances are particularly constructed so that most pruning tests do not apply, e. g., the lune property. Therefore, for these instances the algorithm generates super-polynomially many rectilinear full Steiner trees [855]. The number of full Steiner trees and the total CPU-time grows rapidly, although the structure of the optimal solution does not differ radically from randomly generated instances. To solve instances with 52 terminals one needs almost 200 times as much CPU-time as for randomly generated instances with 100 terminals [823]. However, it is not astonishing that an algorithm for an NP–hard problem has exponential running time for some malevolently constructed instances.

Linear Programming Approach for the Network Steiner Tree Problem. In the following we describe the extension of a linear programming approach for the Steiner tree problem in graphs which achieves the best results on commonly used test environments as the OR-library and SteinLib [79, 489]. It was introduced and developed by Althaus, Daneshmand and Polzin. The algorithm consists of various parts which have been enhanced over the last years [642, 644, 643, 25, 645]. In the following we give a description of the overall scheme.

The general framework of the algorithm is a branch-and-bound approach. In the *branching step* a set of possible solutions is partitioned into two non-empty subsets. In the *bounding step* a lower bound for the value of each of the two subsets is computed. A subset of solutions can be excluded if such a computed lower bound exceeds an upper bound. The main focus of Daneshmand and Polzin actually lies not in the branching step but on computing lower and upper bounds and some special preprocessing steps which are also referred to as reduction methods. Only if this process happens to be blocked, a branching step is performed. In the following section we give the required definitions and introduce the underlying integer program. Afterwards, we introduce the main features of the algorithm. The success of the algorithm lies in the interaction of different components such as the computation of lower and upper bounds and also reduction tests. Each of these components was enhanced during the last years. We will describe the process of enhancement.

Directed Cut Formulation. There are many different integer programming formulations and relaxations of the Steiner tree problem. For an overview and theoretical study see the survey of Daneshmand and Polzin [643]. Here we give only the directed cut formulation used in their implementation.

The Steiner tree problem can also be defined for a directed network $G = (V, A, c)$. Let $T \subseteq V$ be the set of terminals and one terminal $t_1 \in T$ designated as the unique *root*. The *Steiner arborescence problem* is to find an arborescence of minimal total length rooted at r and spanning all terminals, that is, a tree with a directed path from r to each terminal.

Any instance of the undirected Steiner tree problem in networks can be transformed into an instance of the directed Steiner arborescence problem: Replace each undirected edge by two directed edges in opposite directions each with the same weight as the undirected one. Then choose an arbitrary terminal as root.

A *cut* in a directed graph $G = (V, A, c)$ is defined as a partition $C = (\overline{W}, W)$ of V with $\emptyset \neq W \subset V$ and $V = W \dot\cup \overline{W}$. We use $\delta^-(W)$ to denote the set of edges $(v_i, v_j) \in A$ with $v_i \in \overline{W}$ and $v_j \in W$. A cut is called a *Steiner cut* if $r \in \overline{W}$ and $(T \setminus \{r\}) \cap W \neq \emptyset$, that is the cut separates r from at least one of the other terminals in T. The underlying integer program used by Daneshmand and Polzin is a directed cut formulation. It was first introduced by Wong [841].

$$\min \sum_{(v_i, v_j) \in A} c_{ij} x_{ij}$$

$$\sum_{(v_i, v_j) \in \delta^-(W)} x_{ij} \geq 1 \qquad \forall (\overline{W}, W) \text{ Steiner cut} \qquad (6)$$

$$x_{ij} \in \{0, 1\} \qquad \forall (v_i, v_j) \in A$$

The inequalities (6) ensure to get a Steiner arborescence. They force to select for each Steiner cut at least one edge from W to $\overline{W}$. Altogether one gets a arborescence rooted at r spanning all terminals. Unfortunately, their can be exponentially many inequalities.

When we drop the integrality constraints of the integer linear program and solving the resulting LP (called LP relaxation), we get an surprisingly tight lower

bound for the original problem. Daneshmand and Polzin investigated that for all
D-instances of the OR-library[2], which consist of instances of graphs with 1000
nodes each, the solution of the relaxation is equal to that of the original program
[644]. Due to the exponentially many inequalities, one cannot solve this relaxation
directly with an LP-solver. Therefore, other methods had to be developed. We describe two methods to get lower bounds. First a combinatoric algorithm to get a
solution of the dual and second a method called row generation.

Lower Bounds. The directed cut formulation is also defined for undirected
graphs [32]. A primal-dual approximation for constrained forest problems based
on undirected cut formulations includes the Steiner tree problem [336]. Although,
the ratio between the upper and lower bound is two, the empirical results for
lower bounds of the undirected cut formulation are worse than those for the directed cut formulation for which no such theoretical bound was known. Daneshmand and Polzin use the directed cut formulation and alter the algorithm so
that they managed to guarantee a bound of two and also derive good empirical
results.

Let y_W be the dual variable associated with the Steiner cut $(\overline{W}, W)$. Then
the dual to the LP relaxation of the above integer program is given by:

$$\max \sum_{(\overline{W}, W) \text{ Steiner cut}} y_W$$

$$\sum_{W, (v_i, v_j) \in \delta^-(W)} y_W \leq c_{ij} \tag{7}$$

$$y_W \geq 0 \qquad \forall (\overline{W}, W) \text{ Steiner cut.}$$

The meaning behind the inequalities (7) is that the values of the dual variables
which have to be maximized are not allowed to exceed the sum of the costs of the
edges of the corresponding Steiner cut. So the dual variables specify the edges
which have to be used by a Steiner tree.

Wong introduced a dual ascent algorithm for the directed Steiner problem
to compute lower bounds [841]. His approach is based on an equivalent multi-
commodity flow relaxation. Wong's approach is summarized in Algorithm 8.

Although the algorithm empirically computes tight lower bounds, the ratio
between the upper and lower bound can be arbitrarily large. As already mentioned, Daneshmand and Polzin presented an algorithm which combines both
features, empirically tight lower bounds *and* a ratio of two [642]: For each terminal $t_k \in T$ the *component of* t_k is the set of all vertices for which there exists a
directed path to t_k using only edges of zero reduced costs. An *active component*
is a component which does not contain the root. The main idea is to grow the
components as long as they are active. Dual variables corresponding to several
cuts which share the same arc may be increased at the same time. To avoid the
problem of decreasing the reduced costs of arcs which are in the cuts of many

---

[2] The OR-library consists of four problem sets B, C, D, E summing up to 78 instances.

Algorithm 8. DUAL-ASCENT ALGORITHM

1: Set the reduced costs $\tilde{c}_{ij} := c_{ij}$ for all $(i,j) \in A$, the lower bound $lower := 0$ and all dual variables $y_W = 0$.

2: **while** A terminal $t_k \in T \setminus \{r\}$ exists which is not reachable from r by edges of zero reduced costs **do**

3:     Let $W \ni t_k$ be the smallest set such that $(\overline{W}, W)$ is a Steiner cut and $\tilde{c}_{ij} > 0$ for all $(v_i, v_j) \in \delta^-(W)$.

4:     Set $\Delta := \min\{\tilde{c}_{ij}|(v_i, v_j) \in \delta^-(W)\}$.

5:     Set $y_W := \Delta$, $lower := lower + \Delta$ and $\tilde{c}_{ij} := \tilde{c}_{ij} - \Delta$ for all $(v_i, v_j) \in \delta^-(W)$.

---

active components they limit the decrease of dual variables which share a vertex by a constant.

The running time of the dual ascent algorithm is $O(|A| \min\{|A|, |T| \cdot |V|\})$. The variation of Daneshmand and Polzin can be designed to run in time $O(|A| + |V| \cdot \log(|V|))$. The empirical results are impressive: The average gap between lower bound and optimum is 0.4% for the D-instances of the OR-library (containing graphs with 1000 nodes). The average running time is .4s. Unfortunately, for larger instances the algorithm becomes too slow. To get a fast routine to solve the relaxed program they introduced a so-called *row generation* which starts with a subset of constraints of the relaxed primal program as the initial program, solves it and then finds violated Steiner cut inequalities and adds them to the program. This procedure is iterated until no Steiner cut inequality is violated anymore. This idea has already been used before to solve the Steiner tree problem in networks [169, 80, 490].

In 2003 Althaus, Daneshmand and Polzin introduced a new technique for computing lower bounds with relaxations [25]. Their approach, called *vertex splitting*, aims at identifying locations in the network that contribute to the integrality gap and split up the decisive vertices. The transformation is equivalent to the integral solution but the solution of the LP relaxation may be improved. In this publication they also describe new separation techniques as well as shrinking operations, the latter being first mentioned by Chopra and Rao [170]. Separation techniques want to find feasible but fractional solutions to separate whereas shrinking operations want to reduce the graph by shrinking operations.

Reductions. Beasley [78] was the first who came up with reductions for the Steiner tree problem in graphs. Combining them with a Lagrangian relaxation (meaning that some side constraints are omitted but their violation is penalized in the objective function) he was able to compute lower bounds with an average duality gap of approximately 12% for 30 instances with up to 50 terminals, 200 edges, and 100 vertices in total. Three years later Beasley used a shortest spanning tree formulation with additional constraints and solved all of these instances to optimality within one second [436]. Again he applied some reduction test to the instances before solving them. Duin and Volgenant captured the idea of reduction and were able to solve all instances to optimality with the reduction tests they developed even faster [262]. This development shows that instances which seem to be hard to solve can turn out to be easy within a few years. In order to have a platform for comparing algorithms without implementing all reduction tests in advance Duin and Voß developed the so-called *incidence instances* which are hard to reduce by all methods known until then [263]. Daneshmand and Polzin improved known tests and designed efficient realizations of them. Furthermore, they designed new tests and integrated them into their packet. It is essential to have a large arsenal of tests because each test works only for a special type of instance. Therefore, a significant achievement can only be obtained in the interaction of a series of tests.

There are two major classes of reduction tests: The *alternative-based* and the *bound-based* tests. The first class looks for alternative solutions such that the current solution can be pruned away. Here we can distinguish two different ideas. The exclusion tests check whether there is an alternative solution of no greater cost without the current part. The inclusion tests check the converse argument. The bound-based tests in contrast compute a lower bound under the assumption that a certain part of the graph is contained or is not contained in the solution. If such a lower bound exceeds a known upper bound we exclude the considered part. In the following we give an example for each of the two tests.

Alternative-based Reduction. One alternative-based reduction is to delete all edges with length greater than the bottleneck Steiner distance as described before for the geometric Steiner tree problem. This test for networks was introduced by Duin and Volgenant [262]. It was enhanced by Duin [261] and made practical by Daneshmand and Polzin who used the following well-known proposition:

Proposition 1. *Let B be the length of a longest edge in the minimum spanning tree for all terminals. Then every edge (v_i, v_j) with $c(v_i, v_j) > B$ can be removed from the network.*

Bound-based Reduction. On top of their use in exact algorithms, lower and upper bounds can serve to reduce the instance. We can use the dual ascent algorithm or the variant of Daneshmand and Polzin for reductions by the following proposition:

Proposition 2. *Let $G = (V, A, c)$ be a (directed) network and $\tilde{c} \leq c$. Let lower' be a lower bound for the value of any (directed) Steiner tree in $G' = (V, A, c')$ with $c' := c - \tilde{c}$. For each $\tilde{x}$ representing a feasible Steiner tree for G, lower' $+ \tilde{c}^T \tilde{x} \leq c^T \tilde{x}$ holds.*

Assume $\tilde{c}$ to be the reduced cost of the DUAL-ASCENT algorithm, then one can easily observe that the lower bound *lower* provided by the algorithm is the same as *lower'* in G'. Thus, for any $\tilde{x}$ representing a feasible Steiner tree $\tilde{T}$, *lower* $+ \sum_{(v_i, v_j) \in A} \tilde{c}_{ij} \tilde{x}_{ij}$ represents a lower bound for $\tilde{T}$. This observation can be used to compute lower bounds for the value of an optimal Steiner tree under certain assumptions, e. g., that the tree contains a certain non-terminal.

Daneshmand and Polzin give many extensions of these tests which are very effective, for example, they introduced new reduction techniques based on vertex separators using partitioning methods [645].

Experimental Results. Daneshmand and Polzin use as test environment instances of the OR-library and SteinLib [79, 489]. The OR-library is older than SteinLib and more experimental results of other algorithms exist for it. On the three groups of instances of the OR-library the results of Daneshmand and Polzin are impressive. The fastest algorithm due to Koch and Martin [490] before this new implementation solves problems of the instance groups C,D and E of the OR-library[3] in 16, 117 and 1020 seconds in comparison to that of Daneshmand and Polzin in 0.2, 0.3 and 1.4 seconds, respectively. This improvement cannot be explained by the speed up of the hardware (a Sun Sparc 20 and a Pentium-II). Daneshmand and Polzin solve instances with up to 11500 terminals in less than one hour [644]. The largest amount of time for a previously solved instance has been 74s (the E18 of the OR-Library). This stands in a huge contrast to 68000s used by Koch and Martin's algorithm. Moreover, in the publication of 2003 also instances are mentioned that were not solved by other authors before. The largest of these instances has about 52000 terminals [25].

As in the program packet GeoSteiner for the geometric Steiner tree problem, the excellent results are achieved by the interaction of different parts. For both problems, the geometric and the network problem, it was important to design powerful pruning and reduction tests to restrict the size of the search space.

9.3.2   Approximation Algorithms and Heuristics

Even though there are powerful algorithms and implementations which solve the Steiner tree problem exactly, there are also approximations for the problem. However, most of them are only considered from a theoretical point of view. The asymptotic worst case running times can be shown to be polynomial but not that good to reach fast implementations. Most of them are not implemented so far.

The most popular approach is the minimum spanning tree heuristic which was suggested several times, e. g., by Choukmane [171] and by Kou, Markowsky and Berman [496]. Almost all approximation algorithms use the spanning tree approximation as a starting point. Improvements are done in different ways. After introducing this fundamental approach, we present a general approximation framework due to Zelikovsky [857]. This algorithm, initially designed for the Steiner tree problem in graphs, has multiple extensions also for the geometric Steiner tree problem. Most of the approximation algorithms for the Steiner tree problem in networks as well as for the geometric Steiner tree problem use this idea for which various kinds of enhancements were developed. Finally, we

---

[3] The C, D and E instances of the OR-library contain instances with 500, 1000 and 25000 nodes, respectively.

describe a local search heuristic which maintains good performances on experimental test beds when it was published [448].

Minimum Spanning Tree Algorithm. We restrict the illustration of the algorithm to the Steiner tree problem in graphs. Nevertheless, it can also be adapted to the geometric Steiner tree problem.

The minimum spanning tree algorithm (see Algorithm 9) takes as input the distance network. The *distance network* for a graph $G = (V, E)$, a subset $T \subseteq V$ and length function $l : E \to \mathbb{R}_{\geq 0}$ is the complete graph $G_D = (T, E_D)$ on the terminal set with length function $l_D : T \times T \to \mathbb{R}_{\geq 0}$. For each pair of terminals $v, w \in T$ the length $l_D(v, w)$ of the edge between v and w is defined as the length of a shortest (v, w)-path in G.

Algorithm 9. MST ALGORITHM

1: Compute the complete distance network G_D.
2: Compute a minimum spanning tree T_D in G_D.
3: Transform T_D to a subgraph T of the original graph: Replace each edge of $E(T_D)$ by the corresponding shortest path in G.
4: Compute a minimum spanning tree T^* in T.
5: Transform T^* into a Steiner tree by removing all leaves which are not terminals.

Instead of computing a Steiner minimum tree, the idea of the algorithm is to determine the minimum spanning tree for the set of terminals. This gives an approximation of the Steiner minimum tree. The bottleneck of this algorithm is the computation of the distance network. We must compute $O(|T|)$ shortest paths each requiring at most $O(n \log n + m)$. Mehlhorn improves the running time by using instead of the distance network a sparser network while still ensuring that every minimum spanning tree of this sparse network to be also a minimum spanning tree of the distance network [554]. He uses an application of Voronoi regions to graphs and includes an edge between two terminals in the sparser network only if there exists an edge between the Voronoi regions of these terminals. With this we get a running time of $O(n \log n + m)$ for the minimum spanning tree algorithm with an instance of n vertices and m edges [554]. Variations of this heuristic have been tested by de Aragão and Werneck [204].

For the Steiner tree problem in graphs this algorithm delivers a 2-approximation. For the rectilinear and Euclidean Steiner tree problem the bounds are $3/2$ [418] and $2/\sqrt{3}$ [258], respectively. Empirical tests show that these worst-case bounds, although tight for certain instances, are overly pessimistic for typical instances [204].

Greedy Local Search. As input for the algorithm we assume an instance of the Steiner tree problem in networks or of the geometric Steiner tree problem. First, we compute the distance network on the set of terminals as defined above.

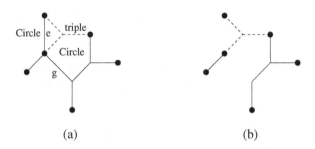

Fig. 9.5. The inserted triple is shown by dashed lines. In (b) the longest edges are removed.

Furthermore, we choose a $k \in \mathbb{N}$ and a selection function $f : T \to \mathbb{R}$ with T the set of terminals. The algorithm (see Algorithm 10) starts with a minimum spanning tree as a first solution. In each step it tries to improve the current solution by selecting a Steiner minimum tree for a subset of the terminals. The subsets are of cardinality at most k. The selection is managed by the function f.

Algorithm 10. GREEDY LOCAL SEARCH

1: Compute the minimum spanning tree for the terminals T (in the distance network).
2: Set $i := 0$.
3: **while** There is an improving full component measured by the selection function f
   do
4:     Choose a subset $\tau_i \in T$ with cardinality $\leq k$ that minimizes f.
5:     Contract the vertices of τ_i.
6:     Set $i = i + 1$.
7: Output the Steiner tree by undoing the contraction of $\tau_0, \tau_1, \ldots, \tau_{i-1}$.

The difference between the various algorithms lies in the choice of k and the selection function f. The selection function measures the estimated *gain* of selecting some subset. This means the improvement is compared to the current solution. Zelikovsky chooses $k = 3$ and defines the function as follows: If we insert the Steiner minimum tree (denoted as $\mathrm{smt}(\tau)$) for a triple τ, then the tree contains two cycles. For each of these cycles choose the longest edge denoted by e and g, respectively. See also Figure 9.5. The selection function is defined as $f(\tau) = l(e) + l(g) - l(\mathrm{smt}(\tau))$. This gives an 11/6-approximation for the Steiner tree problem and the running time is $O(nm + |T|^4)$ for a graph with n vertices and m edges [857].

Berman and Ramaiyer generalize Zelikovsky's approach to full components with cardinality k and achieve a performance ratio of 1.734 for large k [96]. However, this last algorithm gives only a theoretical profit because it is not practicable for large k.

A further improvement by Robins and Zelikovsky takes the *loss* of a Steiner tree as basis for the selection function [677], [678]. The loss was introduced by Karpinski and Zelikovsky [466]. It measures how much length is needed to connect the Steiner points of a full component to its terminals. The idea is to penalize the choice of Steiner points that require long edges to connect themselves to a terminal. The loss Loss(A) of a set of Steiner points A is defined as the minimum length forest in which every Steiner point $v \in A$ is connected to a terminal. The length of the Loss(A) is denoted by loss(A). The second idea now is to take into account not the absolute but the relative difference, i. e., to relate the length of the chosen component to its benefit. Assume that the algorithm has already chosen the full components $\tau_1, \ldots, \tau_i$. The length of the tree after choosing these sets is denoted as mst($K/(\tau_1 \cup \ldots \cup \tau_i)$). Then the selection function measures the loss relative to the benefit of the chosen component:

$$f(\tau) := \frac{\text{loss}(\tau)}{\text{mst}(K/(\tau_1 \cup \ldots \cup \tau_i)) - \text{mst}(K/(\tau_1 \cup \ldots \cup \tau_i \cup \tau))}.$$

The performance ratio of this algorithm is 1.550, but it is mainly of theoretical interest because simpler heuristics achieve also good results and are much easier to implement. Generally, little is known about experimental results with these approaches. Most of them are impractical, i. e., computing the loss of a Steiner tree is quite expensive compared to the expected gain.

Only a variant, called batched-greedy heuristic, of Zelikovsky's greedy algorithm for uniform orientation metrics introduced by Kahng, Măndoiu and Zelikovsky achieves good results [446, 447]. They compute approximations for instances up to 500,000 terminals in less than half an hour. These instances cannot be solved by GeoSteiner. The worst-case running time of the algorithm is $O(n \log^2 n)$. The main difference to Zelikovsky's approach is, that the gain is not updated each time a triple is contracted.

Iterated 1-Steiner Heuristic and Edge-Based Heuristic. The iterated 1-Steiner Heuristic of Kahng and Robins is a simple local search heuristic which was introduced in 1992 [448]. The algorithm starts with a minimum spanning tree for the terminals T and an initially empty set of Steiner vertices I. In each step it checks whether the current solution can be improved by adding a Steiner point v to I. That means to compute the minimum spanning for the set $T \cup I \cup \{v\}$ and remove all Steiner vertices of degree one and two. If the resulting tree is shorter than the previous then add v to I. Otherwise do nothing. The algorithm stops when no Steiner point leads to an improvement of the solution. For quasi-bipartite and rectilinear instances Robins and Zelikovsky proved that this heuristic achieves an approximation ratio of 3/2 [677], [448].

A slightly similar approach which adds in each step an edge and removes the longest edge of the induced cycle was introduced by Borah, Owens and Irwin for the rectilinear Steiner tree problem in 1999 [121]. The algorithm also starts with a minimum spanning tree of the terminals. Then it performs the edge replacements as long as the solution can be improved. See Figure 9.6 for one step of the

Fig. 9.6. Insert the edge e and delete f

algorithm. The running time of this algorithm is $O(n^2)$, or with sophisticated data structures $O(n \log n)$. This approach has better empirical running time than the iterated 1-Steiner heuristic and can be applied to instances with tens of thousands of terminals.

Linear Programming Based Heuristic. In 1999, Măndoiu, Vazirani and Ganley proposed a heuristic which uses as subroutine an algorithm of Rajagopalan and Vazirani who introduced a 3/2-approximation for the metric Steiner tree problem on quasi-bipartite graphs [604, 659]. *Quasi-bipartite graphs* do not contain edges connecting pairs of Steiner vertices. The algorithm of Rajagopalan and Vazirani is based on the linear programming relaxation of the so-called bidirected cut formulation for the metric Steiner tree problem. Măndoiu, Vazirani and Ganley algorithm computes a Steiner tree of a quasi-bipartite subgraph of the original graph using Rajagopalan's and Vazirani's algorithm. The process is iterated with the selected Steiner points as additional terminals. So the algorithm is allowed to consider larger quasi-bipartite subgraphs. This approach has better average running time than the iterated 1-Steiner heuristic and also GeoSteiner. Moreover, this heuristic gives on average better solutions than the iterated 1-Steiner heuristic.

9.3.3   Conclusions

In this section we presented the Steiner tree problem to give an example for Algorithm Engineering. The earlier algorithms can solve only problems with few terminals. Intensive studies of the structural properties of Steiner trees and the behavior of known algorithms led to very good ideas and approaches to solve the problem also for larger real-world instances up to tens of thousands of terminals. An interesting observation is that theoretical improvements do not automatically yield to enhancements of the practical behavior: For the GeoSteiner implementation it was noticed that it was not necessarily good to prune as much full Steiner trees away as possible because the concatenation phase slows down in consequence of this [823]. We see that extensive experimental studies are capable of detecting bottlenecks of algorithms which can systematically be removed. It is also helpful to have common libraries of test instances to get better comparisons of the different implementations. One further conclusion is that up to now all successful algorithms and implementations are improved in all parts of the appropriate algorithm. It does not suffice to improve one detail of the problem to be solved. Excellent results are achieved by good interaction of different methods. In particular, this can be seen by the work of Daneshmand and Polzin who achieve good results due to the interaction of a vast amount of Algorithm Engineering techniques: First the modeling of the problem as an integer linear program based on Steiner cuts, second the different approaches to get good lower and upper bounds, and finally the methods to reduce the problem size by applying preprocessing methods.

We have restricted our consideration to the classical Steiner tree problem without further constraints. As already mentioned, there are lots of variants for the Steiner tree problem as, e.g., the group Steiner tree problem or the node weighted Steiner tree problem. For some of these variants very little is known about the practical performance of algorithms. Here is a further field of research with potential for Algorithm Engineering.

9.4 Voronoi Diagrams

Voronoi diagrams are subdivisions of the plane into nearest neighbor regions with respect to a given set of geometric objects called sites. Figure 9.7 shows a Voronoi diagram of a set of point sites with respect to Euclidean distance. Voronoi diagrams are ubiquitous in geometric computing. Since they have so many applications in different areas, Algorithm Engineering issues have been addressed in a number of research papers on algorithms for computing Voronoi diagrams.

As discussed in Chapters 3 and 6, precision caused robustness problems are a major issue in the implementation of geometric algorithms: Geometric algorithms are usually designed under the assumption that we have exact real arithmetic at hand. As we have seen in Section 3.5.2 of Chapter 3 on "Algorithm Design", straightforward implementations of geometric algorithms produce numerical errors. Geometric algorithms can be very susceptible to those errors because of the strong dependency of combinatorial decisions on numerical results. Inconsistency in these decisions can then lead to all kind of errors as illustrated in [471]. Additionally, many papers on geometric algorithms leave handling of degenerate configurations to the reader. This also holds for papers on algorithms for computing Voronoi diagrams.

We have chosen Voronoi diagrams for this geometric case study, because different approaches to attack precision and robustness problems have been successfully applied to the design and implementation of Voronoi diagram algorithms, culminating in Held's extremely robust VRONI software for Voronoi diagrams for points and line segments of line segments on one hand, and in exact Voronoi diagrams implementations on the other hand. Such implementations for computing exact Voronoi diagrams, even for degenerate input, is offered by the CGAL and LEDA software libraries and J. R. Shewchuck's TRIANGLE software, which computes the Delaunay triangulation, the geometric dual of the Voronoi

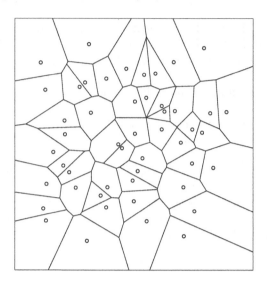

Fig. 9.7. (Part of the) Voronoi diagram of a set of points with respect to Euclidean distance

diagram of a set of points. All these are master pieces in Algorithm Engineering in Computational Geometry.

Before we consider geometric Algorithm Engineering issues regarding the computation of Voronoi diagrams of point sites and Voronoi diagrams of line segments, both for Euclidean distance, we give a more precise definition, discuss applications, and then briefly present standard algorithms.

9.4.1   Nearest Neighbor Regions

Actually, Voronoi diagrams have been reinvented in different areas. Descartes [239] already used them informally in 1644. Voronoi diagrams are also known as Dirichlet tessellations and Voronoi regions as Thiessen polygons. The name Voronoi diagram goes back to a paper by Georgy Voronoi in 1908 [815].

Voronoi diagram partition the plane into nearest neighbor regions with respect to a given finite set of geometric objects, usually points, and a distance function. In the context of Voronoi diagram computation, the given objects are called *sites*. The goal is to compute regions such that all points in a region have the same closest site among the given ones. Figure 9.7 provides an example.

Let S be a set of sites and d be a distance function to measure distance from a point to a site. Let x_i and x_j be sites in S. The set of all points in the plane that have equal distance to x_i and x_j is the *bisector* $B(x_i, x_j)$ of x_i and x_j:

$$B(x_i, x_j) = B(x_j, x_i) = \{\, x \in \mathbb{R}^2 \mid d(x, x_i) \;=\; d(x, x_j) \,\}.$$

The set of points closer to x_i than to x_j is called the *dominance region* of x_i over x_j:

$$R(x_i, x_j) = \{\, x \in \mathbb{R}^2 \mid d(x, x_i) \;<\; d(x, x_j) \,\}.$$

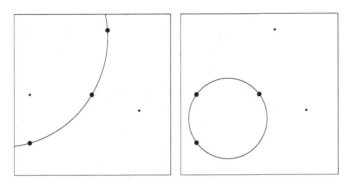

Fig. 9.8. Left: invalid circle (contains a point); right: valid circle (no point enclosed)

The intersection of all dominance regions of x_i over the remaining sites in $\mathcal{S}$ is the *Voronoi region* $VR(x_i)$ of x_i,i. e.,

$$VR(x_i) = \bigcap_{j \neq i} R(x_i, x_j).$$

The *Voronoi diagram* is the set of points belonging to no region, i.e., the set of points that have at least two closest sites. A point with at least three closest sites is a *Voronoi vertex*. A Voronoi vertex v is *degenerate* with respect to $\mathcal{S}$ if v has more than three closest sites in $\mathcal{S}$.

In this case study we consider Voronoi diagrams with respect to the Euclidean metric only. We only consider sets of point sites and sets of line segments and points as sites. For a set of points $\mathcal{S}$, the *Delaunay diagram* is the so-called dual of the Voronoi diagram. Two points $x_i, x_j \in \mathcal{S}$ are connected by the straight line segment $\overline{x_i x_j}$ if and only if their Voronoi regions have a one-dimensional common boundary. If there are no degenerate vertices in a Voronoi diagram, its dual is a triangulation, the *Delaunay triangulation*, and it is the unique triangulation so that the circumsphere of every triangle contains no sites in its interior, cf. Figure 9.8. The Delaunay triangulation has the nice property, that it maximizes the minimum angle over all triangulations of $\mathcal{S}$. Figure 9.9 shows the Delaunay diagram corresponding to the Voronoi diagram shown in Figure 9.7, refined to a triangulation.

Every vertex in the Voronoi diagram (see Figure 9.10(a)) corresponds to exactly one triangle in the Delaunay triangulation (see Figure 9.10(b)). The circumcircle of the triangle has its center in exactly that Voronoi vertex. Therefore, the Voronoi diagram can be obtained from the Delaunay triangulation by replacing each triangle in the Delaunay triangulation with the center of its circumcircle and the three bisectors that meet there. Figure 9.8 shows an illustration of a circumcircle not contributing and a circumcirle contributing to the Delaunay triangulation for the point set used in Figure 9.10.

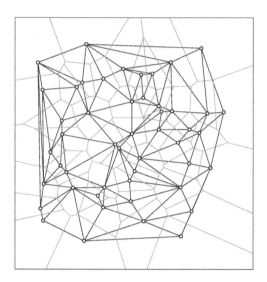

Fig. 9.9. (Part of the) Voronoi diagram of a set of points with respect to Euclidean distance and a corresponding Delaunay triangulation of the point set

9.4.2   Applications

Voronoi diagrams have many applications in various disciplines beyond Computational Geometry. We list only a few of them:

In the Area of Pattern Recognition they can support the layout of Neural Networks by partitioning the input space given by the training patterns (see [128]).

In Art Voronoi diagrams are applicable for creating abstract ornamental designs (see [454]). Kaplan specifically outlines two very useful features of Voronoi diagrams: the conservation of symmetry and the continuity of the output when changing the generating points. This allows for interesting tilings of the plane as well as for smooth, nearly organic animations of tilings.

In Biology, e.g. in the area of ecology and botany, they can help with the simulation and analysis of systems of growing plants. Those plants, being depicted as points in the Voronoi diagrams, are characterized by their coordinates, radii and the type of species. Based on different growing rules for different plants, the interdependencies of plant interactions in a dense system of growing plants are of interest. To study the size-distance and size-area relationships of those living spaces, weighted Euclidean Voronoi diagrams provide an efficient way to model those influences. For example, the area occupied by a plant is computed as the area of the Voronoi region corresponding to this plant (see [320] for the software tool).

In Materials Sciences (see Roberts and Garboczi in [673]) most real cellular solids are random materials, while most of the known theoretical results are for periodic models. To obtain realistic elastic properties for random models

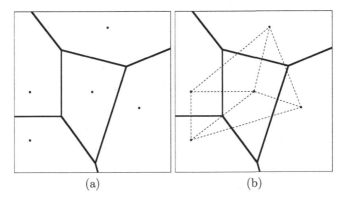

Fig. 9.10. Example Voronoi diagram and Delaunay triangulation

Voronoi diagrams can be used to generate models that more adequately represent the structures of foamed solids. Roberts and Garboczi were able to reveal an even more complex density dependence of the aforementioned elastic properties than predicted by conventional theories that relied only on periodic models.

In Robot Motion Planning Voronoi diagrams can be used for determining paths around obstacles while always maintaining the maximum possible distance to them. A simple approach would be to limit movements along the Voronoi bisectors (see [106] for a more sophisticated idea).

TSP Solving can benefit from the structures known from Voronoi diagrams and Delaunay triangulations as they can be used for heuristic approaches (see [706]).

For further applications we refer the interested reader to Christopher Gold's www.voronoi.com web-site and David Eppstein's Geometry in Action[4] pages on Voronoi diagrams.

9.4.3 Algorithms

Next, we turn to Voronoi diagram computation. Opposite to the previous case study on Steiner trees, polynomial-time algorithms are available. As usual in theory, the algorithms are designed for a machine that can compute exactly with arbitrary real numbers.

Standard geometric algorithm design paradigms have been applied to Voronoi diagram computation and to the construction of the Delaunay triangulation, including the *incremental approach*, the *divide-and-conquer approach*, and the *sweep-line approach*. Let us shortly talk about their basic ideas, before going into details, especially on the caveats of implementing a "robust" algorithm.

---

[4] http://www.ics.uci.edu/~eppstein/gina/voronoi.html

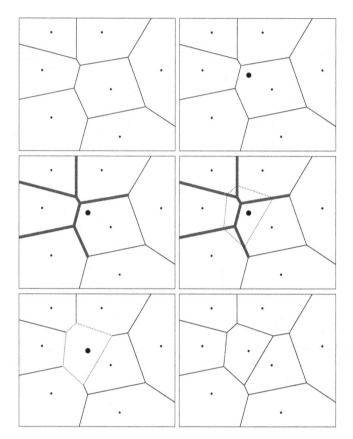

Fig. 9.11. Illustration of the incremental approach (from left to right and top to bottom): Current state, the new point to be inserted, the invalidated Voronoi edges, the Voronoi region of the new point, the Voronoi region after the removal of conflicting bisectors, the updated Voronoi diagram.

Incremental Construction. The idea is well-known: The algorithm starts out with any three sites of the complete problem. For these three sites the Voronoi diagram is trivial. The other sites are added successively and the Voronoi diagram is updated each time until all sites were added (see Fig 9.11).

For each newly inserted site all invalidated Voronoi regions have to be removed and the new partition has to be made. As the algorithms run time clearly depends on the number of regions and edges that need to be updated, it suffers from "bad" insertion orders and can speed up with "good" insertion orders. To minimize the influence of such effects randomization helps a lot.

The Divide-and-Conquer Approach. In 1975, Shamos and Hoey [728] presented the first deterministic worst-case optimal algorithm for Voronoi diagrams. Their approach is based on the divide-and-conquer paradigm, very similar to

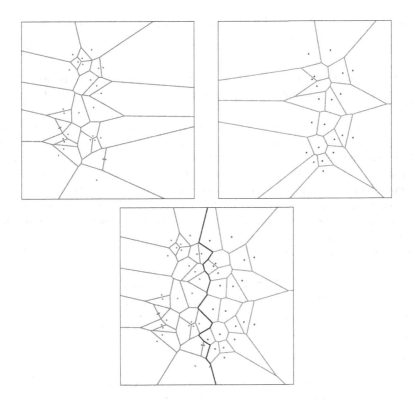

Fig. 9.12. Divide-and-conquer: On top, the left and right point set's Voronoi diagrams and below the resulting (combined) Voronoi diagram with the bisector of the two point sets.

general divide-and-conquer approaches. However, in geometric applications it helps to "divide" in such a way that locality information on the involved geometric objects is preserved. This eases the "merge" step.

1. divide the set of sites into two parts of equal size by a vertical line
2. generate the Voronoi diagram recursively for each part
3. merge the two parts

The interesting steps are the first and the last one. When both can be carried out in $O(n)$ then the overall run time of the algorithm will be in $O(n \log n)$.

After presorting the elements of S by their $x-$ and $y-$coordinates (which requires $O(n \log n)$ time), the dividing line can be chosen easily within constant time, for example by taking the median. This solves the first step.

The merge process then requires the *merging bisector* of the left and right part to be determined in order to form the solution, cf. Figure 9.12. One possible approach utilizes the relation between Voronoi diagrams and the convex hull: The convex hull of a (partial) Voronoi diagrams can be constructed in $O(n)$, as all points with an unlimited Voronoi region are part of the convex hull. Details can be found in [51].

The Sweep-Line Approach. The basic idea with a sweep-line approach is to convert a static n-dimensional problem into a dynamic $(n - 1)$-dimensional problem.

Consider the classic example: The discovery of all intersections of lines segment in the plane. In a sweep-line approach a vertical line L is moved from the left to the right across the plane. A list stores all line segments that L currently intersects in a bottom-up order. When L hits a line segment's endpoint, the line segment is added to or removed from the list, respectively. After each update of the order only pairs of line segments which just became neighbors have to be checked for intersection (instead of a quadratic number of line pairs with the brute-force approach). To apply the sweep-line idea to Voronoi diagrams of points in the plane some more effort is required though, see Figure 9.13 for an illustration.

The interested reader will find more details about the sweep-line method in the original paper by Fortune [294] and in Seidel [721] or in Aurenhammer and Klein [51].

9.4.4   The Implementation Quest

While most algorithms developed in numerical analysis are stable, in the sense that the computed output is close to the correct output for a small perturbation of the input data, most algorithms in computational geometry are neither stable nor robust in this sense. In geometric computing rounding errors can easily lead to inconsistent decisions that the algorithms cannot handle, because it was designed under the assumption of exact arithmetic that excludes such inconsistencies. There are two obvious approaches to deal with numerical problems caused by the discrepancy between theory, here exact real arithmetic, and practice, where inherently inexact floating-point arithmetic is used. Namely, either adopt theory or change practice. The former means to take imprecision into account when designing geometric algorithms, the latter means to enable exact computation in practice. Indeed, this is possible for many classes of problem instances and many geometric algorithms. Both approaches have been successfully applied in the context of Voronoi diagrams.

9.4.5   The Exact Geometric Computation Paradigm for the Computation of Voronoi diagrams

A branching in the execution of an algorithm depends on the sign of some numerical expressions that ultimately depend on some constants and the numerical data in the input only. The computation of the signs of these expressions is usually encapsulated in so-called geometric primitives. Of course, we avoid inconsistent decisions, if we guarantee all decisions, i.e., all sign computations, to be

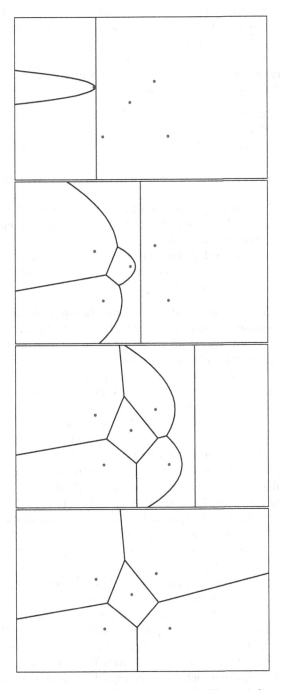

Fig. 9.13. Illustration for the sweep-line approach for Voronoi diagrams of points in the plane

correct. This is the basic idea behind the so-called *exact geometric computation paradigm*: Exact numerical values are not necessary, exact sign computations, and consequently exact decisions, suffice.

Although each geometric algorithm uses different geometric primitives, there are geometric primitives that are used in many geometric algorithms. We provide some examples for geometric primitives:

Coordinate comparison. Does point p have a smaller, the same, or a larger x-coordinate than point q?

Sidedness. Does a point lie on, on the left side, or on right side of a directed line?

In-circle test. Does a point lie inside or outside of a circle defined by three points, or on it?

Order along a bisector. Do we reach the Voronoi vertex of points p, q, and r before we reach the Voronoi vertex of points p, q, and t when walking along the bisector of points p and q in a given direction?

Order of circle event and point event. Is the x-coordinate of the leftmost point of the circumcircle of three points q, r, and s smaller than, equal to, or larger than the x-coordinate of point p?

Such geometric primitives are used in the computation of Voronoi diagrams. For many geometric problems, only rational numbers arise during evaluation of the related geometric primitives, if all input data are rational numbers, too. This holds for the computation of Voronoi diagrams of point sites with Euclidean distance, but unfortunately not, if line segments are involved, because bisectors are non-linear in this case, cf. Figure 9.14, and the coordinates of Voronoi vertices might be irrational algebraic numbers.

Thus, if only rational numbers arise during the geometric computations, a rational number type based on arbitrary precision integers suffices to get numerically correct results and hence correct decisions, thereby guaranteeing correct Delaunay triangulation for point sets and correct combinatorics, i.e., topology, of the Voronoi diagram of a set. Such exact rational number types are provided by the GNU multiple precision library [334] and LEDA [513] for example, see also Chapter 7. However, this approach slows down computation significantly. Karasick et al. [458] report on a slow-down factor of several orders of magnitude when computing Delaunay triangulation of a set of points using a hand-made arbitrary precision rational arithmetic.

Therefore, Karasick et al. [458] already exploit alternative approaches, based on the observation that high numerical precision is required only if the numerical value whose sign we are interested in is close to zero. This is the basic idea of floating-point filters that is discussed in Section 6.7 on "Geometric Algorithms". Their paper was the first approach implementing the exact geometric computation paradigm using speed-up techniques partially based on interval arithmetic in the context of computing Delaunay triangulations and, equivalently, Voronoi diagrams. However, while the approach is similar on an abstract level to the floating-filters, that were introduced and discussed a few years later by Fortune and van Wyk [298] for the computation of Delaunay triangulations, the

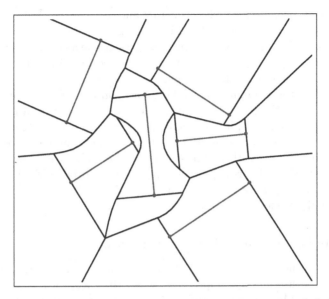

Fig. 9.14. (Part of the) Voronoi diagram of a set of line segments and their endpoints with respect to Euclidean distance

engineering details are quite different. In particular, Fortune and van Wyk used static analysis techniques and integer arithmetic tuned for special applications. Furthermore, they provide an expression compiler to ease the tuning task.

Finally, Shewchuk [731] presented very efficient exact predicates for the computation of Delaunay triangulations, which are based on techniques by Dekker, Knuth, and Priest for extending the precision of floating-point arithmetic. These techniques are discussed in Section 6.7 of the chapter on "Implementation Aspects". In contrast to standard floating-point filters, which switch to an exact arithmetic if the floating-point computation can not be verified by the computed error bound, Shewchuk's predicates use several stages to increase adaptiveness. While this could be achieved by cascaded filters as well, Shewchuk's predicates have the additional advantage that they reuse previous results in later stages. His predicates guarantee exact sign computations as long as intermediate floating-point results are representable. No further a priori information on the numerical data in the input, e.g., integrity in a certain range, is required.

Thanks to such techniques correct Delaunay triangulation software based on the exact geometric computation paradigm is often slowed-down only by a small factor less than two compared to its purely floating-point based counterparts. This requires a word of explanation: For random input points degenerate and nearly degenerate configurations are unlikely, and thus software based on the exact geometric computation paradigm mainly has to verify its floating-point computations at low additional cost. The additional cost is much higher for (most) degenerate and nearly degenerate cases, because now additional, more expensive computations are required. But in this case, we compare apples and oranges anyway, because for such degenerate and nearly degenerate cases, purely floating-point based software will crash or "at best" compute slightly incorrect results. Despite of its algorithmic beauty, the sweep-line algorithm is not the best choice in terms of exact geometric computation, because of the use of geometric predicates with a higher arithmetic demand.

Compared to the computation of Voronoi diagrams of point sets with Euclidean distance in the plane, the arithmetic demand involved in the computation of Voronoi diagrams of line segments in the plane is much higher, especially because algebraic numbers arise. Here, general purpose number types for exact geometric computation with real algebraic numbers like `CORE::Expr` [457] and `leda::real` [141] (as described in Section 6.7.3) could be used. However, some implementations use more restricted number types with better performance for what is actually needed.

9.4.6   Topology-Oriented Inexact Approaches

Algorithms designed for the real RAM model with exact real arithmetic usually can not cope with numerical imprecision when the theoretical exact arithmetic is simply replaced by inherently inexact floating-point arithmetic. Especially for input instances involving degenerate and near degenerate configurations, algorithms designed for exact real arithmetic are very likely to fail. Thus, numerical imprecision has to be taken into account already at the design phase. The so-called topology-oriented approach is an approach pioneered by Sugihara and co-workers [765, 764, 619] in the context of Voronoi diagrams. The basic principle is to rank topological correctness and consistency higher than the result of numerical computations.

When designing according to the topology-oriented approach, first some "topological" properties are selected that every valid solution to a problem instance must have. Preserving these topological properties is the guideline for the algorithm. The properties must be efficiently checkable with combinatorial and topological computation which does not involve any numerical computations. Thus, the checking can be assumed to be correct. The basic part of the algorithm is based on purely combinatorial and topological computation in such a way that the selected properties are maintained. Numerical computations support the combinatorial and topological computation. Numerical results that contradict the results of combinatorial and topological computation are simply refused. The combinatorial and topological computation has priority. Usually, the computed solution contains some numerical data as well, but they are not guaranteed to correspond to the computed combinatorial and topological parts. Since the combinatorial and topological computation has right of way, there are no inconsistencies caused by numerical imprecision.

In order to keep the algorithms simple, the topology-oriented approach does not handle degenerate cases. Since numerical computations are not trustworthy, because they are error-prone, the numerical detection of a degenerate case is not trusted either. Instead, the numerical computation is refused and a non-degenerate topology is computed.

A very strong point of the topology-oriented approach is the lack of assumptions on the precision or the accuracy of the numerical computations. Algorithms designed according to the topology-oriented approach "work" even if all numerical results are replaced by random values! Working means, the computed solutions has the desired topological properties. The numerical data in the output will be garbage, however.

To illustrate the idea, we apply the topology-oriented approach to the construction of the Voronoi diagram of points in the plane [764, 765]. The selected topological properties for the Voronoi diagram of points in the plane are

- (a) every site has its own Voronoi region,
- (b) every Voronoi region is connected, and
- (c) two Voronoi regions share at most one edge.

The algorithm computes the Voronoi diagram incrementally. The basic step from $n - 1$ to n points consists of two parts: (1) finding the Voronoi regions affected by the insertion of the new point, and (2) updating the affected Voronoi regions. Part (1) is supported by numerical computations. By giving combinatorial and topological computations higher priority it is ensured that the part of the Voronoi diagram to be removed is always a tree-like structure. By ensuring this property, the selected topological properties are preserved. Whenever the numerical computations would tell to remove a cyclic subpart, these numerical computation would be refused. Of course, by numerical computations coordinates of Voronoi vertices are computed. There is no guarantee that these coordinates give us a crossing-free embedding of the computed topological structure. However, preserving the topological properties guarantees that such a crossing-free embedding of the computed topological structure indeed exists.

For an illustration of the update step we refer to Figures 9.15 and 9.16. The exact coordinates of the six newly inserted vertices are not important, cf. Figure 9.17.

One could say that the numerical and topological part complement each other by taking turns in solving the problem. That way it is always guaranteed, that the result of the algorithm is *a* topologically correct structure, although it might be (depending on the numerical errors) far away from the "exact" solution. With reasonably accurate arithmetic we will even get *the* topologically correct structure for the given input in many cases. Furthermore, if the algorithm is implemented correctly, the resulting program will never crash. However, since degeneracies are not handled, we never obtain the exact topological structure in the presence of degeneracies (in the output), even if an exact arithmetic is used.

The topological approach is considered attractive, because degeneracies are completely avoided, in contrast to "epsilon-tweaking", where whatever is close to zero is interpreted as zero, i.e., nearly degenerate is considered degenerate, and closeness is determined by some, often mysterious, epsilon. Perturbation also avoids handling degenerate cases. While symbolic perturbation requires exact sign computations, the more recent approach of controlled perturbation [378] by Halperin and Shelton purely relies on floating-point computation. The chosen non-symbolic perturbation must let all carried-out floating-point computations

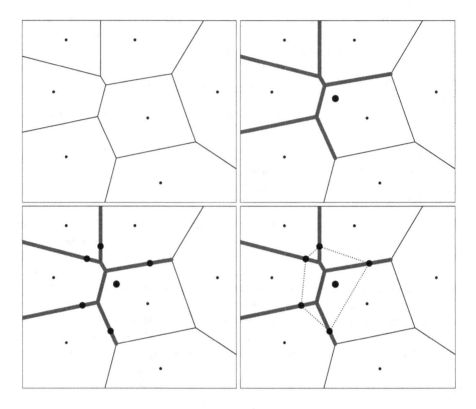

Fig. 9.15. a) Intermediate Voronoi diagram. b) The new point and the Voronoi edges that need to be updated. c) Each of the outer edges obtains a new Voronoi vertex on it. d) The Voronoi regions of the new point consists of these vertices.

be easily verifiable. Thus, floating-point filter would never fail. This approach has been recently applied to the computation of Delaunay triangulations by Funke, Klein, Mehlhorn, and Schmitt [311].

9.4.7   Available Implementations

Both mainstream approaches to tackle precision and robustness problems in geometric computation have been successfully applied to the computation of Voronoi diagrams, including Euclidean Voronoi diagrams for point sets, or equivalently the Delaunay triangulation of the point sets, and for sets of line segments. Regarding point sets the efforts culminate in the code available in the C++ libraries CGAL [151] and LEDA [513] and Shewchuk's TRIANGLE software on one hand and Sugihara's FORTRAN code on the other hand. The former intensively use the filtering techniques discussed above for efficiency while the latter implements a topology-based approach. Regarding sets of line segments the efforts culminate in Karavelas' CGAL implementation and Held's VRONI code. While Karavelas'

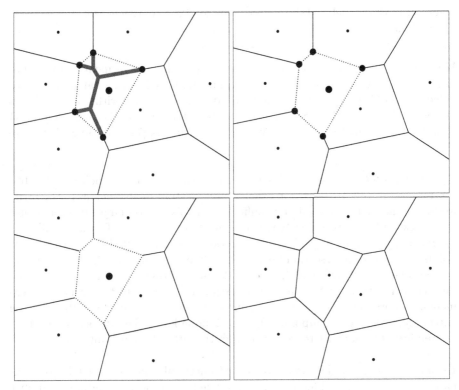

Fig. 9.16. a) New Voronoi region and the skeleton marked for removal. b) Skeleton removed. c) The new point and its Voronoi region. d) The resulting Voronoi diagram.

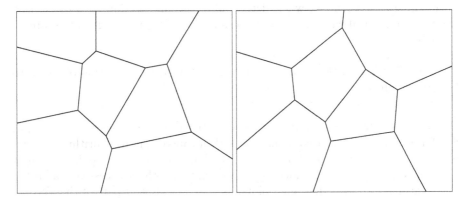

Fig. 9.17. Two different, but topologically equivalent Voronoi diagrams

implementation is based on the exact geometric computation paradigm, VRONI uses the topology-oriented approach as well and therefore does not guarantee utmost accuracy, but a certain topological correctness of the resulting Voronoi diagram. In the sequel we take a closer look at these approaches for line segment Voronoi diagrams.

Karavelas' Implementation. [459] computes the line segment Voronoi diagram in the plane, even for intersecting segments. Based on exact arithmetic provided by CGAL [151] it uses a randomized incremental algorithm and achieves better performance than Seel's *avd* (shortcut for *abstract Voronoi diagrams*) code for Euclidean Voronoi diagrams of line segments [718]. Its main ideas are the following:

Site Representation. When representing intersection points by their coordinates, the number of bits required for exact representation might increase arbitrarily up to exponential size. While *avd* suffers from this fact on larger instances that can quickly fill the available RAM of a machine, Karavelas follows a different approach: Line segments without intersections are represented by their two endpoints. A point of intersection between two line segments is not represented by its coordinates, but by the endpoints of the intersecting line segments. A partial line segment, created by a cut of a line segment with up to two other line segments, is represented by the original line segment's end points as well as by the cutting line segments' endpoints. This technique keeps the number of bits that are required for an exact representation of the sites at a constant level.

Geometric Filtering. The well-known arithmetic filtering at first tries to evaluate a predicate, e.g. sidedness, using a fixed-precision floating-point number type and keeps track of the numerical error. Should the error become too large, the predicate is determined using an exact number type. Geometric filtering now means to test for shortcuts before the numerical evaluation of predicates is activated. For example, when determining the intersection of two line segments no numerical calculations are necessary at all if those segments share an endpoint.

Random Shuffling of the input data is used to avoid bad insertion orders with high probability.

PLVOR as introduced by Imai [425] uses the topology-oriented approach of Sugihara and Iri [764] in combination with an incremental algorithm to compute the Voronoi diagram of a disjoint set of line segments and points. At first *PLVOR* constructs the Voronoi diagram of points and then successively adds the line segments (without their endpoints, as they are already part of the Voronoi diagram of points).

The program features no exceptional rules to handle degeneracies, so they have to be resolved by the topology-oriented approach alone. It is written in Fortran and accepts only integer coordinates.

VRONI has been engineered by Held [385]. It can be seen as a successor of pvd (= Pocket Voronoi diagram), a program by Sethia, Held and Mitchell [725] for computing the Voronoi diagram of line segments that form non-intersecting polygons. The main objectives in the design of VRONI were to create a completely reliable and fast program based on conventional floating-point arithmetic, that can handle any polygonal input of arbitrary size. VRONI is also based on the topology-oriented approach and uses a randomized incremental algorithm as well. The construction of the Voronoi diagram is then a two-split process: Similar to the *PLVOR* code by Imai [425], at first the Voronoi diagram of the endpoints of the line segments (and further points) is computed. The second step then inserts one line segment after another and modifies the existing Voronoi regions appropriately.

In order to ensure the correctness of the resulting Voronoi diagram, the correctness of each single step has to be guaranteed. VRONI achieves this by including the following features:

- a careful implementation of the numerical computations
- an automatic *relaxation of epsilon thresholds* and
- a *multi-level recovery process* in combination with a so-called *desperate mode*.

Numerical Considerations. Typical degeneracies are zero-length edges, partially overlapping edges, vertices on the edges of a polygon as well as (self)intersections. Unfortunately, most of them are the undesired result of algorithmic or numerical problems within the generator software. As advised by the "defensive design" paradigm everything that cannot be influenced by the programmer, e.g., external data, should be treated as unpredictable.

In VRONI at first the duplicate points are removed via a simple scan after sorting them by their x- and y-coordinates. Every input point is then assigned an index in the sorted array of points so duplicate points will have the same index. The intersection point of two lines sharing a common endpoint is revealed easily by these indices. Also the zero-length line segments can be discarded.

Although the topology-oriented approach ensures that the solution fulfills various criteria, it is obvious that the quality of the final output significantly depends on the fidelity of the numerical computations. So additionally to the basic topology checks the following numerical plausibility checks are used:

- When inserting a new Voronoi vertex (= center of a new circumcircle) during the incremental update, this vertex has to lie on each bisector it forced to be cut off (removed bisectors are not considered).
- The clearance distance of the new Voronoi vertex has to lie between the minimum and maximum of those of the previous vertices.
- In the case of an (already inserted) line segment as a generator, the new Voronoi vertex has to lie on the same side of that very line as the vertex it replaced.

Those properties help to detect whether the result is valid or not. If one of them fails the multi-level recovery process is initiated (detailed below).

Relaxation of ϵ-Thresholds. With the numerical errors coming from using standard floating point arithmetic an epsilon has to be given that defines the bound for the question: "Is a given number still equal to zero?" or in terms of geometry: "How far must two points be at least apart for not being considered as the same point?" This user-given bound, called upper bound, together with the minimum epsilon given by the used floating point arithmetic, called lower bound, gives a range for VRONI to work in. When approaching a point in the program where numerical data computation is required, the ϵ-relaxation works as follows:

- Initialize epsilon to the maximum precision (the lower bound).
- Conduct the necessary calculations and check whether they are correct according to the topological properties and the numerical sanity checks.
- If the data is not correct, raise epsilon and repeat the calculation until either the data is considered correct or the upper bound for epsilon is hit.

When the upper bound is reached, "local plausibility checks" (see *Numerical Considerations* above) are conducted. If the relaxation should not succeed the "*Backup Algorithms*" stand in.

Backup Algorithms. The typical routines needed during the computation of the Voronoi diagram include the determination of roots of second-order polynomials as well as solving linear equations. As standard algorithms for those tasks might suffer from instabilities, there exists at least one backup routine in VRONI for every required numerical computation. Those routines are executed instead of the original ones, whenever the input data indicates that the calculation might be numerically unstable. They mostly have a larger run time for the same task, but are designed to avoid any instability by renouncing vulnerable operations like square roots or divisions.

Desperate Mode. VRONI also contains a so-called "desperate mode" that is activated whenever all of the above methods failed. It then tries to extract usable information from already achieved calculations and decides how to continue. If a specific numerical computation did not succeed, then an approximation of the calculation result is determined and used instead. Again special care has been taken not to use any operation that is not defined for floating point numbers. Second, if the numerical computation should succeed but one or more of the following sanity checks fail, the result which fits best is chosen. Finally any violation of topological properties is "healed", by force if necessary. This mode guarantees that VRONI will terminate correctly, whatever happens.

Algorithm 11 provides a schematic overview of the program flow of VRONI.

9.4.8   Conclusions

Voronoi diagrams are an important tool in computational geometry and its application areas. Therefore, the computation of Voronoi diagrams has gained a lot of attention. Both the exact geometric computation paradigm as well as topology-oriented approaches have been successfully applied. Comparing both approaches

Algorithm 11. Schematic program flow of VRONI

1: remove duplicate points
2: remove zero-length edges
3: topologically construct the Voronoi diagram of points
4: **while** (there is a not-yet-inserted line segment left) **do**
5:     insert the new line segment
6:     update the Voronoi diagram topologically
7:     calculate the new vertices' coordinates numerically using the ϵ-relaxation
8:     **if** (a numerical plausibility check fails) **then**
9:         use a backup algorithm instead
10:         **if** (the backup algorithm also fails) **then**
11:             enter DESPERATE MODE

in terms of performance is like comparing apples and oranges. With the topology-oriented approaches you get an approximate structure quickly. However this approach only preserves some essential properties. While most of these approaches are perfectly robust, since they never crash, but always compute some result, there are no guarantees regarding stability, i.e., the quality of the computed result with respect to the actual input data. On the other hand, the exact geometric computation paradigm guarantees exact results, even in the presence of degeneracies. However, this utmost accuracy does not come for free. Especially in the presence of degeneracies it takes time to compute the exact result.

For both approaches it took a lot of geometric Algorithm Engineering to achieve what we have now: A user with inaccurate input data can go for the much more efficient topological approach, while a user more interested in accuracy of the output might prefer to invest more running time to get exact results. This situation is rather rare in computational geometry. Since implementing the exact geometric computation paradigm is much easier with available tools, this approach has gained more attention over the past decades. It allows for a more straightforward implementation and does not require redesigning algorithms in order to deal with imprecision. On the other hand, VRONI nicely illustrates what a clever imprecision-oriented (re)design can achieve.

Chapter 10. Challenges in Algorithm Engineering

Matthias Müller-Hannemann and Stefan Schirra

This final book chapter is meant as a brief reflection on the current status of Algorithm Engineering and its future development. It is devoted to the many challenges this discipline has to face. By *challenges* we mean things that are worthy to invest a significant research effort, and working on these problems promises a high potential impact.

In early 2007, the authors made a poll among colleagues questioning about the most important challenges for Algorithm Engineering. We also asked them about future trends and developments for the discipline they envision. The answers we obtained covered a broad range of issues which we tried to integrate into the following discussion and overview. We acknowledge thankfully contributions by David Bader, Ulrik Brandes, Hervé Brönniman, Dan Halperin, Riko Jacob, Michael Jünger, Ernst Mayr, Cathy McGeoch, Kurt Mehlhorn, Petra Mutzel, Stefan Näher, Hartmut Noltemeier, Knut Reinert, Peter Sanders, Anita Schöbel, Steve Skiena, Anand Srivastav, Raimund Seidel, Berthold Vöcking, and Ingo Wegener. Another valuable source for challenges is the grant proposal by Mehlhorn et al. [556] for the DFG funding initiative on Algorithm Engineering (www.algorithm-engineering.de). Nevertheless, the following compilation describes the personal view of the authors in first place.

We start our discussion with general remarks on the discipline, and then list challenges along the different phases of the Algorithm Engineering cycle. Thus, the order of topics should not be interpreted as a ranking with respect to importance.

10.1 Challenges for the Algorithm Engineering Discipline

According to the French philosopher Bruno Latour, much science-in-the-making appears as art until it becomes settled science [508]. Algorithm Engineering is a quite young and evolving new discipline. Therefore, it is quite natural that it has to face a number of challenges with respect to its own development. The main challenge is probably to further establish Algorithm Engineering as a scientific discipline in algorithmics and more generally in computer science.

In algorithmics, theoretical and experimental research have been to a large extent separated since the 1970s and 1980s, and experimental work in algorithmcs often does not yet get the credit it deserves, although experimentation is an integral part of the process of taking theoretical results to practice. Experimental algorithmics is still often only considered as a substitute where theoretical analysis fails, not as a complementary method to better study what is best suited to solve real-world problems at hand in practice. Still, driven by the need for practical solutions Algorithm Engineering has entered algorithmics over the past decade. Besides classical asymptotic algorithm analysis, there are now more and

M. Müller-Hannemann and S. Schirra (Eds.): Algorithm Engineering, LNCS 5971, pp. 446–453, 2010.
© Springer-Verlag Berlin Heidelberg 2010

more field experiments that measure runtimes on real-world problem instances in order to get more precise information about program performance in practice [549]. But Algorithm Engineering is more than that, e.g. it can also lead to new algorithmic insights.

The most general and ambitious goal of Algorithm Engineering is to close the gap between theory and practice in algorithmics. This by itself is obviously a major challenge as Algorithm Engineering has to make use of the algorithmic knowledge developed in theory and thus has to turn sophisticated methods into (re)usable software. Regarding runtime prediction the gap between asymptotic unit cost analysis and performance on real computers is ever increasing with modern system architectures that have multicore processors and multilevel caches. Engineering practical efficient algorithms for multicore, parallel, and distributed systems is another major general challenge in Algorithm Engineering these days.

10.1.1   Realistic Hardware Models

The demand for experimentation in Algorithm Engineering exists because asymptotic analysis and the models of computation used in theory do not allow for predicting the actual performance in practice accurately. The gap between theory and practice in algorithmics is partially due to a gap between models of computation, like a random access machine with uniform cost measures, and existent computers today. Thus we need more useful models. We need models that are closer to the actual hardware and allow for more accurate performance prediction. Ideally, such better models are still simple enough for design and analysis, but let the algorithm designers tune their algorithms prior to the experimentation phase or might even render the experimentation phase obsolete.

Modern architectures are particularly challenging. With respect to memory hierarchies, the cache-aware and cache-oblivious models are important steps forwards, but they have their limitations as well and still must prove impact on practice.

Use of flash memory is one of the latest developments. Flash memory will either completely replace magnetic hard disks or become at least an additional secondary storage in the near future. Flash memory is similar to RAM with respect to its ability of fast random reads, but also similar to hard disks as a block based device with slow write operations. Since write operations require the erasure of a whole block, and erased blocks wear out, erasures should be spread out almost evenly over the blocks to extend the life time of the chip. This is called *wear leveling* and requires new algorithmic designs, something like "flash-aware" or "flash-oblivious" algorithms. The latter is particularly desired since flash technology still changes very rapidly. Algorithmic research in this area has just started [21].

The key challenge today is the design and analysis of efficient, high-performance algorithms for multicore and parallel processors. The industry has adopted multicore as a mechanism to continue to leverage Moore's Law, and parallel algorithm design now moves from a special niche to the mainstream. Yet the masses of algorithm designs and programmers think "sequentially" and no canonical model of parallel algorithm design is accepted for multicore processors such as the IBM Cell, Intel TeraOps, and other homogeneous and heterogeneous multicore chips. While it is difficult to engineering algorithms for sequential processors due to memory hierarchies, it is even more difficult to incorporate other artifacts such as memory bandwidths, hierarchical systems (multicore, SMP, clusters), transactional memory, heterogeneous cores, speculative multithreading, and so on. The design of good models for parallel and distributed computing that take thread safety into account is quite challenging. It is not clear how Algorithm Engineering will model multiple cores in a canonical fashion and refactor all algorithms into multicore frameworks. This demand will certainly become more important in the near future.

10.1.2   Challenges in the Application Modeling and Design Phase

As for software engineering, which spans both the design and the implementation phase, fostering reuse and extracting code commonality for generic design are primary objectives.

Due to the ubiquitousness of information technology and increasing capacity of storage media, the amount of (measured) data that has to be processed has become huge in many applications. Dealing with such massive data sets is challenging with respect to memory hierarchies. On the other hand, massive data sets are particularly interesting from a more theoretical point of view, because many asymptotically efficient methods developed in theory become relevant for such large problem instances only.

Massive data streams often require that decisions must be made by algorithms that merely make one single pass over the stream. The design of one-pass, space-efficient algorithms is a relatively new area which is likely to benefit from Algorithm Engineering techniques a lot.

But even without the strong data access restriction of one-pass algorithms, large scale instances usually have to be solved in linear (or even sublinear) time. Thus the question is how far can we get if we restrict ourselves to the class of linear time algorithms with small or moderate-size hidden constants, for some appropriate notion of "small" or "moderate-size".

Given that most real problems in practice involve NP-hard or even more difficult problems, algorithmics has developed a large body of approximation algorithms that are guaranteed to find near-optimal solutions, for various definitions of "near". The classical quest is to find the best possible approximation guarantee for a problem which has led to the development of many very complicated algorithms. Here Algorithm Engineering may help if we shift our focus towards drastically simpler and practically applicable algorithms which still come with reasonable performance guarantees. There seems to be a big playground to explore the trade-off between approximation guarantees and efficiency.

Modeling uncertainty is another challenge in the modeling and design phase. For example, real-world data are often subject to uncertainty because of measurement errors. Nevertheless, many algorithms for such applications are designed under the assumption of exact input data, or — at best — by using simplifying assumptions on probability distributions of the input, for example, for the location of a point in a GIS algorithm or for the distribution of processing times in stochastic scheduling.

10.1.3   Challenges in the Analysis Phase

Analogously to the quest for more realistic models of computation a major challenge of the analysis phase is to achieve better performance prediction in practice. This subsumes better analysis techniques for expected running times, gaining more insight and developing better tools for comparison of expected performance, and finding further ways towards explaining well-behavior in practice. The latter includes extending smoothed analysis to other problems, see also Chapter 4. The traditional competitive analysis of on-line algorithms is often way too pessimistic. Here we probably need a new concept and methodology to analyze algorithms in such a setting more appropriately.

Again, modern computer architectures with multicore processors and memory hierarchies and parallel, cluster, and distributed systems pose further challenges for algorithm analysis in Algorithm Engineering. Regarding the analysis of experimental results there is certainly a need for developing good statistical tools for analyzing data. The existing tools are intended to answer different types of questions — for example, techniques intended for fitting curves can be adjusted for use in finding bounds on curves. Probably we should collaborate more closely with statisticians and data analysis experts to find methodologies specifically designed to address the types of questions we find interesting.

Finally, there are algorithm-specific and domain-specific challenges for algorithm analysis, for example, analyzing quality and efficiency of meta-heuristics. Many practical problems are so badly understood that no one is able to formalize the function to be optimized. Often this function can be obtained only by an experiment or by the simulation of the experiment. Then non-specialized randomized search heuristics like local search, taboo search, Metropolis, simulated annealing and all variants of evolutionary and genetic algorithms seem to be the methods of choice. Unfortunately, these methods come typically without any performance guarantee. Therefore, we need to build a theory of randomized search heuristics and to improve the methods to analyze the expected optimization time of these heuristics for various problems.

10.1.4   Challenges in the Implementation Phase

The transition from the high-level pseudo-code description of a sophisticated algorithm or data structure into an efficient implementation often appears to be more difficult than expected. In fact, many algorithms developed in theoretical computer science are regarded as purely theoretical and no attempt has been made to implement them due to the large hidden constants that are involved. With rare exceptions, theory papers specify the running time of algorithms only in big-Oh-notation and do not even specify the approximate size of the suppressed constants.

A typical example for the semantic gap between abstract specification and implementation is a famous $O(nm \log n)$ matching algorithm by Galil, Micali, and Gabow [312] from 1986. This algorithm makes extensively use of sophisticated data structures, in particular of concatenable priority queues. Its first implementation succeeded in 2000 by Schäfer and Mehlhorn [563].

We need further attempts to implement some of the more advanced algorithms that have never been implemented. Quite recently, Tazari and the first author started a project to implement a PTAS suggested by Borradaile et al. [126, 127] for the Steiner tree problem in planar graphs. Our experience with this attempt and our accompanying computational study suggest that we can learn a lot from such endeavors. In this particular case our own expectations of what might be achievable with such an algorithm has been well exceeded in computational experiments with large instances [776].

Even the implementation of relatively easy algorithms can be demanding. Small implementation details can lead to significant differences in the constant factors.

The ability to perform successful experiments is closely related to good software engineering in the implementation phase. Insightful experimentation requires that we are able to exchange data structures and subalgorithms in a most flexible way. In Algorithm Engineering we are not only reusing existing software, but we are also interested in providing our algorithmic solutions in such a way, that they are reusable for us and others. Hence, software libraries that make algorithmic advances available are crucial for the implementation phase. It is getting more and more important that such libraries can exploit modern computer architectures with multicore processors and modern memory hierarchies.

Many people in Algorithm Engineering would prefer such libraries as open source. Chapter 7 discusses what makes a good software library for Algorithm Engineering. In Algorithm Engineering it is specifically important that software libraries are flexible and adaptable and ease the exchange of components. This allows for engineering the combination that is most appropriate for the actual problem instances by experimentation.

10.1.5   Challenges in the Experimentation Phase

Experimental studies should be conclusive. They are not so much interesting by its own, but they should allow a computer scientist to make the right design choices for producing software for a particular problem. The results of experiments should be generalizable and portable. Apparently, this is not so easy to achieve.

We need better, more generally accepted guidelines for experimental setup and hypothesis testing.

In the experimentation phase of Algorithm Engineering choosing the right problem instances for testing is always challenging. For example, often there are several input parameters affecting the performance. Then we have to see how these parameters influence the test results and we have to find appropriate parameter settings and variations thereof for the experiments. Evaluating performance when parameters affecting the performance are changed, and how to compare non-problem-specific methods whose performance depends on many parameters, is a major challenge in Algorithm Engineering. Maybe, there is no general solution for this problem.

Similarly, it is difficult to choose input for testing beyond worst and average cases systematically. What are other relevant and interesting cases and how do we get corresponding problem instances? While we might be able to generate such problem instances artificially, it is usually quite hard to get real-world data with the characteristics we want, if we know what we want at all.

Benchmark test libraries make experimental studies more comparable and should support predictability of algorithmic behavior. In some areas, good collections of meaningful benchmark problem instances are available, especially for hard optimization problems (for example, MIPLIB, TSPLib, SteinLib). In some others, such collections do not exist. It is a striking observation that realistic problem instances are especially rare for certain classes of polynomially solvable problems like network flows or matching. Seemingly no-one knows how to construct typical instances for these problem classes. Likewise, the artificial construction of "hard instances" for many, if not most known algorithmic approaches for efficiently solvable problems would be desirable since the gap between observed performance and predicted worst-case performance is quite large.

Comparability of experimental studies on the same subject and reproducibility of experiments are a must for good Algorithm Engineering. Comparability and reproducibility make Algorithm Engineering research more transparent. Nevertheless, both are often cited as primary challenges in Algorithm Engineering. Reproducibility requires a detailed comprehensive description of what has been done and this usually takes more space than what is available in conference proceedings. Or it requires publication of all the software and data sets. While there are many papers that publish relevant code and problem instances used in the experiments, in computer science, including Algorithm Engineering, it is by far not common practice yet to do so.

Writing good experimental papers is difficult. Experimental results almost ever give rise to further questions which require additional experiments. Thus, it is much harder to finalize an experimental paper, while a theoretical paper can be finished as soon as all proofs are completed. Referees are often in a difficult position. They have, of course, to ensure that a paper is sound and answers the right questions. But they have also to refrain from requesting too many additional experiments.

The ACM Journal of Experimental Algorithmics (JEA) has been initiated with the aim (among others)

> "to distribute programs and testbeds throughout the research community and to provide a repository of useful programs and packages to both researchers and practitioners."

As the publication of programs and test data is not mandatory it seems difficult to encourage authors to do so: looking back to publications of JEA in recent years, it is more the exception than the rule that a paper comes with related resources. The recently added JEA Research Code Repository (www.jea.acm.org/repository) is a repository for code, data, and test files that accompany papers presented at conferences and workshops addressing problems in Experimental Algorithmics. It is intended for those cases where the publisher of the proceedings does not support electronic publication of code and test data. This initiative needs further support by the community.

The sister discipline Mathematical Programming has recently decided to set up a new journal — Mathematical Programming Computation, edited by Bill Cook of Georgia Tech. Its first issue appeared in July 2009. Its review process includes the evaluation and testing of accompanying software. The journal encourages authors to publish their software as open source. Submission of articles describing non-open source software will require that referees are given access to executable codes that can be used to verify reported results. If this policy will be accepted by authors in practice, it would be a big step forward also in Algorithm Engineering.

Finally, it would be nice to have workbenches for experimentation. They should allow non-experts, e.g., more theoretically oriented people, to experiment with various alternatives quite easily in order to get more insight into algorithmic problems and to compare existing solutions with their own. Such workbenches would also enhance reproducibility of experiments for non-experts. However, this rather seems to be a long-term goal. A first project in this direction was ExpLab [389], but unfortunately its further development has been stopped.

10.1.6   Increase the Community!

Like every other scientific discipline, Algorithm Engineering must try to attract the strongest young talents. Successful work in this area requires a fairly broad spectrum of skills, ranging from a strong background in theory, profound knowledge in application modeling and hardware architectures, excellence in software engineering and the implementation of complex algorithms to a good sense for experiments.

Currently, we observe that many talented PhD students go to industry after graduation in Algorithm Engineering and decide against a career in academia. Usually, they can freely choose between several job offers from industry. This may be interpreted as good news in so far as it shows that there is a high demand for people with these skills and may also be seen as a sign that industry acknowledges our attempt to bridge the gap between theory and practice. The truth, however, is probably that the overall demand for computer scientists exceeds the number of available professionals by a great margin. But at the same time, it may be an indication that career opportunities inside academia are not sufficiently attractive. Although this move from academia to industry may have a positive side effect for the dissemination of ideas and concepts of Algorithm Engineering, it certainly bears problems for the development of the discipline.

For example, many promising projects are stopped after the driving forces behind it change their position. In comparison with pure theoretical research, Algorithm Engineering usually requires a much longer time horizon for a research project, since implementation and experiments, as well as several runs through the Algorithm Engineering cycle are very time-consuming.

While theory is typically done by single researchers or by small and only loosely connected groups of researchers working on a short-term basis and with similar background on a specific problem together (for just one common paper), the situation in Algorithm Engineering is quite different. In general, it requires true teamwork and, for the development of efficient algorithmic libraries, also larger groups which work closely together for a longer period. Maybe it could help if we set out an award for the "best algorithmic software of the year".

The fact that the research community of researchers in Algorithm Engineering is still quite small becomes also apparent with refereed conferences. There are only few annual conferences explicitly devoted to Algorithm Engineering. These conferences still have program committees with a considerable fraction of members who are highly respected colleagues in traditional theoretical computer science but have only little own experience with Algorithm Engineering.

Maintaining and updating repositories of benchmark instances is a substantial amount of work which requires some kind of award system to find volunteers. This service for the community should be organized like a scientific journal to ensure long-term availability. Several years ago, in 1999, Andrew Goldberg and Bernard Moret already promoted such an initiative [341], but at that time did not receive enough support to get it really started.

10.2 Epilogue

Our brief discussion of challenges shows that the new paradigm Algorithm Engineering is still in the transition towards an established discipline, but offers several fascinating research opportunities.

Success stories of Google Inc., Celera Corporation, Akamai Technologies Inc., and ILOG Inc. — just to name a few prominent examples of companies whose main products all build to a large extent on strong Algorithm Engineering— clearly demonstrate the potential and importance of this discipline for the development of innovations in almost all current and future technologies. Thus it is highly desirable that the spirit and basic principles of Algorithm Engineering will be spread out from a still small scientific community to industry as soon as possible.

References

1. Abraham, I., Fiat, A., Goldberg, A.V., Werneck, R.F.: Highway dimension, shortest paths, and provably efficient algorithms. In: Proceedings of the 21st Annual ACM-SIAM Symposium on Discrete Algorithms (SODA), pp. 782–793 (2010)
2. Abrial, J.-R.: The B-book: Assigning programs to meanings. Cambridge University Press, Cambridge (August 1996)
3. Abrial, J.-R., Schuman, S.A., Meyer, B.: Specification language. In: McKeag, R.M., Macnaghten, A.M. (eds.) On the Construction of Programs: An Advanced Course, pp. 343–410. Cambridge University Press, Cambridge (1980)
4. Achlioptas, D., Chrobak, M., Noga, J.: Competitive analysis of randomized paging algorithms. Theoretical Computer Science 234(1-2), 203–218 (2000)
5. Achterberg, T., Berthold, T., Martin, A., Wolter, K.: SCIP – solving constraint integer programs (2007), http://scip.zib.de/
6. Achterberg, T., Grötschel, M., Koch, T.: Software for teaching modeling of integer programming problems, ZIB Report 06-23, Zuse Institute Berlin (2006)
7. Ackerman, M.J.: The visible human project - getting the data (2004), http://www.nlm.nih.gov/research/visible/getting_data.html (last update: January 11, 2010)
8. Advanced Micro Devices, Inc., AMD developer central - ATI stream software development kit, SDK (2009), http://developer.amd.com/gpu/ATIStreamSDK/Pages/default.aspx
9. Agarwal, P.K., Arge, L., Danner, A., Holland-Minkley, B.: Cache-oblivious data structures for orthogonal range searching. In: Proceedings of the 19th Annual ACM Symposium on Computational Geometry, pp. 237–245. ACM Press, New York (2003)
10. Agarwal, P.K., Arge, L.A., Murali, T.M., Varadarajan, K., Vitter, J.: I/O-efficient algorithms for contour-line extraction and planar graph blocking. In: Proceedings of the 9th Annual ACM-SIAM Symposium on Discrete Algorithms (SODA), pp. 117–126 (1998)
11. Aggarwal, A., Vitter, J.S.: The input/output complexity of sorting and related problems. Communications of the ACM 31(9), 1116–1127 (1988)
12. Aggarwal, G., Datar, M., Rajagopalan, S., Ruhl, M.: On the streaming model augmented with a sorting primitive. In: Proceedings of the 45th Annual IEEE Symposium on Foundations of Computer Science (FOCS), pp. 540–549 (2004)
13. Agrawal, M., Kayal, N., Saxena, N.: PRIMES is in P. Annals of Mathematics 160(2), 781–793 (2004)
14. Aho, A.V., Hopcroft, J.E., Ullman, J.D.: The design and analysis of computer algorithms. Addison-Wesley Publishing Company, Reading (1974)
15. Ahuja, R.K., Magnanti, T.L., Orlin, J.B.: Network flows: Theory, algorithms, and applications. Prentice Hall, Englewood Cliffs (1993)
16. Ahuja, R.K., Mehlhorn, K., Orlin, J.B., Tarjan, R.E.: Faster algorithms for the shortest path problem. Journal of the ACM 37(2), 213–223 (1990)
17. Ahuja, R.K., Orlin, J.B.: Use of representative operation counts in computational testing of algorithms. INFORMS Journal on Computing 8, 318–330 (1992)

18. AIX versions 3.2 and 4 performance tuning guide (1996),
    `http://www.unet.univie.ac.at/aix/aixbman/prftungd/toc.htm`
19. Ajwani, D., Dementiev, R., Meyer, U.: A computational study of external-memory
    BFS algorithms. In: Proceedings of the 17th Annual ACM-SIAM Symposium on
    Discrete Algorithms (SODA), pp. 601–610 (2006)
20. Ajwani, D., Dementiev, R., Meyer, U., Osipov, V.: The shortest path problem:
    The ninth DIMACS implementation challenge. In: DIMACS series in Discrete
    Mathematics and Theoretical Computer Science, ch. Breadth First Search on
    Massive Graphs, vol. 74, pp. 291–308. American Mathematical Society, Providence
    (2009)
21. Ajwani, D., Malinger, I., Meyer, U., Toledo, S.: Characterizing the performance of
    flash memory storage devices and its impact on algorithm design. In: McGeoch,
    C.C. (ed.) WEA 2008. LNCS, vol. 5038, pp. 208–219. Springer, Heidelberg (2008)
22. Akl, S.G.: Parallel computation: models and methods. Prentice-Hall, Inc., Engle-
    wood Cliffs (1997)
23. Alexandrov, A., Ionescu, M.F., Schauser, K.E., Scheiman, C.: LogGP: Incorpo-
    rating long messages into the LogP model for parallel computation. Journal of
    Parallel and Distributed Computing 44(1), 71–79 (1997)
24. Allen, E., Chase, D., Flood, C., Luchangco, V., Maessen, J.-W., Ryu, S., Steele
    Jr., G.L.: Project Fortress: A multicore language for multicore processors. Linux
    Magazine, 38–43 (2007)
25. Althaus, E., Polzin, T., Daneshmand, S.V.: Improving linear programming ap-
    proaches for the Steiner tree problem. Research Report MPI-I-2003-1-004, Max-
    Planck-Institut für Informatik, Saarbrücken, Germany (2003)
26. Amdahl, G.M.: Validity of the single processor approach to achieving large scale
    computing capabilities. In: Readings in Computer Architecture, pp. 79–81. Mor-
    gan Kaufmann Publishers Inc., San Francisco (1999)
27. Amenta, N., Ziegler, G.M.: Deformed products and maximal shadows of poly-
    topes. In: Contemporary Mathematics, vol. 223, pp. 57–90. American Mathemat-
    ical Society, Providence (1999)
28. Amini, M.M., Barr, R.S.: Network reoptimization algorithms: A statistically de-
    signed comparison. ORSA Journal on Computing 5(4), 395–409 (1993)
29. An, P., Jula, A., Rus, S., Saunders, S., Smith, T., Tanase, G., Thomas, N., Amato,
    N.M., Rauchwerger, L.: STAPL: An adaptive, generic parallel C++ library. In:
    LCPC, pp. 193–208 (2001)
30. Anderson, E., Bai, Z., Bischof, C., Blackford, S., Demmel, J., Dongarra, J., Du
    Croz, J., Greenbaum, A., Hammarling, S., McKenney, A., Sorensen, D.: LAPACK
    users' guide, 3rd edn. Society for Industrial and Applied Mathematics, Philadel-
    phia (1999)
31. Androutsellis-Theotokis, S., Spinellis, D.: A survey of peer-to-peer content distri-
    bution technologies. ACM Computing Surveys 36(4), 335–371 (2004)
32. Aneja, Y.P.: An integer linear programming approach to the Steiner problem in
    graphs. Networks 10, 167–178 (1980)
33. Applegate, D.L., Bixby, R.E., Chvátal, V., Cook, W.J.: The traveling salesman
    problem: A computational study. Princeton University Press, Princeton (2006)
34. Apt, K.: Principles of constraint programming. Cambridge University Press, Cam-
    bridge (2003)
35. Arge, L.: The buffer tree: A new technique for optimal I/O-algorithms. In: Sack,
    J.-R., Akl, S.G., Dehne, F., Santoro, N. (eds.) WADS 1995. LNCS, vol. 955, pp.
    334–345. Springer, Heidelberg (1995)

36. Arge, L.: External memory data structures. In: Meyer auf der Heide, F. (ed.) ESA 2001. LNCS, vol. 2161, pp. 1–29. Springer, Heidelberg (2001)

37. Arge, L.: External memory data structures. In: Abello, J., Pardalos, P.M., Resende, M.G.C. (eds.) Handbook of Massive Data Sets, pp. 313–357. Kluwer Academic Publishers, Dordrecht (2002)

38. Arge, L., Bender, M., Demaine, E., Holland-Minkley, B., Munro, J.I.: Cache-oblivious priority-queue and graph algorithms. In: Proceedings of the 34th ACM Symposium on Theory of Computing (STOC), pp. 268–276. ACM Press, New York (2002)

39. Arge, L., Brodal, G.S., Fagerberg, R.: Cache-oblivious data structures. In: Mehta, D.P., Sahni, S. (eds.) Handbook on Data Structures and Applications. CRC Press, Boca Raton (2004)

40. Arge, L., Brodal, G.S., Toma, L.: On external-memory MST, SSSP and multi-way planar graph separation. Journal of Algorithms 53(2), 186–206 (2004)

41. Arge, L., Chase, J., Vitter, J., Wickremesinghe, R.: Efficient sorting using registers and caches. ACM Journal of Experimental Algorithmics 7(9), 1–17 (2002)

42. Arge, L., de Berg, M., Haverkort, H., Yi, K.: The priority R-tree: A practically efficient and worst-case optimal R-tree. In: SIGMOD International Conference on Management of Data, pp. 347–358 (2004)

43. Arge, L., Goodrich, M.T., Nelson, M., Sitchinava, N.: Fundamental parallel algorithms for private-cache chip multiprocessors. In: Proceedings of the 20th Annual ACM Symposium on Parallel Algorithms and Architectures (SPAA), pp. 197–206 (2008)

44. Arge, L., Procopiuc, O., Vitter, J.S.: Implementing I/O-efficient data structures using TPIE. In: Möhring, R.H., Raman, R. (eds.) ESA 2002. LNCS, vol. 2461, pp. 88–100. Springer, Heidelberg (2002)

45. Arge, L., Toma, L.: Simplified external memory algorithms for planar DAGs. In: Hagerup, T., Katajainen, J. (eds.) SWAT 2004. LNCS, vol. 3111, pp. 493–503. Springer, Heidelberg (2004)

46. Arge, L., Toma, L., Zeh, N.: I/O-efficient topological sorting of planar DAGs. In: Proceedings of the 15th Annual ACM Symposium on Parallel Algorithms and Architectures (SPAA), pp. 85–93. ACM, New York (2003)

47. Arge, L., Vitter, J.S.: Optimal dynamic interval management in external memory. In: Proceedings of the 37th Annual IEEE Symposium on Foundations of Computer Science (FOCS), pp. 560–569 (1996)

48. Arora, S.: Polynomial time approximation schemes for the Euclidean traveling salesman and other geometric problems. Journal of the ACM 45, 753–782 (1998)

49. Arya, S., Mount, D.M.: Approximate nearest neighbor queries in fixed dimensions. In: Proceedings of the 4th Annual ACM-SIAM Symposium on Discrete Algorithms (SODA), pp. 271–280 (1993)

50. Atkinson, A.C.: Plots, transformations and regression: an introduction to graphical methods of diagnostic regression analysis. Oxford University Press, UK (1987)

51. Aurenhammer, F., Klein, R.: Voronoi diagrams. In: Sack, J.-R., Urrutia, J. (eds.) Handbook of Computational Geometry, ch. 5, pp. 201–290. North-Holland, Amsterdam (1999)

52. Avnaim, F., Boissonnat, J.-D., Devillers, O., Preparata, F., Yvinec, M.: Evaluating signs of determinants using single precision arithmetic. Algorithmica 17(2), 111–132 (1997)

53. Babcock, B., Babu, S., Datar, M., Motwani, R., Widom, J.: Models and issues in data stream systems. In: ACM PODS, pp. 1–16 (2002)

54. Bader, D.A., Kanade, V., Madduri, K.: SWARM: A parallel programming framework for multi-core processors. In: 21st International Parallel and Distributed Processing Symposium (IPDPS 2007), pp. 1–8 (2007)
55. Bader, D.A., Madduri, K.: SNAP, small-world network analysis and partitioning: An open-source parallel graph framework for the exploration of large-scale networks. In: 22nd International Parallel and Distributed Processing Symposium (IPDPS 2008), pp. 1–12 (2008)
56. Bader, D.A., Moret, B.M.E., Sanders, P.: Algorithm engineering for parallel computation. In: Fleischer, R., Moret, B.M.E., Schmidt, E.M. (eds.) Experimental Algorithmics. LNCS, vol. 2547, pp. 1–23. Springer, Heidelberg (2002)
57. Bader, M., Zenger, C.: Cache oblivious matrix multiplication using an element ordering based on a Peano curve. Linear Algebra and its Applications (Special Issue in honor of Friedrich Ludwig Bauer) 417(2-3), 301–313 (2006)
58. Baeza-Yates, R., Barbosa, E.F., Ziviani, N.: Hierarchies of indices for text searching. Journal of Information Systems 21, 497–514 (1996)
59. Balzert, H.: Lehrbuch der Software-Technik. Spektrum Akademischer Verlag, Heidelberg (1996)
60. Barr, R.S., Golden, B.L., Kelly, J.P., Resende, M.G.C., Stewart Jr., W.R.: Designing and reporting on computational experiments with heuristic methods. Journal of Heuristics 1(1), 9–32 (1995)
61. Barrett, C., Bisset, K., Holzer, M., Konjevod, G., Marathe, M.V., Wagner, D.: Engineering label-constrained shortest-path algorithms. In: Demetrescu, C., Goldberg, A.V., Johnson, D.S. (eds.) Shortest Path Computations: Ninth DIMACS Challenge, DIMACS Book, vol. 74, pp. 309–319. American Mathematical Society, Providence (2009)
62. Barrett, C., Bisset, K., Jacob, R., Konjevod, G., Marathe, M.V.: Classical and contemporary shortest path problems in road networks: Implementation and experimental analysis of the TRANSIMS router. In: Möhring, R.H., Raman, R. (eds.) ESA 2002. LNCS, vol. 2461, pp. 126–138. Springer, Heidelberg (2002)
63. Barrett, C., Jacob, R., Marathe, M.V.: Formal-language-constrained path problems. SIAM Journal on Computing 30(3), 809–837 (2000)
64. Barták, R.: Constraint programming: In pursuit of the holy grail. In: Proceedings of the Week of Doctoral Students (WDS), Prague, Czech Republic. MatFyz Press (1999)
65. Basili, V.R., Boehm, B., Davis, A., Humphrey, W.S., Leveson, N., Mead, N.R., Musa, J.D., Parnas, D.L., Pfleeger, S.L., Weyuker, E.: New year's resolutions for software quality. IEEE Softw. 21(1), 12–13 (2004)
66. Bast, H., Funke, S., Matijevic, D., Sanders, P., Schultes, D.: In transit to constant shortest-path queries in road networks. In: Proceedings of the 9th Workshop on Algorithm Engineering and Experiments (ALENEX 2007), pp. 46–59. SIAM, Philadelphia (2007)
67. Bast, H., Funke, S., Sanders, P., Schultes, D.: Fast routing in road networks with transit nodes. Science 316(5824), 566 (2007)
68. Bast, H., Weber, I.: Don't compare averages. In: Nikoletseas, S.E. (ed.) WEA 2005. LNCS, vol. 3503, pp. 67–76. Springer, Heidelberg (2005)
69. Batista, V.H.F., Millman, D.L., Pion, S., Singler, J.: Parallel geometric algorithms for multi-core computers. In: Proceedings of the 25th Annual ACM Symposium on Computational Geometry, pp. 217–226. ACM, New York (2009)
70. Batz, V., Delling, D., Sanders, P., Vetter, C.: Time-dependent contraction hierarchies. In: Proceedings of the 11th Workshop on Algorithm Engineering and Experiments (ALENEX 2009), pp. 97–105. SIAM, Philadelphia (2009)

71. Bauer, R., Delling, D.: SHARC: Fast and robust unidirectional routing. In: Munro, I., Wagner, D. (eds.) Proceedings of the 10th Workshop on Algorithm Engineering and Experiments (ALENEX 2008), pp. 13–26. SIAM, Philadelphia (April 2008)

72. Bauer, R., Delling, D.: SHARC: Fast and robust unidirectional routing. ACM Journal of Experimental Algorithmics 14, 2.4–2.29 (2009); Special Section on Selected Papers from ALENEX 2008

73. Bauer, R., Delling, D., Sanders, P., Schieferdecker, D., Schultes, D., Wagner, D.: Combining hierarchical and goal-directed speed-up techniques for Dijkstra's algorithm. In: McGeoch, C.C. (ed.) WEA 2008. LNCS, vol. 5038, pp. 303–318. Springer, Heidelberg (2008)

74. Bauer, R., Delling, D., Sanders, P., Schieferdecker, D., Schultes, D., Wagner, D.: Combining hierarchical and goal-directed speed-up techniques for Dijkstra's algorithm. ACM Journal of Experimental Algorithmics 15(3) (2010)

75. Bauer, R., Delling, D., Wagner, D.: Shortest-path indices: Establishing a methodology for shortest-path problems. Tech. Report 2007-14, ITI Wagner, Faculty of Informatics, Universität Karlsruhe, TH (2007)

76. Bäumker, A., Dittrich, W., Meyer auf der Heide, F.: Truly efficient parallel algorithms: 1-optimal multisearch for an extension of the BSP model. Theoretical Computer Science 203(2), 175–203 (1998)

77. Bayer, R., McCreight, E.M.: Organization and maintenance of large ordered indexes. Acta Informatica, 173–189 (1972)

78. Beasley, J.E.: An algorithm for the Steiner tree problem in graphs. Networks 14, 147–159 (1984)

79. Beasley, J.E.: OR-Library: Distributing test problems by electronic mail. Journal of the Operation Research Society 41, 1069–1072 (1990)

80. Beasley, J.E., Lucena, A.: A branch and cut algorithm for the Steiner problem in graphs. Networks 31, 39–59 (1998)

81. Beckmann, A., Dementiev, R., Singler, J.: Building a parallel pipelined external memory algorithm library. In: 23rd IEEE International Parallel & Distributed Processing Symposium (IPDPS). IEEE, Los Alamitos (2009)

82. Beebe, N.H.F.: GNU scientific library (2001), http://www.math.utah.edu/software/gsl.html

83. Beier, R., Vöcking, B.: Probabilistic analysis of knapsack core algorithms. In: Proceedings of the 15th Annual ACM-SIAM Symposium on Discrete Algorithms (SODA), pp. 468–477 (2004)

84. Beier, R., Vöcking, B.: Random knapsack in expected polynomial time. Journal of Computer and System Sciences 69(3), 306–329 (2004)

85. Beier, R., Vöcking, B.: An experimental study of random knapsack problems. Algorithmica 45(1), 121–136 (2006)

86. Beier, R., Vöcking, B.: Typical properties of winners and losers in discrete optimization. SIAM Journal on Computing 35(4), 855–881 (2006)

87. Ben-David, S., Borodin, A.: A new measure for the study of on-line algorithms. Algorithmica 11(1), 73–91 (1994)

88. Bender, M.A., Cole, R., Raman, R.: Exponential structures for cache-oblivious algorithms. In: Widmayer, P., Ruiz, F.T., Bueno, R.M., Hennessy, M., Eidenbenz, S., Conejo, R. (eds.) ICALP 2002. LNCS, vol. 2380, pp. 195–207. Springer, Heidelberg (2002)

89. Bender, M.A., Demaine, E.D., Farach-Colton, M.: Cache-oblivious B-trees. In: Proceedings of the 41st Annual IEEE Symposium on Foundations of Computer Science (FOCS), pp. 399–409. IEEE Computer Society Press, Los Alamitos (2000)

90. Bender, M.A., Duan, Z., Iacono, J., Wu, J.: A locality-preserving cache-oblivious dynamic dictionary. In: Proceedings of 13th Annual ACM-SIAM Symposium on Discrete Algorithms (SODA), pp. 29–38 (2002)
91. Bentley, J.L.: Multidimensional binary search trees used for associative searching. Communications of the ACM 18(9), 509–517 (1975)
92. Bentley, J.L.: Experiments on traveling salesman heuristics. In: Proceedings of the 1st Annual ACM-SIAM Symposium on Discrete Algorithms (SODA), pp. 91–99 (1990)
93. Bentley, J.L.: Programming Perls. Addison Wesley Professional, Reading (2000)
94. Berberich, E., Eigenwillig, A., Hemmer, M., Hert, S., Kettner, L., Mehlhorn, K., Reichel, J., Schmitt, S., Schömer, E., Wolpert, N.: EXACUS: Efficient and exact algorithms for curves and surfaces. In: Brodal, G.S., Leonardi, S. (eds.) ESA 2005. LNCS, vol. 3669, pp. 155–166. Springer, Heidelberg (2005)
95. Berkeley Unified Parallel C (UPC) Project (2009), http://upc.lbl.gov/
96. Berman, P., Ramaiyer, V.: Improved approximations for the Steiner tree problem. Journal of Algorithms 17, 381–408 (1994)
97. Berretini, E., D'Angelo, G., Delling, D.: Arc-flags in dynamic graphs. In: ATMOS 2009 - Proceedings of the 9th Workshop on Algorithmic Approaches for Transportation Modeling, Optimization, and Systems, Dagstuhl Seminar Proceedings. Schloss Dagstuhl - Leibniz-Zentrum für Informatik, Germany (2009)
98. Beth, T., Gollmann, D.: Algorithm engineering for public key algorithms. IEEE Journal on Selected Areas in Communications 7, 458–466 (1989)
99. Bilardi, G., Pietracaprina, A., Pucci, G.: Decomposable BSP: A Bandwidth-Latency Model for Parallel and Hierarchical Computation. In: Handbook of parallel computing: Models, algorithms and applications. CRC Press, Boca Raton (2007)
100. Bilardi, G., Pietracaprina, A., Pucci, G., Herley, K.T., Spirakis, P.G.: BSP versus LogP. Algorithmica 24(3-4), 405–422 (1999)
101. Binder, R.V.: Testing object-oriented systems: Models, patterns, and tools. Addison-Wesley Professional, Reading (October 1999)
102. Bisseling, R.H.: Parallel scientific computation. In: A Structured Approach Using BSP and MPI. Oxford University Press, Oxford (2004)
103. Bixby, R.E.: Solving real-world linear programs: A decade and more of progress. Operations Research 50, 3–15 (2002)
104. Björklund, A., Husfeldt, T., Kaski, P., Koivisto, M.: Fourier meets Möbius: fast subset convolution. In: Proceedings of the 39th Annual ACM Symposium on Theory of Computing (STOC), pp. 67–74. ACM, New York (2007)
105. Blackford, L.S., Demmel, J., Dongarra, J., Duff, I., Hammarling, S., Henry, G., Heroux, M., Kaufman, L., Lumsdaine, A., Petitet, A., Pozo, R., Remington, K., Whaley, R.C.: An updated set of basic linear algebra subprograms (BLAS). ACM Trans. Math. Software 28(2), 135–151 (2002)
106. Blaer, P., Allen, P.K.: Topbot: automated network topology detection with a mobile robot. In: Proceedings of the 2003 IEEE International Conference on Robotics and Automation, pp. 1582–1587 (2003)
107. Blandford, D.K., Blelloch, G.E., Kash, I.A.: Compact representations of separable graphs. In: Proceedings of the 14th Annual ACM-SIAM Symposium on Discrete Algorithms (SODA), pp. 679–688 (2003)
108. Blazewicz, J., Trystram, D., Ecker, K., Plateau, B. (eds.): Handbook on parallel and distributed processing. Springer, New York (2000)
109. Blitz++: Object-oriented scientific computing, version 0.9 (2005), http://www.oonumerics.org/blitz/

110. Bloch, J.: Effective Java: Programming language guide. Java series. Addison-Wesley, Boston (2001)

111. Bloom, T., Sharpe, T.: Managing data from high-throughput genomic processing: A case study. In: Very Large Data Bases (VLDB), pp. 1198–1201 (2004)

112. Blum, M., Kannan, S.: Designing programs that check their work. Journal of the ACM 42(1), 269–291 (1995)

113. Bodlaender, H.L.: A linear-time algorithm for finding tree-decompositions of small treewidth. SIAM J. Computing 25(6), 1305–1317 (1996)

114. Bodlaender, H.L., Telle, J.A.: Space-efficient construction variants of dynamic programming. Nordic Journal of Computing 11, 374–385 (2004)

115. Bogdanov, A., Trevisan, L.: Average-case complexity. Found. Trends Theor. Comput. Sci. 2(1), 1–106 (2006)

116. Bollobás, B.: Modern graph theory. Springer, New York (2002)

117. Bondi, A.B.: Characteristics of scalability and their impact on performance. In: WOSP 2000: Proceedings of the 2nd International Workshop on Software and Performance, pp. 195–203. ACM Press, New York (2000)

118. Bonorden, O., Gehweiler, J., Meyer auf der Heide, F.: A web computing environment for parallel algorithms in Java. Journal on Scalable Computing: Practice and Experience 7(2), 1–14 (2006)

119. Bonorden, O., Juurlink, B., von Otte, I., Rieping, I.: The Paderborn University BSP (PUB) library. Parallel Computing 29(2), 187–207 (2003)

120. Boost C++ Libraries, version 1.42 (2010), http://www.boost.org

121. Borah, M., Owens, R.M., Irwin, M.J.: A fast and simple Steiner routing heuristic. Discrete Applied Mathematics 90, 51–67 (1999)

122. Borgelt, C., Kruse, R.: Unsicherheit und Vagheit: Begriffe, Methoden, Forschungsthemen. KI, Künstliche Intelligenz 3(1), 18–24 (2001)

123. Börger, E., Stärk, R.: Abstract state machines: A method for high-level system design and analysis. Springer, Heidelberg (2003)

124. Borgwardt, K.H.: The simplex method – a probabilistic analysis. Springer, Heidelberg (1987)

125. Borodin, A., El-Yaniv, R.: Online computation and competitive analysis. Cambridge University Press, Cambridge (1998)

126. Borradaile, G., Kenyon-Mathieu, C., Klein, P.N.: A polynomial time approximation scheme for Steiner tree in planar graphs. In: Proceedings of the 18th Annual ACM-SIAM Symposium on Discrete Algorithms (SODA), pp. 1285–1294 (2007)

127. Borradaile, G., Kenyon-Mathieu, C., Klein, P.N.: Steiner tree in planar graphs: An $O(n \log n)$ approximation scheme with singly-exponential dependence on epsilon. In: Dehne, F., Sack, J.-R., Zeh, N. (eds.) WADS 2007. LNCS, vol. 4619, pp. 275–286. Springer, Heidelberg (2007)

128. Bose, N.K., Garga, A.K.: Neural network design using Voronoi diagrams. IEEE Transactions on Neural Networks 4(5), 778–787 (1993)

129. Brandes, U., Erlebach, T. (eds.): Network Analysis. LNCS, vol. 3418. Springer, Heidelberg (2005)

130. Brodal, G.S.: Cache-oblivious algorithms and data structures. In: Hagerup, T., Katajainen, J. (eds.) SWAT 2004. LNCS, vol. 3111, pp. 3–13. Springer, Heidelberg (2004)

131. Brodal, G.S., Fagerberg, R.: Cache oblivious distribution sweeping. In: Widmayer, P., Triguero, F., Morales, R., Hennessy, M., Eidenbenz, S., Conejo, R. (eds.) ICALP 2002. LNCS, vol. 2380, pp. 426–438. Springer, Heidelberg (2002)

132. Brodal, G.S., Fagerberg, R.: Funnel heap - a cache oblivious priority queue. In: Bose, P., Morin, P. (eds.) ISAAC 2002. LNCS, vol. 2518, pp. 219–228. Springer, Heidelberg (2002)

133. Brodal, G.S., Fagerberg, R., Jacob, R.: Cache oblivious search trees via binary trees of small height. In: Proceedings of the 13th Annual ACM-SIAM Symposium on Discrete Algorithms (SODA), pp. 39–48 (2002)

134. Brodal, G.S., Fagerberg, R., Meyer, U., Zeh, N.: Cache-oblivious data structures and algorithms for undirected breadth-first search and shortest paths. In: Hagerup, T., Katajainen, J. (eds.) SWAT 2004. LNCS, vol. 3111, pp. 480–492. Springer, Heidelberg (2004)

135. Brodal, G.S., Fagerberg, R., Vinther, K.: Engineering a cache-oblivious sorting algorithm. In: Proceedings of the 6th Workshop on Algorithm Engineering and Experiments (ALENEX), pp. 4–17. SIAM, Philadelphia (2004)

136. Brönnimann, H., Burnikel, C., Pion, S.: Interval arithmetic yields efficient dynamic filters for computational geometry. In: Proceedings of the 14th Annual ACM Symposium on Computational Geometry, pp. 165–174 (1998)

137. Brönnimann, H., Emiris, I.Z., Pan, V.Y., Pion, S.: Computing exact geometric predicates using modular arithmetic with single precision. In: Proceedings of the 13th Annual ACM Symposium on Computational Geometry, pp. 174–182. ACM Press, New York (1997)

138. Brönnimann, H., Yvinec, M.: Efficient exact evaluation of signs of determinants. In: Proceedings of the 13th Annual ACM Symposium on Computational Geometry, pp. 166–173. ACM Press, New York (1997)

139. Brooke, A., Kendrick, D., Meeraus, A., Rosenthal, R.E.: GAMS - A user's guide (2006)

140. Brunel, E., Delling, D., Gemsa, A., Wagner, D.: Space-efficient SHARC-routing. In: Festa, P. (ed.) SEA 2010. LNCS, vol. 6049, pp. 47–58. Springer, Heidelberg (2010)

141. Burnikel, C., Fleischer, R., Mehlhorn, K., Schirra, S.: Efficient exact geometric computation made easy. In: Proceedings of the 15th Annual ACM Symposium on Computational Geometry, pp. 341–350. ACM Press, New York (1999)

142. Burnikel, C., Fleischer, R., Mehlhorn, K., Schirra, S.: A strong and easily computable separation bound for arithmetic expressions involving radicals. Algorithmica 27, 87–99 (2000)

143. Burnikel, C., Funke, S., Mehlhorn, K., Schirra, S., Schmitt, S.: A separation bound for real algebraic expressions. In: Meyer auf der Heide, F. (ed.) ESA 2001. LNCS, vol. 2161, pp. 254–265. Springer, Heidelberg (2001)

144. Burnikel, C., Funke, S., Seel, M.: Exact geometric computation using cascading. International Journal of Computational Geometry and Applications 11(3), 245–266 (2001)

145. Bussieck, M.: Optimal lines in public rail transport, Ph.D. thesis, Technische Universität Braunschweig (1998)

146. Butenhof, D.R.: Programming with POSIX threads. Addison-Wesley, Reading (1997)

147. Buyya, R. (ed.): High performance cluster computing: Programming and applications. Prentice Hall PTR, Upper Saddle River (1999)

148. C++ applications (2009),
http://public.research.att.com/~bs/applications.html

149. Camazine, S., Franks, N.R., Sneyd, J., Bonabeau, E., Deneubourg, J.-L., Theraula, G.: Self-organization in biological systems. Princeton University Press, Princeton (2001)

150. Caragea, G.C., Saybasili, A.B., Wen, X., Vishkin, U.: Brief announcement: Performance potential of an easy-to-program PRAM-on-chip prototype versus state-of-the-art processor. In: SPAA 2009: Proceedings of the 21st Annual ACM Symposium on Parallel Algorithms and Architectures, Calgary, Alberta, Canada, August 11-13, pp. 163–165. ACM, New York (2009)

151. CGAL: Computational Geometry Algorithms Library, version 3.4 (2009), http://www.cgal.org/

152. CGAL user and reference manual (2009), http://www.cgal.org/Manual/index.html

153. cgmLIB: A library for coarse-grained parallel computing, version 0.9.5 Beta (2003), http://lib.cgmlab.org/

154. Chakravarti, A.J., Baumgartner, G., Lauria, M.: The organic grid: Self-organizing computation on a peer-to-peer network. IEEE Transactions on Systems, Man, and Cybernetics, Part A: Systems and Humans 35(3), 373–384 (2005)

155. Chamberlain, B.L., Callahan, D., Zima, H.P.: Parallel programmability and the Chapel language. Int. J. High Perform. Comput. Appl. 21(3), 291–312 (2007)

156. Chan, A., Dehne, F.: CGMgraph/CGMlib: Implementing and testing CGM graph algorithms on PC clusters. In: Dongarra, J., Laforenza, D., Orlando, S. (eds.) EuroPVM/MPI 2003. LNCS, vol. 2840, pp. 117–125. Springer, Heidelberg (2003)

157. Chan, A., Dehne, F., Taylor, R.: CGMGRAPH/CGMLIB: Implementing and testing CGM graph algorithms on PC clusters and shared memory machines. International Journal of High Performance Computing Applications 19(1), 81–97 (2005)

158. Chan, T.M., Chen, E.Y.: Optimal in-place algorithms for 3-D convex hulls and 2-D segment intersection. In: Proceedings of the 25th Annual ACM Symposium on Computational Geometry, pp. 80–87. ACM Press, New York (2009)

159. Chandra, R., Menon, R., Dagum, L., Kohr, D., Maydan, D., McDonald, J.: Parallel programming in openMP. Morgan Kaufmann, San Francisco (2000)

160. Chang, E.-C., Choi, S.W., Kwon, D., Park, H., Yap, C.-K.: Shortest path amidst disc obstacles is computable. In: Proceedings of the 21st Annual ACM Symposium on Computational Geometry, pp. 116–125. ACM Press, New York (2005)

161. Chapman, B., Jost, G., van der Pas, R.: Using OpenMP: Portable shared memory parallel programming. MIT Press, Cambridge (2007)

162. Charles, P., Grothoff, C., Saraswat, V.A., Donawa, C., Kielstra, A., Ebcioglu, K., von Praun, C., Sarkar, V.: X10: an object-oriented approach to non-uniform cluster computing. In: OOPSLA, pp. 519–538 (2005)

163. Chazelle, B.: Triangulating a simple polygon in linear time. In: Proceedings of the 31st Annual IEEE Symposium on Foundations of Computer Science, pp. 29–38 (1990)

164. Chazelle, B.: Triangulating a simple polygon in linear time. Discrete Computational Geometry 6, 485–524 (1991)

165. Chazelle, B.: Cuttings. In: Handbook of Data Structures and Applications. CRC Press, Boca Raton (2005)

166. Chen, J., Kanj, I.A., Xia, G.: Improved parameterized upper bounds for vertex cover. In: Královič, R., Urzyczyn, P. (eds.) MFCS 2006. LNCS, vol. 4162, pp. 238–249. Springer, Heidelberg (2006)

167. Cherkassky, B.V., Goldberg, A.V., Radzik, T.: Shortest paths algorithms: Theory and experimental evaluation. Mathematical Programming 73, 129–174 (1996)

168. Chiang, Y.-J., Goodrich, M.T., Grove, E.F., Tamassia, R., Vengroff, D.E., Vitter, J.S.: External-memory graph algorithms. In: Proceedings of the 6th Annual ACM-SIAM Symposium on Discrete Algorithms (SODA), pp. 139–149 (1995)

169. Chopra, S., Gorres, E.R., Rao, M.R.: Solving the Steiner tree problem on a graph using branch and cut. ORSA Journal on Computing 4, 320–335 (1992)

170. Chopra, S., Rao, M.R.: The Steiner tree problem I: Formulations, compositions and extension of facets. Mathematical Programming 64, 209–229 (1994)

171. Choukhmane, E.-A.: Une heuristique pour le probleme de l'arbre de Steiner. RAIRO Rech. Opér. 12, 207–212 (1978)

172. Christofides, N.: Worst-case analysis of a new heuristic for the traveling salesman problem. Tech. Report 388, GSIA, Carnegie-Mellon University, Pittsburgh (1976)

173. Chu, C., Wong, Y.-C.: Fast and accurate rectilinear Steiner minimal tree algorithm for VLSI design. In: ISPD 2005: Proceedings of the 2005 International Symposium on Physical Design, pp. 28–35. ACM Press, New York (2005)

174. Cilk Arts, Multicore programming software (2009), http://www.cilk.com/

175. CLAPACK: f2c'ed version of LAPACK, version 3.1.1.1 (2008), http://www.netlib.org/clapack/

176. Clark, D.R., Munro, J.I.: Efficient suffix trees on secondary storage. In: Proceedings of the 7th Annual ACM-SIAM Symposium on Discrete Algorithms (SODA), pp. 383–391 (1996)

177. Clarkson, K.L.: Safe and effective determinant evaluation. In: Proceedings of the 31st IEEE Symposium on Foundations of Computer Science (FOCS), Pittsburgh, PA, pp. 387–395 (October 1992)

178. Cobham, A.: The intrinsic computational difficulty of functions. In: Bar-Hillel, Y. (ed.) Proc. 1964 International Congress for Logic, Methodology, and Philosophy of Science, pp. 24–30. North-Holland, Amsterdam (1964)

179. Cockayne, E.J., Hewgill, D.E.: Exact computation of Steiner minimal trees in the plane. Information Processing Letters 22, 151–156 (1986)

180. Cockayne, E.J., Hewgill, D.E.: Improved computation of plane Steiner minimal trees. Algorithmica 7(2/3), 219–229 (1992)

181. Coffin, M., Saltzmann, M.J.: Statistical analysis of computational tests of algorithms and heuristics. INFORMS Journal on Computing 12(1), 24–44 (2000)

182. Comer, D.: The ubiquitous B-tree. ACM Computing Surveys, 121–137 (1979)

183. Conover, W.J.: Practical nonparametric statistics. John Wiley & Sons, Chichester (1980)

184. Cook, S.A.: The complexity of theorem-proving procedures. In: Proceedings of the 3rd Annual ACM Symposium on Theory of Computing (STOC), pp. 151–158 (1971)

185. Cook, W.J., Cunningham, W.H., Pulleyblank, W.R., Schrijver, A.: Combinatorial Optimization. Wiley, New York (1998)

186. Coppersmith, D., Winograd, S.: Matrix multiplication via arithmetic progressions. J. Symb. Comput. 9(3), 251–280 (1990)

187. Coppola, M., Schmollinger, M.: Hierarchical models and software tools for parallel programming. In: Meyer, U., Sanders, P., Sibeyn, J.F. (eds.) Algorithms for Memory Hierarchies. LNCS, vol. 2625, pp. 320–354. Springer, Heidelberg (2003)

188. Cordella, L., Foggia, P., Sansone, C., Vento, M.: An improved algorithm for matching large graphs. In: 3rd IAPR-TC15 Workshop on Graph-based Representations in Pattern Recognition (May 2001)

189. The Core library, version 1.7 (2004), http://cs.nyu.edu/exact/core_pages/index.html

190. Cormen, T.H., Goodrich, M.T.: A bridging model for parallel computation, communication, and I/O. ACM Computing Surveys, Article No. 208, 28 (1996)

191. Cormen, T.H., Leiserson, C.E., Rivest, R.L., Stein, C.: Introduction to algorithms, 3rd edn. MIT Press, Cambridge (2009)

192. Corrêa, R., Dutra, I., Fiallos, M., Gomes, F. (eds.): Models for parallel and distributed computation. Theory, algorithmic techniques and applications. Kluwer, Dordrecht (2002)

193. Cosnard, M., Trystram, D.: Parallel algorithms and architectures. PWS Publishing Co. (1995)

194. Courant, R., Robbins, H.: What is mathematics? Oxford University Press, Oxford (1941)

195. Crauser, A., Mehlhorn, K.: LEDA-SM, extending LEDA to secondary memory. In: Vitter, J.S., Zaroliagis, C.D. (eds.) WAE 1999. LNCS, vol. 1668, pp. 228–242. Springer, Heidelberg (1999)

196. Crowder, H.P., Dembo, R.S., Mulvey, J.M.: Reporting computational experiments in mathematical programming. Mathematical Programming 15, 316–329 (1978)

197. Crowder, H.P., Dembo, R.S., Mulvey, J.M.: On reporting computational experiments with mathematical software. ACM Transactions on Mathematical Software 5(2), 193–203 (1979)

198. Culler, D.E., Karp, R.M., Patterson, D., Sahay, A., Santos, E.E., Schauser, K.E., Subramonian, R., von Eicken, T.: LogP: a practical model of parallel computation. Commun. ACM 39(11), 78–85 (1996)

199. Culler, D.E., Singh, J.P., Gupta, A.: Parallel computer architecture - a hardware/software approach. Morgan Kaufmann, San Francisco (1999)

200. Dahl, O.-J., Dijkstra, E.W., Hoare, C.A.R.: Structured Programming. Academic Press, New York (1972)

201. Dall'Osso, A.: Computer algebra systems as mathematical optimizing compilers. Science of Computer Programming 59(3), 250–273 (2006)

202. Dantzig, G.B.: Linear programming and extensions. Princeton University Press, Princeton (1963)

203. Dash optimization – Leading optimization software (2007), http://www.dashoptimization.com/home/products/products_optimizer.html

204. de Aragão, M.P., Werneck, R.F.: On the implementation of MST-based heuristics for the Steiner problem in graphs. In: Mount, D.M., Stein, C. (eds.) ALENEX 2002. LNCS, vol. 2409, pp. 1–15. Springer, Heidelberg (2002)

205. de Berg, M.: Linear size binary space partitions for fat objects. In: Spirakis, P.G. (ed.) ESA 1995. LNCS, vol. 979, pp. 252–263. Springer, Heidelberg (1995)

206. de Berg, M., Cheong, O., van Krefeld, M., Overmars, M.: Computational geometry: Algorithms and applications, 3rd rev. edn. Springer, Heidelberg (2008)

207. de Berg, M., van der Stappen, A.F., Vleugels, J., Katz, M.J.: Realistic input models for geometric algorithms. Algorithmica 34(1), 81–97 (2002)

208. de Kunder, M.: Geschatte grootte van het geïndexeerde world wide web, Master's thesis, Universiteit van Tilburg (2008)

209. de la Torre, P., Kruskal, C.P.: Submachine locality in the bulk synchronous setting (extended abstract). In: Fraigniaud, P., Mignotte, A., Robert, Y., Bougé, L. (eds.) Euro-Par 1996. LNCS, vol. 1124, pp. 352–358. Springer, Heidelberg (1996)

210. Dean, A., Voss, D.: Design and analysis of experiments. Springer Texts in Statistics. Springer, Heidelberg (1999)

211. Dechter, R., Pearl, J.: Tree clustering for constraint networks. Artificial Intelligence 38(3), 353–366 (1989)

212. Dehne, F.: Guest editor's introduction. Algorithmica 24(3-4), 173–176 (1999)

213. Dehne, F.: Guest editor's introduction. Algorithmica 45(3), 263–267 (2006)

214. Dehne, F., Dittrich, W., Hutchinson, D.: Efficient external memory algorithms by simulating coarse-grained parallel algorithms. Algorithmica 36, 97–122 (2003)

215. Dehne, F., Dittrich, W., Hutchinson, D., Maheshwari, A.: Bulk synchronous parallel algorithms for the external memory model. Theory Comput. Systems 35, 567–597 (2002)

216. Dehne, F., Fabri, A., Rau-Chaplin, A.: Scalable parallel computational geometry for coarse grained multicomputers. Int. J. Comput. Geometry Appl. 6(3), 379–400 (1996)

217. Dekker, T.J.: A floating-point technique for extending the available precision. Numerische Mathematik 18(3), 224–242 (1971)

218. Delling, D.: Time-dependent SHARC-routing. In: Halperin, D., Mehlhorn, K. (eds.) ESA 2008. LNCS, vol. 5193, pp. 332–343. Springer, Heidelberg (2008)

219. Delling, D.: Engineering and augmenting route planning algorithms, Ph.D. thesis, Universität Karlsruhe (TH), Fakultät für Informatik (2009)

220. Delling, D.: Time-dependent SHARC-routing. In: Algorithmica (2009); Special Issue: European Symposium on Algorithms 2008 (2009)

221. Delling, D., Geisberger, R., Sanders, P., Schultes, D., Vetter, C.: Exact routing in large road networks using contraction hierarchies. Transportation Science (2009) (submitted)

222. Delling, D., Nannicini, G.: Bidirectional core-based routing in dynamic time-dependent road networks. In: Hong, S.-H., Nagamochi, H., Fukunaga, T. (eds.) ISAAC 2008. LNCS, vol. 5369, pp. 812–823. Springer, Heidelberg (2008)

223. Delling, D., Pajor, T., Wagner, D.: Accelerating multi-modal route planning by access-nodes. In: Fiat, A., Sanders, P. (eds.) ESA 2009. LNCS, vol. 5757, pp. 587–598. Springer, Heidelberg (2009)

224. Delling, D., Sanders, P., Schultes, D., Wagner, D.: Engineering route planning algorithms. In: Lerner, J., Wagner, D., Zweig, K.A. (eds.) Algorithmics of Large and Complex Networks. LNCS, vol. 5515, pp. 117–139. Springer, Heidelberg (2009)

225. Delling, D., Sanders, P., Schultes, D., Wagner, D.: Highway hierarchies star. In: Demetrescu, C., Goldberg, A.V., Johnson, D.S. (eds.) Shortest Path Computations: Ninth DIMACS Challenge. DIMACS Book, vol. 74, pp. 141–174. American Mathematical Society, Providence (2009)

226. Delling, D., Wagner, D.: Landmark-based routing in dynamic graphs. In: Demetrescu, C. (ed.) WEA 2007. LNCS, vol. 4525, pp. 52–65. Springer, Heidelberg (2007)

227. Delling, D., Wagner, D.: Pareto paths with SHARC. In: Vahrenhold, J. (ed.) SEA 2009. LNCS, vol. 5526, pp. 125–136. Springer, Heidelberg (2009)

228. Delling, D., Wagner, D.: Time-dependent route planning. In: Ahuja, R.K., Möhring, R.H., Zaroliagis, C. (eds.) Robust and Online Large-Scale Optimization. LNCS, vol. 5868, pp. 207–230. Springer, Heidelberg (2009)

229. Dementiev, R., Kärkkäinen, J., Mehnert, J., Sanders, P.: Better external memory suffix array construction. ACM Journal of Experimental Algorithms 12(3.4), 1–24 (2008)

230. Dementiev, R., Kettner, L., Mehnert, J., Sanders, P.: Engineering a sorted list data structure for 32 bit keys. In: ALENEX 2004: Algorithm Engineering and Experiments, pp. 142–151. SIAM, Philadelphia (2004)

231. Dementiev, R., Kettner, L., Sanders, P.: STXXL: Standard template library for XXL data sets. Software: Practice and Experience 38(6), 589–637 (2008)

232. Demetrescu, C., Finocchi, I., Ribichini, A.: Trading off space for passes in graph streaming problems. In: Proceedings of the 17th Annual ACM-SIAM Symposium on Discrete Algorithms (SODA), pp. 714–723 (2006)

233. Demetrescu, C., Goldberg, A.V., Johnson, D.S. (eds.): Shortest path computations: Ninth DIMACS challenge. DIMACS Book, vol. 74. American Mathematical Society, Providence (2009)

234. Demetrescu, C., Italiano, G.F.: What do we learn from experimental algorithmics? In: Nielsen, M., Rovan, B. (eds.) MFCS 2000. LNCS, vol. 1893, pp. 36–51. Springer, Heidelberg (2000)

235. Demetrescu, C., Italiano, G.F.: Dynamic shortest paths and transitive closure: Algorithmic techniques and data structures. Journal of Discrete Algorithms 4(3) (2006)

236. DeMillo, R.A., McCracken, W.M., Martin, R.J., Passafiume, J.F.: Software testing and evaluation. Benjamin-Cummings Publishing, Redwood City (1987)

237. Demmel, J., Hida, Y.: Fast and accurate floating point summation with application to computational geometry. Numerical Algorithms 37, 101–112 (2005)

238. National Institute of Standards Department of Commerce and Technology, Announcing request for candidate algorithm nominations for the advanced encryption standard (AES). Federal Register 62(177), 48051–48058 (1997)

239. Descartes, R.: Principia philosophiae, Ludovicus Elzevirius (1644)

240. Deshpande, A., Spielman, D.A.: Improved smoothed analysis of the shadow vertex simplex method. In: Proceedings of the 46th Annual IEEE Symposium on Foundations of Computer Science (FOCS), pp. 349–356 (2005)

241. Dial, R.B.: Algorithm 360: shortest-path forest with topological ordering [H]. Communications of the ACM 12(11), 632–633 (1969)

242. Diestel, R.: Graph theory. Graduate Texts in Mathematics, vol. 173. Springer, Heidelberg (2005)

243. Dietzfelbinger, M.: Primality testing in polynomial time. Springer, Heidelberg (2004)

244. Dijkstra, E.W.: A note on two problems in connexion with graphs. Numerische Mathematik 1, 269–271 (1959)

245. Dijkstra, E.W.: Notes on structured programming, circulated privately (April 1970)

246. DiLascia, P.: What makes good code good? MSDN Magazine 19(7), 144 (2004)

247. Dilley, J., Maggs, B., Parikh, J., Prokop, H., Sitaraman, R., Weihl, B.: Globally distributed content delivery. IEEE Internet Computing 6(5), 50–58 (2002)

248. DIMACS implementation challenges (2006),
     `http://dimacs.rutgers.edu/Challenges/`

249. DIMACS TSP challenge (2006), `http://www.research.att.com/~dsj/chtsp/`

250. Website of Dinkumware's STL implementation (2006),
     `http://www.dinkumware.com/cpp.aspx`

251. Disser, Y., Müller-Hannemann, M., Schnee, M.: Multi-criteria shortest paths in time-dependent train networks. In: McGeoch, C.C. (ed.) WEA 2008. LNCS, vol. 5038, pp. 347–361. Springer, Heidelberg (2008)

252. DOC++ (2003), `http://docpp.sourceforge.net/`

253. Dorrigiv, R., López-Ortiz, A., Salinger, A.: Optimal speedup on a low-degree multi-core parallel architecture (LoPRAM). In: SPAA 2008: Proceedings of the Twentieth Annual Symposium on Parallelism in Algorithms and Architectures, pp. 185–187. ACM, New York (2008)

254. Douglas, C.C., Hu, J., Kowarschik, M., Rüde, U., Weiss, C.: Cache optimization for structured and unstructured grid multigrid. Elect. Trans. Numer. Anal. 10, 21–40 (2000)

255. Drayton, P., Albahari, B., Neward, T.: C# in a nutshell: A desktop quick reference, 2nd edn. O'Reilly & Associates, Inc., Sebastopol (2003)

256. Dreyfus, S.E., Wagner, R.A.: The Steiner problems in graphs. Networks 1, 195–207 (1971)
257. Du, D.-Z., Cheng, X. (eds.): Steiner trees in industries. Kluwer Academic Publishers, Dordrecht (2001)
258. Du, D.-Z., Hwang, F.K.: A proof of the Gilbert-Pollak conjecture on the Steiner ratio. Algorithmica 7, 121–135 (1992)
259. Du, Z., Eleftheriou, M., Moreira, J.E., Yap, C.-K.: Hypergeometric functions in exact geometric computation. Electronic Notes in Theoretical Computer Science 66(1), 53–64 (2002)
260. Duboc, L., Rosenblum, D.S., Wicks, T.: A framework for modelling and analysis of software systems scalability. In: ICSE 2006: Proceeding of the 28th International Conference on Software Engineering, pp. 949–952. ACM Press, New York (2006)
261. Duin, C.W.: Steiner's problem in graphs: reduction, approximation, variation, Ph.D. thesis, Universiteit van Amsterdam (1994)
262. Duin, C.W., Volgenant, A.: Reduction tests for the Steiner problem in graphs. Networks 19, 549–567 (1989)
263. Duin, C.W., Voss, S.: Efficient path and vertex exchange in Steiner tree algorithms. Networks 29, 89–105 (1997)
264. Duran, J.W., Wiorkowski, J.J.: Quantifying software validity by sampling. IEEE Transactions on Reliability R-29, 141–144 (1980)
265. The ECL^{i}PS^e constraint programming system (2007), http://eclipse.crossscoreop.com/
266. ECMA-334 C# language specification (2006), http://www.ecma-international.org/publications/files/ecma-st/ECMA-334.pdf
267. Edelkamp, S., Jabbar, S., Schrödl, S.: External A*. In: Biundo, S., Frühwirth, T., Palm, G. (eds.) KI 2004. LNCS (LNAI), vol. 3238, pp. 226–240. Springer, Heidelberg (2004)
268. Edelsbrunner, H., Mücke, E.P.: Simulation of simplicity: A technique to cope with degenerate cases in geometric algorithms. In: Proceedings of the 4th Annual ACM Symposium on Computational Geometry, pp. 118–133 (1988)
269. Edmonds, J.: Paths, trees, and flowers. Canadian J. Math. 17, 449–467 (1965)
270. Eén, N., Sörensson, N.: An extensible SAT-solver. In: Giunchiglia, E., Tacchella, A. (eds.) SAT 2003. LNCS, vol. 2919, pp. 502–518. Springer, Heidelberg (2004)
271. Eiden, W.A.: Präzise Unschärfe – Informationsmodellierung durch Fuzzy-Mengen. ibidem-Verlag (2002)
272. Eiden, W.A.: Scheduling with fuzzy methods. In: Fleuren, H., den Hertog, D., Kort, P. (eds.) Operations Research Proceedings 2004, Operations Research Proceedings, vol. 2004, pp. 377–384. Springer, Heidelberg (2004)
273. Emiris, I.Z., Canny, J.F.: A general approach to removing degeneracies. SIAM J. Comput. 24(3), 650–664 (1995)
274. Eppstein, D.: Quasiconvex analysis of backtracking algorithms. In: Proceedings of the 15th Annual ACM-SIAM Symposium on Discrete Algorithms (SODA), pp. 788–797. SIAM, Philadelphia (2004)
275. Erikson, C.: Hierarchical levels of detail to accelerate the rendering of large static and dynamic polygonal environments, Ph.D. thesis, University of North Carolina (2000)
276. EXACUS: Efficient and exact algorithms for curves and surfaces, version 1.0 (2006), http://www.mpi-inf.mpg.de/projects/EXACUS/
277. Exploratory data analysis (2006), http://www.itl.nist.gov/div898/handbook/eda/eda.htm

278. Fabri, A., Giezeman, G.-J., Kettner, L., Schirra, S., Schönherr, S.: On the design of CGAL, a computational geometry algorithms library. Software Practice and Experience 30(11), 1167–1202 (2000)

279. Fantozzi, C., Pietracaprina, A., Pucci, G.: Translating submachine locality into locality of reference. In: Proc. 18th Intl. Parallel and Distributed Processing Symp (IPDPS 2004), CD-ROM. IEEE Computer Society, Los Alamitos (2004)

280. Farach-Colton, M., Ferragina, P., Muthukrishnan, S.: On the sorting complexity of suffix tree construction. Journal of the ACM 47, 987–1011 (2000)

281. Farias, R., Silva, C.T.: Out-of-core rendering of large, unstructured grids. IEEE Computer Graphics and Applications 21(4), 42–50 (2001)

282. Fatahalian, K., Knight, T.J., Houston, M., Erez, M., Horn, D.R., Leem, L., Park, J.Y., Ren, M., Aiken, A., Dally, W.J., Hanrahan, P.: Sequoia: Programming the memory hierarchy. In: Proceedings of the 2006 ACM/IEEE Conference on Supercomputing (2006)

283. Fatourou, P., Spirakis, P., Zarafidis, P., Zoura, A.: Implementation and experimental evaluation of graph connectivity algorithms using LEDA. In: Vitter, J.S., Zaroliagis, C.D. (eds.) WAE 1999. LNCS, vol. 1668, pp. 124–138. Springer, Heidelberg (1999)

284. Feigenbaum, J., Kannan, S., McGregor, A., Suri, S., Zhang, J.: On graph problems in a semi-streaming model. In: Díaz, J., Karhumäki, J., Lepistö, A., Sannella, D. (eds.) ICALP 2004. LNCS, vol. 3142, pp. 531–543. Springer, Heidelberg (2004)

285. Ferragina, P., Grossi, R.: The string B-tree: A new data structure for string search in external memory and its applications. Journal of the ACM 46, 236–280 (1999)

286. Fiat, A., Karp, R.M., Luby, M., McGeoch, L.A., Sleator, D.D., Young, N.E.: Competitive paging algorithms. J. Algorithms 12(4), 685–699 (1991)

287. Fiat, A., Woeginger, G.J. (eds.): Online algorithms: The state of the art. Springer, Heidelberg (1998)

288. Fleischer, R., Moret, B.M.E., Schmidt, E.M. (eds.): Experimental Algorithmics. LNCS, vol. 2547. Springer, Heidelberg (2002)

289. http://blog.flickr.net/en/2008/11/03/3-billion/ (2008)

290. Floudas, C.A., Pardalos, P.M.: A Collection of Test Problems for Constrained Global Optimization Algorithms. LNCS, vol. 455. Springer, Heidelberg (1990)

291. Foggia, P.: The VFLib graph matching library, version 2.0 March (2001), http://amalfi.dis.unina.it/graph/db/vflib-2.0/doc/vflib.html

292. Fomin, F.V., Grandoni, F., Kratsch, D.: Measure and conquer: Domination – a case study. In: Caires, L., Italiano, G.F., Monteiro, L., Palamidessi, C., Yung, M. (eds.) ICALP 2005. LNCS, vol. 3580, pp. 191–203. Springer, Heidelberg (2005)

293. Ford, L.R., Fulkerson, D.R.: Flows in Networks. Princeton University Press, Princeton (1963)

294. Fortune, S.: A sweepline algorithm for Voronoi diagrams. In: Proceedings of the 2nd Annual ACM Symposium on Computational Geometry, pp. 313–322. ACM Press, New York (1986)

295. Fortune, S.: Stable maintenance of point set triangulations in two dimensions. In: Proceedings of the 30th Annual IEEE Symposium on Foundations of Computer Science (FOCS), pp. 494–499 (1989)

296. Fortune, S.: Polyhedral modelling with exact arithmetic. In: SMA 1995: Proceedings of the Third ACM Symposium on Solid Modeling and Applications, pp. 225–234. ACM, New York (1995)

297. Fortune, S.: Introduction. Algorithmica 27(1), 1–4 (2000)

298. Fortune, S., van Wyk, C.J.: Efficient exact arithmetic for computational geometry. In: Proceedings of the 9th Annual ACM Symposium on Computational Geometry, pp. 163–172 (1993)

299. Fortune, S., van Wyk, C.J.: Static analysis yields efficient exact integer arithmetic for computational geometry. ACM Transactions on Graphics 15(3), 223–248 (1996)

300. Fortune, S., Wyllie, J.: Parallelism in random access machines. In: Proceedings of the 10th ACM Symposium on Theory of Computing (STOC), pp. 114–118 (1978)

301. Fößmeier, U., Kaufmann, M.: On exact solutions for the rectilinear Steiner tree problem, Tech. Report WSI-96-09, Universität Tübingen (1996)

302. Fößmeier, U., Kaufmann, M.: On exact solutions for the rectilinear Steiner tree problem Part I: Theoretical results. Algorithmica 26, 68–99 (2000)

303. Foster, I.T., Iamnitchi, A.: On death, taxes, and the convergence of peer-to-peer and grid computing. In: Kaashoek, M.F., Stoica, I. (eds.) IPTPS 2003. LNCS, vol. 2735, pp. 118–128. Springer, Heidelberg (2003)

304. Fourer, R., Gay, D.M., Kernighan, B.W.: AMPL: A modeling language for mathematical programming. Brooks/Cole Publishing Company, Monterey (2002)

305. Fox, G., Williams, R., Messina, P.: Parallel computing works! Morgan Kaufmann, San Francisco (1994)

306. Frias, L., Petit, J., Roura, S.: Lists revisited: Cache-conscious STL lists. In: Àlvarez, C., Serna, M. (eds.) WEA 2006. LNCS, vol. 4007, pp. 121–133. Springer, Heidelberg (2006)

307. Friedman, J.H., Bentley, J.L., Finkel, R.A.: An algorithm for finding best matches in logarithmic expected time. ACM Transactions on Mathematical Software 3(3), 209–226 (1977)

308. Frigo, M., Leiserson, C.E., Prokop, H., Ramachandran, S.: Cache-oblivious algorithms. In: Proceedings of the 40th Annual IEEE Symposium on Foundations of Computer Science (FOCS), pp. 285–298. IEEE Computer Society, Los Alamitos (1999)

309. Fuchs, B., Kern, W., Mölle, D., Richter, S., Rossmanith, P., Wang, X.: Dynamic programming for minimum Steiner trees. Theory Comput. Syst. 41(3), 493–500 (2007)

310. Fuchs, B., Kern, W., Wang, X.: The number of tree stars is $O^*(1.357^n)$. Algorithmica 49, 232–244 (2007)

311. Funke, S., Klein, C., Mehlhorn, K., Schmitt, S.: Controlled perturbation for Delaunay triangulations. In: Proceedings of the 16th Annual ACM-SIAM Symposium on Discrete Algorithms (SODA), pp. 1047–1056 (2005)

312. Galil, Z., Micali, S., Gabow, H.N.: An $O(EV \log V)$ algorithm for finding a maximal weighted matching in general graphs. SIAM J. Comput. 15(1), 120–130 (1986)

313. Gamma, E., Helm, R., Johnson, R., Vlissides, J.: Design patterns: Elements of reusable object-oriented software. Addison-Wesley, Reading (1995)

314. Ganley, J.L., Cohoon, J.P.: Optimal rectilinear Steiner minimal trees in $O(n^2 2.62^n)$ time. In: Proc. 6th Canad. Conf. on Computational Geometry, pp. 308–313 (1994)

315. Gansner, E.R., North, S.C.: An open graph visualization system and its applications to software engineering. Software — Practice and Experience 30(11), 1203–1233 (2000)

316. Garey, M.R., Graham, R.L., Johnson, D.S.: The complexity of computing Steiner minimal trees. SIAM Journal on Applied Mathematics 32, 835–859 (1977)

317. Garey, M.R., Johnson, D.S.: The rectilinear Steiner tree problem is NP-complete. SIAM Journal on Applied Mathematics 32, 826–834 (1977)

318. Gärtner, B., Henk, M., Ziegler, G.M.: Randomized simplex algorithms on Klee-Minty cubes. Combinatorica 18(3), 349–372 (1998)

319. Gass, S.I., Saaty, T.L.: The computational algorithm for the parametric objective function. Naval Research Logistics Quarterly 2, 39 (1955)

320. Gavrilova, M.: Weighted Voronoi diagrams in biology (2007), http://pages.cpsc.ucalgary.ca/~marina/vpplants/

321. Website of the GNU GCC project (2006), http://gcc.gnu.org/

322. Gebremedhin, A.H., Lassous, I.G., Gustedt, J., Telle, J.A.: PRO: A model for parallel resource-optimal computation. In: Proc. 16th Int. Symp. High Performance Computing Systems and Applications (HPCS), pp. 106–113. IEEE Computer Society, Los Alamitos (2002)

323. Geisberger, R., Sanders, P., Schultes, D., Delling, D.: Contraction hierarchies: Faster and simpler hierarchical routing in road networks. In: McGeoch, C.C. (ed.) WEA 2008. LNCS, vol. 5038, pp. 319–333. Springer, Heidelberg (2008)

324. Geldermann, J., Rommelfanger, H.: Fuzzy Sets, Neuronale Netze und Künstliche Intelligenz in der industriellen Produktion. VDI-Verlag, Düsseldorf (2003)

325. Gent, I.P., Grant, S.A., MacIntyre, E., Prosser, P., Shaw, P., Smith, B.M., Walsh, T.: How not to do it, Tech. Report 97.27, School of Computer Studies, University of Leeds (May 1997)

326. Gent, I.P., Jefferson, C., Miguel, I.: MINION: A fast, scalable, constraint solver. In: Brewka, G., Coradeschi, S., Perini, A., Traverso, P. (eds.) Proc. 17th European Conference on Artificial Intelligence (ECAI 2006). Frontiers in Artificial Intelligence and Applications, vol. 141, pp. 98–102. IOS Press, Amsterdam (2006)

327. Gent, I.P., Walsh, T.: CSPLIB: A benchmark library for constraints, Tech. Report APES-09-1999, Department of Computer Science, University of Strathclyde, Glasgow (1999)

328. Gent, I.P., Walsh, T.: CSPLIB: A benchmark library for constraints. In: Jaffar, J. (ed.) CP 1999. LNCS, vol. 1713, pp. 480–481. Springer, Heidelberg (1999)

329. Gerbessiotis, A.V., Valiant, L.G.: Direct bulk-synchronous parallel algorithms. J. Parallel Distrib. Comput. 22(2), 251–267 (1994)

330. Geurts, A.J.: A contribution to the theory of condition. Numerische Mathematik 39, 85–96 (1982)

331. Ghezzi, C., Jazayeri, M., Mandrioli, D.: Fundamentals of software engineering. Prentice Hall, New Jersey (1991)

332. Gibbons, P.B., Matias, Y., Ramachandran, V.: Can a shared-memory model serve as a bridging model for parallel computation? Theory Comput. Syst. 32(3), 327–359 (1999)

333. Giegerich, R., Kurtz, S.: From Ukkonen to McCreight and Weiner: A unifying view of linear-time suffix tree construction. Algorithmica 19(3), 331–353 (1997)

334. GMP: GNU Multiple Precision Arithmetic Library, version 4.2.1 (2006), http://www.swox.com/gmp/

335. Goedecker, S., Hoisie, A.: Performance optimization of numerically intensive codes. Society for Industrial and Applied Mathematics, Philadelphia (2001)

336. Goemans, M.X., Williamson, D.P.: A general approximation technique for constrained forest problems. SIAM Journal on Computing 24(2), 296–317 (1995)

337. Gog, S.: Broadword computing and Fibonacci code speed up compressed suffix arrays. In: Vahrenhold, J. (ed.) SEA 2009. LNCS, vol. 5526, pp. 161–172. Springer, Heidelberg (2009)

338. Goldberg, A.V., Harrelson, C.: Computing the shortest path: A* search meets graph theory. In: Proceedings of the 16th Annual ACM–SIAM Symposium on Discrete Algorithms (SODA), pp. 156–165 (2005)

339. Goldberg, A.V., Kaplan, H., Werneck, R.F.: Reach for A*: Efficient point-to-point shortest path algorithms. In: Proceedings of the 8th Workshop on Algorithm Engineering and Experiments (ALENEX 2006), pp. 129–143. SIAM, Philadelphia (2006)

340. Goldberg, A.V., Kaplan, H., Werneck, R.F.: Better landmarks within reach. In: Demetrescu, C. (ed.) WEA 2007. LNCS, vol. 4525, pp. 38–51. Springer, Heidelberg (2007)

341. Goldberg, A.V., Moret, B.M.E.: Combinatorial algorithms test sets (CATS): The ACM/EATCS platform for experimental research. In: Proceedings of the Tenth Annual ACM-SIAM Symposium on Discrete Algorithms, Baltimore, Maryland, January 17-19, pp. 913–914 (1999)

342. Goldberg, A.V., Werneck, R.F.: Computing point-to-point shortest paths from external memory. In: Proceedings of the 7th Workshop on Algorithm Engineering and Experiments (ALENEX 2005), pp. 26–40. SIAM, Philadelphia (2005)

343. Goldberg, D.: What every computer scientist should know about floating-point arithmetic. ACM Computing Surveys 23(1), 5–48 (1991)

344. Goldchleger, A., Goldman, A., Hayashida, U., Kon, F.: The implementation of the BSP parallel computing model on the integrade grid middleware. In: MGC 2005: Proceedings of the 3rd International Workshop on Middleware for Grid Computing, pp. 1–6. ACM, New York (2005)

345. Golden, B.L., Stewart, W.R.: Empirical analysis of heuristics. In: The Traveling Salesman Problem – a Guided Tour of Combinatorial Optimization, pp. 207–249. John Wiley & Sons, Chichester (1985)

346. Goldstine, H.H., von Neumann, J.: Numerical inverting of matrices of high order II. Proc. Amer. Math. Soc. 2, 188–202 (1951); Reprinted in (774, pp. 558–572)

347. Goodrich, M.T., Handy, M., Hudson, B., Tamassia, R.: Accessing the internal organization of data structures in the JDSL library. In: Goodrich, M.T., McGeoch, C.C. (eds.) ALENEX 1999. LNCS, vol. 1619, pp. 124–139. Springer, Heidelberg (1999)

348. Goodrich, M.T., Tamassia, R.: Algorithm design: Foundations, analysis, and internet examples. Wiley, Chichester (September 2001)

349. Goodrich, M.T., Tsay, J.-J., Vengroff, D.E., Vitter, J.S.: External-memory computational geometry. In: Proceedings of the 34th Annual IEEE Symposium on Foundations of Computer Science (FOCS), pp. 714–723 (1993)

350. Govindaraju, N.K., Larsen, S., Gray, J., Manocha, D.: A memory model for scientific algorithms on graphics processors. In: Proceedings of the ACM/IEEE SC 2006 Conference on High Performance Networking and Computing, Tampa, FL, USA, November 11-17, p. 89 (2006)

351. Graham, S., Kessler, P., McKusick, M.: An execution profiler for modular programs. Software - Practice and Experience 13, 671–685 (1993)

352. Grama, A., Gupta, A., Karypis, G., Kumar, V.: Introduction to parallel computing. Pearson Education, London (2003)

353. Grama, A., Kumar, V., Ranka, S., Singh, V.: Architecture independent analysis of parallel programs. In: Proc. Intl. Conf. on Computational Science (ICCS 2001) - Part II, London, UK, pp. 599–608. Springer, Heidelberg (2001)

354. Gramm, J., Guo, J., Hüffner, F., Niedermeier, R.: Automated generation of search tree algorithms for hard graph modification problems. Algorithmica 39(4), 321–347 (2004)

355. Granlund, T.: GMP: The GNU multiple precision arithmetic library. In: Free Software Foundation, Boston, MA (2006)

356. Graphviz: Graph visualization software, version 2.16 (2007),
     http://www.graphviz.org/
357. Greenberg, H.J.: Computational testing: Why, how and how much. ORSA Journal
     on Computing 2(1), 94–97 (1990)
358. Greene, D.H.: Integer line segment intersection (unpublished manuscript)
359. Greene, D.H., Yao, F.F.: Finite-resolution computational geometry. In: Proceed-
     ings of the 27th Annual IEEE Symposium on Foundations of Computer Science
     (FOCS), pp. 143–152 (1986)
360. Gregor, D., Lumsdaine, A.: The parallel BGL: A generic library for distributed
     graph computations. Tech. report, Open Systems Laboratory, Indiana University
     (2005)
361. Grötschel, M., Martin, A., Weismantel, R.: The Steiner tree packing problem in
     VLSI design. Mathematical Programming 78(2), 265–281 (1997)
362. Grubb, P., Takang, A.A.: Software maintenance: concepts and practice, 2nd edn.
     World Scientific, Singapore (2003)
363. GSL: GNU scientific library, version 1.8 (2006),
     http://www.gnu.org/software/gsl/
364. Guibas, L.J., Salesin, D., Stolfi, J.: Constructing strongly convex approximate
     hulls with inaccurate primitives. In: SIGAL 1990, pp. 261–270. Springer, Heidel-
     berg (1990)
365. Gunkel, T., Müller-Hannemann, M., Schnee, M.: Improved search for night train
     connections. In: Liebchen, C., Ahuja, R.K., Mesa, J.A. (eds.) Proceedings of
     the 7th Workshop on Algorithmic Approaches for Transportation Modeling,
     Optimization, and Systems (ATMOS 2007), Internationales Begegnungs- und
     Forschungszentrum für Informatik (IBFI), Schloss Dagstuhl, Germany, pp. 243–
     258 (2007)
366. Gurevich, Y., Kutter, P.W., Odersky, M., Thiele, L. (eds.): ASM 2000. LNCS,
     vol. 1912. Springer, Heidelberg (2000)
367. Gusfield, D.: Algorithms on strings, trees, and sequences. University of Cambridge
     Press, Cambridge (1997)
368. Gustavson, D.B.: The many dimensions of scalability. In: COMPCON, pp. 60–63
     (1994)
369. Gustavson, F.G.: Recursion leads to automatic variable blocking for dense linear-
     algebra algorithms. IBM J. of Research and Development 41(6), 737–756 (1999)
370. Gustedt, J.: External memory algorithms using a coarse grained paradigm. Tech.
     Report 5142, INRIA Lorraine / LORIA, France (March 2004)
371. Gustedt, J., Vialle, S., De Vivo, A.: The parXXL environment: Scalable fine
     grained development for large coarse grained platforms. In: Kågström, B., Elm-
     roth, E., Dongarra, J., Waśniewski, J. (eds.) PARA 2006. LNCS, vol. 4699, pp.
     1094–1104. Springer, Heidelberg (2007)
372. Gutman, R.J.: Reach-based routing: A new approach to shortest path algorithms
     optimized for road networks. In: Proceedings of the 6th Workshop on Algorithm
     Engineering and Experiments (ALENEX 2004), pp. 100–111. SIAM, Philadelphia
     (2004)
373. Gutwenger, C., Mutzel, P.: A linear time implementation of SPQR-trees. In:
     Marks, J. (ed.) GD 2000. LNCS, vol. 1984, pp. 77–90. Springer, Heidelberg (2001)
374. Haigh, T.: Oral history: An interview with, Traub, J.F. (2004),
     http://history.siam.org/oralhistories/traub.htm
375. Hall, N.G., Posner, M.E.: Generating experimental data for computational testing
     with machine scheduling applications. Operations Research 49(7), 854–865 (2001)

376. Halperin, D., Leiserowitz, E.: Controlled perturbation for arrangements of circles. In: Proceedings of the 19th Annual ACM Symposium on Computational Geometry, pp. 264–273 (2003)
377. Halperin, D., Packer, E.: Iterated snap rounding. Comput. Geom. Theory Appl. 23, 209–225 (2002)
378. Halperin, D., Shelton, C.R.: A perturbation scheme for spherical arrangements with application to molecular modeling. In: Proceedings of the 13th Annual ACM Symposium on Computational Geometry, pp. 183–192. ACM Press, New York (1997)
379. Hambrusch, S.E.: Models for parallel computation. In: ICPP Workshop, pp. 92–95 (1996)
380. Hanan, M.: On Steiner's problem with rectilinear distance. SIAM Journal on Applied Mathematics 14, 255–265 (1966)
381. Hansen, P.: Bricriteria path problems. In: Fandel, G., Gal, T. (eds.) Multiple Criteria Decision Making – Theory and Application, pp. 109–127. Springer, Heidelberg (1979)
382. Hart, P.E., Nilsson, N., Raphael, B.: A formal basis for the heuristic determination of minimum cost paths. IEEE Transactions on Systems Science and Cybernetics 4, 100–107 (1968)
383. Hassin, R.: Approximation schemes for the restricted shortest path problem. Mathematics of Operations Research 17(1), 36–42 (1992)
384. Heitmann, C.: Beurteilung der Bestandsfestigkeit von Unternehmen mit Neuro-Fuzzy, Peter Lang, Frankfurt am Main (2002)
385. Held, M.: VRONI: An engineering approach to the reliable and efficient computation of Voronoi diagrams of points and line segments. Comput. Geom. Theory Appl. 18(2), 95–123 (2001)
386. Hendrickson, B., Leland, R.: A multilevel algorithm for partitioning graphs. In: Supercomputing 1995: Proceedings of the 1995 ACM/IEEE Conference on Supercomputing (CDROM), p. 28. ACM Press, New York (1995)
387. Henzinger, M.R., Raghavan, P., Rajagopalan, S.: Computing on data streams. In: External Memory Algorithms, DIMACS Series in Discrete Mathematics and Theoretical Computer Science, vol. 50, pp. 107–118 (1999)
388. Heroux, M.A., Raghavan, P., Simon, H.D.: Parallel processing for scientific computing (software, environments and tools). SIAM, Philadelphia (2006)
389. Hert, S., Kettner, L., Polzin, T., Schäfer, G.: ExpLab - a tool set for computational experiments (2003), http://explab.sourceforge.net
390. Hilbert, D.: Über die stetige Abbildung einer Linie auf ein Flächenstück. Math. Annalen 38, 459–460 (1891)
391. Hildrum, K., Kubiatowicz, J.D., Rao, S., Zhao, B.Y.: Distributed object location in a dynamic network. In: SPAA 2002: Proceedings of the Fourteenth Annual ACM Symposium on Parallel Algorithms and Architectures, pp. 41–52. ACM Press, New York (2002)
392. Hilger, M., Köhler, E., Möhring, R.H., Schilling, H.: Fast point-to-point shortest path computations with arc-flags. In: Demetrescu, C., Goldberg, A.V., Johnson, D.S. (eds.) Shortest Path Computations: Ninth DIMACS Challenge. DIMACS Book, vol. 74, pp. 41–72. American Mathematical Society, Providence (2009)
393. Hill, J., McColl, W., Stefanescu, D., Goudreau, M., Lang, K., Rao, S., Suel, T., Tsantilas, T., Bisseling, R.: BSPlib: the BSP programming library. Parallel Computing 24, 1947–1980 (1998)
394. Hill, M.D.: What is scalability? SIGARCH Computer Architecture News 18(4), 18–21 (1990)

395. Hill, M.D., Smith, A.J.: Evaluating associativity in CPU caches. IEEE Trans. Comput. 38(12), 1612–1630 (1989)
396. Hiller, B., Krumke, S.O., Rambau, J.: Reoptimization gaps versus model errors in online-dispatching of service units for ADAC. Discrete Appl. Math. 154(13), 1897–1907 (2006)
397. Hoare, C.A.R.: An axiomatic basis for computer programming. Communications of the ACM 12(10), 576–580 (1969)
398. Hobby, J.D.: Practical segment intersection with finite precision output. Comput. Geom. Theory Appl. 13(4), 199–214 (1999)
399. Hochstein, L., Basili, V.R., Vishkin, U., Gilbert, J.: A pilot study to compare programming effort for two parallel programming models. Journal of Systems and Software 81(11), 1920–1930 (2008)
400. Hoffman, K.L., Jackson, R.H.F.: In pursuit of a methodology for testing mathematical programming software. In: Mulvey, J.M. (ed.) Evaluating Mathematical Programming Techniques, Proceedings of a Conference held at the National Bureau of Standards, Boulder, Colorado, January 5-6, 1981. Lecture Notes in Economics and Mathematical Systems, vol. 199, pp. 177–199. Springer, Heidelberg (1982)
401. Hoffmann, C.M.: Robustness in geometric computations. Journal of Computing and Information Science in Engineering 2, 143–155 (2001)
402. Hoffmann, C.M., Hopcroft, J.E., Karasick, M.S.: Towards implementing robust geometric computations. In: Proceedings of the 4th Annual ACM Symposium on Computational Geometry, pp. 106–117. ACM Press, New York (1988)
403. Holte, R.C.: Very simple classification rules perform well on most commonly used datasets. Machine Learning 11, 63–91 (1993)
404. Holzer, M., Schulz, F., Wagner, D.: Engineering multi-level overlay graphs for shortest-path queries. In: Proceedings of the 8th Workshop on Algorithm Engineering and Experiments (ALENEX 2006). SIAM, Philadelphia (2006)
405. Holzer, M., Schulz, F., Wagner, D.: Engineering multi-level overlay graphs for shortest-path queries. ACM Journal of Experimental Algorithmics 13, 2.5:1–2.5:26 (2008)
406. Holzer, M., Schulz, F., Wagner, D., Willhalm, T.: Combining speed-up techniques for shortest-path computations. ACM Journal of Experimental Algorithmics 10, 2.5 (2005)
407. Holzer, M., Schulz, F., Willhalm, T.: Combining speed-up techniques for shortest-path computations. In: Ribeiro, C.C., Martins, S.L. (eds.) WEA 2004. LNCS, vol. 3059, pp. 269–284. Springer, Heidelberg (2004)
408. Hooker, J.N.: Needed: An empirical science of algorithms. Operations Research 42(2), 201–212 (1994)
409. Hooker, J.N.: Testing heuristics: We have it all wrong. Journal of Heuristics 1(1), 33–42 (1995)
410. Hoos, H.H., Stützle, T.: SATLIB: An online resource for research on SAT. In: Gent, I., van Maaren, H., Walsh, T. (eds.) SAT 2000, Highlights of Satisfiability Research in the Year 2000. Frontiers in Artificial Intelligence and Applications, vol. 63, pp. 283–292. IOS Press, Amsterdam (2000)
411. Hopcroft, J.E., Kahn, P.J.: A paradigm for robust geometric algorithms. Algorithmica 7(4), 339–380 (1992)
412. Hopcroft, J.E., Tarjan, R.E.: Efficient planarity testing. Journal of the ACM 21, 549–568 (1974)
413. Hou, Q., Zhou, K., Guo, B.: BSGP: Bulk-synchronous GPU programming. ACM Trans. Graph. 27(3), 1–12 (2008)

414. Hougardy, S., Prömel, H.-J.: A 1.598 approximation algorithm for the Steiner problem in graphs. In: Proceedings of the Tenth Annual ACM-SIAM Symposium on Discrete Algorithms, pp. 448–453 (1999)

415. Hu, J., Alpert, C.J., Quay, S.T., Gandham, G.: Buffer insertion with adaptive blockage avoidance. In: ISPD 2002: Proceedings of the 2002 International Symposium on Physical Design, pp. 92–97. ACM Press, New York (2002)

416. Huddleston, S., Mehlhorn, K.: A new data structure for representing sorted lists. Acta Informatica, 157–184 (1982)

417. Hüffner, F.: Algorithm engineering for optimal graph bipartization. In: Nikoletseas, S.E. (ed.) WEA 2005. LNCS, vol. 3503, pp. 240–252. Springer, Heidelberg (2005)

418. Hwang, F.K.: On Steiner minimal trees with rectilinear distance. SIAM Journal on Applied Mathematics 30, 104–114 (1976)

419. Ibarra, O.H., Kim, C.E.: Fast approximation algorithms for the knapsack and sum of subset problems. Journal of the ACM 22(4), 463–468 (1975)

420. IEEE standard for binary floating-point arithmetic, ANSI/IEEE standard 754–1985, Institute of Electrical and Electronics Engineers, New York (1985); Reprinted in SIGPLAN Notices 22(2), 9-25 (1987)

421. Ikeda, T., Hsu, M.-Y., Imai, H., Nishimura, S., Shimoura, H., Hashimoto, T., Tenmoku, K., Mitoh, K.: A fast algorithm for finding better routes by AI search techniques. In: Proceedings of the Vehicle Navigation and Information Systems Conference (VNSI 1994), pp. 291–296. ACM Press, New York (1994)

422. ILOG CPLEX: High-performance software for mathematical programming and optimization (2009), http://www.ilog.com/products/cplex/

423. ILOG CPLEX 11.2 reference manuals (2009), http://www.cplex.com

424. ILOG solver (2009), http://www.ilog.com/products/solver/

425. Imai, T.: A topology oriented algorithm for the Voronoi diagram of polygons. In: Proceedings of the 8th Canadian Conference on Computational Geometry, pp. 107–112. Carleton University Press (1996)

426. Yahoo claims record with petabyte database (2008), http://www.informationweek.com/news/software/database/showArticle.jhtml?articleID=207801436

427. Intel threading building blocks website, http://osstbb.intel.com/

428. Netezza promises petabyte-scale data warehouse appliances (2008), http://www.intelligententerprise.com/showArticle.jhtml?articleID=205600559

429. ISO/IEC 14882:2003 programming languages – C++ (2003)

430. Jackson, R.H.F., Boggs, P.T., Nash, S.G., Powell, S.: Guidelines for reporting results of computational experiments. Report of the ad hoc committee. Mathematical Programming 49, 413–425 (1991)

431. Jacobsen, L., Larsen, K.S.: Complexity of layered binary search trees with relaxed balance. In: Restivo, A., Ronchi Della Rocca, S., Roversi, L. (eds.) ICTCS 2001. LNCS, vol. 2202, pp. 269–284. Springer, Heidelberg (2001)

432. JaJa, J.: An introduction to parallel algorithms. Addison-Wesley, Reading (1992)

433. Jarník, V., Kössler, M.: O minimálních grafech osahujících n daných bodu. Čas. Pěstování Mat. 63, 223–235 (1934)

434. Jazequel, J.-M., Meyer, B.: Design by contract: The lessons of Ariane. Computer 30(1), 129–130 (1997)

435. Jensen, J.R.: Remote sensing of the environment: An earth resource perspective. Prentice-Hall, Englewood Cliffs (2007)

436. Beasley, J.E.: An SST-based algorithm for the Steiner problem in graphs. Networks 19, 1–16 (1989)

437. Johnson, D.S.: A theoretician's guide to the experimental analysis of algorithms. In: Goldwasser, M.H., Johnson, D.S., McGeoch, C.C. (eds.) Data Structures, Near Neighbor Searches, and Methodology: Fifth and Sixth DIMACS Implementation Challenges. DIMACS Monographs, vol. 59, pp. 215–250 (2002)

438. Johnson, D.S., McGeoch, C.C. (eds.): Network flows and matching: First DIMACS implementation challenge. DIMACS Series in Discrete Mathematics and Theoretical Computer Science, vol. 12. AMS, Providence (1993)

439. Johnson, D.S., McGeoch, L.: Experimental analysis of heuristics for the STSP. In: Gutin, Punnen (eds.) The Traveling Salesman Problem and its Variations, pp. 369–443. Kluwer Academic Publishing, Dordrecht (2002)

440. Johnson, D.S., McGeoch, L.A.: The traveling salesman problem: A case study in local optimization. In: Aarts, E.H.L., Lenstra, J.K. (eds.) Local Search in Combinatorial Optimization. John Wiley and Sons, Chichester (1997)

441. Johnson, S.: Lint, a C program checker, Unix Programmer's Manual. AT&T Bell Laboratories (1978)

442. Jones, J.A., Harrold, M.J., Stakso, J.: Visualization of test information to assist fault localization. In: ICSE 2002 International Conference on Software Engineering, pp. 467–477 (2002)

443. Jovanovich, M., Annexstein, F., Berman, K.: Scalability issues in large peer-to-peer networks - a case study of Gnutella. Tech. report, ECECS Department, University of Cincinnati (2001)

444. Juurlink, B.H.H., Wijshoff, H.A.G.: A quantitative comparison of parallel computation models. ACM Trans. Comput. Syst. 16(3), 271–318 (1998)

445. Kaashoek, M.F., Karger, D.R.: Koorde: A simple degree-optimal distributed hash table. In: Kaashoek, M.F., Stoica, I. (eds.) IPTPS 2003. LNCS, vol. 2735, pp. 98–107. Springer, Heidelberg (2003)

446. Kahng, A.B., Măndoiu, I.I., Zelikovsky, A.Z.: Highly scalable algorithms for rectilinear and octilinear Steiner trees. In: Proceedings 2003 Asia and South Pacific Design Automation Conference (ASP-DAC), pp. 827–833 (2003)

447. Kahng, A.B., Măndoiu, I.I., Zelikovsky, A.Z.: Practical Approximations of Steiner Trees in Uniform Orientation Metrics. In: Approximation Algorithms and Metaheuristics. Chapman & Hall/CRC (2007)

448. Kahng, A.B., Robins, G.: A new class of iterative Steiner tree heuristics with good performances. IEEE Trans. Computer-Aided Design 11, 1462–1465 (1992)

449. Kalai, G.: A subexponential randomized simplex algorithm. In: Proceedings of the 24th Annual ACM Symposium on Theory of Computing (STOC), pp. 475–482 (1992)

450. Kalai, G., Kleitman, D.J.: A quasi-polynomial bound for the diameter of graphs of polyhedra. Bulletin Amer. Math. Soc. 26, 315 (1992)

451. Kaligosi, K., Sanders, P.: How branch mispredictions affect quicksort. In: Azar, Y., Erlebach, T. (eds.) ESA 2006. LNCS, vol. 4168, pp. 780–791. Springer, Heidelberg (2006)

452. Kanet, J.J., Ahire, S.L., Gorman, M.F.: Constraint Programming for Scheduling. In: Handbook of Scheduling: Algorithms, Models, and Performance Analysis, pp. 47-1–47-21. Chapman & Hall/CRC (2004)

453. Kanth, K.V.R., Singh, A.: Optimal dynamic range searching in non-replicating index structures. In: International Conference on Database Theory ICDT, pp. 257–276 (1999)

454. Kaplan, C.S.: Voronoi diagrams and ornamental design. In: Proceedings of the First Annual Symposium of the International Society for the Arts, Mathematics, and Architecture, ISAMA 1999, San Sebastián, Spain, June 7-11, pp. 277–283 (1999)

455. Kaplan, H., Shafrir, N.: The greedy algorithm for shortest superstrings. Information Processing Letters 93(1), 13–17 (2005)

456. Karakostas, G.: A better approximation ratio for the vertex cover problem. In: Caires, L., Italiano, G.F., Monteiro, L., Palamidessi, C., Yung, M. (eds.) ICALP 2005. LNCS, vol. 3580, pp. 1043–1050. Springer, Heidelberg (2005)

457. Karamcheti, V., Li, C., Pechtchanski, I., Yap, C.-K.: A core library for robust numeric and geometric computation. In: Proceedings of the 15th Annual ACM Symposium on Computational Geometry, pp. 351–359 (1999)

458. Karasick, M., Lieber, D., Nackman, L.R.: Efficient Delaunay triangulation using rational arithmetic. ACM Trans. Graph. 10(1), 71–91 (1991)

459. Karavelas, M.I.: A robust and efficient implementation for the segment Voronoi diagram. In: International Symposium on Voronoi Diagrams in Science and Engineering (VD 2004), pp. 51–62 (2004)

460. Karger, D., Lehman, E., Leighton, T., Levine, M., Lewin, D., Panigrahy, R.: Consistent hashing and random trees: Distributed caching protocols for relieving hot spots on the world wide web. In: ACM Symposium on Theory of Computing, pp. 654–663 (May 1997)

461. Karlin, A.R., Phillips, S.J., Raghavan, P.: Markov paging. In: Proceedings of the 33rd Annual IEEE Symposium on Foundations of Computer Science (FOCS), pp. 208–217 (1992)

462. Karlsson, B.: Beyond the C++ standard library: An introduction to Boost. Addison-Wesley, Reading (2005)

463. Karmarkar, N.: A new polynomial-time algorithm for linear programming. Combinatorica 4(4), 373–396 (1984)

464. Karp, R.M.: Reducibility among combinatorial problems. In: Miller, R.E., Thatcher, J.W. (eds.) Complexity of Computer Computations, pp. 85–104. Plenum Press, New York (1972)

465. Karp, R.M., Ramachandran, V.: Parallel algorithms for shared-memory machines. In: Handbook of Theoretical Computer Science. Algorithms and Complexity, vol. A, pp. 869–942. Elsevier, Amsterdam (1990)

466. Karpinski, M., Zelikovsky, A.: New approximation algorithms for the Steiner tree problem. Journal of Combinatorial Optimization 1, 47–65 (1997)

467. Karypis, G.: METIS - family of multilevel partitioning algorithms (2007)

468. Karypis, G., Kumar, V.: A fast and high quality multilevel scheme for partitioning irregular graphs. SIAM J. Sci. Comput. 20(1), 359–392 (1998)

469. Kelner, J.A., Spielman, D.A.: A randomized polynomial-time simplex algorithm for linear programming. In: Proceedings of the 38th Annual ACM Symposium on Theory of Computing (STOC), pp. 51–60 (2006)

470. Kettner, L.: Reference counting in library design — optionally and with union-find optimization. In: Lumsdaine, A., Schupp, S. (eds.) Library-Centric Software Design (LCSD 2005), San Diego, CA, USA, pp. 1–10. Department of Computer Science, Texas A&M University (October 2005)

471. Kettner, L., Mehlhorn, K., Pion, S., Schirra, S., Yap, C.-K.: Classroom examples of robustness problems in geometric computations. In: Albers, S., Radzik, T. (eds.) ESA 2004. LNCS, vol. 3221, pp. 702–713. Springer, Heidelberg (2004)

472. Khachiyan, L.G.: A polynomial algorithm in linear programming. Dokl. Akad. Nauk SSSR 244, 1093–1096 (1979)

473. Khronos Group, OpenCL (2009), `http://www.khronos.org/opencl/`

474. Klein, C.: Controlled perturbation for Voronoi diagrams, Master's thesis, Universität des Saarlandes (April 2004)

475. Kleinberg, J., Tardos, E.: Algorithm design. Pearson Education, London (2006)

476. Klingman, D., Albert Napier, H., Stutz, J.: NETGEN: A program for generating large scale capacitated assignment, transportation, and minimum cost flow network problems. Management Science 20(5), 814–821 (1974)

477. Knuth, D.E.: The art of computer programming, 1st edn. Seminumerical Algorithms, vol. 2. Addison-Wesley Professional, Reading (1969)

478. Knuth, D.E.: Structured programming with go to statements. ACM Computing Surveys 6, 261–301 (1974)

479. Knuth, D.E.: The WEB system of structured documentation, Stanford Computer Science Report CS980 (September 1983)

480. Knuth, D.E.: Literate programming. The Computer Journal 27(2), 97–111 (1984)

481. Knuth, D.E.: The Stanford graphbase: A platform for combinatorial computing. ACM Press, New York (1993)

482. Knuth, D.E.: The art of computer programming, 2nd edn. Sorting and Searching, vol. 3. Addison-Wesley Professional, Reading (1998)

483. Knuth, D.E.: The art of computer programming. Fascile 1: Bitwise tricks and techniques; binary decision diagrams, vol. 4. Addison-Wesley Professional, Reading (2009)

484. Knuth, D.E., Levy, S.: The CWEB system of structured documentation, version 3.0. Addison-Wesley, Reading (1993)

485. Köbler, J., Schöning, U., Toran, J.: The graph isomorphism problem: Its structural complexity. Birkhäuser, Basel (1993)

486. Koch, T.: ZIMPL user guide, ZIB Report 00-20, Zuse Institute Berlin (2001), Current version, `http://zimpl.zib.de/download/zimpl.pdf`

487. Koch, T.: Rapid mathematical programming, Ph.D. thesis, Technische Universität Berlin, ZIB-Report 04-58 (2004)

488. Koch, T.: ZIMPL (2008), `http://zimpl.zib.de/`

489. Koch, T., Martin, A.: Steinlib (1997), `ftp://ftp.zib.de/pub/Packages/mp-testdata/steinlib/index.html`

490. Koch, T., Martin, A.: Solving Steiner tree problems in graphs to optimality. Networks 33, 207–232 (1998)

491. Koch, T., Martin, A., Voß, S.: SteinLib: An updated library on Steiner tree problems in graphs, Tech. Report ZIB-Report 00-37, Konrad-Zuse-Zentrum für Informationstechnik Berlin, Takustr. 7, Berlin (2000)

492. Koch, W., et al.: The GNU privacy guard, version 1.4.5 (2006), `http://gnupg.org/`

493. Köhler, E., Möhring, R.H., Schilling, H.: Acceleration of shortest path and constrained shortest path computation. In: Nikoletseas, S.E. (ed.) WEA 2005. LNCS, vol. 3503, pp. 126–138. Springer, Heidelberg (2005)

494. Kontoghiorghes, E.J. (ed.): Handbook of parallel computing and statistics. Chapman & Hall/CRC (2005)

495. Kotula, J.: Source code documentation: An engineering deliverable. In: TOOLS 2000: Proceedings of the Technology of Object-Oriented Languages and Systems (TOOLS 34'00), Washington, DC, USA, p. 505. IEEE Computer Society, Los Alamitos (2000)

496. Kou, L., Markowsky, G., Berman, L.: A fast algorithm for Steiner trees. Acta Inform. 15, 141–145 (1981)

497. Kowarschik, M., Weiß, C.: An overview of cache optimization techniques and cache-aware numerical algorithms. In: Meyer, U., Sanders, P., Sibeyn, J.F. (eds.) Algorithms for Memory Hierarchies. LNCS, vol. 2625, pp. 213–232. Springer, Heidelberg (2003)

498. KProf – profiling made easy (2002), http://kprof.sourceforge.net/

499. Krishnamurthy, B.: Constructing test cases for partitioning heuristics. IEEE Transactions on Computers 36(9), 1112–1114 (1987)

500. Krumke, S.O., Noltemeier, H.: Graphentheoretische Konzepte und Algorithmen. B. G. Teubner (2005)

501. Kühl, D., Nissen, M., Weihe, K.: Efficient, adaptable implementations of graph algorithms. In: Proceedings of the 1st Workshop on Algorithm Engineering, WAE 1997 (1997), http://www.dsi.unive.it/~wae97/proceedings/

502. Kuhn, T.S.: The structure of scientific revolutions. The University of Chicago Press, Chicago (1970)

503. Kumar, V., Grama, A., Gupta, A., Karypis, G.: Introduction to parallel computing: Design and analysis of algorithms. Benjamin-Cummings Publishing (1994)

504. LaMarca, A., Ladner, R.E.: The influence of caches on the performance of sorting. In: Proceedings of the 8th Annual ACM-SIAM Symposium on Discrete Algorithms (SODA), pp. 370–379 (1997)

505. LaMarca, A., Ladner, R.E.: The influence of caching on the performance of sorting. Journal of Algorithms 31, 66–104 (1999)

506. Lane, D., Lu, J., Peres, C., Zitek, E.: Online statistics: An interactive multimedia course of study (2006), http://onlinestatbook.com/index.html

507. LAPACK: Linear Algebra PACKage, version 3.1.1 (2007), http://www.netlib.org/lapack/

508. Latour, B.: Science in action. Harvard University Press, Cambridge (1987)

509. Laura, L., Leonardi, S., Millozzi, S., Meyer, U., Sibeyn, J.F.: Algorithms and experiments for the webgraph. In: Di Battista, G., Zwick, U. (eds.) ESA 2003. LNCS, vol. 2832, pp. 703–714. Springer, Heidelberg (2003)

510. Lauther, U.: An extremely fast, exact algorithm for finding shortest paths in static networks with geographical background. In: Geoinformation und Mobilität - von der Forschung zur praktischen Anwendung. IfGI prints, vol. 22, pp. 219–230 (2004)

511. L'Ecuyer, P.: Simulation of algorithms for performance analysis. INFORMS Journal on Computing 8(1), 16–20 (1996)

512. The LEDA user manual (2009), http://www.algorithmic-solutions.info/leda_manual/

513. LEDA, Library for efficient data types and algorithms, Version 6.2.1 (2009), http://www.algorithmic-solutions.com/

514. Leighton, F.T.: Introduction to parallel algorithms and architectures: Arrays - trees - hypercubes. Morgan Kaufmann, San Francisco (1992)

515. Leiss, E.L.: A programmer's companion to algorithm analysis. Chapman & Hall/CRC (2006)

516. Lengauer, T.: Combinatorial algorithms for integrated circuit layout. Wiley, Chichester (1990)

517. Lennerz, C., Thiel, S.: Handling of parameterized data types in LEDA, Tech. report, Algorithmic Solutions GmbH (1997)

518. Lester, D., Gowland, P.: Using PVS to validate the algorithms of an exact arithmetic. Theoretical Computer Science 291, 203–218 (2003)

519. Levin, L.A.: Universal sequential search problems. Problems of Information Transmission 9(3), 265–266 (1973)

520. Levitin, A.: Introduction to the design and analysis of algorithms. Pearson Education, London (2003)
521. Lewis, B.: Debugging backward in time. In: Proceedings of the 5. International Workshop on Automated and Algorithmic Debugging, AADEBUG (2003), http://www.lambdacs.com/debugger/debugger.html
522. Lewis, H.R., Papadimitriou, C.H.: Elements of the theory of computation. Prentice-Hall, Englewood Cliffs (1981)
523. Li, C., Yap, C.-K.: A new constructive root bound for algebraic expressions. In: Proceedings of the 12th Annual ACM-SIAM Symposium on Discrete Algorithms (SODA), pp. 496–505 (2001)
524. Li, C., Yap, C.-K.: Recent progress in exact geometric computation. In: Basu, S., Gonzalez-Vega, L. (eds.) Proc. DIMACS Workshop on Algorithmic and Quantitative Aspects of Real Algebraic Geometry in Mathematics and Computer Science, March 12-16 (2001)
525. Liang, J., Kumar, R., Ross, K.W.: Understanding KaZaA (2004), http://citeseer.ist.psu.edu/liang04understanding.html
526. Lidor, G.: Construction of nonlinear programming test problems with known solution characteristics. In: Mulvey, J.M. (ed.) Evaluating Mathematical Programming Techniques, Proceedings of a Conference held at the National Bureau of Standards, Boulder, Colorado, January 5-6. Lecture Notes in Economics and Mathematical Systems, vol. 199, pp. 35–43. Springer, Heidelberg (1982)
527. Lindner, T.: Train schedule optimization in public rail transport, Ph.D. thesis, Technische Universität Braunschweig, Germany (2000)
528. Lipton, R.J., Tarjan, R.E.: A separator theorem for planar graphs. SIAM Journal Applied Mathematics 36, 177–189 (1979)
529. Liskov, B., Guttag, J.: Abstraction and specification in program development. MIT Press, Cambridge (1986)
530. Literate programming (2009), http://www.literateprogramming.com
531. Lübbecke, M.E., Desrosiers, J.: Selected topics in column generation. Operations Research 53(6), 1007–1023 (2005)
532. Ma, B.: Why greed works for shortest common superstring problem. In: Ferragina, P., Landau, G.M. (eds.) CPM 2008. LNCS, vol. 5029, pp. 244–254. Springer, Heidelberg (2008)
533. Maggs, B.M., Matheson, L.R., Tarjan, R.E.: Models of parallel computation: A survey and synthesis. In: Proceedings of the 28th Hawaii International Conference on System Sciences, pp. 61–70 (January 1995)
534. Maheshwari, A., Zeh, N.: I/O-efficient algorithms for graphs of bounded treewidth. In: Proceedings of the 12th Annual ACM-SIAM Symposium on Discrete Algorithms (SODA), pp. 89–90, ACM-SIAM (2001)
535. Maheshwari, A., Zeh, N.: I/O-optimal algorithms for planar graphs using separators. In: Proceedings of the 13th Annual ACM-SIAM Symposium on Discrete Algorithms (SODA), pp. 372–381, ACM-SIAM (2002)
536. Makhorin, A.: GNU linear programming kit reference manual version 4.11, Dept. Applied Informatics, Moscow Aviation Institute (2006)
537. Malkhi, D., Naor, M., Ratajczak, D.: Viceroy: A scalable and dynamic emulation of the butterfly. In: Proceedings of the 21st Annual ACM Symposium on Principles of Distributed Computing, pp. 183–192. ACM Press, New York (2002)
538. Martins, E.Q.: On a multicriteria shortest path problem. European Journal of Operational Research 26(3), 236–245 (1984)
539. Matias, Y.: Parallel algorithms column: On the search for suitable models. ACM SIGACT News 28(3), 21–29 (1997)

540. Matoušek, J., Pach, J., Sharir, M., Sifrony, S., Welzl, E.: Fat triangles determine linearly many holes. SIAM Journal on Computing 23(1), 154–169 (1994)

541. Matoušek, J., Sharir, M., Welzl, E.: A subexponential bound for linear programming. Algorithmica 16(4/5), 498–516 (1996)

542. McCarl, B.: McCarl GAMS user guide (2008),
http://www.gams.com/dd/docs/bigdocs/gams2002/mccarlgamsuserguide.pdf

543. McColl, W.F.: Scalable computing. In: van Leeuwen, J. (ed.) Computer Science Today: Recent Trends and Developments. LNCS, vol. 1000, pp. 46–61. Springer, Heidelberg (1995)

544. McColl, W.F., Tiskin, A.: Memory-efficient matrix multiplication in the BSP model. Algorithmica 24(3-4), 287–297 (1999)

545. McGeoch, C.C.: Analyzing algorithms by simulation: Variance reduction techniques and simulation speedups. ACM Computing Surveys 24(2), 195–212 (1992)

546. McGeoch, C.C.: Challenges in algorithm simulation. INFORMS Journal on Computing 8(1), 27–28 (1996)

547. McGeoch, C.C.: Toward an experimental method for algorithm simulation. INFORMS Journal on Computing 8(1), 1–15 (1996)

548. McGeoch, C.C.: Experimental analysis of algorithms. Notices of the AMS 48(3), 304–311 (2001)

549. McGeoch, C.C.: Experimental algorithmics. Communications of the ACM 50(11), 27–31 (2007)

550. McGeoch, C.C., Moret, B.M.E.: How to present a paper on experimental work with algorithms. SIGACT News 30(4), 85–90 (1999)

551. McGeoch, C.C., Sanders, P., Fleischer, R., Cohen, P.R., Precup, D.: Using finite experiments to study asymptotic performance. In: Fleischer, et al. (eds.) [288], pp. 93–126

552. Megiddo, N.: Improved asymptotic analysis of the average number of steps performed by the self-dual simplex algorithm. Mathematical Programming 35(2), 140–172 (1986)

553. Mehl, M., Weinzierl, T., Zenger, C.: A cache-oblivious self-adaptive full multigrid method. Numer. Linear Algebra Appl. 13(2-3), 275–291 (2006)

554. Mehlhorn, K.: A faster approximation algorithm for the Steiner problem in graphs. Information Processing Letters 27, 125–128 (1988)

555. Mehlhorn, K., Meyer, U.: External-memory breadth-first search with sublinear I/O. In: Möhring, R.H., Raman, R. (eds.) ESA 2002. LNCS, vol. 2461, pp. 723–735. Springer, Heidelberg (2002)

556. Mehlhorn, K., Möhring, R.H., Monien, B., Mutzel, P., Sanders, P., Wagner, D.: Antrag auf ein Schwerpunktprogramm zum Thema Algorithm Engineering (2006),
http://www.algorithm-engineering.de/beschreibung.pdf

557. Mehlhorn, K., Mutzel, P.: On the embedding phase of the Hopcroft and Tarjan planarity testing algorithm. Algorithmica 16(2), 233–242 (1996)

558. Mehlhorn, K., Näher, S.: Algorithm design and software libraries: Recent developments in the LEDA project. In: Algorithms, Software, Architectures, Information Processing — Proc. IFIP Congress, vol. 1, pp. 493–505. Elsevier Science, Amsterdam (1992)

559. Mehlhorn, K., Näher, S.: LEDA: A platform for combinatorial and geometric computing. CACM: Communications of the ACM 38, 96–102 (1995)

560. Mehlhorn, K., Näher, S.: From algorithms to working programs: On the use of program checking in LEDA. In: Brim, L., Gruska, J., Zlatuška, J. (eds.) MFCS 1998. LNCS, vol. 1450, pp. 84–93. Springer, Heidelberg (1998)

561. Mehlhorn, K., Näher, S.: LEDA: A platform for combinatorial and geometric computing. Cambridge University Press, Cambridge (November 1999)
562. Mehlhorn, K., Sanders, P.: Algorithms and data structures - the basic toolbox. Springer, Heidelberg (2008)
563. Mehlhorn, K., Schäfer, G.: Implementation of $O(nm \log n)$ weighted matchings in general graphs: The power of data structures. ACM Journal of Experimental Algorithms 7(4), 1–19 (2002)
564. Melzak, Z.A.: On the problem of Steiner. Canad. Math. Bull. 4, 143–148 (1961)
565. Mendelzon, A.O., Wood, P.T.: Finding regular simple paths in graph databases. SIAM Journal on Computing 24(6), 1235–1258 (1995)
566. Meyer, B.: Design by contract, Tech. Report TR-EI-12/CO, Interactive Software Engineering Inc. (1986)
567. Meyer, B.: Applying 'design by contract'. Computer 25(10), 40–51 (1992)
568. Meyer, B.: Object-oriented software construction, 2nd edn. Prentice Hall PTR, Englewood Cliffs (March 2000)
569. Meyer, U., Sanders, P., Sibeyn, J.F. (eds.): Algorithms for Memory Hierarchies. LNCS, vol. 2625. Springer, Heidelberg (2003)
570. Meyers, S.: More effective C++. Addison-Wesley, Reading (1996)
571. Meyers, S.: Effective C++, 3rd edn. Addison-Wesley, Reading (2005)
572. Milenkovic, V.J.: Verifiable implementation of geometric algorithms using finite precision arithmetic. Artif. Intell. 37(1-3), 377–401 (1988)
573. Milenkovic, V.J.: Shortest path geometric rounding. Algorithmica 27(1), 57–86 (2000)
574. Miller, G.L.: Riemann's hypothesis and tests for primality. Journal of Computer and System Sciences 13, 300–317 (1976)
575. Minakawa, T., Sugihara, K.: Topology oriented vs. exact arithmetic - experience in implementing the three-dimensional convex hull algorithm. In: Leong, H.W., Imai, H., Jain, S. (eds.) ISAAC 1997. LNCS, vol. 1350, pp. 273–282. Springer, Heidelberg (1997)
576. Mishra, B.: Algorithmic algebra. Texts and Monographs in Computer Science. Springer, Heidelberg (1993)
577. Mitchell, J.S.B.: Guillotine subdivisions approximate polygonal subdivisions: A simple polynomial-time approximation scheme for geometric TSP, k-MST, and related problems. SIAM Journal on Computing 28(4), 1298–1309 (1999)
578. Mitchell, J.S.B.: A PTAS for TSP with neighborhoods among fat regions in the plane. In: Proceedings of the 18th Annual ACM-SIAM Symposium on Discrete Algorithms (SODA), pp. 11–18 (2007)
579. Möhring, R.H.: Verteilte Verbindungssuche im öffentlichen Personenverkehr – Graphentheoretische Modelle und Algorithmen. In: Horster, P. (ed.) Angewandte Mathematik, insbesondere Informatik – Beispiele erfolgreicher Wege zwischen Mathematik und Informatik, pp. 192–220. Vieweg (1999)
580. Möhring, R.H., Müller-Hannemann, M.: Complexity and modeling aspects of mesh refinement into quadrilaterals. Algorithmica 26, 148–171 (2000)
581. Möhring, R.H., Müller-Hannemann, M., Weihe, K.: Mesh refinement via bidirected flows: Modeling, complexity, and computational results. Journal of the ACM 44, 395–426 (1997)
582. Möhring, R.H., Schilling, H., Schütz, B., Wagner, D., Willhalm, T.: Partitioning graphs to speed up Dijkstra's algorithm. In: Nikoletseas, S.E. (ed.) WEA 2005. LNCS, vol. 3503, pp. 189–202. Springer, Heidelberg (2005)
583. Mokbel, M.F., Aref, W.G., Kamel, I.: Analysis of multi-dimensional space-filling curves. Geoinformatica 7(3), 179–209 (2003)

584. Moret, B.M.E.: Towards a discipline of experimental algorithmics. In: Goldwasser, M.H., Johnson, D.S., McGeoch, C.C. (eds.) Data Structures, Near Neighbor Searches, and Methodology: Fifth and Sixth DIMACS Implementation Challenges. DIMACS Monographs, vol. 59, pp. 197–213. American Mathematical Society, Providence (2002)

585. Moret, B.M.E., Shapiro, H.D.: Algorithms and experiments: The new (and old) methodology. Journal of Universal Computer Science 7(5), 434–446 (2001)

586. Moret, B.M.E., Shapiro, H.D.: An empirical assessment of algorithms for constructing a minimal spanning tree. In: Computational Support for Discrete Mathematics. DIMACS Series in Discrete Mathematics and Theoretical Computer Science, vol. 15, pp. 99–117 (1994)

587. Morin, P.: Coarse grained parallel computing on heterogeneous systems. In: Proc. 1998 ACM Symp. on Applied Computing (SAC 1998), pp. 628–634. ACM Press, New York (1998)

588. Morrison, D.R.: PATRICIA: Practical algorithm to retrieve information coded in alphanumeric. Journal of the ACM 15, 514–534 (1968)

589. Motwani, R., Raghavan, P.: Randomized algorithms. Cambridge University Press, Cambridge (1995)

590. Mount, D.M.: ANN programming manual (2006),
http://www.cs.umd.edu/~mount/ANN

591. MPFI, Multiple precision floating-point interval library, version 1.3.4-RC3 (2006),
http://gforge.inria.fr/projects/mpfi/

592. MPFR, A multiple precision floating-point library, version 2.2.0 (2005),
http://www.mpfr.org/

593. MTL: The matrix template library, version 2.1.2-22 (2005),
http://www.osl.iu.edu/research/mtl/

594. Müller–Hannemann, M., Schnee, M.: Finding all attractive train connections by multi-criteria Pareto search. In: Geraets, F., Kroon, L.G., Schoebel, A., Wagner, D., Zaroliagis, C.D. (eds.) Railway Optimization 2004. LNCS, vol. 4359, pp. 246–263. Springer, Heidelberg (2007)

595. Müller–Hannemann, M., Weihe, K.: Pareto shortest paths is often feasible in practice. In: Brodal, G.S., Frigioni, D., Marchetti-Spaccamela, A. (eds.) WAE 2001. LNCS, vol. 2141, pp. 185–197. Springer, Heidelberg (2001)

596. Müller-Hannemann, M.: High quality quadrilateral surface meshing without template restrictions: A new approach based on network flow techniques. International Journal of Computational Geometry and Applications 10, 285–307 (2000)

597. Müller-Hannemann, M., Peyer, S.: Approximation of rectilinear Steiner trees with length restrictions on obstacles. In: Dehne, F.K.H.A., Sack, J.-R., Smid, M.H.M. (eds.) WADS 2003. LNCS, vol. 2748, pp. 207–218. Springer, Heidelberg (2003)

598. Müller-Hannemann, M., Schwartz, A.: Implementing weighted b-matching algorithms: Insights from a computational study. ACM Journal of Experimental Algorithms 5, 8 (2000)

599. Mulmuley, K., Vazirani, U.V., Vazirani, V.V.: Matching is as easy as matrix inversion. Combinatorica 7(1), 105–113 (1987)

600. Munagala, K., Ranade, A.: I/O-complexity of graph algorithms. In: Proceedings of the 10th Annual ACM-SIAM Symposium on Discrete Algorithms (SODA), pp. 687–694 (1999)

601. Murtagh, B.A.: Advanced linear programming. McGraw-Hill, New York (1981)

602. Musser, D.R.: Introspective sorting and selection algorithms. Software: Practice and Experience 27(8), 983–993 (1997)

603. Muthu Muthukrishnan, S.: Data streams: Algorithms and applications. In: Foundations and Trends in Theoretical Computer Science, vol. 1(2). NOW (2005)
604. Măndoiu, I.I., Vazirani, V.V., Ganley, J.L.: A new heuristic for rectilinear Steiner trees. In: ICCAD 1999: Proceedings of the 1999 IEEE/ACM international conference on Computer-aided design, Piscataway, NJ, USA, pp. 157–162. IEEE Press, Los Alamitos (1999)
605. Myers, N.C.: Traits: A new and useful template technique. C++ Report 7(5), 32–35 (1995)
606. Näher, S.: Delaunay triangulation and other computational geometry experiments (2003), http://www.informatik.uni-trier.de/~naeher/Professur/research/index.html
607. Näher, S., Zlotowski, O.: Design and implementation of efficient data types for static graphs. In: Möhring, R.H., Raman, R. (eds.) ESA 2002. LNCS, vol. 2461, pp. 748–759. Springer, Heidelberg (2002)
608. Nanevski, A., Blelloch, G., Harper, R.: Automatic generation of staged geometric predicates. Higher-Order and Symbolic Computation 16, 379–400 (2003)
609. Nannicini, G., Delling, D., Liberti, L., Schultes, D.: Bidirectional A* search for time-dependent fast paths. In: McGeoch, C.C. (ed.) WEA 2008. LNCS, vol. 5038, pp. 334–346. Springer, Heidelberg (2008)
610. Naor, M., Wieder, U.: Novel architectures for P2P applications: The continuous-discrete approach. In: SPAA 2003: Proceedings of the Fifteenth Annual ACM Symposium on Parallel Algorithms, pp. 50–59 (2003)
611. Nemhauser, G.L., Wolsey, L.A.: Integer and combinatorial optimization. John Wiley & Sons, New York (1988)
612. Nemhauser, G.L., Wolsey, L.A.: Integer programming. In: Nemhauser, G.L., et al. (eds.) Optimization, pp. 447–527. Elsevier North-Holland, Inc., New York (1989)
613. Nethercote, N., Seward, J.: Valgrind: A program supervision framework. Electronic Notes in Theoretical Computer Science 89(2), 44–66 (2003)
614. Nielsen, B.K., Winter, P., Zachariasen, M.: An exact algorithm for the uniformly-oriented Steiner tree problem. In: Möhring, R.H., Raman, R. (eds.) ESA 2002. LNCS, vol. 2461, pp. 760–772. Springer, Heidelberg (2002)
615. Nodine, M.H., Goodrich, M.T., Vitter, J.S.: Blocking for external graph searching. Algorithmica 16(2), 181–214 (1996)
616. Nodine, M.H., Vitter, J.S.: Deterministic distribution sort in shared and distributed memory multiprocessors. In: Proceedings of the 5th Annual ACM Symposium on Parallel Algorithms and Architectures, pp. 120–129 (1993)
617. NVIDIA Corporation, CUDA zone – the resource for CUDA developers (2009), http://www.nvidia.com/cuda/
618. OGDF — open graph drawing framework (2008), http://www.ogdf.net
619. Oishi, Y., Sugihara, K.: Topology-oriented divide-and-conquer algorithm for Voronoi diagrams. CVGIP: Graphical Model and Image Processing 57(4), 303–314 (1995)
620. Okasaki, C.: Red-black trees in a functional setting. Journal of Functional Programming 9(4), 471–477 (1999)
621. O'Neill, R.P.: A comparison of real-world linear programs and their randomly generated analogs. In: Mulvey, J.M. (ed.) Evaluating Mathematical Programming Techniques, Proceedings of a Conference held at the National Bureau of Standards, Boulder, Colorado, January 5-6. Lecture Notes in Economics and Mathematical Systems, vol. 199, pp. 44–59. Springer, Heidelberg (1982)
622. Orlin, J.B.: On experimental methods for algorithm simulation. INFORMS Journal on Computing 8(1), 21–23 (1996)

623. Overmars, M.H., van der Stappen, A.F.: Range searching and point location among fat objects. Journal of Algorithms 21(3), 629–656 (1996)
624. Owre, S., Shankar, N., Rushby, J.M.: PVS: A prototype verification system. In: Kapur, D. (ed.) CADE 1992. LNCS, vol. 607, pp. 748–752. Springer, Heidelberg (1992)
625. The Oxford BSP toolset, version 1.4 (1998), http://www.bsp-worldwide.org/implmnts/oxtool/
626. Page, L., Brin, S., Motwani, R., Winograd, T.: The Page-Rank citation ranking: Bringing order to the web (1999), http://ilpubs.stanford.edu:8090/422/1/1999-66.pdf
627. Pan, V.Y., Yu, Y., Stewart, C.: Algebraic and numerical techniques for the computation of matrix determinants. Computers and Mathematics with Applications 34(1), 43–70 (1997)
628. Papadimitriou, C.H., Steiglitz, K.: Combinatorial optimization. Dover Publications, Inc., New York (1998)
629. Parnas, D.L., Clements, P.C.: A rational design process: How and why to fake it. IEEE Trans. Softw. Eng. 12(2), 251–257 (1986)
630. Paterson, M., Frances Yao, F.: Efficient binary space partitions for hidden-surface removal and solid modeling. Discrete & Computational Geometry 5, 485–503 (1990)
631. Patterson, D.A., Hennessy, J.L.: Computer organization and design. In: The Hardware/Software Interface, 3rd edn. Morgan Kaufmann Publishers Inc., San Francisco (2005)
632. Paul, W.J., Bach, P., Bosch, M., Fischer, J., Lichtenau, C., Röhrig, J.: Real PRAM programming. In: Euro-Par 2002: Proc. 8th International Euro-Par Conference on Parallel Processing, pp. 522–531. Springer, Heidelberg (2002)
633. PBGL: The parallel boost graph library, version 0.7.0 (2009), http://www.osl.iu.edu/research/pbgl/
634. Space-filling curve, http://en.wikipedia.org/wiki/Space-filling_curve (last visited 15.2.2009)
635. Peano, G.: Sur une courbe qui remplit toute une aire plane. Math. Annalen 36, 157–160 (1890)
636. Pietracaprina, A., Pucci, G., Silvestri, F.: Cache-oblivious simulation of parallel programs. In: Proc. 8th Workshop on Advances in Parallel and Distributed Computational Models (CD). IEEE Computer Society, Los Alamitos (2006)
637. Pion, S., Yap, C.-K.: Constructive root bound for k-ary rational input numbers. In: Proceedings of the 19th ACM Symposium on Computational Geometry, pp. 256–263. ACM Press, San Diego (2003)
638. Pisinger, D.: Algorithms for knapsack problems, Ph.D. thesis, University of Copenhagen, Dept. of Computer Science (1995)
639. Pizzonia, M., Di Battista, G.: Object-oriented design of graph oriented data structures. In: Goodrich, M.T., McGeoch, C.C. (eds.) ALENEX 1999. LNCS, vol. 1619, pp. 140–155. Springer, Heidelberg (1999)
640. Plauger, P.J., Stepanov, A.A., Lee, M., Musser, D.R.: The C++ Standard Template Library. Prentice-Hall, Englewood Cliffs (2000)
641. Pohl, I.: Bi-directional search. In: Meltzer, B., Michie, D. (eds.) Proceedings of the Sixth Annual Machine Intelligence Workshop, vol. 6, pp. 124–140. Edinburgh University Press, Edinburgh (1971)
642. Polzin, T., Daneshmand, S.V.: Primal-dual approaches to the Steiner problem. In: Jansen, K., Khuller, S. (eds.) APPROX 2000. LNCS, vol. 1913, pp. 214–225. Springer, Heidelberg (2000)

643. Polzin, T., Daneshmand, S.V.: A comparison of Steiner relaxations. Discrete Applied Mathematics 112, 241–261 (2001)

644. Polzin, T., Daneshmand, S.V.: Improved algorithms for the Steiner problem in networks. Discrete Applied Mathematics 112, 263–300 (2001)

645. Polzin, T., Daneshmand, S.V.: Practical partitioning-based methods for the Steiner problem. In: Àlvarez, C., Serna, M. (eds.) WEA 2006. LNCS, vol. 4007, pp. 241–252. Springer, Heidelberg (2006)

646. Pratt, V.R.: Every prime has a succinct certificate. SIAM Journal of Computing 4, 214–220 (1975)

647. Prechelt, L.: An empirical comparison of seven programming languages. Computer 33(10), 23–29 (2000)

648. Priest, D.M.: On properties of floating point arithmetics: Numerical stability and the cost of accurate computations, Ph.D. thesis, University of California at Berkeley (1992)

649. Procopiuc, O., Agarwal, P.K., Arge, L., Vitter, J.S.: Bkd-tree: A dynamic scalable kd-tree. In: 8th International Symposium on advances in Spatial and Temporal Databases, SSTD, pp. 46–65 (2003)

650. Prokop, H.: Cache-oblivious algorithms, Master's thesis, Massachusetts Institute of Technology (1999)

651. Pyrga, E., Schulz, F., Wagner, D., Zaroliagis, C.: Experimental comparison of shortest path approaches for timetable information. In: Proceedings of the 6th Workshop on Algorithm Engineering and Experiments (ALENEX 2004), pp. 88–99. SIAM, Philadelphia (2004)

652. Pyrga, E., Schulz, F., Wagner, D., Zaroliagis, C.: Towards realistic modeling of time-table information through the time-dependent approach. In: Proceedings of ATMOS Workshop 2003, pp. 85–103 (2004)

653. Pyrga, E., Schulz, F., Wagner, D., Zaroliagis, C.: Efficient models for timetable information in public transportation systems. ACM Journal of Experimental Algorithmics, Article 2.4, 12 (2007)

654. Raab, S., Halperin, D.: Controlled perturbation for arrangements of polyhedral surfaces (2002),
http://acg.cs.tau.ac.il/danhalperin/publications/
dan-halperins-publications

655. Rabin, M.O.: Mathematical theory of automata. In: Proceedings of the 19th ACM Symposium in Applied Mathematics, pp. 153–175 (1966)

656. Rabin, M.O.: Probabilistic algorithm for testing primality. Journal of Number Theory 12, 128–138 (1980)

657. Rahman, N., Cole, R., Raman, R.: Optimized predecessor data structures for internal memory. In: Brodal, G.S., Frigioni, D., Marchetti-Spaccamela, A. (eds.) WAE 2001. LNCS, vol. 2141, pp. 67–78. Springer, Heidelberg (2001)

658. Rahman, N., Raman, R.: Analysing the cache behaviour of non-uniform distribution sorting algorithm. In: Paterson, M. (ed.) ESA 2000. LNCS, vol. 1879, pp. 380–391. Springer, Heidelberg (2000)

659. Rajagopalan, S., Vazirani, V.V.: On the bidirected cut relaxation for the metric Steiner tree problem. In: Proceedings of the 10th Annual ACM-SIAM Symposium on Discrete Algorithms (SODA), pp. 742–751 (1999)

660. Rajasekaran, S., Reif, J. (eds.): Handbook of parallel computing: Models, algorithms and applications. Chapman & Hall CRC Computer & Information Science. CRC Press, Boca Raton (2007)

661. Ramachandran, V.: Parallel algorithm design with coarse-grained synchronization. In: International Conference on Computational Science, vol. 2, pp. 619–627 (2001)
662. Ramsey, N.: Literate programming simplified. IEEE Softw. 11(5), 97–105 (1994)
663. Rardin, R.L., Lin, B.W.: Test problems for computational experiments – issues and techniques. In: Mulvey, J.M. (ed.) Evaluating Mathematical Programming Techniques, Proceedings of a Conference held at the National Bureau of Standards, Boulder, Colorado, January 5-6, vol. 199, pp. 8–15. Springer, Heidelberg (1982)
664. Ratnasamy, S., Francis, P., Handley, M., Karp, R., Schenker, S.: A scalable content-addressable network. In: Proceedings of the ACM SIGCOMM, pp. 161–172. ACM Press, New York (August 2001)
665. Ratschek, H., Rokne, J.: Exact computation of the sign of a finite sum. Applied Mathematics and Computation 99, 99–127 (1999)
666. Raymond, E.S.: The art of UNIX programming. Pearson Education, London (2003)
667. Reinders, J.: Intel threading building blocks: Outfitting C++ for multi-core processor parallelism. O'Reilly Media, Inc., Sebastopol (2007)
668. Reinelt, G.: TSPLIB—a traveling salesman problem library. ORSA Journal on Computing 3(4), 376–384 (1991)
669. Reis, G.D., Mourrain, B., Rouillier, F., Trébuchet, P.: An environment for symbolic and numeric computation. In: International Congress of Mathematical Software ICMS 2002 (April 2002)
670. Reynolds, C.W.: Flocks, herds, and schools: A distributed behavioral model. Computer Graphics 21(4), 25–34 (1987)
671. Rice, J.R.: A theory of condition. SIAM J. Num. Anal. 3, 287–310 (1966)
672. Richardson, D.: How to recognize zero. Journal of Symbolic Computation 24(6), 627–645 (1997)
673. Roberts, A.P., Garboczi, E.J.: Elastic moduli of model random three-dimensional closed-cell cellular solids. Acta Materialia 49(2), 189–197 (2001)
674. Robertson, N., Sanders, D.P., Seymour, P., Thomas, R.: Efficiently four-coloring planar graphs. In: Proceedings of the 28th ACM Symposium on Theory of Computing (STOC), pp. 571–575. ACM Press, New York (1996)
675. Robertson, N., Seymour, P.D.: Graph minors. XIII: The disjoint paths problem. J. Comb. Theory Ser. B 63(1), 65–110 (1995)
676. Robertson, N., Seymour, P.D.: Graph minors. XX. Wagner's conjecture. J. Comb. Theory Ser. B 92(2), 325–357 (2004)
677. Robins, G., Zelikovsky, A.: Improved Steiner tree approximation in graphs. In: Proceedings of the 11th Annual ACM-SIAM Symposium on Discrete Algorithms (SODA), pp. 770–779 (2000)
678. Robins, G., Zelikovsky, A.: Tighter bounds for graph Steiner tree approximation. SIAM Journal on Discrete Mathematics 19(1), 122–134 (2005)
679. Röglin, H., Vöcking, B.: Smoothed analysis of integer programming. In: Jünger, M., Kaibel, V. (eds.) IPCO 2005. LNCS, vol. 3509, pp. 276–290. Springer, Heidelberg (2005)
680. Rossi, F.: Constraint (logic) programming: A survey on research and applications. In: Selected papers from the Joint ERCIM/Compulog Net Workshop on New Trends in Constraints, pp. 40–74. Springer, London (2000)
681. Rossi, F., Petrie, C., Dhar, V.: On the equivalence of constraint satisfaction problems. In: Aiello, L.C. (ed.) ECAI 1990: Proceedings of the 9th European Conference on Artificial Intelligence, pp. 550–556. Pitman, Stockholm (1990)

682. Rossi, F., van Beek, P., Walsh, T. (eds.): Handbook of constraint programming. Elsevier, Amsterdam (2006)

683. Rowstron, A., Druschel, P.: Pastry: Scalable, decentralized object location, and routing for large-scale peer-to-peer systems. In: Guerraoui, R. (ed.) Middleware 2001. LNCS, vol. 2218, pp. 329–350. Springer, Heidelberg (2001)

684. Rump, S.M., Ogita, T., Oishi, S.: Accurate floating-point summation part I: Faithful rounding. SIAM Journal on Scientific Computing 31(1), 189–224 (2008)

685. Rump, S.M., Ogita, T., Oishi, S.: Accurate floating-point summation part II: Sign, K-fold faithful and rounding to nearest. SIAM Journal on Scientific Computing 31(2), 1269–1302 (2008)

686. Saad, Y.: Iterative methods for sparse linear systems, 2nd edn. Society for Industrial and Applied Mathematics, Philadelphia (April 2003)

687. Sagan, H.: Space-filling curves. Springer, Heidelberg (1994)

688. Salesin, D., Stolfi, J., Guibas, L.J.: Epsilon geometry: building robust algorithms from imprecise computations. In: Proceedings of the 5th Annual ACM Symposium on Computational Geometry, pp. 208–217. ACM Press, New York (1989)

689. Saltelli, A., Tarantola, S., Campolongo, F., Ratto, M.: Sensitivity analysis in practice: A guide to assessing scientific models. John Wiley & Sons, Chichester (2004)

690. Samet, H.: The quadtree and related hierarchical data structures. ACM Computing Surveys 16(2), 187–260 (1984)

691. Sametinger, J.: Software engineering with reusable components. Springer, Heidelberg (1997)

692. Sanchis, L.A.: On the complexity of test case generation for NP-hard problems. Information Processing Letters 36(3), 135–140 (1990)

693. Sanders, P.: Presenting data from experiments in algorithmics. In: Fleischer, et al. (eds.) [288], pp. 181–196

694. Sanders, P.: Algorithm engineering - an attempt at a definition. In: Albers, S., Alt, H., Näher, S. (eds.) Efficient Algorithms. LNCS, vol. 5760, pp. 321–340. Springer, Heidelberg (2009)

695. Sanders, P.: Algorithm engineering — an attempt at a definition using sorting as an example. In: Blelloch, G., Halperin, D. (eds.) ALENEX 2010, pp. 55–61. SIAM, Philadelphia (2010)

696. Sanders, P., Egner, S., Korst, J.H.M.: Fast concurrent access to parallel disks. In: Proceedings of the 11th ACM-SIAM Symposium on Discrete Algorithms (SODA), pp. 849–858 (2000)

697. Sanders, P., Schultes, D.: Highway hierarchies hasten exact shortest path queries. In: Brodal, G.S., Leonardi, S. (eds.) ESA 2005. LNCS, vol. 3669, pp. 568–579. Springer, Heidelberg (2005)

698. Sanders, P., Schultes, D.: Engineering highway hierarchies. In: Azar, Y., Erlebach, T. (eds.) ESA 2006. LNCS, vol. 4168, pp. 804–816. Springer, Heidelberg (2006)

699. Sanders, P., Schultes, D., Vetter, C.: Mobile route planning. In: Halperin, D., Mehlhorn, K. (eds.) ESA 2008. LNCS, vol. 5193, pp. 732–743. Springer, Heidelberg (2008)

700. Savage, J.E.: Models of computation, exploring the power of computing. Addison-Wesley, Reading (1998)

701. Savage, J.E., Zubair, M.: A unified model for multicore architectures. In: Proceedings of the 1st International Forum on Next-Generation Multicore/Manycore Technologies, IFMT 2008, Cairo, Egypt, p. 9 (2008)

702. Schamberger, S., Wierum, J.M.: A locality preserving graph ordering approach for implicit partitioning: Graph-filling curves. In: Proc. 17th Intl. Conf. on Parallel and Distributed Computing Systems, PDCS 2004, ISCA, pp. 51–57 (2004)

703. Schirra, S.: A case study on the cost of geometric computing. In: Goodrich, M.T., McGeoch, C.C. (eds.) ALENEX 1999. LNCS, vol. 1619, pp. 156–176. Springer, Heidelberg (1999)

704. Schirra, S.: Robustness and precision issues in geometric computation. In: Sack, J.R., Urrutia, J. (eds.) Handbook of Computational Geometry, pp. 597–632. Elsevier, Amsterdam (January 2000)

705. Schirra, S.: Real numbers and robustness in computational geometry. In: 6th Conference on Real Numbers and Computers, Schloss Dagstuhl, Germany (November 2004) (invited lecture)

706. Schmitting, W.: Das Traveling-Salesman-Problem - Anwendungen und heuristische Nutzung von Voronoi-Delaunay-Strukturen zur Lösung euklidischer, zweidimensionaler Traveling-Salesman-Probleme, Ph.D. thesis, Heinrich-Heine-Universität Düsseldorf (1999)

707. Schneider, S.: The B-method: An introduction. Palgrave (2002)

708. Schorn, P.: Robust algorithms in a program library for geometric computation, Ph.D. thesis, ETH: Swiss Federal Institute of Technology Zürich, Diss. ETH No. 9519 (1991)

709. Schorn, P.: An axiomatic approach to robust geometric programs. J. Symb. Comput. 16(2), 155–165 (1993)

710. Schrijver, A.: Theory of linear and integer programming. John Wiley & Sons, Inc., Chichester (1998)

711. Schultes, D.: Route planning in road networks, Ph.D. thesis, Universität Karlsruhe (TH), Fakultät für Informatik (February 2008)

712. Schultes, D., Sanders, P.: Dynamic highway-node routing. In: Demetrescu, C. (ed.) WEA 2007. LNCS, vol. 4525, pp. 66–79. Springer, Heidelberg (2007)

713. Schulz, F.: Timetable information and shortest paths, Ph.D. thesis, Universität Karlsruhe (TH), Fakultät für Informatik (2005)

714. Schulz, F., Wagner, D., Weihe, K.: Dijkstra's algorithm on-line: An empirical case study from public railroad transport. In: Vitter, J.S., Zaroliagis, C.D. (eds.) WAE 1999. LNCS, vol. 1668, pp. 110–123. Springer, Heidelberg (1999)

715. Schulz, F., Wagner, D., Weihe, K.: Dijkstra's algorithm on-line: An empirical case study from public railroad transport. ACM Journal of Experimental Algorithmics 5 (2000)

716. Schulz, F., Wagner, D., Zaroliagis, C.: Using multi-level graphs for timetable information in railway systems. In: Mount, D.M., Stein, C. (eds.) ALENEX 2002. LNCS, vol. 2409, pp. 43–59. Springer, Heidelberg (2002)

717. Sedgewick, R.: Implementing quicksort programs. Communications of the ACM 21(10), 847–857 (1978)

718. Seel, M.: Eine Implementierung abstrakter Voronoidiagramme, Master's thesis, Universität des Saarlandes (1994)

719. Segal, M.: Using tolerances to guarantee valid polyhedral modeling results. In: SIGGRAPH 1990: Proceedings of the 17th Annual Conference on Computer Graphics and Interactive Techniques, pp. 105–114. ACM Press, New York (1990)

720. Segal, M., Séquin, C.H.: Consistent calculations for solids modeling. In: Proceedings of the 1st Annual ACM Symposium on Computational Geometry, pp. 29–38. ACM Press, New York (1985)

721. Seidel, R.: Constrained Delaunay triangulations and Voronoi diagrams, Report 260 IIG-TU Graz, pp. 178–191 (1988)

722. Seidel, R.: The nature and meaning of perturbations in geometric computing. In: Enjalbert, P., Mayr, E.W., Wagner, K.W. (eds.) STACS 1994. LNCS, vol. 775, pp. 3–17. Springer, Heidelberg (1994)

723. Sellappa, S., Chatterjee, S.: Cache-efficient multigrid algorithms. Int. J. High Perform. Comput. Appl. 18(1), 115–133 (2004)

724. Sen, S., Chatterjee, S.: Towards a theory of cache-efficient algorithms. In: Proceedings of the 11th ACM-SIAM Symposium on Discrete Algorithms (SODA), pp. 829–838 (2000)

725. Sethia, S., Held, M., Mitchell, J.S.B.: PVD: A stable implementation for computing Voronoi diagrams of polygonal pockets. In: Buchsbaum, A.L., Snoeyink, J. (eds.) ALENEX 2001. LNCS, vol. 2153, pp. 105–116. Springer, Heidelberg (2001)

726. Seti@home (2006), http://setiathome.berkeley.edu

727. Website of SGI's STL implementation (2006), http://www.sgi.com/tech/stl/

728. Shamos, M.I., Hoey, D.: Closest-point problems. In: Proceedings of the 16th Annual IEEE Symposium on Foundations of Computer Science (FOCS), pp. 151–162. IEEE Computer Society, Los Alamitos (1975)

729. Sheskin, D.J.: Handbook of parametric and nonparametric statistical procedures. CRC Press, Boca Raton (2007)

730. Shewchuk, J.R.: Companion web page to [731], http://www.cs.cmu.edu/~quake/robust.html

731. Shewchuk, J.R.: Adaptive precision floating-point arithmetic and fast robust geometric predicates. Discrete and Computational Geometry 18, 305–363 (1997)

732. Shier, D.R.: On algorithm analysis. INFORMS Journal on Computing 8(1), 24–26 (1996)

733. Sibeyn, J.F.: From parallel to external list ranking, Technical Report MPI-I-97-1-021, Max-Planck Institut für Informatik (1997)

734. Sibeyn, J.F., Kaufmann, M.: BSP-like external memory computation. In: Bongiovanni, G.C., Bovet, D.P., Di Battista, G. (eds.) CIAC 1997. LNCS, vol. 1203, pp. 229–240. Springer, Heidelberg (1997)

735. Siegel, S.: Nonparametric statistics for the behavioral sciences. McGraw-Hill, New York (1956)

736. Siek, J.G., Lee, L., Lumsdaine, A.: The Boost graph library. Addison-Wesley, Reading (2002)

737. Siek, J.G., Lumsdaine, A.: The matrix template library: A generic programming approach to high performance numerical linear algebra. In: Caromel, D., Oldehoeft, R.R., Tholburn, M. (eds.) ISCOPE 1998. LNCS, vol. 1505, pp. 59–70. Springer, Heidelberg (1998)

738. de Moura, E.S., Navarro, G., Ziviani, N., Baeza-Yates, R.: Fast and flexible word searching on compressed text. ACM Transactions on Information Systems 18(2), 113–139 (2000)

739. Singler, J.: Graph isomorphism implementation in LEDA 5.1, version 2.0 (2006), http://www.algorithmic-solutions.de/bilder/graph_iso.pdf

740. Singler, J., Sanders, P., Putze, F.: MCSTL: The Multi-Core Standard Template Library. In: Kermarrec, A.-M., Bougé, L., Priol, T. (eds.) Euro-Par 2007. LNCS, vol. 4641, pp. 682–694. Springer, Heidelberg (2007)

741. Skiena, S.S.: Who is interested in algorithms and why? Lessons from the Stony Brook algorithms repository. In: Mehlhorn, K. (ed.) Algorithm Engineering, pp. 204–212. Max-Planck-Institut für Informatik (1998)

742. Skiena, S.S.: The algorithm design manual, 2nd edn. Springer, New York (2008)

743. Skillicorn, D.B., Talia, D.: Models and languages for parallel computation. ACM Computing Surveys 30(2), 123–169 (1998)

744. Sleator, D.D., Tarjan, R.E.: Amortized efficiency of list update and paging rules. Communications of the ACM 28(2), 202–208 (1985)

745. Smale, S.: On the average number of steps of the simplex method of linear programming. Mathematical Programming 27, 241–262 (1983)

746. Smith, W.D.: How to find Steiner minimal trees in Euclidean d-space. Algorithmica 7, 137–177 (1992)

747. Snir, M., Otto, S.: MPI – the complete reference: The MPI core, 2nd edn. MIT Press, Cambridge (1998)

748. Sommerville, I.: Software engineering, 8th edn. International Computer Science Series. Addison-Wesley, New York (2006)

749. Spielman, D.A., Teng, S.-H.: Smoothed analysis of algorithms: Why the simplex algorithm usually takes polynomial time. Journal of the ACM 51(3), 385–463 (2004)

750. Spirakis, P.G., Zaroliagis, C.D.: Distributed algorithm engineering. In: Fleischer, R., Moret, B.M.E., Schmidt, E.M. (eds.) Experimental Algorithmics. LNCS, vol. 2547, pp. 197–228. Springer, Heidelberg (2002)

751. Splint – secure programming lint, version 3.1.2 (2007), http://splint.org/

752. Spolsky, J.: User interface design for programmers. Apress, Berkeley (2001)

753. Sprent, P., Smeeton, N.C.: Applied nonparametric statistical methods. Chapman & Hall/CRC (2001)

754. Stallman, R.M., et al.: GCC, the GNU compiler collection, version 4.3.3, source code (2009), http://gcc.gnu.org/

755. Stepanov, A.A., Lee, M.: The standard template library, Tech. Report HPL-95-11, Hewlett Packard (November 1995)

756. Website of STLport (2006), http://www.stlport.org/

757. Stoica, I., Morris, R., Karger, D., Kaashoek, F., Balakrishnan, H.: Chord: A scalable peer-to-peer lookup service for internet applications. In: Proceedings of the 2001 ACM SIGCOMM Conference, pp. 149–160 (2001)

758. Strassen, V.: Gaussian elimination is not optimal. Numerische Mathematik 13, 354–356 (1969)

759. Stroustrup, B.: The C++ programming language, special edition. Addison-Wesley, Reading (2000)

760. Stroustrup, B.: A brief look at C++ox (January 2006), http://www.artima.com/cppsource/cpp0x.html

761. STXXL: Standard template library for extra large data sets, version 1.2.1 (2008), http://stxxl.sourceforge.net/

762. Sugihara, K.: A robust and consistent algorithm for intersecting convex polyhedra. Comput. Graph. Forum 13(3), 45–54 (1994)

763. Sugihara, K., Iri, M.: A solid modelling system free from topological inconsistency. J. Inf. Process. 12(4), 380–393 (1989)

764. Sugihara, K., Iri, M.: A robust topology-oriented incremental algorithm for Voronoi diagrams. Int. J. Comput. Geometry Appl. 4(2), 179–228 (1994)

765. Sugihara, K., Iri, M., Inagaki, H., Imai, T.: Topology-oriented implementation - an approach to robust geometric algorithms. Algorithmica 27(1), 5–20 (2000)

766. Suijlen, W.J.: BSPonMPI (2006), http://bsponmpi.sourceforge.net/

767. Sun, X.-H., Ni, L.M.: Another view on parallel speedup. In: Supercomputing 1990: Proc. ACM/IEEE Conf. on Supercomputing, pp. 324–333. IEEE Computer Society, Los Alamitos (1990)

768. Sutcliffe, G., Suttner, C.B.: The TPTP problem library - CNF release v1.2.1. Journal of Automated Reasoning 21(2), 177–203 (1998)

769. Sweedyk, Z.: A $2\frac{1}{2}$-approximation algorithm for shortest superstring. SIAM Journal on Computing 29(3), 954–986 (1999)

770. Tamassia, R., Vismara, L.: A case study in algorithm engineering for geometric computing. International Journal of Computational Geometry Applications 11(1), 15–70 (2001)

771. Tarjan, R.E.: Efficiency of a good but not linear set union algorithm. J. ACM 22(2), 215–225 (1975)

772. Tarjan, R.E.: Updating a balanced search tree in $O(1)$ rotations. Information Processing Letters 16(5), 253–257 (1983)

773. Tarjan, R.E.: Amortized computational complexity. SIAM Journal on Algebraic and Discrete Methods 6(2), 306–318 (1985)

774. Taub, A.H. (ed.): John von Neumann collected works. Design of Computers, Theory of Automata and Numerical Analysis, vol. V. Pergamon, Oxford (1963)

775. Tazari, S., Müller-Hannemann, M., Weihe, K.: Workload balancing in multistage production processes. In: Àlvarez, C., Serna, M. (eds.) WEA 2006. LNCS, vol. 4007, pp. 49–60. Springer, Heidelberg (2006)

776. Tazari, S., Müller-Hannemann, M.: Dealing with large hidden constants: Engineering a planar Steiner tree PTAS. In: ALENEX 2009, pp. 120–131. SIAM, Philadelphia (2009)

777. Tennent, R.D.: Specifying software. Cambridge University Press, Cambridge (2002)

778. The BlueGene/L Team, An overview of the BlueGene/L supercomputer. In: Proc. ACM/IEEE Conf. on Supercomputing, pp. 1–22 (2002)

779. Thiel, S.: The LEDA memory manager, Tech. report, Algorithmic Solutions GmbH (August 1998),
`http://www.algorithmic-solutions.info/leda_docs/leda_memmgr.ps.gz`

780. Thorup, M.: Integer priority queues with decrease key in constant time and the single source shortest paths problem. Journal of Computer and System Sciences 69(3), 330–353 (2004)

781. Toledo, S.: A survey of out-of-core algorithms in numerical linear algebra. In: External memory algorithms, pp. 161–179. American Mathematical Society, Providence (1999)

782. TPIE: A transparent parallel I/O environment (2005),
`http://www.cs.duke.edu/TPIE/` (version from September 19, 2005)

783. Trefethen, L.N., Bau III, D. (eds.): Numerical linear algebra. Society for Industrial and Applied Mathematics, Philadelphia (1997); MR1444820 (98k:65002)

784. Tufte, E.R.: The visual display of quantitative information. Graphics Press (1983)

785. Tukey, J.W.: Exploratory data analysis. Addison-Wesley, Reading (1977)

786. Turing, A.M.: Rounding-off errors in matrix processes. Quarterly Journal of Mechanics and Applied Mathematics 1, 287–308 (1948); Reprinted in [787] with summary and notes (including corrections)

787. Turing, A.M.: Pure mathematics. Collected Works of A. M. Turing. North-Holland, Amsterdam (1992); Edited and with an introduction and postscript by J. L. Britton and Irvine John Good. With a preface by P. N. Furbank

788. The universal protein resource, UniProt (2007), `http://www.uniprot.org/`

789. Valiant, L.G.: A bridging model for parallel computation. Commun. ACM 33(8), 103–111 (1990)

790. Valiant, L.G.: General purpose parallel architectures. In: Handbook of Theoretical Computer Science. Algorithms and Complexity (A), vol. A, pp. 943–972. Elsevier, Amsterdam (1990)

791. Valiant, L.G.: A bridging model for multi-core computing. In: Halperin, D., Mehlhorn, K. (eds.) ESA 2008. LNCS, vol. 5193, pp. 13–28. Springer, Heidelberg (2008)

792. Valiente, G.: Algorithms on trees and graphs. Springer, Heidelberg (2002)

793. Frank van der Stappen, A.: Motion planning amidst fat obstacles, Ph.D. thesis, Department of Computer Science, Utrecht University (March 1994)

794. van Emde Boas, P.: Preserving order in a forest in less than logarithmic time and linear space. Information Processing Letters 6, 80–82 (1977)

795. van Emde Boas, P., Kaas, R., Zijlstra, E.: Design and implementation of an efficient priority queue. Mathematical Systems Theory 10, 99–127 (1977)

796. van Heesch, D.: The Doxygen website (2009),
http://www.stack.nl/~dimitri/doxygen/

797. van Hulzen, J.A., Hulshof, B.J.A., Gates, B.L., van Heerwaarden, M.C.: A code optimization package for REDUCE. In: Proceedings of the ACM-SIGSAM 1989 International Symposium on Symbolic and Algebraic Computation, pp. 163–170 (1989)

798. van Leeuwen, J. (ed.): Handbook of theoretical computer science. Algorithms and complexity, vol. A. Elsevier/MIT Press (1990)

799. van Leeuwen, M.A.: Literate programming in C: CWEBx manual, Report AM-R9510, Centrum voor Wiskunde en Informatica, Department of Analysis, Algebra and Geometry, Stichting Mathematisch Centrum, Amsterdam, The Netherlands (1995)

800. Vandervoorde, D., Josuttis, N.M.: C++ templates: the complete guide. Addison-Wesley, Reading (2003)

801. Veldhuizen, T.L.: Expression templates. C++ Report 7(5), 26–31 (1995)

802. Veldhuizen, T.L.: Arrays in Blitz++. In: Caromel, D., Oldehoeft, R.R., Tholburn, M. (eds.) ISCOPE 1998. LNCS, vol. 1505, pp. 223–230. Springer, Heidelberg (1998)

803. Venners, B.: Joshua Bloch: A conversation about design (An interview with effective Java author, Josh Bloch by Bill Venners) (January 2002), First Published in JavaWorld,
http://www.javaworld.com/javaworld/jw-01-2002/jw-0104-bloch.html

804. Vershynin, R.: Beyond Hirsch conjecture: walks on random polytopes and smoothed complexity of the simplex method. In: Proceedings of the 47th Annual IEEE Symposium on Foundations of Computer Science (FOCS), pp. 133–142 (2006)

805. Vigna, S.: Broadword implementation of rank/select queries. In: McGeoch, C.C. (ed.) WEA 2008. LNCS, vol. 5038, pp. 154–168. Springer, Heidelberg (2008)

806. Vishkin, U., Caragea, G.C., Lee, B.C.: Models for Advancing PRAM and Other Algorithms into Parallel Programs for a PRAM-On-Chip Platform. In: Handbook of parallel computing: Models, algorithms and applications. CRC Press, Boca Raton (2007)

807. Visone: Analysis and visualization of social networks, version 2.3.5 (2008),
http://visone.info/

808. Vitter, J.S.: External memory algorithms and data structures: Dealing with massive data. ACM Computing Surveys 33(2), 209–271 (2001)

809. Vitter, J.S.: Algorithms and data structures for external memory. Foundations and Trends in Theoretical Computer Science. NOW Publishers (2008)

810. Vitter, J.S., Shriver, E.A.M.: Algorithms for parallel memory I: Two level memories. Algorithmica 12(2-3), 110–147 (1994)

References

811. Vitter, J.S., Shriver, E.A.M.: Algorithms for parallel memory, I/II. Algorithmica 12(2/3), 110–169 (1994)
812. Vleugels, J.: On fatness and fitness – realistic input models for geometric algorithms, Ph.D. thesis, Department of Computer Science, Utrecht University (March 1997)
813. von Neumann, J., Goldstine, H.H.: Numerical inverting of matrices of high order. Bull. Amer. Math. Soc. 53, 1021–1099 (1947); Reprinted in (774, pp. 479–557)
814. von zur Gathen, J., Gerhard, J.: Modern computer algebra, 2nd edn. Cambridge University Press, Cambridge (2003)
815. Voronoi, G.: Nouvelle applications des paramètres continus à la theorie des formes quadratiques. J. Reine Angew. Math. 134, 198–287 (1908)
816. Wagner, D., Willhalm, T.: Geometric speed-up techniques for finding shortest paths in large sparse graphs. In: Di Battista, G., Zwick, U. (eds.) ESA 2003. LNCS, vol. 2832, pp. 776–787. Springer, Heidelberg (2003)
817. Wagner, D., Willhalm, T., Zaroliagis, C.: Dynamic shortest path containers. In: Proceedings of ATMOS Workshop 2003, pp. 65–84 (2004)
818. Wagner, D., Willhalm, T., Zaroliagis, C.: Geometric containers for efficient shortest-path computation. ACM Journal of Experimental Algorithmics 10, 1.3 (2005)
819. Wallis, P.J.L. (ed.): Improving floating-point programming. Wiley, London (1990)
820. Wang, J.: Average-case computational complexity theory. In: Selman, A.L. (ed.) Complexity Theory Retrospective, in Honor of Juris Hartmanis on the Occasion of His Sixtieth Birthday, July 5, 1988, vol. 2. Springer, Heidelberg (1997)
821. Warme, D.M.: A new exact algorithm for rectilinear Steiner minimal trees, Tech. report, System Simulation Solutions, Inc., Alexandria, VA 22314, USA (1997)
822. Warme, D.M.: Spanning trees in hypergraphs with applications to Steiner trees, Ph.D. thesis, Computer Science Dept., The University of Virginia (1998)
823. Warme, D.M., Winter, P., Zachariasen, M.: Exact algorithms for plane Steiner tree problems: A computational study, Tech. Report TR-98/11, DIKU, Department of Computer Science, Copenhagen, Denmark (1998)
824. Warme, D.M., Winter, P., Zachariasen, M.: GeoSteiner 3.1, DIKU, Department of Computer Science, Copenhagen, Denmark (2003),
     http://www.diku.dk/geosteiner/
825. Weidendorfer, J.: Performance analysis of GUI applications on Linux. In: KDE Contributor Conference (2003)
826. Weihe, K.: A software engineering perspective on algorithmics. ACM Computing Surveys 33(1), 89–134 (2001)
827. Weihe, K., Brandes, U., Liebers, A., Müller-Hannemann, M., Wagner, D., Willhalm, T.: Empirical design of geometric algorithms. In: Proceedings of the 15th Annual ACM Symposium on Computational Geometry, pp. 86–94 (1999)
828. Weinard, M., Schnitger, G.: On the greedy superstring conjecture. SIAM Journal on Discrete Mathematics 20(2), 502–522 (2006)
829. Whaley, R.C., Petitet, A., Dongarra, J.J.: Automated empirical optimization of software and the ATLAS project. Parallel Computing 27(1-2), 3–35 (2001)
830. Wikipedia (2010),
     http://en.wikipedia.org/wiki/Wikipedia:Modelling_Wikipedia's_growth
831. Wilkinson, J.H.: Rounding errors in algebraic processes. In: IFIP Congress, pp. 44–53 (1959)
832. Wilkinson, J.H.: Error analysis of floating-point computation. Numer. Math. 2, 319–340 (1960)

833. Wilkinson, J.H.: Rounding errors in algebraic processes, Notes on Applied Science, No. 32, Her Majesty's Stationery Office, London (1963); Also published by Prentice-Hall, Englewood Cliffs, NJ, USA (1964); Translated into Polish as Bledy Zaokraglen w Procesach Algebraicznych by PWW, Warsaw, Poland (1967); And translated into German as Rundungsfehler by Springer-Verlag, Berlin, Germany (1969); Reprinted by Dover Publications, New York (1994)

834. Wilkinson, J.H., Reinsch, C.H. (eds.): Handbook for automatic computation. Linear Algebra, vol. 2. Springer, Heidelberg (1971)

835. Williams, R.: FunnelWeb user's manual. University of Adelaide, Adelaide, South Australia, Australia (1992)
    ftp.adelaide.edu.au/pub/compression/pub/funnelweb

836. Williams, T.L., Parsons, R.J.: The heterogeneous bulk synchronous parallel model. In: Proc. 15th Intl. Parallel and Distributed Processing Symp. (IPDPS 2000), Workshops on Parallel and Distr. Processing, pp. 102–108. Springer, Heidelberg (2000)

837. Wilson, P.R., Johnstone, M.S., Neely, M., Boles, D.: Dynamic storage allocation: A survey and critical review. In: Baker, H.G. (ed.) IWMM-GIAE 1995. LNCS, vol. 986, pp. 1–116. Springer, Heidelberg (1995)

838. Winter, P.: An algorithm for the Steiner problem in the Euclidean plane. Networks 15, 323–345 (1985)

839. Winter, P., Zachariasen, M.: Euclidean Steiner minimum trees: An improved exact algorithm. Networks 30, 149–166 (1997)

840. Wolsey, L.A.: Integer programming. John Wiley & Sons, Chichester (1998)

841. Wong, R.T.: A dual ascent approach for Steiner tree problems on a directed graph. Mathematical Programming 28, 271–287 (1984)

842. Woodcock, J.C.P., Davies, J.: Using Z: Specification, proof and refinement. Prentice Hall International Series in Computer Science (1996)

843. Li, X., Zhang, X., Kubricht, S.A.: Improving memory performance of sorting algorithms. ACM Journal of Experimental Algorithmics 5(3) (2000)

844. Yap, C.-K.: A geometric consistency theorem for a symbolic perturbation scheme. J. Comput. Syst. Sci. 40(1), 2–18 (1990)

845. Yap, C.-K.: Symbolic treatment of geometric degeneracies. J. Symb. Comput. 10(3-4), 349–370 (1990)

846. Yap, C.-K.: Towards exact geometric computation. Comput. Geom. Theory Appl. 7(1-2), 3–23 (1997)

847. Yap, C.-K.: Fundamental problems of algorithmic algebra. Oxford University Press, Oxford (2000)

848. Yap, C.-K.: Robust geometric computation. In: Goodman, J.E., O'Rourke, J. (eds.) Handbook of Discrete and Computational Geometry, 2nd edn., pp. 927–952. Chapmen & Hall/CRC, Boca Raton (2004)

849. Yap, C.-K., Mehlhorn, K.: Towards robust geometric computation. In: Fundamentals of Computer Science Study Conference, Washington DC, July 25-27 (2001)

850. Yeh, T.-H., Kuo, C.-M., Lei, C.-L., Yen, H.-C.: Competitive analysis of on-line disk scheduling. Theory of Computing Systems 31, 491–506 (1998)

851. Yellen, J., Gross, J.L.: Graph theory and its applications. CRC Press, Boca Raton (1998)

852. Yildiz, M.C., Madden, P.H.: Preferred direction Steiner trees. In: GLSVLSI 2001: Proceedings of the 11th Great Lakes symposium on VLSI, pp. 56–61. ACM Press, New York (2001)

853. Yoon, S.-E., Lindstrom, P.: Mesh layouts for block-based caches. IEEE Trans. Visualization and Computer Graphics 12(5), 1213–1220 (2006)

854. Yourdon, E.: Flashes on maintenance from techniques of program structure and design. Techniques of Program Structure and System Maintenance, QED Information Science (1988)

855. Zachariasen, M.: Rectilinear full Steiner tree generation. Tech. Report TR-97/29, DIKU, Department of Computer Science, Copenhagen, Denmark (1997)

856. Zachariasen, M., Rohe, A.: Rectilinear group Steiner trees and applications in VLSI design. Mathematical Programming 94, 407–433 (2003)

857. Zelikovsky, A.Z.: An 11/6-approximation algorithm for the network Steiner problem. Algorithmica 9, 463–470 (1993)

858. Zeller, A.: Why programs fail – a guide to systematic debugging, 2nd edn., Dpunkt (2009)

859. ZIB optimization suite (2009), http://zibopt.zib.de/

860. Ziegler, J.: The LEDA tutorial (2006), http://www.leda-tutorial.org/

861. Zokaities, D.: Writing understandable code, Software Development, 48–49 (2001)

862. Zumbusch, G.: Parallel multilevel methods. Adaptive mesh refinement and load-balancing. Teubner (2003)

Subject Index

absolute error, 109
abstract
    factory, 263
    model, 159
    problems, 1
abstraction, 17
    level, 17, 20
accounting method, 135, 136
accuracy, 26, 347, 350
ad hoc network, 195
adaptability, 12, 238
adaptive rounding, 147, 150
Advanced Encryption Standard (AES),
    61
adversary, 10, 141
aggregate analysis, 135, 136
Akamai Technologies, Inc., 13
ALENEX, 7, 328
algebraic
    identity, 258
    modeling language, 9, 17, 30,
        49–53
    number, 309, 436, 438
        real, 279
algorithm
    approximation, 6
    certifying, 243–245
    design, 6, 9, 19
    external memory, 11
    geometric, 14
    greedy, 65
    library, 291
    linear time, 3
    offline, 139, 179
    online, 15, 138–141
    pencil-and-paper, 5
    randomized, 15
    sublinear, 3, 15
    sweep-line, 323
Algorithm Engineering, V, IX, XIV,
        2, 4–7, 9, 11–19, 21, 26–28,
        49, 50, 53, 55, 57–59, 63,

        73, 89, 159, 200, 219, 235,
        237–239, 250, 262, 263, 267,
        273, 284, 325–327, 353–355,
        360, 389, 390, 393, 399, 410,
        411, 426–428, 445–453
    cycle, 6, 15, 325, 326
    process, 27
Algorithmics, 1, 8
    classical, 2
all-pairs shortest paths (APSP), 390
`alldifferent` constraint, 45
Amdahl's law, 210, 249
amortized
    analysis, 9, 130, 134–140
    cost, 135, 137
AMPL, 49
analysis, 2, 4, 6, 23, 325
    amortized, 9, 130, 134–140
    average-case, 9, 128, 130,
        132–134, 140, 192
    experimental, 5, 174, 325
    graphical, 368–375, 381
    of requirements, 8
    probabilistic, 152, 155, 159
    sensitivity, 22
    smoothed, 10, 128, 130,
        140–159, 449
    statistical, 337, 368, 375–381
    theoretical, 4, 326, 328
    worst-case, 9, 128, 130–132,
        168, 172
antithetic variate, 338
application, 3, 6, 430
    development, 1
    domain, 1
    real-world, 6, 22
approximation, 26, 160, 364, 409
    algorithm, 2, 6, 333, 422
    ratio, 370
    scheme, 2
APX-hard, 164
arbitrary position, 4